HEALTH PSYCHOLOGY
HYMIE ANISMAN

Los Angeles | London | New Delhi
Singapore | Washington DC | Melbourne

SAGE was founded in 1965 by Sara Miller McCune to support the dissemination of usable knowledge by publishing innovative and high-quality research and teaching content. Today, we publish over 900 journals, including those of more than 400 learned societies, more than 800 new books per year, and a growing range of library products including archives, data, case studies, reports, and video. SAGE remains majority-owned by our founder, and after Sara's lifetime will become owned by a charitable trust that secures our continued independence.

Los Angeles | London | New Delhi | Singapore | Washington DC | Melbourne

For Yakov, Binyamin and Edgge

Los Angeles | London | New Delhi
Singapore | Washington DC | Melbourne

SAGE Publications Ltd
1 Oliver's Yard
55 City Road
London EC1Y 1SP

SAGE Publications Inc.
2455 Teller Road
Thousand Oaks, California 91320

SAGE Publications India Pvt Ltd
B 1/I 1 Mohan Cooperative Industrial Area
Mathura Road
New Delhi 110 044

SAGE Publications Asia-Pacific Pte Ltd
3 Church Street
#10-04 Samsung Hub
Singapore 049483

Editor: Luke Block
Editorial assistant: Katie Norton
Production editor: Imogen Roome
Marketing manager: Alison Borg
Proofreader: Leigh C. Timmins
Cover design: Wendy Scott
Typeset by: C&M Digitals (P) Ltd, Chennai, India
Printed and bound in Great Britain by Ashford
Colour Press Ltd

Library of Congress Control Number: 2015948860

British Library Cataloguing in Publication data

A catalogue record for this book is available from
the British Library

ISBN 978-1-4739-1897-9
ISBN 978-1-4739-1898-6 (pbk)

Contents

About the author   xi
Preface   xii
Acknowledgments   xiv
Companion website   xv

1 Health psychology described   **1**

Getting there from here   2
Dealing with coordinated systems   2
Evidence-based practice   4
What do we mean when we say 'health psychology'?   4
Psychosomatic illness   6
A continuum between wellness and illness   7
Vulnerability versus resilience   8
Illness comorbidities   10
Health psychology globally   11
Encouraging behavioral change   19
Including biopsychosocial perspectives of illness   22
Summary   23

2 Methodological approaches in health psychology   **25**

Linkages to illness   25
Research using animal models   26
Research in humans: Experimental studies   29
Regression approaches   32
Epidemiology   36
Program evaluation   38
Data synthesis   39
Caveats on methodology   40
Summary   41

3 Biological systems and functioning   **43**

Multiple converging systems   44
A genetics primer   44
Gene × environment interactions   47
The nervous system   51
Autonomic nervous system   56
Endocrine systems   56
Hormones associated with the stress response   57
Eating and energy-related hormones   58
Sex hormones   61
Growth factors   66
Immune functioning   67
The enteric nervous system and the microbiome   72
Summary   76

4 The stress process   **77**

Defining stress and moderating factors   77
Attributes and dimensions of stressors   78
Stressor appraisals   79
Characteristics of stressors   82
Previous stressor experiences   88
Social support   94
Stressor effects across the life span   97
Collective and transgenerational trauma   105
Instruments used to assess stressor experiences, appraisals
and coping   108
Summary   111

5 Neurobiological stress responses   **112**

Stressor-provoked neurobiological changes as an adaptive response   113
Neurotransmitter variations   113
Hormonal changes elicited by stressors   120
Stress and energy balances   126
Sex hormones   128
Oxytocin   130
Growth factors   132
Stress and immunity   134
Summary   138

6 Healthy behaviors, unhealthy behaviors, and behavioral change   **140**

Gaining a foothold   141
Treatment of illness   141

Individualized treatment strategies   141
Intervention approaches   144
Risk factors related to health and disease   151
Cultural and ethnic differences   155
Gender differences   156
Behavioral change means health change   157
Changing attitudes, changing behaviors, and barriers to change   158
Psychosocial and cognitive perspectives of health behaviors   162
Harm reduction programs   174
Summary   175

7 Life-style factors   **176**

Keeping the motor running   177
Exercise   177
Nutrition   180
Eating-related processes   182
Overweight and obesity   183
Making changes   193
Health foods and the expansion of neutraceuticals   198
Public health and public policy   202
Sleep   203
Sleep disorders   207
Accidents at work and at home   209
Summary   211

8 Cardiovascular illnesses and related disorders   **212**

Getting to know the heart   213
The cardiovascular system   213
Diseases of the heart   215
Hypertension   215
Coronary artery disease   217
Factors that promote heart disease   219
Personality factors   227
Physiological stress responses in relation to heart disease   228
Pharmacological treatments of heart disease   231
Chronic obstructive pulmonary disease   236
Stroke   238
Summary   243

9 Diabetes   **244**

The broader health impact of diabetes   245
Type 1 diabetes   245
Type 2 diabetes   246

Genetic contributions   247
Stressors and type 2 diabetes   249
Inflammatory factors in type 2 diabetes   250
Gestational diabetes   253
Dealing with diabetes   254
Summary   257

10 Immune-related disorders   **259**

Immunity and illness   261
Allergies   261
Infectious diseases   264
Sexually transmitted infection   273
Life-style factors in relation to immune functioning and well-being   274
Autoimmune disorders   277
Summary   288

11 Cancer   **289**

Filling in a few blanks   290
What is cancer and how does it develop?   291
Genetic contributions   293
Environmental contributions   297
Viral factors   298
A stress–cancer link   299
Eating and cancer   304
Exercise and cancer   305
Sleep and cancer   306
Cancer treatment and psychological factors   306
Broad consideration regarding cancer treatment   313
Treatment methods   316
Summary   321

12 Pain   **322**

The ubiquitous malady   323
Defining pain   323
Pain assessments   325
Psychological consequences of chronic pain   326
Psychological factors related to pain perception   327
Psychosomatic (psychogenic) pain   331
Neurophysiology of pain processes   332
Pain management   335
Psychological manipulations to deal with pain perception   338
Hypnosis   341

Alternative medicine   343
Summary   344

13 Addiction   **345**

The breadth of addiction   346
Defining addiction   346
A broad view of addiction   347
Factors leading to addiction   348
Multiple neurochemical components associated with addiction   350
Why are addictions as persistent as they are?   355
A link between propensity for eating and drug addiction   357
Putting things together   358
Treatment strategies   360
Social cures as means to beat addiction   365
Drug treatments to curb addictions   366
Summary   368

14 Major physical illnesses   **370**

Features of chronic illness   371
Quality of life   371
Adjustment to chronic illness   372
Appraising and coping with illness   375
Stigma   379
Self-perceptions   382
Summary   383

15 Dealing with illness   **384**

Recognizing illness symptoms and what needs to be done   385
Recognizing warnings and health risks   385
Illness perceptions and beliefs   386
Relation between the patient and the health provider   389
Obtaining medical care   400
Summary   404

16 Caregiving, death, and grief   **406**

Looking at end of life   407
Caregiving   408
The dying process   410
End-of-life care   413
Physician-assisted death   415
Loss and grieving   417
Summary   419

17   From molecules, to individuals, to communities, to policy   **420**

Integrating genetic, neurobiological, and psychosocial processes:
Eliminating silos   421
Translational research   422
Instigating policy change   426
Summary   429

References   430
Index   508

About the Author

Hymie Anisman received his PhD in 1972 (University of Waterloo), and has been a Professor at Carleton University, Ottawa, since that time, while also holding an adjunct appointment with the Institute of Mental Health Research (Royal Ottawa Hospital). Professor Anisman was a Senior Ontario Mental Health Research Fellow (1999–2006), is a Fellow of the Royal Society of Canada, and has held a Canada Research Chair in Neuroscience since 2001. The principle theme of his research has concerned the influence of stressors on neurochemical and neuroendocrine systems, and how these influence psychological (anxiety, depression) and physical (immune-related and neurodegenerative) disorders. His work has spanned animal models to assess stress-related pathology as well as studies in humans to assess stress, coping, and appraisal processes. In this regard, he has assessed the impact of chronic strain emanating from discrimination and stigmatization on well-being, depression, and PTSD among refugees from war-torn regions and among Aboriginal groups that suffered childhood traumatization, distress associated with abusive relationships and life transitions, as well as the transmission of trauma effects across generations. In addition to sitting on the editorial boards of several journals and on numerous grant panels, Professor Anisman has published more than 400 peer-reviewed journal papers and book chapters, as well as several review papers within neuroscience and psychology journals, and has edited two books, one dealing with stress processes and the second concerning psychoneuroimmunology. As well, he has published two books dealing with Stress and Health. One of these, published by SAGE, was meant as a textbook for university students, and the other was written for lay audiences. His research has been funded by the Canadian Institutes of Health Research (CIHR), The Natural Sciences and Engineering Research Council of Canada (NSERC), the Ontario Mental Health Foundation (OMHF), the Canadian Foundation for Innovation (CFI), and the Canada Research Chairs program (CRC).

Preface

'And all the king's soldiers and all the king's men couldn't put Humpty together again.' This simple children's rhyme dates back to the late eighteenth century, although in a somewhat different version from that of today's quatrain. There have been all sorts of interpretations of this rhyme, some with political and others with religious implications. This kid's rhyme can also offer lessons that are relevant for health psychology, although these aren't particularly profound. The last line essentially tells us that when things are badly broken, repairing them can be very difficult or even impossible. So, obviously, it's not a good idea to let either ourselves or Humpty get to that point. The very first lines tell us that it's also a bad idea to sit on dangerous ledge, especially if you have a round butt. Phrased somewhat differently, don't put yourself at risk needlessly. I don't mean to blame the victim, but Humpty obviously wasn't the smartest egg in the basket.

Sickness is something we all encounter, often on multiple occasions. Some illnesses just happen and we can't readily attribute their occurrence to any particular events, and nobody is to blame. Sometimes, bad things simply happen either because of particular genes that have been inherited, or events and factors that develop as a result of bad luck or fate. In other instances, our health can be undermined by factors that we're unaware of, and weren't inflicted on us with malevolent intent (e.g., widespread use of pesticides decades ago), although there are also instances in which we are placed in jeopardy owing to the willful behavior of others (manufacturers of cigarettes who, of course, claim that we had the choice to smoke or not to do so). There are other illnesses, such as bacterial or viral infections, that typically aren't attributable to the misbehaviors of others (although in some instances viral or bacterial carriers may not be taking precautions to preclude germs from being passed along), but some people might not be blameless as they hadn't taken precautionary measures (e.g., vaccination) to limit the chance of contracting the illness. Finally, there are a huge number of preventable illnesses that hit us owing to our own behaviors, including overeating, not exercising, drug use, or engaging in risky behaviors, much like Humpty did.

This book will focus on how psychological and behavioral processes can help individuals develop greater resilience so that they can overcome, or at least deal effectively, with various illnesses. There will be a focus on preventive measures that can be adopted so that the occurrence of illness will be limited. To be sure, we might not always be successful in preventing or overcoming every pathological condition through psychological and life-style changes, but at the least, stress can be diminished and quality of life can be enhanced.

To achieve these goals, the book is organized into sections, each comprising several chapters. The initial two chapters provide general background about health psychology and what it entails, as well as the methodological approaches that have been used in the field, together with several caveats regarding research issues that might be encountered. For some of the topics covered it is necessary to have a basic understanding of biological processes that feed into health and illness. Thus, Chapter 3 is meant as a primer relevant to genetic processes as well as various biological systems (neurotransmitter functioning in the brain, hormonal systems, immune processes, and microbiota) that are pertinent to health processes. Given that stressful experiences are fundamental to the provocation or exacerbation of so many illnesses, the next two chapters focus on stress-related processes, considering behavioral and cognitive mechanisms (Chapter 4) and neurobiological functioning (Chapter 5). This is followed by a discussion of still other factors that affect health outcomes (Chapter 6 and 7), including the adoption of healthy behaviors (e.g., prevention versus treatment) and life-style factors (exercise, diet, sleep). The ensuing six chapters get into nitty-gritty issues related to specific illnesses. These chapters focus on the promotion or advancement of heart disease, diabetes, immune-related illnesses, cancer, chronic pain, and addictions, which come about owing to genetic, experiential, and behavioral factors. In each of these chapters approaches to treatment are covered, including those of a medical and behavioral nature. Chapter 14 is concerned with chronic diseases, their consequences, and what to do about them. Chapter 15 provides a discussion concerning how to deal with illness, including doctor–patient relations. The impact of chronic illness on family members engaged in caregiving as well as factors related to the dying process, including the right to die, are covered in Chapter 16. Finally, Chapter 17 deals with the translation of research to practice and policy.

With this book come supplementary (electronic) materials. These include some recommended readings in the form of journal articles and websites that offer interesting information that is provided in excellent formats. As well, with so much happening on internet sites that involve video formats, for each chapter I've provided links that are relevant to that chapter. There may well be better videos available, but of those I've screened, these stood out as getting across the message I wanted. In some instances they have an interesting angle or a different spin on a standard topic, or they are particularly well crafted and entertaining, but in each case they have considerable teaching value.

Acknowledgments

I lucked-out over the years in having some terrific collaborators, particularly Zul Merali and Kim Matheson, who were instrumental in modifying the research approaches I adopted and the questions that were asked. There were many other colleagues and friends that I was fortunate to have worked with who directly influenced the material included in this book. Shawn Hayley Alfonso Abizaid, Barbara Woodside, Michael Hildebrand, Matt Hollahan, Natalina Salmaso, and John Stead were instrumental in affecting the research mentioned related to physiological processes; Alex Haslam, Cath Haslam, and Nyla Branscombe similarly influenced my perspectives concerning social psychological studies. My long-time friends Arun Ravindran and Owen Kelly were influential in affecting the approach used in covering issues related to treatment practices, and Aviva Freedman provided many insightful ideas.

I've also been lucky to have had many impressive graduate students and postdoctoral fellows who worked with me on this volume, often carrying the heavy load. I won't name them all (as I have elsewhere) as the list is fairly long. However, Marie-Claude Audet, Amy Bombay, Robyn McQuaid, Opal McInnis, and Rob Gabrys contributed directly to this book's formation, and together with Marc Bedard, Robbie Woods and Angela Paric were exceptionally kind in volunteering their time in proofing the manuscript and making suggestions for change. I also had the benefit of several wonderful undergraduate students, Kasia Szyskowics, Mary Sedrak, Hannah Robson, and Eloise Racine, who told me when the material was too light-weight, too complex, too boring, or simply unnecessary. I'm especially indebted to Jerzy Kulczycki and Marzena Sieczkos who have worked with me for about 20 years, taking care of my lab, and mentoring my students, and made it possible for all the good things that have happened.

Alex Haslam was instrumental in getting me to write this book, and my first editor at SAGE, Michael Carmichael, together with Keri Dickens, helped shape its direction. Luke Block, Katie Norton, and Imogen Roome continued supporting and facilitating its composition, as well as seeing that my life was made simple and free from headaches. I'm greatly indebted to them for their efforts in this book coming about. My own research over the years, and my approach in this book, couldn't have been done without the help and support of the Natural Science and Engineering Research Council of Canada, the Canadian Institute of Health Research, the Ontario Mental Health Foundation, the Canadian Foundation for Innovation, and the Canada Research Chairs program.

Finally, Simon, Rebecca, Jessica, Max and Maida, as well as Simon and Helen, have had a lot to do with the evolution of this product.

Companion Website

Health Psychology is supported by a wealth of online resources for both students and lecturers to aid study and support teaching, which are available at https://study.sagepub.com/anisman

For students:

- Watch author-selected **videos** to give you deeper insight into select concepts within Health Psychology, building on context to foster understanding and facilitate learning
- **Interactive quizzes** allow you to test your knowledge and give you feedback to help you prepare for assignments and exams
- Free access to **scholarly journal articles**, chosen to deepen your knowledge and reinforce your learning of key topics

For instructors:

- **Testbanks** containing questions related to the key concepts in each chapter can be downloaded and used in class, as homework or exams
- **PowerPoint slides** featuring figures and tables from the book, which can be downloaded and customized for use in your own presentations

1 Health Psychology Described

THE TYRANNY OF ILLNESS

All chronic illnesses are distressing, and each chronic illness has its own unique distressing characteristics. That might not sound as elegant as Tolstoy's Anna Karenina ("Happy families are all alike; every unhappy family is unhappy in its own way"), but it's just as true. Many illnesses aren't fatal (periodontal disease, skin problems, such as psoriasis and eczema), but can be socially embarrassing, undermining self-esteem and self-efficacy, and disrupting social and professional functioning. Other chronic conditions can be more physically devastating, and can take a significant toll on the emotional well-being of those affected as well as on their families. These conditions may be stable or they can be progressive (worsening in small steps, possibly with stable periods intervening between bouts). Initially individuals function properly on a day-to-day basis, though the individuals' abilities will become impaired as the disease worsens (e.g., arthritis, lupus erythematosus, Parkinson's disease, heart disease). Illnesses such as type 2 diabetes are deceptive; they might not initially have significant repercussions, even if they require marked life-style changes, but can have drastic repercussions in the development of other disorders. Still other illnesses are associated with brutal treatments, might lead to death (cancer, heart disease, HIV), are physically incapacitating (e.g., amyotrophic lateral sclerosis (ALS), paralysis, stroke), or might steal the individual's very core (Alzheimer's disease and other forms of dementia). As well, chronic conditions that involve psychological and cognitive functioning (depression, schizophrenia, addiction) are often accompanied by social stigma that can be as devastating as the illness itself, and have been associated with the development of several physical illnesses. Some illnesses (viral illnesses or bacterial infection) seemingly appear out of the blue ("one day I was well, and then, bam, I was sick") because some martyr decided it was OK to go to work while suffering flu symptoms. Other illnesses might develop, in part, because of our own unhealthy behaviors, or because of unfortunate accidental occurrences.

(Continued)

(Continued)

The cause, nature, and trajectories of illnesses differ appreciably, as do the needs of the affected person, which vary yet again over the course of the illness. These conditions differ in the degree to which a person is reliant on others and the extent to which they are able to use coping strategies to help them adjust to the illness and to deal with other negative life experiences that are encountered. What they have in common, however, is that they all influence the individual's quality of life, and to an extent they can all be influenced by psychosocial factors.

GETTING THERE FROM HERE

Many texts on health psychology begin with the fundamental question of "What is health psychology?" We'll get to that shortly, but before we do, it might be better to consider, however briefly, the general processes by which mental and physical health might come to be impaired, or conversely, what factors contribute to the maintenance of a high level of well-being. Once we get past this general framework, many complex issues that we'll be dealing with will make more sense and be easier to absorb. This chapter will:

- introduce several basic definitions and concepts related to health psychology
- consider key variables that influence or determine physical and psychological health
- introduce the idea that seemingly different illnesses can be related to one another, being determined by common neurobiological processes as well as the individuals' experiences and behaviors
- indicate that treatment of illnesses ought to consider individual difference factors and that personalized (individualized) treatments are necessary in the treatment of many illnesses.

DEALING WITH COORDINATED SYSTEMS

A holistic perspective

Each of the body's organs has its own specific functions, but directly or indirectly, they have the capacity to communicate with one another. Just as the left hand needs to know what the right hand is doing, the brain needs to know what the gut or the immune system is up to, and peripheral organs are also affected by what the brain does. There are multiple routes, or highways, through which this occurs. Our blood supply, which travels through every aspect of the body, carries assorted messages to the brain and other organs. Likewise, the peripheral nervous system, endocrine systems, immune processes, and even gut bacteria (microbiota) profoundly influence one another and also affect brain functioning. Thus, our general well-being, and the development of specific pathological conditions, might reflect the changes of multiple processes. This holistic perspective dictates that in adopting treatment strategies for various illnesses, it might not be sufficient simply to deal with the specific organ or system affected, but to take a broader perspective and treat multiple dimensions of the individual, including their psychological state. This doesn't mean that a heart or kidney problem can be cured by a brain manipulation, but it does imply that the physical illness can, one way or another, have psychological ramifications that influence general well-being and can hinder the effectiveness of treatments. Accordingly, treatment options should not be limited to treating the failing organ, as there may be advantages to also treating the psychological processes that are being assaulted. As we'll see, adopting this approach might not only have effects on the course of an illness, but will also influence the patient's treatment *compliance* (the individual's propensity to follow medical advice), and the course of recovery.

As we go through the successive sections of this book, the impact of various psychosocial and developmental influences on biological systems will be considered in relation to illness. This will not only include how psychological factors and physical illnesses are interwoven, but also how psychological treatments can be used to facilitate healing (or in some instances dying well). Throughout this book, it should be kept in mind that we're dealing with interconnected systems, even if this isn't expressed every time we cover a particular issue.

Multiple concurrent or sequential influences

Even if it seems as if an illness occurred suddenly, its insidious development may have resulted from poor health-related behaviors that had been adopted for a long time. Problems in regulating sugar (glucose) levels leading to type 2 diabetes as well as the build-up of plaque that contributes to heart disease may reflect the confluence of many inputs that evolved over decades. Even illnesses that appear among individuals *at risk* (e.g., those who are particularly vulnerable to a given pathology, possibly owing to genetic influences or early life experiences) may involve a second set of factors whose actions also develop with time. These can include the cumulative effects of exposure to *toxins* (naturally occurring substances produced in living organisms), *toxicants* (agents created or released into the environment, such as herbicides, insecticides, fungicides, rodenticides, and even food additives), the adoption of bad health behaviors, the use of certain drugs, or experiencing multiple or chronic life stressors.

Our well-being, as it turns out, is not only influenced by fairly recent events, such as those experienced in the last few weeks or months, but also events that happened years earlier. Indeed, early life experiences, whether good or bad, can have marked effects on the trajectory of neurobiological, behavioral, and emotional development, which might render people more or less vulnerable (or resilient) to a pathology that could potentially materialize years later. It's not just the early postnatal experiences that have such effects, and indeed, as we'll see, prenatal experiences (stemming from events mom encountered while pregnant) can have enduring postnatal consequences. In fact, intergenerational effects can come about owing to stressors or toxicants, so that we might be affected by our parents' experiences, and we, in turn, might pass these features on to our own children. Beyond these influences, community and government agencies may facilitate the establishment of particular social and educational services, promote health-related behaviors, or limit the presence of toxicants or other dangers. As much as we can all benefit from community actions geared toward healthy living, too often this is hindered by obstacles to progressive actions.

EVIDENCE-BASED PRACTICE

Besides examining what works in aiding well-being, we'll also consider some often used treatments that aren't particularly effective. This will include treatments that were developed with good intentions but failed to be effective, those that are outright scams (there are so many of these that we'll only touch on a few) and treatments that are based on beliefs, no matter how many people share them, that simply don't stand up to scientific analysis (e.g., which supplements or natural products are or aren't beneficial). *Evidence-based practice* refers to the enhancement of decision making and treatment stemming from rigorous research that meets the criteria for valid and reliable methodological consideration, and interpretation of findings based on equally rigorous criteria. This typically entails *quantitative analyses* in which hard data are obtained and examined with respect to how strong the effects actually are, given the number of participants or samples assessed and the variability within the data collected (Hjørland, 2011). In other instances, the approach might involve *qualitative analyses* in which narratives are obtained through participant interviews and specific themes are sought within these expositions. This approach may be a useful addition to quantitative measures, typically expanding on aspects that might not be picked up through the numbers alone (Denzin & Lincoln, 2005). As well, in certain instances, hard data might be virtually impossible to obtain, necessitating reliance on qualitative findings with the understanding that these can occasionally be misleading (e.g., making false assumptions regarding causality as in the case of researchers concluding that longevity among certain isolated groups is based solely on their diet), promote inappropriate generalizations, or might be frankly wrong.

WHAT DO WE MEAN WHEN WE SAY 'HEALTH PSYCHOLOGY'?

Health psychology defined

With this long preamble behind us, we're finally able to consider what health psychology is about. Teaching and research in psychology had traditionally focused on normal and abnormal behaviors, identifying the factors that lead to cognitive and emotional disorders, the neurobiological mechanisms responsible for them, as well as methods to attenuate the symptoms of psychological disorders. To an appreciable extent, the possibility that psychological factors could influence physical illnesses was largely overlooked at one time, and correspondingly little attention was devoted to the prospect that psychological interventions and treatments could be used in relation to physical illnesses. A shift in this regard evolved with reports that physical illnesses, such as heart disease, gastric ulcers, immune-related disorders, and diabetes, could be influenced by environmental and psychosocial triggers. This view was subsequently reinforced by findings that biological substrates associated with physical disorders, including gene actions related to neuro-biological processes, could be influenced by early life experiences and psychosocial processes. More than this, however, psychological techniques could be used to diminish symptoms of physical illnesses, and behavioral interventions could go a long way in precluding some diseases from ever appearing.

As these developments were unfolding, it also became apparent that the multiple silos that existed within behavioral and brain sciences (e.g., between psychiatry and neurology, as well as between social/developmental psychology and neuroscience) had hindered the identification of causes of illnesses and effective treatment strategies. Thus, increased efforts were made to integrate these disciplines, or at least to take down the silos that separated them. By its very nature, health psychology is a multidisciplinary field that incorporates information from varied aspects of the social and life sciences, and has been at the forefront in the development of research and treatment strategies that represent the conjoint influences of psychosocial (including psychological, behavioral, and cultural factors), neurobiological, and genetic factors in relation to varied physical illnesses. This field is now at an exceptionally exciting phase with the promise not only of explaining how psychosocial factors come to affect physical illnesses, but also in the development of psychologically-based treatment strategies to foster well-being and attenuate existent illnesses.

Psychological factors can directly or indirectly affect physical well-being. For instance, stressful events or being a chronic worrier can influence biological processes that promote heart disease, or affect life-style factors (sleeping, eating, drug use, smoking) that come to affect health. Although some health psychologists have focused on psychological factors in relation to health outcomes, others have been concerned with the impact of psychosocial, socioeconomic, neurobiological, and genetic factors, as well as prenatal and early life experiences, in determining well-being. By example, a researcher might ask whether a particular psychological event triggers hormonal changes, which then affects immune system functioning, and ultimately leads to illness. Alternatively, it may be of interest to determine why a particular event had varied effects across individuals. Were some people better at coping with stressors, did they have stronger biological systems, possibly because they inherited the right set of genes, or were they simply younger and thus more resilient? The point is that there may be many facets that link a given event and a particular pathology, and at the end of the day, research from various sources, using different approaches, might be necessary to identify these linkages.

Clinical health psychology

Having obtained the necessary information, clinical health psychologists might apply it to the development of therapeutic strategies aimed at diminishing physical illnesses or interventions to prevent or delay the occurrence of pathological conditions. The data may also be transmitted to health care providers and educators, and to Public Health agencies focusing on relations between psychosocial factors and health outcomes at a community or population level. In the latter regard, the research information might also be provided to policy makers and other government officials, so that recommendations can be made that apply to whole communities (e.g., benefits of exercise in relation to heart disease) or that target a subset of individuals who might be at risk. This not only includes those with pre-existing health conditions, older individuals, and pregnant women, but also individuals working in particular types of job that dispose individuals to pathology.

Behavioral medicine

Health psychology and behavioral medicine are often thought of interchangeably as both involve the integration of biological, behavioral, and medical sciences in the prediction and modification of illnesses. Behavioral medicine, as the term implies, is focused on *treatments of illness* using techniques that involve a biological and psychosocial approach, such as hypnosis, biofeedback, occupational therapy, and rehabilitation medicine (Matarazzo, 1980), rather than relying strictly on the standard medical model. For instance, disorders related to substance abuse, hypertension, heart disease, diabetes, pain reduction, insomnia, and obesity, all fall into a category in which the symptoms can be altered by behavioral adjustments. Aside from dealing with illnesses directly, behavioral medicine has similarly been concerned with the relationship between patient and doctor, treatment compliance, and has involved cognitive, behavioral, and psychodynamic approaches in remedying physical disturbances. Health psychology and behavioral medicine have, clearly, ventured into one another's waters, and ultimately, the difference between the two might be a matter of semantics, although behavioral medicine is more closely tied to medical disciplines.

PSYCHOSOMATIC ILLNESS

Development of psychosomatic illness

It had long been suspected that psychological processes, especially anxiety and stress, could cause physical illnesses to develop or worsen (e.g., lower back pain, migraine headache, irritable bowel syndrome) (Levenson, 2006). In general, *psychosomatic illnesses* fall into several categories, including those where (1) a mental illness and a medical illness are both present, and each negatively affects the other, (2) a psychiatric problem (e.g., depression, anxiety, post-traumatic stress disorder (PTSD)) develops as a result of a medical illness, such as cancer, or its treatment, and (3) a psychiatric disturbance is expressed through physical problems (e.g., pain), as in the case of bullied children and adolescents who might exhibit varied physical disturbances (Gini & Pozzoli, 2013).

Somatoform disorders

Somatoform disorders are physical illnesses that are solely provoked by psychological factors, and thus psychological treatments might be effective in ameliorating symptoms. Somatoform disorders can appear in several varieties, as described in Table 1.1. On occasion, an illness might be viewed as a somatoform disorder, only to be reconsidered and later viewed as a medical condition that can be exacerbated by psychological factors. It had at one time been thought that peptic ulcers were a consequence of stressful experiences, but it was later discovered that this condition was provoked by particular bacteria (*Helicobacter pylori*) (Marshall, 1990). As many people carrying the bacteria were actually ulcer-free, the view evolved that bacteria and mental factors (stressors) jointly contributed to ulcers. Similar confusion existed concerning whether psychological factors alone were responsible for *Irritable Bowel Syndrome* (IBS) or whether a combination of physical and psychological factors was at play in the development of this condition (Whitehead et al., 2002).

Table 1.1 Somataform disorders

Body dysmorphic disorder: individuals exhibit excessive and undue focus on a minor physical (or imaginary) flaw.

Somatization disorder: physical disturbances, such as headaches or gastrointestinal complaints, are expressed in the absence of a physical cause.

Hypochondriasis: individuals are obsessed with the possibility of developing or having a serious illness (e.g., being overly concerned that recent headaches are due to a brain tumor, or a sprained back muscle might be a symptom of lung cancer).

Conversion disorder: neurological symptoms (related to movement and senses), but in the absence of any known physical cause. In some cases the symptoms can be exceptionally marked and may even include blindness, paralysis, or seizures.

The presence of somatoform and psychosomatic disorders can cause enormous distress, which may be exacerbated when others believe that the person isn't actually ill, but instead is thought of as being highly neurotic. In some instances, this is compounded because of a lack of medical evidence supporting the presence of illness, although the failure to find signs of illness might reflect the poor sensitivity of the tests, rather than an issue related to the patient. With greater understanding of the biological processes that are responsible for pathological conditions, as well as how brain processes interact with peripheral mechanisms in promoting physical illnesses, diseases that were once seen as sketchy are increasingly being viewed as legitimate biologically-based illnesses (e.g., chronic fatigue syndrome).

A CONTINUUM BETWEEN WELLNESS AND ILLNESS

It is often assumed that being well and being ill lie on a continuum from absolutely great health to being dreadfully ill. From one perspective this might be how it is, as individuals can feel varying degrees of illness. Yet, an apparently healthy person can, unbeknownst to them, become progressively less healthy because their arteries are slowly becoming blocked, but physical symptoms don't appear until things have gone very far. Likewise, a person with cancer might be unaware of this until the tumor has grown to the point that it affects daily functioning. On the surface these people had been perfectly fine, but shortly thereafter they were at the other end of the continuum. Should this occur, their ability to contend with the situation may be influenced by their psychological, physical, and financial resources.

Becoming ill can act as a profound stressor that undermines an individual's self-reliance and sense of independence, shatters illusion of invulnerability, and frequently forces life-style changes to be adopted. It can also diminish the person's ability to work and to take care of dependents, cause financial problems, and in some instances the illness or its treatment may produce considerable pain. The distress associated with illness can lead to psychological disorders, such as depression, anxiety, and PTSD, and in some instances the multiple hardships endured, coupled with the individual's progressively diminishing capacities, may cause the formation of a new identity that comprises 'the sick person'. A major component of health psychology has been to develop and facilitate the implementation of strategies that prevent the erosion of good health, including the behavioral and emotional disturbances that can disrupt an individual's recovery from illness.

VULNERABILITY VERSUS RESILIENCE

Vulnerability to illness is usually taken to mean the susceptibility of an individual to develop certain psychological or physical disturbances in response to external or internal triggers. Most people will recognize that vulnerability to colds is increased when we are tuckered out, getting little sleep, eating poorly, and feeling stressed, so that immune functioning is compromised. Vulnerability to certain cancers or heart disease is also high if an individual happens to have certain genes, and this vulnerability can be still greater in the presence of particular environmental events.

Ordinarily, our biological systems might operate well and the risk of illness is low or moderate. However, when an excessive load is placed on the system, irrespective of whether this involves increased physical or psychological strain, a weak link in our armor may eventually give way, leaving us more likely to become ill. The specific illness that develops will be determined by the particular weaknesses that are present in any given individual. For one person it might have to do with a deficiency of a specific aspect of their immune system, for another it may involve a cardiovascular factor, or it might involve neurobiological processes responsible for psychological integrity (Anisman et al., 2008). Knowing that an individual is at high risk (vulnerable) to a particular illness could potentially be instrumental in helping that person devise behavioral strategies to diminish the odds of becoming ill. But, identifying the specific biological processes that make individuals vulnerable to an illness, or identifying which environmental triggers cause illnesses to occur in a subset of high-risk individuals, is one thing; getting individuals to change their behavioral methods to avert illness is another thing entirely.

Resilience is usually meant to reflect an individual's propensity to overcome an illness, although it can also be used to refer to the ability of an individual to withstand the effects of stressful events that would ordinarily lead to a pathological condition. Vulnerability and resilience are often mistakenly taken to sit at opposite ends of a continuum, but the absence of vulnerability doesn't necessarily mean that resilience reigns, any more than not having any financial debts make us rich. Individuals can have numerous attributes that make them resilient to all sorts of challenges, but there may be one simple feature that makes all the resilience in the world meaningless. An individual may have taken the best care of themselves and appear remarkably fit, but a brain aneurysm or a gene mutation that favors a cancer developing can erase all that's healthy about them. Conversely, an individual who is at risk for illness owing to the presence of certain genes or particular experiences, or a combination of the two, can in the presence of a supportive social relationship, or perhaps having religious beliefs that allows them to endure bad times, overcome some of the obstacles that would otherwise lead to illness.

What makes individuals resilient is both simple and exceptionally complex, as it may entail multiple factors that need to be brought together in precisely the right mix (see Figure 1.1). Some investigators have pointed to resilience as coming from the presence of neuronal processes that favor positive feelings as well as optimism, altruism, social bonding, adaptive social behaviors, and appropriate responses to fear-related situations (Charney, 2004). Resilience might also come from having a strong social identity, being positively connected to others, and having an effective social support network (C. Haslam et al., 2008; Jones et al., 2012). To this one can also add that resilience entails having a positive perspective on life, accepting change, maintaining control, spirituality, as well as particular cognitive abilities, such as being adaptable and flexible in response to changes (e.g., Belsky & Pluess, 2013; Rutter, 2013). Certain personality dimensions may likewise contribute to resilience, including high levels of self-esteem, self-efficacy, optimism, mastery, self-empowerment, hardiness, hope, and an internal locus of control. A constellation of other elements enter the resilience mix, including numerous genetic factors and having positive early life experiences (with enough mild stressors encountered to imbue us with hardiness) as well as our socioeconomic status (SES).

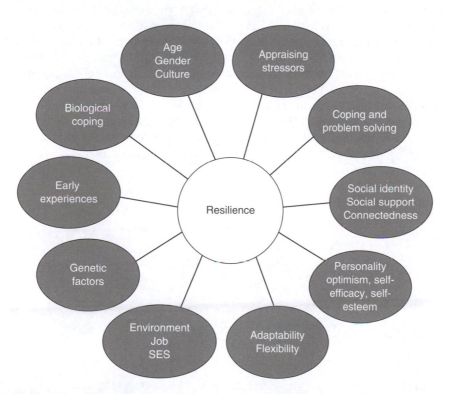

Figure 1.1   Our ability to deal with challenging experiences so that illness is either precluded or overcome may be related to a constellation of biological, environmental, experiential, and psychosocial factors. Shown in Figure 1.1 are a few of the many variables that affect resilience, each of which involves multiple components. By example, 'biological coping' may involve several hormones, neurotransmitters, growth factors, and immune elements, whereas personality dimension includes variables such as locus of control, self-empowerment, hardiness, and many others. Clearly, it is difficult to identify which variables are most important in accounting for the ability to withstand diverse challenges, especially as each may call on different resilience factors, be dependent on contextual factors, and can vary yet again across situations and over the lifespan. No doubt, the resilience factors listed may also interact with one another in promoting well-being.

ILLNESS COMORBIDITIES

It's bad enough to have developed a serious illness but, as depicted in Figure 1.2, many illnesses may be linked (*comorbid*) with one another so that when one particular illness occurs, it might be predictive of others developing. By example, depressive illness has been associated with the occurrence of diabetes, heart disease, various immune-related disorders, cancer, addictions, occurrence of head trauma and concussion, obesity, and even neurodegenerative disorders such as Alzheimer's and Parkinson's disease (Anisman et al., 2008). It might be thought that having one of these physical illnesses encourages depression, either because of the malaise experienced, or perhaps because individuals have been confronted by their own weaknesses or mortality. However, depression often precedes the physical illness, and thus it could be argued that the distress associated with being depressed may have led to one of these physical illnesses. It is equally possible that the antecedents of depression, which could entail stressful experiences, also provoked the physical disorders. Similarly, depression and a particular physical illness may share one or more common neurobiological mechanisms, so that when one illness appears it's more likely that another will also occur (Anisman et al., 2008). For instance, the presence of inflammation within the body, brought on by any number of factors, including stressful experiences, may encourage the development of both heart disease and depression (Frasure-Smith et al., 2009). Alternatively, comorbidities may evolve sequentially owing to multiple processes; inflammation may lead to metabolic syndrome, which then promotes diabetes, which favors the development of heart disease.

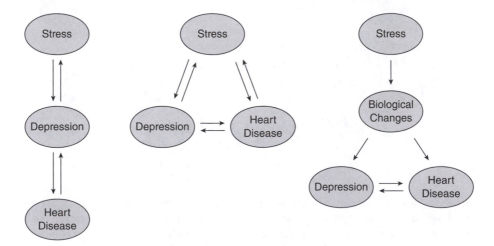

Figure 1.2   Different routes by which comorbid illness evolve. Stress could cause depression, which promotes heart disease, or conversely, the appearance of heart disease might promote depression. A second possibility is that stress causes both depression and heart disease, and both these conditions could influence one another. It is equally possible that stressful events promote particular biological disturbances that engender both illnesses, and these biological factors could serve as predictors (biomarkers) of subsequent illness.

The fact that illnesses are linked to one another has several important implications. If depression *causes* heart disease, then it would be of obvious benefit to quickly and efficiently treat the depression in an effort to preserve proper heart functioning. If, however, depression doesn't cause heart disease, but instead both are determined by some common factor, then we ought to treat the depression, but also determine what the common elements comprise, and on this basis adopt interventions to diminish the likelihood of heart disease developing. There's yet another important element related to comorbidities. Depression has been associated with a doubling (or even quadrupling) of heart-related disturbances (Halaris, 2009), and thus physicians ought to keep a watchful eye on patients who have been depressed, as it could serve as a warning (a marker) of problems that could lie ahead if life-style changes aren't undertaken.

BIOMARKERS OF ILLNESS

Wouldn't it be convenient if a computer-like read-out could be produced that could inform physicians of what illnesses their patients are apt to develop some time in the future? In this way, the physician might not only be prepared to treat them when symptoms first appeared, but might be able to encourage preventive steps so that the illness would never actually develop. If patients are informed that 'smoking causes cancer', it might not discourage their smoking simply because the concept doesn't trigger cognitions of 'personal risk'. Besides, it's fairly likely that the individual will have the misguided belief that 'it won't happen to me'. However, if this read-out flashed an alarm indicating that although the occurrence of lung cancer over a life time is on average 1 in 15, this particular person's likelihood of developing cancer is 20 times greater, and that it likely will happen fairly soon, their behavior would be more likely to change. Risk in this instance no longer refers to some ephemeral concept, but is based on the individual's own biological marks.

In fact, there are many read-outs based on behavioral and biological markers that can tell us how likely a person is to develop certain illnesses. For instance, particular genetic factors (or mutations) might be present that can act in this capacity, and the presence of specific biological constituents in blood (e.g., the presence of inflammatory factors) could be a biomarker for several illnesses. These biomarkers might not only be exceptionally useful in informing the individual (or their treating physician) about their vulnerability to illness, but may also inform the appropriate treatment strategies that would be most suitable.

HEALTH PSYCHOLOGY GLOBALLY

Changing patterns of illness

There are different ways one can evaluate the health of a population. We could simply determine how long people live on average, or how long people live without infirmities, or we might ask what percent of children die before a certain age (e.g., in the first year of life). But, no matter how it is sliced, there will be reasons to believe that the measure used isn't optimal. By example, people within two countries could appear to be equally healthy and thus should live equally long. But, in fact, the average life span is 10 years shorter in one than in the other. Simply knowing this, however, might tell us fairly little about what can be done to actually make things better, although it tells us that in the short-lived population there is room for enhancement, and might encourage the identification of the differences that exist between the groups that could account for the shorter life span. Among other things, one would want to know what specific illness conditions are most common. What feeds into these illnesses (e.g., environmental factors, viruses, life-styles, as well as food and water safety), and are certain individuals more likely to develop these illnesses? Once these and many other questions have been addressed, the information can be used to recommend and foster remedial actions.

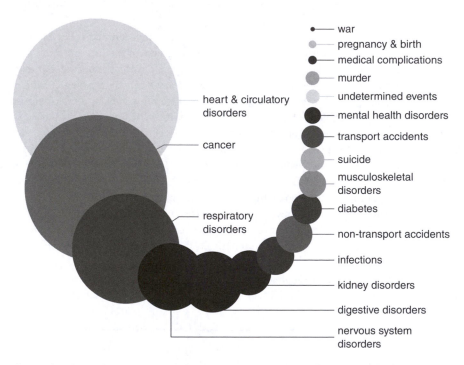

Leading cause of death in perspective

Figure 1.3   Within the UK heart diseases beat out cancer, respiratory illnesses, and infections, and actually account for more deaths than numerous other conditions combined. This same pattern is apparent within Europe and North America. However, the patterns of illness have been changing, particular in underdeveloped and newly developing countries.

Source: Britain's National Health Service, www.nhs.uk/Tools/Pages/NHSAtlasofrisk.aspx

Within the West the illnesses as well as the causes of death that are most common are fairly similar across countries. The main causes of death, depicted in Figure 1.3, vary appreciably with age. Under the age of 1 year, death is most often a result of congenital anomalies or premature birth, whereas between the ages of 1 and 44 unintentional accidents, homicides, and suicide are the main causes of death. With greater age, heart disease and cancer make up the greatest causes of death. The supplementary materials that come with this book show this breakdown in greater detail.

Global health

In an effort to assess how populations fare over time, studies are sometimes conducted to ask simple questions that comprise "What are the greatest causes of death (or disability), have these been changing over time, and what are the implications of this for policy changes at the local, national or international level?" One might also ask about the Global Burden of Disease (GBD), going beyond consideration of the greatest causes of death and disability, but taking into account the average duration of *disability-adjusted life years* (DALYs). This amounts to evaluating *years lost owing to premature mortality* (YLL), and also provides an index of the *years lived with disability* (YLD) (Murray, 1994). In addition, it is usually important to know whether the situation related to particular diseases is stable or changing over the years, and to identify the source of any changes. In underdeveloped countries where Westernization (or industrialization) has been occurring, one might expect that contagious illnesses would decline with better health care and the availability of vaccines, whereas illnesses related to factors such as obesity might be increasing owing to changing diets.

It is no easy matter to identify the sources of disabilities across regions or countries, categorizing these across various types of illness and accident, and to do so over many years. This obviously requires large numbers of participants and many researchers to collect, input, and analyze the data. However, such an '*epidemiological*' approach, as we'll see, provides important clues concerning what needs to be done to enhance quality of life and enhance longevity. An intensive investigation of this sort was conducted to assess a wide variety of diseases and injuries (291 of them) in 21 regions world-wide, and assessing the changes that occurred between 1990 and 2010/2013. This permitted fundamental global, national, and regional analyses of conditions such as HIV, tuberculosis, malaria, obesity, maternal mortality, and death early in life. Not surprisingly, health was elevated in wealthier nations (or geographically richer areas within Western nations) more than in poorer countries, including regions of Eastern, Central, and Western sub-Saharan Africa (e.g., Murray et al., 2014). Overall, the burden of diseases shifted away from premature death (among children under 5 years of age) and years lived with disability. As well, the impact of some diseases, particularly communicable diseases, declined in favor of non-communicable illnesses, although in sub-Saharan Africa, communicable diseases, as well as maternal, neonatal, and nutritional disorders, persisted as the most prominent causes of disease burden. Heart disease became the top ranked cause of death, followed by lower respiratory infections (even though its overall occurrence had declined), stroke, diarrheal diseases (despite a reduction by 51%), and HIV/AIDS. As well, mental illnesses, such as major depression, have been increasing, and it won't be long before they're within the top 5; indeed some researchers maintain that by 2020 it will be the number 1 burden of disease, surpassing heart disease. Likewise, musculoskeletal disorders and diabetes have been increasing markedly, and will certainly present a challenge in coming years. Given that most DALYs varied across regions, and the burden of disease changed with the passage of time, policy considerations and applied efforts need to be in step with these changes, focusing not only on diseases that are present and increasing in frequency, but also on those that are emerging.

MONEY DOESN'T BUY HAPPINESS, BUT IT KEEPS HUNGER FROM THE DOOR

The silly expression 'money doesn't buy happiness' gets under my skin. Pop authors write about it, pointing occasionally to the incidents of the spoiled children of the very rich who go through life abusing those around them, and sometimes even sinking into poverty because they're basically inept at everything other than spending the money made for them. There's also research showing that beyond some point, more wealth doesn't lead to greater happiness. I believe that on occasion, when the rich come face to face with poverty they use that expression to assuage their guilt, or they might do so to appease the poor. The poor say this as well, possibly to hold in check their envy or to rationalize their circumstances.

The American Psychological Association commissioned surveys to find out what stresses Americans (2014). Not surprisingly, financial worries topped the list. In the preceding month 72% of Americans had felt stressed about their financial state, of which 22% reported extreme stress, and the situation had gotten worse over the preceding 7 years. What's more, 75% of Americans believed that the stress they felt contributed to their feeling irritable, angry, anxious, demotivated, overwhelmed, tired, and depressed.

Of course, we've known for years that financial concerns are bad for our mental health, and poverty can also be a kiss of death, so to speak, in relation to physical health. For instance, within a major Canadian city, children born into the lowest income group (bottom 20%) had a life span 0–15 years shorter than those in the wealthiest 20%. In yet another city, infant death was doubled in the most financially deprived groups, obesity was similarly elevated, emergency department visits or physical problems increased by almost this amount, and mental health problems more than tripled. If this is the case in a Western country where all sorts of amenities are available, even to the poor, how much worse is it in third world countries? Ask these people if money would buy them happiness, or perhaps thwart sadness that might otherwise be present.

Figure 1.4 depicts the leading causes of death in the world according to the World Health Organization (WHO). In this instance, however, the causes, of death are sorted by low, medium, and high income countries. Heart disease, stroke, cancers, and chronic obstructive pulmonary disease (COPD) are the top causes of death in wealthy nations, but the shift in middle and low income countries is notable and has obvious implications for policies that need to be adopted. This said, even among Western countries there are huge disparities regarding health and causes of death in relation to socioeconomic status (SES). We'll see this repeatedly with many illnesses, likely stemming from the contribution of multiple factors, ranging from diet, exercise, education, and even access to medical help.

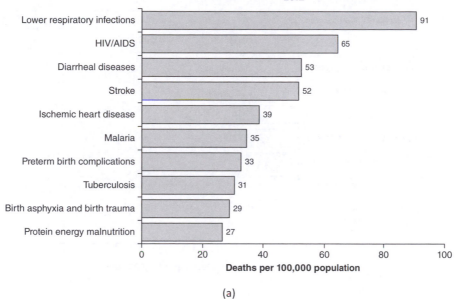

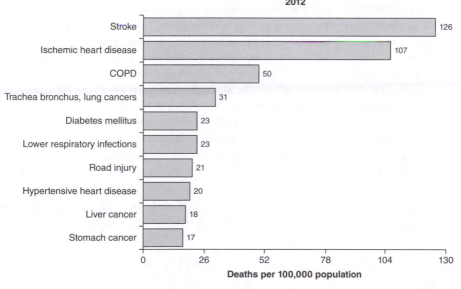

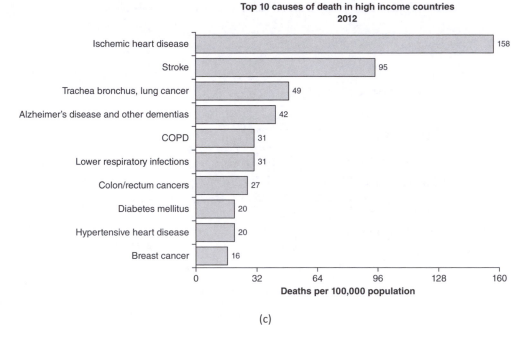

(c)

Figure 1.4   Causes of death vary as a function of a country's income. In low income countries (a) some of the causes of death hardly register on the scale of lethal factors in middle or high income countries, although all countries share stroke and heart disease as major causes of death. In poorer countries, diarrheal diseases, birth-related problems, and malnutrition rate high in causes of death (appearing on this top 10 chart), whereas cancers are more prevalent in richer countries. About 100 years ago the major health concerns and causes of death comprised infectious diseases, such as influenza, typhoid fever, cholera, and polio, in part because fewer people lived long enough to die of heart disease, cancer, or dementia. In the latter part of the twentieth century, however, noncommunicable diseases such as heart disease and cancer increased markedly, and diseases that had hardly been of major concern began to appear in great numbers (e.g., lupus erythematosus, rheumatoid arthritis, inflammatory bowel diseases multiple sclerosis, celiac disease, diabetes, Alzheimer's and Parkinson's disease). These illnesses have been appearing throughout the world, and noncommunicable diseases. Environmental poisons, as well as eating the wrong foods, lack of exercise, and other poor life-style choices (e.g., smoking), have likely been responsible for this shift. The threat of communicable diseases continues nonetheless and, as we'll see, there's reason to fear their return in more vicious forms.

Source: Reprinted from Fact Sheets, Fact Sheet 310, World Health Organization, The top 10 causes of death, page 2, copyright (2014), www.who.int/mediacentre/factsheets/fs310/en/, (accessed on: 21/07/2015)

The data presented in Figure 1.4 make it clear that diseases experienced are linked to the wealth of countries. But, there's a bit more to it than that. Life expectancy (determined in 2011) has been linked to how much each country spends on health programs. It's not surprising that the more money spent the longer the life span, with diminishing returns at the upper end of the curve.

Particularly interesting, however, are some of the anomalies that are present in Figure 1.4. Despite the huge spending of the US, the life span of its citizens are nowhere near the top of the curve. Likewise, Russia falls below a number of other countries that spend the same amount. There are also a group of countries near the top of the curve that spend moderately on health care, but have the longest living people. Does this have to do with their genes, the life-styles adopted, a healthier environment, or some other factors?

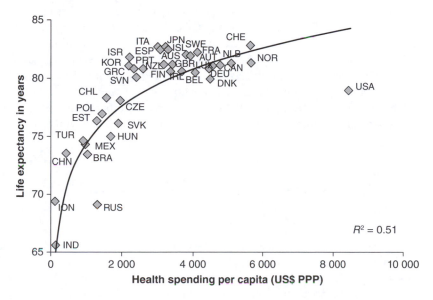

Figure 1.5   The relationship between health spending on a per capita basis and projected life span for children born in 2011.

Source: Organisation for Economic Co-operation and Development (OECD) (2013). *Health at a Glance 2013: OECD Indicators*. Paris: OECD Publishing. http://dx.doi.org/10.1787/health_glance-2013-en

Life span changes

With changes of health-related behaviors that have been widely adopted, together with improved regulations enacted concerning environmental toxicants and other risk factors, life span increased dramatically, accompanied by more years free from serious health problems (i.e., increased 'health-span'). According to the Centers for Disease Control and Prevention (CDC) (2015a, Life expectancy), within the US, a male and female child born in 1930 could have expected to live to 58.1 and 61.6 years, respectively. By 1950 this had increased to 65.6 and 71.7; a child born in 1990 could expect to live to 71.8 and 78.8, and in 2010 it was 76.2 and 81.1. These numbers vary across countries, so that life expectancy in EU countries is currently slightly longer than in the US, and in the former Soviet Bloc countries life span is a few years shorter. In many sub-Saharan African countries life span had increased appreciably over the years, but then dipped markedly beginning about 1990, largely due to HIV/AIDS, and life span in these countries still falls behind Western countries by almost 20–30 years.

Despite the decline of some illnesses, the picture isn't entirely rosy. Type 2 diabetes, for instance, has been increasing at an alarming rate in parallel with the 'obesity epidemic', although there have been indications that its growth has been leveling off (Danaei et al., 2011). There is also increasing concern regarding *emerging infectious illnesses*, such as West Nile virus, SARS, AIDS, Lyme disease, various forms of influenza, and Ebola virus, appearing and becoming progressively more threatening (Taylor et al., 2001). Some diseases that had been identified years earlier have suddenly cropped up in greater frequency and might pose a substantial threat. For example, one illness that appears somewhat like polio (but for the moment has been attributed to enterovirus D68) infected well over 1100 children in the US, and over 100 experienced paralysis (as of March, 2015), and the forecast for the coming year is murky. According to the National Institute of Allergy and Infectious Diseases (NIAID) and the Institute on Science for Global Policy (2015), we're also facing the threats of *re-emerging infections*, such as measles and drug-resistant tuberculosis, which had waned and are now reappearing. No doubt, drivers of this increased risk have included increased population size, increased urbanization, easier movement of people and commodities, coupled with the adoption of poor health behaviors.

CLIMATE CHANGE AND ILLNESS

The hazards of climate change have been broadly discussed, and regardless of whether or not it's occurring as a result of humans, even modest increases of temperature will have enormous repercussions. We primarily hear about changes in weather (polar vortices, typhoons/hurricanes, floods), leading to altered food supplies and crop failures, and diminished land mass as sea levels rise. Extreme weather also takes a toll on health, and deaths can be provoked when temperatures rise too high or fall too low. Curiously, we hear much less about the potential for climate change affecting the development and spread of particular diseases through our food and water as well as through insects, rodents, birds, and even large mammals, such as deer. As well, with increasing temperatures salmonella and other bacteria will have a greater opportunity to grow and will affect increasingly more of our food supply. We can also count on heavy rains causing overflow from sewage plants that can affect our water supplies, and animal feces in flooded areas will end up in rivers creating further contamination and the occurrence of several types of parasite (Karl et al., 2009). We've already been seeing an increase in diseases carried by insects, such as Lyme disease donated by ticks, and West Nile virus passed on by mosquitos. More recently, another mosquito-transmitted illness, chikungunya virus (which causes abrupt fever accompanied by severe joint pain, as well as muscle pain, headache, nausea, fatigue, and rash), has been moving northward and has reached North America, and we can probably count on more such illnesses following.

Technically, these illnesses aren't due to health behaviors being ignored, but they do fall into the class of preventable illnesses. Enacting appropriate preventive measures in a community or even in a country can be difficult, and it will obviously take much more to derail global warming.

ENCOURAGING BEHAVIORAL CHANGE

Health psychology has been involved in the development of strategies to encourage behavioral change, which can be fundamental in preventing the onset of illnesses (e.g., finding ways to get people to stop smoking is obviously a better strategy than trying to treat lung cancer after it has developed). It has also been involved in developing methods to facilitate adherence to recommended treatments or behavioral styles (e.g., ensuring that diabetic individuals maintain healthy life-styles, including proper sleep, eating and exercise, and having them remember to take their medications). Encouraging behavioral change involves more than just telling smokers not to smoke or those who are overweight not to eat certain foods. Changing well-entrenched behaviors is difficult, and there have been misinformed strategies adopted to do so using simplistic solutions (e.g., reminding gambling addicts through pop-up messages on slot machines "don't bet beyond your limits") that, at best, have only transient positive effects, if any at all.

In order to have people maintain appropriate life-styles, health psychologists have tried to understand why so many people engage in irrational behaviors that are clearly not in their best interests. Why, despite all the warnings, do people smoke, fail to be vaccinated when a flu pandemic is about to hit, or continue to engage in unprotected sex? Knowing the reasons for these counterproductive behaviors may be a first step in the development of strategies that will lead to behavioral change. In some instances, problems arise almost entirely owing to unique characteristics of the individual and thus treatments necessarily focus on this person. In other cases, problems might have arisen because people hadn't recognized, or minimized, the risk of their behaviors (those who come from the 1960s era were less aware of the dangers of alcohol and tobacco relative to individuals today; conversely, those born later in the twentieth century may be unaware of how dreadful measles can be). Thus, as a starting point, treatment and intervention strategies require education and effective communication in an effort to circumvent the multiple barriers that might limit the adoption of good health practices.

VACCINE HESITANCY

There can hardly be a soul that isn't aware that vaccines have made us safe from diseases that rampaged across the world in earlier times. In most parts of the world polio is no longer the threat that it had once been, smallpox and diphtheria are largely gone, and measles, mumps, and rubella have been relatively rare in Western countries (Roush et al., 2007), although in poor countries measles killed almost 150,000 people and a still greater number were disabled in some manner. Interestingly, some vaccines, such as that for influenza, may have yet another benefit in that they may act against heart disease, particularly among high-risk patients (Udell et al., 2013). Still, lack of knowledge and

(Continued)

(Continued)

false information that had been published in scientific journals (and since retracted) and fueled by the media, have led some individuals to believe that vaccination (or ingredients of vaccines, such as thimerosal, which acts as a preservative) could be dangerous to children and might be a key factor for the development of autism. Well-meaning parents have opted to agree with actors or politicians rather than physicians and scientists, and have chosen not to have their children vaccinated against diseases in the fear that they may actually be causing them harm. It's puzzling that actors would be chosen as their trusted source of information, as it's unlikely that they learned much about medicine or health while at acting school. Besides, should we even believe that there's sincerity in what they're saying? They are, after all, actors! It seems that even if "Gwyneth Paltrow is wrong about everything" (Caulfield, 2015), people are able to identify with her as she embodies what some people would like to be like, and thus are more apt to believe what she says.

Of course, this doesn't explain why people have become progressively less trusting of scientists, or why messages from scientists might have lost their luster. Perhaps scientists have been sending the wrong message, or are getting tangled up in the weeds and don't transmit their messages properly. It's equally possible that frequent inconsistent findings reported by scientists or increasingly more common article retractions have undermined trust in scientists. It's more likely, however, that people might be willing to trust scientists, provided that these people don't have preconceived notions regarding specific issues, and thus choose to listen to others who share their misguided beliefs (confirmation bias). People often come into situations with a wide range of biases that encourage certain positions being adopted and others rejected, and attempting to change these characteristics amounts to rowing into the current. In fact, providing them with the straight goods – namely scientific evidence that vaccines aren't dangerous – may backfire, making people stronger in their resolve to avoid vaccination (Nyhan et al., 2014). This difficulty is compounded by the fact that like many people, they may be overly confident concerning their own knowledge, and even underestimate what they don't know (Mannes & Moore, 2013).

It probably should be acknowledged that there may be several factors that foster vaccine hesitancy, and not all individuals behave as they do for the same reasons. Among some people, vaccine hesitancy might not be based on rational processes, as reflected by erratic behaviors in which individuals agree to one type of vaccination, but not another. In other instances, individuals might want to take control of their own lives, but this autonomy ought to mean becoming properly informed and doing the right things. At the same time, as people become more informed, they may also become less trusting or confident concerning establishment pronouncements, and might thus become more readily influenced by ideas outside the norm, including opinions that go against vaccination (Larson et al., 2015). Perhaps no amount of coaxing, cajoling, shaming, or threats will turn the tide on strong opinions. The person probably best equipped to get parents to have their kids vaccinated is their pediatrician. In this regard, the pediatrician is more likely to obtain a positive response if the request is phrased purposefully ("Well, we have to do some shots") than when it is presented as an uncertain choice ("What do you want to do about those shots?"). At the end of the day, it is difficult to push parents to vaccinate their kids, and hopefully there will be self-corrections that will lead to appropriate behaviors being adopted. Legislation by governments might work in this regard, but it could be argued that the better approach might be to adopt the position of "Don't push the river: It flows by itself."

Changing patterns of health delivery: Curing health care systems

The effectiveness of health care systems is not just influenced by doctors, nurses, and other health professionals who are at the front line delivering services to those in need, but also by policy makers who have considerable influence on how services are distributed and provided. Health delivery is not simply a matter of building more and larger medical facilities, but determining the specific needs of the population, and then making sure that the resources are available to meet these needs. If the population is aging, then more resources will be needed to deal with diseases of aging, and if infectious diseases have been rampant, then resources to limit spread of infection and to provide vaccines will be necessary. Likewise, training programs will be required so that expert staff are available, and this would have to be initiated years before the actual needs were present.

Policy makers have been instrumental in making use of information that dictates how health services should be delivered. This might mean creating small clinics in rural areas as well as in cities, in an effort to relieve the burden on emergency services. Likewise, home care delivery might be required to diminish the use of hospital beds for noncritical issues. However, there's much more to policy changes than simply determining how health services are delivered. For a long time, for instance, cancer treatments were moving forward inexorably slowly and the frequency of these illnesses was not declining. Several observant medical scientists realized that environmental factors were having a profound effect on the emergence of some cancers and thus increasing efforts, not without some resistance, were made to promote interventions (rather than simply relying on treatments once illnesses had developed) to curb behaviors that were self-injurious. For this to have occurred, scientific data were required that could inform policy makers what was needed to prevent the occurrence of illness. Having obtained the relevant data, large-scale community-based campaigns could be undertaken to convince people to behave responsibly, such as getting people to stop smoking or sitting in the sun to get a gorgeous tan, and to adopt positive health behaviors such as eating the right foods and exercising. Such programs have saved individuals from the distress of illness and the tyranny of invasive treatments.

Medical acceptance

Despite the silos that long separated various health disciplines from one another, it eventually became clear that psychological factors could affect the development of some physical illnesses, as well as the course of illness recovery. It also became apparent that in many respects patients would do better when treatment of their physical health was accompanied by treatments that preserved their psychological well-being. Thus, a fundamental role of health psychology has been to develop behavioral strategies that limit the course of an illness or prevent it from happening at all. Of course, psychological changes might be relatively ineffective in moderating some illnesses, but even in these cases an individual's general well-being can be influenced by interventions that facilitate effective coping (Melamed, 1995). The inclusion of health psychologists on treatment teams that focus on complex, serious illnesses was reinforced by reports that patients who received relevant counseling were more satisfied with treatment, more likely to follow the instructions given regarding what to do following treatment, and their well-being was enhanced accordingly.

Focus on the patient

Adopting novel policies and practices have been successful, to a degree, but too often have failed to consider the desires of the patients themselves. Not only is patient satisfaction enhanced when they have a say over their treatments, but in some instances their health may improve as well (Mergl et al., 2011). At the very least, it allows them to feel as if they have control over their destiny as opposed to having to adopt the role of the sick, helpless victim. Thus, as we'll see later in more detail, there has been increasing emphasis on the patient and doctor making treatment decisions together. This alliance can also be useful in encouraging patient compliance with treatments, or to discourage them from engaging in wacky therapies offered by charlatans.

In the case of complex illnesses that involve difficult and lengthy procedures, whole teams of specialists treat the patient. Treatment of diabetes might include a family physician and an endocrinologist, as well as a dietician. Likewise, treatment for cancer may include an oncologist, surgeon, pain specialist, nurse, social worker, and psychologist. Many physicians acknowledge the importance of psychosocial factors in facilitating recovery from some illnesses or simply in coping with them, but the infiltration of these views into medical treatments wasn't rapid. A systematic review of interventions within hospital settings concluded that although much is still uncertain about the best practices to adopt, quality of care is enhanced when a collaborative approach is adopted that involves multidisciplinary teams, and when the unique requirements of each patient are recognized (Conry et al., 2012).

Positive outcomes have also been seen when programs are explicitly established to prepare patients for imminent surgery and focusing on strategies to facilitate recuperation following surgery. Whereas decades ago patients were often largely unaware of what was in store for them, they now are informed about what to expect following surgery so that they feel more in control of their lives, are plagued less by uncertainty, and they don't always have to be on the alert thinking "is this pain normal?" As well, owing to the high frequency of re-hospitalization, there has been a marked increase of transitional care programs, both prior to and following release from hospital (e.g., Stamp et al., 2014). Once more, health psychologists play an important role in demonstrating how psychological interventions and treatments can diminish negative effects associated with illness, enhance quality of life, and facilitate recuperation from illness.

INCLUDING BIOPSYCHOSOCIAL PERSPECTIVES OF ILLNESS

Multiple biological processes underlying pathology

Whether we're dealing with psychological or physical illnesses, disturbed biological processes of one sort or another are involved. Illnesses can develop owing to certain cells not doing their job efficiently, as in the case of pancreatic beta cell malfunctioning leading to diabetes, runaway growth of certain cells culminating in cancer, or immune cells messing up and turning on the self to promote an autoimmune disorder. In each instance a series of changes may have occurred that caused biological processes to behave in ways they shouldn't, culminating in pathology.

Unfortunately, tracking the processes that promote these cellular disturbances and then finding remedies is difficult, especially as multiple factors typically come together to promote illness. We can approach the problem at many levels of analyses. The behavior of cells can be assessed (e.g., How do pancreatic beta cells respond in the presence of particular treatments?), or we can go deeper into cells to assess how activation of receptors influence the *intracellular* (within the cell) processes that eventually affect illness. We can also consider how different brain systems (networks) come into play in determining psychological processes that eventually affect illnesses involving peripheral organs.

Implications for treatment

In many instances we know about the cascade of biological changes responsible for a particular pathology, and although we can dampen the symptoms of the illness or even hinder its progression, we might not be able to actually exact a cure. Simply diminishing symptoms obviously isn't the preferred outcome, but failing the availability of an actual cure, being able to limit symptoms, and perhaps causing a pause in illness progression can be a fairly good result. For the patient experiencing intractable pain, simply eliminating this pain is a blessing, and later the mechanisms involved in producing the pain can be considered. Although this might be a reasonable outcome, at least in the short run, continued treatments may have their own negative side effects and thus better remedies need to be established.

How we view the processes that govern the appearance of illness may have a lot to say concerning how it is treated. If we view an illness as being solely of physiological origin, then we can expect that its treatment would be based on a standard medical model (e.g., through drug treatment or surgery). In contrast, if psychological factors were also seen as affecting the sickness process, then psychological intervention or treatment strategies might be adopted as well. As effective as this might be during early phases of an illness, once it was fully developed, psychological factors might be less relevant in its curtailment. By example, if heart disease were promoted by stressful events or eating unhealthy foods, then training people to diminish their stressor appraisals or to use effective coping methods, as well as to eat proper foods, might have a positive effect on illness progression. However, if the illness has been well entrenched, say in the form of blood vessels being extensively blocked, changes of life-style might delay further damage, but might be less likely to undo the damage already created.

SUMMARY

Identifying the sources of illnesses could potentially lead to ways of limiting health disorders and providing optimal treatment strategies. We've known for years that negative early life experiences, poor diet during development, substandard education, poverty, and its cousin social inequality, limit well-being, but the struggle to produce changes in this regard has moved in baby steps. Curiously, we often look to poor countries as being particularly victimized by poverty and inequality, but it isn't necessary to go so far afield when it's plentiful in our own back yard.

Health psychology focuses on how our behaviors and life-styles can affect well-being, and how to promote behavioral change that can produce positive outcomes. It's fine to encourage change of health-related behaviors, but much more will be needed in the mid- and long term, especially as the factors that affect our health and well-being are broad and involve multiple tiers of society, business, and government. Our health is not only affected by the behaviors in which we, as individuals, engage, but also by the multiple environmental disturbances that come about simply based on population size, the behaviors of large groups of people, and by industry. Often, unfortunately, we have the attitude of "so what if I conserve and recycle, there are so many others, including whole countries that aren't doing their bit, and my little drop in the sea won't go far." At an individual level the attitude might be that "I'm so far overweight that losing 10 kg won't make much of a difference" or "I've been smoking so many years, and the damage is already done, so why quit now?" This counterfactual thinking obviously is a bad first step to behavior change. When the problems go beyond the behavior of any one individual and requires new ways for communities to behave, engendering change is certainly more difficult.

LUCY SPEAKS

There is a Peanuts cartoon in which Lucy threatens Linus with a fist, saying "These five fingers . . . individually, they're nothing. But when I curl them together like this into a single unit, they form a weapon that is terrible to behold!"

Linus quickly surrenders and then addressing his fingers says "Why can't you guys get organized like that?"

In the context of organized efforts to enhance health, we might ask the same question that Linus does.

2 Methodological Approaches in Health Psychology

SO MANY WAYS TO BE RIGHT AND SO MANY TO BE WRONG

A misguided scientist (yes, they do exist) trains a common house fly through instrumental conditioning to jump on command. "Jump, fly!" he says, and it cooperates and does so. He then callously removes its two front legs and again repeats "jump fly!", and it does, although with some difficulty. He removes the next two legs and once again the fly, with still more difficulty, obeys the command. Finally, after removing the last two legs and saying "jump, fly!" the fly lays there, unmoving. The scientist concludes in his log book "removing all six legs from a fly causes it to become deaf".

He could repeat this procedure countless times and it would always lead to the same outcome. The finding is reliable! However, the conclusion is not necessarily valid. Whereas a valid finding ought to provide reliable results, reliable results aren't always valid.

LINKAGES TO ILLNESS

In assessing the link between any number of factors and the presence or emergence of pathology, a variety of approaches can be adopted. Some links to pathology have been made through animal experimentation as the nature of the necessary procedures is too intrusive to be conducted in humans. This said, some of the distressing events endured by humans can't be conducted in animals for ethical reasons. Animal studies have an additional advantage over human studies as they allow for the manipulation of genes (e.g., through selective breeding or by genetic engineering comprising the deletion or insertion of genes) that can be linked, alone or in combination with other genes or environmental events, to particular pathological outcomes.

Studies in humans vary widely in the approaches that are adopted, with many evaluating correlations between events, whereas others assess the changes induced by particular treatments.

These studies often differ in the specific questions being addressed. In one instance, the focus of the research might be to determine the relationship between an event (e.g., early experiences) and an outcome (e.g., emergence of diabetes), and whether this relationship varies in the presence of other variables, such as personality factors. A second investigation might similarly focus on whether a relationship exists between events and particular illnesses, but the primary objective might be to identify specific biological substrates (e.g., genetics, hormonal factors) associated with the pathology. Still other experimental questions are of a more causal nature, asking whether particular manipulations can ameliorate pathology, and whether this occurs selectively in some people (based on genetic factors present) or in unique circumstances. While most studies are highly informative, they can't possibly address all the questions that need to be answered. Science is a dynamic process that involves the accumulation of various bits of data in the hope that these can be integrated (or disentangled) to provide a cohesive story. With the systematic appraisals of many studies, a relatively accurate picture can be deduced concerning the processes responsible for a particular disease condition. This chapter is intended to provide:

- a broad overview of research methods in animals and humans
- a distillation of the value of animal studies in relation to human disturbances
- an overview of varied experimental and correlation methods in health-related research
- warnings about problems that can be encountered in conducting and evaluating research.

RESEARCH USING ANIMAL MODELS

Working across species

Researchers working with animals to determine the processes leading to a disease and its treatment want their animal models to be valid indices of what occurs in humans. It is often thought that animals higher on the phylogenetic scale (evolutionary tree), such as monkeys, are better approximations of humans than are rodents. This may be correct in many instances, but other species are considered to be appropriate models of human conditions. Considerable congruity exists across species with respect to organs associated with diseases and some of the processes that lead to pathological outcomes, and as much as 98% of the human genome is conserved in mice. It is relevant, as well, that the simplicity of neurobiological systems in some species, such as planaria (flat worms), permits observations to be made that aren't readily achieved in more complex species. Thus, health-related research can often get by through evaluating lower species, such as rodents, provided that they prescribe to several basic assumptions to assure the validity of their model. Validity in this context refers to a scientist actually measuring or modeling what they think they're measuring or modeling (Anisman & Matheson, 2005).

Validity of animal models of illness

Assessing human disorders through animal models can be done at several levels of analysis from molecules, the single cell, cell–cell interactions, and system interactions. For an animal model to be considered a valid reflection of a human condition, several fundamental criteria ought to be met, although as we'll see, in some situations this isn't possible. It ought to go without saying that animals should be well maintained and free of distressing experiences. This is obviously necessary for ethical reasons, but also because discomfort experienced may change animal behavior, vulnerability to pathology, as well as responses to treatments that should ameliorate illness. With this as a fundamental caveat, Table 2.1 provides the criteria necessary to model human disturbances (Anisman & Matheson, 2005).

Table 2.1 Criteria for valid animal models of human illness

- the symptoms of a human disorder ought to be recapitulated in the animal model
- treatments that ameliorate symptoms in humans ought to do so in the animal model
- treatments that are ineffective in humans should be ineffective in animals
- manipulations that promote or exacerbate symptoms in humans should also have these actions in the animal model
- the presumed mechanisms underlying a disorder ought to operate in this capacity in both species.

Caveats concerning animal models of human illness

In some research projects that are attempting to model a disorder in humans, all the criteria can't be met. Take the case of autism, in which we don't know what mechanisms are responsible for the illness, nor do we know how to treat the disorder. As a result, it's difficult to develop a valid model and consequently animal research that could potentially be relevant might be held back. Indeed, this is the case for most pathological conditions; when researchers first start out to assess pathologies in animals there is likely to be insufficient information available to assure that the model is valid. Still, if the many characteristics of the animal are consistent with the established criteria, it's possible that the model will provisionally be acceptable. Understandably, conclusions in these circumstances are limited, but as further research is conducted the usefulness of the model system will be either rejected or accepted.

In attempting to model human psychiatric disorders, such as depression or schizophrenia, some of the symptoms in humans can be recapitulated in animals, but we can't model the syndrome as a whole. For instance, what does a very sad mouse look like, or how will we know that a mouse has experienced a hallucination? Yet, these limitations don't preclude the possibility of evaluating other symptoms that characterize the disorders and identifying possible biological processes that lead to illnesses. Despite impressive efforts to develop valid and precise animal models, there isn't a guarantee that the behaviors in the model actually reflect a valid index of the human illness. In a sense, this is reminiscent of a jury trial in which a defendant is found to be 'not guilty', but this doesn't necessarily mean that the defendant is actually innocent.

Research based on studies in animals has gone a long way in identifying causes of some disease states and defining treatments to manage or eliminate them. At the same time, we shouldn't fool ourselves into thinking that these studies are free of problems. Failures to replicate results are not uncommon, sometimes because of subtle differences in procedures. Even using methods as identical as they can possibly be, effects can differ across laboratories, and mice obtained from different sources can also yield very different results (Wahlsten et al., 2006).

A research commentary published not long ago (Begley & Ellis, 2012) reported on multiple failures to replicate a very large number of preclinical studies dealing with cancer therapies. The studies were selected for examination because they appeared to be of sufficient merit to become the target of future research to develop cancer treatments. There are so many variables that can affect research outcomes and one would reasonably expect some failures to replicate earlier findings, but they reported that only 11% (6 of 53 studies) could be repeated successfully. A similar study coming from the Bayer laboratories examining cancer models likewise indicated that only 25% of the studies assessed could be validated to the extent that they could justify further research with these models (Prinz et al., 2011). Failure to replicate findings could occur because the originally reported studies were tainted or the data were fabricated, the most positive findings were selectively reported, small numbers of animals were used so that the reliability was diminished, or seemingly small differences in the procedures between studies led to divergent outcomes.

CONSIDERATIONS CONCERNING THE VALIDITY OF ANIMAL MODELS OF PATHOLOGY

The European Commission workshop that focused on the use of animals in medical research concluded that despite the positive attributes of animal-based research, greater synergy needs to be developed between basic science researchers and clinicians. In this regard, considerable attention was devoted to the frequent failures to repeat earlier findings successfully. It was suggested that:

- More opportunities be provided for the publication of negative results. In fact, preclinical studies ought to be reported irrespective of outcomes, so long as the study was conducted in a scientifically rigorous manner. Typically, only positive findings are published in scientific journals, and as a result one could mistakenly conclude, based on a few positive outcomes with a given treatment, that a cure is at hand, when in actuality there have been many failures to attain a positive effect, but these go unpublished. This obviously doesn't only apply to studies in animals, as the very same problems are inherent in human studies.

- In published papers, links should be made to journal articles in which findings differ from those initially reported, especially those considered 'landmark' studies.

- Opportunities should be created for trainees, technicians, and colleagues to discuss troubling or unethical behaviors, and possibly to report these without the fear of negative consequences to them.

- Dialogue between physicians, scientists, patient advocates, and patients should be encouraged, as scientists will benefit from learning about clinical reality, and physicians ought to have an understanding of the challenges and limitations of preclinical studies. Both will certainly gain from the concerns expressed by patients, as this could influence whether or not patients will adhere to treatment protocols that are offered.

RESEARCH IN HUMANS: EXPERIMENTAL STUDIES

Randomized control trial (RCT)

A *randomized control trial* (RCT) is one in which participants are randomly assigned to groups, one of which receives an experimental treatment, whereas the second is similarly treated but is given a control treatment that ought to have little, if any, effect on its own. In clinical trials of drug treatments, irrespective of the illness that is being treated, participants in one condition will receive the active drug, and those in the other will receive a placebo (an inert chemical that ought to have no effect, although, as we'll see later, placebos can have very profound consequences). In other studies where a novel compound is being tested, the control condition may entail a previously used drug that has positive effects, thereby permitting researchers to determine whether the new compound yields better outcomes or fewer negative side effects. In these instances, it is preferable that a double-blind procedure is used so that neither the experimenter nor the participant is aware of which treatment was received (of course, to avoid biases, having the participants and experimenters naïve as to the treatment condition is also preferable in studies that do not involve drug treatments). Once the effectiveness of a treatment is determined in double-blind studies, later experiments might address other questions (e.g., assessing optimal doses or side effects), and an open label trial may be used in which patients and the clinicians know what was administered. The assumption in each case is that if some treatment is applied that leads to particular outcomes, then a *causal* connection may exist between the two.

Table 2.2   Clinical trials

In the development of new drugs, medical devices or gene therapies, a series of steps is necessary before they can go to market for use in humans.

Preclinical studies. These studies are conducted in animals to determine the safety of the treatments and the range of doses that are appropriate. The preclinical experiments also evaluate toxicity, side effects, adverse outcomes, and *pharmacodynamics* (what effect the drug has on the body and brain, including its carcinogenic effects and potential actions on reproduction).

Phase I. A small number (10–15) of human test participants receive a low dose of the drug to determine its safety, the optimal route of administration (e.g., pill or injection), impact on the body (pharmacokinetics), and what the body does to the drug (pharmacodynamics), including drug absorption, distribution, metabolism, and excretion.

(Continued)

Table 2.2   (Continued)

Phase II. The effectiveness of the treatment is assessed and the safety of the drug at various doses is monitored in a moderate number of participants (20–80), and side effects are documented. Side effects can be common or occur in a very select number of individuals, or might only appear with chronic use, and in some instances might not appear for years. In essence, there are limits to what Phase II trials can determine.

Phase III. The effectiveness and safety of the treatment is assessed using relatively large sets of participants (1,000–3,000), and are tested at several centers. In this phase the drug can be compared to other commonly used treatments. Does it have faster action, greater positive effects, and fewer negative consequences? Double-blind clinical trials allow for unbiased evaluations of drug efficacy and the occurrence of undesirable side effects.

Phase IV. Once the drug is on the market it continues to be assessed (post-marketing studies) to identify potential long-term effects, including benefits and risks. In some instances adverse effects might only be detected at this phase, leading to box (or black box) warnings indicating that the drug carries serious risks for adverse events, or the drug may be withdrawn from the market.

Factorial designs

The questions that need to be answered are often more complex than just whether one treatment is superior to another. For example, are the observed effects more effective in males than in females, or do they vary with any of a large set of experiences, such as earlier trauma, life-style factors, the availability of social support, or the presence of a particular gene mutation? In such studies, for example, a given treatment or a control manipulation can be administered to participants, some of whom are males and other females, and of these individuals a portion will have encountered particular experiences, whereas others won't have. Thus, multiple variables can be considered within an experimental design to determine whether these variables have additive effects or whether one variable acts synergistically (multiplicatively) or antagonistically with other variables. In some instances, it might be desirable to evaluate participants at various times relative to a given treatment. This can be done by testing independent groups at these times, or testing the same participants repeatedly over some preset times (this is usually referred to as a within-subject or repeated measures design). Usually, there are a limited number of factors that can or should be studied at any one time, not only because the experiments can become too large and unwieldy, but also because in some situations, the data obtained might become too complex to be interpretable.

Quasi-experimental design

In some instances a quasi-experimental design is used, which is essentially the same as a more usual RCT, except that participants aren't randomly assigned to groups, but instead are assigned to conditions on the basis of particular characteristics (e.g., being at low versus high risk for an illness). Several types of quasi-experimental design can be used (Trochim & Donnelly, 2007), the most common being one in which participants with a particular condition or characteristic are tested before and after a treatment (or no treatment) is administered, and evaluations are made as to whether pretest and post measures differ as a function of the treatment. A second quasi-experimental design might have participants assigned to one condition or another based on pretest scores on some variables. For instance, the experimenter might want to evaluate the effectiveness of a cardiac medication or a social intervention based on pretest scores that indicate whether participants have high or low levels of a particular hormone. This might simply be done on the basis of some cut-off measure so that those showing scores above the mean are assigned to one group and those below the mean are assigned to the second group. You'll recognize that this isn't all that satisfactory given that two individuals who differ slightly on a specific dimension might end up being assigned to groups as if one were in a high-risk category and the other not. As we'll see shortly, in many cases, there are better methods of doing this.

Retrospective analyses

Investigators might wish to determine the antecedent events or experiences that were related to some people developing an illness. To this end, a simple approach comprises a *retrospective* study, in which past experiences are recorded based on the individual's recall or in response to specific questions, and then relating these to their current state or illness. By example, a researcher interested in whether stressful experiences were linked to breast cancer might ask a group of women in treatment (or those in remission) and women without any illness about the stressors they had previously encountered. If they find a relation between the presence of breast cancer and reports of previously encountered stressors, it doesn't imply that one event caused the other, but the researchers might believe that they're on the right track in uncovering the root of breast cancer.

No doubt you'll recognize that the linkage between events and outcomes in this case are tenuous. Can we really trust that people have accurate memories of the past? They most certainly don't, as we know from the studies conducted to unveil false memory syndrome, which was a scourge for so many families when therapists, through subtle suggestions, were able to alter an individual's recall of events (Loftus, 2005). Indeed, any number of factors can alter recall or perceptions of the past, and the individual's current illness might bias their perspectives of the past. Some patients may look for a source for their illness, something to blame it on (good people, after all, shouldn't suddenly get ill. Should they?), whereas others might be generally negative as a result of their illness and thus may see the past through this dark lens. Clearly, when individuals are asked about previous events, their recall or perceptions might not be an accurate reflection of what had actually occurred. To overcome such problems, researchers might ask about more recent events that might be linked to disease, such as those that occurred in the past 2 or 5 years and have someone else, such as a family member, confirm that these negative events actually occurred. Aside from the fact that these memories may also be tainted, the events of the past 2 years may be relevant to some illness, such as depressive disorders, but they might be less likely to contribute to other illnesses, such as cancer, in which the first tumor cells may have appeared many years earlier.

Longitudinal and cross-sectional studies

An approach superior to retrospective analyses is the longitudinal (*prospective*) analysis. Here again, the question of interest might be whether a given experience (e.g., maintaining a particular life-style, being in an abusive relationship, or receiving a treatment to diminish diabetic risk factors) is linked to the emergence of particular illnesses or changes of illnesses with the passage of time. In prospective studies, participants are tracked for some time, periodically assessing whether and to what extent particular changes have developed and subsequently determining whether these events were linked to the later development of illness.

The prospective study can involve a large number of participants in whom assessments are made as to whether certain variables are more or less likely, alone or in unique combinations, to be related to pathology. Alternatively, one can focus on individuals who do or do not have certain characteristics or experiences (e.g., the presence of particular risk factors), and then assess the subsequent development of a disease. In studies where certain experiences of interest are uncommon, targeting these individuals is necessary in order to have a large enough sample to provide meaningful results. As ideal as these approaches are, it can take many years before answers are obtained, and it is not unusual to have a high *attrition* (drop-out) rate as participants may have moved location, or simply found that participating had become a chore. Moreover, it is possible that drop-outs will result in the sample being one that is biased (e.g., those participants who are ill may be most likely to drop out).

The alternative to the longitudinal study is the cross-sectional design in which independent sets of participants of interest are obtained at various times after a particular experience (e.g., either soon afterward, 1, 5, 10, or 20 years later) and compared to individuals who had not experienced these events. Obviously, attrition will be diminished, but the data obtained may not be as precise as in the longitudinal study since differences between groups might not simply be due to changes that occur over time, but instead reflect the impact of the previous event of interest having occurred at various 'historical times'. The social stigma associated with being gay 20 years ago was likely to be different than it was 5 years ago, and thus differentially related to later illness development.

REGRESSION APPROACHES

Simple correlational studies

A common methodology used in both human and animal studies is to determine whether two factors are related, often as a first step in identifying complex interactions that exist between many variables. Initially, the questions asked are seemingly straightforward, such as "Is poverty or exposure to environmental pollutants early in life related to the subsequent appearance of a physical pathology, such as heart disease?" or "Are certain diets related to the appearance of diabetes?" However, the appearance of a given illness may be related to multiple factors. For instance, heart disease might be related to the presence of particular genes, but the relationship might be stronger among individuals who have also encountered chronic stressful experiences, have particular personality traits, adopted specific diets, or experienced mood disorders. Thus, more complex correlational analyses can be conducted that consider multiple factors.

Table 2.3   Correlation versus causation

It might be observed, for instance, that poor self-esteem and depression are highly correlated. This finding, as informative as it might be, doesn't mean that they are 'causally' related. Even if there were a causal connection between the two, it is often difficult to determine its directionality. In essence, is it that impoverished self-esteem caused depression or that depression caused disturbed self-esteem, or is there a third factor, such as stressful experiences, that promoted both negative self-esteem and depression? Despite every researcher knowing this, we sometimes fall into the trap of expressing causal connections between events simply because we believe that they ought to occur this way. This said, there are conditions in which the accumulation of evidence might lead us to conclude a causal relationship between correlational data (e.g., the link between smoking and lung cancer). Hill (1965) offered a series of recommendations regarding how seriously a causal connection should be considered based on correlational data, although at the end of the day none of these can assure that causal relations actually do exist.

1. **Strength**: A small correlation between variables does not imply a causal connection, but neither does it imply that a causal effect is not present. As the association between the two increases, so does the likelihood of a causal relation.

2. **Consistency**: Replicable findings across situations and by different investigators make it more likely that the effects observed are genuine.

3. **Specificity**: Causation might be considered if a relationship appears with a disease in a specific population at a specific site, provided that no other likely explanation is available. In essence, the more specific the link between a particular factor and an outcome, the more likely it is that this connection is causal.

4. **Temporality**: The presumed cause must precede the outcome (e.g., viral exposure must precede illness symptoms). In some instances, a delay may be expected between the two and this should occur in a well-defined manner.

5. **Biological gradient**: Most often, a gradient should exist so that greater exposure should promote greater outcomes. There are instances, however, in which the relationship is not linear so that any amount of exposure leads to an outcome. In other instances, the relationship is an inverse one, or one that is quadratic (U- or inverse U-shaped).

6. **Plausibility**: Being able to hypothesize, in advance, a plausible mechanism between cause and outcome adds strength to the causal inference.

7. **Coherence**: When the data are consistent under controlled laboratory conditions and those collected in the field, the likelihood of a causal relationship is enhanced.

8. **Analogy**: Similar factors ought to be related to comparable outcomes.

9. **Experiment**: Ultimately, experiments need to be conducted in which the presumed causal factors are manipulated and outcomes assessed.

Multiple correlations, cluster analysis, and hierarchical regression analysis

In assessing the relationships between an illness, antecedent experiences, and biological factors, a *correlation matrix* would be created to determine which of many variables are linked to one another.

It might be discovered that several factors are related to the presence of the illness, and thus further statistical methods, such as *cluster analysis*, would be conducted to determine whether several variables, as a group (*cluster*), might be more predictive of (more highly related to) pathology than knowing about only one factor. Likewise, one could conduct *hierarchical regression analyses* to determine whether several variables have additive (or interactive) value in predicting an outcome variable. In essence, this type of analysis tells us whether knowledge concerning a second or third variable provides predictive power above and beyond that of a single variable.

Moderating effects

The relationship between two variables can be influenced (*moderated*) by another variable. By example, in a study of cardiovascular illness it might be predicted that diet would be linked to heart disease, but this relationship might depend upon whether or not individuals had been chronically stressed. In this instance, an experimenter might choose to determine the average (mean or median) stress experienced by participants, and then assign those individuals who scored above the mean to one group and those below the mean to the other. As indicated earlier, this is intuitively unsatisfactory, as two individuals who differed by a slight amount (around the mean) could end up in different groups ('stressed' versus the 'non-stressed' condition). Hierarchical regression analysis gets around this problem as the moderating influence of the stressor is considered using the whole range of stressor scores. Thus, in the example we've been using it can be determined whether the relationship between diet and exercise is consistent irrespective of stressor experiences or whether stressor encounters of varying degrees were accompanied by changing relationships between diet and heart disease. In effect, moderation assesses *under what conditions* the relationship between two variables occurs (see Figure 2.1).

Mediated effects

There are occasions on which researchers might suspect that the correlation between two variables is *mediated* by a third variable. Once more, let's turn to the case of a correlation between stressful events and the later development of heart disease. The researcher might suspect that stressful events are related to heart disease that develops later in life and that this was in some way linked (mediated) to inflammatory processes that were elevated in the presence of stressors. If this were the case, then if we 'statistically controlled' for the influence of inflammatory processes (in a sense, eliminating the contribution of inflammatory factors from the equation), the correlation between stressful events and subsequent heart disease ought to disappear or be reduced. In contrast, if inflammatory factors were irrelevant, then the correlation between stressful experiences and heart disease would be unaffected when we controlled for inflammatory factors (Preacher & Hayes, 2008). Thus, if a variable mediates the relationship between two other variables, there is a better understanding of *how that correlation occurs*. Finding a mediated effect doesn't necessarily mean that these variables are causally related to one another, but it might prompt experimental studies to assess whether these factors were causal agents for the illness.

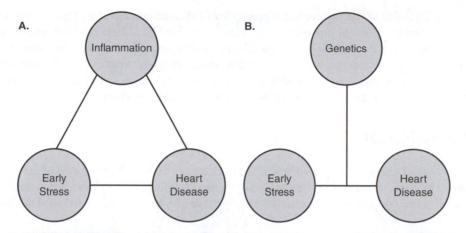

Figure 2.1 Mediated and moderated models. Early stressful experiences (e.g., neglect or abuse) might be correlated with increased risk for heart disease developing many years later. If it is believed, as depicted in A (left-hand portrait), that this occurs through a process that involves activation of the immune system (inflammation), then an analysis can be conducted to determine whether the correlation between stress and heart disease is altered when controlling for inflammation. If this relation declines, then we can assume that the link between early stress and heart disease occurred through inflammation, whereas no change of the correlation would suggest that the link between stress and heart disease is a direct one. The right-hand side of the figure (B) provides a model in which the relation between early stress and heart disease is 'moderated' by a genetic factor. This means that the link between the variables is strong when a particular genetic factor is present, but not when other genetic conditions prevail.

Moderated mediations

We can go still further with regression analyses to determine whether several variables act as mediators of a particular outcome, as well as whether a given mediated effect is evident only under certain conditions. For instance, is the mediated effect we just discussed regarding stress, inflammation, and heart disease always present or does it occur in males and not females (or vice versa) or in the presence of particular genes? These *moderated mediations* once again do not imply causal connections between variables, but they can be very important in predicting the characteristics of individuals who are most likely to exhibit vulnerability to illness, or conversely characteristics of individuals who might be most helped by certain treatments.

Structural equation modeling

Mediated and moderated models, as we've discussed them, are fairly simple (although it might not sound that way), but sometimes questions that need to be asked can become an order of magnitude more complex. The researcher might, for instance, believe that a sequence of events, occurring in parallel or in series, is related to particular outcomes. By example, it might be expected that in the presence of certain genes, stressful early-life experiences may be associated with a negative personality style that is accompanied by a propensity to alienate other people. This, in turn, might be associated with less social support being obtained from friends, and increased occurrence of an illness. In this instance a sequence of mediated (and moderated) relations might be expected, and the paths through which events are related are determined through *structural equation modeling*. As this sequence of events was described it sounded very causal, but once more, this analytical tool only tells us about patterns of correlations and not causal connections.

EPIDEMIOLOGY

Epidemiological research focuses on how often diseases occur in different groups of people, and possibly why these diseases occur (Porta, 2014). With this information in hand, strategies can be developed to limit or prevent illness as well as help those who have already developed the illness.

CHANGING TIMES, CHANGING APPROACHES

Epidemiology has a remarkably exciting history, so much so that small snippets of this history have appeared as books and movies. Like so many other medically related issues, attributes of epidemiology date back to Hippocrates. His analyses of diseases led him to distinguish those that were 'epidemics' being 'visited upon' a population and those that were 'endemic', essentially being present within the population without external input being needed to sustain it.

More recent history saw John Snow, a British physician, tracking down the cause of cholera epidemics by demonstrating disease clusters within select parts of London, originating from water supplied by the Southwark Company. He was thus able to end the epidemic by removing the pump handles (where water was contaminated) and adding chlorine to water. Others like Snow, including Ignaz Semmelweis, had much to do with reducing mortality. In the mid-1800s Puerperal fever (a fever that occurred following childbirth or miscarriage owing to infection of female reproductive organs brought about by unhygienic medical staff or by medical equipment that hadn't been cleaned) was common, and fatal in somewhere between 10–15% of cases. In 1847 Semmelweis successfully reduced this rate simply by instituting the practice of washing with chlorinated lime solutions. This wasn't popular (How dare he suggest that the hands of doctors needed washing?) and was often ignored, but with the discovery of antiseptics by Lister in 1865, the practice returned in full force. Semmelweis became progressively more depressed as he fought his battles with institutionalized medicine of the times, and was forced into a medical asylum where he was beaten by guards after trying to leave, and died two weeks afterward owing to either internal injuries or gangrene brought on by the beatings.

Later pioneers in epidemiology included figures such as Ronald Ross, who won the Nobel prize for the suggestion that malaria was brought about by a greyish mosquito (a bit of controversy occurred as some felt that Giovanni Battista Grassi deserved half the prize). Janet Elizabeth Lane-Claypon made her mark by, among other things, being involved in the development of cohort studies and case-control studies, and Anderson Gray McKendrick was involved in the development of mathematical methods in epidemiology. Sir Richard Doll and Austin Bradford Hill together made the connection between cigarette smoking and lung cancer.

Today, many arrows have appeared in the epidemiologists' quiver as they work collaboratively with experts in related fields. These comprised the possibility of identifying biomarkers present within an individual, sampled in blood or saliva or specific tissues, which can tell us whether individuals are at risk for particular illnesses. What is critically important from these biomarker approaches is to recognize that a great deal of individual variability exists regarding illnesses and vulnerability to them. Indeed, 'the unique disease principle' proposes that the development of a disease state across individuals may comprise processes that differ from one individual to the next (Ogino et al., 2012, 2013), and thus treatments for diseases need to be individualized. In an effort to deal with today's scientific reality, a subfield of epidemiology evolved, now termed molecular pathological epidemiology (MPE), which focuses on analyses of the multiple molecular processes related to individual differences associated with pathology, including interactions between genetic factors, as well as changes of gene expression in response to environmental influences (Spitz et al., 2012).

Epidemiological questions and approaches

Research linking genetic factors, experiences, and environmental factors to illnesses can be conducted within the general population, or within *target populations* who are already at risk (e.g., older individuals if the investigator were interested in heart disease, women if the focus were on autoimmune disorders, or different amounts of cigarette smoking if the topic of interest were lung and other cancers). In addition to identifying the key factors that are associated with people becoming ill, medical epidemiological studies can determine whether particular relations are widespread or unique to a particular region or country. Epidemiological analyses may also involve monitoring (*surveillance*) of time trends to determine which diseases are waning and which are increasing, so that proper policy decisions can be made regarding population health strategies. Unlike studies conducted within laboratory settings, epidemiological studies are based on what happens within natural settings (*in situ*), and as a result, the ability to control what variables influence specific situations is lost. At the same time, by being able to assess events *in situ*, it becomes possible to evaluate the interactive effects of several variables and to discern how these play out over time. In considering the benefits of one approach over another, it's good to keep in mind the general rule of thumb that 'relevance is inversely related to rigor' and the researchers get to choose their poison.

Epidemiological data related to health may come in a variety of different forms, such as the frequency of mortality, morbidity (incidence or prevalence of a disease), disability, birth defects or childhood deaths, or use of hospital or care services. The epidemiologist might assess the *prevalence* of an illness, which is an index of how many people within a fixed number are affected (e.g., 200 of 1,000 people are affected, so the prevalence is 20%). Alternatively (or in addition), there might be an interest in the *incidence* of a disease, which refers to either the number of new cases that appear within a given population or the number of new cases that occur over a set period of time. The term '*risk*' refers to a combination of the two, defined as the frequency of illness in a set population over a predetermined period of time.

Case control studies

Several methods can be used to identify the factors that might have resulted in a particular disease. *Case control studies* compare those individuals with a particular illness to those who do not with the objective of identifying the factors (e.g., experiences, toxicant exposure, genetic factors) responsible for individuals becoming ill (Forgues, 2012). The data obtained in this instance will tell us the *odds* that a particular factor may have made one group more likely to become ill, while not discounting the role of the many other factors that could have influenced the development of pathology.

Cohort studies

A second common method comprises *cohort studies* in which sets of individuals who are thought to be similar in most respects, but differ on particular dimensions (e.g., life-styles), are followed for an extended period to determine whether they differ with respect to the development of specific illnesses. Given the multiple factors that affect people, appreciable variability can be expected in outcomes, and so to obtain meaningful data a large number of individuals need to be assessed. As well, these studies may be undermined by some of the same factors that negatively affected case control studies. Despite such limitations, cohort research has uncovered the sources for a variety of illnesses and has warned us of emerging diseases.

PROGRAM EVALUATION

In an ideal research world it would be possible to evaluate the influence of given variables on specific outcome measures across multiple venues. However, field studies often encounter problems where this can't readily be done. For instance, one might want to evaluate whether particular health programs are effective (e.g., a team approach versus individual doctors), and whether they differ across different segments of the population. However, assessing the relative merits of the team versus single physician approach might be confounded if the doctors in the single physician approach differ on some dimension from doctors included in the team approach. As well, it might be that team treatments are conducted in one hospital, whereas the single doctor approach is delivered in a second hospital. So, not everything in the two groups is identical, and the influences of specific doctors and specific hospitals are confounded with other factors. There isn't much choice in some situations and experimenters have to make do with what they have. They can try to repeat the studies in several hospitals using several doctors, but in the end, the data won't be as clean as one would like. Nevertheless, analyses can be conducted based on common outcome variables in which strict quantitative analyses aren't fully relied upon. Given the limitations, program evaluations might rely on *focus groups* (opinions obtained from small collectives under each condition), detailed interviews, or other qualitative approaches. It's not the perfect solution, but in some instances it simply has to do.

DATA SYNTHESIS

Meta-analyses

With the proliferation of research it became progressively more difficult to synthesize the data obtained, especially as in some instances the research didn't yield the same findings or conclusions. Studies often differed in significant ways that could contribute to such disparities. Furthermore, in some studies the number of participants were fairly small (20 or 30 respondents), but in others the sample might have been very large, often reaching several thousand. Do we place the same value on studies irrespective of size?

Meta-analyses have become an increasingly popular way of reviewing and organizing large swaths of research. This entails a statistical procedure in which the outcomes of multiple studies are considered, not simply on the basis of whether a particular effect was provoked by a given treatment, but on the basis of the *effect size* in each study (i.e., the strength of associations that exist between variables), as well as the number of participants in that study. In this way, an estimate can be obtained regarding how meaningful the results are, what can be expected under various sets of conditions, and what key variables might act as mediating or moderating factors that could affect outcomes (Walker et al., 2008).

In conducting meta-analyses, investigators will specify the criteria used for including or excluding particular studies (e.g., those that involved prospective approaches might be included and those that used retrospective analyses excluded). As investigators might use different criteria for including studies in their analyses, the conclusions derived can also differ. Although it might be tempting to accept the conclusions of meta-analyses at face value, the outcomes of such analyses are only as good as the studies included and the specific variables considered.

Systematic reviews

Papers that review literature in a particular field to account for factors responsible for disease states are meant to provide other researchers with an up-to-date appraisal of the published work in a field and/or to integrate large chunks of research into particular frameworks. *Systematic reviews* have become more common, incorporating data based on a strict set of criteria (Harden et al., 2004). These analyses follow rigorous guidelines concerning which questions should be addressed, how to frame the question, identifying the relevant work that should be included or excluded, and how to assess the quality of the research considered in the review (Khan et al., 2003). If the information can be obtained through quantitative analyses, then that's certainly desirable, but analyses can also rely on qualitative studies in which data are derived from an analysis of individual narratives. For instance, in describing certain situations or events, predetermined questionnaires might not ask 'the right questions', and often what individuals say, when given the opportunity, adds considerable insight into issues. As well, systematic reviews might look into methodological considerations of studies, and it is not unusual to have separate raters make these evaluations. The weight placed on various studies is thus determined by the perceived goodness of the studies. The popularity of these reviews is seen from the breadth of issues that have been covered, including clinical treatments for just about any illness one could think of, social and public health interventions, the adverse effects of various treatments, the economic factors associated with treatments (or lack of treatments), and cost–benefit analyses related to the risks associated with particular treatments relative to the consequences of not treating (Petticrew & Roberts, 2006).

CAVEATS ON METHODOLOGY

Caveats associated with simple experimental designs

We've already mentioned several important issues that need to be considered in any scientific research study. These included the need for controlling experimental conditions, and the importance of considering different cultures and both sexes in research and treatment options (as we'll see in later chapters). The importance of random assignment to different conditions is of obvious importance, but once again, it is important to appreciate that in some instances it may be difficult to recruit participants who represent random segments of the population. For instance, if questionnaires were mailed out about sexually-transmitted diseases or drug-related problems, one might find that those with such problems might be reluctant to participate. Likewise, in an experiment in which participants are recruited to examine the impact of earlier psychological or physical abuse in relation to later illness, individuals who had experienced abuse previously and have volunteered for the study may be a select set of individuals who are actually willing to reveal their abusive experience. It's unlikely that they represent all people who were in abusive situations, and indeed, it's possible that their responses might differ from those who were more reticent to volunteer, possibly because their experiences were more traumatic (Hernán et al., 2004).

Similar issues might affect other types of experiments, including those that examine the effectiveness of drug remedies for particular illnesses. Researchers might have obtained patients to assess the effectiveness of a new drug therapy in the treatment of depressive disorders. The patients may have been carefully selected so that other illnesses were not present and no other drugs were on board, and then assigned to either the drug or a placebo condition, matched on the basis of factors such as age and gender, and all sorts of other important variables. But, we would still need to ask who these patients were, given that a large portion of depressed individuals fail to seek help. Indeed, those who do come forward as volunteers might be the most motivated to get better, the least affected by the stigma associated with mental illness, or perhaps not as ill as others. Thus, conclusions derived from these studies need to be considered cautiously.

Power issues

The *power* of a test refers to the ability to detect a statistically significant difference between groups, given the variability present between participants within each condition, and the number of participants in the samples. Thus, if we know how great the variability is likely to be (based on our own previous research), then we can calculate the number of participants that will likely be needed in the study to detect an effect of a particular size. Ordinarily, studies with a small number of participants might lack the power to detect significant effects (Cohen, 1988). Thus, there are instances where non-significant effects are observed and investigators conclude that the treatment in question actually had little effect when, in fact, the power they had was simply insufficient to detect potential treatment differences that might have existed. Conversely, investigators might have conducted studies with only a small number of participants, but observed significant outcomes that might not actually be reliable. As we've seen, one investigator might report a significant group difference based on an experiment with a small number of participants, but other studies using a larger number of participants might fail to detect this difference. Which study results are we to accept? Having a larger number of participants doesn't necessarily make the study a better one or more valid, but, other things being equal, the study with the larger number of participants will win out.

Understanding variability

In any experiment, the performance of participants within a particular group will differ from one another, and the difference observed is referred to as *variability*. Some of this variability may have to do with the characteristics of the procedures themselves, and even the behaviors of the experimenter may contribute to the variability observed. Obviously, in any experiment we try to limit extraneous sources of variance to the extent that this is possible. However, we can only be so effective in doing this.

Aside from variance attributable to the procedures used, characteristics of the participants, their genes, previous experiences, and any number of other individual differences could influence variability. Thus, experimenters seeing the variability, and provisionally identifying factors that contribute to this, might conduct further studies to determine whether particular experimental conditions have effects that are unique to some individuals. Experimenters may also take note as to whether comparable variability appeared in each of the groups, or whether it occurred to a greater extent in experimental groups. The latter outcome could occur simply because as scores go up, so does the range of scores. But, once again, it could mean that our treatment has effects only on some people or only some of the time, and so we might entertain another experiment to identify why only some participants show a particular outcome. For example, does an anti-cancer or antidepressant medication only have positive effects among individuals with a certain genotype? Alternatively, does the effectiveness of a treatment to stop smoking vary as a function of impulsivity, according to the extent of cravings, or as the reason for people being motivated to change? Whatever the case, the variability observed may provide important hints as to 'next steps' in conducting research.

SUMMARY

There are many routes that can be taken to get from point A to point B, and often there are multiple means of transportation that can be used. Typically, we'd like to take the trip through the shortest and fastest route, preferably sitting in the most comfortable seats. This is exactly the case with respect to health-related research. As much as we'd like to get answers quickly, this isn't always possible. We might not be able to get from A to B directly, and instead have to board 'puddle-jumpers' that make many stops on route, and there isn't a first-class section on the plane.

Numerous approaches have been developed to link particular factors and the development of pathological conditions as well as the best treatment options to deal with these conditions. Some are based on animal studies (e.g., preclinical studies) that lead to experimental human trials of varying sizes and complexities; others comprise correlational studies that determine whether simple (or complex) relations exist between variables. Some studies comprise investigations that can be completed fairly quickly, whereas others are detailed and lengthy prospective studies, involving a large number of participants, conducted over many years. Our knee-jerk response is to assume that the latter studies have more value and validity than do smaller and less intensive studies, but it doesn't always work this way. The best evidence of a study's value is, of course, whether an original finding can be successfully replicated, although failures in this regard could occur owing to numerous legitimate reasons. With so many studies having been conducted, often with variable results, meta-analyses and systematic reviews are fundamental in the integration of multiple data sets so that a perspective can be reached as to what effects particular treatments have and whether these always (or usually) occur, or are present only under particular conditions.

3 Biological Systems and Functioning

OTHER WORLDLY

There are lots of things that I'd like to know, but that I don't have the capacity to understand or the opportunity to look into. There are also things that would be nice to know, but as I don't actually need to know these things, I don't dwell on them. When I would say to my dog "We'll save this tasty treat for tomorrow", did she know what I meant and think "Tomorrow! I want it now". I assume she had the capacity to understand the concept of the future as she would hide things (from the sneaky cat) for later retrieval, but I don't think this would stand up to scientific scrutiny. I'm also puzzled by natural selection. I don't question evolution; I just don't get some aspects of it. I'm OK with the giraffes and long necks part, it's what came before that which puzzles me, especially the part about the development of internal organs and systems. For us to stay alive all of our organs and their systems need to be operational. If the heart, or kidneys, or lungs fail us, the end point is exactly the same – death of the organism. Does this also mean that over the course of evolution these different systems developed in parallel, since the absence of any one of these could lead to the organism never being born or hatched? Maybe, there had been only a few organs that had multiple functions, which then became more specialized as subsystems developed and gained their (partial) independence.

We don't have to go this far back to realize how complex biological processes can be. If all our cells start off the same, how is it that some of them become lymphocytes or neurons or kidney cells, and then behave accordingly? Then again, why do some of these cells get really messed up, becoming cancer cells that seem to feel that they can go anywhere they like and create a new colony (metastasis)? Furthermore, when we look into the machinery present within single cells of our bodies and brain, and examine how cells came to be able to communicate with one another, we need to wonder whether something so complex could have really evolved through natural selection, which necessarily involved trial and error until things were, to quote Goldilocks, 'just right'. Then again, what are the alternatives?

(Continued)

(Continued)

I suppose, aliens could have seeded the planet with all sorts of stuff that would come to make all the animals, so that they would evolve, two by two. God could have created the heavens and earth and all the lowly critters, then got bored and went off to create more exciting galaxies and worlds, leaving us to our own devices. Physicists might know the answers to these questions, especially as some of them are proposing the existence of multiple universes occupying the same physical space, and even that we can exist on several planes concurrently. Their talk about multi-universes frustrates me enormously, given that I can't even understand much about the one I'm apparently in, although 'the me' that might be present in another universe might have better insights on this.

MULTIPLE CONVERGING SYSTEMS

Our ability to do all the things that we do is dependent on multiple processes all interacting with one another in precisely the right way at precisely the right time. Our brain holds sway on other systems which reciprocally affect brain functioning. This multidirectional communication requires considerable coordination within and between multiple systems. To an extent, this involves the influence of genetic factors that lay down the working drawings for these systems, which can be modified by experiences and environmental factors. This chapter provides a surface appreciation of:

- genetic processes that might contribute to the organization and functioning of systems that govern our functioning
- how the brain and its neuronal connections operate to affect various aspects of behavior and functioning of other body systems
- the contribution of growth factors (*neurotrophic factors*) to the formation and strengthening of new neuronal connections and the elaboration of neural circuits (*neuroplasticity*)
- the contribution of our endocrine systems to assure that metabolic processes are working as they should and what happens when they fail to do so
- how our immune system protects us from foreign particles that seem intent on harming us
- the involvement of gut bacteria, our *microbiota*, in determining our health and well-being.

A GENETICS PRIMER

A glance at Mendelian inheritance

Before getting into neurobiological systems, we'll first consider genetic processes that govern their functioning. You'll probably recall that your physical, biological, and behavioral characteristics (*phenotypes*) are determined, to an extent, by the genes you inherited from your parents (*genotype*).

One *allele*, or gene component, was inherited from your dad and one from your mom, and these could appear as either dominant or recessive. If you carried a dominant allele it alone would determine your phenotype, regardless of whether the other allele was dominant or recessive. The recessive phenotype would only appear if both alleles were recessive. Let's imagine for a moment that hair color was determined by a single gene just as the color of pea plants (yellow versus green) might be. If your parents carried only the dominant gene for dark hair they would have this hair color, and so would you because you inherited only the genes for dark hair. Likewise, if both your parents carried the recessive allele, then you would have inherited only recessive alleles. If both your parents were *heterozygous*, carrying both a dominant and recessive allele, they would still be dark haired as the dominant gene for this trait was present. However, as you would inherit one allele from each of your parents, you could potentially inherit the recessive allele from each of your parents, and thus your hair color would differ from that of either of your parents. That example might be fine for pea plants and for simple phenotypes, but a given gene might not be fully dominant, and thus even if you carry the dominant gene, you might not fully resemble the dominant phenotype. As we'll see repeatedly, as well, complex behaviors and complex illnesses don't involve single genes, but instead involve the additive or interactive effects of many genes (*polygenic effects*). It also appears that the influence of genes can be moderated by environmental events. For that matter, environmental factors can alter the expression of genes themselves. Obviously, there's more to inheritance than the brief description offered here, and many good texts are available to explain this further (e.g., Carey, 2003).

SCIENCE MAGIC

In the olden days, back when I was a kid in high school, it was understood that genotype influenced phenotype, but it was less clear how this actually came about. Particular genes were inherited and, seemingly through magic, particular traits and vulnerabilities somehow emerged. Most people never gave a thought to the processes by which this came about, even less than they considered how signals came through wires to create pictures on a TV screen. However, for those in fields related to health and well-being, including behavioral sciences, it is useful to understand at least some of the processes by which genes come to have the effects that they do, and to appreciate how the environment can, in some instances, dictate the actions of these genes.

The 23 pairs of chromosomes in humans each comprise coiled DNA made up of a very large number of small particles (varying from 100,000 to 3.75 million) referred to as nucleotides. These nucleotides are guanine (G), adenine (A), cytosine (C), and thymine (T), and the sequence of these bases provides the information that makes us what we are. Much as letters in the alphabet when strung together form words, in sets of three these nucleotides form amino acids, a series of which make up genes and regulatory elements of these genes that determine protein synthesis. Figure 3.1 provides a brief description of the flow of this process.

(Continued)

(Continued)

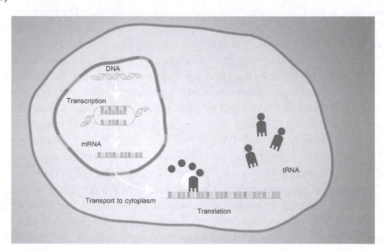

Figure 3.1   The DNA, which includes the various genes, serves as a template for the 'transcription' of RNA so that it is essentially identical to the DNA. The presence of particular proteins, referred to as transcription factors, unwind the DNA strand that normally exists in the shape of a double helix. At this point, RNA polymerase transcribes (copies) a single strand of DNA into a single strand of RNA, referred to as messenger RNA (mRNA), which crosses into the cytoplasm of the cell (outside the cell's nucleus). Once in the cytoplasm, a form of RNA, referred to as transfer RNA (tRNA), together with ribosomes, will engage in 'translation' in which lengthy chains of amino acids (made up of a sequence of nucleotides) form a protein. This is a dynamic process with new proteins being formed all the time, and it's these proteins that govern our phenotype. This doesn't only include those factors that determine our physical characteristics, but also the formation of hormones and enzymes as well as various factors that contribute to the creation of other complex neurobiological chemicals. In essence, by affecting chemical processes, the activity of genes influences the functioning of our various organs. The formation of proteins also affects ongoing behavior and the responses that are emitted when challenges are encountered, and they play a considerable role in the evolution of illnesses. Modified from http://ghr.nlm.nih.gov/handbook/howgeneswork/makingprotein.

More than 99% of our genome is common across all people, thus accounting for our many similarities. Certain genes, comprising about 1% of DNA, contain the information that contributes to the formation of all of our phenotypes, but a sequence of amino acids, referred to as promoter or regulatory region, tells the primary gene when to turn on or off, or even when to interact with other genes. As well, these regulatory processes can be affected by environmental events, such as stressors or toxins, so that the genes' influence on neurobiological processes, such as hormone production, can be altered. In effect, contrary to the old view that the effects of genes are more or less fixed, features of the environment may influence what these genes will actually do (Rands et al., 2014). A large portion of DNA carries what is referred to as junk DNA because it has no known function, although this doesn't exclude the possibility that some functions will be discovered.

GENE × ENVIRONMENT INTERACTIONS

It had been thought at one time that for better or worse, whatever genes an individual inherited was what they were stuck with. This was hardly questioned and the great debates seemed to revolve around how much of a given phenotype was determined by genes and how much was the product of environment. Indeed, our *phenotypic variance* (P_v) was thought to reflect a combination of the variance contributed by our genes (G_v) plus our environment (E_v) plus the variance attributable to the gene × environment interaction. Although that sounds fairly reasonable, it turned out to be far too simplistic, since the expression of a gene can be influenced by the environment in which an organism is raised or tested. Studies of inbred strains of mice, in which every mouse of a given strain is identical to every other mouse (essentially being identical twins), have indicated that although they generally share behavioral phenotypes, even small environmental differences (e.g., where animals are bred) can create a marked divergence in the behavioral profiles that are evident (Crabbe et al., 1999). Furthermore, as we'll see shortly, the environment can actually cause a change of gene functioning itself.

Twin research methodology

One approach to evaluate the extent to which a trait is genetically inherited is through twin studies. *Monozygotic* (identical) twins share all of their genes, whereas *dizygotic* (non-identical; fraternal) twins share only half their genes, and so one would expect that if a phenotype were primarily determined by genes, the phenotypic correlation between monozygotic twin pairs would be greater than among dizygotic twins. However, this relationship could also be affected by how twins were raised, particularly as monozygotic twins are often treated alike to a greater extent than are dizygotic twins, perhaps because they look alike and are, in a sense, interchangeable (Joseph, 2003). To dissociate the contribution of genes and environment to behavioral phenotypes, studies were conducted comparing phenotypes of identical twins that had been raised together versus those twins that had been raised apart (e.g., Elder et al., 2012). As useful as this paradigm might be, the conclusions that could be drawn were limited by a number of factors. Foremost in this regard is that the environment of twins reared apart is not actually entirely non-identical. It wasn't as if one twin went into a good and the other into a modestly poor environment. In the main, twins end up in fairly similar middle- or upper-class homes. Furthermore, identical twins that had been raised apart had shared an intrauterine environment, and thus might have experienced a more similar prenatal environment than did fraternal twins.

Twin studies have been used to assess *heritability* in relation to many phenotypes (i.e., the extent to which a given characteristic or trait in a population is attributable to genetic differences). These have included physical pathologies, such as heart disease, various types of cancer, diabetes, addiction (alcohol, smoking), and just about any other physical and psychological disorder that can be thought of. As well, studies have explored heritability in relation to social attitudes (e.g., socialism, abortion, gay rights, racial segregation), as well as dispositional and ideological orientations (neuroticism, agreeableness, religious fundamentalism, right-wing authoritarianism). Despite the many studies conducted to identify genetic contributions to personality factors on the basis of twin studies, in the main there has only been limited agreement concerning the contribution of genetic factors in this regard (Balestri et al., 2014). With advances in molecular genetics, particularly the ability to identify particular genes and gene mutations, twin studies have to a considerable extent been supplanted by alternative approaches tying specific genes to particular phenotypes.

Gene polymorphisms

The 20,000 or so genes that we carry are made up of approximately 3 billion nucleotide bases, and the precise sequence of these nucleotides are the same in each of the 10 trillion cells that are formed over the average life span. The transcription of DNA to mRNA is fairly complex, and almost every cell in a given individual ought to have an identical sequence of bases. In fact, nature has seen fit to include a proofreading process to limit the occurrence of errors (*mutations*), but with so much going on it is understandable that some errors will occur (Bertram, 2000). Some of these *mutations* (permanent changes of the sequence of nucleotides that comprise a gene) can be fairly extensive, as in the case of large *deletions*, *amplifications* (in which sections of the gene are duplicated), or *translocations* (the movement of a gene fragment from one location to another chromosome), or they can appear fairly innocuous, amounting to a change of a single nucleotide. A mutation, or a change of the gene sequence, that appears in a significant portion of the population (more than 1%) is referred to as a *polymorphism*, and those that involve only a single nucleotide are referred to as *single nucleotide polymorphisms* (SNP; pronounced snip). Mutations might occur owing to environmental influences (*acquired mutations*), such as ultraviolet radiation from the sun, or the presence of other toxic elements. Should these mutations occur within sperm or egg, they can be transmitted to the next generation (*inherited mutations*).

Change of a single nucleotide might not sound as if it's very serious, and indeed it isn't if this 'mutation' occurs on an unimportant portion of a DNA strand. But, if it occurs at some important portion of the gene, then changing just one nucleotide, just like changing one letter or word of a sentence can alter its entire meaning, the function of the gene can be entirely altered. For instance, a change of a single nucleotide or amino acid may alter the functional effects of the gene so that certain proteins (e.g., hormones or hormone receptors) may not form as they should.

One approach to link specific genes and phenotypes has made use of the ability to identify the presence of particular SNPs. Specifically, attempts have been made to determine whether individuals with or without a particular SNP display different phenotypes. However, given the vast number of cells formed, and the complexity of each DNA strand, it shouldn't be surprising that a large number of mutations may occur, and several SNPs may even be present in a single gene. The frequency of SNPs varies with the length of the chromosome, numbering within the tens of thousands on each, reaching as high as 100,000 on some chromosomes. By virtue of the sheer number of SNPs that each of us carry, it is exceedingly difficult to link specific polymorphisms to particular phenotypes, especially as complex behaviors likely involve multiple genetic contributions. Still, this approach has afforded researchers the opportunity to do this, although this involves using a very large cohort. However, some of the early studies linking SNPs to psychopathology weren't replicated readily, possibly because of biases inherent in studies that involved a small number of participants.

The complexity of linking particular SNPs to phenotypic outcomes is compounded by several factors. The appearance of a given SNP may vary across cultures or societies. By example, a mutation on the gene for a particular hormone receptor (oxytocin) might appear at a rate of about 20% among Euro-Caucasians, but within Asian populations it is far more frequent, reaching 70–80% (Kim et al., 2011), and the influence of a SNP in one cultural group may differ from those involved in a second cultural group. Also, as we'll see, a given SNP might interact with other genetic variations as well as with environmental or experiential factors (e.g., Caspi et al., 2003). Essentially, the presence of a particular genetic factor may represent a component, a vulnerability factor in a sense, but a particular outcome might not appear until a second hit, such as a stressor or toxicant, was encountered. This sort of interaction is not uncommon, and a two-hit hypothesis of this nature has been proposed in relation to depressive disorders, certain types of cancer, Parkinson's disease, and stroke recovery (e.g., Carvey et al., 2006; Caspi et al., 2003).

MUTATIONS IN HOSTILE ENVIRONMENTS

The term 'mutation' brings up the thought of some creature like the Hulk or Ninja Turtle, or something that's quite negative. Yet, mutations may well be an essential component of evolution and may have actually been responsible for making us as fit as we are. When bacteria, such as Escherichia coli (E. coli), were exposed to a challenging environment that comprised either potential starvation or the presence of an antibacterial agent (antibiotic) that could kill them, the rate of mutation (mutagenesis) in the E. coli genes increased appreciably (bacteria, like other organisms, carry genes). In essence, features of the bacterial genes might have changed in an effort to adapt to the relatively hostile conditions present (Amar et al., 2012). Ordinarily, when an antibiotic was present, most bacteria would be destroyed. However, if there were a great number of different bacteria present (bacterial diversity), or if there were bacteria that had mutated so that they could survive the antibacterial onslaught, they might have contributed to the formation of new bacterial colonies carrying the mutation and would be more resistant should the antibiotic again be present. Thus, mutations can serve as a survival mechanism for the bacterial species, and the more mutations that occur, the greater the likelihood of species survival. Mutations could similarly proliferate in humans with increasingly more hostile environments, and those that enhanced fitness would be most likely to be preserved within the gene pool and passed down across generations (Nei, 2013). In essence, challenges favor the preservation of certain mutations, which is a fundamental driving force for evolution.

Epigenetics

There are several common misconceptions regarding the influence of genes on behavior. How often do we hear the notion that a person inherited particular genes and thus they necessarily will express some sort of phenotype? To an extent this is accurate, but genes often don't act alone, nor are the phenotypic effects of genes immutable. While some genes contain the information for the formation of a phenotype, as described earlier, the nearby gene promoter region tells the primary gene when it ought to turn on or off, and whether a gene should be interacting with other genes. Thus, some genes serve to define a phenotype, whereas aspects of a promoter gene act as the instruction manual that guides the gene's action. If the actions of these promoter genes change, which can occur through the influence of the environment or experiences, then the actions of genes that give rise to a particular phenotype can be altered.

The notion that both genes and environment contribute to phenotypes is hardly new, but what hadn't been expected was that experiential and environmental factors would actually influence how genes were expressed. Specifically, it seems that under some conditions (e.g., in response to stressors, the presence of particular toxicants, or even some foods), *epigenetic* changes may occur in which the actions of some genes or their promoters may be suppressed, but without altering the DNA sequence (Bird, 2007; Szyf et al., 2005). In effect, the gene itself was unaltered, but its functioning was turned off.

Epigenetic changes may come to influence many biological processes (hormones and hormone receptors, growth factors, immune elements) and might thereby contribute to a variety of psychological disorders, such as depression, PTSD, and addiction (Maze et al., 2010; Mehta et al., 2013) as well as physical disease states, such as many forms of cancer, heart disease, and autoimmune disorders. Given that epigenetic changes, like mutations discussed earlier, can instigate disease processes, there have been efforts to fight illnesses, such as cancer, through drug treatments that could reverse (reprogram) these destructive epigenetically-derived disturbances. However, as this could end up having negative consequences on non-cancerous cells, targeting these treatments appropriately may turn out to be difficult. Furthermore, there may be a large number of epigenetic changes associated with a given pathology (Labonté et al., 2013), making it difficult to identify which are causally linked to outcomes, which are provoked by the pathology, and which might simply be bystanders. The presence of epigenetic marks that occur in concert with pathology, even if they are not causally involved in the illness, may nevertheless be significant as they could serve as biomarkers to predict the occurrence of later pathology (Kundakovic et al., 2015).

Epigenetics and intergeneration actions

Epigenetic effects are not only significant because of their effects on gene expression and disease processes, but also because they can occur owing to events that occurred prenatally and early in development (Szyf et al., 2005) and can persist over the course of an organism's life, giving rise to later behavioral or physical changes (Essex et al., 2013). Moreover, if the epigenetic changes occur within germ line cells (egg or sperm), then they can be transmitted from one generation to the next. In effect, biological and behavioral effects elicited in a given individual as a result of environmental triggers (psychosocial factors or what mom eats) can be recapitulated in their children and grandchildren (Franklin et al., 2010; Lillycrop, 2011). Pesticides, such as methoxychlor (which, ironically, was a replacement for the highly dangerous pesticide DDT until it was banned in the US in 2003 because of its actions on hormone systems), which has known epigenetic actions, can have effects that appear over several generations (Manikkam et al., 2014). As such, the increase of diseases we are seeing today could actually be due to events experienced by our forebears.

As negative experiences, such as social strife and poverty, can profoundly influence the course of development and can serve to increase vulnerability to pathology, it has been said that "society itself should be considered 'an environment' that through epigenetic actions can affect cognitive, emotional, and physical health" (Branscombe & Reynolds, 2015: 10). It is particularly significant that despite the persistence of epigenetic changes, they are modifiable so that even if a gene is silenced, this can be reversed. Such changes have been achieved through drug interventions, but can perhaps emerge through positive nurturing (Weaver et al., 2005).

THE NERVOUS SYSTEM

Through networks of billions of neurons that are able to talk to one another in a highly coordinated manner, our central nervous system (CNS), which comprises the brain and spinal cord, is fundamental for sensory processes, motor outputs, cognitive functioning, memory, emotions, as well as processes associated with primitive drives (eating, thirst, sex, sleep) and energy regulation. In addition, the brain also influences its cousin, the peripheral nervous system, including autonomic activity that controls involuntary functioning (e.g., heart activity, digestion), and profoundly influences immune and hormonal processes.

Neuronal system

Our many neurons have thousands of branches, which have their own smaller branches coming off of them, and each of these has many, many synapses. With all this wiring running all over the place, one would think it would be a hodge-podge of circuits, held together by some neuronal duct tape. However, brain wiring is actually highly organized, with large and small tracts going off to different places in a predetermined, genetically encoded manner. For the sake of simplicity, we're often told that various brain regions serve different functions. To a considerable extent this is correct, but in dealing with complex behaviors or pathological conditions, we can pretty well be assured that these are determined by *neuronal systems* that involve several brain regions operating sequentially or in parallel. For example, a syndrome such as post-traumatic stress disorder (PTSD) may involve brain regions governing fear (aspects of the amygdala), memory of the trauma (hippocampus), and judgment and appraisals (aspects of the prefrontal cortex). Likewise, addictions may involve areas associated with anxiety (aspects of the amygdala), cognitive processes and impulsivity (prefrontal cortex), and reward processes (nucleus accumbens) (e.g., Kalivas & Volkow, 2011). Indeed, even seemingly basic functions, such as eating or sex, are influenced by systems involving interconnections between multiple brain regions.

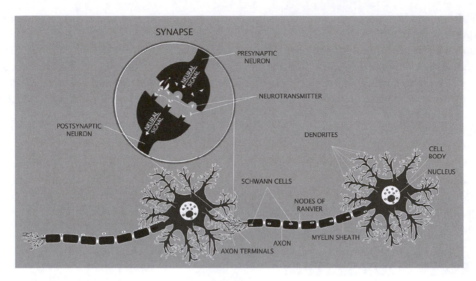

Figure 3.2   Depiction of a neuron. Each of the many billions of neurons in the brain has a primary, lengthy tentacle, termed an *axon* coming from its cell body (*soma*), which is essential for transmitting information to other cells (see Figure 3.2). A neuron also has many smaller tentacles coming from it, referred to as *dendrites*, which are responsible for receiving information. Minute electrical stimuli can be generated within an axon, so that where it meets the dendrites of an adjacent postsynaptic neuron (referred to as a *synapse*), the electrical pulse will cause a chemical (*neurotransmitter*) to be released from the axon terminals that will stimulate *receptors* present on the dendrites or cell body of this next neuron. In the main, each neuron contains one type of chemical (although more than one can occur in some instances), but because many receptors are present, each of which can be stimulated by a different neurotransmitter, messages can be received from a great number of different types of neurons.

Brain cells and how they function: Neurotransmission

Neuronal functioning involves a large number of neurotransmitters, including norepineph-rine, dopamine, serotonin, acetylcholine, GABA, glutamate, as well as neuropeptides such as β-endorphin, dynorphin, and encephalin. To this point, more than 100 neurotransmitters (or potential neurotransmitters) have been discovered, and for many of these several different receptors have been identified. Neurotransmitters can have different functional effects across brain regions, and the presence of these receptors, like the neurotransmitters themselves, can either decrease or increase, depending on conditions experienced. Obviously, with such a great array of neurotransmitters and receptors, and so many neurons in play at any given time, con-siderable coordination is needed. To this end, in addition to neurotransmitters that excite the activity of other neurons, in order to diminish sources of noise and to regulate the degree of neuronal activity transmitters are present, such as GABA, that act in an inhibitory capacity, essentially causing certain cells to be quiet while others are active (Anisman et al., 2008).

The various neurotransmitters and their receptors across brain regions serve in different ways. Within limbic brain regions (e.g., hippocampus, amygdala, and prefrontal cortex) they may be associated with emotions, executive functioning (appraisals, decision making), and memory processes, whereas in hypothalamic nuclei (e.g., paraventricular nucleus, arcuate nucleus) they interact with several hormones to affect basic functioning, such as energy regulation, feeding, and sexual behavior. A given neurotransmitter may have multiple functions, depending upon the brain region involved. By example, dopamine activation within the ventral tegmentum and the nucleus accumbens is associated with reward processes, and excessive activity of particular dopamine receptors in cortical regions is accompanied by schizophrenia, whereas a loss of dopamine within another brain region, the substantia nigra, is associated with Parkinson's disease. It similarly appears that the action of norepinephrine at the locus coeruleus is involved in vigilance, in the amygdala it can be associated with fear memories, and at the hypothalamus it may serve in the regulation of autonomic functioning. Thus, in describing the action of these and each of the other transmitters we'll discuss, it's essential to distinguish between the brain regions in which they are acting. In fact, there are occasions in which a drug is administered to reverse particular neurological disturbances by stimulating a neurotransmitter in one region, only to have other disturbed behaviors emerge because the drug also affects brain regions that hadn't been impaired at the outset. For instance, administration of a drug to increase dopamine to attenuate symptoms of Parkinson's disease may promote gambling addiction because the drug also affects reward processes related to dopamine functioning within the nucleus accumbens.

Receptor functions

When a neurotransmitter is released from vesicles present at the terminal region of an axon, it travels across the synaptic cleft to stimulate receptors that are present on an adjacent neuron (*postsynaptic neuron*), which causes its activation. For most neurotransmitters and hormones there may be several types of receptors present and when stimulated they may each have different effects on a variety of outcome measures. In addition to the receptors present on the adjacent neuron, located at the presynaptic end of each axon are receptors, termed *autoreceptors*, which, upon being stimulated by the neurotransmitter that has been released, have the effect of telling the neuron to slow down the production of the neurotransmitter. Thus, as the amount of neurotransmitter released into the synapse increases, these autoreceptors are more likely to be triggered, and, through this feedback process, the neurotransmitter production is self-regulated. In addition to being affected by these *endogenous* factors (those ordinarily present within the body or brain), an increase or decrease of neurotransmitter functioning can be accomplished through *exogenous* administration (introduced from an external source) of drugs that either stimulate or block receptors. Agents that directly stimulate receptors, essentially acting much like the neurotransmitter, are termed *agonists*, whereas those that bind to the receptor and prevent stimulation from occurring are referred to as *antagonists*.

Turnover and reuptake

In considering the relationship between neurotransmitter functioning and the emergence of pathology, it's not sufficient to simply know how much of a particular transmitter is present, but also how much neurotransmitter is actually produced and released (*turnover*), which specific receptors are being triggered, how they might affect and be affected by specific hormones or other neurotransmitters, and where in the brain these changes are occurring.

Having been released from storage vesicles at the terminals of axons and stimulated postsynaptic receptors, the neurotransmitter needs to be eliminated. Some of the transmitter is degraded by enzymes present in the synaptic cleft, but in the case of many transmitters it can also be transported back into the cell (by a transporter mechanism) through a process called *reuptake*, thereby making it available for later reuse (our own little environmentally-friendly recycling plant). The longer the neurotransmitter stays in the synaptic cleft, the greater the chances are that a receptor will be stimulated. Accordingly, the efficiency of the neurotransmitter can be increased by pharmacologically increasing its time in the synaptic cleft. This can be achieved by inhibiting enzymes that ordinarily destroy the transmitter or, alternatively, by inhibiting the reuptake of the transmitter back into the neuron. The latter process is how drugs, such as the selective serotonin reuptake inhibitors (SSRIs) used in the treatment of depression, might have their effects (Zhou et al., 2007), although there's a good chance that the antidepressant actions might come from other actions of these agents.

NEUROLOGICAL VERSUS MENTAL DISORDERS

The boundaries between a disorder and what constitutes a mental disorder are vague. In general, though, neurological disorders comprise those that involve structural, biochemical, or electrical abnormalities in the brain, spinal cord, or other nerves, which promote varied symptoms (depending on the brain region involved), such as altered levels of consciousness, confusion, paralysis, seizures, poor coordination, muscle weakness, pain, and loss of sensation. Relatively common neurological disturbances include Alzheimer's disease, Parkinson's disease, epilepsy, amyotrophic lateral sclerosis (ALS), stroke, brain tumors, migraine (and other headache disorders), multiple sclerosis, neuroinflammation, trauma to the nervous system, neurological disorders that occur as a result of malnutrition, conditions that involve sensory, motor, or learning disabilities (e.g., agnosia, aphasia, ataxia, apraxia), as well as childhood conditions such as autism and attention deficit hyperactivity disorder (ADHD). These are only a portion of the long list of neurological disorders provided by the National Institute of Neurological Disorders and Stroke.

Mental disorders are more commonly considered to be those that involve changes of how a person feels, thinks, perceives, or acts, often varying with the social context. Unlike some neurological disorders, which typically involve gross neuronal damage, mental disorders might not be accompanied by such frank damage, and more often involve disturbances of neuronal activity. Thus, mental disorders might not always be as readily diagnosed, and often are determined on the basis of behavioral analyses rather than discrete physical characteristics. A wide variety of mental disorders exist, ranging from disturbances of mood and anxiety, personality, sleep, eating, and sexual behaviors, as well as developmental and conduct disorders. Most often, these conditions are treated through behavioral therapies or drug treatments, although other options, such as transmagnetic brain stimulation, electroconvulsive stimulation, and surgical procedures (e.g., deep brain stimulation through electrical pulses to specific brain regions), have been used.

Psychiatric and neurological impairments both involve and can be influenced by neuronal disturbances, as well as psychological and social processes. More than this, traumatic brain injury can give rise to fear and anxiety associated with PTSD, just as it may be a risk factor for dementia (Gardner et al., 2014). Moreover, disorders such as PTSD, schizophrenia, depressive disorders, bipolar disorder, and obsessive compulsive disorder are all accompanied by structural brain changes, including the diminished size of several brain regions (White et al., 2012). Despite their overlapping features, psychiatric and neurological disorders have lived and been treated in different silos, but there have been repeated calls for better integration between these fields (Insel et al., 2010).

Glial cells

The brain's second type of cell, known as *glial* cells, had at one time not been a focus of great interest, only receiving occasional lip service. These cells were thought to be 'the help', serving as support cells, providing nutrients and taking away debris, and hence weren't considered as being directly related to cognitive processes. However, it became apparent that glial cells do much more, being fundamental in the clearance of neurotransmitters from the synaptic cleft, thereby preventing damaging effects attributable to a build-up of some transmitters, such as glutamate. As well, within some brain regions they can act like neurons in the transmission of information (Newman, 2003).

Several types of glial cells have been identified that serve in different capacities. *Oligodendrocytes* are involved in the *myelination* of neurons (myelin forms a sheath around axons) that allows for the rapid propagation of electrical signals down the axon (in the periphery, Schwann cells serve in this capacity). *Astrocytes*, the most abundant type of glial cell, are involved in maintaining ion balances within fluid outside brain cells, and play a fundamental role in the repair of brain and spinal cord neurons. They are also smarter than we thought, and are able to communicate with neurons by the release of particular neurotransmitters (e.g., GABA, glutamate) (Allen & Barres, 2005). More than this, astrocytes have another exceedingly important function. Specifically, they begin to form neurons in areas of the brain damaged by stroke, and in this way may be important for repair of brain damage (Kokaia & Lindvall, 2012; Magnusson et al., 2014).

Still another type of glial cell, *microglia*, are constantly in search of potentially damaging factors, such as plaque and infectious agents, and they typically eliminate those that pose a risk to neurons (Rivest, 2009). Although their role is meant to be one of protecting the brain through the release of chemicals that trigger inflammation (as we'll see later in this chapter, inflammation may reflect an adaptive response), microglia can also have some very negative effects (Ekdahl et al., 2009). Specifically, if the inflammatory response elicited by microglia becomes too great, neuro-destructive actions may ensue, thereby promoting neurodegenerative disorders, such as Alzheimer's and Parkinson's disease, as well as mood-related disorders (Litteljohn & Hayley, 2012).

AUTONOMIC NERVOUS SYSTEM

Sympathetic and parasympathetic activity

The autonomic nervous system (ANS) is the portion of our nervous system which regulates body organs and processes over which we don't have voluntary control (e.g., heart, gut, stomach). The primary brain region involved in the regulation of the ANS is the medulla oblongata. Other brain regions involved in regulating the ANS include the hypothalamus, which is involved in eating and drinking, and the amygdala, which is related to emotional responses.

The ANS comprises two subsystems, the *sympathetic* nervous system (involving the release of epinephrine, also referred to as adrenaline), which is responsible for activating various organs (e.g., stimulating the sympathetic system will increase the heart rate), and the *parasympathetic* system (involving the release of acetylcholine), which acts against the actions of the sympathetic system (e.g., Brodal, 2004). These complementary systems ordinarily are in balance with one another, but occasionally environmental triggers will instigate changes so that sympathetic activity predominates, as observed in response to emotionally arousing events that produce an increase of blood pressure and heart rate. In other instances the compensatory antagonistic system may be overly active, and thus blood pressure and heart rate may become inordinately low.

ENDOCRINE SYSTEMS

Hormones share several characteristics with neurotransmitters, serving as chemical signaling molecules that are released by a cell or by a gland in response to external or internal signals (e.g., changes of glucose levels or in response to stressors). Whereas neurotransmitters travel very short distances to excite receptors on adjacent neurons, hormones can enter the bloodstream and then travel to distal sites where they trigger specific receptors present on cells. Some hormones, referred to as *endocrine* hormones, are released directly into the bloodstream, whereas *exocrine* hormones are secreted directly into a duct and then flow either into the bloodstream or spread from cell to cell by diffusion. Furthermore, several hormone-like substances are manufactured within the brain and can act as if they were neurotransmitters that activate particular types of receptors. These receptor types are present in differing concentrations across brain regions, and may have very diverse functions or even opposing actions.

Hormones and what they do

Hormones are manufactured and released from different sites (as described in Tables 3.1–3.4), and have different functions. They may be involved in the operation of metabolic processes, cell growth and cell death (apoptosis), stress reactions, eating and energy balances, sexual characteristics and behaviors, and they can influence brain functioning. Moreover, dysfunction of hormone systems can lead to various illnesses and might contribute to the sex differences that have been related to illnesses, such as heart disease and autoimmune disorders (Lleo et al., 2008).

HORMONES ASSOCIATED WITH THE STRESS RESPONSE

As stressful events affect various psychological and physical disorders, considerable attention has been devoted to the involvement of stress-related hormones in these pathological conditions. Once again, these hormones don't act in isolation of other processes, and can interact with other hormones or with brain neurotransmitter systems in determining behavioral and physical well-being and illnesses. Thus, even though we often consider the role of hormones in relation to various conditions, the potential cross-talk between diverse systems should be kept in mind.

HPA responses

Among the most examined stress systems are those related to autonomic nervous system functioning (e.g., epinephrine and norepinephrine), and those of the *hypothalamic-pituitary-adrenal (HPA)* system (see Table 3.1). We'll cover this in greater detail in Chapter 5, but for the moment, it is suffice to say that stressors cause activation of brain processes that instigate the release of *corticotropin releasing hormone* (CRH) from the hypothalamus, which stimulates the secretion of *adrenocorticotropic hormone* (ACTH) from the pituitary gland that lies at the base of the brain. The ACTH enters the bloodstream and upon reaching the adrenal gland it stimulates the release of *cortisol* (in rodents, *corticosterone*, rather than cortisol, is released). Activation of this system facilitates our ability to deal with challenges but, in some instances, problems might arise, especially when hormone release is excessive and occurs over a protracted period, ultimately promoting pathological outcomes, including neurodegenerative disorders. It is important to underscore that these are only some of the many hormones altered by stressors. Moreover, virtually every hormone affected by stressors is also affected by other variables, including those related to eating and energy regulating processes, and indeed, these hormones are all known to have multiple actions.

Table 3.1 Hormones related to stress responses

Secreted hormone	Biological effect	Behavioral outcome
Corticotropin-releasing hormone (CRH)	Formed in the paraventricular nucleus of the hypothalamus, as well as several limbic and cortical regions. Stimulates ACTH release from the pituitary gland.	Involved in stress responses, promoting fear and anxiety, and contributes to eating processes. In addition to being fundamental to stress responses, it diminishes food intake and increases metabolic rate.
Adrenocorticotropic hormone (ACTH)	Formed in the anterior pituitary gland. Stimulates corticosteroid (glucocorticoid and mineralocorticoid) release from adrenocortical cells.	Stress responses elicited are primarily due to actions on adrenal corticoids.

(Continued)

Table 3.1   (Continued)

Secreted hormone	Biological effect	Behavioral outcome
Arginine vasopressin (AVP)	Released by both the paraventricular and supraoptic nucleus: promotes water reabsorption and increased blood ACTH.	Together with CRH, may synergistically increase stress responses. Influences social behaviors.
Cortisol (corticosterone in rodents)	Released from the adrenal gland. Has anti-inflammatory effect, promotes release and utilization of glucose stores from liver and muscle, and increases fat storage.	Prototypical stress hormone; influences defensive behaviors, affects memory processes, stimulates caloric intake, and may promote preference for high calorie foods under stressful circumstances (stimulates consumption of comfort foods).
Mineralocorticoids (e.g., aldosterone)	Released from the adrenal gland. Stimulate active sodium reabsorption and passive water reabsorption, thus increasing blood volume and blood pressure.	Increased aldosterone influences salt and water balance. Excessive sodium and water retention leads to hypertension. Low levels of aldosterone leads to a salt-wasting condition evident in Addison's disease.
Epinephrine (EPI) (adrenaline) and norepinephrine (NE) (noradrenaline)	Produced in the adrenal gland (medulla) and within sympathetic neurons; increases oxygen and glucose to the brain and muscles; promotes vasodilation; increases catalysis of glycogen in liver and the breakdown of lipids in fat cells; increases respiration and blood pressure; suppresses bodily processes (e.g., digestion) during emergency responses; influences immune system activity.	Elicits fight or flight response. In the brain, EPI and NE have multiple behavioral actions related to defensive behaviors (e.g., vigilance, attention).
Beta-endorphin	Secreted from several sites, such as the arcuate nucleus.	Inhibits perception of pain.

EATING AND ENERGY-RELATED HORMONES

Several hormones play a fundamental role in energy regulation processes and balances, being involved in either the initiation of eating or its cessation. These same hormones are also integrally involved in stress responses and may contribute to stress-related psychological disorders. Many of these hormones are referred to in Table 3.2. In addition, there are several other hormones that are associated with *metabolic responses* (storage or use of nutrients), including growth hormone, prolactin, and thyroid hormones.

Table 3.2 Hormones related to energy regulation and eating

Secreted hormone	Biological effect	Behavioral outcome
Leptin	Produced by fat cells. Influences neurons in hypothalamic regions.	Reduces food intake and appetite, and increases energy expenditure.
Ghrelin	Produced in gut. Affects same brain regions as leptin, but in an opposite manner. Influences brain regions associated with reward.	Stimulates food intake and appetite, while reducing energy expenditure. Enhances reward-seeking behaviors; modulates stress responses.
Insulin	Produced by beta cells in the pancreas. Regulates fat and carbohydrate metabolism. Involved in getting glucose from the blood into various body cells and storing it as glycogen.	In brain, insulin stimulates hormones that reduce food intake.
Bombesin (appears in humans as neuromedin B [NMB] and gastrin releasing peptide [GRP])	Produced in gut and in several brain regions.	Acts as a satiety peptide (signals when individual is full) and is released in response to stress, thereby promoting anxiety.
Neuropeptide Y (NPY)	Produced by the gut and in several brain regions, including the hypothalamic arcuate nucleus. Increases vasoconstrictor actions of norepinephrine.	Increases food intake and reduces physical activity; increases energy stored in the form of fat; blocks nociceptive (noxious) signals to the brain; acts as an anxiolytic agent.
Orexin (hypocretin)	Produced within the lateral hypothalamus, but orexin receptors are found throughout the brain.	Involved in appetite, as well as stress and reward processes, arousal, and wakefulness.
α-Melanocyte stimulating hormone (α-MSH)	Produced in the arcuate nucleus of the hypothalamus. Acts as an agonist of melanocortin (MC-3 and MC-4) receptors in the brain, including stress-related regions.	Reduces appetite, increases energy expenditure as modulated by leptin.
Agouti-related peptide (AGRP)	Produced in the arcuate nucleus (by same cells that produce NPY), and serves as a natural antagonist of MC-3 and MC-4 receptors.	Increases appetite and reduces energy expenditure. Modulated by leptin and ghrelin.
Glucagon-like peptide-1 (GLP-1)	Produced in the gut. Important in stimulating insulin release.	Acts in brain to reduce appetite and to diminish functioning of reward processes.

Leptin

The discovery of the hormone *leptin* has been considered among the most important research findings in the field of energy balance. Produced primarily by *adipocytes* (fat cells), this hormone enters circulation and then, by affecting the brain and peripheral organs, reduces food intake, increasing energy expenditure and reducing adiposity (fat) (Zhang et al., 1994). Leptin also influences HPA axis activity, and promotes the release of neurotransmitters such as serotonin and dopamine, thereby inhibiting reward-seeking behaviors and affective tone related to feeding, and mood states (Abizaid et al., 2014; Fulton et al., 2006). Leptin isn't alone in serving as a satiety signal (i.e., a stop signal), as other less studied hormones, such as *neuromedin B* (NMB) and *gastrin-releasing peptide* (GRP), also serve in this capacity, and they too have effects on emotional processes (Moody & Merali, 2004).

Ghrelin

Opposing the actions of leptin, elevated levels of ghrelin are associated with increased food consumption (Abizaid & Horvath, 2008). The levels of ghrelin increase just before meal-time, presumably signaling us to eat (or acting as a preparatory response for food we're about to eat), and then declines after we've eaten. Dysfunction of ghrelin functioning is related to disturbed energy and feeding processes, in that elevated ghrelin occurs in anorexia and bulimia nervosa, whereas binge eating was associated with decreased ghrelin (Geliebter et al., 2005).

Like other eating-related peptides, ghrelin activates dopamine neurons that are involved in reward processes, and could thus be an intermediary step for the rewarding feelings derived from food (Abizaid, 2009). In fact, eating was increased by ghrelin injected directly into the ventral tegmental region of the brain, which is involved in reward processes, whereas ghrelin antagonists had the opposite effect. Ghrelin also directly stimulates *orexin* receptors in the lateral hypothalamus (orexin is a hormone that has been associated with food craving), as well as cells in several other hypothalamic nuclei. Furthermore, in humans, ghrelin administration increased food-related imagery and stimulated reward pathways, thus implicating ghrelin in appetitive responses to *incentive* cues (i.e., visual and olfactory cues that had been associated with reward) that promote food cravings (Schmid et al., 2005).

Insulin

The main job of insulin is to have cells in the body take up glucose from the blood, and then store it as glycogen. When insulin is absent or when the response to insulin is diminished, glucose won't readily be taken up into cells, leading to diabetes. In addition, insulin interacts with cortisol, as well as leptin and other regulatory hormones that have been implicated in the development of obesity and metabolic disturbances associated with chronic stressors. Clearly, multiple processes play into eating behaviors; some stimulate hunger or satiety, or influence energy production and use, whereas others influence the rewarding value obtained from food and contribute to the cravings we feel for some of these.

SEX HORMONES

Estrogen and testosterone

Often referred to as *gonadal steroids*, sex hormones in males comprise *androgens* (primarily testosterone, as well as androstenedione, dehydroepiandrosterone, and dihydrotestosterone), and in females these consist of *estrogens* (primarily estradiol, and also estriol and estrone) as well as *progesterones*. As indicated in Table 3.3, testosterone is formed in the testis, and to a lesser extent in the adrenal glands. Estrogen is formed in the ovaries following stimulation by *follicle-stimulating hormone* (FSH), although smaller amounts of estrogen can also be formed by other tissues and by fat cells (Nelson & Bulun, 2001).

Table 3.3 Sex hormones

Secreted hormone	Biological effect	Behavioral outcome
Testosterone	Male steroid hormone produced in the testis in males and ovaries in females. To a lesser extent is produced in adrenal glands. Involved in the development and sexual differentiation of brain and reproductive organs. Fundamental in secondary sexual features, including body hair, muscle, and bone mass.	Associated with sexual behavior and libido. Linked to aggressive and dominant behaviors.
Dehydroepiandrosterone (DHEA)	In males, produced in adrenals, gonads, and brain. Acts as an anabolic steroid to affect muscle development.	Acts like testosterone. Has been implicated in maintaining youth.
Estrogens (estrone, estradiol, estriol)	Estradiol is predominant of the 3 estrogens produced in the ovaries. Principle steroid regulating hypothalamic-pituitary ovarian axis functioning. Involved in protein synthesis, fluid balances, gastrointestinal functioning and coagulation, cholesterol levels and fat depositions. Affects bone density, liver, arterial blood flow, and has multiple functions in the brain.	Influences female reproductive processes and sexual development. Important for maternal behavior, maintaining cognition, as well as anxiety and stress responses.
Progesterone	Formed in the ovary; precursor for several hormones; involved in triggering menstruation, and for maintaining pregnancy (e.g., inhibits immune response directed at embryo); reduces uterine smooth muscle contraction; influences resilience of various tissues (bones, joints, tendons, ligaments, skin).	Influences female reproductive processes and sexual development. Affects maternal behavior, disturbs cognitive processes. Has anti-anxiety actions.

(Continued)

Table 3.3   (Continued)

Secreted hormone	Biological effect	Behavioral outcome
Luteinizing hormone (LH)	Produced in the anterior pituitary gland. In females, an 'LH surge' triggers ovulation and development of the corpus luteum, an endocrine structure that develops from an ovarian follicle during the luteal phase of the estrous cycle.	Behavioral changes associated with estrogen or testosterone are elicited indirectly through actions on other steroids.
Follicle stimulating hormone (FSH)	Secreted from the anterior pituitary gland; regulates development, growth, pubertal maturation, and reproductive processes. Together with LH it acts synergistically in reproduction and ovulation.	Behavioral changes associated with estrogen or testosterone are elicited indirectly through actions on other steroids.

Estrogens are, of course, best known for their role in the development of female secondary sexual characteristics (e.g., breasts), in the regulation of the menstrual cycle, and a surge of estrogen promotes *luteinizing hormone* release, which triggers ovulation. Figure 3.3 shows some of the hormonal changes that occur over the menstrual cycle, depicting the relation to body temperature, lining of the uterus, menstruation, and ovulation. But, as indicated in Table 3.3, there's much more to estrogen's action than that. Estrogens are also involved in stimulating sexual receptivity, metabolic process, increasing fat stores, stimulation of endometrial growth (associated with menstruation), and enhancing uterine growth, and together with progesterone maintains the uterus lining for the implantation of a fertilized egg (Christensen et al., 2011). As well, estrogen enhances bone formation and reduces bone resorption, and bone weakness is often observed after menopause. Beyond these actions, estrogen also affects cardiac and lung functioning, and may influence hormone-dependent cancers (Rosano & Panina, 1999).

As the levels of sex hormones decline at menopause, and various negative symptoms begin to emerge (e.g., diminished bone density), hormone replacement therapies became popular in an effort to mitigate these outcomes. Particular attention was delivered to what were referred to as compounded 'bioidentical hormones' that were said to have precisely the same chemical and molecular structure as hormones that are 'naturally' made in the body. The use of hormone therapy generally declined with reports that this form of treatment could have severe adverse effects. It seems, however, that hormone replacements are still being used, often in the form of the bioidentical hormones that can be obtained through the internet or directly from suppliers, even though these compounds have not received approval from the Federal Drug Administration (FDA). In fact, many of the treatments purchased from these sources may not provide accurate amounts of hormone, may have serious health consequences, and many women using these compounded hormones are unaware of the health risks they're placing on themselves (Pinkerton & Santoro, 2015).

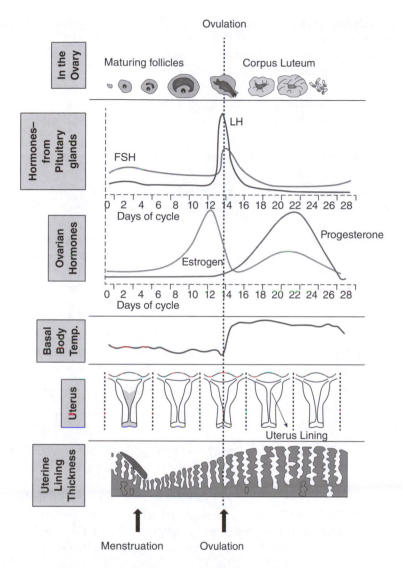

Figure 3.3 Variations of hormones from the pituitary gland (follicle stimulating hormone (FSH) and luteinizing hormone (LH)) as well as estrogen and progesterone) over the menstrual cycle, together with changes of body temperature, uterine status, menstruation, and ovulation.

('What happens menstrual cycle hormone ovary basal body Uterus' www.pcosjournal.com)

The production of testosterone is influenced by hypothalamic and pituitary processes, and can be affected by psychological factors. Much like its female counterpart, testosterone is pivotal in the production of male reproductive organs (testis, prostate) as well as the development of secondary male features, such as the growth of body hair, muscle growth, and bone density, and has been linked to dominance challenges and aggressive behaviors (Sapolsky, 2005; Sapolsky et al., 2000). Testosterone may have important implications for health, and low levels of this hormone have been associated with heart disease, just as they have been associated with mood changes; hormone replacement treatments have been used to counter these effects. Although testosterone is essential for male development, it is also formed in females, and when levels are too low, vulnerability to obesity increased, as did body fat and heart disease (Fagman et al., 2014).

JUICING

Most people, especially those who follow sports, might be aware that anabolic and androgenic steroids have been used by athletes to gain an advantage over their competitors, and even young people have been using these agents in an effort to get a head start. At high doses these steroids contribute to the development of muscles, and hence greater strength and enhanced athletic performance. It's unfortunate for users that these steroids have a considerable down side, negatively influencing the heart and liver, creating immune system disturbances, and skin (complexion) problems. Moreover, steroids also affect brain neurotransmitters, thereby influencing emotional and cognitive functioning. As much as they can have negative consequences in adults, still more profound negative consequences can occur in adolescents, in whom frontal cortical functioning is still developing, which can obviously have long-term repercussions.

Prolactin

Although estrogens and androgens have received the greatest attention in relation to sex-related behaviors and development, other hormones also contribute in this regard. The prime function of *prolactin*, which is released from the anterior pituitary, is that of promoting lactation. Prolactin is stimulated by suckling in mammals, and among birds by tactile and visual stimuli from the nest, eggs, or chicks themselves. In addition to maternally-related behaviors, prolactin also contributes to several other essential biological processes, including sexual behavior and sexual pleasure, eating-related processes, pain perception, and responses to emotional stressors.

'BREAST IS BEST'

Humans are the only species in which women can opt not to breast feed their infants and substitute this with formulas. Breast feeding occurs across countries and cultures, but tends to be more common in non-industrialized countries, possibly because of the costs of alternatives. In some countries paid leave and workplace accommodations have made it easier for mothers to breast feed, but even so, many women choose not to do so or engage in breast feeding for limited amounts of time. In a detailed review of this topic it was concluded that this method of feeding infants has multiple benefits (Jonas & Woodside, 2015). We've all heard that breast feeding may help bonding by causing the release of hormones, such as oxytocin, but it has multiple other important functions. Jonas and Woodside pointed out that breast milk contains nutrients such as fat, protein, vitamins, and minerals, and long chain polyunsaturated fatty acids that contribute to the development of cognitive and motor processes. Furthermore, breast milk contributes to growth factors and hormones that affect neurodevelopment, as well as immunoglobulins important to prevent some infections. As a result, relative to bottle-fed infants, those who were breast-fed were less likely to develop respiratory tract infections, problems associated with the gastrointestinal tract, obesity, diabetes, and childhood leukemia and lymphoma (e.g., Amitay & Keinan-Boker, 2015). Extended duration of breast feeding was also accompanied by enhanced cognitive abilities in children. Whether these effects stemmed from the biological changes that come from breast feeding or were secondary to other factors is uncertain.

It's not just the infant who gains from breast feeding. Jonas and Woodside pointed to the benefits gained by the mom, including reduced risk of later breast and ovarian cancer, metabolic disorders, type 2 diabetes, and anxiety. These moms were also more sensitive to their children's requests, reflected by brain changes elicited by the cries of their children. Furthermore, meta-analyses have pointed to this practice diminishing risk for several illnesses in moms, such as type 2 diabetes (e.g., Jäger et al., 2014). However, here again, intervening variables could influence the observed differences between breast- versus bottle-fed infants.

Not all scientists agree that breast is best, intimating that many studies supporting that view were beset by procedural problems. In general, white infants were more likely to be breast-fed than were black infants, which was linked to household income and education, and thus could have been the critical link to well-being. When these factors were controlled for in statistical models of data collected from the National Longitudinal Study of Youth, which tracked individuals from 1986 through 2010, it seemed that the advantages of breast feeding were absent (Colen & Ramey, 2014).

Within the US, 75% of new mothers initially breast feed their children, but owing to several factors, by the time the child is 6 months of age, only 13% do so exclusively. Yet, both the World Health Organization and American Academy of Pediatrics recommend exclusive breast feeding for the first 6 months of life, and combined breast and formula feeding until 1 or 2 years of age. The US Surgeon General has provided a list of recommendations for mothers and employers so that breast feeding is facilitated (www.surgeongeneral.gov/library/calls/breastfeeding/index.html).

Oxytocin

The hormone oxytocin is released during childbirth as well lactation, and is thought to be important in mother–child attachment formation. Beyond this, oxytocin has also been implicated as being fundamental for other prosocial behaviors, such as love, generosity, altruism, empathy, sacrifice, the motivation to be with others (social motivation), and even the ability to infer the emotions of others based on their facial cues (McQuaid et al., 2014). When oxytocin receptors are altered (through a gene polymorphism) individuals may be less responsive to socially-related environmental triggers (Cardoso, Orlando et al., 2014; Insel & Young, 2001), may see the world as more threatening, and might have a tendency to be less generous (Campbell, 2010).

There has been a considerable increase in public interest regarding oxytocin, fueled by the media, which refer to it as 'the love hormone'. Given its role in social interactions, social identity, and trust (Kosfeld et al., 2005), this hormone may have a pronounced influence on many attributes related to interpersonal interactions as well as our abilities to use social factors in helping us deal with stressors. While not denying a role for oxytocin in promoting prosocial behaviors, as we'll see in Chapter 5, it has been suggested that oxytocin may have a darker side in relation to behavioral outputs, depending on different contexts and interactions with other hormone and neurotransmitter processes (McQuaid et al., 2014).

GROWTH FACTORS

Growth factors (*neurotrophins*) comprise substances that are fundamental for cellular growth and proliferation, as well as cellular differentiation (the latter allows cells to become specialized and to engage in particular functions), and can promote the development and growth of new neurons (Huang & Reichardt, 2001). So, contrary to the long-held belief that whatever neurons you had at birth was the maximum you would ever have, there is the possibility that in some brain areas new cells can be born, although the number is likely to be relatively small. Still, if these cells could be encouraged to develop, then ways might be established to treat disorders that stem from neuronal loss.

The best known and most widely studied aspect of neurotrophins is their capacity to enhance *neuroplasticity*, generally referring to formation of synaptic connections and the strengthening of these connections owing to experiences, learning and memory, thinking, and emotional responses. With continued experiences these neurotrophins allow for increased communication between neurons and the creation of increasingly sophisticated neuronal networks. The most widely studied growth factor in relation to psychological processes is brain-derived neurotrophic factor (BDNF). This growth factor can be disturbed by environmental challenges, such as stressful events, and thus in addition to affecting memory processes it has been implicated in a variety of psychological disorders, such as depression and PTSD (Duman & Monteggia, 2006), which we'll hear more about in Chapter 5.

Yet another growth factor, basic fibroblast growth factor (FGF-2), operates much like BDNF. This growth factor is also affected by stressful events, and may influence neurogenesis within the hippocampus, and could thus influence memory processes and mood states (Molteni et al., 2001). Numerous other growth factors have been identified, each of which has specific functions, although there is considerable overlap in what they do. Table 3.4 presents a listing of some of these growth factors and their presumed functions.

Table 3.4 Growth factors

Neurotrophin	Biological effect	Outcome
Brain-derived neurotrophic factor (BDNF)	Supports survival of neurons; encourages growth and differentiation of new neurons; promotes synaptic growth.	Influences memory processes, stress responses, mood states.
Basic fibroblast growth factor (bFGF or FGF-2)	Involved in neuroplasticity; formation of new blood vessels; protective actions in relation to heart injury; essential for maintaining stem cell differentiation.	Contributes to wound healing; neuroprotective; diminishes tissue death (e.g., following heart attack); related to anxiety and depression.
Nerve growth factor (NGF) and family members Neurotrophin-3 (NT-3) and Neurotrophin-4 (NT-4)	Contributes to cell survival; growth and differentiation of new neurons. Fundamental for maintenance and survival of sympathetic and sensory neuron; axonal growth.	Survival of several types of neuron; new neuron formation from stem cells; related to neuron regeneration, myelin repair, and neurodegeneration. Implicated in cognitive functioning, inflammatory diseases, in several psychiatric disorders, addiction, dementia as well as in physical illness, such as heart disease, and diabetes.
Insulin-like growth factor 1 (IGF-1)	Secreted by the liver upon stimulation by growth hormone (GH).	Promotes cell proliferation and inhibits cell death (apoptosis).
Vascular endothelial growth factors (VEGF)	Signaling protein associated with the formation of the circulatory system (vasculogenesis) and the growth of blood vessels (angiogenesis).	Creates new blood vessels during embryonic development, encourages development of blood vessels following injury, and creates new blood vessels when some are blocked. Muscles stimulated following exercise. Implicated in various diseases, such as rheumatoid arthritis, and poor prognosis in relation to breast cancer.

IMMUNE FUNCTIONING

The immune system's job is that of protecting us from all sorts of potential foreign invaders in the form of bacteria, viruses, and a constellation of other microorganisms that seem intent on harming us. In order to be able to do its job effectively, the immune system needs to be able to distinguish between what is part of the self from that which isn't, and then get rid of the foreign particles. The immune system is capable and tough, but it's obviously limited in some respects given that we often do develop illnesses. Viral and bacterial infections are common, as are endemic illnesses and epidemics, and the risk of pandemics seems to be a pervasive threat. Cancers appear to be able to get around our immune defenses, diseases such as HIV/AIDS do their dirty work by causing our immune response to be compromised, allergic reactions occur when aspects of our immune system become too pronounced, and sometimes our own immune system, like a traitorous best friend, can turn on us so that an *autoimmune disorder* develops (i.e., where the immune system attacks the self). Some people seem to have particularly effective immune systems that are well equipped to deal with challenges, but what is it that makes them this way? Is this connected to the genes inherited or to life-style factors? Do neurotransmitter and hormonal processes affect immune functioning, and does immune functioning also affect CNS processes and hence encourage the development of psychological disorders?

How the immune system operates

To consider these questions, an understanding of how the immune system works is necessary, even if this is at a very rudimentary level. The immune system is often described as being analogous to an army equipped with different regiments that go into the battle at different times. Some troops, based on their experience, are responsible for recognizing the enemy and also recognizing the self so that attacks aren't misdirected (friendly fire). Troops are needed at the front lines with the intent of slowing down the enemy advance, and more specialized, stronger troops are brought up to go into the battle should the first line of defense be breached. Communication between different cells within the immune system is necessary so that more troops can be brought to the front lines, so that they enter the battle at the right time, and so that they disengage and return to the barracks once the battle is won.

Innate and acquired immunity

The immune system begins to develop prenatally, and at birth can fend off some challenges, although immune system functioning still has some way to go before it's ready for a ruthless environment filled with multiple threats. During the course of prenatal development, immune cells learn about tissues that are part of the self, and thus when they encounter foreign particles postnatally, their '*innate immunity*' is critical in identifying what's part of the self and, by exclusion, what is foreign (e.g., Medzhitov, 2007). After birth, as immune cells come into contact with foreign materials, further learning occurs about foreign matter, which is referred to as '*adaptive*' or '*acquired*' immunity (Pancer & Cooper, 2006). When our immune cells first encounter a virus we might become ill as it takes some time for an immune response to be mounted and the enemy engaged. However, having learned about foreign particles (*antigens*), should they again be encountered, a greater and faster immune response (*secondary immune response*) is mounted so that the virus is destroyed before we become ill (Janeway et al., 2005).

Monocytes, neutrophils and macrophage

Travelling through our bodies are several types of white blood cells responsible for identifying and destroying foreign particles (Roitt et al., 2001). Of these, *neutrophils* and *monocytes*, which are particularly abundant, respond quickly to bacteria. Monocytes will leave the bloodstream and convert to *macrophages*, which remove dead cells as well as attacking and engulfing microorganisms, a process referred to as *phagocytosis*. After gobbling up foreign particles, macrophages break them down and present a portion of them to other immune cells (e.g., *lymphocytes*), some of which have the capability of recognizing whether or not the particle is foreign.

Lymphocytes

Lymphocytes come in several varieties, including T and B cells formed in the thymus and bone marrow, respectively. In addition, they are present in lymph nodes, spleen, and lungs, which serve as secondary lymphoid organs. One form of T cell, the *T helper* (Th) cell, is responsible for recognizing the foreign particles presented to them by macrophages. Once this recognition has occurred, the Th_1 cells (a form of Th cell) will inform *T cytotoxic* cells of this, causing them to multiply rapidly (this is what causes glands to swell) and then act against the virus. Being devious, viruses ordinarily infiltrate body cells and use their machinery to multiply within the cell, after which they burst forth to infect other cells. To counter this, T cells will bind with infected cells, rupture the cellular membrane and inject enzymes into it (a processes referred to as *lysis*), thereby causing the viral contents to be destroyed. Thus, when this '*cellular*' immune response is instigated, T cells are destroying whole factories of virus producers. Once the job of getting rid of the foreign particle has been completed, yet another type of T cell, referred to as Treg cells, are responsible for getting cytotoxic T cells to stop their attacks. At the same time, certain Th cells, notably Th_2 cells, release anti-inflammatory cytokines that act against the pro-inflammatory actions that had been instigated by Th_1 cells.

In addition to destroying invaders through T cytotoxic cells, Th cells also excite *B cells* which multiply prodigiously and go into battle to fend against foreign invaders. The B cells do this through the production of *antibodies* or *immunoglobulin* molecules (abbreviated Ig) that recognize foreign particles based on earlier experiences, trap and mark them, and then call upon other agents (*complement factors*) to help complete the job of destroying them. This process is frequently called *humoral immunity* because the substrates involved in this immune response are found in body fluids (or humors). The B cells secrete several classes of immunoglobulin molecules (IgA, IgD, IgE, IgM, and IgG) that have somewhat different functions, reside in different places, and are called upon at different times. Thus, they differ with respect to which antibodies meet antigens first and, correspondingly, they are activated at different times over the course of an immune response being mounted.

Natural killer (NK) cells

Yet another type of immune cell that acts like a front-line defender is the *natural killer* (NK) cell, which seem to have learned about the self during prenatal development. These cells travel through the body just as T cells do, and serve to destroy virally infected cells or those that have become cancerous. These aren't the strongest immune cells, despite their threatening name, but are fundamental in keeping infection from becoming excessive, thus allowing for the build-up of more powerful T cells to come into action at an appropriate time.

Immunological memory

One of the most important features of T and B cells is that they may develop an *immunological memory* of a foreign particle that had been encountered. When this particle or one that is sufficiently similar to it is again met some time later, a rapid and robust immune response is mounted so that the illness typically doesn't develop. When T and B cells are primed or *sensitized* to respond in a particular way, they undergo *clonal* expansion (increased multiplication, also termed *proliferation*) and each of their progeny behave in the same particular way, thus leading to a powerful immune response. As well, *passive immunity* can occur, which comprises the transfer of humoral immunity as in the form of maternal antibodies from a pregnant woman to the fetus. There are instances, however, in which immune memory might not help us avoid illness. Specifically, a virus may be successful in hiding (e.g., within nerve cells) and may re-emerge at some later time, perhaps in a different form. For example, shingles (herpes zoster) may develop among those who had had chickenpox years earlier.

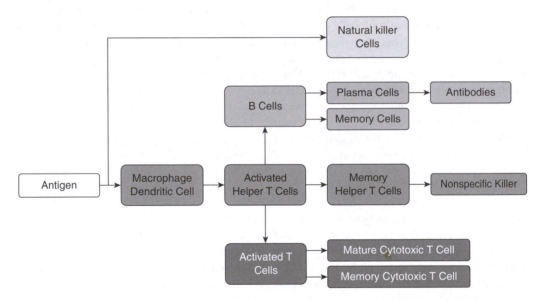

Figure 3.4 Following exposure to an antigen (or pathogen), an immune response is mounted. This comprises a rapid activation of natural killer cells, and a sequence of changes in which macrophages gobble up the foreign particles, digest them, and then present them to T helper cells that decide whether they are part of the self or a foreign substance. In the latter instance, T and B cells are informed, which then multiply. Activated T cells will mature and then destroy foreign particles present within cells, whereas B cells do so through secreting antibodies that bind with the antigen indirectly, causing its destruction. Once the threat is removed, another form of T helper cell, together with T regulatory cells (Treg), will act to quiet the immune response. Some of the T and B cells will retain a memory of the foreign particle so that a more rapid and stronger response is mounted should this threat reappear at a later time.

Cytokines

Just as neurons within the brain communicate with one another, so do immune cells, although the nature of the communication is less elaborate or sophisticated. Communication between these cells occurs through the release of signaling molecules, *cytokines*, which are manufactured within immune cells and in brain microglia (O'Shea & Murray, 2008). In the periphery these cytokines cause the growth and differentiation of lymphocytes, and exert a regulatory effect on them (much like the growth factors discussed earlier). In the context of research related to health psychology, the best known cytokines are interleukin (IL)-1β, IL-6, tumor necrosis factor-α (TNF-α), and interferons (IFN), all of which encourage inflammation and are thus referred to as pro-inflammatory cytokines. Tight regulation of immune and cytokine functioning is essential given their role in our survival. The Goldilocks principle applies in this regard (not too hot, not too cold; not too little, not too much), and immune functioning is managed through the balance of pro- and anti-inflammatory cytokines (e.g., IL-4 and IL-10), which vary over the course of an infection. Pro-inflammatory cytokines ought to predominate initially and during the main part of infection, but once the foreign particles have been eliminated, anti-inflammatory cytokines should become more prevalent in an effort to dissuade T cells from continuing in an attack mode.

Cytokine–endocrine interactions

Immune functioning is also regulated through the influence of various hormonal processes. Endocrine and immune factors signal one another, and reciprocal balances exist to keep their functioning within a particular range (Blalock, 1994). In this regard, cortisol, the hormone that is integral to the stress response, plays an especially significant role. It is activated by inflammatory stimuli and, conversely, it can dampen inflammatory immune functioning (Sternberg, 2006). When cortisol is increased, but remains within *physiological levels*, meaning it is within the 'normal' range observed in response to challenges, it sets a cap on immune functioning so that it doesn't become excessive. At *pharmacological levels*, induced by exogenous administration of the hormone (or drug treatments), the considerably higher cortisol levels may have an immunosuppressive action. Thus, alone or in combination with other agents, it has been used in treating illnesses where high levels of immune system actions are harmful. Cortisol isn't alone in serving in this regulatory capacity; epinephrine, CRH, melanocortin, thyroid hormones, as well as estrogen and progesterone all have immunomodulatory actions (Blalock, 2005).

Cytokine–brain interactions

It had long been thought that the brain was 'immunologically privileged' in the sense that it was independent of immune functioning. However, just as CNS processes may come to affect immune functioning, an activated immune system may influence brain functioning. Immune cells can communicate with the brain through cytokines, which, despite their large size, directly or indirectly affect neurotransmission (Nadeau & Rivest, 1999). Indeed, in several respects the actions of inflammatory factors on brain functioning are akin to the effects of stressful events. This has contributed to the suggestion that the brain interprets peripheral immune challenges as if they were stressors, thereby promoting symptoms of mood and anxiety-related disorders as well as several neurological disturbances (Anisman & Merali, 1999). Cytokines appear within the brain (some more than others), possibly coming from the periphery, but they can also be generated by microglia resident within the CNS. In response to physical and chemical insults (e.g., concussion, seizure, cerebral ischemia, chemically induced brain lesions), and systemic challenge with bacterial agents or viruses, as well as strong stressors, cytokine expression within the brain increases appreciably (Anisman et al., 2008). The increased cytokine presence might act in a protective or a reparatory capacity; however, if their levels become excessively high, they might instead have destructive actions (Rothwell & Luheshi, 2000). The important point for the moment is that complex interactions exist among immune, hormonal, and brain neurochemical systems, which can then influence behavioral outcomes; and conversely, brain processes can affect each of these systems (Maier & Watkins, 1998).

Challenges to immunological functioning

There are occasions where the capacity of the immune system to protect us may be compromised. Chronic stressful experiences, for instance, could impair T, B, and NK cell multiplication, as well as their proficiency in eliminating foreign threats. Such effects can be elicited in animals by exposing them to predator odors, social aggression, or social instability, and in humans similar changes accompany psychologically stressful experiences, such as ostracism, relationship difficulties, job strain, and illness (Kemeny & Schedlowski, 2007; Slavich, Way et al., 2010).

It is hardly surprising that poor diet and loss of sleep may also affect immune system functioning and may thus contribute to the development or exacerbation of illnesses (Irwin, 2015). These life-style factors can also interact with stressful experiences to further influence the development of illness, and stressful events themselves will affect eating, sleep, and exercise, thereby making the effects of stressors that much worse. In Chapter 10 we'll be dealing with illnesses associated with impaired immunity and we'll come back to this topic in greater detail.

THE ENTERIC NERVOUS SYSTEM AND THE MICROBIOME

Our skin and immune factors that are present wherever entry to the body is possible (eyes, nose, mouth) protect us from the potential bad players that are lurking about. In a way, the good bacteria in the gut as well as immune factors that are present serve in a similar capacity. Stuff that gets to our tummy might not be all that clean, and bacteria that we have inherited (usually from mom during pregnancy and during actual delivery) serve as a barrier against microorganisms that threaten us.

The enteric brain

Within fields such as psychology and neuroscience, the focus of research has been on the brain and autonomic and immune systems, and much less attention had been devoted to the '*enteric nervous system*', which refers to the nervous system associated with the gut. In fact, many people are surprised at the notion that there's anything brain-related concerning the gut. Yet, the gut contains millions of neurons that communicate through many of the same neurotransmitters that are found in the brain. The enteric system runs through tissue that lines the esophagus, stomach, small intestine and colon, and is able to influence brain functioning, just as the brain influences gut functioning (Gershon, 2000). Further, messages to the brain may occur through different routes, such as through stimulation of the *vagus nerve*, which extends from the viscera to the brain stem. Gut hormones, such as ghrelin, can also affect brain activity, thereby influencing hunger and obesity (Suzuki et al., 2010) and, as we saw earlier, may also influence mood and reward processes.

Microbiota

Our intestine isn't a pristine place; it contains 100 trillion microorganisms of about 500–1,000 different bacterial species. The word 'bacteria' elicits negative connotations related to infection, and indeed some gut bacteria can be very bad for us, but some also come in a good form that keeps us well. Despite the great number of species that exist within the gut, about 30% comprise four key species – *B. thetaiotaomicron*, *B. vulgatus*, *B. distasonis*, and *B. fragilis* – which are probably particularly important in determining well-being (Sears, 2005). Gut bacteria are involved in the digestion of foods – including those that the stomach and gut couldn't effectively digest, fighting against microorganisms that could produce negative consequences, the production of vitamin K, enhancement of fat storage, as well as contributing to the production of gut-associated lymphoid tissue and augmentation of immune functioning (Sears, 2005). Moreover, gut microbiota and its genome (*microbiome*) are fundamental in determining energy balance, and can affect several hormones, neurotransmitters, and immune factors. The metabolic functioning of gut microbiota is extensive and essential, to the extent that gut bacteria, collectively, have been referred to as 'a forgotten organ' (O'Hara & Shanahan, 2006).

The immune system in the gut has a tough balancing act to perform. On the one side it must respond to challenges in the form of pathogens, but on the other it must also be nonresponsive to food antigens and the microflora that are *commensal* (i.e., those bacteria that act in a positive symbiotic fashion with other factors). It seems likely that gut bacteria have evolved to maintain diversity, thereby increasing their ability to fight off a greater variety of bad bacteria that could appear, but concurrently act cooperatively with good bacteria. In fact, when times get tough (e.g., being in a low oxygen environment), gut bacteria even secrete substances that facilitate the survival of other bacterial species (Heinken & Thiele, 2015).

Gut and immunity

As in the case of so many of our other functions, multiple players are involved in shaping and maintaining intestinal immunity, including nutrition, short chain fatty acids, particular vitamins, cytokines, collaboration between specific types of immune cells, and commensal microflora (Spencer & Belkaid, 2012; Veldhoen & Brucklacher-Waldert, 2012). An animal can survive without the presence of gut bacteria, but their ability to withstand immunological challenges, for instance, will be markedly diminished (Rakoff-Nahoum et al., 2004). It also appears that among rodents born entirely germ-free, normal immune development that occurs postnatally is hindered, lymphoid disturbances will appear, and the balance between various aspects of the immune system will be thrown off, culminating in pathological vulnerabilities. In a like fashion, antibiotic treatments early in life can alter the microbiome and thus have long-term ramifications on well-being. Further, the vertical transmission of microbial protection that comes with vaginal birth may be precluded through Caesarean delivery, thus leaving offspring vulnerable to illness (Peterson et al., 2015). There are, to be sure, several other elements that determine the microbial functioning of a newborn organism. This includes the specific foods that had been consumed by mom while she was pregnant as well as her general health and her use of medications, such as antibiotics.

It seems that a continuous battle persists between good bacteria in our gut and those that are harmful. Some of the good bacteria come from the food we eat and others are released by the epithelial cell layer (these line both the cavities and surfaces of structures), and even a modest increase shifts the balance to the good guys (Schluter & Foster, 2012). We are also blessed with a gene (dubbed SIGIRR), which stimulates immune responses that act against bad bacteria forming colonies that negatively affect health. However, disruptions of SIGIRR by antibiotics can cause the battle for supremacy to move toward the bad bacteria (Sham et al., 2013).

Illnesses related to microbiota alterations

When the balance between good and bad bacteria favors the bad, metabolic dysfunctions can arise (e.g., insulin resistance), inflammatory bowel disorder can be provoked (Sanz et al., 2015), as can colorectal cancer (Louis et al., 2014). The influence of gut bacteria doesn't stop there, having been implicated in other disturbances ranging from chronic fatigue syndrome, fibromyalgia, mood disorders, alcoholism, and heart disease (Galland, 2014). Bacterial enzymes can also produce metabolites, such as D-lactic acid and ammonia, which can be toxic to neurons. It has also been reported that about 90% of the serotonin found in our periphery (only a small portion exists in the brain where it acts as a neurotransmitter) is formed in the digestive tract, some of which is made by bacteria (Yano et al., 2015). The peripheral serotonin may play a role in the promotion of illnesses such as irritable bowel syndrome, osteoporosis, and heart disease. Similarly, eating disorders, such as anorexia nervosa and bulimia, are influenced by specific proteins made by bacteria that affect eating (Tennoune et al., 2015).

Fortunately, *probiotics* (ingested microorganisms believed to have beneficial effects) and *prebiotics* (chemicals that promote the growth of microorganisms) can attenuate chronic disorders of the gut (DuPont & DuPont, 2011), and can influence obesity and metabolic syndrome (Delzenne et al., 2011). For that matter, changes of gut bacteria early in life can have persistent effects on health. For instance, when female mice that were genetically at risk for type 1 diabetes were treated with normal gut bacteria from adult mice, the likelihood of diabetes developing was reduced by 85%. This was accompanied by an increase of testosterone (which it will be recalled is present in females, although to a lesser extent than in males), and appeared to be essential for the effects of the gut bacterial treatment to be effective (Markle et al., 2013). It is of interest, as well, that gut bacteria can be passed from a mom to her child (e.g., through breast feeding). In a pregnant woman, good gut bacteria can affect those present in the fetus but, by the same token, among pregnant women using antibiotics, the loss of good bacteria will be felt by both mom and the fetus. During delivery the infant obtains further good bacteria present in the mom's birth canal, and it has been maintained that differences are apparent between babies born vaginally and those born through C-section, which can have lasting health repercussions (Bäckhed et al., 2015).

ANTIBIOTIC JEOPARDY

Antibiotics have been used for decades to deal with bacterial infections. These were at one time the wonder drugs that could do what no other drug could, but their effectiveness has diminished as increasingly more bacteria have become resistant to these agents. There's a second issue that needs to be considered in relation to the effects of antibiotics, namely that they not only kill potentially harmful bacteria, but also destroy good bacteria. When the balance of these bacteria shifts to the bad side, vulnerability to infection is increased. One particular condition, Clostridium difficile (C. difficile) infection has become rampant, most often appearing among hospital patients who had been treated with antibiotics. C. difficile is not uncommon, with 3 million new cases being reported each year, accompanied by 100,000 deaths, and has become increasingly more frequent within the community (i.e., outside hospitals). Several antibiotics can be used to treat C. difficile, such as *Metronidazole* and *vancomycin*, with about comparable efficacy (Drekonja et al., 2011), but the problem may reoccur. New treatments may be around the corner, at least based on animal studies in which two immunization treatments mustered a strong response by anti-toxin antibodies (Baliban et al., 2014).

Probiotics have become increasingly popular, so that some people might choose to use natural probiotic treatments to eliminate C. difficile, but in general this strategy isn't particularly useful, and is not recommended for use, even as an add-on to standard medication (Pillai & Nelson, 2008). Not long ago, variants of C. difficile emerged that were more destructive and were resistant to some antibiotics, probably owing to people overusing antibacterial agents. In these cases, fecal microbiota obtained from a healthy donor are transplanted (in a liquefied and purified form, most often by colonoscopy or through the nasogastric route) to the affected individual, thereby reestablishing the colony of good bacteria, leading to success almost 90% of the time (Brandt et al., 2011). For those who are squeamish about treatment through colonoscopy or through a nasogastric tube, new delivery methods involving acid-resistant capsules have allowed for oral administration (Youngster et al., 2014). It seems, however, that full fecal transplants might not be needed as a small set of bacteria that alter the composition of bile acids may be sufficient to do the trick. Specifically, a cocktail containing the bacteria C. scindens and three other bacteria that partially attenuate C. difficile, effectively eliminated C. difficile (Buffie et al., 2015). So, that's the poop on this issue.

There is some good news in our war against bacteria. Perhaps more companies will come out against using animals loaded with antibiotics, people might become more educated and stop using antibiotics when they get the sniffles, especially as antibiotics don't work against viruses, and thus antibiotic resistance might develop less readily. Better antibiotics might also be created, although many drug companies have dropped out of the antibiotic chase. There may also be changes afoot as to how antibiotic resistance is determined and infections treated. Ordinarily, this amounts to

(Continued)

(Continued)

taking some material from an infected area (or from blood or urine) and allowing resident bacteria to multiply in the presence of particular antibiotics. If they don't multiply, then the antibacterial agent will likely be a good one to treat the infection. However, if bacteria continue to multiply irrespective of the antibiotic present, then we're dealing with a resistant strain. This is all fine, except that it takes 16–24 hours to obtain results. New technologies allow for this to be reduced to 3–4 hours by determining whether antibiotics cause bacterial structure to change (Choi et al., 2014). If this approach pans out, same-day treatment will be possible for people with some sort of infection.

SUMMARY

The many behaviors in which we engage involve intricate and sensitive communication between neuronal processes. This is evident in the varied neurotransmitter functions that occur within and between brain regions, as well as interactions with hormone systems and the autonomic nervous system. It's also clear that considerable communication occurs between the brain and the immune system, and in this regard mood states and other stress responses could affect immune ability, and, conversely, immunological processes can affect brain functioning. Even gut-related systems have been considered to be a player in the complex interactions that govern immune, endocrine, and brain functioning, and thus behavioral outputs.

As we'll see in ensuing chapters, the functioning of these highly integrated systems are influenced by multiple external factors (stressors, diet, psychosocial experiences). Although we often attempt to identify individual factors that contribute to health disturbances, and then develop psychological tools to attenuate them, the very fact that so many systems interact with one another should, if nothing else, point to the complexities that are encountered in determining the development and course of illnesses, as well as how to attenuate them through behavioral methods. There are many routes by which environmental factors can impact endogenous processes leading to a pathological condition, and, as a result, a given treatment may be effective in attenuating symptoms of an illness in some individuals or under some condition, but not others.

4 The Stress Process

THE MOST PREDICTABLE THING ABOUT STRESSORS IS THAT THEY'RE UNPREDICTABLE

Although there are few certainties in life, we can pretty well count on meeting all sorts of stressful events. They can be isolated incidents, or they might occur in threes, sixes or twelves, perhaps becoming chronic and intractable, seemingly going on forever. Some will appear as social stressors involving family or friends, whereas others might involve financial strains or problems with health. What's also fairly certain is that events interpreted as stressful by one person might not be similarly appraised by a second, and even if they were viewed in the same way, entirely different methods might be used to cope.

There's yet another certainty concerning stressors. Specifically, there's no shortage of experts on the topic, offering strategies to diminish your feelings of distress. Massage, acupuncture, yoga, relaxation therapy, deep breathing, meditation, herbals, chiropractic, time management, exercise, pet therapy, music, cognitive therapy, mindfulness, anti-anxiety meds, antidepressants, spirituality, Tai chi, and chai tea. There's also advice offered through magazines written by some person who claims that stress can be relieved in just 10 minutes through 'being present' (I'm not sure what this even means). There are certainly some beneficial ways of dealing with stressors, but there's clearly an awful lot of cow-paddy as well.

In fact, there isn't any single best way of dealing with all stressors. Effective ways of coping vary across situations and over time, and just as a lot of frogs might need to be kissed before meeting Prince (or Princess) Charming, trying more than a single strategy might be necessary to beat the effects of stressors. More than anything, individuals need to be flexible in relation to how they deal with challenges, and they ought to be prepared to seek help.

DEFINING STRESS AND MODERATING FACTORS

What is it that makes some stressors more aversive than others, and what are the factors that make them so difficult to deal with? Why is it that we differ so broadly in how stressors affect us? What are some of the consequences of stressors on our psychological and physical well-being, and how do these come about? I've previously written about these topics in considerable detail (Anisman, 2014), and so only an abbreviated version is provided here. In this chapter we'll consider several of these questions, focusing on:

- the characteristics of stressors that make them more or less aversive
- how we appraise stressors
- how our appraisals (and misappraisals) come to affect coping efforts
- individual factors, such as age, sex, personality, that alter the way stressors are perceived or dealt with
- the short- and long-term consequences of stressors, as well as the source for intergenerational effects of collective trauma.

ATTRIBUTES AND DIMENSIONS OF STRESSORS

Stressor, stress, and distress

In assessing the consequences of stressors on health, we need to consider several characteristics of stressful events that make them seem more or less aversive than others. So that we're all working from the same playbook, let's first define a few terms. '*Stressor*' refers to a stimulus or event that is appraised as being negative. The *stress response*, often just referred to as '*stress*', is an outcome that can be reflected by emotional, behavioral, or biological changes that occur in response to a stressor, possibly in an effort to deal with it. The term '*distress*' will be used to refer to biological and psychological states or responses that develop as a result of the stressor becoming overwhelming or failure to deal with or adapt to it effectively.

Psychogenic and neurogenic stressors

There are an astounding number of different stressful experiences that can be encountered, each with their own unique features and consequences. In general, we can divide these as falling into several categories. *Processive* stressors, which involve cognitive (information) processing, may comprise *psychogenic* stressors, referring to those that are of a psychological origin (e.g., loss of a loved one, public humiliation), or *neurogenic* stressors that are of a physical nature (e.g., burns, cancer-related pain). Not surprisingly, psychogenic and neurogenic stressors will often have different behavioral and emotional consequences and will differentially influence brain neuronal processes, and as a result they can have important implications in the treatment of pathological conditions (Merali et al., 2004).

Stressors that involve interpersonal events, such as the death of a loved one or family problems, might promote responses that are distinct from those involving achievement-related adverse events, such as school- or business-related problems (Mazure et al., 2000). Moreover, whereas social stressors may have more profound effects in women than in men, job strain and competition may have greater consequences in men, and women may be more likely to encounter stressors than are men (Kendler et al., 2001). Unlike despair, which might arise owing to stressful events that have already occurred (e.g., loss of some sort), stressors that are anticipated (e.g., the dread of seeing the bully in the schoolyard, anticipation of imminent surgery) are more likely to be accompanied by anxiety (Harkness, 2008). Still, other anticipatory stressors, especially if they are ambiguous in nature (e.g., the pilot of your plane announcing that 'we have to return to the airport' without further explanation) might be accompanied by heightened anxiety and vigilance, as well as disorganized cognitions while the situation plays out. Some stressors involve an evaluative component (e.g., where individuals are appraised, as in the case of public speaking or experiencing a job interview), or a social component (e.g., a falling-out with your best friend), which elicits strong emotional responses, such as feelings of shame, and they may be particularly apt to cause neurobiological changes (Dickerson & Kemeny, 2004). Although the effects of many stressors are fairly transient, those that instigate shame and public humiliation may be remarkably powerful, engendering life-long negative consequences (Robinaugh & McNally, 2010).

Systemic stressors

We are consciously aware of most stressors encountered, although subtle cues, especially those associated with previously experienced stressors, may have effects even if they seem to go unnoticed. Psychogenic and neurogenic stressors are all in some sense tangible (i.e., we can detect them physically or psychologically), but we can also encounter *systemic* stressors of which we're unaware, such as the presence of bacterial or viral challenges as well as disturbances of gut microbiota (intestinal bacteria). These challenges can influence brain neurochemical processes much like processive stressors do, and may be instrumental in promoting mood disorders related to anxiety and depression (Anisman et al., 2008). Unlike psychogenic and neurogenic stressors, which permit the opportunity for us to deal with them in some fashion, systemic stressors can behave like silent, insidious marauders that surreptitiously disturb physical and psychological health.

STRESSOR APPRAISALS

Primary and secondary appraisals

One of the fundamental views concerning stress processes, as described in Figure 4.1, links appraisal of stressful events to how we cope with these challenges, and how these influence well-being (Lazarus & Folkman, 1984). Appraisals of stressors vary considerably across individuals. By example, two individuals required to update their computer skills in a week-long set of lectures may have very different perspectives. One might see this as a chore that will cost them time away from their job, whereas the other might see this as a challenge in which a small investment of time will allow for considerable gains later on. These different appraisals might have been influenced by previous experiences in dealing with both similar and dissimilar events. Alternatively, they might have been the product of the individual's specific beliefs, self-perceived abilities, as well as personality dimensions related to self-efficacy, intolerance for uncertainty, hardiness, optimism, trait negative/positive affect, and extraversion and neuroticism (Anisman & Matheson, 2005; Hemenover & Dienstbier, 1996). When appraisals comprise a threat of harm/loss, negative emotions such as anxiety or anger may ensue, whereas appraisals that entail challenge and opportunity may elicit positive emotions, such as exhilaration and eagerness, and hence positive well-being.

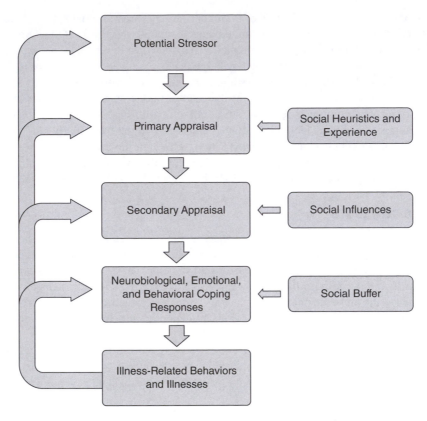

Figure 4.1   When we first encounter a novel, potentially stressful event, we make a primary appraisal of this event or stimulus, asking whether it represents a threat or risk to our well-being. We might then make a secondary appraisal, and consider whether we have the coping resources necessary to meet the demands placed on us. Once we know where we stand, we will endorse specific coping responses to deal with the challenge. At most steps along this process, social factors may influence appraisals or coping. Social heuristics (simplified appraisals based on experiences) can alter the way we initially appraise an event, and social influences can alter the secondary appraisals that are made. Likewise, social buffers (social coping) can influence the adoption of other coping methods. If individuals are able to make accurate appraisals and enlist effective methods of coping, stressor-related problems ought to be relatively limited. In contrast, making appraisal errors or adopting poor coping methods may favor the development of pathological conditions.

Appraisals, misappraisals, and heuristics

In a series of papers, Kahneman and Tversky (e.g., Kahneman & Tversky, 1996; Tversky & Kahneman, 1974) proposed a theoretical model related to decision making that has considerable significance regarding stressor appraisals. Fundamental to their model is that decisions are often made on the basis of information that is easily accessed as a result of earlier experiences or by previously established rules or shortcuts (*heuristics*). These strategies or shortcuts are influenced by several factors that comprise associative coherence, attribute substitution, and processing fluency. *Associative coherence* refers to the stimulus or event being consistent with our preconceived or *primed* 'intuitions'. Specifically, based on previous experiences or perhaps things we've heard in the past, we might form particular expectancies about a person or an event, which then influence our later appraisals. The second component, *attribute substitution*, means that when we have made a judgment about something, we might form further unconscious attributes about this stimulus. By example, if I have the impression that Rebecca is a charitable person, even though I know absolutely nothing more about her, I might also believe that she is kind, warm, and easy to get along with. The third element, *processing fluency*, refers to our subjective impression concerning the relative ease/difficulty associated with a particular appraisal – the easier it is to make a particular judgment, the more likely it is that it will be adopted.

PRIMES AND ANCHORS IN APPRAISALS AND DECISION MAKING

The view was offered that dual systems operate in making decisions; an automatic or Fast Thinking system (System 1) and a more cognitively based, Slow Thinking system (System 2) (Kahneman, 2011). The automatic, fast thinking system is 'primed' to react in a particular way in response to environmental events in decision-making situations. Our previous experiences, or even things we had been told about, can prime us to react in a particular way and might be especially important in stressful situations that call for fast responses. But, when relatively complex decisions need to be made, the cognitively-oriented slow thinking System 2 is called upon, possibly to override the fast System 1 responses that would otherwise be adopted (thereby precluding blunders).

We often find ourselves in ambiguous situations and we might lack the knowledge or experience to make proper appraisals that are necessary for appropriate decisions. This might entail something as straightforward as buying a used car, but you haven't got a clue about cars or what to offer. Alternatively, a government agency pronounces that the risk of illness stemming from a particular virus is high, but given your lack of knowledge on the topic you might be uncertain regarding what actions to take. To guide our decision making, we often look for 'anchors' that we can use to help us appraise the situation and make decisions. These anchors might comprise the asking price for a car or it might amount to something as prosaic as something that 'some guy said' or perhaps on what your friends or others are doing (social comparisons).

Unfortunately, even under excellent conditions, our appraisals aren't always accurate, and when we're stressed our ability to make proper appraisals may be compromised. Likewise, when our mood is bad, our appraisals of a situation are more likely to be negative, and, conversely, when things are generally going well and our spirits are up, our appraisals will be positive, and even situations that are patently negative might appear manageable. Essentially, the ways we appraise events are not only influenced by past experiences and by the anchors that are currently available, but, for better or worse, they can also be colored by our current mood.

CHARACTERISTICS OF STRESSORS

Stressful experiences can differ from one another across multiple dimensions, and their impact may be related to several of its characteristics. Most obviously, the consequences of a stressor will be related to its perceived severity, so that, other things being equal, the worse the stressor is perceived to be, the greater the negative impact it can have on well-being. However, it's not just severe stressors that can have negative repercussions, as even day-to-day minor stressors can have damaging effects. There are also instances in which stressors can have positive effects, producing an activating effect so that we can deal better with what's in front of us. The anxiety present before a public performance, provided that it is within a manageable range, may favor better outcomes. It is also the case that modest stressors can be instrumental in children learning how to cope with challenges and thus diminish the negative consequences of stressors that might subsequently be met (Katz et al., 2009).

To be sure, different stressors may have effects that vary appreciably, and it's difficult to make comparisons between different types of stressful events. Is loss of a loved one more stressful than experiencing a severe debilitating illness? Is financial loss more distressing than daily public humiliation? Each is terribly aversive and each is uniquely terrible in its own way, and there is little point in suggesting that one is worse than the next. As the saying goes, 'at night all black cows look alike'. Still, there are several fundamental principles that may be considered in predicting the types of event that can lead to more or less negative outcomes.

WORRYING: THE MIND NEVER RESTS

Some people just generally seem to think negatively, often being worriers or ruminators, whereas others are more likely to put a positive spin on events. The brain's responses to events among these two types of individuals seem to be quite different from one another. When participants were shown a negative image (a masked man holding a knife to a woman's throat) but asked to put a positive spin on the situation, the worriers tended to be less able to do this and brain imaging indicated a worsening of their negativity. It seems that negativity is an inherent characteristic that is difficult to change, and attempts at forced reappraisals can have counterproductive consequences (Moser et al., 2014). There are ways of changing negative thinking (e.g., cognitive behavioral therapy), but simply telling your distressed buddy "hey, think positively" probably won't be helpful.

It is understandable that the arousal, anxiety, and worry (and the neurochemical changes that accompany these emotions) are often taken in a pejorative sense. Yet, these emotions and the accompanying neurobiological changes may be highly adaptive, keeping individuals vigilant and ready to respond should a stressful situation escalate. These emotions become problematic primarily if a persistent state of arousal develops, possibly as a result of the belief that a threat is imminent all or most of the time, and might thus confer increased illness vulnerability (Hemenover & Dienstbier, 1996; McEwen & Morrison, 2013).

Stressor controllability

Among the most important attributes of stressors that make them more or less aversive concerns their controllability. It had been suggested that when animals experienced stressful events over which they had no control, cognitive changes emerged that impaired later performance in situations where they were required to escape from aversive stimuli (Maier & Seligman, 1976). These animals were thought to have learned that "nothing I do matters", essentially developing a cognitive schema of '*helplessness*', and in subsequent behavioral tests, even when escape from a stressor was possible, they failed to make attempts at controlling their own destinies. The impact of the initial uncontrollable stressor experience disturbed the animal's capacity to perform well in diverse situations, impaired new learning, diminished the animal's capacity to gain pleasure in tests where animals were required to work for rewards, and elicited a behavioral profile reminiscent of depression (Zacharko & Anisman, 1991). If, however, animals first learned that control over events was possible, they were *immunized* against the effects of subsequent uncontrollable stressor experiences so that behavioral disturbances were not apparent (Seligman et al., 1975). The clinical application of such findings is consistent with the view that if individuals first develop the mindset that they could control their destiny, they might be immunized against the adverse consequences of subsequently encountered uncontrollable events.

Studies initially conducted with animals gave rise to the notion that stressor controllability was pertinent to the development of human pathologies, including depression (Abramson et al., 1978; Alloy et al., 2008) and illnesses that might be comorbid with mood disorders. However, it was not universally accepted that these outcomes were due to cognitive changes that comprised feelings of helplessness, but instead, stemmed from a constellation of brain neurochemical changes that favored the development of behavioral deficits (Zacharko & Anisman, 1991). It could be argued that these neurochemical changes were a reflection of the helplessness engendered by uncontrollable events, but in some instances predictions based on a helplessness model don't comfortably map onto those associated with a neurochemical explanation. As we'll see in Chapter 5, neurochemical explanations concerning the effects of stressors have become progressively more complex and have had implications for treatment that go beyond those offered by a helplessness perspective.

Appraisals and attributions in relation to helplessness

Some people who experience stressful events succumb to illnesses, whereas others appear to be *resilient* and are able to get through the most horrid tragedies, or are able to bounce back from stress-related illnesses. So what is it that makes individuals so different, and what can this teach us in helping those who fall victim to stress-related disorders? One view, stemming from a helplessness perspective, is that the attributions and appraisals that individuals make regarding stressful events largely determine their impact (Abramson et al., 1978). It was proposed that individuals differ on three appraisal dimensions related to *locus of control* (beliefs concerning whether the outcomes of our actions are contingent on our own behaviors or factors that are outside our personal control), which can influence the development of helplessness. When individuals encounter a stressor, say failing at a particular task at school or at work, they frequently form attributions as to why this occurred. These attributions can be internal ("I'm not very good at math") or external ("the professor made the dopiest exam that had nothing to do with what he taught us"); they can be stable or unstable ("I've never been very good at math and never will be" versus "I should have worked harder at math, and I'll turn it around next time"); and they can be specific or global ("I'm not very good at math, but I have lots of other skills" versus "I'm not good at math or any other academic subjects"). Those who make negative external, stable, global attributions concerning their inabilities will develop negative expectations of what they can expect in the future, as well as develop broad feelings of inadequacy and poor self-esteem, culminating in feelings of helplessness and depression.

To be sure, the negative cognitions that lead to depression entail more than just attributions that individuals bring to particular situations, but might reflect negative appraisals and a general dysfunctional pattern of thinking (Beck & Dozois, 2011). These behavioral and cognitive styles might have arisen owing to the confluence of negative early life experiences, children's modelling of parental cognitive styles, and negative inferential feedback that comprises the tendency to attribute negative events to stable and widespread causes (Alloy et al., 2008). Thus, while not diminishing the potential role for stressor uncontrollability in relation to pathology, the effects of stressful experiences on the evolution of many pathological conditions go beyond that of acute, uncontrollable stressful events that are able to create feelings of helplessness.

Unpredictability and uncertainty

There are some events that we can count on experiencing, although their appearance may be either predictable or *unpredictable*. At the end of each school term it is predictable that there will be an exam period, but what specific questions will appear on the exam is less predictable. There are also stressors whose occurrence is *uncertain*, meaning that we don't know whether the event will actually occur (Will this flu that's been going around in Asia turn into a pandemic that affects most of us?). An uncertain event can also be unpredictable in that we may not know whether it will occur, but if it does, we might not know when it will happen. In general, the stressfulness of a situation increases with its unpredictability and uncertainty (Koolhaas et al., 2011).

THE VOICE OF DOOM AND GLOOM

Individuals, especially adolescents or those of university age, are often impulsive and they also frequently have a sense of invulnerability. As naïve as their perspective might be, they seemingly behave (and believe) as though bad things might happen to others, but will be less likely to happen to them. An optimism bias of this sort doesn't exclusively occur in younger individuals, being apparent among many people across numerous situations. Individuals seem to believe that relative to others they are at reduced odds of developing a severe illness, such as breast or prostate cancer, and that the possibility of being infected by a potential virus at some time in the future is also reduced (Taha et al., 2013, 2014). People not only had a sense of personal invulnerability, but they also believed that their close friends were less likely to contract an illness relative to the general population ('immunity by proxy'). Yet, if individuals thought that an acquaintance or family member had contracted the illness, then their own sense of invulnerability diminished. This type of bias is common, likely contributing to the unhealthy behavior of sun worshippers and smokers who might believe that 'it won't happen to me'.

For a time, news reports had indicated that the Ebola virus in parts of Africa was seemingly out of control. Thousand had been infected and many had died. Projections were that many more people would become infected before things got better. A poll conducted by the Harvard School of Public Health indicated that most people in the US knew relatively little about the Ebola virus, with about two-thirds believing that Ebola spreads easily and one-third believing that there was an effective treatment for the illness. There seems to be something particularly scary about Ebola, more so than many other viral illnesses. About 40% of people thought that the virus would spread to the US, and about 26% believed that they or their family members might become sick. Ebola far away was taken far more seriously than H1N1, which was in our backyards and homes, and actually killed many more people than Ebola had.

Stressful events that are certain allow us to prepare, whereas uncertainty leaves us confused about which way to turn and we might not even be sure if we should be engaging in particular behaviors to ward off the threat (My child has spiked a fever of 103°F, but I'm not sure whether this is serious or not, so do I rush to the ER or will I look stupid doing so?). Although uncertainty usually favors the emergence of negative stress responses, as we'll discuss in Chapter 15, in the context of illness in which treatment efforts have failed to stall the fatal course of a disease, it may be possible to capitalize on uncertainty as it allows people to maintain hope, despite the likelihood of the worst coming true (Mishel, 1999).

GAMBLING WITH FATE

People differ with respect to their 'intolerance of uncertainty', a trait characteristic in which individuals typically express elevated anxiety and distress in response to uncertain stressors, and persistently seek information in an effort to obtain proper information and thus reduce uncertainty. At the other end of the spectrum are those who seem to prefer that fate simply take its course, and actually prefer not to become enmeshed in the drama. There are instances in which individuals may or may not have inherited a particular gene that might influence the odds of developing a disease. Women with a family history of breast cancer attributable to a particular gene mutation (e.g., BRCA1 or BRCA2) might be inclined to be tested to determine whether they have inherited this gene, and thus feel as if they can exert some control over their lives. For instance, they might choose to undergo a double mastectomy and ovariectomy, thereby diminishing the possibility of developing breast or ovarian cancer. Others, in contrast, prefer not to know and are seemingly able to compartmentalize these thoughts and go on with life. However, where is the cut-off between feeling 'safe' and feeling sufficiently 'at risk' to take actions to thwart uncertain events? How certain (or uncertain) must a woman be that she will develop a form of cancer before she decides to take preventative action. This certainly varies across individuals, depending, for instance, on their tolerance for uncertainty and situational factors (e.g., does the woman have children who would be affected by her decision?).

Ambiguity

Related to uncertainty and unpredictability is the ambiguity of a threat. Ambiguous situations are those in which the available information is murky so that one might become suspicious that some bad event could occur, but be reluctant to become overly reactive. Thus strong responses are held in abeyance pending better information becoming available. It isn't unusual for individuals to develop physical symptoms that aren't sufficiently coherent to prompt them to seek medical attention, but are nevertheless worrisome. People will sometimes do nothing in the hope that the vague symptoms will simply disappear, but depending on their intolerance of uncertainty they might decide to see a physician. Of course, when symptoms are vague it's difficult for a physician to form a diagnosis and he/she will likely send the person off for tests that might cast some light on the situation.

When we encounter situations that involve a degree of risk, but in which ambiguity or unknowability are prominent, neuronal activity increases markedly in brain regions involved in decision making (Bach et al., 2009). Our brain seems dissatisfied with ambiguity, and neuronal activity may increase in an effort to make sense of this situation, especially among individuals with high intolerance for uncertainty. From the Kahneman and Tversky perspective, under these ambiguous conditions it is likely that a *representative heuristic* would be adopted in making an appraisal (i.e., appraising the situation based on other previous similar situations), and then acting accordingly.

Complexity

Some situations may become terribly complex, and it is difficult to decipher all the options before us, let alone make choices regarding the most appropriate way forward. When this occurs, and we're not blessed with a brain sufficiently adept to work out all the possible combinations, what we tend to do, as Kahneman indicated, is consider the problem in a simpler way or search for a simple solution to the problem (such as go with the opinion of our ingroup).

CHOOSING NOT TO CHOOSE

In his book *Paradox of Choice*, Schwartz (2004) points out that we like the idea of having choices, but having too many choices can be distressing. For instance, given too many options, individuals might think less about what they could gain from making a particular choice, and instead might focus more on missed opportunities that come from making other choices. Likewise, the tyranny of having too many choices may cause feelings of dissatisfaction with choices made. In a sense, when many choices are available that are equally palatable, as when choices are complex, people get stuck in their tracks and might make no choice at all. My friend tells me that a standard routine in her business is to provide customers with several options, so that they can get what's suitable for their kid. As it turns out, some individuals are readily overwhelmed by the choices, and their response is often "I think I'll go home and think about it". She fumes at this: "She's going home to think about it! What's there to think about? She's not making a critical decision like should I choose mastectomy versus lumpectomy". She says that she used to offer fewer choices, carrying only the single product that she believed was best. Although customers almost invariably followed store recommendations, they weren't fully satisfied unless they had choices.

Volatility

A characteristic of some threats is their volatility, in that features of the situation can change quickly and unpredictably. This type of threat is encountered in combat situations and among first responders, but hasn't been as widely studied in relation to stressors in other milieus. Some stressors encountered might get progressively worse or diminish systematically, and in either case we have the opportunity to adapt to the demands placed on us. However, there are instances in which stressors don't follow a predictable trajectory and go from a minor fire to a full-blown conflagration in just an instant. A headache shows up as an 'anomaly' on a brain scan, which can turn out to be an aggressive tumor based on a follow-up biopsy. One moment the person was perfectly healthy, and then they weren't, all in the blink of an eye. Clearly, this is very hard to deal with, and we need to be prepared, be nimble in using particular coping strategies, and have social networks that are ready and able to come to our side when the need arises.

ILLUSIONS AND DELUSIONS REGARDING STRESSORS

Many of us are deluded in thinking that we are in some way able to control our destinies, and that life has a predictable flow, and so we make plans for the future and behave as if we can reliably predict what's in store for us. Of course, with even a little bit of thought we realize that the predictability and controllability of life events are illusions (or delusions) that we adopt. It's obviously not for nothing that expressions have arisen that become folk-wisdom. Woody Allen's comment "If you want to make God laugh, tell him about your plans" adequately interprets the expression "mann tracht unt got lacht" – People think (plan) and God laughs.

Faulty assumptions concerning the degree of control we have over our lives might, unfortunately, leave us less prepared to deal with unpredictable, ambiguous, and volatile stressful situations when they do arise. Sudden unexpected illness, or events that affect whole communities (terrorists attacks, wars, nuclear plant meltdowns, hurricanes, famines, and floods) might catch us by surprise, and our ability to deal with these events might not be as direct and useful

(Continued)

(Continued)

as they would be if there had been an opportunity to prepare. In considering stock market investments, Taleb (2010) suggested that any given event that can shake the market is rare, which he refers to as a black swan, but given the number of potential events that can happen, it's unlikely that market shake-ups can entirely be avoided. Likewise, although any single traumatic event that we could personally encounter might occur infrequently, the sheer number of potentially negative events that are possible makes it unlikely that we'll get away entirely unscathed. In fact, 50–60% of individuals, even those of college age, reported that they had encountered traumatic events sufficiently severe to fill them with fear and horror. This brings us to the obvious question of what we ought to do about this. Is it possible to take pre-emptive steps so that we're relatively flexible in dealing with diverse events as they occur, or do we simply accept situations for what they are?

PREVIOUS STRESSOR EXPERIENCES

Stress sensitization

The stressors that we encounter are often moderate and transient, and not long after they've passed they might be banished from consciousness. As brief as a stressor might be, however, some events can haunt us for extended periods. This can occur as a result of encountering reminders of the event, whereas in other instances, such as experiencing public shame or humiliation, where we are diminished in the eyes of others, diminished feelings of the self might be incorporated into an individual's self-schema. As described by Nolen-Hoeksema (1998), although a stressor experience might have been transient, the rumination that follows may be far more persistent and can be exceptionally damaging.

How we appraise events may be influenced by our previous stressor experiences. Individuals who have experienced a traumatic event may subsequently be more cautious in relation to potentially stressful stimuli, and reminders of these experiences may have profound psychological and physical repercussions. These persistent effects of stressors likely come about owing, in part, to the brain's neuroplasticity. It will be recalled that in response to experiences, synaptic connections between neurons can be established and further strengthened as these experiences occur again. More than this, as we'll see in more detail in Chapter 5, stressful experiences may result in changes in the sensitivity or reactivity of neuronal processes, referred to as *sensitization*, so that later stressors will re-induce neuronal activation, thereby altering behavioral responses (Anisman et al., 2003). In fact, although fairly strong stressors may be needed to provoke a first episode of depression, the recurrence of illness can be brought about by relatively small challenges (Kendler et al., 2000) or even by reminders of stressful experiences (Monroe & Harkness, 2005).

Chronic stressors and allostatic overload

Some stressors may be encountered repeatedly and their nature might not vary appreciably over time, and thus we might be able to find ways to adapt to or deal with them. However, we might also encounter chronic challenges that are unpredictable and vary over time. As well, some chronic stressors, such as illnesses or caregiving for a person with psychological or physical disturbances, can have multiple secondary effects that are uncontrollable, unpredictable, and uncertain, making them that much more aversive and much more likely to affect us in the most negative ways. Whether we meet multiple stressors, or a stressor that causes continued rumination (or the individual is the ruminative type or disposed to chronic worrying), when brain regions associated with stress never have the opportunity to be recuperate, pathological outcomes may ensue (e.g., Yan et al., 2013).

TIME-OUT FROM STRESSORS

Through active or passive processes, the effects of stressors on biological systems ought to dissipate and hence negative outcomes are forestalled or entirely prevented. When reminders of the event are intermittently encountered, however, the dissipation of pathological processes is precluded (Maier, 2001). For individuals experiencing pervasive, continuous, ongoing stressors, such as those associated with war or stigmatization, their impact is doubly disastrous because they may lack safe places that would allow for healing and recovery to occur.

As we'll see, many neurotransmitter, endocrine, immune, and peripheral nervous system changes occur in response to stressors. These biological changes, which are usually activated fairly quickly, are essential to maintain stability within biological systems, while simultaneously providing resources needed to deal with external threats. These neurobiological adaptations, referred to as allostasis, operate together with behavioral, cognitive, and social processes to maintain our well-being. Allostasis is much like homeostasis, but because of the urgency of many stressful situations, it involves rapid mobilization of biological resources. As much as this is highly adaptive, when these mechanisms are engaged for protracted periods, *allostatic overload* may be experienced, wherein neurobiological circuits become overly taxed or might themselves have negative secondary repercussions on brain and body systems. As a result, vulnerability to a range of illnesses may be increased, including heart disease, immune-related disorders, neurodegenerative illnesses as well as psychological disturbances (McEwen, 2000). In addition to challenges that impact on us directly, insidious challenges comprising sustained social disturbances, social conflict, and poverty can engender what McEwen and Wingfield (2003) referred to as 'type 2' allostatic overload, which can markedly influence well-being and may require changes of social structures to prevent the development of pathology.

Cumulative stressor experiences

Most of us will experience stressors on multiple occasions, which may have cumulative effects that affect our health. The accumulation of stressors, such as living in a poor social environment, social isolation, and emotional disturbances may favor the processes that contribute to the development and progression of physical illnesses (Steptoe & Kivimäki, 2013). When multiple stressful events begin during childhood, including events secondary to childhood maltreatment and disturbed home environments, the odds of developing depression, suicidality, and drug abuse, as well as comorbid physical illnesses such as diabetes, are appreciably elevated in adulthood (Dube et al., 2003). Many of these illnesses such as heart disease, diabetes, and immune-related disorders don't simply appear overnight, but reflect the accumulation of small changes that develop over an extended period.

SURE ENOUGH, STRESS MAKES YOU OLD BEFORE YOUR YEARS

Some effects of chronic strain might be detectable by evaluating patterns of neurobiological changes (e.g., altered daily neurobiological rhythms), but in the main, the effects of chronic stressors aren't easily detected based on simple biological markers. Not long ago, evidence emerged that stressor experiences might have effects on telomeres, the caps that protect the tips of chromosomes, much like plastic aglets that protect a shoe lace from unravelling. With each replication of a cell these telomeres become shorter, so that with age the shortening of the telomeres will result in the cells being unable to replicate or dying (Sanders & Newman, 2013).

It is especially pertinent that stressful experiences are also accompanied by a reduction of the length of telomeres, and in a sense can be a marker of both aging and cumulative stressor experiences. Telomere length has been associated with stressful encounters during childhood, including maternal violence, verbal or physical assaults, or even witnessing domestic disputes (Entringer et al., 2011). Likewise, adult stressor experiences and reduced social support, lower optimism, and elevated physiological stress reactivity were accompanied by shortening of telomere length (Zalli et al., 2014), as were poor life-styles, smoking cigarettes, and high alcohol consumption (Bendix et al., 2014). Shorter telomere length has been related to a variety of age-related diseases, such as diabetes and heart disease, and appears to be dose-dependently related to early-life stressors in the sense that greater stress is accompanied by more pronounced illness (Price et al., 2013). Shortened telomere length is also linked to childhood adversities and lower socioeconomic status, which was linked to poorer health (Cohen et al., 2013). Given that stressors and poor life-styles are accompanied by reduced telomere length, is it also the case that positive life-styles are accompanied by increased telomere length? There have been reports indicating that moderate exercise increased telomere length, but this was attenuated with too much exercise (Ludlow et al., 2013), which, as we'll see later, may also be accompanied by poorer health outcomes.

It is uncertain whether telomere changes that have been observed were responsible for age- or stress-related health disturbances, although this claim has been made (see Chapter 11 dealing with cancer), but they might serve as a marker for their occurrence. Much like rings on a tree can inform us about its age and experiences (e.g., past weather conditions), telomere length can provide indications of past stressors, although the length of the telomeres doesn't tell us when the stressors occurred or what they comprised.

Coping processes

Having identified and appraised a stressor and deemed it to be a threat, particular coping strategies will be called upon in an effort to eliminate it or to diminish its impact. The coping strategies we use may vary across situations, but might be guided by our disposition to cope in particular ways (i.e., style of responding). Many coping methods can be used to deal with stressors, but they generally fall into about 15 coping methods that can be conceptualized within three broad classes: problem-, emotion-, and avoidant-focused coping. Often-used coping strategies within each of these three categories are described in Table 4.1, which I adopted from an earlier book that dealt with stress and coping (Anisman, 2014). In examining this table, you'll see that most coping methods were assigned to one category or another. However, many coping methods don't fall comfortably into a particular category, but instead serve in multiple capacities, depending on the context, and their role may also vary over the course of a lengthy stressor experience.

Table 4.1   Coping strategies

Problem-focused strategies

Problem solving: Finding methods that might deter the impact or presence of a stressor.

Cognitive restructuring (positive reframing): Reassessing or placing a new spin on a situation so that it may take on positive attributes. This can entail finding a silver lining to a black cloud.

Finding meaning (benefit finding): A form of cognitive restructuring that entails individuals finding some benefit or making sense of a traumatic experience. This might involve private, emotional, or cognitive changes, or active efforts so that others will gain from the experience.

Avoidant or disengagement strategies

Active distraction: Using active behaviors (working out, going to movies) as a distraction from ongoing problems.

Cognitive distraction: Thinking about issues unrelated to the stressor, such as immersing ourselves in our work, or engaging in hobbies.

(Continued)

Table 4.1   (Continued)

Denial/emotional containment: Not thinking about an issue or simply convincing oneself that it's not particularly serious.

Humor: Using humor to diminish the distress of a given situation.

Drug use: Using certain drugs in an effort to diminish the impact of stressors.

Emotion-focused strategies

Emotional expression: Using emotions, such as crying, anger, and even aggressive behaviors, to deal with stressors.

Other-blame: Comprises blaming others for adverse events. This is used to avoid being blamed, or as a way to make sense of some situations.

Self-blame: Blaming ourselves for events that occurred.

Rumination: Continued, sometimes unremitting thoughts about an issue or event, or replaying the events and the strategies that could have been used to deal with events.

Wishful thinking: Thinking what it would be like if the stressor were gone, or what it was like in happier times before the stressor had surfaced.

Passive resignation: Acceptance of a situation as it is, possibly reflecting feelings of helplessness, or simply accepting the situation without regret or malice ('it is what it is').

Religion

Religiosity (internal): A belief in God to deal with adverse events. This may entail the simple belief in a better hereafter, a belief that a merciful God will help diminish a negative situation.

Religiosity (external): A social component of religion in which similar minded people come together (congregate) and serve as supports or buffers for one another to facilitate coping.

Social support

Social support seeking: Finding people or groups who may be beneficial in coping with stressors. This common coping method is especially useful as it may buffer the impact of stressors and also serve multiple other functions in relation to stressors.

Stressor-provoked mood changes, such as depression, are often accompanied by high levels of emotion-focused coping and low levels of problem-focused efforts. As a result, it is often thought that emotion-focused coping methods are maladaptive, whereas problem-focused methods are preferable. In many instances this is the case, but this is far too simplistic. An emotional coping strategy that comprises verbal and nonverbal messages concerning one's emotions might reflect a request for help. As well, emotional coping can be used in acknowledging, exploring, and understanding emotional responses to challenges, and in emotionally charged situations it might be beneficial in helping individuals come to terms with their feelings, thereby diminishing distress (Stanton et al., 1994).

In some situations, especially when events are seemingly out of the individual's control, such as dealing with a terminal illness, problem-solving efforts might be of little benefit. Attempting to cope through problem-solving efforts may offer individuals the illusion that they have some control over their life, but it might be more effective to use avoidant coping methods (distraction) so that they can function effectively on a day-to-day basis. When a stressor is sufficiently severe, our capacity to cope through problem solving may also be disturbed as people might have difficulty planning and initiating actions. Furthermore, unlike non-stressed individuals, who, when placed in a problem-solving situation, ordinarily take the simplest approach to reach a solution, highly stressed individuals frequently engage in excessively complex strategies, despite not being able to articulate why they chose these strategies. In effect, stressful events may influence the way we deal with situations, moving us away from purposeful, conscious approaches to those that might not be particularly productive.

Although we've seen that there isn't a best single strategy to deal with all situations, there are certainly some people who are better able to deal with stressors than others. Several factors might feed into this ability, including being able to make appropriate appraisals of the situation. It is also essential to appreciate that any given coping strategy typically isn't used in isolation of others, and multiple coping methods are often used concurrently. Individuals who are best at dealing with stressors are those who are relatively adept in using particular coping strategies in conjunction with one another (Matheson & Anisman, 2003). By example, although rumination has frequently been associated with depressive illness (Nolen-Hoeksema, 1998), this occurs primarily when individuals adopt negative rumination in which other emotion-focused strategies (self-blame, recrimination, emotional expression) are co-expressed. Among individuals who are not depressed, stressors may lead to rumination, but this strategy may be accompanied by problem- and emotion-focused strategies, as well as cognitive disengagement (e.g., Things are bad right now, and I need to carefully consider the options I have available, or perhaps consult with some friends to find a way out of this jam) (Kelly et al., 2007). There is reason to believe that individuals who are skilled at using a relatively broad range of coping strategies, and who are flexible in their choice of coping methods, being able to shift from one strategy to another as the situation requires, may be best suited to deal with stressors. Furthermore, the use of particular coping strategies may vary over time following a stressor's first appearance (Tennen et al., 2000), and being able to adapt appropriate coping combinations as the stressor situation plays out may be advantageous. Those individuals with a narrow range of coping methods, especially if they are rigid in abandoning ineffective coping strategies, will likely be at a disadvantage and most likely to fare poorly (Cheng et al., 2014).

Finding meaning and personal growth

In response to mild or moderate stressors, we might put a particular spin on the situation as a way of coping. Cognitive restructuring, as described earlier, might comprise finding something positive in a negative situation, but this likely won't do the trick in response to very strong stressors. In such instances, cognitive restructuring may take on a different form, termed post-traumatic growth (also referred to as finding meaning or benefit finding). Having lived through a traumatic experience, individuals might try to make sense of the event and actually find some benefit from the experience (Davis et al., 1998). Survivors might use the experiences as a learning opportunity to improve their physical and mental health, or they may engage in a particular cause in an effort to spare others from similar experiences. In many cases we've seen successful national campaigns come out of such tragedies, such as creating laws against drunk driving or establishing programs to treat diabetes, spinal cord damage, Parkinson's disease, and mental illness, although in other cases positive outcomes have been limited (e.g., banning assault weapons).

At an individual level, those living through a severe trauma, such as dealing with cancer, might recognize positive implications of their experience or feel that they have grown from the experience (Sherman et al., 2010).

The struggle to survive an illness or the challenge of taking on large corporations that are viewed as being responsible for deaths due to negligence lend themselves to finding meaning. Yet, as much as a person might want to find meaning in horrible events, this might not always pan out. Searching for meaning ('meaning-making efforts') and arriving at a meaning ('meaning made') may be independent of one another, and not every person in search of meaning finds it (Park, 2010). For that matter, continued, unsuccessful efforts to find meaning might be indicative of an unhealthy preoccupation with an adverse event. In essence, finding meaning might only be effective to diminish distress for a subset of people and might not be useful across all situations. Meaning obtained through caregiving or by promoting research to treat specific illnesses can be psychologically healing. It's something else entirely to find meaning in relation to a person who died when drunkenly driving off the road, or death that occurred as a result of some freak act of nature, such as being hit by lightning.

COPING THROUGH RELIGION

There are topics that, as soon as they're raised, cause great controversy or condemnation, and for some individuals the value of religion sometimes falls into this category. There are many people who believe that religion is inherently bad or foolish, but for others it's an effective strategy to deal with stressful experiences. It's a core component of their identity, and it can serve as an effective coping strategy, providing comfort, especially when all else has failed (Pargament, 2001). Provided that it isn't an exclusive alternative for dealing with illness (e.g., simply praying that a cancer will disappear isn't a great curative method), religion can help to diminish health disturbances that might be elicited by stressors (Weber & Pargament, 2014). Religion also fosters a system of beliefs that allows individuals to find meaning in an experience (Park, 2010), and may limit feelings of hopelessness as events might be 'under God's control'. Beyond these attributes, religion might provide a social support network from like-minded people to promote solace and peace of mind and may also facilitate problem-focused coping (Ysseldyk et al., 2010). Spirituality has indeed been linked to lower depression and correspondingly greater neuronal density within brain regions, such as the prefrontal cortex and hippocampus (L. Miller et al., 2014), although there have also been reports that religion in late life was accompanied by hippocampal atrophy (Owen et al., 2011).

SOCIAL SUPPORT

Social support is among the most effective ways of dealing with stressful situations. Having support might be instrumental in eliminating stressors, but failing this, it could serve to buffer against some of the adverse psychological effects that might otherwise occur, and might promote physical health and recovery from illness (Carod-Artal & Egido, 2009). Social support can also diminish stressor-elicited hormonal and immunological changes that might have adverse consequences (Heinrichs et al., 2003), and attenuate stressor-provoked neuronal activity changes within the right prefrontal cortex and amygdala (Taylor et al., 2008).

Multiple coping functions can be provided through social support, which may vary with particular personality characteristics and change over the course of a stressor experience (DeLongis & Holtzman, 2005). For instance, when first diagnosed with a severe illness, an individual might rely on social support for problem solving (e.g., get advice, finding alternative treatment strategies) and for support. As the disease progresses, the social support may be combined with emotional coping that entails having someone to talk to about feelings, and, still later, the instrumental aspects of the support (e.g., trips to hospital) may become more apparent. Over the course of the illness, especially when things reach the bleakest point, social support may be used for comfort and finding peace.

SUPPORT AND POSITIVE PSYCHOLOGY

If negative events cause health problems, can we expect that positive events will encourage good health? There is reason to believe that pleasant emotions may be accompanied by better immune functioning than that apparent among those experiencing negative events (Barak, 2006) and that having an optimistic personality allows for better regulation of stress hormones (Jobin et al., 2014). In line with such findings, a 15-year prospective study indicated that positivity was accompanied by a lower risk for chronic heart disease, even taking into consideration other risk factors. Moreover, positive mood among individuals with an already established illness was predictive of lower levels of mortality (Chida & Steptoe, 2008).

Interventions based on positive psychology enhanced well-being and diminished depressive mood (Bolier et al., 2013). As well, maintaining a positive mood can facilitate the adoption of proper health behaviors, and may diminish some adverse neurobiological effects of stressors (just as having social support can act in this capacity), and when individuals do become sick they might be more likely to adhere to recommended treatments. However, in relation to chronic, progressive diseases, where damage is already extensive, as in the case of heart disease, it is less certain whether adopting a positive mood can turn back the clock and instigate a cure.

Limits of social support and unsupportive relationships

As useful as social support typically is, especially when it comes from a welcome source, such as a group or person with whom we strongly identify, it might not always be the ideal way of coping. A person might want independence and hence might not wish for external support or, alternatively, seeking support might reflect a sign of weakness in some cultures and hence might be eschewed. Furthermore, individuals might not wish for support as it might make them feel indebted, which might create a burden for them (indeed, there are people who, after doing a good deed, can't help themselves, following this up with "hey, remember, you owe me big time", which entirely undoes their good behavior).

There are researchers and clinicians who believe that positive psychology and social support are all well and good, and can be a useful auxiliary treatment for dealing with illnesses, but don't provide a cure. For that matter, there is some question about the meaningfulness of data that have been obtained in some studies. For instance, there have been reports that social support is accompanied by enhanced immune functioning, but we need to question whether this actually translates into improved health. A 10% or 20% rise of immune functioning, although statistically significant, might not reflect appreciably greater ability to fight infection or cancer. In essence, in considering the influence of positive psychology, or any other treatment to ameliorate illnesses, it is essential to distinguish between effects that are statistically significant from those that are practically meaningful.

Unsupportive relations

Occasionally, a person who seeks support might have their request rebuffed, or encounter a response that is not helpful. Such responses might comprise laying blame (e.g., "well you should have thought of that" or "there's two sides to every story"), bumbling (essentially not knowing what to say), minimizing or forced optimism ("don't worry, everything will work out alright"), as well as disconnecting or distancing themselves (they seem not to want to hear about it or pretend not to have seen you). These *unsupportive interactions* seem to be more damaging than simply not having support, and are prominent in making negative situations worse (Ingram et al., 2001). The negative effects of such interaction on health outcomes have been seen in relation to discriminatory events (McQuaid et al., 2014), among women in abusive dating relationships (Matheson et al., 2007) as well as those affected by HIV/AIDS (Song & Ingram, 2002). The negative consequences of unsupportive events can be exceptionally damaging in relation to severe illness, as we'll see in Chapter 14. It's especially unfortunate that occasions of unsupportive actions not only occur at a personal level, but also appear in relation to group behaviors. As Martin Luther King indicated, "In the end we will remember not the words of our enemies, but the silence of our friends", or as Elie Wiesel put it, ". . . to remain silent and indifferent is the greatest sin of all". These statements aren't nearly as harsh as those found in Dante's ninth circle of hell, which is reserved for those engaged in betrayal or treachery.

Social rejection and ostracism

Of the many stressors that can be encountered, social rejection (ostracism) is one of the most powerful. Ostracism comes in many forms, with discrimination being the most pernicious, but it also comes in other demeaning ways. Members of a group often feel as if they comprise a unified social entity (*entitativity*), and having individuals who negatively represent them (e.g., they're not cool) might promote a '*black sheep effect*', in which outliers are denigrated in an effort to preserve the good standing of the group as a whole (Eidelman & Biernat, 2003). Targeted rejection can undermine self-esteem and promote or exacerbate depressive mood. Adolescents can be fairly mean to one another (e.g., bullying), and it isn't uncommon for them to form new relationships, and in doing so dump earlier friends, who might feel ignored, rejected, diminished, or ostracized. The negative feelings of rejection are also apparent in relation to online social exclusion, especially as it can be made apparent for all to see that a person has been defriended on a social media site.

Within a laboratory context, social rejection has been assessed through 'cyberball', a computer game in which a virtual ball is tossed between three icons, one of which is controlled by a participant, whereas the other two are controlled through a computer, and not by actual people as the study participant believes (Blackhart et al., 2007). At first, the ball is passed between the players equally, but soon the two computer-driven icons pass the ball to one another, leaving out the participant. Even though this is a game, with little at stake for the participant, it elicits negative ruminative thoughts, altered mood, hostility, and elevated cortisol levels (McQuaid et al., 2015). As well, functional magnetic resonance imaging (fMRI) imaging indicated that ostracism in this situation promoted increased neuronal activity within the dorsal anterior cingulate cortex (Eisenberger et al., 2003), not unlike the effects of a physical stressor (Eisenberger, 2012). Thus, it was suggested that emotional and physical pain may involve overlapping neural circuits. In a sense, positive social interactions may be a fundamental need (like food or water) and our brain responds to social pain so that we can make the proper adaptive responses to thwart social challenges.

STRESSOR EFFECTS ACROSS THE LIFE SPAN

Altering life trajectories

The malleability or the plasticity of the brain is evident throughout life, but it is especially profound during early-life periods, so that stressors encountered at this time may have particularly poignant effects. Freud was an early advocate of the notion that stressful experiences at one time in life could have effects at later times. His theorizing obviously preceded our understanding of neuroplasticity, and the concept of sensitization hadn't yet been developed, but he nevertheless understood that stressful experiences could instill profound and lasting effects, serving as 'an agent still at work'.

CHAOTIC LIFE TRAJECTORIES

Many individuals believe that they had experienced 'turning points' that influenced the trajectory that their lives took. These turning points can be unique to particular individuals or they can be universal in the sense that large numbers of people had the same experience and were affected in a similar same way (Wheaton & Gotlib, 1997). These turning points can be influenced by age, gender, and the context in which these occurred, as well as by previous stressor experiences.

In a book meant for the lay person, which includes a discussion related to life trajectories, turning points, and happenstance, I use a game of billiards (pool) as a metaphor for 'chaos theory' that might be relevant to life changes stemming from seemingly small events (Anisman, 2015). In a game of pool 15 balls of various colors are aligned to form a triangle at one end of a pool table. A player at the other end of the table strikes a white cue ball, which smashes into colored balls

(Continued)

(Continued)

sending them careening in various directions. If a second shot (a do-over) were permitted, it would similarly travel across the table, but its trajectory might be off by a slight amount, say 1°. The trajectory of this ball would diverge from the first with the distance travelled, hitting the 15-ball pack of colored balls at a slightly different point. In both instances the balls would go off in different directions, but where they came to rest would differ in the two instances. Even a very small deviation at the point of origin, a mere 1°, would engender markedly different outcomes. As the pool balls careened about the table, a ball might have ended up in a pocket or, alternatively, it might have been headed for a pocket, but another ball struck it, altering its route. It's equally possible that by chance the cue ball might have had its course diverted so that it ended up in a pocket, which in pool is not a good outcome at all.

This is reminiscent of chaos theory; minuscule differences at the outset can produce greater and greater differences as we move outward in time or distance from the initial event. Secondary effects associated with these divergent paths create still greater differences, and predictions of the future thus become exceedingly more difficult. However, irrespective of where the white ball hit the pack, if one were to place the cue (stick) diagonally on the table with the narrow end pointing at an end pocket, those balls that ran into the cue with enough momentum would roll down it and into the pocket (Do you get the feeling that I know too much about pool and spent some unproductive time at it when I was younger?).

Turning to human behavior, we can make some probabilistic statements that likely won't be met with considerable opposition. For instance, negative early-life events will likely, but not necessarily, lead to adverse outcomes, whereas positive events will lead to better outcomes. This said, regardless of the individual's early experiences or the genes that had been inherited, the consequences aren't fixed in stone, and later events can, for better or for worse, serve as turning points that alter life trajectories, much like placing a cue diagonally across the pool table can do so. Negative early environments, sickness, poverty, and so many other factors can push individuals in bad directions, but the effects of negative circumstances can sometimes be undone or prevented.

Prenatal experiences

It's long been known that women who consume particular drugs during pregnancy place the fetus at risk for malformations (*teratogenic effects*). Although public perceptions of the teratogenic consequences of various agents had at one time focused on blatant physical abnormalities, they can also comprise altered mental development as well as neuropsychiatric conditions that might not be accompanied by obvious structural malformations. The magnitude of a teratogenic effect is influenced by the dosage of the teratogen, and are typically more pronounced the earlier in pregnancy the teratogens are encountered, although they can have effects at other times as well. Vulnerability to the negative actions of a teratogenic agent may also depend on the genotype of the fetus and the ability of the agent to come into direct contact with the fetus.

We usually think of teratogens as agents that were inhaled or ingested or perhaps applied to the skin (e.g., certain medications or alcohol), although they should be viewed more broadly. Environmental toxicants that are encountered on a daily basis, such as second-hand smoke or pollutants encountered in larger cities or industrialized regions, as well as PCBs (polychlorinated biphenyls) and even common household chemicals, can potentially affect the developing fetus. Likewise, what mom eats or fails to eat may profoundly affect the offspring. Viral challenges can also have profound effects on the fetus, and stressful events encountered during pregnancy can affect the physical and psychological well-being of the offspring, often persisting into adulthood (Beydoun & Saftlas, 2008).

Prenatal resources

Ideally, the fetus ought to go through its development without hazards being encountered, but this isn't always the case, especially if mom isn't knowledgeable about prenatal care (e.g., in the use of drugs or teratogenic agents), but unlucky events can also occur that threaten the well-being of the fetus. Typically, pregnant women in high income countries see physicians about 50% more often than non-pregnant women do, and there's a relatively large cohort who tend not to seek medical help or advice. Numerous factors contribute to this, many of which are linked to poverty (living in distressed neighborhoods or those with higher rates of unemployment, low family income, uninsured status), low education level, and an array of maternal factors (young maternal age, non-marital status, planned pattern of prenatal care, late recognition of pregnancy) (Feijen-de Jong et al., 2012). Too often children of mothers with these characteristics are more likely to experience fetal distress and will start off life with some physiological disadvantages.

Prenatal stressors

Prenatal stressors aren't limited to those that comprise trauma, such as war-time experiences, but also include workplace stressors, psychological abuse, discrimination and bereavement, and, in rodents, even witnessing another rat being stressed was sufficient to induce profound morphological disturbances in brain regions of subsequently born pups (Mychasiuk et al., 2011). Predictably, the negative repercussions on the developing fetus are especially notable if a woman encountered multiple psychological stressful experiences (Robinson et al., 2011). Clearly, it would be of considerable benefit to find methods of diminishing the distress experienced by pregnant women. In some instances this isn't possible, but having a nurturing and positive postnatal environment can undo some of the adverse effects of prenatal stressors, making it that much more important to provide adequate support programs for distressed mothers and their infants (Luby et al., 2013).

In humans, strong stressors experienced during pregnancy increase the risk of premature delivery and low offspring birth weight, just as such an outcome is more frequent among women experiencing high levels of anxiety or depression (Staneva et al., 2015) or those who smoke, drink alcohol, or use cocaine (Parazzini et al., 2003). As well, altered levels of several hormones have been associated with prenatal stressors and premature delivery, which may be accompanied by delayed fetal neuromuscular and nervous system maturation, diminished grey matter volume, and impaired mental development (Sandman et al., 2011). These children may develop cognitive disturbances (e.g., delayed language development, attention deficit hyperactivity disorder), as well as emotional problems (e.g. fearfulness and anxiety) that are first manifested during childhood, often carrying through into adulthood (Glover, 2011). Moreover, epidemiological studies indicated that these experiences were linked to physical illnesses, such as disturbed cardiovascular regulation (Mastorci et al., 2009), type 1 diabetes (Virk et al., 2010), and metabolic syndrome that might foreshadow adult type 2 diabetes (Rinaudo & Wang, 2011). Elevated production of both pro- and anti-inflammatory cytokines related to these events could potentially influence later psychological disorders (Entringer et al., 2008), as well as vulnerability to allergies, asthma, and infectious diseases (Nielsen et al., 2011). In fact, among humans who had experienced prenatal distress, their adult profile of cortisol and ACTH was in line with that associated with PTSD, leading to the suggestion that they were particularly vulnerable to this disorder, as well as other psychological disturbances in the face of adult stressor experiences (Entringer et al., 2009). Consistent with this view, treatments that simulate some of the actions of stressors, such as administration of the synthetic glucocorticoid betamethasone (used in an effort to promote maturation in fetuses at risk of preterm delivery), influenced infant temperament and behavioral reactivity (Davis et al., 2011).

Prenatal viral challenges

Just as activation of the inflammatory immune response can trigger hormonal and brain neurotransmitter alterations that can have long-term repercussions, prenatal viral challenges also affect later pathology in the offspring. Fetal exposure to syphilis, rubella, herpes simplex, toxoplasmosis, and other viruses may elicit various morphological disturbances, and could potentially be involved in provoking learning disabilities. There has also been growing evidence of a link between prenatal viral experiences and the emergence of psychiatric disturbances, such as schizophrenia (Brown, 2011; Meyer & Feldon, 2009).

Identifying causal connections between prenatal viral infection and the subsequent emergence of pathology is understandably challenging and this is especially true of the link to schizophrenia, which might not emerge until late adolescence. This is further hampered by the fact that viral and bacterial challenges can have multiple biological consequences, making it difficult to identify links between specific immunological challenges and particular neurobiological changes that lead to a psychopathological condition. Nonetheless, prenatal infection in rodents promoted brain morphological changes linked to schizophrenia, such as diminished size of cortical and hippocampal regions, as well as altered dopamine activity and receptor functioning (Meyer & Feldon, 2009). The dopamine changes were apparent irrespective of whether pups were raised by the mother that had experienced infection during pregnancy or a surrogate mother (following birth), suggesting that the prenatal experience, rather than those associated with postnatal maternal care, was fundamental in the provocation of later behavioral disturbances. It is especially interesting that the schizophrenia-like effects of prenatal infection were not apparent soon after birth, but, as in humans, emerged during the adolescent period (Meyer et al., 2008) and could be attenuated by antipsychotic medications that act on dopamine functioning.

Consistent with the data obtained from animal studies, the occurrence of viral epidemics in humans (rubella, influenza, toxoplasma gondii, and herpes simplex virus type 2) was related to a considerable increase (500–700%) in the birth of children who later developed schizophrenia (Brown, 2011). Although viral insults and the resulting inflammatory changes could potentially affect neuronal processes that provoke schizophrenia, other factors might also be related to this outcome, including febrile (fever) responses, malnutrition, and fetal hypoxia secondary to infection (Brown, 2011). In a review of this literature, Harvey and Boksa (2012) pointed out that prenatal infection has been associated with numerous pathological conditions, including not only schizophrenia, but also autism, cerebral palsy, epilepsy, and Parkinson's disease. Thus, they suggested that prenatal and early postnatal infection might act as a general vulnerability factor for neurodevelopmental disorders, but other factors govern which specific illness will emerge.

AUTISM AND IMMUNITY

Autism may be instigated by genetic factors, and possibly by prenatal or early-life factors. It is possible that autism is linked to immunologically-related processes, but this line of inquiry has an exceptionally tainted background, largely owing to controversial reports by Andrew Wakefield, a British physician and medical researcher, who claimed that MMR (mumps, measles, rubella) vaccination led to autism. It turned out that Wakefield's claims were fraudulent and his published work, such as that in the prestigious journal *Lancet*, has been withdrawn. When his report was first published, it had huge repercussions as parents stopped immunizing their children, thus leaving them vulnerable to diseases.

There probably isn't a single factor that leads to all instances of autism. Fetal experiences or those that occur early in life (e.g., very premature birth and the concordant hypoxia that goes with it) might contribute to this disorder, as might epigenetic changes (Zhubi et al., 2014). Among those with autism, microglia, astroglia, and cytokine levels are elevated, possibly reflecting chronic inflammation owing to the genes for inflammation being continuously switched on (Angelidou et al., 2012). It might not be that a virus itself is causing autism as much as the strong immune response in the pregnant mother causes this outcome or that mothers of children with autism have particular antibodies that can bind to fetal brain proteins, thereby causing damage. To be sure, these are simple correlations that don't address causal links, but they do raise the possibility of autism being associated with immune cells turning against the fetal brain.

Early-life challenges

Childhood experiences, ranging from those that are positive and nurturing through to trauma and toxic environments, shape developmental trajectories, so that behavioral and neurobiological processes are markedly affected, and vulnerability to illnesses in adulthood may be altered. Indeed, children who experience a trauma are more likely to develop pathological illnesses, such as depression and PTSD (Kendler et al., 2004). Such early experiences can be 'programmed' into various neurochemical, hormonal, and immunological processes so that individuals become more likely to be affected by later stressor experiences. This might reflect changes in the reactivity of biological systems, and could also affect how individuals appraise or cope with challenges (Compas et al., 2001). They might become less trusting, have difficulties forming social relations, experience disturbed self-regulation, and adopt poor life-style choices, any of which could aggravate disturbed neurobiological processes (Miller et al., 2011).

When the term early-life stressor is used, people might incorrectly think of traumatic experiences that involve sexual or physical abuse, and pay inadequate attention to psychological abuse, which can also have devastating short- and long-term consequences. The latter form of abuse includes neglect, withholding affection, parental problems (e.g., mental illness, addiction), family disturbances, and poverty (Harkness et al., 2006), which occurs in almost half of children and adolescents (Bethell et al., 2014). The consequences of very negative early experiences vary broadly, taking the form of disrupted school performance, impaired decision making and diminished ability to form and maintain close relationships, increased stress reactivity, resistance to fear responses being extinguished, the development of depression and anxiety (Callaghan & Richardson, 2011), and vulnerability to physical illnesses (Shonkoff et al., 2009). In fact, childhood adversity has been associated with premature death, and among individuals who experienced two or more traumas, the death rate prior to the age of 50 increased by about 60%, even after controlling for education, social class, alcohol and tobacco consumption, and psychological disorders (Kelly-Irving et al., 2013).

It's a bit puzzling that experiences in infancy or early childhood can have the profound long-term psychological effects that they do, especially as we ordinarily don't have any memories of these times of our lives. Early theorists struggled with this dilemma, finally suggesting that such memories were assigned to the unconscious, but nonetheless affected behaviors. More recent explanations include the possibility that owing to neuroplasticity or epigenetic changes, negative experiences alter the sensitivity or reactivity of neuronal processes, leading to exaggerated responses to later challenges. As described earlier, a life-time of stressors can have cumulative adverse effects that favor the development of pathological outcomes, especially if the effects of stressor experiences were 'embedded' during childhood and then exacerbated by further stressor encounters (McGowan & Szyf, 2010). Because of the brain's plasticity, early experiences are, in a sense, the seeds laid down that might bloom at later times.

Altered appraisals and coping

Stressors experienced early in life could potentially influence self-perceptions (e.g., self-blame, mastery, self-esteem) and the way individuals appraise events, as well as foster the development of warped cognitions and a negative cognitive style, ultimately affecting the coping strategies used to deal with later stressors. In this regard, instead of adopting methods that potentially could eliminate stressors, children who experienced negative early-life stressors displayed greater reliance on avoidant and emotion-focused coping or strategies characterized by risk-taking, confrontation, and the release of frustration (Compas et al., 2001; Shonkoff et al., 2009). Many facets of coping aren't well developed in children, and strong or repeated stressors may result in attempts to understand why negative experiences are happening to them. Their beliefs might then be internalized so that they become stable, and are attributed to their own shortcomings, and if these impaired appraisals and coping methods are carried into adulthood, they can affect vulnerability to pathological states.

Tolerable versus toxic challenges

Not all early-life adversities have negative long-term consequences. Whereas 'toxic' challenges (e.g., extreme poverty, psychological or physical abuse, neglect, maternal depression, parental substance abuse, and family violence) might be aligned with later emergence of psychopathology, modest ('tolerable') stressors encountered early in life could potentially facilitate learning how to appraise and cope with such events (Shonkoff et al., 2009). Tolerable stressors might also prime essential biological systems so that later challenges will engender moderate neurochemical changes that facilitate coping efforts.

Adolescence and early adulthood

Transitions from one phase of life to another call upon the ability to adapt to new circumstances and social demands. Adolescence is a phase in which enormous social changes occur; young people have a need to 'fit in', find a peer group with whom they feel comfortable and that will accept them, and sexual stirrings become more prominent. These challenges are also apparent as young people move from high school to university. Old social networks and romantic relationships may be left behind and new ones formed. This is accompanied by the development of an adult-like identity, in which there's a need for social, economic, and emotional independence, which in some instances collides with the reality of the loss of important social support systems. The resulting distress may contribute to university-aged individuals frequently experiencing clinical levels of major depression and anxiety disorders, which have been estimated as approaching 25% (Mackenzie et al., 2011). The frequency of these disorders may actually be higher as they often go undiagnosed, in part owing to shame and the fear of stigmatization. For some individuals, the transition is as seamless as it is exciting, but for many others it is destabilizing, distressing, and lonely.

Transitions are influenced by the availability of good social buffers, the individual's connectedness, as well as personality factors (self-mastery, self-esteem). In addition, transitions to and from adolescence are also biologically driven, being accompanied by the reorganization of neuronal and hormonal systems, and stressful events during these times are apt to produce changes of certain brain neurotransmitters, as well as disturbances in the development of nerve cell growth within the hippocampus (Kovalenko et al., 2014). In rodents, the adolescent (juvenile) period is an especially sensitive one, and stressors encountered during this time have pronounced and lasting effects on vulnerability to stressor-related pathological outcomes. Is also important for rodent socialization, and social instability at this time may be particularly apt in disrupting brain development and may affect memory processes, including fear-based memories (McCormick et al., 2011). This also seems to occur in humans, as fear responses established during adolescence are difficult to overcome, and it was estimated that 75% of adult fear-related disorders have their roots in anxiety that developed at earlier ages (Uys et al., 2006).

BEING LONELY IN A CROWDED ROOM

Most people will, at one time or another, have felt isolated and lonely, but most often these feelings are fairly transient. However, when they are chronic, feelings of loneliness can be pervasive and all-encompassing, creating extreme distress and feelings of being disconnected and apart from others. Being alone and having feelings of loneliness can be adaptive and advantageous under some circumstances and in some contexts, but for a social species such as our own, loneliness is often linked to depression and fairly pronounced physical and psychological disturbances (Cacioppo et al., 2015), and among older individuals loneliness has been associated with dementia (Holwerda et al., 2014) and is a risk factor for all-cause early mortality (Luo et al., 2012).

Middle years

By the time an individual is in their middle years (35–55), they likely have established or begun to establish a family, have a job and responsibilities, and achieved a degree of contentment.

This time of life may be accompanied by good emotional regulation, practical intelligence and a sense of mastery. But, it doesn't always work out that way, and some individuals might experience health problems, including serious chronic illnesses. As well, they might have to deal with aging parents who need to be attended to, children who are a challenge, financial hardships, relationship problems, and job strain. Thus, a clash may exist between the virtues that develop with age and the downside that accompanies heavy responsibilities and other stressors. At midlife people ought to be able to see all that they've achieved, and have a sense of what they would still like to accomplish. It can be disturbing and disheartening to realize that life goals and expectancies are unmet and will continue so.

As much as it's a cliché, hardships experienced might encourage a 'mid-life crisis' in 10–25% of men and women. The individual's realization that they are aging, their physical abilities are declining, and they are trapped in an undesirable situation, may promote personal turmoil that leads to changes in personal goals, life-style, and life course (e.g., Rosenberg et al., 1999). This can amount to career and job changes, new or deeper religious experiences, seeking new creative outlets, simplification and streamlining of life, and seeking new directions. In some instances, individuals may feel trapped as a result of financial and family responsibilities, prompting a desire to escape from these responsibilities, and junking any excess baggage. Self-destructive behaviors may emerge, such as increased drug and alcohol use, irritability, the desire for a sexual affair, and generally doing things that could lead to problems for themselves and for those who depend on them.

Older age

"Old age", as the actress Bette Davis said, "ain't no place for sissies". If you believe television commercials, old age represents the 'golden years' when we no longer have to trudge to work daily, and instead can take nice walks on sandy beaches. This may be true for some individuals, but for others, aging comes with the deterioration of biological systems, leading to heart, kidney, liver, and lung diseases, endocrine-related illness (e.g., diabetes), and neurodegenerative diseases seeming to be constant threats. With age, our capacity to fight off illness is diminished, and life stressors as well as past poor life-style choices may now express themselves. Not only might this decay reflect diminished functioning of biological resources to deal with stressors, but it appears that in some instances adaptive neurobiological changes, once set in motion, tend to persist for too long. Regulatory processes to shut systems down might not be operating well, favoring the development of allostatic overload and increased vulnerability to pathology (McEwen & Gianaros, 2011).

With the emergence of illness come repeated visits to different doctors, and sometimes dehumanizing medical procedures that could potentially encourage further stress-related illness. To make things still more distressing, older individuals may experience a loss of control and independence, and have to rely on others. Difficulties in mobility means a reduction of usual social activities and contacts, and often social support systems have deteriorated owing to a loss of friends who predeceased them or moved away, and dispersal of family members who have taken employment or other opportunities elsewhere. As social networks dissipate, loneliness, which is distressing for individuals of any age, becomes chronic, thereby exacerbating illness vulnerability (Perissinotto et al., 2012).

If all of this weren't more than enough, aged individuals might experience unsupportive inter-actions (often being patronized, talked down to, dismissed, and made to feel invisible or made to feel like a burden) and stigmatization. Is it any surprise that depression rates in older people are as high as they are, and that drug use to treat mood problems or sleep disturbances have soared? While not intended solely for older people, Maya-Angelou fittingly wrote

Alone, all alone

Nobody, but nobody

Can make it out here alone.

COLLECTIVE AND TRANSGENERATIONAL TRAUMA

Beyond the intergenerational effects of stressors being passed on through epigenetic processes, 'collective trauma' that had historically been experienced by a group, can be passed down across generations by word of mouth or through writings. There are many instances of cumulative emo-tional and psychological wounding being experienced by groups over generations, leading to profound disturbances of psychological and physical health, as we've seen among Aboriginal Peoples (Brave Heart, 2003). Among other things, collectively experienced traumas have social and psychological trajectories that can impact family and community dynamics, resulting in dis-turbed social functioning as well as an erosion of leadership, basic trust, social norms, morals and values (Bombay et al., 2009, 2014a).

Why would trauma experiences of forbears have such dramatic effects on their children or grandchildren? To explain this, Marion Hirsch (2001) suggested that although they hadn't wit-nessed the traumatic events directly, children 'remember' the experiences of their parents or grandparents in the form of narratives and images with which they grew up. Hoffman (2004) like-wise indicated that verbally or through nonverbal communication, which so often is a remnant of severe trauma, the children of survivors learn from the past and fill in the blanks as necessary. The consequences of collective traumas can wane over generations, being kept in mind primarily through rituals and symbols (e.g., holidays and remembrance days), and as much as there might be the belief that the group has 'recovered', the feelings about these events may be close to the surface. If there was any hope for collective, historical trauma being pushed aside, current experi-ences of discrimination act as powerful reminders of the many indignities committed against their group and effectively prevent healing (Evans-Campbell, 2008; Whitbeck et al., 2004).

Beyond these influences, severe cultural trauma, such as wars as well as dislocation second-ary to conflict, can have profound social repercussions, including the impoverished conditions that follow, limited care of children, disrupted education and social rules, and deterioration in the way individuals cope with later stressors (Bombay et al., 2014a, 2014b). In some instances traumatic experiences affect an individual's mental health, and the capacity to serve as a good parent may be impaired, thereby affecting health risks in their children. Unfortunately, as adults, these children may also have poor parenting skills, which will affect the next generation (Bombay et al., 2014b).

COLLECTIVE HISTORICAL TRAUMA

There's no question that traumatic events can have exceedingly negative consequences on survivors as well as on their children. But some groups were able to move forward, whereas others seemed less able to do so, and instead experienced a decline of functioning over generations. By example, the life trajectory was very different for children of Indigenous People of North America who suffered for generations at the hands of European colonizers, relative to the children and grandchildren of Holocaust survivors, whose ancestors similarly experienced multiple collective historical traumas. To be sure, the children of trauma survivors, including those of the Holocaust, were reported to be at increased risk for illnesses, such as PTSD (Yehuda et al., 2001), but in other instances they seemed to have been more resilient (Barel et al., 2010).

So, what is it that makes one set of individuals that experienced collective trauma resilient to the effects of later stressors, whereas another group might succumb to further hardships? The question itself may be inappropriate as comparisons between the collective, historical trauma experienced across groups may not be meaningful, as each trauma may be unique and each has its own consequences (Kirmayer et al., 2014). Still, at least some of the reasons for the continuing problems can hardly be missed, but fixing these is far more difficult.

Aboriginal Peoples within Canada, Australia, and the United States encountered multiple collective historical traumas, with forced attendance at Indian Residential Schools representing a recent, long-lasting, and severe event. Several generations of children (over a period of more than 100 years) were taken from their homes and housed in government- and church-run institutions where they were physically, sexually, and psychologically abused, their pride demolished, and made to feel ashamed of their culture. This was accompanied by their communities and culture being undermined, and when they eventually returned to their homes they were faced with poverty and limited child care. The residential school experience encouraged lateral violence (i.e., toward other children) that continued to be expressed once the children had left the Indian Residential Schools (Bombay et al., 2014a). The multiple adversities fostered poor community government, made much worse by short-sighted and inadequate federal government policies, planning, financing, and education, and the opportunity for proper healing wasn't realized. The net result was that life for many Aboriginal people improved only marginally, and in many communities the hardships grew progressively more alarming. In essence, the state of Aboriginal Peoples might not just be a consequence of the collective traumas that had been endured, but was compounded by subsequent poverty, mistreatment, stigma, shame, and a loss of identity.

The experiences of Jews during the Holocaust are so repugnant they can hardly be absorbed by those who weren't witness to the events. Despite these experiences, and the flagrant prejudices and unsupportive responses received, Holocaust survivors, often with support from their communities, had opportunities in new homes, and as a result they frequently thrived and flourished. The life of the children of Holocaust survivors was consequently very different from that of the Aboriginal children. For some survivors, the trauma might have made them that much more caring in regard to their children (perhaps overly-protective), and might have influenced their values, including those relevant to social and educational issues, and they frequently reported many close friend and family relations, elevated appreciation of life, more spirituality, greater personal strength, and new priorities in life. Like Holocaust survivors themselves, their children might have engaged in behaviors that helped them find meaning and contribute to their community (Greene et al., 2012). As well, the experiences of their parents or grandparents in some fashion may have prepared them for trauma or hardened them so that they were better able to deal with trauma. It is of particular significance that having a strong social identity and being with like-minded supportive individuals might have facilitated coping (Barel et al., 2010).

The attitudes of offspring of collective historical trauma have been changing, which might give rise to better outcomes. Despite the "soul wound" created by collective trauma among Aboriginal Peoples, as Brave Heart (2003) described it, the realization of just how profound previous injustices had been has encouraged shame and humiliation to be replaced by anger and social activism so that increased collective efforts have emerged among groups to control their own destinies. Even the thought of being perceived as being diminished in some fashion is absolutely abhorrent to them. Still, the problems that had been created for Aboriginal Peoples by European colonizers have been deep and wide within some communities, so that one hardly knows where to begin in making changes. It is certain that a Band-Aid here and a bit of antiseptic there won't get rid of a severe endemic disease.

Personality

A considerable portion of the variability regarding responses to stressors is determined by relatively fixed personality *traits* that might have developed as a result of genetic factors, socialization that occurred in early life, as well as other experiences. Some personality variables might affect the way we appraise or cope with stressors, whereas others might make us more sensitive or reactive to stressors. Just as an individual's locus of control influenced how a failure experience might be interpreted and hence affect later behavior, some individuals, such as high risk takers, frequently tend to get into situations that create considerable distress. There are also those who seem to generate social stressors through their insecurities, depressive symptoms, or an inability to deal with uncertainty. As well, neuroticism, as defined through the Five Factor Model of personality, which largely comprises emotional instability reflected by the disposition to experience unpleasant emotions (anger, anxiety, depression, or vulnerability), is linked to a person's stress responses (Vollrath, 2001).

Several personality factors have been identified that could determine to what extent resilience exists in the face of stressors. Individuals who approach challenging situations optimistically may have very different perspectives and realize better outcomes than do individuals who enter it with a pessimistic outlook. This has been observed in relation to health challenges, such as breast cancer in females and radical prostatectomy in men (Carver & Connor-Smith, 2010; Carver et al., 1993). Likewise, an individual's *self-efficacy* (the belief that tasks can be accomplished and difficulties resolved through one's own efforts) can moderate the impact of stressors on well-being. There are many additional personality factors that are relevant to how we deal with stressors, but we won't go through these here. For the moment, the important point is that the response to stressful events may be determined by individual characteristics that are brought to any given situation.

Sex

Several illnesses are more common in women than in men. Major depression occurs about 2–3 times more often in women, varying with the subtype of depression being considered (Piccinelli, 2000). Anxiety disorders and PTSD in response to traumatic events similarly develop more readily in women (Tolin & Foa, 2006), and some physical illnesses, such as autoimmune disorders (in which the immune system attacks the self) are far more common in women than in men. Hormonal factors no doubt contribute to these differences, as do stress-related brain neurochemical alterations (Cahill, 2006). Beyond this, gender differences exist with respect to socialization processes that promote certain behavioral coping styles being adopted, and women often carry a greater load than do men, being more responsible for the home and children, as well as caregiving for other family members (e.g., aging parents). Whether it's fruit flies or humans, genetic factors, brain architecture, and behavioral/social processes might account for the gender differences in stressor-related health disturbances (Jazin & Cahill, 2010).

Despite some stress-related illnesses being more common in women than in men, the view has been expressed that women are in fact tougher and more resilient than are men (Pratchett et al., 2010). Although the gap has been declining, women still outlive men in both industrialized and non-industrialized countries. This could stem from characteristics secondary to women having two X chromosomes, or it might reflect testosterone cutting short the lives of men. Alternatively, several life-style factors, such as relatively more smoking, drinking, and eating foods that promote elevated cholesterol levels, as well as the use of poor coping strategies (internalizing rather than letting go and externalizing), may favor the male's earlier death.

INSTRUMENTS USED TO ASSESS STRESSOR EXPERIENCES, APPRAISALS AND COPING

The arsenal of tests used to assess stressful experiences, appraisals and coping methods is fairly extensive. Some procedures have been used to assess the effects of stressors and coping in response to general events, whereas others were used to evaluate the effects of specific stressors, such as abusive experiences or loss, on the development of illness. Moreover, some coping measures evaluated general coping styles, whereas others were used to assess the specific coping strategies endorsed to deal with particular types of event.

Daily hassles

Stressors can be so severe as to render individuals virtually incapacitated, but even trivial day-to-day annoying events that might appear as minor annoyances can have cumulative effects on well-being, especially if they appear against a background of powerful life challenges (Cheng & Li, 2010). You might know the distressing feeling of having to deal with a major stressor that entirely strains your psychological stamina, only to have some minor, annoying distraction raise its ugly little head, forcing you to redirect some of your psychological resources from the more important challenges. Yet it is also possible that in the context of a major chronic stressor, minor hassles might have very little effect on outcomes, perhaps because their significance seems negligible in the greater scheme (McGonagle & Kessler, 1990).

Ordinarily, juggling multiple demands might be part of an individual's repertoire, but having too many balls in the air may cause the entire act to fall apart. For those who generally are less able to deal with multiple issues concurrently, overload will likely occur more readily and hence behavioral dysfunction may evolve. Indeed, 'daily hassles' have been linked to depression, and even to irritable bowel syndrome and diabetes, although this doesn't necessarily mean that the hassles caused the pathology, as those who are already ill may be more sensitive to day-to-day annoyances (Ravindran et al., 1999).

The *Hassles and Uplifts Scale* (Kanner et al., 1981) was developed to assess the impact of daily annoyances in relation to well-being. This scale asks individuals to indicate which hassles of a fairly long list they've experienced recently, and how severe they were (e.g., social obligations, concerns about owing money, too many responsibilities, and problems with aging parents). Similar instruments were subsequently developed that focused on particular groups (e.g., caregivers) or circumstances (e.g., transition to university). These scales are fairly lengthy and broad, allowing for determination of an overall hassle score, but they can also be used to assess specific types of hassles that might provide information as to whether certain types of events are especially cogent in relation to pathology. After all, different hassles, such as those related to a partner, friend, or family member, could lead to different outcomes relative to those related to work, health, or financial strains. As an alternative to using the daily hassles scale, daily diaries can be requested of respondents in the form of brief statements or by responding to specific questions. Yet another index, the *Daily Life Experiences Checklist* (DLE), considers the desirability and meaningfulness of events that fall into several domains – work, leisure, family, friends, and financial (Stone & Neale, 1982), and might be useful in determining links between minor events and illness.

Major life stressors

Several scales were developed to assess the link between major life stressors and the development of pathology. One approach to assess the stress–pathology relationship focused on measuring the social adjustment required in response to varied life events over a prescribed time period (e.g., 6 months or 1 year) (Holmes & Rahe, 1967). Other scales were more concerned with major life stressors experienced over a set period of time, with the severity of any particular event being based on responses previously obtained from a normative group of participants (Paykel et al., 1971). Still other instruments considered particular types of stressor, such as traumatic events experienced at a particular age (e.g., the Traumatic Life Events Questionnaire; Kubany et al., 2000). As well, questionnaires have been developed to consider specific stressful events, including those related to marital and family relations (Moos & Moos, 1981), and various aspects related to the workplace (Moos, 1981).

As enlightening as the data obtained have been using these scales, in several respects the data and conclusions derived weren't entirely satisfying. These scales were based on recall of past events, and, as indicated in Chapter 2, retrospective analyses are burdened by several biases. Furthermore, evaluating the impact of stressors in relation to normative data might not provide a valid portrayal of the stressor's severity. Using the Social Readjustment Scale, for instance, 'death of a child' receives a score of 100, which is as distressing as it gets, and lower scores are given for other stressors, such as 'pregnancy' (40), 'trouble with in-laws' (29), 'changes in work hours' (20), 'revisions of personal habits' (24). The summed scores provide an index of the stressor severity experienced by an individual. On the surface this makes sense, but what it implies is that getting pregnant, changing personal habits, altering work hours, and having issues with your in-laws might be more disturbing (or life changing) than death of one's child. The deficiencies of such questionnaires are also problematic given that they don't consider the context in which a stressor had occurred. Does divorce have the same impact when it was long expected (and desired) relative to that felt when a partner drops the other person unexpectedly and takes off with their 'office friend'?

A frequently used alternative to major life events scales has been the *Perceived Stress Scale* (Cohen et al., 1983). This is a self-report instrument that taps into several attributes of stressor experiences, particularly how unpredictable, uncontrollable, and overloaded respondents find their lives. Several variants of this scale were developed, including a 4-item version that is preferred for telephone interviews, which necessarily must be brief.

Stress interviews have been used as an adjunct or alternative to questionnaire methods. These procedures might uncover subtle features that would otherwise be missed, but they may be subject to problems of interpretation and retrospective biases, and scoring interviews might be prone to biases on the part of the investigator. Still, qualitative data may be an excellent adjunct for the quantitative information obtained from more standard rating scales and allows the researcher or clinician to identify the presence of particular stressors that may be risk factors for pathological outcomes. Qualitative measures, in general, might not be useful for comparisons between individuals, but they allow for a richer description of stressful events encountered, provided that interviewers have been appropriately trained to collect the essential information (Wethington et al., 1995).

Stressor appraisals

When individuals are asked what stressors they have previously encountered, they are essentially being asked to make an appraisal concerning what they considered stressful in their own experience. But, more specific information (e.g., severity of the experience) can be obtained through scales that explicitly assess their appraisals. One frequently used scale for this purpose is the *Stress Appraisal Measure* (SAM) (Peacock & Wong, 1990), which measures three components of primary appraisals (challenge, threat, and centrality), as well as secondary appraisals comprising the resources the individual has available to contend with a particular event.

Coping with stressors

The link between an individual's coping ability and the emergence of pathology has received considerable attention, and several coping scales were developed, each of which have their own advantages and drawbacks. The *Ways of Coping Questionnaire* (WOC) asks individuals to describe a recently encountered stressor and assesses the degree to which individuals use particular coping methods (e.g., emotion versus problem-focused strategies) in response to this event (Folkman & Lazarus, 1988). Alternative coping measures, the *Coping Orientation to Problem Experience inventory* (COPE; Carver et al., 1989) and the *Survey of Coping Profile Endorsement* (SCOPE; Matheson & Anisman, 2003), measure multiple coping strategies that fall into problem-focused coping (e.g., planning), emotion-focused coping (e.g., self-blame), and avoidant-focused coping (e.g., denial). These questionnaires ask participants how they would cope with stressors in general (coping styles) or in response to specific events (strategies), and a variant of the SCOPE asks participants to indicate the degree to which they believed their coping method to be effective, which provides an index of secondary appraisals. In addition to these scales, several coping measures were developed that focused on specific situations (e.g., Quality of Social Support Scale) or specific illnesses (e.g., Mental Adjustment to HIV Scale, Mental Adjustment to Cancer scale).

SUMMARY

Few researchers or clinicians would argue against the notion that stressful events contribute to the emergence or exacerbation of pathology, and hinder recovery from illness. It is equally certain, however, that outcomes in any given individual would be difficult to predict given the enormous number of different types of stressor that can be experienced, many of which may vary yet again in their specific characteristics (controllability, predictability, ambiguity, uncertainty, chronicity, and previous experiences with stressors). Moreover, the response to stressors varies with age, sex, personality variables, as well as the appraisal and coping methods that individuals use. No doubt, some of these variables may interact with other factors (e.g., genetic contributions), thereby determining vulnerability to illnesses. Because individuals may differ in relation to what their weak link might be, analyses that attempt to tie stressful events to particular pathological conditions might find that although stressors increase all-cause morbidity (and mortality), the ability to predict specific illnesses might prove challenging.

5 Neurobiological Stress Responses

MISSION UNLIKELY

Let's play a make-believe game. You're a visitor from another planet who is given the task of creating humans that can survive on their own once you leave to go create new worlds elsewhere. You might first decide that the organism you create needs to be able to move about, obtain energy to continue to do this, be able to reproduce, and you might even think of making this new organism a social one so that they will help one another along the way. On the surface, all this seems fairly straightforward. You invent legs (and arms), organs such as the stomach and heart, as well as reproductive organs. Would you have thought of making a systematically organized brain that could do all that our own brain is capable of doing? One that was responsible for so many cognitive functions and which had an indirect role in affecting each of the other organs? The heart is fairly complex, as are the digestive processes that convert food into energy, but they don't come remotely close to the intricate features of the brain, which comprise whole networks of neurons so that coordination occurs between different aspects of our behavior. These neuronal processes allow us to appraise situations, make decisions, have the ability to learn and remember events, and how to behave in various situations. As well, by influencing the autonomic nervous system, the brain affects the functioning of our body organs, such as the heart, which, in turn, is necessary for effective brain functioning. Likewise, two-way communication occurs between the brain and the immune system, and with our microbiota, which protect us from unwelcome invaders. To make sure that this organism can deal with novel challenges that might be met, would you have thought of creating methods wherein functionally advantageous traits remained with the organism and others were cropped from its repertoire? Given all these intricacies, would you have been able to do something as dramatic as this using your already functioning brain? As it happens, teams of human engineers are now trying to do just this, only better, through robotics. One day, it's feared (by some), that these manufactured robots may take over, leaving humans as their inferiors. Their abilities won't be hampered by pointless emotions, such as guilt or remorse, or even empathy and trust, unless the engineers figure out how to create a soul.

STRESSOR-PROVOKED NEUROBIOLOGICAL CHANGES AS AN ADAPTIVE RESPONSE

Just as we might attempt to cope with stressors through behavioral methods, several biological systems are fundamental in helping us deal with insults. Some effects of acute stressors prime us to be more aware and resourceful in dealing with challenges, and several hormones and neurotransmitters likewise serve in this capacity. As well, various growth factors are activated that facilitate neuroplasticity so that we're more prepared to deal with stressors that may be encountered at some later time (Kirby et al., 2013). Our biological responses can only go so far in protecting us from stress-related pathologies. As adaptive as many of these biological responses might be, as indicated earlier, if they persist long enough, or if levels of particular neurochemicals are too high, cellular damage may occur. Moreover, individual difference factors and experiences determine how we perceive and cope with stressors, and they may also be fundamental in determining the biological consequences that occur. After reading this chapter you should be familiar with:

- the impact of stressors on several hormonal, neurochemical, and immunological processes
- the contribution of stress-related biological changes to the emergence of physical and psychological disturbances
- the conditions under which stressors have the most prominent effects on these processes
- the moderating effects of several experiential and organismic variables in determining the impact of stressors on biological functioning and hence on well-being.

NEUROTRANSMITTER VARIATIONS

Considerable research in humans has been conducted assessing the hormonal changes in blood or saliva that are instigated by stressors. However, the opportunities to conduct detailed analyses of stressor-provoked brain neurochemical changes, including the many factors that moderate these actions, have been fairly limited. As a result, much of the information obtained regarding the influence of stressors on neurobiological processes has come from studies in animals. These studies have been informative in detailing the biological effects of stressors and the contribution of a variety of moderating factors on these processes, but at the same time there is a limit concerning what research in rodents can tell us, particularly in view of the complex cognitive changes that occur in stressed humans.

Several neurotransmitters across brain regions are affected by stressful experiences, serving to blunt the psychological impact of the stressor, facilitate the ability to appraise events, augment effective coping, prepare the organism to adapt or contend with continued challenges, and modify the actions of still other biological processes that could otherwise produce adverse outcomes (Anisman et al., 2008). Although most stressors engage several common neurobiological systems, a degree of selectivity is present in that psychological stressors that involve higher-order processing (such as learned threats) engage neural circuits that differ from those that involve innate threats, and these may differ from those activated by physical (neurogenic) or systemic insults (Merali et al., 2004). We won't go through all of the neurochemical changes introduced by stressors, but instead we'll consider those most commonly assessed, and point out some of the key factors that influence their functioning.

Norepinephrine, dopamine, and serotonin

In contending with stressors we don't simply rely on neurochemical changes, but also engage behavioral responses to minimize the negative effects that could arise. In essence, our ability to deal with stressors occurs through both biological and behavioral processes, and it seems that psychological factors surrounding the stressor situation may influence neurochemical functioning, and conversely, neurochemical activity will affect emotional and cognitive processes (Puglisi-Allegra & Andolina, 2015).

Upon being confronted by a stressor there may be uncertainty as to whether it will be brief or prolonged, and whether the organism has control over the situation. Adaptive neurobiological processes can't simply dilly-dally while the brain tries to work out the various attributes of the situation. Thus, survival might require rapid and bold defensive neurobiological responses, and as information is obtained regarding the characteristics of the stressor (e.g., controllability, chronicity), these responses can be adjusted accordingly. Figure 5.1 depicts what is presumed to occur under various stressor conditions with respect to the production (*synthesis*) and release (*utilization*) of neurotransmitters, such as norepinephrine, dopamine, and serotonin (collectively referred to as *monoamines*). These monoamine changes have been observed in brain regions fundamental to vegetative or basic life processes (e.g., hypothalamus) as well as in those associated with appraisals and executive functioning (prefrontal cortex) and reward processes (nucleus accumbens) (Bland et al., 2003), and might thus lend themselves to the emergence of psychological and physical disturbances. The sequence of events described in Figure 5.1 is meant as a general framework. The stressor-provoked neurochemical changes will vary in relation to the characteristics of the organism, such as age, gender, and genetic factors (Anisman & Matheson, 2005). Furthermore, the effects of stressors on these neurotransmitters vary across brain regions, and other neurotransmitters might not behave in this fashion.

Monoamine receptor changes

In addition to the frank changes of monoamine turnover and levels, stressors can also influence various receptor subtypes. In some brain regions, the functioning of particular receptors may be either *up-* or *down-regulated*, and this may vary over time following a stressor. For instance, if a particular system is at risk of becoming too active, then it might be beneficial for the receptors to down-regulate to preserve stability. It also seems that controllable and uncontrollable stressors may have different effects on receptor functioning. By example, an uncontrollable stressor regimen that gave rise to impaired behavioral responding was accompanied by increased expression of particular serotonin receptors (5-HT_{1B}) within the dorsal raphe nucleus (Neumaier et al., 1997). Aside from 5-HT_{1B} receptors, stressors will also have marked effects on other serotonin receptor subtypes (e.g., 5-HT_{1A}, 5-HT_{2A}, 5-HT_{2C}), which can affect multiple behavioral outputs. The stressor-related receptor changes are not limited to those involving serotonergic processes, having been observed in relation to norepinephrine, dopamine, as well as opioids. The receptor variations may be responsible for different cognitive, emotional, and behavioral outcomes, and have been implicated in the emergence of varied pathological conditions (Arnsten et al., 2015).

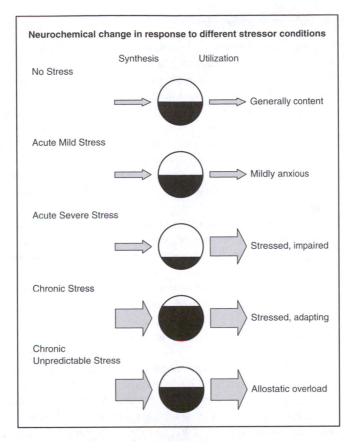

Figure 5.1 The synthesis, utilization, and levels of serotonin, norepinephrine, and dopamine in several brain regions, such as the prefrontal cortex and hippocampus, are markedly affected by stressors. Ordinarily, in the absence of a stressor, transmitter synthesis (production) and release (utilization) are in balance with one another, and hence the levels of the transmitter stored inside the presynaptic neuron (shown inside the circle) remain stable. When a mild or moderate stressor is experienced, the utilization of the transmitter increases so that the organism will be better equipped to deal with the challenge. This is accompanied by elevated synthesis of the neurotransmitter, and thus the level of the transmitter remains stable. As the severity of the stressor increases, particularly when behavioral methods of dealing with the stressor are unavailable, the burden of coping rests more heavily on biological systems. Under these conditions, the utilization of the transmitter increases, and if this becomes sufficiently pronounced, synthesis of the neurotransmitter might not keep pace with utilization (more is being used than produced) and as a result the absolute level of the neurotransmitter declines. If the stressor persists (chronic stressor), further adaptive changes may occur so that the organism is able to deal with events. Among other things, a compensatory increase in synthesis occurs, possibly because of autoreceptor down-regulation (so that the message of 'make more' continues), and as a result, the stored levels of the neurotransmitter will normalize, and may even come to exceed control levels. To preclude negative consequences of excessive neural activation, postsynaptic receptor functioning may be down-regulated (number or sensitivity of receptors declines), protecting against potential adverse effects. This doesn't mean that all is well, however, as the elevated synthesis and utilization can go on for only so long. Eventually, the adaptive processes may be overwhelmed (allostatic overload), especially when a chronic stressor occurs on an unpredictable and variable basis. Under such conditions, the development of pathology is most likely to occur.

Sensitization of monoamine changes

The monoamine changes provoked by acute stressors are usually transient, persisting for a matter of minutes or a few hours, being longer-lasting in older animals and in certain strains of mice, and they can be relatively long-lasting in response to social stressors (e.g., social defeat) (Audet et al., 2010). This should not, however, be misinterpreted to suggest that once neurotransmitter activity has normalized, things have entirely returned to normal. The initial stressor may result in the *sensitization* of a neurochemical system or related receptors (Anisman et al., 2003) so that when animals are subsequently re-exposed to a challenge, the monoamine changes may occur more readily and might be more pronounced. Conversely, if animals had first been trained in a situation where control over a stressor was possible, they seemed to be 'immunized' against the neurochemical disturbances that would otherwise be elicited by a subsequent uncontrollable event (Bland et al., 2003).

This sensitization effect is not simply a matter of the animal learning about a specific stressor so that its reappearance triggers particular memories that elicit the neurochemical changes. Indeed, the sensitization is apparent even when the re-exposure experience involves a stressor that differs from that previously encountered. For that matter, 'cross-sensitization' effects have been reported so that among stressed animals exaggerated responses are later apparent in response to drugs that affect monoamines, such as amphetamine or cocaine, and even to challenges of an immunological nature (Anisman et al., 2003). Likewise, if animals were initially treated with cocaine or amphetamine, later responses to stressors were greatly augmented, potentially increasing the propensity for stress-related disorders.

The sensitization elicited by stressors is not restricted to monoamine variations, having been observed with respect to other transmitters and hormones. How this sensitization comes about hasn't yet been entirely worked out, but the mechanisms underlying sensitization could well vary for different neurotransmitters. For example, sensitization of serotonin neuronal activity within the raphe nucleus may involve variations of CRH_2 receptors (Maier & Watkins, 2005), whereas the cross-sensitization between stressors and amphetamine could involve glutamate processes. Furthermore, the initial treatment may promote increased fibroblast growth factor (FGF-2) essential for the neuronal plasticity that encourages responses to later challenges (Flores & Stewart, 2000). Whatever the mechanism, the sensitization and cross-sensitization effects that occur may have ramifications for psychological and physical well-being long after the initial stressor experience.

Chronic stressors: Adaptation versus allostatic overload

What happens to our neurochemical systems when we encounter stressors on a chronic basis? Do we adapt to such experiences, or do the negative effects of stressors become progressively more damaging? From both a behavioral and a neurochemical perspective, both outcomes could occur. As well, not all neurochemical systems operate in an identical fashion and while a diminished response may occur with respect to one system, an elevated response could potentially occur within a second. Likewise, whatever effects are observed may be specific to particular brain regions so that an adaptation may be evident in one, but not in another.

It is remarkable how many different adaptive responses occur in dealing with stressors, and how different checks and counterchecks occur in an effort to maintain allostasis. Indeed, the decline of monoamine levels that occurs when acute stressors cause utilization to exceed synthesis might not be evident in response to chronic stressors. As a challenge continues, a compensatory increase of neurotransmitter synthesis may occur, meeting the high rate of utilization, and so the monoamine levels may normalize. This may be highly adaptive in the medium term as it allows the organism to deal with ongoing challenges. It is tempting to believe that under these conditions the organism has weathered the storm and that things are under control. In fact, however, this is hardly the case as increased utilization and receptor activation that persist for an extended period not only place an excessive load on critical systems, but have secondary effects that favor negative outcomes (e.g., excessive cortisol release may result in cell loss within the hippocampus) (McEwen, 2007) and may ultimately contribute to a variety of illnesses, including neurodegenerative disorders (Goldstein, 2011). This allostatic overload is still more apt to occur when the chronic stressor doesn't readily allow for adaptation (e.g., when the stressor occurs on an intermittent, unpredictable basis leading to still greater neuronal activity), and, as in other instances, genetic factors and previous stressor experiences, particularly those encountered early in life, may influence vulnerability (or resilience) in response to challenges (e.g., Gardner et al., 2009).

LIMITS TO NEURONAL ADAPTATION FROM A SIMPLER PERSPECTIVE

The way our neurons function in response to varied stressor experiences isn't unlike the changes that we see in people as they deal with assorted life challenges. On a week-to-week basis we spend our money to make numerous purchases (much like a neuron uses a neurotransmitter) and every few weeks our bank account is blessed with incoming funds (synthesis) from our job. Occasionally, unexpected expenses can be incurred that must be dealt with, but our savings are limited. This might mean cutting back on some luxury items, delay in getting a second-hand car to replace the one that's about to be junked, and maybe even selling off some nonessential stuff at a garage sale. Should we encounter yet another financial problem, the burden we face becomes still heavier, so that we might have to take on some additional part-time work to keep our bank balance stable (akin to a compensatory increase of neurotransmitter synthesis), and this year's vacation plans will have to be abandoned (limit utilization). Still, on the surface, things generally look OK; the electricity hasn't been cut-off and the kids are still getting lunch money, but there's hardly a crack of daylight between the demands we're facing and financial disaster. Simply because we're getting by doesn't imply that everything is back to normal. Psychological and physical strain has increased, our work–life balance is toast, and there's far less room to maneuver financially given that our time and resources are taken up. Should yet another emergency arise, we're really in trouble. Mortgage rates might go up, the roof shingles or washing machine might need to be replaced, or some sort of illness might develop that interferes with our ability to maintain our job. Contending with unpredictable stressors outside our control, often hitting us one after another, can eventually undermine our adaptive abilities, causing damage to both mental and physical health.

Glutamate

Glutamate, the most abundant excitatory neurotransmitter in the brain, is an important element in synaptic plasticity and hence in memory processes, and together with its receptors has been essential in determining a variety of other behaviors, ranging from pain perceptions (Hildebrand et al., 2014) through to psychiatric disorders, such as schizophrenia and depressive illness (e.g., Sanacora et al., 2012). As with so many brain systems, a balance exists between excitatory glutamate functions and that of the inhibitory neurotransmitter, GABA, and these actions may be modulated by various peptide hormones. It is clear that glutamate release may be increased by stressors and contributes to the establishment and retention of fear responses (Davis & Walker, 2014) as well as stressor-related psychopathologies (Popoli et al., 2012).

A wide assortment of receptors exist that can be stimulated by glutamate, falling into two broad classes, generally referred to as ionotropic and metabotropic, each of which has several receptor subtypes. Two types of receptor within the ionotropic family, NMDA and AMPA, have received particular attention as both are elevated in response to stressors (Marrocco et al., 2014), and there have been indications that early-life stressful events can persistently alter NMDA-receptors (Ryan et al., 2009). The impact of stressors on glutamate functioning, coupled with reports that antidepressant medications may influence glutamate release (Musazzi et al., 2013), has generated interest in targeting glutamate in the treatment of depression.

The increased focus on glutamate involvement in affective illness was fueled by reports that ketamine, a glutamate antagonist that is used as an anesthetic and analgesic in veterinary medicine, as well as a street drug (where it is known as special K), can produce powerful antidepressant effects even among patients who had been treatment resistant. Moreover, these effects occur after a very brief time (e.g., 1 hour), rather than requiring several weeks of treatment, as in the case of standard antidepressants (Serafini et al., 2014). Aside from its actions on glutamate functioning, ketamine also causes rapid effects on the growth hormone BDNF that enhances neuroplasticity, which may turn out to be responsible for the antidepressant effects observed (Duman, 2014). Whatever the case, findings such as these have made it clear that perspectives of depression that strictly focus on monoamines are outdated. Indeed, a paradigm shift has been occurring in relation to psychopathology so that instead of thinking simply in terms of too little or too much of a neurotransmitter or altered receptor number or sensitivity, some pathological conditions are seen as reflecting a change of neuroplasticity.

γ-Aminobutyric acid (GABA)

Unlike the biogenic amines and glutamate, which have excitatory actions, GABA acts as an inhibitory neurotransmitter within the mammalian central nervous system (CNS), functioning as a brake so that neuronal activity of other systems is properly regulated. Once again, the actions of GABA on behavioral output are determined by the types of receptor that are activated. Anxiety-provoking situations are accompanied by elevated levels of GABA in plasma and cerebrospinal fluid, and GABA release in the brain was increased in response to certain stressors (de Groote & Linthorst, 2007). As well, stressors that occur chronically alter the characteristics of $GABA_A$ receptors, and could thereby influence anxiety (Poulter et al., 2010). As in the case of other neurotransmitters and hormones, GABA functioning in response to negative events may be influenced by earlier stressor experiences. In this regard, stressors encountered early in life or during adolescence affect the trajectory of biological processes related to GABA functioning, and may contribute to basal and stressor-elicited levels of anxiety that carry through to adulthood (Jacobson-Pick et al., 2008).

Imaging studies in humans have confirmed that in response to threats, GABA activity declined relative to the activity apparent during a safe period (Hasler et al., 2010). Paralleling such findings, GABA concentrations were reduced in frontal cortical regions of depressed patients (Sanacora et al., 2004), and characteristics of GABA receptors in depressed humans who died by suicide were disturbed relative to those of individuals who had not been depressed and had died as a result of factors other than suicide (Merali et al., 2004). These imaging and postmortem studies are all of a correlational nature and so they don't tell us whether the GABA disturbances led to the pathological outcomes or whether the GABA changes were secondary to the distress related to depression. Yet, given the profound effects of stressors on GABA functioning in animals, coupled with findings that GABA manipulations can alter anxiety- and depressive-like behaviors, it is likely that the variations of the neurotransmitter are causally linked to the mood changes. This said, GABA certainly doesn't act alone in affecting mood states, serving with serotonin, CRH, and other transmitters in eliciting these outcomes (Waselus et al., 2005). As well, $GABA_A$ receptor expression may be altered by ovarian hormones, such as progesterone, possibly being a source for sex differences that exist with respect to depression and anxiety (Maguire & Mody, 2007).

Cannabinoids

Cannabis (marijuana) has long been known to promote a calming effect (although in a subset of individuals it can have the opposite type of action), but it's only been in the past decade or so that the neurobiological processes associated with cannabis use have come to be better understood. Naturally occurring molecules (*endocannabinoids*; eCBs) that bind to specific cannabinoid receptors (e.g., CB_1 and CB_2) have been identified within several brain regions. The psychoactive component of cannabis, *Δ9-tetrahydrocannabinol* (THC), binds to such receptors, giving rise to some of the drugs' effects (Hill et al., 2010). It is of particular significance that activation of the eCB system and the CB_1 receptors can regulate the release of several neurotransmitters that influence stress reactions, and was thus proposed as a novel drug target to ameliorate anxiety-related disorders (Gunduz-Cinar et al., 2013). Consistent with this view, administration of a CB_1 agonist directly into the basolateral amygdala diminished stressor-induced HPA activation, and it seems that eCB system functioning might contribute to the consolidation of stressor-provoked emotional memories (Hill et al., 2010).

Two naturally occurring brain endocannabinoids, *anandanine* (AEA) and *2-arachodonoyl-glycerol* (2-AG), may be fundamental for both basal and threat-elicited anxiety (Hill & Tasker, 2012). Specifically, AEA is thought to act as a gatekeeper that allows us to remain mellow, but also contributes to anxiety in response to stressor experiences. The 2-AG system also kicks in when stressors are encountered, but it does so a bit later and, among its other actions, it serves to attenuate stress responses. In effect, the stress response doesn't simply fade with the passage of time, but instead involves active neuronal processing that is governed by 2-AG. Persistent anxiety from this perspective might involve high levels of AEA functioning or the absence of a 2-AG response that is needed to turn off anxiety.

HORMONAL CHANGES ELICITED BY STRESSORS

Many hormones are fundamental in dealing with stressors (e.g., cortisol, CRH, ACTH, NPY, vasopressin, prolactin, endorphins, enkephalins, norepinephrine, somatostatin, melatonin), some of which have been found to influence (and be influenced by) psychological and physical illnesses, and could potentially affect the course of recovery.

Cortisol/corticosterone responses

Acute stressor effects

Within seconds of a stressor being encountered neurons within frontal cortical regions make appraisals of the event, and very quickly thereafter the autonomic nervous system is activated, so that peripheral organs are prepared to deal with the challenge (e.g., the epinephrine release increases heart rate and blood pressure, thereby increasing oxygen supply to various organs). As illustrated in Figure 5.2, through a series of steps involving the hypothalamus and pituitary gland, stressors cause the release of cortisol (corticosterone in rodents) from the adrenal gland. The cortisol enters the bloodstream and reaches a variety of target tissues, eliciting multiple positive effects, as described in the text box.

The cortisol rise is typically proportional to the severity of the stressor as is the time needed for *normalization* to occur (i.e., how long it takes before cortisol returns to its resting level). Effective cortisol regulation, like that of any other hormone, neurotransmitter, or immune factor, is essential for well-being. This not only means that appropriate release of various substances occurs in response to challenges, but also that this release ceases when the challenge has terminated. Upon reaching the brain, cortisol stimulates neurons in the hypothalamus and hippocampus, which terminates further HPA activation. This self-regulating (negative feedback) loop is fundamental for the integrity of this system, as persistent cortisol release may have damaging effects. In particular, the sustained release of cortisol will continuously stimulate glucocorticoid receptors present on hippocampal cells, eventually causing damage to them. As the hippocampus is a fundamental component of the shut-down mechanism, damage to these cells will allow further cortisol release, producing still greater hippocampal cell loss, and as this cycle continues cognitive disturbances may emerge. With aging, cortisol levels ordinarily rise, but this rise and the potential hippocampal cell loss can be aggravated by stressors that promote sustained cortisol elevations, leading to still greater cognitive problems (McEwen & Gianaros, 2011). As important as cortisol may be for our functioning, it seems that there can be too much of a good thing, and under some conditions cortisol can have negative consequences.

Corticoid changes elicited by stressors may be particularly notable if animals initially encounter a stressor early in life or during the prenatal period. These persistent actions of stressors may reflect the plasticity and sensitization of stress systems, possibly involving changes of glutamate receptors, or they may come about through epigenetic processes (e.g., Szyf, 2011). Whatever the case, it appears fairly certain that corticoid changes that occur in response to stressors encountered early in life can affect later psychological and physical functioning.

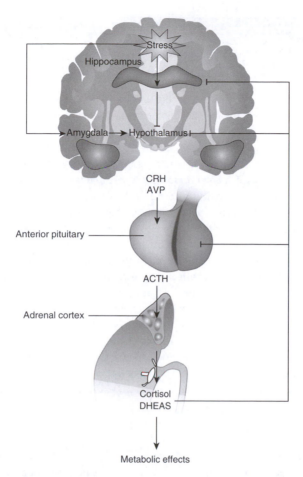

Figure 5.2 Stressors induce the activation of several brain regions, such as the prefrontal cortex and amygdala, which are involved in appraisal of stressful events. When an event is judged to be a threat, the paraventricular nucleus (PVN) of the hypothalamus is stimulated (shown by the lines ending in arrows). This causes the release of CRH from cells at the ventral (bottom) portion the hypothalamus, the median eminence, resulting in the pituitary gland being stimulated and adrenocorticotropic hormone (ACTH) being released. The ACTH enters the bloodstream and eventually reaches the adrenal glands (situated just above the kidneys), stimulating the release of cortisol (corticosterone in rodents). The cortisol enters the bloodstream and affects a variety of target organs. It also reaches the brain where it inhibits actions within the hypothalamus and hippocampus (depicted by blunted endings rather than arrows), thereby inhibiting the release of CRH, and thus brings cortisol release to a stop.

Source: http://www.nature.com/nrendo/journal/v8/n1/fig_tab/nrendo.2011.153_F1.html Papadopoulos and Cleare (2012) *Schematic representation of the hypothalamic-pituitary-adrenal (HPA) axis,* 'Nature Reviews Endocrinology' 8, 22–32 (January 2012)

HOW CORTISOL (CORTICOSTERONE) HELPS US DEAL WITH STRESSORS

Having been released into the bloodstream, cortisol increases blood sugar (derived from substrates such as lactate and glycogen in the liver and in muscle) and aids in the metabolism of fats, carbohydrates and proteins. As well, it sets a limit on the immune activating effects of stressors that could have damaging effects. Aside from these regulatory actions, cortisol may influence neuronal functioning in several brain regions, thereby affecting memory processes (Wingenfeld & Wolf, 2014).

In describing the actions of many hormones that are fundamental in dealing with stressors, Sapolsky et al. (2000) indicated that cortisol can act in several different ways. It allows other stressor-provoked hormonal changes to be expressed or amplified (permissive actions). It can also stimulate or suppress the actions of other hormones or biological factors (e.g., immune functioning), depending on the specific conditions present. Cortisol can also facilitate an organism's ability to deal with impending stressors (preparative action), and may influence neuroplasticity, thereby contributing to the sensitization of processes that affect later responses to stressors. As a result of the actions of cortisol, agents that affect this hormone, such as hydrocortisone, prednisone, prednisolone, and dexamethasone, have seen wide clinical use. Among other things, these drugs have been used to diminish allergic reactions and to inhibit inflammatory responses in an effort to manage disorders in which the immune system attacks certain parts of the self, as well as to limit tissue rejection that could occur following organ transplantation and in graft-versus-host disease (where the transplanted tissue, the graft, attacks the recipient or host).

Chronic stressor effects

An adaptation-like effect may occur in response to chronic stressors so that the corticosterone (cortisol) response is less pronounced. As in the case of the neurotransmitter changes associated with stressors, the adaptation occurs readily if the stressor is consistent across sessions, but not when the stressor appears intermittently and unpredictably, and when the nature of the stressor varies over days (Anisman et al., 2008). On the surface, it seems as if the ability of the HPA system may be diminishing with repeated stressor exposure, but this is hardly the case. Although the adaptation may be apparent in response to a particular stressor being encountered repeatedly, should a new or particularly relevant stressor appear, an exaggerated neuroendocrine response may occur, suggesting that brain-related appraisal processes contribute to the seeming down-regulation of the corticosterone response (Uschold-Schmidt et al., 2012). Apparently, the 'adaptation' is specific to particular events or stimuli, rather than reflecting a decline in the capability of a corticoid response being mounted. Once again, this reflects a highly adaptive response; it would be counterproductive for an adaptation to develop to all stressors simply because animals had adapted to one type of stressor, and so despite a progressive reduction of corticosterone release, the HPA system is ready to respond to significant stimuli should they be encountered.

Stressor-provoked cortisol changes in humans

There seems to be an erroneous belief concerning the effects of stressors on cortisol in humans, likely based on the pronounced changes of corticosterone frequently reported in rodents (200–800% increases are common, depending on stressor severity). In humans, the changes of cortisol elicited by stressors are modest; reminders of previous negative experiences can elicit small cortisol elevations in blood, anticipation of academic exams hardly affect cortisol at all, and even fairly dramatic stressors, such as anticipation of heart surgery, produce cortisol changes of about 30–50% (Michaud et al., 2008). In contrast, threats to our social identity, such as sexism or racial discrimination (Matheson & Anisman, 2012), as well as public speaking, can promote greater cortisol elevations (Michaud et al., 2008). For instance, the Trier Social Stress Test (TSST), in which participants engage in public speaking to a small panel of judges, followed by a verbal arithmetic test, elicits marked increases of plasma or saliva cortisol levels, usually of about 50–200% (Kirschbaum et al., 1993). Furthermore, in response to chronic or severe stressors that lead to PTSD, cortisol levels fall below that of nonstressed individuals (Yehuda, 2002).

This begs the question as to why obviously profound life stressors have effects on cortisol that are so much smaller than those produced in laboratory situations. In part this might be related to when the cortisol was measured relative to the stressor. In the case of academic exams or impending surgery, cortisol was determined in anticipation of the stressor, whereas in situations like the TSST, cortisol was determined in blood (or saliva) taken *after* the stressor test. It seems that the cortisol response might be more closely aligned with experiencing a stressful event, rather than simply anticipating its occurrence. In addition, stressors may be particularly effective in triggering cortisol changes if they comprise uncontrollable *social-evaluative threat*s (e.g., when an audience evaluates the person being stressed), which elicit emotions such as shame (Dickerson & Kemeny, 2004). Likewise, anger associated with stressful events or recollection of these events (e.g., such as having been in an abusive dating relationship) were linked to the appearance of elevated cortisol (Matheson & Anisman, 2012), although the anger in this instance was accompanied by embarrassment and shame ("I'm so embarrassed I can't stand myself – I'd like to just kick myself around the block"). In essence, the cortisol response elicited by these stressors may be linked to the emotional responses that they elicit, rather than being a direct response of the stressor.

Consistent with the stress buffering effects of social support, the availability of social support may limit some of the effects of stressors, including the cortisol changes that are promoted in laboratory challenges, such as the TSST. At the same time, in tests like the TSST, cortisol levels are elevated irrespective of whether audience members are supportive or unsupportive, indicating that concerns about being evaluated outweigh the positive attributes of having support (Taylor et al., 2010). In fact, when women were tested in the TSST with their male partner present to offer social support, their cortisol levels were exaggerated relative to those seen when he was not present even if he was viewed as being supportive (Kirschbaum et al., 1995). Despite being perceived as a source of support, he also might have added to the evaluative threat.

Cortisol in relation to trauma

Particularly telling findings concerning HPA functioning are seen in response to different types of challenges among individuals who had previously experienced trauma. Ordinarily, CRH released from the hypothalamus causes an increase in the secretion of ACTH from the pituitary gland, which then causes adrenal cortisol release. Likewise, when a person is injected with CRH, it causes the release of ACTH, just as endogenous CRH acts this way. However, among depressed women who had been abused when they were young, the ACTH release in response to a CRH challenge was diminished, pointing to down-regulated HPA functioning. Yet, upon being exposed to a social evaluative threat, such as public speaking (the TSST), their ACTH response was exaggerated (Heim et al., 2008). Similarly, relatively low levels of cortisol were observed among women who had experienced psychological and/or physical abuse in a dating relationship and exhibited symptoms of PTSD. However, a much exaggerated cortisol response was elicited when these women encountered reminders of their abusive experience (Matheson & Anisman, 2012).

These findings make sense from an adaptive perspective. Following trauma, elevated and prolonged (or frequent) cortisol elevations could result in the HPA system being overly taxed or secondary damage could be provoked in other brain regions (allostatic overload). As such, down-regulation of HPA activity could be beneficial, but at the same time it would be counter-productive if this occurred non-selectively as there may be times when cortisol elevations are necessary. The best of both worlds is that down-regulated HPA functioning occur, but in the presence of particularly relevant cues or those that elicit strong emotional responses, the mechanisms responsible for the down-regulated HPA response would be overridden, allowing for an especially marked cortisol release. Once more, it seems that the fundamental physiological responses elicited by stressors can be regulated by psychological processes.

The morning cortisol response

Cortisol levels vary over the course of the day (diurnal cortisol variations), being relatively high in the morning, declining towards the afternoon and evening, reaching their nadir at about 11:00 at night, and then begin a progressive rise. More discrete analyses revealed a fairly significant hormone change (measured in saliva) during the first 30 minutes following awakening, during which cortisol typically rises by about 40%, and then declines just as quickly (Schmidt-Reinwald et al., 1999). This cortisol rise is particularly marked among individuals who are dealing with ongoing or recent stressors (Schlotz et al., 2004), and the cortisol decline progresses more slowly in those experiencing distress, as well as among individuals with low social positions or experiencing poor health. Thus, the morning cortisol rise has been taken as an index of distress that individuals are experiencing in their daily lives.

The positive correlation between feelings of distress and the increased morning cortisol response was not evident among individuals who had either experienced a traumatic stressor that led to PTSD or experienced excessive or prolonged strain (e.g., job-related burnout or fatigue and exhaustion related to distress). To the contrary, in these instances the diurnal cortisol profile may be flattened so that morning cortisol levels are reduced, whereas evening cortisol levels are elevated. Although this might simply reflect a disruption of ordinary HPA functioning, it might reflect an adaptation to prevent the adverse effects of prolonged cortisol elevations that could accrue if a chronic stressor is persistent or a traumatic stressor encourages prolonged rumination (Michaud et al., 2008). Unfortunately, getting participants to take saliva samples reliably and accurately on awakening, before eating or brushing their teeth (both may affect cortisol levels in saliva), is difficult, thus undermining the usefulness of the morning cortisol procedure.

Corticotropin releasing hormone (CRH)

Besides being a key hormone in the HPA loop, CRH is present in several brain regions where it has actions relevant to both stress and eating processes. For instance, the release of CRH from different aspects of the amygdala was implicated in the acquisition, expression, and extinction of fear responses (LeDoux, 2000). Further to this, while fear involves activation of the central nucleus of the amygdala, general anxiety is maintained by an extended portion of the amygdala, the bed nucleus of the stria terminalis (Lee & Davis, 1997). Stressors also influence CRH in prefrontal cortical regions and the hippocampus, which contribute to appraisals, decision making, and memory, and stressor-related CRH changes can affect locus coeruleus activity, which is thought to be involved in vigilance (Hammack et al., 2003). Given the widespread CRH variations elicited by stressors, we can count on them being involved in many of the behavioral and cognitive effects that ensue.

CRH receptors

Treatments that increase CRH may induce anxiety and, conversely, administration of a CRH receptor antagonist attenuates the anxiety or depressive-like behavior provoked by a stressor. However, these outcomes are predicated upon the specific types of CRH receptor that are engaged. The elevated anxiety associated with overproduction of CRH was prevented in genetically engineered mice with one type of CRH receptor (CRH_1) deleted or by pharmacologically antagonizing this receptor subtype (Muller et al., 2003), indicating its involvement in anxiety. The contribution of CRH_2 receptors in this regard is less certain, but the view was entertained that the two CRH receptor subtypes mediate different aspects of stress responses. Whereas CRH_1 receptors might contribute primarily to emotional responses, CRH_2 receptors might be more aligned with the regulation of coping responses (Liebsch et al., 1999). Alternatively, CRH_1 receptors may be important in the regulation of executive functions, conscious experience of emotions, attention, and learning about emotions, whereas CRH_2 receptors are more involved in characteristics necessary for survival, such as feeding, reproduction, and defense. From this perspective, patients presenting with anxiety and depression might benefit primarily from drug treatments that target CRH_1 receptors, whereas eating disordered patients, for instance, would be more appropriately treated with drugs that affect CRH_2 receptors. There is still considerable uncertainty concerning how the receptor subtypes are involved in stressor-related behavioral outcomes, but once this has been clarified, improved treatment strategies for anxiety-related disorders might be developed.

Neuropeptide Y

Neuropeptide Y (NPY) elevations in response to stressors may be an important contributor to resilience (Sah & Geracioti, 2013). It came to attention with reports that in relatively severe stressor situations, soldiers with high levels of NPY were less apt to demonstrate PTSD (Sah et al., 2014). In line with such findings, anxiety levels were elevated in rodents genetically engineered to lack NPY receptors (Heilig, 2004), whereas administration of NPY diminished the propensity for stressor-provoked PTSD-like outcomes (Serova et al., 2013). Given the involvement of NPY in stress responses, it has been assessed as a potential biomarker to predict resilience related to surgical recovery (Graham & Becerril-Martinez, 2014).

STRESS AND ENERGY BALANCES

Intuitively, stress and eating processes ought to be seen as acting antagonistically to one another. It would, after all, be counterproductive for animals to continue their search for food if a predator were nearby. In humans, severe stressors typically diminish food consumption, and in some individuals this also occurs in response to moderate stressors. In others, however, moderate and mild stressors will have the opposite effect, promoting food consumption, and may be instrumental in the production of obesity. It also appears that drugs that reduce anxiety (e.g., benzodiazepines) typically have the effect of increasing eating and, conversely, treatments that reduce eating can promote anxiety. For pharmaceutical companies, it has been difficult to develop anti-anxiety treatments that do not encourage weight gain.

CRH and cortisol

For animals in the wild, eating is an inherently dangerous activity. Critters approaching the watering hole need to be wary of being ambushed by predators, and even predators need to be careful as prey can also harm the predator. Thus, it makes sense that food seeking and eating would be accompanied by elevated CRH release (Merali et al., 1998). The increased eating that sometimes accompanies moderate stressor experiences might come about in an effort to cope with stressors, but it also appears that biological processes provoked by stressful events may contribute to this outcome. Specifically, the CRH release elicited by a moderate stressor promotes dopamine activation within the nucleus accumbens, thereby making rewards more salient or more reinforcing. Thus, should the individual be inclined to eat, this tendency will be strengthened by the dopamine changes. This is less likely to occur, in contrast, if the stressor is severe, as the marked increase of CRH release that occurs will no longer promote an increase of dopamine release, and behaviors will shift away from appetitive responses and toward defensive responses, such as anxiety and vigilance (Lemos et al., 2012).

EATING TO COPE

Despite the biological imperative to stop eating in the context of a threat, there are many people who will tell you "I eat when I'm stressed", and when they do, it's not just any food that they go for. They prefer high carb foods, yummy ice cream, cookies, chips, and just about any taste-good food. Rarely, if ever, will the words be heard "I'm stressed out. A nice celery stick or some radishes would really hit the spot right now". The foods sought in response to distressing circumstances are comfort foods that might temporarily make individuals feel better, and, in a sense, eating these foods serves as a way of coping. Alternatively, stressors might instigate chemical changes in the brain and body that promote food craving, and we might be particularly drawn to a fast caloric fix provided by sugars and carbs. If nothing else, these comfort foods might be instrumental in providing energy to facilitate coping with psychological stressors, and the biological changes provoked by comfort foods might also diminish anxiety that might otherwise occur.

An interesting and influential perspective linking stress responses and eating was based on the relationship between stressor-elicited changes of both CRH and cortisol and subsequent food choices (Dallman, 2010). In particular, the corticoid elevations associated with stressors were thought to increase food intake, and in the presence of insulin the preference for high calorie foods was enhanced still further. Under these circumstances the salience of pleasurable or compulsive activities (ingesting sucrose, fat) is increased, and yummy comfort foods might thus instigate still greater pleasure than they would otherwise. The linkages that seemed to exist among stress, cortisol and altered metabolic processes, eating, and the preference for comfort foods led Dallman to suggest that these factors contribute to the current obesity epidemic. What makes her perspective especially interesting and significant is that stressor-elicited corticoids also contribute to the redistribution of stored fat, so that it preferentially appears as abdominal fat depots. As we'll see in ensuing chapters, the bulging tummy that occurs in relation to stressor-elicited eating, owing to the release of cytokines from fat cells present, may contribute to heart disease and immune-related disorders.

INSULIN, THE STRESS RESPONSE, AND REWARD PROCESSES

Insulin is best known for its involvement in glucose being taken up into cells, and in the development of diabetes, but through its actions in mobilizing energy stores, it enables adaptive responses necessary to deal with stressors. Insulin has yet another fairly important action in relation to stress and eating, being able to excite dopamine neurons within brain regions involved in reward processes (Könner et al., 2011), thereby affecting the hedonic or pleasurable component of eating. With the reduced insulin sensitivity resulting from chronic stressors the circuits that engender pleasure associated with food might become disturbed (Egecioglu et al., 2011), thus diminishing food consumption. It is ironic that this comes about only after insulin functioning is impaired, as a reduction in the positive and soothing actions of comfort foods might have done more good before metabolic syndrome or type 2 diabetes had actually developed.

Hormones directly involved in eating initiation and cessation

Leptin and ghrelin

The key hormones involved in eating processes, leptin and ghrelin, are influenced by stressors and contribute to features of stress-related disorders, such as depression and anxiety (Andrews & Abizaid, 2014). In response to acute stressors both ghrelin and leptin increase, which may persist with chronic stressors. This could potentially give rise to 'leptin resistance', so that leptin will fail to signal 'stop eating', and thus stressor-provoked eating will persist. Furthermore, ghrelin activation in response to acute stressors may diminish anxiety, thereby allowing animals to maintain 'appropriate' food-seeking behavior so that energy will be available to deal with challenges, despite the presence of danger (Spencer et al., 2012). The view was also offered that ghrelin or leptin–ghrelin interactions facilitate coping that acts against depressive-like states (Abizaid et al., 2014; Chuang & Zigman, 2010). In line with this suggestion, depressive-like behavioral disturbances and corticosterone elevations provoked by stressors in rodents could be antagonized by leptin administration (Stieg et al., 2014).

In contrast to the effects of stressors in animals, the data concerning the connection between leptin, ghrelin, and depressive states in humans have been equivocal (Chuang & Zigman, 2010). Why incongruity exists between animal and human studies isn't certain. However, as leptin, ghrelin, cortisol, and other hormones are entwined in stress responses, it may be essential to determine how they come together to affect stressor responses, rather than evaluating their actions independently of each other. Given the array of hormones involved in eating and stress responses, it has been considered that they might each have different functions in relation to depression, with some contributing primarily to the neurovegetative features of the illness (e.g., eating, sleeping), whereas others might contribute more to mood features (Abizaid et al., 2014).

SEX HORMONES

Men and women often exhibit very different responses to stressors, and the prevalence of some stress-related illnesses, such as anxiety and depression, are much more frequent in women. Beyond differences in the behavioral and emotional responses to stressors, men and women may also exhibit different responses to stressors owing to the influence of sex hormones.

Estrogen and testosterone

In rodents, females generally exhibit more pronounced stressor-elicited corticosterone elevations than do males, possibly through the influence of gonadal hormones (Toufexis et al., 2014). As well, stressor-elicited neuronal activity in brain regions that govern behavioral and cognitive responses to stressors (e.g., frontal, cingulate, and piriform cortices) are more pronounced in female rodents than in males, varying with the estrous cycle, thus implicating sex hormones in moderating these outcomes (Cahill, 2006). In both sexes, stressors encountered in early life or adolescence exert especially pronounced effects on the later development of hormonal processes, and may influence brain development owing to interactive effects with several hormones and neurotransmitter systems. This said, the plasticity of the developing brain also provides the opportunity for the negative effects of stressors to be diminished through positive experiences.

The gender differences in response to stressors in animals are to an extent recapitulated in humans. Stressor effects in women vary with the estrous cycle, with cortisol responses being most pronounced during the latter part of the menstrual cycle (*luteal phase*), during which the hormone progesterone is very high (Kirschbaum et al., 1999), and may also vary following menopause (Kajantie & Phillips, 2006). Stress-arousing stimuli also elicited especially marked neuronal activity in stress-relevant brain regions (amygdala, orbitofrontal cortex) of women, and once more these effects were most pronounced during the early *follicular* phase (prior to ovulation) (Goldstein et al., 2005). It seems that estradiol can limit HPA axis activity, whereas progesterone (which peaks during the latter half of the cycle) may promote disturbed negative glucocorticoid feedback. Aside from estrogen and testosterone, other variables contribute to sex differences in the stress response, and these may vary yet again with the nature of the stressor experienced. For instance, in response to emotionally arousing stimuli, the left and right amygdala operate differently in males versus females (Williams et al., 2005), and sex differences of dopamine functioning have been observed, which may be linked to differences in addiction potential between men and women (Lynch et al., 2002).

Stress and reproduction

Stressed females are typically less likely to engage in *proceptive* behaviors (courting, or those behaviors that lead to sex) and they're less inclined to respond to male overtures (*receptivity*). Sexual behavior among males is often altered as well, although it might take a bit more distress for males to lose interest. Essentially, stressful periods promote anxiety and distractions so that individuals are less able or motivated to focus on sexual behaviors, and they may experience a bit of anhedonia.

In addition to disturbed proceptive and receptive behaviors, among females the suppressive effect of stressors on reproduction itself might arise owing to disrupted ovulation (gonadal hormone production likewise occurs in males) and uterine disturbances necessary for implantation of a fertilized egg (Wingfield & Sapolsky, 2003). As well, stressors promote the secretion of the opioid peptide β-endorphin, which increases *gonadotropin inhibitory hormone* (GnIH), leading to reduced release of luteinizing hormone, thereby promoting infertility (Cameron, 1997). When the gene for GnIH was knocked out, reproductive behavior was normalized (Geraghty et al., 2015), pointing to its fundamental role in determining the stressor effects.

As with so many other hormonal and behavioral disturbances, stressors experienced early in life may influence later adult sexual behavior, possibly owing to enduring disturbances of estrogen receptors. Even fairly moderate stressors, or being exposed to mild infection, diminished receptivity among females, as well as behavioral responsiveness to estradiol and progesterone in adulthood (Ismail et al., 2011). Likewise, stressful events experienced during the prenatal period can affect later adult sexual behaviors (Pereira et al., 2006), and prenatal stressors, including infection, can disrupt later maternal behaviors.

Prolactin

Technically, prolactin is not a sex hormone, but instead is involved in maternal behaviors. Stressors provoke a reduction of prolactin levels, which could disturb ongoing parental efforts. Although this could place offspring in jeopardy, in the context of strong threats, the reduced prolactin may favor the survival of the parent who would, for a while at least, be less focused on her offspring (Angelier & Chastel, 2009). Prolactin receptors are present in several stress-sensitive brain regions, such as the central amygdala and the nucleus accumbens, raising the possibility that this hormone is involved in emotional responses. Of particular significance is that during the peripartum period (i.e., before or a short period following delivery) prolactin levels or prolactin receptor variations contribute to the attenuation of behavioral and neuroendocrine stress responses that might be disadvantageous for the offspring (Torner & Neumann, 2002).

STRESSING MOM VERSUS STRESSING HER PUPS

Although HPA activity in rodents is very responsive to stressors, its functioning is blunted during lactation. A critical feature for this was that the mom and her pups had to have been in contact with one another within the preceding few hours. In the absence of this contact, the effects of stressors on HPA functioning in the moms were not attenuated (Walker, 2010). It is important for stress hormone responses to be inhibited during the lactation period, so that excessive corticosterone does not reach the fetus or pups (postnatally through the mother's milk). However, there are occasions in which corticosterone will increase in a nursing mother. Unlike the response evident when the threat was directed at mom, when the threat was directed at offspring more resources were placed at mom's disposal to ensure offspring survival, including a marked rise of corticosterone (Walker, 2010). Messing with mom is one thing, but messing with her pups is something else entirely.

OXYTOCIN

Moderation of the stress response

In view of oxytocin's presumed role in prosocial behaviors, it would be expected that this hormone might operate to diminish the impact of stressors by encouraging social coping. In fact, oxytocin administration to humans (as a nasal spray) attenuated cortisol stress responses (Cardoso, Kingdon et al., 2014) and reduced anxiety in response to an interpersonal stressor, even among individuals with low emotional regulatory abilities (Quirin et al., 2011). Such findings led to the suggestion that oxytocin might be useful in treating stress-related psychological disturbances (Koch et al., 2014).

Early-life experiences

Stressful early experiences, including those related to maternal care and emotional abuse, may affect oxytocin during adulthood (Heim et al., 2009), possibly owing to epigenetic effects (Cushing & Kramer, 2005). Early-life social stressors that modified oxytocin levels could also provoke lasting consequences on prosocial behaviors, such as bonding and trust, and thus influence the ability to contend with further psychosocial challenges. Given the importance of oxytocin in social interactions, it is especially interesting that oxytocin levels were greatly altered among women who had experienced childhood abuse, whereas a nonsocial stressor in the form of childhood cancer elicited lesser effects (Pierrehumbert et al., 2010). As prenatal stressors in rodents also disrupted later social interactions in adulthood, which could be attenuated by oxytocin administered directly to the amygdala, it is likely that the link between prenatal stressors, oxytocin changes, and social interactions is a causal one (Lee et al., 2007).

Tend and befriend versus tend and defend

Males and females share many common methods of coping, although distinct differences also exist in this respect. It has been proposed that a key gender difference related to coping is that female behaviors are often characterized by a 'tend and befriend' approach, including nurturing behaviors to facilitate self-protection and that of close others, and the development and maintenance of social connections. This tend and befriend feature of women, which includes altruism (helping fellow group members despite a cost to oneself), is thought to be influenced by oxytocin together with opioid peptides and gonadal hormones (Taylor et al., 2000).

In view of the influence of oxytocin on prosocial behaviors, coupled with the importance of social support as a key coping method, oxytocin may be linked to our well-being by virtue of it favoring social support seeking to deal with stressors (Cardoso et al., 2013). Consistent with a role for oxytocin in affecting stress responses, a gene polymorphism was identified on the oxytocin receptor (OXTR), which could potentially influence prosocial behaviors and thus alter stress responses. As described by McQuaid et al. (2014), this gene was related to cortisol responses elicited by social stressors and was associated with social support seeking in stressful situations.

As much as it sounds reasonable to attribute a 'tend and befriend' characteristic primarily to women, prosocial behaviors attributed to oxytocin are also seen in males. However, males are also more likely to exhibit an evolutionarily significant 'tend and defend' characteristic. This involves *parochial altruism*, in which they are true to their own group members, but they also warn and defend one another in relation to other groups (Israel et al., 2012). In effect, although oxytocin may instigate cooperation in males, it may also be linked to defense-motivated noncooperative attitudes and behaviors (De Dreu, 2012).

Oxytocin increases sensitivity to social stimuli

Instead of seeing oxytocin as a purely prosocial hormone, another view has emerged which suggests that oxytocin doesn't simply act in this capacity, but might operate to increase sensitivity to social stimuli. In the presence of elevated oxytocin, positive social interactions would be viewed as more significant, and negative social interactions would similarly be viewed as more negative (Ellenbogen et al., 2013; McQuaid et al., 2013). From this vantage, oxytocin might not always have the positive effects often attributed to it, and in the face of negative events (e.g., early-life mistreatment), high oxytocin might result in more damaging outcomes than would otherwise occur. Conversely, among those with an oxytocin dysfunction, these abusive events would not have the negative consequences that would normally be expected (McQuaid et al., 2013). Likewise, in the presence of genes associated with high levels of oxytocin, high interpersonal stressor levels predicted elevated depression, but this did not occur in the presence of a polymorphism that ought to have reduced the level of this hormone (Tabak et al., 2015). Further to this, following a breach of trust, women who had received oxytocin through a nasal spray were less forgiving than placebo-treated participants, suggesting that the betrayal was perceived as being more profound in those treated with oxytocin (Yao et al., 2014). In light of such findings, the idea of including oxytocin for the treatment of depression might have a downside. In particular, if the levels of this hormone were not diminished in depressed patients, the high levels of oxytocin that would result from administration of this hormone might make individuals overly sensitive to negative social cues. For that matter, given the warped appraisals characteristic among depressed individuals, even neutral social stimuli would be more likely to be negatively misinterpreted.

GROWTH FACTORS

Growth factors, including BDNF, FGF-2, and GDNF, have been implicated in stress-related mood disturbances, such as depressive illness. In rodents, strong acute stressors or reminders of these stressors reduced BDNF in limbic brain regions that have been associated with mood states (Duman & Monteggia, 2006). The reductions of BDNF within the hippocampus also varied with chronic stressor treatments, especially if this comprised a series of different challenges (Grønli et al., 2006), just as such a regimen was most closely aligned with mood disorders.

The reduction of hippocampal BDNF elicited by stressors has reinforced the view that depressive illness might stem from growth factor changes rather than neurotransmitter alterations, as previously thought. However, the involvement of BDNF in depression may be more complex than initially considered. Other than the hippocampus, stressors do not uniformly induce growth factor reductions in stress-sensitive brain regions that have been implicated in underlying depression. Indeed, stressful events increased BDNF mRNA expression in several aspects of the prefrontal cortex (anterior cingulate, prelimbic, and infralimbic), and long-lasting BDNF elevations were seen in the ventral tegmentum, a brain region that has been associated with reward processes (Fanous et al., 2010). Likewise, within the anterior cingulate cortex, which is involved in the processing of emotionally salient events as well as in decision making, BDNF expression was elevated to a greater extent after controllable rather than uncontrollable stressors (Bland et al., 2007), possibly indicating that BDNF was in some fashion related to new learning related to the controllable situation rather than being a consequence of the stressor.

The variations of stressor-related BDNF changes across brain regions may be aligned with different aspects of emotional and cognitive functioning and may interact with neurotransmitters, such as serotonin, in determining depression (Martinowich & Lu, 2008). There is also reason to suppose that while hippocampal BDNF might be involved in the memory of negative events, the changes within the prefrontal cortex might contribute to the strengthening of cognitive and behavioral responses associated with depression (e.g., the negative thinking and poor appraisals that are commonly seen). Although this suggestion is highly provisional, the available data suggest, if nothing else, that determining the relation between stressors, BDNF, and the emergence of pathology won't be simple. There's still much that isn't understood concerning the linkages between BDNF and illnesses, including to what extent the effects of stressors are tied to gender, which is essential given the disproportionate frequency of depression in females. Furthermore, BDNF is only one of the several growth factors that has been associated with depression, FGF-2 having also been linked to psychiatric illness (Evans et al., 2004), and it is uncertain how several growth factors may interact in eliciting behavioral changes.

Influence of early-life experiences

As we've seen, stressors encountered early in life can either disturb or enhance later responses to stressors. Moderate stressors experienced during early life and adolescence may facilitate the ability to deal behaviorally with later stressors, possibly through increases of neurotrophic factors. In essence, mild stressors might prime growth factor functioning, encouraging synaptic plasticity, thereby facilitating the ability to contend with subsequently encountered challenges. Conversely, severe or toxic early-life stressors that disturb growth factor functioning may disrupt neuroplasticity, consequently undermining the development of behavioral coping methods and favoring later psychopathology.

Both prenatal and early postnatal stressor experiences may have enduring effects on the expression of BDNF and FGF-2 within the brain, possibly being related to epigenetic factors (Roth et al., 2009). Likewise, stressors experienced by a pregnant rodent may influence FGF-2 in her unborn pups and may affect their later responses to stressful events (Fumagalli et al., 2005), rendering them more vulnerable to a depressive-like condition. Beyond these psychiatric impairments, FGF-2 has also been implicated in disturbances associated with hypoxia (reduced oxygen) that follows from very premature birth, including mild to moderate cognitive delay and increased incidence of neuropsychiatric conditions, such as anxiety, attention deficit hyperactivity, and autism spectrum disorders (Salmaso et al., 2014).

STRESSOR-RELATED CHANGES OF BRAIN MORPHOLOGY

Among children who had experienced physical abuse or neglect, the volume of the amygdala and hippocampus was reduced (Hanson et al., 2015), and such changes were particularly notable with cumulative stressor experiences (Frodl & O'Keane, 2013). Such brain changes were associated with disturbed coping and social support that have been linked to the development of PTSD, as well as to epigenetic changes that produce lasting effects on stress hormones (Mehta et al., 2013). In this regard, the impact of stressors on brain size has also been linked to gene × stressor interactions. Among adults who experienced stressors such as unemployment, financial loss, accidents, serious illnesses, divorce, or loss of a loved one, hippocampal size was diminished provided that they also carried a gene mutation related to BDNF, serotonin reuptake, or an enzyme involved in degrading norepinephrine (COMT), all of which have been related to depressive states and high stressor reactivity (Rabl et al., 2014).

Aside from hippocampal reductions, the size of the prefrontal cortex might also be diminished with chronic stressor experiences. This may be accompanied by cognitive and behavioral changes wherein decision-making abilities were altered so that individuals tended to fall back on previously established behavioral strategies (i.e., biases, habits), rather than framing and adopting new approaches. On the positive side, the brain changes and disturbed decision-making abilities associated with stressors normalized as the stressor experiences receded (Soares et al., 2012).

STRESS AND IMMUNITY

Stressful experiences can influence the ability of immune cells to deal effectively with antigenic challenges, but the nature of the changes observed vary with several attributes of stressors, and a given stressor may not affect all aspects of immune functioning in the same way. Still, several general conclusions can be made concerning the impact of stressors on immune functioning. Specifically, immune changes are dependent on the severity and chronicity of the stressor experienced (Dhabhar, 2009), as well as several experiential, developmental, and organismic factors described earlier (Audet et al., 2014). Although immune changes often accompany physical trauma, such as burns, the effects of stressors aren't simply due to tissue damage, as psychological stressors, such as loneliness and disturbed social stability, can elicit immune alterations (e.g., Pressman et al., 2005).

Effects of acute and chronic stressors in animals

Stressors can alter various aspects of immune functioning, including the absolute number of immune cells in circulation, the rate at which immune cells proliferate, and their ability to kill pathogens (*cytotoxicity*). Predictably, stressors also influence immune responses to bacteria and viruses, and the time for wound healing to occur (Godbout & Glaser, 2006). These outcomes vary with the severity of the stressor in that relatively mild challenges may augment immune functioning, whereas intense stressors will compromise immune functioning. From an adaptive perspective, an acute stressor might be expected to instigate an immune surge to deal with an ongoing threat. Concurrently, nonessential functions, such as digestion or reproduction, ought to be suppressed. As the severity or chronicity of the stressor increases, both primary and secondary immune responses (the powerful response that occurs when an animal is re-exposed to an antigenic challenge) may be compromised, leading to greater illness vulnerability (Dhabhar, 2009; Sorrells et al., 2009).

STRESS-RELATED SKIN 'BLEMISHES'

Immune changes can influence skin conditions, which although transient and not life-threatening, can take their toll on an individual's self-esteem and well-being. Skin eruptions might appear in the worst possible place just before an important social event. This might not be the only occasion when blemishes appear, but anyone affected this way will remember it well and assume some sort of causal relationship between the skin problem and the significance of the event. In fact, stressors of moderate severity and anticipation of stressors may inhibit skin healing following exposure to an irritant, such as allergic contact (e.g., akin to poison ivy), and may influence atopic dermatitis (eczema) psoriasis, rosacea, and acne (Lin et al., 2014). These effects likely come about owing to hormonal changes that affect immune processes and hence skin health and healing (Madva & Granstein, 2013).

The notion that moderate acute stressors would enhance immune functioning, whereas severe or chronic stressors would have the opposite effect, is intuitively appealing, but at the same time it has puzzling elements. For animals in the wild, stressors don't occur on an occasional basis, but appear repeatedly in different forms – danger of predators, food shortages, and climactic change (it is, after all, a jungle out there) – which ought to favor elevated cortisol levels and hence suppressed immune functioning. As well, stressors in the form of social defeat or disruption of social hierarchies, especially if these occur on a continuous basis, could undermine the immune system's capability of mounting an effective response. Although animals at the bottom of a social hierarchy may experience continued distress, and are understandably at risk for immune disturbances, this doesn't mean that animals at the top of the social hierarchy get away unscathed, as they too exhibit marked immune alterations (Audet et al., 2010). Being the emperor means having to continuously look over your shoulder to see who's stealthily coming up from behind (Sapolsky, 2005).

As the challenges persist, immune disturbances may become more pronounced, but once again compensatory changes may develop, varying as a function of whether the stressor occurs on an uncontrollable, variable, and unpredictable basis. As we saw earlier, with continued stressor experiences glucocorticoid levels may be reduced and/or receptor sensitivity may diminish, and as a result the immunosuppressive effects of glucocorticoids decline (Powell et al., 2013). Given the many different challenges that animals experience in their natural habitat, it's a delicate bit of juggling that allows for sufficient corticosterone functioning to deal with stressors, and yet not impair immune functioning.

STERILE INFLAMMATION

Although we usually think of inflammation as an essential component in the immune system's battle against invasive pathogens, inflammation also occurs in response to trauma, chemically induced injury, and ischemia, despite the absence of any challenging microorganisms. This 'sterile inflammation' is accompanied by the recruitment of various immune cells and the production of pro-inflammatory cytokines (Chen & Nuñez, 2010). Among its other talents, the immune system is able to detect danger through 'danger (or damage) molecular pattern molecules' (DAMPs) that can initiate immune responses and prolong them once they are present. However, the persistent elevation of DAMPs and various immune factors in response to pollutants, ionizing radiation, or tobacco smoke could give rise to increased levels of 'reactive oxygen species', a by-product of cellular metabolism, which can lead to tissue damage. As well, sterile inflammation may also be associated with heart disease and may contribute to the growth of cancer cells, an overwhelming inflammatory response in patients with acute lung injury, the development of multi-organ failure, and even dementia (Fleshner, 2013).

Stressor effects in humans

Studies in humans assessing the impact of stressors on immune functioning have largely relied on blood measures to determine levels of various immune substrates or immune changes that are elicited by *in vitro* challenges (e.g., NK cytotoxicity or lymphocyte proliferation induced by a foreign substance). Functional outcomes have also been assessed through analyses of time for wounds to heal, or susceptibility to viral infection. There have also been studies that have assessed the effects of stressors on responses to vaccines, which in essence are viral threats (although the threat has been inactivated) that the immune system will recognize (Yang & Glaser, 2002).

In such paradigms, acute psychological stressors have increased immune functioning (e.g., Pace et al., 2006), whereas chronic stressors, such as caregiving (e.g., for a partner with Alzheimer's disease), have disrupted immune activity (Glaser et al., 1999; Slavich & Irwin, 2014), possibly owing to hormonal changes associated with these stressors (Fonareva & Oken, 2014). It was likewise observed among medical students that the stress of academic examinations was accompanied by reduced T cells and diminished efficacy of memory T cells (Maes, 1999), and life stressors limited the production of antibodies ordinarily associated with immunization (Cohen et al., 2001). Consistent with other neurobiological responses, immune efficacy was affected by early-life negative experiences (Miller et al., 2011), and toxic stressors, such as severe poverty, may be accompanied by epigenetic changes that affect immune functioning (Lam et al., 2012). In addition, altered immune system functioning has been linked to several personality and emotional factors. For instance, NK cell activity was particularly low among individuals who were hostile, especially negative, and who engaged in high levels of rumination or expressed depressive mood states (Kiecolt-Glaser et al., 2002; Zoccola et al., 2014).

Cytokine variations

Cytokines essential for communication between immune cells and in promoting inflammatory responses are markedly affected by stressors and are altered in mood disorders (Dantzer et al., 2008). In rodents, the production of pro-inflammatory cytokines, such as IL-1β in blood, are increased by stressful events, and several days of social disruption promoted greater amounts of IL-1β and TNF-α in lymphoid organs, such as the spleen and lung. The rise of pro-inflammatory cytokines is soon followed by elevated anti-inflammatory cytokines, presumably to maintain a balance between different cytokine subtypes (Anisman et al., 2008).

In humans, levels of IL-1β in blood are too low to be reliably detected, and thus most studies of blood cytokines focused on changes of IL-6 and TNF-α. Psychological stressors, such as public speaking, exercise, or caregiving, were accompanied by elevated IL-6 production and increased presence of the inflammatory marker C-reactive protein that was released from the liver, the latter being especially notable when participants were asked to dwell on their stressful experiences (Zoccola et al., 2014). However, elevated immune and cytokine functioning is not apparent in response to severe, chronic stressors, such as that experienced by parents of children experiencing cancer (Miller et al., 2002). Furthermore, in association with the chronic distress of caregiving, dysregulation may occur in the balance between pro- and anti-inflammatory cytokines, thereby favoring the emergence of disease conditions (Glaser et al., 2001). It seems fairly certain that stressors can impair immune functioning and chronic challenges are particularly adept in promoting pathological outcomes.

Personality, emotion, and cytokine variations

Just as personality factors moderate the influence of stressors on hormonal processes and vulnerability to stressor-related illness, individual characteristics, such as hostility, attributional style, and extraversion-introversion, influence stressor-provoked cytokine variations (Segerstrom, 2000). Optimism, which has been linked to enhanced health and well-being, is accompanied by limited stressor-provoked cytokine variations (Brydon et al., 2009). Likewise, disruptive cytokine responses ordinarily elicited by stressors are limited among people with higher self-esteem (K. O'Donnell et al., 2008), but were more pronounced among individuals who felt low in social status (Derry et al., 2013). It was similarly reported that the rise of blood IL-6 and the anti-inflammaory cytokine IL-10 elicited by a public speaking stressor was linked to feelings of shame or anger (Danielson et al., 2011). In essence, just as cytokine responses to stressors are subject to moderation by personality factors, these effects can also be linked to the emergence of particular emotions.

LINKING CYTOKINES TO DEPRESSIVE DISORDERS

One approach to treat some forms of cancer (e.g., malignant melanoma) and hepatitis C has been through the administration of the cytokine interferon-α, and other forms of this cytokine have been used to abate the course of multiple sclerosis. Speaking to the causal link between inflammatory cytokines and psychological disorders, approximately 40–50% of treated patients developed severe depression, often sufficiently intense to require treatment cessation. This outcome was most common among individuals who were considered at relatively greater risk for depressive illness, but these actions could be attenuated by antidepressant medications (Capuron & Miller, 2011; Raison et al., 2006).

Although several processes were considered to explain how interferon-α came to produce depression, one that has received considerable support was that this cytokine stimulates an enzyme, indoleamine-2, 3-dioxygenase (conveniently referred to as IDO), that indirectly reduces the production of serotonin. More than this, however, IFN-α is also involved in the production of metabolites (3-hydroxy-kynurenine and quinolinic acid), which can have neurodestructive effects, thereby leading to depression (Dantzer et al., 2011; Wichers et al., 2005), and might also influence the development of neurodegenerative diseases such as Huntington's, Parkinson's, AIDS, and dementia (Hartai et al., 2005).

There is another aspect regarding interferon that is interesting. In naïve mice, IFN-α seemed to have hardly any observable behavioral effects and fairly limited neurochemical actions. This isn't overly surprising as not every manipulation that affects mice has similar effects in humans, and vice versa. However, in this instance, if mice had been moderately stressed (e.g., through social disruption), the effects of IFN-α were greatly increased (Anisman et al., 2007). This may be pertinent from a clinical perspective as humans undergoing cytokine immunotherapy are typically under considerable strain, and the depression elicited by the treatments might reflect the synergistic (multiplicative) actions of the cytokine and the ongoing stressor conditions.

Brain cytokine variations

The effects of stressors on cytokine levels or production are not limited to peripheral processes, but may also occur in the brain, although the changes may be very different from the profile seen peripherally (Anisman et al., 2008; Miller et al., 2009). In rodents, acute stressors provoke an increase of inflammatory cytokines, especially if the stressor occurs on the backdrop of an immune challenge (Gibb et al., 2013). Furthermore, when animals are re-exposed to a stressor sometime after an initial challenge, the cytokine response may be greatly exaggerated, even when this has involved a very different stressor (Johnson et al., 2002). Thus, encounters with a stressor may prime immune factors or brain microglia to respond more vigorously to later challenges, and the excessive cytokine release could potentially lead to pathological outcomes (Anisman et al., 2003).

Cytokine-induced neurochemical changes in the brain

The significance of brain cytokine variations is apparent from the multiple actions that they can have on neuronal processes. Among other things cytokines give rise to several brain neurochemical changes that can influence normal behavioral functioning as well as pathophysiological conditions. In many respects, immune and cytokine challenges elicit brain neurochemical changes that are reminiscent of those engendered by strong stressors, such as increasing monoamine utilization in the prefrontal cortex, central amygdala and hippocampus, GABA and glutamate within limbic and hypothalamic regions, and growth factors in the hippocampus (Audet & Anisman, 2013; Hayley et al., 2005). Moreover, at least some of these actions, such as the increase of serotonin turnover in the prefrontal cortex elicited by the cytokine interferon-α, could be attenuated by pretreatment with a nonsteroidal anti-inflammatory drug (Asnis et al., 2003). Likewise, the monoamine changes ordinarily elicited by stressors were precluded by inhibiting the actions of IL-1β, and the behavioral and neuroendocrine effects of a chronic mild stressor were not apparent among mice that were genetically engineered so that IL-1β receptors were deleted. These mice also did not display the reduction of hippocampal neuroplasticity that otherwise accompanied stressor treatments (Goshen et al., 2008). Findings such as these led to the suggestion that the brain interprets inflammatory immune activation, much like it does other stressor challenges (Anisman & Merali, 1999). Of course, bacterial and viral infections don't promote cognitive appraisals of the challenge like those produced by psychogenic stressors. They might nevertheless affect processes that could affect later appraisals of events, and by virtue of effects on neurochemical processes, immune and cytokine alterations could affect mood states.

SUMMARY

Stressors have effects on many neurotransmitters, hormones, growth factors, and elements of the immune system, and if a given system is vulnerable to being sufficiently disturbed, then pathology may arise. It also seems that certain stress-sensitive responses (e.g., inflammatory immune activation) may affect several different illnesses (e.g., heart disease, diabetes, depression), accounting for the frequent comorbidities that exist between disorders.

We've only touched on some of the effects of stressors on biological processes and many of the variables that can influence them. Nonetheless, it is certain that several biological systems work in tandem with one another, and it can be difficult to disentangle their relative roles in relation to stressor-provoked pathological outcomes. It similarly appears that behavioral and cognitive processes have a say in at least some of the biological changes introduced by stressors, and thus it's a fairly reasonable bet that psychological manipulations to reduce distress, at least in some instances, can have positive effects on health. This certainly brings to the front the notion that in treating physical illnesses, it might often be of considerable benefit to treat the psychological ramifications of the disease.

6 Healthy Behaviors, Unhealthy Behaviors, and Behavioral Change

PREVENTION COULD ELIMINATE THE NEED FOR CURE

"An ounce of prevention is worth a pound of cure" has become a tired cliché that dates back to the thirteenth century, although the expression is often attributed to Benjamin Franklin. Like so many other bits of folk wisdom, it developed based on experiences and common sense.

In his book *The Emperor of all Maladies: A biography of cancer* (2010), Siddhartha Mukherjee describes some of the efforts that had historically been made and the approaches used in treating cancer. After describing the dehumanizing experiences that cancer patients endured (and still do, but less so than in the past), he recounts the observations of Percival Potts concerning scrotal cancer that occurred at unusually high frequencies among boys who had been chimney sweeps, and the subsequent observations of Henry Butlin who noted that scrotal cancer was far less frequent if chimney sweeps wore protective clothing. Reports such as these galvanized fields such as epidemiology and preventive medicine that sought to identify environmental (and other) factors linked to diseases, and how to develop strategies to prevent these disorders from occurring. Eventually, rather than focusing simply on treatment of illness, the pendulum swung a bit more to the side of illness prevention. This transition is still ongoing, but didn't occur without some resistance. In fact, it wasn't until about 50 years ago that attention was devoted to cancer epidemiology, and in several other fields it's been still slower to emerge. Today, many preventive measures are recommended to tackle diseases, such as finding ways to reduce environmental toxicants and diminish stress, maintaining a proper work–life balance, exercising daily, eating and sleeping right, stopping smoking, and staying out of direct sunlight. There's little doubt that these are all excellent preventive strategies, and there's also little doubt that there are a considerable number of people who don't follow this advice.

GAINING A FOOTHOLD

There has been the perception that the development of illnesses may just be a matter of bad luck. A person might be the victim of random gene mutations coming together in a way that makes particular illnesses, such as cancer, more likely to occur. This could certainly be possible in some instances, but it doesn't rule out the possibility that healthy behaviors act against illnesses occurring, whereas the adoption of unhealthy behaviors have the opposite effect. To gain leverage in sustaining good health, and to facilitate the prevention of illnesses, having people change their behavioral styles may be particularly beneficial. This chapter is aimed at dealing with these issues, focusing on:

- risk factors related to disease conditions
- psychosocial factors that favor the development of illness
- the effectiveness of intervention strategies to limit the development of illness
- various strategies to instigate health-related behavior change
- the best methods to deal with pathological conditions, with emphasis placed on individualized treatment strategies.

TREATMENT OF ILLNESS

Treatments of disorders are typically delivered on a first-come-first-served basis, unless the illness is considered to be an emergency (or the individual has 'protectzia', meaning they are well connected). Often, the treatment comprises *time-limited therapy*, amounting to an *episode of care* that may involve multiple treatment sessions or until some level of success has been reached. In some cases *enhanced therapy* is necessary, in which supplemental strategies are provided in an effort to amplify or extend the benefits attained from a single episode of care. This can entail continued treatment to reach a desirable level of symptom relief for the patient (or an alternative treatment being administered). It may be used in an effort to limit recurrence of a disorder, or the occurrence of comorbid illnesses that could otherwise emerge. Finally, *continuing care*, including supportive and social therapies, is provided for illnesses that are long-lasting, including those for which there is no cure.

INDIVIDUALIZED TREATMENT STRATEGIES

A theme that has appeared repeatedly throughout this text concerns individual differences that exist with respect to illness vulnerability. We can pretty well count on some individuals being particularly vulnerable to pathological outcomes, with the nature of the illness being dictated by biological weak links that might be present. Appreciable differences similarly exist regarding the efficacy of treatments for most illnesses; some people seem to be able to overcome illnesses readily, whereas among others illness features seem to linger for protracted periods. What makes one individual more resilient than another might comprise a long list of personality factors, experiences in dealing with challenge, and the presence of particular hormonal, neurotransmitter or growth factors, as well as genetic influences.

Individualized (personalized) treatments based on endophenotypic analyses

For several reasons, individuals with an apparently similar illness may respond differently to particular treatments. By example, breast cancer can take any of several forms and may involve different genetic and hormonal processes, and thus will be responsive to different treatments. Accordingly, a biopsy is conducted to identify the characteristics of the cancer, which informs treatments that should be used. Similarly, features of illnesses, such as the presence or absence of particular symptoms or biological characteristics, might signify that they will be more or less responsive to a given treatment. Whether it's cancer, heart disease, psychological disturbances, or any of several other illnesses, there isn't a single treatment that's suitable for everybody. Accordingly, there have been efforts to establish *individualized* (personalized) treatments based on identifying specific features of the illness.

The *endophenotypic* approach to defining and treating illnesses has largely been a reaction to the repeated failures to treat patients effectively. The notion has been that instead of considering an illness as a broad syndrome, an illness ought to be deconstructed and treatments applied in light of specific features of the illness (Gottesman & Gould, 2003). The endophenotype was thought to reflect the 'measurable' aspects that link genetic factors and illness, including biochemical (e.g., endocrine, neurotransmitter, immunological, microbial), neuroanatomical, neuropsychological, cognitive, or behavioral factors. Having established the specific linkages that exist to an illness, it may be possible to determine whether particular factors predict the most efficacious treatment strategies. By example, a substantial database has been established (Griffith et al., 2013) that detailed 2,600 genes and 6,300 drugs that target these genes (6,700 genes were also in the database waiting to be linked to specific drugs) to determine whether certain drugs will be particularly

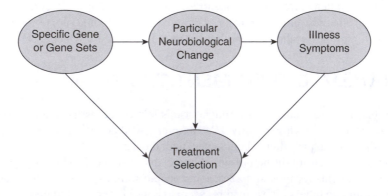

Figure 6.1   Endophenotypic approach: Treatments for a given illness are not simply based on an illness being diagnosed, but instead are dependent upon the specific characteristics that are identified as being present. These include specific genes that may lead to particular neurobiological alterations, which can elicit the emergence of identifiable symptoms. Based on these indices, treatment strategies are adopted on an individual basis.

efficacious in treating illnesses given the presence of specific genes or gene combinations. With so many drugs and a still greater number of genes, finding meaningful matches is exceedingly difficult, especially as some genes associated with an illness or its treatment may not involve causal connections. Still, it would be remarkably important to be able to say with certainty that individuals with a given illness who carry a particular gene will be best treated with treatment X, whereas if they carry some other gene, then they're most likely to benefit from treatment Y.

Endophenotypes in relation to psychiatric disorders

The idea of linking specific genes to diseases, which then determine treatment strategies, has been used for some time in treating cancer and heart disease, but it is still a relative newcomer in dealing with psychiatric disorders. Increasingly, more research is being conducted to identify biomarkers that predict illnesses or that can be used to identify effective treatment methods. This said, the usefulness of the endophenotypic method may be constrained by a lack of precision regarding diagnostic criteria and family history of an illness, difficulties in identifying genetic markers for the emergence of pathology, and the potentially prohibitive cost of personalized treatments (Alda, 2013).

In 2013 the American Psychiatric Association released the *Diagnostic and Statistical Manual of Mental Disorders*, Fifth Edition (*DSM-5*), which is meant to provide a detailed and systematic description of the symptoms of various psychiatric disorders so that all physicians would be using the same playbook in making their diagnoses. However, the *DSM-5* was met with considerable resistance, particularly from those who saw classification systems as being inherently counter-productive. Patients, it was felt, should be treated on the basis of specific symptoms, as well as genetic and other biomarkers, rather than on the basis of broad labels. The National Institutes of Health, whose primary mandate concerns health-related research, developed the NIMH Research Domain Criteria (RDoC), which comprises a different framework for how to diagnose and treat various psychiatric illnesses (Cuthbert & Insel, 2013).

Several features of the RDoC distinguish it from other categorization systems. This framework considers five levels of analysis related to motivational, cognitive, and social domains (see supplementary online material). These comprise Negative Valence Systems (i.e., responses to aversive threats or events), Positive Valence Systems (responses to stimuli or events perceived to be rewarding), Cognitive Systems (related to cognitive control, attention, perception, memory, response selection), Systems for Social Processes (attachment, social communication, self-perception, perception and understanding others), and Arousal/Regulatory Systems (arousal, sleep). Each of these domains is considered at several levels of analysis comprising genes, molecules, cells, neural circuits, physiological processes, behaviors, and self-reports. In this way it is possible to assess assorted symptoms of an illness and link these to specific biological elements. Following this approach it may eventually be possible to tie specific symptoms or aspects of a syndrome to particular biological markers, which can inform treatment strategies.

The RDoC perspective has received considerable support (Casey et al., 2013), but it isn't flawless (Frances, 2014). There may be too much room for measurement error that could affect diagnoses, too much emphasis placed on biological measures, and biological dispositions might not translate well to particular behavioral phenotypes (Lilienfeld, 2014). There may also be conceptual flaws in the perspectives adopted in the RDoC approach (Kirmayer & Crafa, 2014). Specifically, 'normality' as a biomedical construct is defined on the basis of what is statistically common or average in a population, but normality in one culture may not be applicable in a second social or cultural context. Furthermore, dynamic interactions occur among biological, developmental, and psychosocial processes that culminate in normal versus pathological conditions, and these may also be context- and culturally-dependent. For instance, healing processes that are relevant to North American Aboriginal Peoples might not map on well to those typically offered to Euro Caucasians. In the development of treatment strategies it is as valid and important to ask what biological processes occur in the brain as a result of social support and trust as it is to ask what occurs in response to stressful events that are thought to contribute to psychological disturbances (Kirmayer & Crafa, 2014). In essence, analyses of the development and treatment of psychopathological disorders ought to be done in the context of an individual's social identity, family, and community.

INTERVENTION APPROACHES

We place a premium on health, and considerable efforts have focused on the development of medications, treatment and rehabilitation programs, training health care specialists of every variety, and in establishing local clinics and large hospitals. Indeed, health care is among the greatest costs for many Western countries, and a considerable portion of national incomes is spent on health care.

Social and physical determinants of health

As much as effective treatments for illness are essential, it is preferable to develop early *interventions* to prevent the emergence of diseases. To this end, it is necessary to identify the multiple social and physical (environmental) factors that influence health outcomes.

Many of the psychosocial and physical determinants of health are presented in Table 6.1, which is adapted and modified from HealthyPeople.gov (2015). Although determinants of health are largely determined by individual behaviors, this table makes it clear that well-being is also affected by economic stability, education, social- and community-related factors, health and health care accessibility, as well as our built environment. In well-meaning but nonetheless misguided efforts, governments have adopted intervention strategies to enhance well-being, often by simply changing a few practices in single domains (e.g., changing features at schools). Having children obtain better schooling is clearly desirable, but when they don't have access to economic stability, safe foods, physical and psychological safety, and are exposed to toxic social environments, one could hardly expect miraculous outcomes. For interventions to be successful, multiple basic needs must be addressed concurrently.

Table 6.1   Social and physical determinants of health (from HealthyPeople.gov)

- Economic stability

  - Diminishing poverty
  - Enhancing employment
  - Maintaining food security
  - Assuring housing stability

- Education

  - Early childhood education and development
  - High school graduation
  - Language and literacy
  - Opportunities for higher education
  - Acquiring useful trades

- Social and community context

  - Social identity
  - Social cohesion
  - Civic participation
  - Perceptions of discrimination and equity
  - Incarceration/institutionalization
  - Public safety
  - Social norms

- Health and health care

  - Health education and literacy
  - Affordable health care and medicines
  - Access to prenatal care
  - Access to health care
  - Access to primary care
  - Healthy living for older people

- Neighborhood and built environment

  - Access to healthy foods
  - Diminishing toxicants
  - Diminishing crime, violence and fear
  - Creating safe green space
  - Healthy and sustainable environmental conditions

- Policy making

  - Laws diminishing toxicants
  - Taxation on products with inherent risks
  - Traffic and vehicle safety
  - Diminishing populations risks

- Biological factors

  - Age
  - Sex
  - Health status
  - Inherited factors
  - Family history of disease

As well, the success of health-related programs might be dependent on establishing ways of appropriately measuring and monitoring social factors and health relative to the policies and interventions created. This entails assessing the consequences of social factors across lifetimes and generations as well as across contexts, applying and evaluating multidimensional interventions, and determining and addressing when political will is a barrier in the translation of knowledge into action (Braveman et al., 2011).

Types of intervention strategy

With healthy life-styles becoming more common, the frequency of many diseases has been declining, as have mortality rates, and overall life span has increased, often reflected in a good life, not just a long life. Prevention programs come in several different formats (Weisz et al., 2005). *Universal prevention* approaches have been instituted in which particular strategies are meant to deal with risks, regardless of any given person's vulnerability (e.g., vaccination programs), as have *selective prevention* programs, in which certain groups are targeted because they are at elevated risk and hence more apt to develop certain diseases. This has included individuals who show early signs of a disorder, but who don't meet the criteria for a clinical diagnosis (cognitive decline as a prelude to Alzheimer's; metabolic syndrome that could presage diabetes) or individuals who engage in high-risk behaviors (e.g., needle users are at elevated risk of developing HIV/AIDS and hepatitis C). As much as this seems like an eminently reasonable approach, in cases such as diabetes and heart disease individuals at 'average risk' make up more than half of the affected population, and thus it is advantageous to target entire populations rather than just those who are at high risk (Rose, 1985). This would require an enormous number of physicians and nurses to follow patients on a regular basis, and although it could potentially be done, it might not be practical or affordable.

The goal of prevention approaches is not simply to diminish the occurrence of illness and to extend life span, but to enhance disability-free survival. To a significant extent, prevention programs have done exactly this, although admittedly, there's room for improvement. As already mentioned, this would entail greater efforts at health promotion, behavioral change, and harm reduction procedures. A first line of defense to reach desired health goals ought to involve the mobilization of health practitioners who have the greatest contact with patients, but it's unfortunate that some practitioners haven't received the training relevant to intervention strategies. Besides, interventions would only be effective if people actually showed up before they were ill (annual check-ups), but the common attitude is 'Why bother going if I'm feeling fine?. As we've already seen, poverty also interferes with people seeking help when they're sick, and it's still less likely that they'll seek help when they're well. Clearly, effective prevention programs require the inclusion of multiple processes and considerable coordination, as well as the affordability and accessibility of these health care efforts (Walsh & McPhee, 1992).

Broad interventions

Research that can improve health has flourished, and the data have frequently found their way into public policies. Various agencies are responsible for making sure that toxic substances (e.g., lead, certain bacteria, acids, steroids) don't appear in our water or air, efforts are made to ensure that food supplies are kept free of bacteria that could make us ill, potential hazards have been banned from household items and children's toys and clothes. Behaviors such as drinking and driving, selling illicit drugs (especially to kids), driving without wearing a seat belt, or smoking in restaurants or other public venues are all forbidden for the public good, and, eventually, legislation might make it illegal for companies to spew out carbon. It's less likely that legislation within the US will be enacted any time soon to prevent any dufus from carrying a firearm.

THE ONE PERCENT DOCTRINE

When do we take actions to limit the possible effects of environmental or psychosocial contaminants that could affect our health? Likewise, when should we adopt particular behaviors that could prevent later illnesses from occurring? When the issue arose as to the likelihood of terrorist groups seeking to obtain nuclear weapons, and what should be done about it, then US Vice President Dick Cheney suggested that in response to 'low-probability, high-impact events', even if there is only a 1% chance of them occurring, we should be treating them as if they were certainties. After all, a single failure of that magnitude could have repercussions that would be so enormous as to dwarf anything else. One could argue that this 'one percent doctrine' is not only reasonable, but to do otherwise would be inviting treachery.

The case can be made that this doctrine should be applied to prevention strategies and the adoption of health behaviors. There are issues related to climate change, environmental toxicants, failure to adopt appropriate healthy behaviors, and the engagement of great numbers of high-risk behaviors, that have much more than a 1% risk of creating havoc. We might want to take immediate steps to make things right, but our actions can have multiple downstream, unintended consequences, and there are issues that need to be considered before we jump too quickly.

Let's change the context of this discussion somewhat, if for no other reason than to put it into a realistic context. In emergency rooms doctors and nurses are faced with dilemmas on a daily basis. When several cases come into the ER at about the same time, who gets helped first? Instinctively, the response might be that the most seriously injured should be the first to be dealt with. This is, of course, appropriate, but within limits. If the injuries the person has sustained are so severe that recovery is virtually impossible, then it might make more sense to deal with another serious case where there is hope for recovery. In fact, dealing with the more seriously injured victim first might reduce the chances of survival of the somewhat less injured patient. Understandably, making this call is exceptionally difficult and, equally understandable, it might not always be correct. Policy makers who deal with prevention strategies face somewhat similar challenges. Initiating new preventive measures can be expensive and time consuming, so which of many that are encountered should be dealt with first? In a sense, it amounts to a cost–benefit analysis. If we spend X on preventing

(Continued)

(Continued)

heart disease that kills Y number of people, does this provide more benefit than treating cancer that affects fewer people, but takes up more resources? Likewise, should funds go into depressive disorders which occur at a lower rate than heart disease, but is projected to become the greatest burden of illness by 2020?

Let's use a still different example. What if a particular environmental pollutant might have negative effects in 1% of the population, but as initiating a campaign to eliminate the toxin is inordinately expensive, should we take these preventive steps? You might say yes, but what if this means cutting back on other health-related procedures, such as cancer treatments, and what if you were the person who is cut out of these treatments? So, although the 1% doctrine makes perfect sense, it isn't always a viable route that can be taken in illness prevention programs.

Self-initiated interventions and screening

As we age it's almost inevitable that more illnesses will affect us. Some health problems hit individuals out of the blue (e.g., a burst aneurysm), whereas others have an insidious onset, possibly foreshadowed by hints that things aren't quite right. In many cases steps can be taken to 'catch' illnesses before they're fully developed so that treatments will be most effective. To this end, various *screening* procedures have been developed. By example, breast cancer occurs at a fairly high frequency among women, particularly if they have a family history of breast cancer. For women at elevated cancer risk, greater scrutiny is called for, including earlier screening for breast cancer. It had been thought that a mammogram (essentially an x-ray picture of breast tissue) might detect breast cancer early (Mandelblatt et al., 2009), but there has been some controversy as to the effectiveness of mammograms. Still, as of 2014 the National Cancer Institute has been recommending mammograms for women between the ages of 40 and 74. Obviously, with an increasing number of risk factors, the need for a mammogram increases accordingly.

SENSITIVITY VERSUS SPECIFICITY

Lex, the drug-sniffing dog from Bloomington, Illinois, may be very motivated, but he was declared not to be particularly competent. It seems that Lex has signaled the presence of drugs in 93% of cases, but he's been wrong almost as often (40%) as he's been right. Nevertheless, his handler still thinks that Lex is a very, very good dog, and both are still on the job.

Let's go back a few years when airports were hiring people to watch radar screens to detect airplanes coming in so that mishaps wouldn't occur. Job candidates were tested to assess their accuracy in detecting blips on a screen and to evaluate their ability to respond to potential accidents. As depicted in Table 6.2, at one extreme was the individual who always responded to two blips as if a collision was imminent (much like Lex the dog) and had one or both pilots initiate evasive maneuvers. This individual might have prevented many collisions, but might have caused other problems by recklessly announcing multiple false alarms. At the other extreme was the person who never seemed perturbed, never called out any false alarms, but also never saw imminent collisions. Obviously, neither would be the right person for the job. This difficult task calls for accuracy with respect to 'true positives', which means saying that a hit will occur when it actually will, and a low number of true negatives, meaning that they believe a hit won't occur when, in fact, such a hit doesn't happen.

Table 6.2 Graphic description of the outcomes that could occur using a 'signal detection' paradigm

	Signal present	Signal absent
Response emitted	Hit (true positive)	False alarm
No response	Miss	Correct rejection

All of our medical tests work on this principle as well. Tests ought to have a high degree of sensitivity (true positive) in which the proportion of positive responses maps onto correct identification of an illness (saying an individual is ill when they actually are ill), as well as high specificity (true negative), in which patients diagnosed as not being ill are actually not ill. Unfortunately, neither sensitivity nor specificity is 100% in most tests. Sometimes, true illnesses are missed (termed false negatives) and at other times a patient is diagnosed with an illness when, in fact, no illness is present (termed a false positive or false alarm). The fact is that there is a trade-off between sensitivity and specificity. The more accurate a test is in picking up abnormalities, the more likely it is that false alarms will occur. This is exactly the case for mammograms. The sensitivity of a mammogram depends on the size of tumor, how conspicuous it is, the density of the breast tissue (tumors are more difficult to detect with increasing tissue density), the quality of the image, and the interpretive abilities of the radiologist reading the scan, and thus alternative screening methods may be needed (e.g., Kerlikowske et al., 2015). The sensitivity of a mammogram, overall, is fairly good (bordering on 80%), but false negatives do occur, which has been very bad news for patients, as well as for insurers, as this was the source of many medical malpractice suits.

The situation among men who have had a prostate-specific antigen (PSA) test done to detect prostate cancer is somewhat different than it is for women undergoing mammography. The test often fails to detect the presence of cancer, and the levels of the prostate-specific antigen can increase in the presence of urinary tract infection or enlarged prostate; hence the incidence of false positives is high, causing many individuals undue alarm (Thompson et al., 2004). Given that many prostate cancers are very slow-growing, there has been a move against the use of PSA testing. In the end, the usefulness of the test comes down to the relative risk–benefit ratio. What is the upside of the test, and what is the potential downside? The same can also be said of some treatments. How far should we be going in treating an individual with extreme measures given how long their life will be extended, and what their life will be like during this time? In the case of prostate cancer, it seems that surgery to remove the prostate saves 1 out of 20 lives, but can dramatically disrupt quality of life. So, in effect, 19 out of 20 patients *might* have done better if they had been left alone.

As we'll discuss in Chapter 11 in dealing with cancer, there are other screening procedures that ought to be adopted by both men and women as they age. One of these is colorectal cancer screening for those over the age of 50, especially as this is among the most common forms of cancer, and is second to lung cancer with respect to mortality (Smith et al., 2014). The procedure is mildly embarrassing, fairly inconvenient, and a bit intrusive, as it involves having a lengthy tube inserted into the rectum and moved through the large intestine to determine the presence of polyps or adenomas and to remove them. Educational efforts to get people to undergo the test have only been moderately successful, but testing has been seen more likely to be adopted when it is aligned with current social norms (Sieverding et al., 2010), or consistent with common health beliefs (Cyr et al., 2010).

Myths and misconceptions regarding screening

The first misconception about screening is that these procedures are 100% accurate. As we have seen, neither sensitivity nor selectivity is always perfect. The second myth that needs to be done away with is that early detection always leads to a better prognosis. This is often true, but some illnesses, unfortunately, don't have a cure or even a way of slowing them down, and so detecting illness early won't have any benefits and might simply encourage anxiety and distress, although for some people at high risk for certain illnesses, not knowing may actually be more stressful.

Often, early detection does mean enhanced treatment response and greater odds of survival. But, we can be fooled by statistics in relation to what is referred to as '*lead-time bias*'. Once more, an example will portray this best. Let's assume that in a set of identical twins the onset of a particular disease occurs, unbeknown to them, when both are 40 years of age. One twin happened to go in for screening and the illness was uncovered when she was 45, and as a result she is immediately treated. However, the illness continues to progress slowly and frank symptoms become apparent when she is 55, and she eventually dies at the age of 60. Thus, she lived 20 years from the time of the illness first occurring, 15 years from the time of detection, and 5 years following symptoms appearing. Her co-twin procrastinates for some time, but finally, at the age of 50, she goes in for screening and the illness is detected. She too is treated immediately, but her symptoms also appear at the age of 55 and she dies at 60. In both instances frank symptoms appeared at the age of 55, and death followed 5 years later. However, one could conclude that the first twin lived for 15 years after detection, whereas the second twin lived only 10 years after detection. So, if the effectiveness of screening is assessed in relation to post-screening survival, the false impression could be obtained that screening was accompanied by early detection and enhanced survival.

Another bias that is encountered is the '*length bias*'. Slowly developing illnesses are more likely to be detected early than those that progress quickly simply because the illness is there for a longer time, and hence the opportunity to detect it is increased. Thus, if one were to measure the time from detection to death, keeping in mind that detection of quickly progressing illnesses would usually occur only once individuals were symptomatic, it would be concluded that early detection was associated with longer survival, even though this was simply a result of the rate of illness development.

Finally, a bias also exists as to who gets screening and who doesn't. People who are screened for illnesses tend to be more educated, better off financially, and more likely to engage in health behaviors than are individuals who aren't screened, and as a result they live longer. In essence, screening and other factors are confounded with one another, but the conclusion might nevertheless be made that people who are screened for an illness have a better prognosis than people who aren't screened.

The problem of overdiagnosis

Despite some of the myths and misperceptions about screening, there's little question that these procedures have been important in detecting illnesses early, often leading to more effective treatment. But, let's not fool ourselves into thinking that these tests aren't without other problems. Aside from issues related to specificity and selectivity, there has been the danger of too much testing and, with it, the risk of *overdiagnosis*, which basically refers to the diagnosis of a disease condition that won't actually reach the point of causing frank symptoms. In part, this has been encouraged by the perspective that new methodologies are better than older methods, even if at times they aren't. As well, in an effort to avoid the possibility of litigation for having missed a problem that was present, physicians have been at pains to tread cautiously, thus ordering increasingly more tests.

Despite the advantages that have emerged with the proliferation of new diagnostic tools, too often their use may be unnecessary. For instance, those at a low risk for a particular illness would likely not receive much benefit from having expensive and intrusive tests conducted (Moynihan et al., 2014). Furthermore, as we've seen in the case of prostate testing and mammograms, false alarms may occur that elicit anxiety, and in some instances people may be harmed by treatments. It has been recommended that physicians request testing on the basis of dispassionate assessments of medical evidence, and patients need to be made aware of the risks of overdiagnosis, including the practical benefits versus the risks of tests and treatments. This is especially the case as people tend to overestimate the benefits of treatment and/or underestimate the potential harms that can be created (Hoffmann & Del Mar, 2015).

RISK FACTORS RELATED TO HEALTH AND DISEASE

Risks and risky behaviors

What do we mean when we use the terms 'hazard' and 'risk'? A *hazard* refers to the possibility of something causing harm, whereas *risk* refers to the probability of harm occurring when someone actually does something that can create problems. Cigarettes can be a hazard. It doesn't matter whether they're on the store shelf, in your glove compartment or in your pocket, they carry the possibility of causing harm and are thus considered a *hazard*. When a person takes a cigarette out of the packet, places it between their lips, lights it and inhales, then we're talking about the *risk* or probability of the cigarette causing harm (Ropeik, 2002).

Health risk assessment refers to the processes involved in estimating the probability of adverse health effects occurring in relation to particular events or conditions. Various factors go into this equation, such as life-style (whether a person smokes, drinks alcohol, exercises, and what they eat), demographic features (age, sex), whether they're single or married, and whether they've had particular illnesses or if certain illnesses have appeared in their family, as well as basic physiological data (e.g., blood pressure, cholesterol levels, weight, waist circumference, and in some instances a bit more is required, such as albumin levels in urine) (Schoenbach, 1987). Insurance companies use such information to predict how long you're apt to live, whether you'll need a lot of coverage to maintain your health, and thus whether it's a smart move on their part to offer insurance (and at what rate). Environmental protection agencies are also interested in risk factors, but for other reasons. They might want to know what types of health problems may be caused by environmental chemicals and radiation, what are the safe levels of toxicants, and how long we can be exposed to certain levels before our health is jeopardized. They also want to know whether some people are more susceptible to environmental challenges because of age, gender, genetics, pre-existing health conditions, and ethnic practices. Furthermore, to what extent are some people more likely to encounter environmental stressors because of their socioeconomic status, their workplace, and their leisure activities? For health psychologists, risk factors are largely in line with these same concerns, but they also focus on the adoption of behavioral changes that can diminish risks to health.

Sins of omission, sins of commission and illness despite not sinning

Some genetic mutations might promote illness irrespective of the presence or absence of other factors. Other illnesses, in contrast, develop as a result of behaviors that individuals adopt. They choose to smoke, they choose to drink alcohol excessively, they choose to engage in unsafe sex, and they choose to eat all the wrong foods. Thus, when negative outcomes occur, the attitude of others is that this person, because of their sins of commission, has themself to blame for their weakness and the illness, although, as we'll see later, this may be an overly simplistic conclusion.

There are also risks that occur because we fail to do certain things. We might choose not to put on sun screen because we want to get a deep brown color, or we choose not to be vaccinated against an imminent flu epidemic, or choose not to wear a helmet when bicycling. These are all sins of omission and they can be just as dangerous, and they're also very common. Other risks have nothing to do with our own behaviors, and we can be victimized by the unhealthy behaviors of others. Second-hand smoke from the guy sitting next to us, all manner of environmental toxicants floating around, or being exposed to someone who gets on an airplane or comes to work despite having a viral illness that they thoughtlessly spread to others, are all events and stimuli that we encounter that jeopardize our well-being despite our own innocence.

Blaming the victim

Because sins of commission (smoking) and those of omission (not being vaccinated) are sometimes viewed a being a result of the individual's risky (or thoughtless) behaviors, the sinners are sometimes made to suffer doubly the consequences of their (in)actions. If a smoker and nonsmoker both develop heart disease, will they be treated the same by health professionals, or will the nonsmoker get preferential treatment? In essence, the smoker is being given the message that they're the source of their own problems and so now they get to suffer the consequences. However, isn't it possible that the 65-year-old with heart disease was born to a family where everyone smoked, and maybe they had a genetic constitution that favored smoking or addiction? Perhaps they worked in an environment where everyone smoked, or they might come from a poor part of town where the probability of smoking was higher than in the more affluent areas, and so it was fairly likely that they too would try smoking, and before you could say 'Bob's your uncle', they were hooked. As we'll see in Chapter 13 in discussing addiction, drugs, such as alcohol or cocaine, and perhaps even cigarettes, might 'overwhelm' cognitive control circuits that might otherwise limit drug intake. In essence, these agents undermine rational thinking, just as we might see in any other mental illness (Volkow et al., 2010), allowing for addiction to persist. So, do we now punish them still further by offering them less than first-rate medical care?

THE PROBLEM WITH NICOTINE

Nicotine may not be all that bad. It becomes a problem because nicotine is typically delivered to the bloodstream through cigarettes! In fact, nicotine itself may have several benefits. It was implicated as having protective effects on some neurological conditions, such as Parkinson's disease and mild cognitive impairment, Tourette's syndrome and schizophrenia (Barreto et al., 2015; Roh & Evins, 2012). It's especially interesting that although nicotine is often considered to be highly addictive, unlike the response to alcohol and cocaine, it's very difficult to get animals hooked. However, if nicotine is combined with several elements present in cigarettes, then self administration in rodents becomes far simpler. Thus, nicotine might only be addictive in the presence of tobacco or some of its constituents. We'd like to avoid, as the expression goes, throwing the baby out with the bath water, but it's not unusual to find that all sorts of treatments that are ineffective in one context are not considered for other potential uses. Yet we know of all sorts of remedies that have been given new life to treat conditions for which they weren't originally intended. Perhaps it's time to reconsider the benefits of nicotine and use it wisely.

Unintended consequences and benefits

On some occasions particular policies or procedures that have been adopted may have *unanticipated* and *unintended consequences*. A policy might be established to limit alcohol consumption, for instance, only to have alcohol sales continue underground. The appearance of unintended consequences has been recognized for centuries, but it was only much later that Merton (1936) formalized this concept and offered reasons for its occurrence, as described in Table 6.3.

Table 6.3 Sources of unintended consequences

- Ignorance that makes it unlikely that all outcomes could be predicted
- Problems being inappropriately analyzed or approaches to problems adopted that may have been appropriate in the past, but not for current situations
- Tendency to favor short-term gain without appropriate consideration of long-term consequences
- Basic values interfering with certain behaviors even if these are unfavorable
- Fear or panic causing steps to be taken in anticipation of a problem emerging, even if this problem would never have emerged.

More recent perspectives have considered that our behaviors, much like alterations of ecosystems, can have ramifications that are far removed from what had ever been envisaged (e.g., mosquito repellant used on netting in parts of Africa to reduce malaria, leading to resistance to the repellants so that the mosquito problem becomes greater; treatments to reduce cocaine addiction causing an increase in heroine addiction). Related to unexpected consequences are *unexpected drawbacks*, which amount to an unforeseen side effect of the action taken. For instance, a worker's union may successfully increase pay for its members, but this puts the price of the product too high, and as a result sales decline, losses are incurred by the employer, and the workers lose their jobs when the plant closes. In some instances, actions can lead to *perverse results* in which solutions for specific problems can make situations worse. When antidepressant agents (SSRIs) were found to be associated with increased suicide risk among adolescents, governments issued a warning to avoid offering these drugs to young people. This, however, resulted in a decline of outpatient visits (*ambulatory care*) and a commensurate increase of suicides in young people (Katz et al., 2008).

Just as certain actions can elicit negative unintended consequences, it is possible that unanticipated benefits may evolve, as in the case of drugs developed for one purpose having positive effects for other conditions. For instance, the pain reliever acetylsalicylic acid (aspirin) may serve as an anticoagulant and thus may be useful in relation to heart disease. In this regard, there are many pharmacological agents that have been developed for one purpose, only to have far more effective actions in other domains.

Risk compensation

Campaigns of every variety have been instituted in an effort to have people diminish health risks. However, even when these programs appear to be successful, they might not actually have the benefits we might have expected. According to '*risk compensation*' theory, people generally adjust their behavior in response to the appraised risks present. When risks are perceived to be high, individuals behave more carefully and, conversely, when risks are perceived to be low, they tend to be less careful. A corollary of this is that people may behave as if having adopted a safety measure gives them a pass to engage in other riskier behaviors (*Peltzman effect*). For instance, people who wear seatbelts often behave as if they're OK driving faster and closer to the car in front of them. Likewise, drivers with anti-lock breaking systems drive at higher speeds and brake later than they might otherwise and thus the benefits of this braking system is reduced. Wearing helmets emboldens skiers to traverse hills more quickly and engage in riskier behaviors than those without helmets (e.g., Specht, 2007). One also observes similar outcomes in relation to risky sexual behaviors. When penicillin was introduced as an effective treatment of gonorrhea and syphilis, the rates of these illnesses declined precipitously, only to make a subsequent comeback. In part, this might have been due to changes in attitude toward sex, but it is also possible that with the assurance of the illnesses being treatable, condoms were more likely to stay in drawers or wallets. As much as efforts are made to have people adopt positive health-related behaviors, our nature is to find ways to counter these efforts at our own peril.

CULTURAL AND ETHNIC DIFFERENCES

Marked race, ethnic and cultural differences exist in the occurrence of several psychiatric and physical illnesses, including cancer, hypertension, diabetes, ischemic heart disease, stroke, and various mental health conditions (e.g., Kuller, 2004). Some of these differences may be related to the adoption of behaviors relevant to health. For instance, some immigrant groups may be less apt to have the bad health behaviors of non-immigrants (eating large meals high in bad stuff), possibly reflecting the values inherent in their culture; however, with time and acculturation, they too might adopt negative health behaviors (Joshi et al., 2014).

It is also likely that through a process of natural selection (including epigenetic changes), some groups may have become less vulnerable to particular illnesses and perhaps more vulnerable to others. The ethnic and cultural differences reported aren't merely an interesting side note, but may have important implications concerning how illnesses develop and what treatment strategies might be most useful. For instance, when a health difference between subgroups of individuals is detected, it offers the opportunity to determine whether this stems from genetic differences, life-style (e.g., diet) or climactic factors, poverty, and education, thus offering clues concerning illness prevention and treatment strategies.

Groups also differ with respect to their help-seeking behaviors, and are differentially sensitive to being diminished by having to reach out to others (Talebi et al., 2013). There are many other health-related differences that are relevant to diverse cultural groups, and perhaps it shouldn't be surprising that the treatments most effective in one culture might not be as effective in a second. This has been apparent in response to drugs that influence cardiovascular processes, psychiatric disorders, and pain medication (Burroughs et al., 2002), possibly being related to genetic differences and those associated with drug metabolism (Yasuda et al., 2008). In light of these differences, the intervention or treatment strategies adopted ought to be culturally specific, but this isn't normally done.

Behaviors considered unusual in Western cultures may not be seen in this manner in other cultures. There is indeed some question as to whether the diagnostic criteria for mental illnesses in Western society are applicable to Aboriginal Peoples (e.g., in Australia, Canada, and the US) and hence the approaches that are useful for Euro Caucasians might not be the same in these cultures. In some communities mental health problems may be described or understood as well as expressed in ways that are very different from those of others (Kirmayer, 2012).

For instance, among Aboriginal Peoples, well-being might reflect a balance between physical, mental, emotional, and spiritual aspects of life (Waldram et al., 2006), and thus the optimal treatment methods among these groups might differ from those used in other cultures, even if the underlying phenomenology is likely to be the same as in other cultures (Beals et al., 2005). This said, on occasion, the collision of cultural values may become problematic, as in the case of standard medicines with known positive effects (e.g., in some types of childhood cancer) being abandoned in favor of more traditional healing practices. As much as one would hope that the traditional approaches would be effective, sometimes storybook endings aren't in the cards.

GENDER DIFFERENCES

Researchers working with mice and rats have favored using males over females. Although we ought to have known that outcomes of particular treatments might differ between the sexes, the behavior of females was thought to be more variable (possibly being linked to their 4.5 day estrus cycle), or because it was naïvely assumed that the outcomes evident in males would also apply to females. We now know that some sex differences related to physiology and behavior are dramatic, as are the conditions that lead to particular disease states, and the treatments for disorders that are effective in one gender might not produce comparable positive outcomes in the other. As we'll see in later chapters, many illnesses occur preferentially in females (mood and autoimmune disorders), whereas others are more apt to occur in males (e.g., stroke); and there are illnesses, such as schizophrenia, that occur more often in males at 10–25 years of age, but become more common in females at 25–35 years of age, and by 40–50 the difference is slanted toward women to an even greater extent (Baldwin & Srivistava, 2015).

Despite some illnesses occurring more frequently in females, they outlive males by several years. This appears attributable, in part, to greater attention to health behaviors among women, being more willing to have an annual health check, seeking advice from their medical practitioner, attending education sessions, and obtaining information regarding illness prevention (Deeks et al., 2009). Likewise, women are more likely to be screened for gender-specific illnesses than are men, and are less likely to engage in unhealthy behaviors, such as smoking, drinking, lack of exercise, and risky behaviors. Aside from these life-style factors, males and females may differ appreciably in their appraisals and methods of coping with stressors. Social support is sought more readily by women than by men and they have more close confidants. Countering this, however, is that they also experience more frequent and variable stressors, and are often left carrying the burden of caregiving, trying to complete work-related tasks while taking care of a family, and having to deal with workplace inequalities.

As greater female longevity occurs across many species (Grodstein et al., 1997), it is unlikely that this arises simply owing to the adoption of good health behaviors, and it seems that biological influences add 1–2 years onto the lives of women (Luy, 2003). Among other things, having two X chromosomes may be advantageous (or perhaps having a Y chromosome is disadvantageous) (Christensen et al., 2001) and particular hormones (Grodstein et al., 1997) may enhance health.

YES! WE BEAT OUT THE WOMEN

As the website puts it, every year the Darwin awards are given out to "commemorate those who improve our gene pool by removing themselves from it". Put slightly more simply, the awards are given to those who die in the most stupid ways. By a wide difference, males have won these awards more often than have females. The www.darwinawards.com site is now asking readers to offer their views as to why this sex difference occurs. Is it due to males being more dispensable than females from an evolutionary perspective (one male can, after all, father children with many females in a short time span), or is it that more males than females simply fall into the category of 'the village idiot'?

BEHAVIORAL CHANGE MEANS HEALTH CHANGE

The last few decades have witnessed increasing awareness of the need for health promotion, and physicians increasingly counsel their patients on how to prevent illnesses. Aligned with physicians are specialists who prescribe particular life-style changes to deal with potential or actual illnesses (trainers to help with exercise for those at risk for heart disease, dieticians specializing in diabetic diets, physiotherapists to help with ongoing physical difficulties). As well, community and national organizations have initiated or joined campaigns to provide individuals with information regarding health hazards, and legislative bodies have enacted laws to prohibit unhealthy behaviors (e.g., smoking in public places, prohibiting cell phones and texting while driving) and encourage healthy behaviors (use of seat belts).

As praiseworthy as these health promotion efforts have been, their usefulness is only as good as their capacity to instill effective *health behaviors*, and for these to become *health habits*. Despite the broad awareness of the benefits of life-style changes, preventable illnesses, such as diabetes and heart disease, occur at a very high level. In their review of this issue, Bauer et al. (2014) indicated that within the United States these outcomes could largely be attributed to tobacco use, excessive alcohol consumption, poor diet and physical inactivity (and the associated obesity), uncontrolled high blood pressure, and hyperlipidemia (high bad cholesterol and triglyceride levels), all of which could be modified at both the individual and population level. To be sure, it's best that healthy behavioral styles be instilled when people are young (Cohen et al., 1990), but they can be developed at later times, becoming autonomous behaviors so that it is uncomfortable not to engage them. The Institute of Medicine (IOM)/ National Academy of Sciences (NAS) has provided a report on the best practices to promote behavioral change that could lead to enhanced well-being and diminished illness. As described by Solomon and Kington (2002), this report offers a series of recommendations to inform behavioral and social science research, and subsequent reports have issued several additional recommendations (see Table 6.4).

Table 6.4   Promoting health: Intervention strategies from social and behavioral research

---

- Greater attention ought to be devoted to social and behavioral determinants of disease, injury, and disability.
- The engagement of education, social support, laws, incentives, and behavior change programs are necessary to promote proper health behaviors.
- The focus of programs should include multiple levels of influence simultaneously, involving not only individuals, but also families, communities, and nations.
- Consideration should be given to unique needs of target groups (based on age, gender, race, ethnicity, social class).
- Sustained change should be aimed for, even if this requires many years to establish.
- Multiple societal sectors (e.g., law, business, education, social services, and the media) should be engaged in health promotion efforts.
- Recognition that interventions are shaped by social, political, and economic systems as well as the availability and access to resources that facilitate good health behaviors.
- Interventions ought to consider integration of behavioral, psychosocial, and biomedical approaches to engender behavior change.
- Efforts should be made to identify and target individuals at particular risk for illness.
- New technological developments should be adopted that could be used to facilitate intervention and treatment.
- Personal, social, and environmental circumstances are dynamic (ever changing) and there is a need for intervention approaches to be equally adaptable.
- Increase attention and recognition of the need for effective and durable health-related decision-making processes and the development of effective health communications.
- Research in health and behavioral change must have a strong translational component so that best practices and policies can be implemented.

CHANGING ATTITUDES, CHANGING BEHAVIORS, AND BARRIERS TO CHANGE

There's hardly a person who is unaware that 'butting out', eating properly, and diminishing alcohol consumption are behaviors that will extend life. This begs the question as to why so many people have failed to adopt better life-style choices. It's fine to have good intentions in relation to health, but these need to be coupled with appropriate behaviors, and often community groups and government policies can be useful in encouraging behavioral change.

Primary prevention entails intercessions so that problem behaviors will not arise. These may take the form of educational methods but, as we'll see, there may be more effective approaches as individuals frequently are aware of the hazards inherent in their behaviors, but for a variety of reasons opt not to change them. In general, there aren't fixed rules or predictors that are relevant to changing every poor health-related behavior. Some health behaviors might not be adopted because they're 'inconvenient' (e.g., working out, being vaccinated), whereas in other instances, such as living in an impoverished neighborhood, fewer resources might be available for various health needs, such as prenatal health care services or cardiac rehabilitation for those who have experienced a cardiac event (Braveman & Gottlieb, 2014). Increasing accessibility to resources can provide opportunities to engage in improved health-related behaviors (Lemstra et al., 2013), more so in the latter instance.

ARE THEY GIVING US A LITTLE NUDGE OR A GREAT BIG PUSH?

Policy makers can have an enormous impact on the adoption of health behaviors, provided that the approaches used are well thought out and don't alienate those who need help. They can do this by applying penalties (using the stick), offering rewards (reduced premiums for insurance or reduced taxes), or facilitating self-monitoring or self-regulation. Another option is to simply 'nudge people' in the 'right' direction, which can be done through subtle advertising, or by getting people to follow what they are led to believe others are doing (Thaler & Sunstein, 2008). At first blush, this seems like a reasonable option to produce behavioral change but, as indicated by Mols et al. (2014), the ethics of this have been questioned (e.g., who gets to decide when and concerning which issues we should be nudged in a particular direction). Nudge is thought to be effective because people are inclined to follow the lead of others and to capitulate to social norms. The nudge strategy, in a sense, assumes that people are often incapable of making proper decisions, which is true to an extent, as Kahneman and Tversky (1996) have explained, or that they should be more engaged in adopting particular behaviors, and thus need a little help. However, many people might be put off by this paternalistic 'Big Brother' approach, and when they discover that they've been manipulated they may recoil, feeling that they've been duped, and they might even view this as a breach of trust. In effect, the 'nudge' might be viewed as a 'shove' (Mols et al., 2014). There is also uncertainty concerning whether subtle maneuvering associated with 'nudge' is sufficient to deal with 'wicked problems', such as addictions, having children vaccinated, or adopting controversial government policies on a variety of issues. There may be better approaches, such as relying on the influence of shared identities that facilitate the internalization of social norms, which might thus have broader and more enduring effects.

Intentions versus actions

If we want information concerning people's attitudes and behaviors we can simply ask them, and hope that their responses aren't a reflection of the answers that they consciously or unconsciously think we want to hear (*demand characteristics*), aren't affected by other social demands or biases, or efforts to cover up for their self-perceived shortcomings. Unfortunately, self-reports are notoriously unreliable, and what participants say they might do in relation to health behaviors may have only a modest bearing on what they actually do (Sheeran, 2002). So, if I were to ask if you brushed your teeth every morning and evening, or washed your hands before exiting a washroom, I'd guess that many more of you would answer 'yes' than the number who actually do. Likewise, if I were to ask whether individuals intend to be vaccinated in the face of the next potential pandemic, a fair number of people who say that they would, will actually fail to do so. As we know, talk is cheap and intentions don't necessarily add up to actions.

Bridging the intention–behavior gap

The gap between intention and action may be fairly broad, but can be diminished by having 'implementation intentions' become more salient. Individuals ought to make their goals clear ("I intend not to smoke any more" versus "I intend not to smoke eventually"), and form specific plans that go beyond intentions (explicitly planning where and how behaviors will be changed) (Gollwizer, 1999). By being prepared to act in particular ways in defined circumstances, individuals will be more likely to recognize these as opportunities to act on their intentions (Webb & Sheeran, 2007), and the likelihood will increase that the desired behaviors will automatically be activated (Parks-Stamm et al., 2007). In training programs where individuals will likely meet threatening or dangerous conditions (e.g., readying troops for combat, or first responders to aid accident victims), realistic practice runs will facilitate responses when the occasion actually arises. In the same way, thinking out intentions to act in relation to health behaviors may prepare individuals to take the necessary steps when the time comes.

Encouraging health behaviors through education

One of the most common approaches to improving health habits has involved attempts to educate people concerning the hazards of particular behaviors and that point to the upside of endorsing behavioral change. We've known for decades that it isn't just the content of the message that is important in promoting behavioral change, but also how this message is delivered, and who is actually delivering the message. For a time, messages intended to change poor health behavior relied on creating fear (the negative consequences of drug use or campaigns to stop smoking by pointing to gruesome lung tissue at autopsy). But, this type of message may cause people to tune out and may have an effect opposite to that intended (Becker & Janz, 1987), and even when it has a positive effect, it is often transient.

It was considered that when the message is provided in a form that emphasizes the benefits of certain behaviors (quitting smoking may give you extra years to enjoy your family), more effective outcomes might be realized relative to messages that emphasize the negative (you'll die early if you keep smoking), a phenomenon often referred to as the '*framing effect*'. Yet, despite positive messages being 'perceived' to be more effective than negative messages, the nature of the message didn't reliably influence the behavior of health consumers. To be sure, there was considerable variability across studies, and the effectiveness of the message may vary with situational factors, but more was evidently needed to induce behavioral change (Akl et al., 2011).

A message regarding health change should obviously come from a credible individual, the message itself should be simple, brief, and to the point, and the recommendations offered should be clear and firm. This includes emphasis on the potential, realistic consequences of not engaging in certain behaviors (breast self-examination) and the potential consequences of negative behaviors being maintained (cigarette smoking). Although the message should be strong, if it is excessively so, it may have little effect, particularly if the message is going to an audience that is not inclined to follow the advice offered (as we've seen in the push to have parents allow their children to be vaccinated). Here, logical arguments ought to consider the opinions of the other person. One could point to cigarette smoking promoting lung problems, while acknowledging that although smoking could help reduce their distress, on balance, the negatives outweigh the positives. Factors such as *self-affirmation* (the tendency to react less defensively to information that contradicts or is threatening to their sense of self by reflecting on personally-relevant or meaningful values; Steele, 1988) may influence the effect of health messages on intentions and behavior (Sweeney & Moyer, 2015). When people were guided through a self-affirmation exercise, individuals might have been more inclined to act on this advice, and it was even reflected by greater neuronal activity in brain regions associated with decision making (Falk et al., 2015).

GOT THE MESSAGE, BUT DID YOU TRUST IT?

With so much research having been done in relation to the effectiveness of messages in promoting attitude and behavioral change, one would think that health organizations would have methods to do this effectively. Unfortunately, these agencies have experienced multiple road blocks in this respect. In some instances the information is relatively straightforward and isn't controversial, such as the value of exercising, or the benefits of not smoking. In other instances, however, the messages people receive are inconsistent, as in the case of which foods are best for us and which diet regimes are most apt to produce positive results. This leaves people bewildered regarding the right steps to be taken, and it might also undermine the trust that people have regarding the messages that they receive.

When individuals are confronted by an ambiguous threat, their appraisal of risk and their subsequent health behaviors may be influenced by health information obtained from medical professionals and also from public health agencies, which is often filtered through the media. To a significant extent, these appraisals might be determined by the individual's perceived risk of being affected (Brug et al., 2009), coupled with the trust they have in the source of information. In the case of pandemic threats, only 60% of respondents trusted the government to have priorities consistent with the needs of the general public, and still fewer (50%) believed that the government actually had the ability to deal with a pandemic. During the avian flu of 2005, earlier false alarms were recalled (mad cow, SARS), and as a result a new 'imminent' threat was not taken as seriously as it should have been (Elledge et al., 2008). It's been said that the effectiveness of the Centers for Disease Control's (CDC) warnings concerning avian flu was diminished ('flu fatigue') as a result of the government having "exhausted its quota of scary utterances" in relation to other threats (Sandman, 2009).

With an emerging threat that hasn't been well studied, as occurred when H1N1 first came on the scene, medical officials may not have all the information, and hence have limited answers

(Continued)

(Continued)

concerning what ought to be communicated to the general public. It wasn't initially known how severe the potential pandemic would be and what mortality rate might be expected, so health officials had to navigate cautiously between minimizing and catastrophizing about a potential hazard, but still be able to make informative statements regarding potential risks (Sandman, 2009). Erring on the side of caution in such instances is likely the best call. Despite the risks posed by H1N1, however, only about 40% of people were vaccinated. 'Vaccine hesitancy' was associated with distrust of the media and the government (Taha et al., 2013), which was exacerbated by the confluence of several factors that added to this distrust (or perhaps lack of confidence would be a more appropriate way to put this). Vaccine development was slow, initially making for insufficient vaccine availability, and long lines had to be endured to receive the treatment. The hesitancy was also encouraged by uncertainty regarding the vaccine's safety, especially as there hadn't been sufficient time to fully evaluate it. The media sensationalized these issues, reminding people of potential side effects of vaccinations, including the possibility of other conditions developing, such as Guillain-Barre Syndrome, and there were wild rumors – all false – indicating the adverse reactions that could stem from flu vaccination. Even though the media was generally not trusted, and many people felt that their sensationalizing was over the top (Taha et al., 2013), the media certainly capitalized on the phony stories in order to capture public attention. Likewise, it's not unusual for some government agencies to feed the public incomplete information, or to put a particular spin on it, possibly in an effort to minimize worry and panic. The result has been that individuals are less likely to simply 'trust blindly', and instead they take personal control over decision making (Hobson-West, 2007), even if these decisions are based on inaccurate information.

PSYCHOSOCIAL AND COGNITIVE PERSPECTIVES OF HEALTH BEHAVIORS

Several theoretical models have been offered to change health-related behaviors. Some have focused on cognitive and affective processes that might drive behavior change, whereas others have been based on the assumption that behavioral change occurs through a series of distinct steps (stages), and that by capitalizing on an understanding of these steps it should be possible to help individuals modify their behaviors (Schwarzer, 2008).

Models based on social cognition

Social-cognitive perspectives concerning behavioral change assume that many factors act together in promoting the adoption of unhealthy behaviors or the failure to adopt healthy behaviors. Although the past can't be undone, the ramifications of the past can be influenced by modifying beliefs, attitudes, intentions, and actions, and several models were proposed to institute health-related behavioral change.

The Health Belief Model

This perspective, which has been among the most widely adopted (Becker, 1974), considers two fundamental elements related to health behavior. Specifically, does the person perceive a health threat, and if so, do they believe that certain behaviors will attenuate the threat? In essence, individuals might ask themselves whether they are vulnerable to an illness, and whether the severity of an illness would vary if they continued to engage in their current behaviors. Furthermore, what benefits would be accrued if they changed their behaviors, and what are the perceived costs or barriers to engaging in the behaviors? If individuals think that a negative health outcome would be severe and that they might be affected, coupled with the beliefs that the benefits of health behaviors in preventing the illness would be substantial and that the barriers to adopting those behaviors are low, then they would likely adopt the behaviors.

Two additional elements were subsequently added to this model, which were deemed important to behavioral change. The first comprised 'cues to action', which refers to the specific triggers that cause a health action to be endorsed, including internal cues (e.g., throat or chest discomfort among smokers) or external cues (dirty looks from others, or advice received through education programs). The second essential component to produce behavioral change entailed *self-efficacy*, which amounts to the person's confidence or belief that they can successfully engage and succeed in certain behaviors (Rosenstock et al., 1988).

A detailed analysis that included cross-sectional and prospective studies indicated that perceived susceptibility and severity of illness, as well as benefits of and barriers to action, were related to behavior change, with costs/barriers being most predictive (Janz & Becker, 1984). Subsequent analyses largely confirmed these findings, but indicated that individuals were primarily focused on what the behavioral change could do for them and at what cost, and that outcomes varied in relation to whether prevention versus treatment behaviors was being considered, as well as whether the treatment involved drug-taking regimens or other actions (Carpenter, 2010).

This model has been predictive of health behaviors in relation to a fairly wide range of conditions, including health screening programs, smoking and alcohol consumption, preventive dental care, dieting, and self-management of chronic illnesses. However, as already said, predicting behavioral change and actually finding ways of accomplishing the change may be entirely separate. Thus, the usefulness of the Health Belief Model has been criticized as being largely descriptive, and not offering specific strategies for changing health-related actions. As well, the model does not address attitudes and beliefs that could determine whether or not a behavior would be engaged, and whether the behavior to be changed is one that is socially acceptable or unacceptable (e.g., smoking). There is also little concern regarding economic factors that might either enhance or hinder the adoption of certain behaviors, and insufficient consideration has been given to differences between behaviors that reflect addictions (or strong habits) and those behaviors that are not as well entrenched.

Protection Motivation Theory

Protection Motivation Theory (PMT; Rogers, 1983), which is related to the Health Belief Model, was developed in an effort to account for behavior that occurs in response to fear-promoting health threats. Fundamental to Protection Motivation Theory is that behavior change is related to individual vulnerability and supposed severity of outcomes, together with the presumption that recommended actions will reduce the threat (*response efficacy*) and that these can be successfully performed (*self-efficacy*). Meta-analyses confirmed that each of these components predicted intentions and/or behavior, with self-efficacy being most cogent (Milne et al., 2000).

Self-efficacy Theory in relation to health behaviors

According to Social Cognitive Theory (SCT) advanced by Bandura (1986), learning to achieve particular goals in a social context involves dynamic and reciprocal interactions between the person, the context, and their behavior. Having a sense of personal control will facilitate behavioral change, and in this regard previous experiences will influence expectations and whether a specific behavior will be engaged. Of course, for behaviors to be performed effectively, the individual must not only know what to do, but how to do it, which they can learn through instrumental processes (i.e., learning from the consequences of their behaviors) and by observing and then reproducing the actions of others (*modeling*). Individuals will eventually form expectations of their behaviors and will anticipate potential outcomes even before they actually behave in particular ways. This will also influence confidence in relation to their ability to engage in particular behaviors successfully (*self-efficacy beliefs*), the actual goals that individuals set for themselves, the time and effort that will be expended to this end, and ultimately whether health behavior change will be initiated (DeVellis & DeVellis, 2000).

Although self-efficacy is generally viewed as being essential for behavior change, it should be considered that this characteristic can vary in relation to specific domains (Schwarzer, 2008). By example, individuals wishing to lose weight might perceive themselves as being capable of engaging in exercise, but they might feel less control in resisting certain foods. Tools have been developed to assess self-efficacy associated specific behavioral features, which can be used by counselors in an effort to facilitate behavior change.

The Theory of Reasoned Action and the Theory of Planned Behavior

The Theory of Reasoned Action (TRA; Ajzen & Fishbein, 1980) was initially developed to predict *intentions* to engage in a behavior at a specific time and place. This perspective was formulated on the basis of research suggesting that behavioral intentions, such as those relevant to health change, are influenced by attitudes regarding the engagement of particular behaviors and the likelihood that the behavior will lead to the expected outcomes. If a behavior is evaluated positively, and individuals believe that they have the power to either facilitate or limit a given behavior, and that others believe that they should engage in that behavior (social norms), then the intention to act will be increased.

This position was subsequently modified with the recognition that intention doesn't necessarily translate into action. This Theory of Planned Behavior (TPB; Ajzen, 1991) considered that not all behaviors can be initiated readily and multiple factors will determine the adoption of these behaviors. Perceived behavioral control, which incorporates the ease (or difficulty) in performing the behavior, as well as earlier experiences that might be pertinent to a given situation, together with attitudes and subjective norms, were seen as affecting behavior change.

Implicit in the model is that individuals have the resources necessary to engage in the behavioral change, but is this actually the case in all situations? Behavioral intentions can be moderated by factors such as the individual's previous experiences, fears that might be present, social influences, mood state, and financial problems that could be incurred by engaging in change. So, as much as we might believe that individuals have self-will, actually being able to exercise it can be difficult. As well, even if an individual is motivated and intent on change a particular behavior, this can be fleeting, making it essential to consider how to maintain the motivation during the lag between intention and action.

Stage models

Transtheoretical Model

The guiding principle of the Transtheoretical Model (TTM) is that most people don't change their behaviors readily, especially if these comprise well-entrenched habits. Changing these behaviors requires small steps, with different strategies being adopted to help individuals move from one stage to the next. This model suggests that to achieve proper behavioral change individuals move through five stages, as described in Table 6.5 (Prochaska, 1994). The approach was initially used help people quit smoking, but has since been used far more broadly and several variants of this model were developed (De Vries & Mudde, 1998).

Table 6.5   Stages of change within the Transtheoretical Model (TTM)

Precontemplation – The individual does not intend to take action in the near future (within the next 6 months), and might not even be aware that their behavior could be harmful. At this stage, most people underestimate the gains that could be obtained through behavioral change, and over-emphasize the negatives that would come from a change of behavior.

Contemplation – With the recognition that their behavior may be harmful, individuals are at a point where they intend to engage in healthy behavior relatively soon (within the next 6 months). They typically have a balanced view of the benefits and difficulties of behavior change, but despite their realistic perspective they might still display reluctance to engage in change.

Preparation (Determination) – Individuals are prepared to take action within the next 30 days. They may have come to the realization that behavioral change will enhance their well-being, and may already have taken small steps in this direction (e.g., given up smoking for a day).

Action – Having recently changed their attitudes and some behaviors, individuals are encouraged to maintain and move forward with that behavior change. During this period, individuals might alter their unhealthy behaviors and acquire new healthy habits.

Maintenance – Once individuals have maintained a behavior change for more than 6 months and intend to continue in this fashion, they are said to be in a maintenance stage. Relapse continues to be difficult to avoid, and considerable work may be needed to prevent this. However, should this occur, individuals are encouraged to maintain their motivation.

According to the TTM perspective, for change to occur *decisional balance* is necessary in which individuals come to the realization that the advantages of change outweigh the disadvantages. Furthermore, individuals must have the confidence that they are capable of initiating and maintaining changes, and should have methods or strategies to facilitate the initiation and maintenance of behavior change. The latter, referred to as *processes of change*, comprises 10 features that are described in Table 6.6.

Table 6.6   Processes of change

1. *Consciousness raising*: Enhanced awareness about the healthy behavior, which is obtained through various sources, including educational programs.
2. *Dramatic relief*: Negative emotional responses occur as a result of unhealthy behaviors, whereas inspiration and hope is obtained through adoption of healthy behaviors.
3. *Self-reevaluation*: Self-reappraisal and realization that healthy behavior is part of who the individual wants to be.
4. *Environmental reevaluation*: Reappraisals in which individuals realize how their unhealthy behaviors affect others and the impact of change in this regard.
5. *Social liberation*: Appreciating that society is supportive of healthy behavior.
6. *Self-liberation*: Committed to change behavior based on the belief that adopting healthy behavior is possible.
7. *Helping relationships*: Finding supportive relationships that encourage change.
8. *Counter-conditioning*: Substituting healthy behaviors and thoughts for unhealthy behaviors and thoughts.
9. *Reinforcement management*: Rewarding positive behavior and reducing the rewards associated with negative behavior.
10. *Stimulus control*: Re-engineering the environment so that reminders and cues are present to support and encourage healthy behavior, and concurrently removing cues that prompt unhealthy behavior.

The TTM approach, although popular in some quarters, has encountered its share of criticism (Sutton, 2000). Among other things, TTM falls short in that it doesn't provide standardization regarding what is meant by each stage, the causal connections among different constructs are unclear, correlational data supporting TTM are often misinterpreted to imply causality, and there is confusion regarding how a stage model can be tested (e.g., Herzog, 2005). Furthermore, the model pays scant attention to the environmental or social context in which change occurs (e.g., socioeconomic status), including the contribution of cues that promote craving. This model has also been criticized on the basis of reports that stage-based intervention strategies (e.g., to diminish smoking and eating disorders) were actually no more effective than other approaches (Riemsma et al., 2003). Finally, TTM works on the assumption that individuals go through logical decision-making processes and then form coherent systematic plans. However, as we've seen, decisions are not necessarily based on accurate appraisals or logical thinking, and these problems can be exaggerated under stressful conditions. This said, for some individuals the approach has worked.

Most researchers and clinicians are aware that no approach is equally effective for all individuals, and, like many other treatments, TTM might be better suited for some than others.

Behavioral and cognitive methods of altering health behaviors

Learning principles in relation to behavioral change

For as long as kids have had dogs, it's been known that if a particular behavior is rewarded, that response will be more likely to reoccur. If, in contrast, the behavior was followed by something the dog didn't like, then the behavior would soon disappear. This knowledge was formally framed as 'the law of effect' by Thorndike in 1911 (kids had no call to give this phenomenon a name). It was probably noticed by kids that a cue that had been paired with a tasty treat, such as the container in which dog treats were kept, would elicit begging and globs of saliva dripping from Grover's mouth. Pavlov noted this involuntary response (salivation) to cues associated with food, which came to be referred to as a 'classically conditioned' response that was governed by the autonomic nervous system. It was also found subsequently that if a cue was paired with a painful stimulus, then this cue would also come to elicit involuntary responses that seemed to be reminiscent of fear and anxiety.

Just as certain behaviors could be established by pairing a response with a reward, it was also possible to eliminate (or inhibit) these conditioned responses through *extinction*. This amounted to not giving the animal a reward for making a particular instrumental response and pretty soon it would cease making the response. Likewise, if a cue was no longer followed by reward, the classically conditioned salivation (i.e., in response to the cue) would disappear. These basic procedures, together with several other principles related to learning processes, became fundamental in the establishment of behavior change methods within applied and clinical settings.

Exposure therapy and systematic desensitization

Extinction of responses by withholding rewards can be achieved readily, but it is more difficult to achieve when the responses to be eliminated comprise fear and anxiety. Specifically, animals (and humans) will initiate these responses well before they have the opportunity to actually find out that not doing so wouldn't have negative consequences. By example, if a student who is afraid of public speaking (e.g., giving class presentations) avoids courses in which these presentations are required, s/he might never know whether or not their fear had diminished over the years as they never allowed themselves to be in that situation. For extinction to occur in this instance, it might be necessary for the negative cues or situations to be experienced by the individual so that they can learn that nothing bad will transpire.

Understandably, suddenly '*flooding*' individuals with anxiety-provoking stimuli to induce extinction might be a bit much for them to handle. So, in a therapeutic context, this '*forced exposure*' occurs in small, graded steps, through a procedure known as '*systematic desensitization*' (Wolpe, 1968). This procedure effectively diminishes fear and anxiety, and has frequently been used to eliminate phobias, as well as in diminishing symptoms of obsessive compulsive disorder (OCD) as it facilitates the development of tolerance to the anxiety associated with not engaging in the compulsive behavior.

Behavior modification and applied behavior analysis

In a clinical setting, the term 'behavior modification' (now more commonly termed 'applied behavior analysis'; ABA) usually refers to changing behavior through instrumental methods. This includes the promotion of particular behaviors through positive and negative reinforcement and the reduction of certain behaviors through extinction or punishment (Mulick, 2006). This procedure has been used to alter behavior across a wide spectrum of conditions (e.g., ADHD, recidivism among young and adult offenders, smoking reduction), although criticisms have been leveled at the inappropriate use of punishment or aversion therapy to elicit behavioral change, particularly given that only short-lasting effects are obtained by punishment.

Cognitive approaches consider the appraisals that individuals make concerning events around them. If the objective, for instance, is to reduce alcohol consumption or cigarette smoking, then individuals need to appreciate to what extent their lives are controlled by their addictions. Are they aware of the strength of their cravings, the behaviors they undertake to get their fix, and the emotional changes that occur as a function of whether or not they have had their fix? In essence, this method counts on individuals being realistic about their abilities of *self-observations* and *self-monitoring* so that they become aware of what promotes their craving, and how to reduce it. This might entail the use of a diary, recording everything to do with their behavior, including details about their feelings (e.g., cravings, anxiety), the conditions and surroundings associated with engaging in their habit, and the responses that occurred once they had their fix. By monitoring themselves, people would diminish their intake of unhealthy substances, but the changes observed were fairly transient (Meichenbaum, 1977).

Self-reinforcement, self-punishment, and contingency contracting

The notion of *self-control* is key to cognitive therapeutic strategies related to health and the therapist's job is to help individuals learn to appraise situations properly and then to take control so that their actions are focused on issues that are distressing or problematic. Related to self-control is *self-reinforcement*, in which individuals reward themselves for maintaining certain behaviors (e.g., if I don't smoke today, then I treat myself with something positive, or I get to eliminate something that is bothering me). Alternatively, individuals might engage in *self-punishment* when they engage in behaviors that should be eliminated (taking away something that the individual likes or having the individual lose a predetermined amount of money when they commit an infraction, e.g., smoke a cigarette). A combination of self-reward and self-punishment, predictably, is more efficacious than either treatment alone.

The findings stemming from such approaches led to the development of *contingency contracting*, wherein a person desiring to make changes in their life might make a deal (contract) with another person (friend, therapist) in which they will be rewarded for certain behaviors and punished for others. For instance, a father might make a deal with his kid(s) that when either of them uses a swear word they have to put 25 cents in a jar to be given to a charitable cause. In addition to being used to diminish unwanted behaviors, it has also been used successfully to help with patient compliance in regard to illnesses (Cupples & Steslow, 2001).

Cognitive restructuring

Related to the preceding approaches were those that sought to alter individuals' cognitions and responses regarding particular events. This approach, referred to as *cognitive restructuring*, focuses on an individual's internal monologues, so that these are framed in a positive and constructive manner, rather than the negative spin that the individual might put on their abilities (Meichenbaum & Cameron, 1974). So, a monologue that consists of "I can't beat it. The need for a drink is just too strong" is replaced with "Alcohol is affecting my entire life. But, this nothing little liquid isn't going to beat me", followed by positive self-statements "Once I've beaten the cravings I'll have time and energy to do the things that are important to me". To have people engage in internal monologues or self-talk, a therapist might model the behavior so that their client will follow their lead. Initially the client will self-talk out loud following the lead of the therapist, and then in small steps the self-talk will go to a whisper and eventually it will be fully internalized.

Cognitive restructuring is aided by having individuals do homework assignments (behavioral assignments), such as keeping a list of things that tempted them away from their health goals, which can later be discussed with the therapist. This gives the individual the opportunity to see their problems more objectively and, in this sense, they have more control over the situation. As well, cognitive therapies can also include training new coping methods, such as *social skills training* or *assertiveness training*, which might be helpful in social situations.

Cognitive behavioral therapy

As the name implies, *cognitive behavioral therapy* (CBT) is a therapeutic approach based on behavioral therapy, cognitive therapy, and a combination of the two. Beck (1970), one of the most influential theorists involved in the development of CBT, viewed the cognitive system as involving both primitive and mature characteristics. The primitive system is fundamentally unrealistic and idiosyncratic, and when it predominates, psychopathology may develop. Among depressed individuals the primitive cognitions may be expressed as cognitive distortions, as well as automatic thoughts or images that focus on negativity, deprivation, hopelessness or self-debasement. Individuals with anxiety-related problems might also display disturbed cognitions, but these might focus on imminent danger related to a specific or generalized stimulus. These negative cognitions are frequently experienced automatically and invade the conscious experience of depressed or anxious individuals, often manifesting as cognitive distortions, and are likely to disturb appraisals and coping methods.

Typically, CBT is undertaken to reduce dysfunctional behaviors, cognitions, and emotions through a goal-oriented, systematic procedure in which individuals are encouraged to challenge inappropriate and counterproductive beliefs, and for dysfunctional attitudes and belief systems ('*schemas*') responsible for the generation of disturbed automatic thoughts to be dealt with systematically. In doing so, cognitive errors and distortions (e.g., *overgeneralizing, magnification of negatives, minimization of positives*, and *catastrophizing*) are replaced with a realistic and effective perspectives, thereby limiting self-defeating behavior and emotional distress (Beck et al., 1979).

Early in the course of treatment patients will realize that their appraisals of threats are not entirely realistic, and are both impractical and counterproductive. Knowing this, however, isn't sufficient to solve the problems, and it is necessary to replace the disturbed cognitions with those that are functionally more effective. This 'quieting' of the primitive (automatic) cognitive system can be achieved by the therapist helping the patient identify these thoughts and then come up with more realistic and more favorable alternatives. Individuals are encouraged to question and test their potentially counterproductive assumptions, evaluations, and beliefs, and to deal directly with uncomfortable issues and find new approaches to dealing with them. Through the various steps of cognitive therapy, coupled with homework assignments to facilitate the identification of cognitive distortions and to deal with them, changes in thoughts ought to precipitate a change in disturbed beliefs, feelings (affect), and actions. It is common for CBT to incorporate other therapeutic methods (e.g., relaxation training, exposure therapy), depending on the nature of the condition or behavioral change being considered. This approach comes with a degree of flexibility, allowing for modifications of basic procedures as the situation demands, and the clinician's preferences and experiences come into play in deciding the specifics of the therapy.

Most often, CBT is used on a one-on-one basis, but for some illnesses a group therapy approach can be effective. There have also been indications that internet-delivered cognitive behavior therapy can be useful (Rice et al., 2014), although only a modest number of studies have been conducted to assess this, and it may be premature to recommend this fully. As well, a guided self-help approach has been developed, but its usefulness is uncertain.

Although CBT was initially used to treat depressive disorders, it subsequently proved to be effective in the treatment of posttraumatic stress disorder (PTSD), as well as various anxiety and eating disorders (e.g., Koucky et al., 2013), and was even effective in treating children with PTSD and depression (Gillies et al., 2013). Beyond these psychological illnesses, CBT has successfully been used to treat problems related to dieting, insomnia, and substance abuse (e.g., Taylor & Pruiksma, 2014), and as an adjunct treatment to diminish the distress associated with physical illnesses, such as multiple sclerosis, epilepsy, HIV, and cancer.

Despite its effectiveness, and the fact that it has been recommended as the treatment of choice for some conditions, patients sometimes reject CBT as a mode of treatment. Some individuals might feel that it's a bit on the hokey side (not everyone cares for 'talk therapy', and some patients prefer the ease and privacy obtained through meds), or it may be more time consuming than they would like, requiring attendance to sessions over about 12 weeks, and to actively engage in homework. Some therapists have rejected CBT because of high non-response and high drop-out rates, and it was suggested that CBT is effective primarily in individuals who have the belief that it can help them and are thus prepared to invest in this approach.

Mindfulness

Mindfulness (also referred to as mindfulness meditation) has become increasingly popular as a way of diminishing stress, and its use has been extended to deal with many pathological conditions. As a therapeutic strategy, mindfulness was developed from a combination of CBT and meditation-centered practices and traditions (Brown & Ryan, 2003; Kabat-Zinn, 1990), with its fundamental goal being the redirection of an individual's thoughts from unpleasant external issues (social conflicts or other stressors) toward moment-to-moment internal processes (Kabat-Zinn, 1990). This entails having individuals become aware of events in the present moment (and not ruminating about the past or worrying about the future), and not being judgmental about them. As a result, individuals will be less likely to fixate and ruminate on nonproductive thoughts, and instead will have the opportunity to observe events as they unfold, and to appreciate physical and emotional responses these situations elicit, but without making attributions (e.g., blame) that might have negative consequences. Ordinarily, when individuals engage in negative rumination, they imprison themselves in a self-perpetuating loop that undermines effective coping and promotes depression and further rumination. Extricating oneself from this loop through *'reperceiving'* (a shift in perspective involving self-regulation, cognitive and behavioral flexibility, and clarification of values) may allow individuals to diminish distress and depressive mood (Brown & Ryan, 2003; Kabat-Zinn, 1990; Segal et al., 2002).

Stress reduction and altered coping

Differences exist in the degree to which mindfulness is part of a person's trait profile, and can be assessed through the Mindful Attention Awareness Scale (MAAS) or the Five Facet Mindfulness Questionnaire (FFMQ). Some individuals have mindful characteristics as part of their basic repertoire, and tend to be less vulnerable to depression and other stress-related disorders, and generally report better health-related quality of life (Whitaker et al., 2014). Although traits are often thought to be relatively fixed characteristics, mindfulness can be increased in an effort to reduce feelings of distress and stressor-related conditions through either *mindfulness-based stress reduction* (MBSR; Kabat-Zinn, 1990) or *mindfulness-based cognitive therapy* (MBCT; Segal et al., 2002). By promoting current moment awareness, mindfulness disrupts automatic, habitual thoughts and behavioral patterns, replacing them with momentary evaluations based on greater thought, without judgment or cognitive elaboration. This might also facilitate the focus on pertinent aspects of a stressful situation, rather than being overwhelmed by multiple extraneous factors, including past or future concerns, and individuals might consequently become less likely to make incorrect, negative attributions concerning stressors, thereby enabling them to use effective coping methods.

By being aware of one's thoughts and emotions, and being able to make appropriate appraisals of stressors as they unfold, individuals would be more likely to tailor their coping strategies to suit specific situations. Indeed, mindfulness was linked to creative solutions to deal with problems and persistence in dealing with difficult tasks, as well as adoption and maintenance of flexible coping strategies in dealing with challenges (Sugiura, 2004). Beyond this, however, the positive effects observed may also stem from increased self-acceptance, mood regulation, and attention control that make for improved ability to deal with day-to-day events as well as diminishing guilt and self-criticism that might otherwise evolve in association with some stressors or pathological conditions (Anderson et al., 2007). Aside from reducing negative appraisal, enhancing awareness mindfulness might also facilitate the appreciation of positive events experienced. In view of the varied benefits of mindfulness training, it has been extensively used in the treatment of a broad range of psychological problems, and has also been used to influence physical illnesses or the psychological ramifications of such illnesses, including the diminution of migraine headache, and in the management of distress associated with cancer, multiple sclerosis, and cardiovascular health (e.g., Gotink et al., 2015).

FLAVOR OF THE MONTH OR SOMETHING MORE?

Mindfulness has become the darling of the decade with respect to treatment of stress-related states, but we shouldn't fool ourselves into believing that it's more than it is. Like any other treatment, it isn't useful for everyone. In fact, a systematic review and meta-analysis concluded that moderate evidence was available supporting its effectiveness in the treatment of anxiety, depression, and pain, and the evidence of its effectiveness in relation to improved mental health quality of life (QoL) was limited. Furthermore, there was insufficient evidence or low evidence concerning the impact of mindful meditation on positive mood, attention, substance use, eating habits, sleep, and weight. More damning still, there was no evidence indicating that mindful meditation programs were any better than drug treatments, exercise, and other behavioral therapies (Goyal et al., 2014). All this said, it ought to be considered that like any other psychological treatment, it isn't meant for every-body and thus considerable variability can be expected pertaining to the efficacy of this procedure.

Biological correlates

The benefits of mindfulness were apparent in relation to physiological indices of distress, being accompanied by reduced blood pressure, diminished levels of the inflammatory marker C-reactive protein, and reversal of cytokine elevations in patients being treated for cancer (Witek-Janusek et al., 2008), as well as reducing chronic inflammation that can lead to several illnesses (Rosenkranz et al., 2013). Moreover, brain changes occur in association with mindfulness training, including alterations within several prefrontal cortical regions, the amygdala, striatum, and anterior cingulate cortex, which are associated with mood and emotional regulation, perspective taking, and various executive functions and attention (Tang et al., 2015). It is generally believed that mindfulness training may promote neuroplastic changes in brain processes involved in the regulation of attention, emotions, and self-awareness, and at the same time could result in the decoupling of connectivity associated with undesirable outcomes (e.g., between brain regions involved in executive functioning and pain perception, as well as between craving-related brain regions and those that are activated by cues related to smoking).

Yoga

Like mindfulness, yoga is thought to have multiple health benefits, such as facilitating weight reduction and blood pressure, as well as risk of heart disease, diabetes, and immune-related disorders (Balaji et al., 2012). It has been suggested that effects of this nature come about because of the actions of yoga in diminishing pro-inflammatory cytokine activity (Kiecolt-Glaser et al., 2010) and in reducing high levels of autonomic nervous system activity, as well as through effects on GABA functioning that acts against stress-related disorders (Streeter et al., 2012). It is still relatively early to make definitive statements regarding the effectiveness of yoga in ameliorating clinical levels of anxiety, just as this is the case for mindfulness. If nothing else, these practices attract unique populations and the data might not be generalizable to others.

The social cure: Change through social identity

Our behaviors, including those that promote good health, are often influenced by social norms and our social identity (Tarrant et al., 2012). We have a drive to evaluate our opinions and abilities, and when objective means aren't available to do so, we make comparisons to those of other people (Festinger, 1954). More than this, the need or desire to fit with other group members who are similar to us might guide our attitudes and behaviors, as would our self-esteem, social status, mood, the presence of threats, and competitiveness. Based on social comparison theory, it might be expected that if my ingroup engages in certain behaviors, then I will too (Oraby et al., 2014). If they use seat belts so will I, if they stop smoking then I will too, and if they choose to receive a flu vaccine then it's likely that I'll do the same. In promoting health behaviors, as in creating fads, perhaps a good approach is to have the most influential people, the trend setters, get on board and, through social comparisons, others will follow.

For most of us, our social identity is exceptionally important in many ways, and these identities can serve in our ability to deal with problems, particularly given that our identity influences whether and from whom social support is obtained. Indeed, the absence of social support and social connectedness (reflected by the number and quality of an individual's relations) has been associated with increased frequency of stress-related pathological outcomes. As we saw earlier, the absence of social connections may result in loneliness, which itself is stressful and can lead to poor health, whereas having strong social relationships is accompanied by longer life and greater ability to contend with illnesses (Cruwys et al., 2013). For that matter, having even a single strong connection has been found to diminish the risk of dying in the ensuing year, and the risk further declined with an increasing number of social connections (Cruwys et al., 2014). Experiences that include social connections are so basic to our functioning that they promote brain neurochemical processes much like those that are elicited by other rewarding stimuli, whereas threats to connectedness may activate neural circuits that are interpreted much like other threats to well-being (Eisenberger & Cole, 2012).

Not every social relationship is equally effective or useful, but when individuals have a 'shared identity', the effectiveness of support is enhanced (Best et al., 2014). It's presumably for this reason that *support groups* in which members share an identity (e.g., parents of children with heart problems; family members of those who died through suicide) are particularly effective in helping individuals get through difficult times. In their persuasive review, Jetten et al. (2014) indicated that key to social connectedness was that sharing meaningful identities would enhance the likelihood that individuals would adopt the group's core values, which can guide their own behaviors. Moreover, sharing with like-minded group members can facilitate individuals learning from one another, and in large groups the social connectedness can facilitate cultural knowledge. Thus, having many social relations and connections can be beneficial, and support that comes from those with shared values can offer a 'social cure' in preventing some illnesses and in dealing with others (Jetten et al., 2012).

It is unfortunate that those most in need of social connections may have the hardest time obtaining them. For instance, the stigma of mental illness represents a considerable barrier in this regard, and among older individuals, maintaining contacts can be difficult owing to physical or mental disturbances, or because friends have moved to other places. Therapists or social workers can have a significant impact on an individual's well-being simply by facilitating the maintenance of earlier connections and through the development of new, empowering identities. There are, to be sure, instances where connectedness and social identity can cause problems (e.g., hanging out with the 'wrong' crowd, as your parents likely told you, can be harmful). Likewise, our social group, even with the best intentions, may get us to engage in what are likely to be unhealthy or counterproductive behaviors. For instance, parents who are anti-vaxxers often appear in clusters. This clustering might reflect their reinforcement of one another's belief, or it might be that individuals of the same mind ended up living in the same communities.

GIVING VERSUS RECEIVING: 'HELPER'S HIGH'

While we're on the topic of social cures, there's another issue that ought to be mentioned that often falls by the wayside. Whether it comprises volunteering or charitable giving for particular causes, or 'random acts of kindness' such as giving a bit of money to a homeless person, positive behaviors might create a feeling of well-being in the giver and may diminish emotional distress. As expected, charitable giving has been associated with improved health and reduced mortality risk, and volunteering among seniors was accompanied by reduced symptoms of depression, fewer functional limitations, enhanced cognitive abilities, better self-reported health, and lower mortality (N.D. Anderson et al., 2014).

Although giving creates positive feelings, these are more apt to appear when prosocial spending is directed at those with whom we have strong social ties (Aknin et al., 2011). The positive effects of giving have been seen across cultures, including within groups that are isolated and relatively primitive, as well as among young children, leading to the view that we have evolved so that giving is rewarding (Aknin et al., 2013). Although the data are still a bit limited, providing social support (just as receiving it) engages some of the same neural circuits associated with feelings of reward (Eisenberger, 2013). Likewise, it was found that when individuals with altruistic tendencies made a charitable donation, brain regions involved in reward processes were activated, but this was less prominent among those who offered charity for more self-interested reasons. There's a further bonus related to charitable giving in that it may bring like-minded people into contact with one another, which could result in the formation of a supportive social group that might serve as a stress buffer.

HARM REDUCTION PROGRAMS

Harm reduction approaches, also referred to as harm minimization policies, are geared to '*manage*' behaviors that are unhealthy or very risky, such as engaging in unsafe sex and recreational drug use (Inciardi & Harrison, 2000). However, the nature of the harm reduction approach necessarily varies as a function of the problem being confronted. Harm reduction programs undertaken to encourage safe sex by educating young people about risks and how to limit them have been successful in diminishing unwanted pregnancies as well as sexually transmitted diseases, including HIV, which was not achieved simply through abstinence-only programs (Johnson et al., 2011). In contrast, programs based on educating people about risks were ineffective in relation to drug abuse, which required a very different approach.

Programs to manage addictions have involved multipronged methods that entailed educational campaigns, the establishment of needle exchange centers where individuals could safely use drugs, as well as heroin maintenance programs in which medical prescriptions for pharmaceutical heroin were provided. The notion was that these 'safe sites' would allow for the presence of medical staff and treatment referrals, information about drugs, provision of sterile injection equipment, and places where risks were generally diminished. Likewise, heroin maintenance programs could benefit users by permitting greater drug safety (e.g., limiting use of tainted drugs), enhance the health and social circumstances of users, and concurrently reduce government expenses secondary to policing, incarceration, and health interventions (Haasen et al., 2007). Opioid replacement therapy (ORT) was also instituted, in which heroin was replaced with drugs such as methadone or buprenorphine. These agents have longer lasting effects, but with diminished euphoric actions, hopefully reducing craving and hence drug use (Amato et al., 2005). There have also been efforts to provide homeless people in shelters with managed alcohol availability in an effort to reduce consumption, provide safety, diminish encounters with police, and reduce emergency room visits (Podymow et al., 2006).

Despite the benefits created through harm reduction programs, they have encountered considerable push-back. Tolerating risky or illegal behavior, it was argued, sends the (wrong) message that such behaviors are acceptable, and it was argued that these programs don't actually reduce harm over the long term. Further, they might give the false impression that there is such a thing as responsible ways to use drugs, thereby misleading people about the inherent dangers of drug use. Other adversaries of the harm reduction approach argued that this philosophy, at its core, suggests that substance use is unpreventable, a view that is both fatalistic and faulty. It is conceivable that there is some validity to these various claims, but they have little in the way of scientific backing, and they don't offer useful alternatives.

SUMMARY

Approaches to health-related issues have evolved so that progressively better methods of treatment have been advanced. An endophenotypic approach and personalized medicine might augment treatment of physical illnesses through psychological approaches just as they have done using other treatment methods. Likewise, increased use of interventions, at the individual and community levels, will enhance life span and quality of life, and if illnesses do occur, healthy life-styles might facilitate the effectiveness of treatments.

Often, however, getting people to change their life-styles isn't easy. This may require that people accept that their current behaviors are counterproductive and dangerous, but this is not sufficient to actually have behavioral change occur. The individual ought to be ready to change and willing to take actions to this effect. Even then, behavioral change is difficult to sustain. Temptations assail us from all sides, and fighting against strong cravings can be exceedingly difficult. Nevertheless, strategies have been developed to facilitate change and to maintain effective health behavior despite the devil in us trying to get the upper hand.

7   Life-style Factors

DOING NOTHING IS SIMPLER THAN DOING SOMETHING

Whether it's eating the wrong foods or not obtaining enough exercise, poor life-style habits can increase vulnerability to certain disease conditions, and those who fail to take proper steps might at some time experience considerable remorse. We've heard it repeatedly from health professionals, teachers, and parents, and we're even assaulted by it through the media to the extent that the message is sometimes ignored or an eye-roll performed that amounts to "gimme a break". Others, however, take health behaviors very seriously; they work-out regularly, eat and sleep well, and maintain a proper balance between different activities. Engaging in proper health care behaviors needs to be approached systematically and consistently so that it becomes part of a routine, a habit that once instilled sticks with the individual. If good health behaviors haven't been instilled when a person is young, it's somewhat more difficult to establish later. So, if you're a couch potato who believes it's sufficient to work-out your thumbs by texting friends, then you can try blaming your Mom or Dad for not raising you right.

When we fail to alter unhealthy behavioral ways, the problem can be of our own making, but there are extraneous factors that foster or even encourage these failures. The temptations we face on a daily basis are remarkable. Not only has choice of high-calorie, high-fat foods increased dramatically over the years, but the portions offered in some restaurants are enormous. That expression "Can I supersize that for you?" ought to be changed to either "Hey buddy, want some more lard on your butt and gut?" or "Hi, can I offer you the opportunity for earlier death?". But, to eat properly, we need to know what a healthy diet comprises. It seems that every other month there's another report that partially contradicts the last as to what's good for us and what's not. At one time butter was bad for us and margarine was good, then margarine turned out to be bad, and butter was somewhat better. Seven glasses of water a day was good as it flushed our system, but then we were told that it wasn't actually necessary. Carbs are the devil's product, fat foods are a curse to the heart. Yet, according to the top nutrition advisory panel of the US, cholesterol that had for about 40 years been considered a no-no, now appears not to be so bad after all, although it's still a problem for those with diabetes or those who are at risk for heart disease. Many of us had believed that to maintain heart health we should be avoiding foods with saturated fats and instead consume foods with polyunsaturated fats, but it now seems that there isn't actually a convincing case to be made for this (Chowdhury et al., 2014), although it would be a good idea to stay away from trans fats.

Diet regimens often seem to contradict one another, and the diet gurus and scientists themselves seem to be in disagreement, all passionately pushing their perspectives. When so many variants of a story confront us, when information is inconsistent and ambiguous, and it's unclear who can be trusted (if anybody), then it's no wonder that we're confused as to what's best for us. *'Once doubt sets in, certainty rarely returns'.*

KEEPING THE MOTOR RUNNING

Maintain a car well, provide regular oil changes, rotate the tires, and check for problems periodically, and it can last long a long time, and could one day be one of those antique cars that collectors crave and drive only on special occasions. Run the car ragged over dirt roads littered with pot holes, keep the engine revved for extended periods, and fail to perform proper maintenance, and you can pretty well count on it finding its way to the scrapyard sooner. Like our cars, we also need to be well maintained. There's no question that our health-related behaviors will have a considerable impact on how well and how long we live, and whether or not we'll need to go into the 'people service station' to have emergency repairs performed. In this chapter we'll examine:

- the primary health behaviors that ought to be adopted
- the relation between life-style factors (exercise, nutrition, sleep) and well-being
- the processes by which these life-style factors might influence various types of illness
- the factors that limit the adoption of healthy life-styles, and hints will be provided that might help getting around the roadblocks.

EXERCISE

Benefits of exercise

Aerobic exercises comprising low-intensity physical activities (distance running, bicycling, jogging) involve free oxygen use to meet energy demands, and hence stimulate and strengthen the heart and lungs (McArdle et al., 2006). Anaerobic exercises, which comprise strength training, enhance muscle capacity and are thus efficient for burning fat. In the period between 2003 to 2014 the time spent exercising has increased appreciably among a large portion of the population. A recent article in *The Economist*, however, indicated that this was not apparent in the poorest segment, which is likely due to several factors, including accessibility to facilities and time to engage in exercise. As indicated in this article, exercise is now close to being a luxury good.

The benefits of regular exercise are evident in relation to improved heart health and greater longevity, whereas a lack of exercise has negative effects that are greater than those usually attributed to obesity (Ekelund et al., 2015). Aside from increasing the strength of the heart and lowering bad cholesterol, regular *moderate* exercise diminishes obesity, diabetes, and osteoporosis, and also enhances aspects of immune functioning and may be accompanied by lower occurrence of some forms of cancer (e.g., Walsh et al., 2011; Warburton et al., 2006a, 2006b). In fact, women who had engaged in moderate exercise during adolescence (amounting to as little as 1.33 hours each week) were at a 15% reduced risk of subsequently developing cancer and at a 13% reduction of all cause mortality.

Many people are seemingly unaware of just how sedentary their life-style is, and it isn't unusual for those who have not been maintaining a work-out schedule to be at a loss as to where to begin. Some exercise, even light or moderate activity, is better than none, and among men with coronary artery disease this was associated with reduced risk of death from any cause (Wannamethee et al., 2000). The exercise needn't be vigorous, and even moderate exercise (say, 30 minutes of exercise daily) was sufficient to reduce mortality risk by a third (Arem et al., 2015). Importantly, even for those who engage in exercise, simply sitting for extended periods of time has been associated with increased mortality stemming from heart disease, cancer and diabetes (Biswas et al., 2015). Sedentary behaviors need to be avoided so that sitting for 30 minutes or more ought to be broken up by occasional walks.

Cognitive benefits

Beyond affecting physical illnesses, exercise has also been associated with improved slow-wave sleep, enhanced synaptic plasticity and growth of new neurons, and augmented cognitive ability (e.g., Hamer & Steptoe, 2009; Hamer, Sabia et al., 2012). Exercise has also been found to diminish anxiety and depression, although in fairly severe depression where individuals find it hard to get sufficiently motivated to get out of bed, pushing them to exercise isn't productive and might be better suited as an adjunct to other forms of treatment. Beyond these mood-related changes, the augmented brain functioning associated with aerobic exercise training is associated with improved attention and information processing speed, executive functioning, and memory, although these effects are only modest. It may be that positive effects are most apparent in those individuals, such as older people, in whom neuronal functioning ordinarily declines (but before any dementia is present) and among other high-risk populations, such as those with cardiovascular problems (Sjösten & Kivelä, 2006). In effect, even if regular exercise and motor skills training only enhance cognitive abilities to a limited extent, that can limit the cognitive decline otherwise associated with aging, although little positive effect may be obtained in reversing dementia (Öhman et al., 2014).

Neurobiological processes that govern exercise-related psychological effects

The way in which exercise comes to have positive effects, beyond the obvious cardiovascular actions, have yet to be fully elucidated, although there has been considerable interest in the possibility that growth (neurotrophic) factors, including BDNF, IGF-I, VEGF, and GDNF, contribute in this regard (Cotman et al., 2007). As well, exercise may affect neural circuits related to stressors, thereby 'reorganizing' them so that when stressors are later encountered, these neuronal processes are less likely to over-react, ostensibly by allowing for activation of the inhibitory neurotransmitter GABA (Schoenfeld et al., 2013).

From illicit to beneficial

The neurotrophic factor erythropoietin (EPO), which received a bad rap because of its illicit use by athletes involved in endurance sports (e.g., long-distance cycling), increases red blood cells that carry oxygen to the brain and elsewhere. Treatments that diminish depression, such as antidepressant medication or electroconvulsive shock, were accompanied by elevated EPO within the hippocampus (Girgenti et al., 2009), thereby increasing BDNF expression, and could potentially reduce depression. Thus, the view was offered that EPO could have clinical utility as an adjunct or add-on treatment for depression (Hayley & Anisman, 2013).

Road blocks to exercise and getting around them

If you ask people why they don't exercise, it's likely that the response you'll hear will comprise "I just don't have the time", "at the end of a tough day I just don't have the energy", or "I just fell out of the habit". It's also common for people to begin exercising, but then drop out, for any number of reasons. They might not have been motivated for the right reasons (e.g., wanting to look buff rather than feel good), unattainable goals were set, the chosen activity wasn't right for them, the routines became boring, too much was expected too soon, bad influences or a self-defeating attitude undermined continuation, injuries had been sustained, or, once again, it's simply easier to do nothing than to do something.

Some of these excuses are legitimate, but most fall into the 'my dog ate my homework' category. However, steps can be taken to encourage participation and diminish attrition, including several based on the common excuses used not to exercise. Among other things, the right attitude or personality will be helpful. Individuals with a high degree of self-efficacy or who appreciate that they can determine their own fates (self-determination) and take control (Teixeira et al., 2012) will fare better than others. Thus, programs that aren't limited to exercise alone but also include efforts to enhance self-efficacy or self-determination should be more effective and have fewer drop-outs than those that don't. Likewise, high enjoyment and preference for physical activity makes for high levels of participation (Salmon et al., 2003), and drop-out will be lessened if individuals select the right activity, vary them to reduce boredom, and make them fun. Significant to success is being able to do the work-outs with others who are reciprocally encouraging. The health value of group exercise beyond that gained from individual efforts is limited (Floyd & Moyer, 2010), but it may be effective in diminishing attrition. Finally, it shouldn't be the least surprising that the more convenient and accessible the exercise location, the more likely it is that individuals will continue with the program. When communities focus on making resources available, exciting, and safe, it's likely that a greater number of individuals will participate in exercise programs.

The health care worker's role in promoting exercise

Despite the known health benefits of exercise, some physicians might fail to advise patients to maintain an exercise regimen, unless of course they exhibit signs of illness, such as diabetes or metabolic syndrome, which can be influenced by exercise. There have been efforts to include exercise counseling in medical training, but a systematic review concluded that there is little evidence indicating that improvements in physician training has an appreciable bearing on recommendations to patients (Dacey et al., 2014).

Difficulties engaging in appropriate activities are notable among older individuals who might be frail and whose aerobic and musculoskeletal fitness is limited, making it that much more important for them to have help in engaging in exercise. For them, a training program ought to begin with flexibility exercises, hopefully leading to resistance and then aerobic exercises (Warburton et al., 2006b). Not surprisingly, adherence to exercise regimens has been linked to being healthy, elevated economic status, and older people with better cognitive ability and fewer depressive symptoms (Picorelli et al., 2014). However, as adherence to exercise programs can be problematic, it is advantageous to encourage exercise in the form of walking, which can be achieved readily in a group of individuals with shared identities (C. Haslam et al., 2014).

NUTRITION

At any given moment we're all burning energy (calories), more so when we're moving around than when we're sitting in front of a computer or vegging on the sofa watching TV. Proteins are being used up continuously, and certain important brain and body chemicals are being reduced. Ideally, the foods we consume replenish energy stores that have been used, and help various organs operate properly. However, as most of us know, not every food is equally useful or healthy.

MISUNDERSTANDING LABELS

Don't misread those nifty little nutrition facts found on virtually every food product. They inform you about the usable energy in a product in the form of calories, but what they don't inform you about is the fact that the calories obtained are influenced by the extent to which the food is processed. Essentially, as far as our biology is concerned, highly processed foods (usually softer and more tasty) are like partially digested foods, so that our system has a simpler time processing them. Because fewer calories are burned during digestion of processed foods, they are more likely to lead to weight gain, whereas the same food item in a raw form might help with weight loss.

Food types

Nutrients that are considered to be 'healthy food' are those that contain dietary fiber, heart-healthy oils, and low-fat proteins (the latter obtained from fish, poultry, legumes, nuts, and seeds), and not foods that are heavily processed and replete with preservatives, sugar, and sodium. Approximately half of our calories ought to come from carbohydrates through whole-grain foods, fresh fruits, and vegetables. Fruits and veggies provide vitamins and minerals, and supply quick energy in the form of simple carbs, whereas foods that provide fiber, such as whole grains and fresh produce, facilitate digestion and stimulate bowel functioning. As well, low-fat proteins are essential for the creation of strong muscles without necessarily creating cholesterol-building fat.

There's a very long list of foods that are bad for us, such as those that increase low-density lipid proteins (bad cholesterol), particularly trans fats found in fried or fast foods, doughnuts, cookies, and other baked goods. Needless to say, sugar from desserts can have some negative effects, and sugar-sweetened beverages are definitely not needed. Efforts have been made to substitute sugars with artificial sweeteners, but these can also have negative effects. By virtue of their actions on gut microbes, they might actually encourage metabolic syndrome, and thus obesity and diabetes (Suez et al., 2014). Eating the right foods can't guarantee that we'll lead longer lives, but it does reduce the risk of death by illnesses such as chronic heart disease (Fung et al., 2001).

YES, VIRGINIA, THERE IS A SANTA CLAUS, AND BAMBI LIVES IN THE FOREST WITH HER BABIES

Even with the frequent confusion regarding what is good for us and what isn't, the benefits derived from certain foods were broadly accepted. For instance, we were advised to sample from different food groups to be assured of obtaining the minerals and vitamins that would keep us healthy. Moreover, we had been led to believe that the needs of the body ought to be supplemented by vitamins, even in megadoses, especially to deal with colds and other illnesses. A generation of kids were fed their daily dose of multivitamin supplements, and as cannibalistic as it might seem, kids couldn't get enough of chomping down on Barney and Wilma, and parents felt good doing the right thing for their kids.

For individuals with vitamin deficiencies there's little question that vitamin supplements are beneficial, but in the absence of such deficiencies it was less certain whether these vitamin supplements actually had any beneficial effects. Some studies suggested that certain vitamins could diminish the risk for heart problems or the occurrence of some forms of cancer, but others revealed little benefit (Bazzano et al., 2006). Likewise, although it had been believed that multivitamins might have cognitive benefits among older individuals, well-controlled, longitudinal studies concluded that this wasn't the case (e.g., Grodstein et al., 2013). Moreover, multivitamin use wasn't accompanied by a change in mortality risk (Macpherson et al., 2013). With the uncertainty surrounding vitamin supplements, individuals might say "well, vitamins may or may not improve my health, but I'll continue to use them since they couldn't be harmful". Now we're told that older women taking daily diet supplements of iron, copper, magnesium, zinc, or multivitamins are at somewhat increased risk of death (Mursu et al., 2011), daily vitamin E use is accompanied by a 17% greater risk of prostate cancer (Klein et al., 2011), and excessive vitamin A can cause the 'forgetting' of antigens by the immune system, thus allowing infections to occur for which we had previously developed immunity (Rob et al., 2015). These findings are consistent with reports linking intake of large amounts of supplements with increased cancer risk; endometrial cancer was related to excessive use of omega-3 fatty acids, colon cancer was linked to excess folate, lung cancer to beta carotene supplementation, and high doses of selenium to prostate and skin cancer.

EATING-RELATED PROCESSES

As food is a basic need, it might be expected that food selection and engagement in eating would primarily be governed by physiological processes. Yet eating can be provoked even if "we're really not all that hungry". We might have difficulty resisting foods that are visually appealing, or the smell of a charcoal broiled steak (at least among those who are omnivores). As we discussed in Chapter 4, stressors can diminish the tendency to eat among some individuals, but in many others it promotes craving for comfort foods rich in carbs, likely owing to interactions between hormones (ghrelin, leptin) and reward processes in the brain. Having considered these neurobiological mechanisms earlier, we'll now consider the processes by which digestion occurs and how foods come to affect multiple physiological processes.

Digestion

Digestion, which occurs through both mechanical and chemical means, is the process through which food is broken down, permitting its absorption into blood and cells and the formation of energy stores. Mechanical digestion begins when food is chewed and moistened, making subsequent phases of digestion easier. Saliva secreted by the salivary glands is necessary for this process as it contains *amylase* that serves as the initial step in the digestion of starch. The food is then formed into a bolus, a round, soft, moist mass that goes down the esophagus and into the stomach by contraction and relaxation of muscles (*peristalsis*). Upon reaching the stomach, gastric juice containing hydrochloric acid and the powerful enzyme *pepsin* begins the process of protein digestion, which is accompanied by peristalsis within the stomach wall that enhances the mixing of food with digestive enzymes.

After 1–2 hours a thick liquid (*chyme*) is formed, which enters the first section of the small intestine (*duodenum*), where digestive enzymes from the pancreas break down protein, fat, and carbohydrates, and the liver releases *bile* to help break down fats. The resulting mish-mash travels through the small intestine where digestion continues, incorporating bile released from the gall bladder. After the chyme is fully digested, nutrients present are absorbed into the blood as it moves through the small intestine, after which the remainder enters the large intestine where water and minerals are reabsorbed into the blood, and what's left is eliminated by defecation.

Consequences of enzyme or hormone disturbances

Protein, fat, and carbohydrates are digested by somewhat different chemical processes, culminating in different end points in relation to what products are produced. These are all complex processes, and disturbances can occur so that ill feelings come about. For instance, a deficiency of *lactase*, which is responsible for breaking down lactose into glucose and galactose, results in *lactose intolerance*, requiring people to stay off milk and related products. It also appears that if energy-storing lipids (e.g., fats, cholesterol, monoglycerides, diglycerides, triglycerides, phospholipids) are too high, which is referred to as *hyperlipidemia*, the risk for heart-related illnesses and diabetes is increased. Similarly, high good and low bad cholesterol levels have been associated with altered amyloid levels, a protein that contributes to the development of Alzheimer's disease (Reed et al., 2014).

Of the various substances that are fundamental to digestion and energy production, one of the most studied is *insulin*, which we'll discuss more in our discussion of diabetes in Chapter 9. Insulin is produced by beta cells within the pancreas and is fundamental for cells in the liver, muscle, and

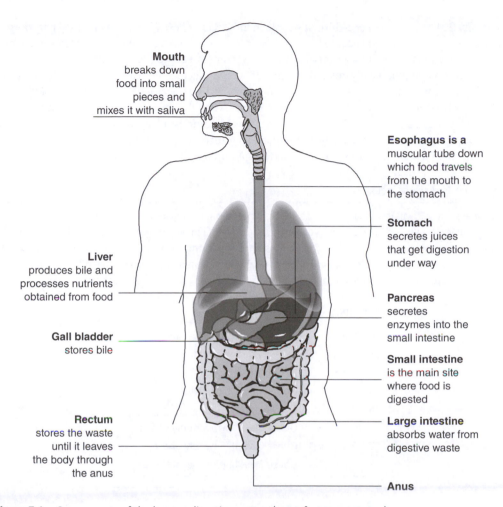

Mouth
breaks down
food into small
pieces and
mixes it with saliva

Esophagus is a
muscular tube down
which food travels
from the mouth to
the stomach

Stomach
secretes juices
that get digestion
under way

Liver
produces bile and
processes nutrients
obtained from food

Pancreas
secretes
enzymes into the
small intestine

Gall bladder
stores bile

Small intestine
is the main site
where food is
digested

Rectum
stores the waste
until it leaves
the body through
the anus

Large intestine
absorbs water from
digestive waste

Anus

Figure 7.1   Components of the human digestive system (www.factmonster.com)

fat tissue to take up *glucose* from the blood and then convert it to *glycogen*, which is stored in the liver and muscles, and it concurrently prevents the utilization of fat as an energy source. However, when insulin is not being produced or is too low, as occurs in diabetes, glucose isn't removed from the blood and the resulting excess of glucose can be toxic to cells, thus necessitating strict diets and medications to control blood sugar levels.

OVERWEIGHT AND OBESITY

The breadth of obesity

The term 'obesity epidemic' has been tossed around so frequently it has become a cliché, but this doesn't make it any less critical. According to the Centers for Disease Control and Prevention (CDC), as of July 2014, more than one-third of people in the US are obese (Ogden et al., 2014), leading to medically-related costs that neared $150 billion in 2008 (and have no doubt increased since then). As the incidence of obesity was very high even in younger people (aged 2–19), there's a reasonable likelihood that medically-related issues will persist. According to a report from the Overseas Development Institute in the UK (Keats & Wiggins, 2014), obesity has increased globally from 23% to 34% over the period 1980 to 2008. To some extent this increase in Western countries has reached a plateau since 2002–2003, but in developing countries it has continued, likely stemming from a combination of factors, especially increasing income, which has allowed individuals the opportunity to consume processed foods and adopt other Western life-styles.

Table 7.1   Body mass index

Body mass index (BMI) is an index of relative weight based on an individual's mass and height. To determine your own body mass index, you can use the formula in which BMI = mass (kg)/(height (m))^2. If you're more comfortable using inches and pounds, then the formula is similar, but involves multiplication by a constant: BMI = mass (lb)/(height (inches))^2 × 703. On the basis of the BMI derived from this measure, people can be classified as being within the normal range, or either over or underweight.

BMI range	Classification
less than 15	Very severely underweight
15.0–16.0	Severely underweight
16.0–18.5	Underweight
18.5–25	Normal (healthy weight)
25–30	Overweight
30–35	Obese Class I (Moderately obese)
35–40	Obese Class II (Severely obese)
> 40	Obese Class III (Very severely obese)

Neurobiological correlates of obesity

Given the involvement of dopamine in reward processes, it is tempting to suggest that in some people altered dopamine functioning might encourage eating and hence obesity. There have also been indications that the brain's opioid system, which also influences reward processes, may be fundamental in producing such an outcome. In this respect, obesity has been accompanied by a reduction of opioid receptors in brain regions associated with reward, and thus increased eating might occur to compensate for reduced pleasure ordinarily obtained (Karlsson et al., 2015).

Aside from actions related to reward processes, over-eating can occur through other mechanisms. For instance, a single mutation on a gene for the neurotrophin brain derived neurotrophic factor (BDNF) results in this growth factor being diminished, resulting in disturbed leptin and insulin signaling, so that messages to stop eating will not be received (Liao et al., 2012) and obesity will ensue. It has become apparent, however, that there are many genes that could contribute to over-eating and obesity. A whole genome analysis identified 97 sites associated with obesity, although the functions of many of these still aren't known. Nonetheless, it appeared that many of these genes in some way contributed to body fat distribution, and could be important for illnesses such as metabolic syndrome, diabetes, and heart disease (Locke et al., 2015; Shungin et al., 2015).

MICROBIOME AND DIGESTION

Our diet can very quickly affect our gut microbiome (David et al., 2014), serving to break down foods and facilitating the absorption of those that are ordinarily indigestible (Cummings & Macfarlane, 1997). Having some of the 'right' bacteria might help keep individuals lean, and many of these bacteria can be strengthened by eating foods that are rich in fiber. When fiber isn't available for microbes to consume, they may die off or, alternatively, they may begin to feed on the mucus lining that serves to maintain the gut wall and keep it healthy. Some foods, such as modest amounts of wine, may increase the presence of *P. pentosaceus* CIAL-86, which has the capability of sticking to the intestinal wall where it fights against bad bacteria (Garcia-Ruiz et al., 2014). In general, however, for individuals who don't have the right assortment of bacteria, staying lean and staying healthy can be a struggle. Thus, gut bacteria have become a target to help individuals deal with obesity. For instance, modified bacteria that express therapeutic factors can be included in the microbiome to either diminish eating or to alter metabolism, thereby lowering food intake, adiposity, and insulin resistance (Z. Chen et al., 2014). Some families of bacteria, such as Christensenellaceae, appear in greater numbers among thin individuals than in people who are heavy, and it seems that these bacteria aren't just correlates of body size, but may causally contribute to this. Specifically, when bacteria associated with slimness were transferred to mice, weight gain was diminished relative to mice that hadn't received this transplantation (Goodrich et al., 2014). In theory, Christensenellaceae could be useful in reducing weight, but we're not at that point yet.

Gut bacteria differ between males and females, with some bacterial species predominating over others, and these may be differentially affected by diet. There is reason to believe that these sex differences may be related to hormonal factors (estrogen, in particular) interacting with gut microbes. It is conceivable that diet in men and women will also have different effects on illnesses related to bacteria, and thus diets meant to treat particular disturbances need to be tailored specifically for men and women (Bolnick et al., 2014).

Obesity and illness

There is considerable evidence pointing to a link between dietary factors, obesity, and the occurrence of diabetes, heart disease, atherosclerosis, and hypertension (Mraz & Haluzik, 2014). Although these disorders have received particular attention, obesity was also associated with an increase of gastrointestinal and esophageal cancers as well as those related to breast, renal, gastrointestinal, and reproductive cancers (Calle et al., 2003; Yang et al., 2009), possibly owing to hormonal, inflammatory, and metabolic changes. In fact, in 2014 the American Society of Clinical Oncology (ASCO) indicated that obesity is among the most unrecognized preventable causes of cancer (Ligibel et al., 2014). The impact of obesity doesn't stop there, as it might be accompanied by difficulties in the delivery and efficacy of chemotherapy in the treatment of some cancers (Lashinger et al., 2014), and has been associated with elevated recurrence of illness as well as increased risk of complications related to surgery and anesthesia. In fact, poor diet and obesity in children may contribute to the premature development of adult diseases (heart disease, hypertension, fatty liver, osteoporosis).

Some people would, no doubt, wish to believe that being overweight might not have the negative consequences of frank obesity. Sadly, being overweight in middle age typically cuts about 3.1 and 3.3 years off the life of males and females, respectively, and is still greater (5.8 and 7.1 years) if males and females are obese (Peeters et al., 2003). As we'll see when we discuss immune-related disorders, heart disease, and diabetes in later chapters, inflammatory factors present in abdominal fat (i.e., the fat around the gut) favors the development of these illnesses, whereas the relation is less pronounced for fat localized at the hips and thighs. Obesity has also been associated with increased recruitment of immune cells into the central nervous system (CNS), potentially contributing to activation of microglia and the provocation of neurologic disorders (Buckman et al., 2014).

I'M OK, BUT THAT OTHER GUY IS DEFINITELY SCREWED

Not every overweight person will be prone to developing pathological conditions related to obesity. In a longitudinal study of more than 43,000 participants, almost half the individuals classified as obese didn't suffer from high blood pressure, insulin resistance, diabetes, low good cholesterol, high bad cholesterol, or high triglycerides. These individuals had a 38% lower risk of early death from any cause relative to obese individuals who had two or more of these markers of poor health (McAuley et al., 2012).

An important meta-analysis of 97 studies that included 2.88 million people indicated that the relationship between weight and obesity was dependent on the extent of the person's obesity. Being overweight or moderately obese (BMI of 25–30 and 30–35, respectively) was not associated with increased mortality. However, mortality rates were appreciably elevated among individuals who were more obese, reflected by a BMI of more than 35 (Flegal et al., 2013). Such findings have fueled the perspective that "I may be overweight, but I'm perfectly healthy", and has even allowed individuals to maintain the poor life-styles that got them to where they are. The rationalization that "obesity doesn't necessarily increase vulnerability in a subset of people" hardly implies that any given person is one of the lucky people who is not negatively affected by being overweight. An informative study that tracked about 2,500 men and women in the UK for 20 years revealed that about one-third of obese people initially were deemed to be healthy based on their blood pressure, fasting blood sugar, cholesterol, and insulin resistance. However, even among these 'healthy obese' people, risk factors eventually developed, so that after 10 years 40% were deemed to be unhealthy obese, and after 20 years more than 50% fell into this category (Bell et al., 2015). So, someone overweight or slightly obese might well be healthy today, but not at some time from today.

Obesity versus healthy eating

When we refer to healthy eating, this means more than just picking the right foods. It entails the establishment of proper eating habits, which, like most habits, involves breaking away from old routines and creating new ones. However, it's neither smart nor realistic to expect changes at the drop of a hat, and some setbacks will be encountered. Thus, we might want to progress in baby steps, changing one thing at a time, such as substituting a tasty but unhealthy food with a more healthy, good-looking salad, and to make sure the portions are sized for a typical person. It's not necessary to ban the yummy good foods entirely, but if a person does indulge, then feeling guilty and distressed over this can drive them to further eating of taboo foods. They should also be aware that the neuronal message to stop eating takes some time to get from the stomach, to the intestine, to the bloodstream, and then to the brain. So, they ought to eat slowly, chew food well, and stop eating before they are full, thus allowing the 'stop eating' message to register in their brain. Snacks during the day are also a good idea to limit sugar spikes and will likely prevent subsequent gorging.

A DIFFERENT TYPE OF EATING DISORDER

Some people, having obtained relief from minor ailments (e.g., heartburn or serious problems of digestive processes) by altering their diet, become very dedicated to eating healthily. Sometimes, they go a bit over the top, adopting every new fad – gluten free, lactose free, wheat free, and frequent cleansings, to the extent that they may become ill and malnourished. This syndrome, referred to as 'orthorexia' (Koven & Abry, 2015), which has yet to be included in the DSM, not only includes an obsessiveness regarding healthy foods, but also intolerance towards the views of others in this regard. Whether this is a genuine eating disorder or an obsession isn't certain, but it's highly likely that these people don't make for good dinner companions.

Roadblocks to eating properly and maintaining healthy food habits

Difficulties in obtaining accurate information

Most of us get a fair bit of information concerning healthy and unhealthy foods from the media (including internet sources), but unfortunately the information is often confusing and contradictory and opinions seem to change much too often. In fact, there's a fairly good chance that the information being obtained is biased in one direction or another or is simply not based on scientifically reliable sources. Aside from obtaining information from these unreliable sources, people might choose to base their behaviors on what their friends tell them, and they too might have received their information from unreliable sources.

The amount of information available pertinent to diets and the right foods to eat is overwhelming. Discussions of complex topics, such as how different foods might affect biological processes related to health, are everywhere. Some information is useful, but in other instances it is transparently incorrect, but pushed dogmatically with hardly a shred of scientific data to back the claims. On occasion there may be references to a scientific paper, published in some obscure journal that has little credibility. Unfortunately, the confusion concerning which foods are best for us is perpetuated because nutrition scientists keep altering their opinions, thus creating doubts regarding recommendations offered by professionals (Nagler, 2014).

HARD TO BELIEVE ANYTHING WE READ

An opinion piece in the *British Medical Journal* presented intriguing observations concerning the influence of diet on health that likely will not be well received by some diet gurus (Smith, 2014). In fact, it was suggested that ". . . bold policies have been based on fragile science, and the long-term results may be terrible". Among other things, the point is made that disease processes (e.g., in relation to heart disease and cancer) are the culmination of genetic factors and poor health behaviors that occurred over many years, and thus analyses based on eating behaviors measured over relatively short periods are not only exceedingly difficult to make sense of, but the conclusions drawn are inaccurate. Besides, most people don't stick to one diet regimen, changing the eating patterns over time, making it difficult to attribute health outcomes to any particular foods.

It has been pointed out (e.g., Ioannidis, 2013) that studies of nutritional intake, determined by questionnaires, yielded results in which participants reported caloric intake that seemed to be "incompatible with life", and thus there ought to be discomfort about the reliability of such findings. The point was also made that virtually any food product one can think of has been evaluated in regard to their link to potential illness development, and a search of the literature indicates that almost every possible outcome has been reported. In their critique of the issue, Schoenfeld and Ioannidis (2013) indicated that some published reports have even made outlandish claims that small amounts of particular nutrients will diminish the occurrence of cancer. Pulling no punches, they also suggested that "implausible results that are 'too good to be true' still threaten nutritional research on many fronts, including survey measurements, observational associations, treatment effects in randomized trials, and estimates of the impact on populations" (Ioannidis, 2013; Schoenfeld & Ioannidis, 2013). Not to be entirely negative, Ioannidis (2013) indicated that randomized trials that involve a relatively large number of participants, typically assessing broader diets, have been encouraging, but these studies need to concurrently consider other variables, such as psychosocial and socioeconomic factors.

We've heard repeatedly that foods high in saturated fats are bad for heart functioning, and that benefits could be obtained by replacing these with polyunsaturated fats (PUFAs) (Schwab et al., 2014). However, others have indicated that there aren't any benefits obtained from PUFAs (Chowdhury et al., 2014). Just about everyone agrees that trans fats (artificially produced unsaturated fats) and foods that are converted into high glucose (i.e., those having a high glycemic index), should be replaced by protective foods, such as vegetables and a Mediterranean diet (Mente et al., 2009). This said, in a persuasive book, Teicholz (2014) comes down on the side of those suggesting that there are actually benefits to consuming fats. She makes important points, including that there is flimsy science being conducted, sometimes funded by groups with vested interests (e.g., large food companies), raising suspicions about biases in the data. She also makes the valuable point that in many studies benefits may be gained with respect to heart disease by reducing fat, but this doesn't necessarily translate to all-cause mortality. So, although reducing fats can enhance heart health, there may be a cost in terms of other illnesses emerging.

A comprehensive report on food-related issues, amounting to 571 pages (and hence too long for most of us to digest), was recently released. The Scientific Report of the 2015 Dietary Guidelines Advisory Committee (2015) has much to offer. It outlines the links between diet and numerous chronic illnesses, helpful life-style interventions, and considers other life-style behaviours that influence well-being. It also informs health promotion and disease prevention strategies at both the individual and population levels.

Dealing with temptation

Several factors favor poor eating habits being maintained, and it's obviously important to determine whether anything can be done to overcome them. The obvious first issue is that the sight and aroma of some foods act as reminders that promote craving among dieters, much like certain cues will cause cravings in a drug addict. To be sure, salads can be made to look nice, and those that are colorful and contain all sorts of different ingredients can be enticing, and some people will prefer these over heavy rich deserts. For so many others, however, a healthy salad simply doesn't evoke the same emotional responses or cravings as those elicited by decadent foods. In fact, among some the presentation of yummy foods in commercials may instigate neuronal activation within brain regions associated with feelings of reward, and in adolescents who exhibited such a response, their BMI increased over a 1-year period (Yokum et al., 2014). As we'll see, there is some overlap in the biological processes associated with food and drug cravings, and too often our brain control mechanisms abdicate their responsibility. As Oscar Wilde put it, "*I can resist everything except temptation*".

Developing preferences

Why do we like particular foods as much as we do? In the case of sweets, it's possible that our preference is hard-wired from birth. It may be a biologically significant preference, as these foods provide a rapid source of energy, and may be important in physical development. As well, because sugars can act as pain relievers in children (Pepino & Mennella, 2005), the evolution of this trait might have been favored by natural selection. While not denying the importance of innate genetic factors in determining the preference for sweet and salty tastes, as well as the rejection of both sour and bitter tastes, we also learn to prefer particular foods and not others based on positive and negative experiences and contexts associated with these tastes. Thus, the adoption of healthy diets will depend on the availability of particular foods, child-feeding practices endorsed (Birch, 1999), the ease of obtaining energy-dense foods rich in sugar, fat, and salt, as well as advertisements that promote these food choices.

TRAINING A SMARTER FOOD BRAIN

We may be born with the potential to prefer certain foods over others, but considerable training may also have gone into reinforcing certain preferences. Eventually, certain food choices, or eating carb-rich foods in response to stressors, become a 'habit'. In fact, these habits might be responsible for driving the cravings (or mindless eating that doesn't involve craving) for particular foods. Our food choices may also be determined by experiences. Those born in the mid-1900s or before can tell you that whole milk was the norm, and their first taste of 2% milk elicited a "yech" response, much as you might now respond to a glass of skim milk. Over time and with experiences, individuals adapted to 2% milk, and then 1%, and for most people whole milk is now distasteful, seeming too thick and sticky.

To an extent, drug and gambling addictions share features with 'eating addictions', including activation of the neuronal processes that govern the positive compulsive behavioral responses elicited by contextual cues (Hebebrand et al., 2014). As in the case of drug addictions, the selection of unhealthy but good-tasting foods may promote certain neural connections related to rewarding feelings becoming progressively strengthened with repeated experiences. In this regard, among obese children, swirling sugar around in their mouth caused particular brain regions to become active to a greater extent than in non-obese children. How this heightened response came about isn't certain, but it might nevertheless contribute to obesity being carried into adulthood (Boutelle et al., 2015). On the positive side, these connections can be undone. Among overweight individuals in whom tasty foods elicited neuronal changes in brain regions that regulate reward processes, 6 months in a weight loss program resulted in previously non-preferred foods eliciting such responses, whereas tasty, unhealthy foods were accompanied by diminished neuronal responses (Deckersbach et al., 2014). What is particularly important is that this program didn't simply aim at having individuals go on a diet, but rather focused on changing their preferences, which might make all the difference in a diet program.

Social influences

A further hurdle that needs to be dealt with in relation to poor eating, or conversely to promote healthy eating, consists of what our friends do in this regard. We've seen how powerful social identity can be in determining our behaviors, and if our friends eat poorly, then we might do so too, much as if it were a social contagion (Christakis & Fowler, 2013). Likewise, if our ingroup values certain behavioral or physical characteristics, then we might follow suit and our behaviors will be governed accordingly. Hang with the wrong people at your own peril.

TREATING UNHEALTHY FOODS AS THEY SHOULD BE

As obesity has grown to the extent that it has, very strong efforts may be needed to curb this problem. In an editorial in the *Canadian Medical Association Journal*, Fletcher and Patrick (2014) indicated that although health services and clinical intervention strategies need to target individuals, this isn't enough. Individual and group behavior ought to be addressed and modified through community-based interventions, and public policies need to be established that influence social and environmental factors that affect obesity. At the moment the voices of food manufacturers and packagers encourage us to eat more and with less hesitation, but there's hardly a sound in opposition. Going a step beyond suggestions provided by the Public Health Agency of Canada, Fletcher and Patrick recommended the establishment of mandates (by government institutions) to reduce the sale of high-calorie beverages and to limit portion sizes, and that this could be done through regulation and taxation, much in the same way that governments regulate cigarette and alcohol sales. In real-world situations, individuals who are obese are, in fact, required to pay a higher premium for health insurance, and their dislike for this, no matter the reason, seems to have little bearing on the costs.

In getting people to change their behaviors, one approach is to provide incentives for weight loss, whereas a second is to apply punishments for misbehavior. When participants were placed in a situation where they could receive a lower health insurance rate if they were of the right weight versus a higher rate when they were overweight, they understandably preferred the former approach ('carrot') rather than the latter ('stick'). But, it wasn't the money that counted most in their choice. Instead the punitive approach was a turn-off, although participants who expressed a dislike for overweight people were oddly content to apply the stick plan for their heftier associates (Tannenbaum et al., 2013).

Diet and exercise

There's no question that dieting is not sufficient to promote lasting weight loss. Instead, multiple life-style changes are needed, which includes the adoption of an exercise program. Indeed, a 30-year prospective study showed that certain life-style factors, including exercise and healthy eating, were associated with reduced occurrence of diabetes, vascular disease, dementia, and all-cause mortality (Elwood et al., 2013). Unfortunately, once individuals become obese, they may find it more difficult to exercise, and they might be embarrassed to do so in public venues, thereby limiting their ability to lose the weight. Moreover, for the person who is just a bit overweight, a decline of 5 or 10 pounds is very noticeable and they are rewarded by seeing the difference when they put on a pair of pants that had previously been tight, and thus they might continue their exercise regimen; whereas for the obese person, a similar weight loss might hardly be noticeable (what psychophysiologists call a JND or 'just noticeable difference'), and the reward for effort will be harder to come by, thus making it difficult to sustain the motivation to exercise.

Stressor-related eating

Stressful experiences, as discussed earlier, can promote eating in a subset of individuals, and has been reported frequently among adolescents. As we've seen, individuals appraise and respond to stressors differently, and there are some types of stressor (e.g., moderate intensity) that are closely aligned with increased eating. Among adolescents, family conflict and disruption, together with financial concerns, are related to obesity in females, whereas risky maternal behaviors have been linked to greater weight in males (Hernandez & Pressler, 2015).

Stress and ghrelin

A hurdle for those wishing to reduce their weight concerns their reaction to stressful events. Although severe stressors will typically reduce eating, some people will increase their propensity to eat when stressed, self-medicating to diminish their sorrow through ice cream, potato chips, cookies, chocolate, or any of a number of other 'quick fixes'. As indicated in Chapter 5, stress and eating are entwined so that activation of stress systems will suppress those associated with feeding and, predictably, anxiety-reducing pharmacological treatments, such as benzodiazepines, increase food consumption (e.g., Merali et al., 2006). As a matter of fact, neurochemical stress responses, particularly dopamine and CRH, have also been implicated in food intake and drug abuse, and hormones such as leptin and ghrelin, which are best known for their actions on eating processes, have marked effects on stress responses (Patterson et al., 2013).

Not everyone responds identically with respect to ghrelin, which seems to vary as a function of whether or not individuals were the type who tended to eat when highly emotional. When these so-called 'emotional eaters' were subjected to a stressor, the endocrine message of "go ahead and eat" was activated, but it didn't turn off readily when it should have (Raspopow et al., 2010). As it happens, ghrelin also stimulates dopamine functioning in brain regions associated with reward processes (Abizaid et al., 2006), thus when emotional eaters indulged themselves in tasty foods in the face of stressors, the positive effects obtained may have been potentiated, possibly causing eating to increase when similar situations were subsequently encountered.

ADULT OBESITY STEMMING FROM EARLY-LIFE TRAUMA

Negative early-life experiences have been associated with several pathologies that appear during adulthood, and can have a powerful effect on the development of obesity (Hemmingsson et al., 2014). On average, negative early-life experiences were accompanied by a 34% increase of adult obesity, and a 50% increase of obesity was associated with severe abuse. It was suggested that early-life stressors might give rise to negative thoughts and emotions, poor mental health, and neuroendocrine changes that feed into appetite regulation, metabolism, as well as disturbed cognitive functioning and sleep, all of which encourage the development of obesity. As such, we might need to think of obesity in a broader sense and multiple approaches, including counselling, might be needed to diminish its presence.

Stress, stigma and eating

Individuals who are overweight might find it difficult to break the stress-eating cycle owing to the considerable stigma related to their weight, often beginning when they were young and following them throughout life. The stigma doesn't just come in the form of snide comments, but also in the form of unsupportive or insensitive comments from friends ("you don't really need that piece of cake" or "the best exercise is pushing away from the table") or being bullied, first in the schoolyard and later at the workplace. These experiences are obviously stressful, and for emotional eaters they may aggravate eating problems. This double whammy can be still more pronounced as a large number of overweight individuals are also at increased risk for depressive illness, and in all likelihood this will take the form of atypical depression characterized by reverse neurovegetative symptoms, such as increased eating.

Set point and famine preparedness

It's not unusual for individuals to go onto a diet in an effort to shed weight, successfully lose a few kilos, only to fall back into poor eating patterns, followed again by a stint of dieting. Each of us has a 'set point' so that when we fall below a particular weight our body adjusts by altering metabolic processes in an effort to increase weight, and concurrently it prompts us to increase eating. But let's take a closer look at what occurs when a diet is adopted. When dieters start to lose weight, their metabolic rate is slowed, likely in order to sustain energy (body cells, after all, don't realize that the person was intentionally dieting and respond as if there was a famine). This 'famine mode' may continue, however, even after normal eating has been reinstated, and consequently calories won't be burned off as quickly, resulting in a rapid weight gain even in the absence of over-eating. In fact, even skipping meals may be sufficient to instigate metabolic changes that cause increased inflammatory changes and storage of fat (Kliewer et al., 2015).

These metabolic problems become accentuated with repeated efforts to diet, making it progressively more difficult to maintain weight loss. In fact, individuals may gain more weight than had been lost initially, making it questionable whether dieting is the right solution (Mann et al., 2007). This view was reinforced by reports that genetic polymorphisms exist that promote eating, but they might only be unmasked when individuals go on a diet (Aberle et al., 2008). Despite the clearly negative effects of yo-yo dieting, intermittent days of fasting, consisting of eating 25% of their usual calorie intake, could elicit changes of gene expression that have been associated with longevity, possibly because intermittent fasting activates reparatory processes (Wegman et al., 2015). Alternatively, fasting, as well as caloric restriction, can influence inflammatory processes, and hence several diseases otherwise provoked by elevated inflammation might be precluded (Youm et al., 2015).

MAKING CHANGES

Various factors might encourage people to adopt a diet. For some, it might be to feel and look better in their own eyes and likely in the eyes of others, or they might have come to realize that their continued poor eating habits might be a health risk, especially if a family history exists for particular illnesses, such as diabetes or heart disease. Regardless of the reason, the motivation to change is essential for success, coupled with a person's self-efficacy in resisting eating when yummy, unhealthy foods are available (Shin et al., 2011).

Diet programs to lose weight

By far, the most common way of losing weight has come through dieting, and the many programs available each promise to be better than the others. Some programs focus exclusively on dieting, or a combination of exercise and dieting, whereas others focus on changing life-styles in a very broad way (including lessons on how to cook nutritious and good-tasting meals). Better programs will capitalize on some of the issues we've already discussed to provide favorable outcomes for their clientele, but diet programs could be especially effective if they allow, and even foster, group activities. As we've seen repeatedly, social support is important to reach certain goals, and having individuals work in pairs or in groups is in line with this, especially as this may result in people maintaining their diet. Reporting back to fellow dieters on achievements in losing weight, and receiving their applause, also goes a long way in maintaining diets, and is fundamental in having individuals stick with the program.

SO, WHICH DIET SHOULD I USE?

Most of the branded diets (i.e., those that are trade-marked) focus on reducing carbs (Atkins, South Beach, Zone), fat consumption (Ornish, Rosemary Conley), or moderation of macronutrients (Biggest Loser, Jenny Craig, Nutrisystem, Volumetrics, Weight Watchers). It's often difficult for individuals to choose the diet that is best but, as it turns out, for obese individuals each of the diets were effective after controlling for exercise and social support received (Johnston et al., 2014). After 6 months and 12 months, each of the diets led to marked weight reductions, which was consistent with reports from the American Heart Association, the American College of Cardiology, and the Obesity Society (Jensen et al., 2014; Ryan & Kushner, 2010). The important element in attaining weight loss was that individuals adhered to the diet, regardless of which was selected. However, the problem with diets is that cravings and culturally-relevant issues (that involve the use of particular foods) limit adherence, and it is thus up to participants to evaluate which diet will be the least challenging for them given their own predilections.

Most studies that assessed the influence of diets considered weight change over relatively narrow time frames. As it turns out, within 1 year, two-thirds of people will regain the weight they had lost previously, and about 95% will regain their weight within 5 years, and sometimes the weight gain exceeds the initial weight loss. One would hope that combining diet with exercise would attenuate the weight regain, but this doesn't seem to be the case (Dulloo & Montani, 2015). If one considers over-eating in a manner like that in which we consider addictions, it will be realized that there aren't magic elixirs that will solve the problem. Instead, multiple and pronounced life-style changes and social support processes are needed to limit weight regain, and individuals may need 'booster shots' in the form of reentering the diet program periodically before appreciable weight loss is sustained.

Therapeutic approaches for weight reduction

Losing weight is half the battle. Keeping the weight off for sustained periods is the other half (the much bigger half). Many programs were developed to change eating habits and to promote weight change, often being effective in reducing weight and modifying life-style in the short run, and some have even been successful in having individuals maintain their altered life-style and reduced weight for years. Several approaches were based on the stages of change model, cognitive behavioral therapy (CBT), and interpersonal therapy, and weight loss could be influenced by altering cognitive appraisals and stress responses (Van Dorsten & Lindley, 2011). Likewise mindfulness meditation has been used in the treatment of binge eating and emotional eating, although mixed findings were observed (Katterman et al., 2014). The fact that these approaches diminish distress is clearly important given that stressful life events may contribute to eating, and also because dieting and related programs can be stressful themselves.

Enhancing behavioral change approaches to promote weight loss

As we saw in Chapter 6, several procedures have been advanced to promote behavior change, but there are elements that are especially noteworthy in relation to weight loss efforts. Specifically, it has been suggested that weight loss programs start with 'motivational interviewing', which allows an analysis of the individual's past failures to lose weight, their current motivation, as well as features that are important for success, such as 'perceived autonomy' (Teixeira et al., 2012). Likewise, it may be helpful to have individuals keep track of what they eat and under what conditions they do so, as well as appraise what they actually ate relative to what they thought they had eaten. Too often, individuals seem to be unaware of their mindless eating and may even have the mindset that amounts to "if I eat off somebody else's plate, then the calories belong to them, not me".

In promoting behavior change, individuals are asked to change the foods that surround them, buying healthy foods for home and making them easily accessible, and simultaneously ridding themselves of high-fat, high-calorie foods. Coupled with this is training to eat at only one place, preferably under a specific set of conditions, and thus grazing and thoughtless snacking will be less likely to occur. They are also trained so that their response to stressors moves away from eating and toward better ways of coping. As well, attitudes toward food, and about the ability to lose weight are altered. Self-efficacy regarding the potential for weight loss is encouraged (I can do this successfully) as is satisfaction with what has been achieved at various steps. As a result, intrinsic motivation will be enhanced and the rewards for successes will promote further change (Warziski et al., 2008), including the incorporation of exercise in weight loss routines. To be sure, not every method uses each of these components, and will vary in relation to who is guiding the treatment.

The potential benefits of these approaches notwithstanding, some procedures, such as CBT, are time-consuming and only a modest number of individuals can effectively be treated in this way. With weight-related issues being problematic for so many people, approaches based on relatively intensive procedures might prove to be inadequate, and there is a need for the development of community-based approaches to increase healthy life-styles (Van Dorsten & Lindley, 2011).

Having social support

To deal with the many psychological obstacles to diminishing bad habits, support from friends and family is important, especially as they can serve as active helpers and coaches. Indeed, when family members engage in a program to change, the chances of success improves for both adults and children (Epstein et al., 2013). For that matter, when meals were eaten as a family, downstream coping methods were enhanced, thereby limiting eating disorders and other unhealthy behaviors (e.g., eating disorders, smoking) (Franko et al., 2008). The efficacy of group-related factors is not restricted to the family unit, and the promotion of healthy *community life-styles* has been linked to higher quality of diets and diminished BMI (Pitts et al., 2015).

THE BROWNING OF WHITE FAT

Fat comes in two forms, white fat and brown fat. Brown fat is easily burned energy and thus, in theory, we should be able to lose this form of fat readily, thereby reducing weight. As babies we have loads of brown fat, but as we mature, this changes so that white fat is abundant, whereas brown fat is hardly present. In 1985 an earthquake hit Mexico City that left more than 10,000 people dead, but there were also some surprising survivors. Among them was a group of infants who had been trapped in the rubble, but who nevertheless survived for days. These infants, "niños del sismo", or the "children of the earthquake", as they're known (they're also referred to as "miracle babies of Mexico City"), might have survived as a result of a miracle, or it might have resulted from their high levels of brown fat providing a source of energy despite the absence of food.

As adults, when our fat is primarily of the white rather than the easily burned brown variety, it's relatively difficult to lose weight. As it happens, obesity has also been associated with increased levels of peripheral serotonin (which is separate from the serotonin found in the brain), possibly because it inhibits brown fat activity. As Western diets promote serotonin availability, particularly as we age, obesity can be exacerbated. Help may eventually arrive in combatting obesity by altering serotonin and hence brown fat functioning. Indeed, mice genetically engineered to be deficient in an enzyme that forms serotonin (tryptophan hydroxylase 1) were protected from obesity even when fed a high-fat diet, and they were also less likely to develop insulin resistance owing to greater energy expenditure and by burning sugar present in brown fat (Crane et al., 2015). Yet another approach has involved the development of methods to coax fat stem cells, which would normally turn into white fat, to become brown fat cells (Moisan et al., 2015).

Some hypothalamic neurons that are involved in eating processes also seem to be involved in converting white fat to brown fat. The attachment of a sugar molecule (O-GlcNAc) to neurons of the hypothalamus that are associated with hunger can influence this, and can even prevent obesity in mice who are maintained on a high-fat diet (Ruan et al., 2014). Eventually, approaches might be developed to increase the 'browning of white fat', but this itself won't be a replacement for exercise to lose weight, given that exercise has many other functions.

Starting at a young age

Childhood and adolescent obesity have sky-rocketed, with fully one-third of children in the US being overweight (Ogden et al., 2014), and the numbers in Canada and the UK are on a par with these. Poor eating and obesity among school-aged children are frequently carried into adulthood and can lead to significant health problems, such as heart disease, type 2 diabetes, stroke, several types of cancer, and osteoarthritis (e.g., Daniels et al., 2005; Freedman et al., 2007), likely made worse by having to face considerable stigma and bullying. In fact, signs of impending heart disease, such as elevated blood pressure and lipid levels, can be detected in overweight adolescents (Sinha et al., 2002), and being overweight during childhood is predictive of heart disease or stroke in adulthood (Baker et al., 2007). As well, excessive eating can lead to a nonalcoholic steatohepatitis (NASH), a liver condition that occurs owing to excessive fat in the liver, which in about 30% of cases leads to liver failure, liver cancer, and death. Indeed, NASH is currently the second most common reason for liver transplants. In view of the many problems that can occur, strong efforts have thus been made to prevent childhood obesity and it has been recommended that school curricula ought to encourage the development of healthy eating, physical activity, and body image. Moreover, the nutritional quality of food provided in schools ought to be improved, and creating environments and cultural practices that favor the development of healthier food choices should be encouraged (Waters et al., 2011).

Meds to curb eating

Many pharmacological treatments have been advanced in an effort to promote weight reduction. Amphetamines were an early favorite, but they had side effects and addiction potential that resulted in their abandonment. During the same period fenfluramine, which promotes serotonin release, was marketed as a weight-reducing agent, but it had only short-lasting weight-reducing effects. It was subsequently combined with another weight-reducing agent, phentermine, but the combined compound fenfluramine/phentermine, which was referred to by the cutesy name of fen-phen, caused vitral valve dysfunction and pulmonary hypertension (Connolly et al., 1997).

More recently, lorcaserin (Belviq), which also acts on the serotonergic system, serving as a 5-HT_{2C} receptor agonist, received approval as an anti-obesity agent. It is effective in reducing weight by 5–10% in a great number of people, although some were unaffected by the treatment. For the moment it hasn't been found to have the negative ramifications of its precursors, and, as it happens, it may also have potent effects in reducing some forms of addiction (Higgins et al., 2013). Yet another strategy to reduce eating has been to fool the body into mistakenly thinking it had already eaten (although it may be more difficult to fool the brain). In this instance, the drug fexaramine causes the release of bile acids into the intestine after people have eaten. Although bile is primarily involved in digestion, it causes cessation of eating, lowering of blood sugar and cholesterol, and increase of brown fat (Fang et al., 2015). It's too soon to know whether the drug will make it to market, but the findings using this approach make it clear that there may be multiple routes to get to a given point.

. . . . AND I'LL HAVE A DIET SODA WITH THAT

You've probably seen, as have I, a substantially obese person carrying a tray with two hamburgers, fries, maybe a slice of pie or a muffin, and a diet soda. The impression left is that because they're having a diet drink they feel free to indulge in a substitute for the few missing calories. There's little

(Continued)

(Continued)

question that sugary drinks are unhealthy, being a leading factor in the development of diabetes. In fact, even one can of sugary drink a day increases diabetes risk by 20%. It turns out, however, that diet drinks may also have some negative effects (other than on food choices) and long-term use of diet drinks can have bad effects on belly size for other reasons. Among older individuals, diet soda consumption was linked to increased waist size, with the more consumed the greater the belly bulge, to the extent that heavy users gained about 3 inches on their waist (Fowler et al., 2015). Consumption of diet soda on a regular basis was also accompanied by increased occurrence of type 2 diabetes (Sakurai et al., 2014), although it is possible that such effects might be related to health status, weight, or weight changes before enrolment in the study (De Koning et al., 2011).

It is believed that the effects of diet sodas weren't simply due to changes in other food habits. In humans gut bacteria were altered by artificial sweeteners (Suez et al., 2014) and studies in mice confirmed that artificial sweeteners increased their propensity to develop glucose intolerance, whereas this wasn't apparent if mice had their water laced with sugar. However, if particular bacteria in the gut were killed off, then glucose intolerance was prevented, pointing to gut bacteria as being the culprit for the diabetic actions of diet drinks. It is probably still premature to make definitive conclusions regarding the processes linking diet soda, weight increases, and diabetes, and whether particular gut bacteria play a role in mediating these relations.

Bariatric surgery

For extreme obesity, bariatric surgery has been Plan B when other methods didn't lead to significant weight loss. This surgery comes in different forms, such as reducing the size of the stomach using a *gastric band* (placing an inflatable silicone band around the top portion of the stomach), or through removal of a portion of the stomach (*sleeve gastrectomy*), or by resecting and re-routing the small intestines to a small stomach pouch (*gastric bypass surgery*). There are several variants of the procedures, as well as combination techniques. These procedures promote significant weight loss, which diminish heart problems, diabetes and mortality, and reduced depression associated with obesity, but the latter action is typically only transient (Booth et al., 2015). Each approach is effective, but there has been a shift toward sleeve gastrectomy owing to the relative effectiveness and safety of the procedure, which can be performed *laparoscopically* (Freitas & Sweeney, 2010). Regardless of the approach, surgical complications can occur, ranging from leaks, '*dumping syndrome*' that comprises bloating or post-meal diarrhea, as well as infection.

HEALTH FOODS AND THE EXPANSION OF NEUTRACEUTICALS

There are certain topics that garner lots of opinions, even from those who know very little. Some topics seem not to be especially touchy, at least on the surface, but nevertheless elicit considerable disagreement. One of these concerns the issue of whether natural products, such as those found at health food stores, are better for our health than manufactured products. There's no question that many of our effective medicines come from naturally occurring plants or other substances. Penicillin came to us, thanks to Alexander Fleming, who determined that the Penicillium mould secreted an antibacterial substance. Aloe vera is used for the treatment of burns, *Taxol* initially derived from the bark of the Pacific yew tree is used in the treatment of various estrogen-related solid tumors, opium from the opium poppy is a powerful pain reducing agent, *digitalis* obtained from several types of plants is used as a heart stimulant, and aspirin in the form of *salicylic acid* derived from willow and myrtle plants has been used as an anti-inflammatory and pain suppressant for millennia. In recent years the hallucinogenic agent *psilocybin*, which is obtained from 'magic' mushrooms, has been used to quiet negative emotions, and it is being assessed in the treatment of several psychological disorders, such as OCD, cluster headaches, depression, and anxiety, and it has been used to help bring new perspectives to people with terminal cancer.

There is a strange notion that if it grows on trees or bushes, or comes directly from the ground, it must be good for us, never mind that plants often have some nasty chemical means of protecting themselves from herbivorous animals that can also affect humans. As well, although strychnine and digitalis in very low doses can have positive effects for some conditions, these plant-derived agents can be lethal at somewhat higher doses. Furthermore, coumarin, ephedra, and calamus oil are natural products that have been banned for health reasons and, while sugars and salt are natural too, we know full well that in excess they can have bad effects on our health. There are mushrooms that are poisonous, and poison hemlock, poison ivy, poison oak, and poison sumac haven't been named as they have for no reason. Risk of bleeding can be elicited by ginko, and individuals with diabetes should not be taking Asian ginseng, and there is a list of substances that should not be used by people undergoing chemotherapy or those with cardiac problems. Ask anyone with allergies to pollen or ragweed what they think of the notion of plant derivatives being universally positive. Some people who swear by varied natural food supplements are also adherents of other seemingly natural ways of obtaining good health, and we can only hope that the fad for colon cleansing, a very dangerous practice that causes bloating, nausea, electrolyte imbalances and possible kidney failure, is at its end.

Over the past decades the spread of herbal medicines to treat all manner of illness has been remarkable (Eisenberg et al., 1998). Echinacea has been used to treat the common cold for ages, even though limited data have supported this claim. In fact, a meta-analysis of 24 randomized control trials concluded that Echinacea effects varied widely across studies, and at best reduced the risk of catching a cold by 10–20% (Karsch-Völk et al., 2014). Ginseng root was reported to have multiple positive effects, including being an aphrodisiac and cure for sexual dysfunction in men, as well as in the treatment of type 2 diabetes (beats me how those two go together). Black tea has likewise been touted as a treatment for diabetes, and green tea was said to limit the progression of chronic lymphatic leukemia (and other cancers), and the severity of atherosclerosis, diabetes, and liver disease. Other plants or plant extracts are praised for antibiotic and anti-inflammatory actions and their ability to reduce stress-related heart problems, attenuate the intestinal side effects of chemotherapy, diminish the course of Alzheimer's disease, diminish the risk of dying of cancer or heart disease, and making you smarter. Incidentally, if you had actually believed that these foods and supplements would make you smarter, and you're still consuming them, then we can probably conclude that they haven't been working for you.

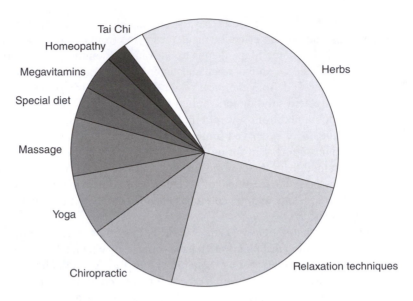

Figure 7.2   Types of complementary and alternative medicine used by US consumers

Source: Tachjian et al., 2010. Use of Herbal Products and Potential Interactions in Patients With Cardiovascular Diseases. J Am Coll Cardiol. 2010 Feb 9; 55(6): 515–525. Data from Tindle HA, Davis RB, Phillips RS, Eisenberg DM. Trends in use of complementary and alternative medicine by US adults: 1997–2002. Altern Ther Health Med. 2005

The standard natural remedies, such as fish oil tablets, ginko biloba, St John's wort, and ginseng, are still being used, but appear to have passed their 'best before date' and have been replaced by herbals of newer sorts. We can expect many more new natural products to appear on the shelves of health food stores, large supermarkets, as well as apothecaries, simply because they aren't being marketed as drugs, and thus haven't had to go through the rigorous, expensive, and time-consuming processes required before a drug can enter the market. You'd think that these compounds would have to meet the tests that other medicines do before they are taken seriously (Firenzuoli & Gori, 2007), or at least demonstrate that they have effects beyond that of a placebo. Not only don't these requirements apply, adequate information isn't typically provided regarding when these natural products should be used, at what doses, and whether there are contraindications that should be considered (e.g., might the compound be dangerous for some people, such as those taking particular medications?). There are also issues that need to be addressed pertaining to the purity, quality, chemical stability, and active constituents of the product (Ernst, 2002), given that quality control related to health is typically absent.

As a result of the lax policies regarding herbal remedies relative to drug treatments, a wide range of supplements have been offered that have little or no genuine value. For that matter, in some countries, such as the UK, information is absent concerning the safe use for more than 90% of products even though some carry considerable risk (e.g., Raynor et al., 2011). Worse still, many natural supplements have little medicinal value in them (frequently being nothing more that some rice or wheat-like substance). There have also been reports of weight loss products and sports supplements being laced with stimulants (e.g., DMBA) so that those taking the treatment will believe that it's actually doing something for them (rather than 'to them'). Some of these compounds, despite being promoted by guys with titles (e.g., Dr) before their names, can cause heart problems, disorders of the nervous system, and even death.

In some instances rigorous trials have been undertaken to evaluate herbal products, but firm conclusions regarding their efficacy haven't always been possible. Although St John's wort (Hypericum perforatum) was purportedly effective in treating mild or moderate depression and had fewer side effects than SSRIs, a systematic review indicated that this herbal medication has minimal positive effects in large trials, while in some smaller trials effects have been detected (Linde et al., 2005). More damaging still are studies sponsored by the National Center for Complementary and Alternative Medicine (NCCAM) that indicated that this substance was no better than a placebo in treating depressive disorders (Hypericum Depression Trial Study Group, 2002). Despite the obvious problems associated with the use of these alternative treatments, it's probably premature to discard them entirely. But, their acceptance ought to be predicated on hard data being collected using legitimate scientific methods, free from biases and other flaws in experimental procedures. There is a middle ground between standard and alternative medicines in the form of '*integrative medicine*', which reflects the confluence of evidence-based medicine and alternative approaches. What it really amounts to is that if standard medication hasn't been effective in diminishing symptoms, then seeking an alternative or a combination treatment would be appropriate.

VOODOO SCIENCE

It's more than a bit curious that despite the lack of data, and many studies that don't meet appropriate scientific standards (Li et al., 2014), people frequently turn to alternative medicines, including Traditional Chinese Medicine (TCM). This might stem from a lack of confidence or trust in standard medicines, especially when the cause and cure for illnesses are uncertain. For that matter, among some people there is the inherent belief that TCM products actually get to the root of problems rather than simply masking symptoms of illness.

Several reviews have suggested that TCM treatments, alone or in combination with traditional therapies, can be effective in dealing with many psychological, neurological, and cardiac illnesses, such as depression, Parkinson's disease and heart failure (Y. Zhang et al., 2014; Zhou & Wang, 2014). Often, however, manufactured compounds, including some based on TCM, were an order of magnitude more powerful than their natural equivalents. This is not to say that combinations of 'natural products' wouldn't yield exciting synergies, but defining what these combinations would comprise will require an enormous number of clinical trials, and even then the chance of success would be marginal.

(Continued)

(Continued)

One of the greatest scams in the alternative health domain is that of homeopathy, which has been around for some time, and has made inroads in treatment methods among some groups. This may have occurred because of it being labelled an 'alternative medicine' or possibly because people can be fooled. This approach, initially established by Samuel Hahnemann in 1796, suggests that a substance that causes illness symptoms can also be used to cure people who are sick (a doctrine that argues that 'like cures like'). In a way this does make sense, and in other contexts, we do use dead viruses as vaccines to prevent illness stemming from later exposure to a live virus.

In the case of homeopathy, however, there's a catch, a bait and switch as it were. Specifically, based on the symptoms expressed, personality features, and psychological condition displayed by a person, a particular substance is selected that will be used in treatment. The selected curative is then diluted, and diluted again, and again, repeatedly, so that in the end, the resulting solution will have none or hardly any of the original molecules, but that doesn't matter a wit, since it is argued that the molecules present will have a 'memory' of the original solution! This product is then given to the person who expects to be healed, and having paid for the treatment, cognitive dissonance may enhance the standard placebo effect (Ernst, 2002). The failure of homeopathy to produce health benefits has been reported in original papers, systematic reviews, and meta-analyses, examining numerous illnesses including cold and flu, asthma, arthritis, chronic fatigue syndrome, eczema, cholera, malaria, and heroin addiction. It also is of no value as an alternative to vaccines, but this hasn't stopped homeopaths from doing a brisk business capitalizing on the fears of others. Even though homeopathic treatments likely won't get rid of illness (beyond placebo effects), the upside is that they won't have nasty side effects either (it's only water, after all).

At one time, there were about 14,000 homeopathic physicians within the US and 22 schools offered degrees in the subject. Many of these schools have since closed, but in some countries they remain, and treatments are covered by universal health care policies. Despite the sketchy practices, there are line-ups of wanna-be doctors wishing to obtain 'accreditation' to offer homeopathic treatments.

If you shop at a large health food store you've no doubt seen homeopathic medications and books on their shelves. You might even have asked someone in the store for help, which is particularly ironic. Asking a grocery clerk for health advice is about as useful as asking your physician for good food recipes. Pseudoscience abounds on the shelves and there's no shortage of suckers who converge on these shops to get their fix.

PUBLIC HEALTH AND PUBLIC POLICY

Community efforts have been useful in altering health behaviors, but efforts beyond the community will be necessary to deal with the current obesity epidemic (Van Dorsten & Lindley, 2011). Governments have become more involved in regulating some practices, such as requiring indications of the contents of various foods as well as in making specific recommendations as to what is good for the individual, and indicating, in general, what is not. However, this is a tough battle to win given that the food industry is able to spend fortunes in promoting their sugar-filled breakfasts, multiple fast treats, and fast-food outlets that often target children. The food industry giants have acknowledged some responsibility for the health of their customers, but actually do little to promote healthy living (Nestle, 2006). They have, in fact, been instrumental in eliminating the World Health Organization recommendations to limit free (added) sugars to 10% or less of energy in their products. As strong as the food lobbies are, the cost of health care related to obesity may become sufficiently great to require government action to change policies.

SLEEP

Neurobiological components

Like other basic needs, such as eating and drinking, sleep is essential for our well-being (Dresler et al., 2014). The occurrence (timing) of sleep is controlled by internal clocks (zeitgebers) present in the brain, with the *suprachiasmatic* nucleus located within the hypothalamus being a primary component involved in regulating this process (Grandin et al., 2006). Sleep has also been linked to serotonin produced in the *anterior raphe nucleus* which projects to the *preoptic* portion of the anterior hypothalamus. Stimulation of the latter region inhibits the neuronal network responsible for wakefulness (Zeitzer, 2013). Beyond the involvement of serotonin, adenosine has been implicated in sleep processes. *Adenosine*, a molecule that is involved in energy regulation processes (Bailey et al., 2014), is ordinarily produced through the degradation of *adenosine triphosphate* (ATP). With increasing neuronal and glial activity within the brain, large amounts of ATP (stored in the form of glycogen) are consumed and hence correspondingly high levels of adenosine are produced. As adenosine levels increase, particular types of adenosine receptors are triggered, engendering non-REM (NREM) sleep. During these less active brain periods, glycogen energy stores recover, resulting in a decline of adenosine levels. The concentration of this molecule within the brain increases with extended periods of wakefulness and declines with sleep, but adenosine seems to be causally involved in this relation, as sleepiness can be induced by administering adenosine.

Features of sleep

Sleep is often characterized as comprising two broad components, rapid eye movement (REM sleep) and non-rapid eye movement (NREM or non-REM sleep), with each type involving specific physiological features. About 20 different neuropeptides and other neurotransmitters have been implicated in the induction of sleep and the switch between sleep and wake states. These neuropeptides are controlled by and also influence the integration and control of *circadian cycles* (processes with an approximately 24-hour cycle), neuronal functioning, and energy homeostasis, and are also influenced by stressors and various illnesses (Richter et al., 2014).

NREM and REM sleep

NREM sleep involves four stages. NREM stage 1 sleep is that point at which we're between sleep and wakefulness, where muscles are still active, and we can be easily awoken. Brain activity, measured through an *electroencephalogram* (EEG), slows down so that fewer oscillations or electrical spikes appear (7–13 Hz; the term Hz (hertz) is defined as one cycle/second) and the amplitude of brain waves becomes larger. This rhythm, often referred to as *alpha* waves is also seen when people have their eyes closed and are relaxed, as well as during meditation. In the next phase, NREM stage 2 or light sleep, electrical activity in the brain slows further, characterized by a *theta* rhythm, in which oscillations occur at a frequency of 3–7 Hz and greater amplitude. This pattern is occasionally interrupted by brief (1–2 sec) periods of high-frequency waves (8–14 Hz referred to as *sleep spindles*), coupled with a fast, high-amplitude wave form called a *K-complex* that seems to be linked to brief awakenings, sometimes owing to external stimuli. The passage into deep sleep, referred to as stage 3, is characterized by *delta* waves in which slow (0.5 to about 3–4 Hz) electrical activity is present, occasionally interrupted by sleep spindles and K-complexes. This stage lasts about 10 minutes, during which there is very little response to external stimuli, although significant events, such as the sound of a crying baby or the person's named being called, will cause awakening. Finally, stage 4, the deepest phase of sleep, during which most body repair occurs, makes up just 15–20% of the sleep cycle. This stage is characterized by particularly slowed delta waves, slowed breathing and heart rate, lower blood pressure, as well as lower brain temperature. Sleep periods also occur during which rapid eye movements (REM) are present, and this *paradoxical* sleep is accompanied by an EEG pattern very like that seen during wakefulness. This REM profile, which occurs while we are dreaming, likely involves the interplay between nuclei in the brainstem, limbic brain regions, several cortical areas, and the hypothalamus (Fraigne et al., 2014).

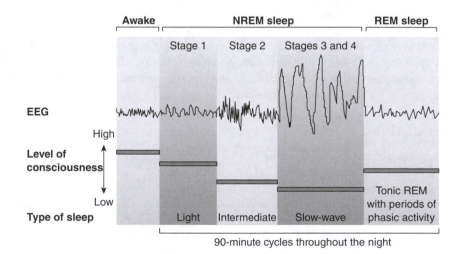

Nature Reviews | Immunology

Figure 7.3   Relations between type of sleep, levels of consciousness, and EEG profile

Source: www.nature.com

GETTING RID OF GARBAGE

Sleep has many important functions related to the recovery of biological elements that have declined during the course of a day, and thus a lack of sleep favors the development of both psychological and physical pathology. As well, there has been the view that during sleep and dreaming we get rid of the 'brain garbage' that might have accumulated during the day (e.g., unimportant memories or trivial synaptic connections). It turns out that sleep may involve elimination of garbage in yet another form. During sleep, openings between cells increase, possibly owing to shrinkage of glial cells, permitting rapid flow of cerebrospinal fluid through the brain and spinal cord, thereby allowing toxins to be removed. It was observed in mice that exogenously administered beta-amyloid, a substance that has been implicated in Alzheimer's disease, could be moved out of the brain more readily during sleep, leading to the suggestion that this could have ramifications relevant to neurological disorders (Mendelsohn & Larrick, 2013). Consistent with such reports, in humans the accumulation of beta-amyloid in the prefrontal cortex has been related to NREM slow wave activity as well as impaired memory consolidation (Mander et al., 2015).

Functions of sleep and health disturbances related to sleep problems

Cognitive disturbances

During periods of wakefulness, the strength or number of synaptic connections between neurons increases, which entails the use of considerable energy, and restoration of these processes is necessary. During sleep, brain activity slows and down-scaling of synapses occurs so that recently strengthened synapses are more prominent, thereby enhancing performance during later wakefulness (Tononi & Cirelli, 2003). As sleep is essential for processes related to brain neuroplasticity, lack of sleep may give rise to hippocampal atrophy and related cognitive impairments (Joo et al., 2014), such as deficits in attention, learning and memory, executive function, decision making, memory consolidation, and performance in situations that call for making proper stressor appraisals and coping responses (e.g., McCoy & Strecker, 2011). Sleep is also important for the production of factors used to support brain functioning, such as myelin (Bellesi et al., 2013), and sleep disturbances may be associated with neurological disorders. In fact, retrospective analyses of medical records indicated that the development of Parkinson's and Alzheimer's disease were preceded by REM sleep problems 15 or more years earlier (Claassen et al., 2010).

Emotional regulation

Aside from these cognitive functions, sleep is essential for emotional regulation. Loss of sleep promotes increased reactivity to further stressors, elevated impulsivity, the amplification of negative appraisals and emotions coupled with elevated amygdala neuronal activity (Yoo et al., 2007), a cortisol profile akin to that of stressed individuals (Guyon et al., 2014). More than this, sleep loss may alter neuronal processes related to appraisals of rewarding stimuli, including those linked to food, which might contribute to increased preference for high-calorie foods and over-eating (Greer et al., 2013). As well, owing to prefrontal cortical changes associated with disturbed sleep, appraisals may be altered so that rewards obtained are over-valued (e.g., in monetary situations), whereas losses are under-valued (Venkatraman et al., 2007). Obviously, this can influence risky decisions that individuals make, and can potentially be a component of excessive gambling and relapse in relation to other addictions. Fundamentally, one unhealthy behavior may promote yet another unhealthy behavior.

Psychological disorders

In a detailed review of the literature pertaining to the effects of sleep on neurobiological, behavioral, and emotional processes, Goldstein and Walker (2014) outlined the processes by which sleep loss, and particularly that of REM sleep, affects homeostatic brain processes and the emotional and social repercussions that follow. In this regard, strong stressors were linked to sleep alterations, particularly REM sleep (Kim & Dimsdale, 2007), and could thereby affect mood state. As multiple neurobiological processes are affected by both stressors and by sleep loss, including those related to synaptic plasticity and hormonal and neurotransmitter processes, the combination of stressors and subsequent sleep loss may have especially pertinent actions on psychological functioning (Grønli et al., 2014).

It's not just REM sleep that's important in relation to psychological disturbances. Continuously waking individuals during stage 4 NREM sleep will also provoke hormonal dysregulation and altered circadian cycles. As such, sleep disturbances may be accompanied by symptoms of psychopathology (Tkachenko et al., 2014), and psychological disturbances, such as PTSD, may be accompanied by sleep problems. For instance, nightmares and insomnia are common among individuals with PTSD, and as in anxiety disorders, sleep disturbances may aggravate PTSD symptoms (Pillar et al., 2000).

Physical illnesses

During sleep periods, most of our biological systems are in an anabolic state, meaning that skeletal and muscular systems are in the process of being rejuvenated, hormones and neurotransmitters are being replenished, and the capacity of the immune system to meet challenges is being enhanced (Vyazovskiy & Harris, 2013). Conversely, a lack of sleep was associated with diminished immune functioning, altered cytokine functioning, and increased occurrence of common colds and flu, as well as other immune-related conditions. It seems that some messenger molecules of the immune system, notably IL-1β and TNF-α, can promote or modulate sleep (Imeri & Opp, 2009), possibly as an adaptive response to facilitate recuperation. Thus, when extended sleep occurs, there is reason to be suspicious that this might be indicative of something being amiss (Cappuccio et al., 2010), and elevations of inflammatory factors could potentially be used as an illness biomarker (Irwin, 2015).

In addition to immune-related alterations, the loss of sleep stemming from worry was predictive of increased cardiovascular disease and all-cause mortality, possibly owing to increased activity of the inflammatory processes (Patel et al., 2009) or to changes of health behaviors (Hamer, Kivimäki & Steptoe, 2012). Loss of sleep quality, even without changes of sleep duration, has also been related to insulin resistance, impaired glucose tolerance, and increased risk of type 2 diabetes (Copinschi et al., 2014), and disturbed sleep may limit diet regulation owing to altered leptin and ghrelin levels, which favor the development of diabetes (Copinschi et al., 2014). Sleep and diabetes also have reciprocally detrimental effects (Martins et al., 2008), which could be an added provocation in the development of cardiac disease.

Sleep and eating

Sleep and eating circuits have overlapping elements, possibly involving the hypothalamic hormone orexin (Rolls et al., 2010), and it has been suggested that weight loss programs ought to include proper sleep as part of the package (Chaput & Tremblay, 2012). The link between sleep and eating is supported by reports that individuals who have slept poorly are more likely to make poor food choices, possibly because sleep loss reduces neuronal activity within the frontal cortex and insular cortex (Greer et al., 2013). In addition, events that undermine internal clocks may promote obesity and type 2 diabetes (Coomans et al., 2013), potentially stemming from alterations of eating-related hormones leptin and ghrelin (Copinschi et al., 2014). In fact, sleep problems can have enduring effects, such that sleep disturbances in adolescence may increase the risk for cardiovascular disease in later adulthood (Narang et al., 2012).

SLEEP DISORDERS

Some of us fall asleep readily, whereas others have a much tougher time falling or staying asleep. Sleep disorders are not uncommon, but are often neglected, even though they might signal important brain disturbances, including those associated with Alzheimer's disease (Anderson, 2014).

Narcolepsy

This condition, which occurs in about 1 of 200 people, is characterized by excessive sleepiness during the day and may appear as a sudden need for sleep, sometimes occurring on several occasions within a day. When this occurs, individuals will go almost directly from wakefulness to a state of REM sleep, without passing through the usual NREM sleep stages. The source for narcolepsy isn't certain. However, it has been associated with genes that control immune functioning and could be triggered by immune activation associated with viruses (Partinen et al., 2014), possibly being related pro-inflammatory cytokines, such as IL-1, which induce sleep, likely as part of a recuperative process.

Parasomnias

This condition refers to disturbing experiences during sleep, such as nightmares that cause individuals to wake up frightened or anxious. Night terrors, a form of parasomnia that occurs in children, should be distinguished from nightmares. During such episodes, screaming and crying may occur, and sometime eyes are open and physical gestures may be made. Night terrors, unlike nightmares, typically occur during stage 3 and stage 4 non-REM sleep. Upon awakening, there is little or no recall of the dream, although heart rate and blood pressure may be elevated, and other signs of autonomic activation, such as sweating, may be present as well.

A variant of parasomnia that is fairly common in children is *somnambulism,* in which sleep-walking occurs during non-REM sleep. Children seem to grow out of this as they get older, and sleep-walking is infrequent in adults. The behavior occurs during deep stage 4 non-REM sleep, and it is difficult to awaken a person at this time (contrary to myth, it is not dangerous to wake a person who is sleep-walking) (Hughes, 2007). When a person is awoken during this phase of sleep, the body might seem to be awake but without full brain awakening. Thus, a person might engage in behaviors such as getting a snack, yet not be fully aware that they were doing this. Some people may go so far as to engage in sleep-driving, which has now become an issue for the courts as legal claims have been made in the belief that some medications, such as zolpidem (traded under several names, such as Ambien), elicited these behaviors (Daley et al., 2011).

Sleep apnea

This disorder entails pauses in breathing or infrequent or shallow breathing (*hypopnea*), during sleep, which can last for a matter of 10–15 seconds, but may also stretch for minutes, occurring anywhere from 5 to 30 times a night. Chemoreceptors present in the blood ordinarily detect elevations of carbon dioxide as a result of pauses in breathing, which signal the brain so that the individual awakens, breathes to restore oxygen, and promptly falls asleep again. This may happen repeatedly during the night, and as individuals with sleep apnea frequently aren't aware of their condition, fatigue and sleepiness may be their constant companion. Because complete sleep may not be obtained, apnea experienced over many years may lead to mood-related disorders, diabetes, heart and some types of liver disease (e.g., Morgenstern et al., 2014; Rosenzweig et al., 2015).

Sleep apnea can often be diminished by weight loss, diminishing consumption of alcohol or muscle relaxants, quitting smoking, and in some instances benefits are obtained by sleeping on the side or in a reclining position. When simple remedies fail, a monitor can be used so that the individual is automatically awoken when breathing ceases for lengthy times. Alternatively, dentists can construct an oral appliance, essentially a mouthpiece that changes the position of the lower jaw, causing the airway to open. If this isn't effective, then devices can be obtained to create *continuous positive airway pressure* (CPAP) in order to keep the pathway open (Vennelle et al., 2010).

Circadian rhythm sleep disorders

About 3% of people experience circadian rhythm sleep disorders (CRSD), although this could be an underestimation as it may be confused with other sleep problems (Kim et al., 2013). These CRSDs can take the form of normal sleep, but occurring sooner or later than that of most people. The sleep problem can also take the form of circadian cycles slowly and gradually changing, which can occur in sighted people, but is more common among those who have lost their sight (Sack et al., 1992). Frequent international travelers will often experience disturbed sleep patterns (jet lag) and among flight crews this can have adverse health consequences (Kim & Lee, 2007). Likewise, sleep problems are experienced by those who work night shifts. In this instance, individuals often attempt to sleep soon after work, which is very different from others who sleep during the period before going to work. Thus, these individuals will begin their work shift having been up for many hours, potentially resulting in work-related or automobile accidents (Ftouni et al., 2013). More than this, shift work undertaken on a long-term basis has been associated with illnesses such as cardiovascular diseases, gastro-intestinal disorders, obesity, disturbed glucose metabolism and metabolic syndrome, immune disturbances, and some types of cancer (Kim et al., 2013).

ACCIDENTS AT WORK AND AT HOME

Virtually everyone is aware that accidents are a major source of disability and death, and many governments have taken steps to limit the occurrence of accidents, including 'root cause analyses', in an effort to limit future accidents. According to the WHO in their Global Status Report on Road Safety 2013 (World Health Organization, 2013), the greatest number of deaths occurs in low and middle income countries. In the UK this number is relatively small, amounting to 3.7 deaths per 100,000 people, somewhat greater in Canada (6.8/100,000), while in the United States it amounts to 11.4/100,000 (or about 35,000 deaths overall). In some countries the death toll is considerably greater, being 18.6 in the Russian Federation, while South Africa, Iran, and Iraq all see somewhat more than 30 deaths/100,000. Within Western countries, the frequency of accidents leading to death and injury is greater among individuals from lower rather than higher socioeconomic backgrounds, and young males are particularly adept at getting into these accidents. These numbers, however, are dwarfed by the 20–50 million people who suffer non-fatal injuries, often leading to life-long disabilities. The good news is that the worldwide incidence of injuries stemming from accidents has declined appreciably (21%) since 1990. A WHO road traffic injuries fact sheet lists some of the problems that continue to exist. These comprise excessive driving speed, drinking and driving, being distracted (use of cell phones, texting), and failure to use seat belts or child restraints, or helmets when riding on a motorcycle (World Health Organization, 2014g).

Like road accidents, those that occur in the workplace are frequent, reaching about 337 million a year, with 2.3 million deaths according to the International Labour Organization (ILO), but the risk of injury at home exceeds that in the workplace. Fire safety, electrical safety, risks related to heating and cooking, accidental poisoning (associated with medicines and cleansers), absence of bath mats in showers and rails on staircases, as well as do-it-yourself and home-gardening ventures are all sources of death and injury. Because so many injuries involve children, pediatricians have urged new parents to take appropriate precautions, and government agencies have instituted many safety rules. Various government health and safety agencies have likewise put a premium on informing people of these hazards and have legislated changes that manufacturers must follow. Finally, the combination of older homes that have inherent risks and some behaviors on the part of those who think they can fix things (when, in fact, they can't) leads to numerous home accidents.

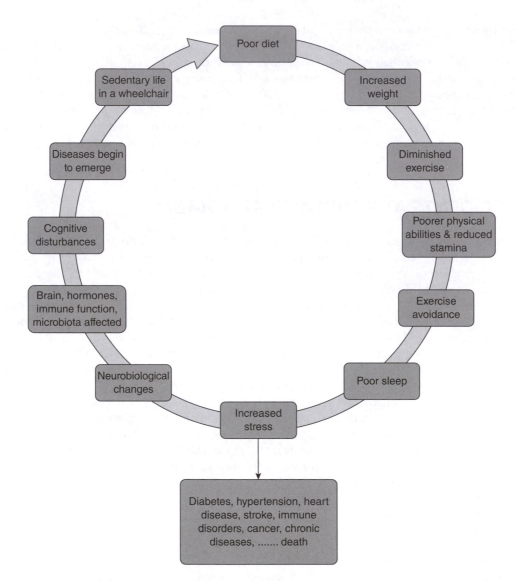

Figure 7.4 Poor life-styles are interlinked so that adoption of one poor behavior may have cascading effects on other aspects of life. In this figure these are shown as occurring sequentially and in a circle, but they could just as easily be viewed as a downward spiral. As well, the cascade of changes begins with poor food choices, but these needn't be the starting point. Initial sedentary behaviors could lead to mindless eating and other poor behavioral choices could follow. Similarly, the order of events might not be sequential, but instead may involve several factors interacting with one another to produce negative outcomes. It should also be considered that the impact of these many factors might also vary with prenatal and early-life experiences, genetic factors, previous stressors encountered and any number of other factors.

SUMMARY

There's little question that adopting inappropriate life-styles can have enormous negative effects on well-being. As depicted in Figure 7.4, one poor life-style choice can lead to another, which leads to another, ultimately undermining essential biological systems, and ultimately the emergence of many types of disease conditions. This might lead to a shorter life span and a poorer health span. In contrast, exercise, proper food choices and effective ways to lose weight if necessary, limiting stress, and obtaining enough quality sleep, all have essential effects on our health. In some instances, changes of poor behaviors can be accomplished fairly readily, but if particular behaviors are well entrenched, they can be difficult to modify. For this to occur, individuals need to be ready to change, meaning that they acknowledge the necessity and are prepared to take the needed actions, and believe they have the capacity to make changes. But even then, change might be fleeting and rigorous treatment programs may be needed (witness the lengths necessary in some instances to have people lose weight). At the end of the day, as much as individuals would like to believe that behavior change is largely due to their own self-efficacy, positive behavioral outcomes may be influenced by their social groups, their own identity in this regard, community initiatives, and broad government policies.

8 Cardiovascular Illnesses and Related Disorders

STILL THE MOST COMMON WAY TO DIE

Cardiovascular or circulatory diseases are the most common causes of death worldwide, amounting to more than 20% in most Western countries. In the US, one person will have a coronary event every 26 seconds, and about every minute one person will die as a result of a heart problem. Based on these statistics, the incorrect impression might be formed that the heart just isn't up to the job it's supposed to do. But consider that every day, day after day, beginning early in gestation, the heart beats and continues to do so for 80 or so years, which amounts to about 2.5–3 billion beats over the course of a lifetime. It receives 'dirty', de-oxygenated blood from the body, sends it to the lungs, where carbon dioxide is removed and oxygen absorbed, before being returned to the heart, from which the newly oxygenated blood is pumped to various body organs that depend on it.

All things considered, the heart seems like a tough organ that works very well, provided that it isn't abused and is well maintained. With age, like any other motor or pump, the effectiveness of the heart begins to wane, and in some instances plaque can build up in blood vessels. This occurs gradually and most people might be entirely unaware that this is occurring, but at some point they might notice that they run out of steam more readily, require rest after short periods of physical work, or perhaps even experience a twinge of chest pain. Despite considerable trepidation and regret for not having taken better care of their heart earlier, sometimes, with a bit of coaxing, a person will visit a physician. They might learn that they need a bit of a tune-up in the form of meds, altered diet, or behavioral methods to help heart functioning, or if arteries are very blocked it might be necessary to have a stent inserted or by-pass surgery performed. It could have been worse, of course, as many individuals discover that there is a problem only when they have a heart attack.

The incidence of deaths and hospitalization related to heart disease and stroke has declined in the past decade, despite the fact that there have been no great treatment breakthroughs during this time (Krumholz et al., 2014). It's likely that these outcomes reflect many moderately improved treatments (better meds and medical devices), and we might also be seeing the benefits of changing life-styles, enhanced quality of care, and earlier identification of potential problems.

GETTING TO KNOW THE HEART

Heart and circulatory diseases are to an extent preventable disorders, or at the least their appearance can be delayed. In this regard, a set of factors comprising elevated cholesterol levels, diabetes, hypertension, obesity, and smoking account for about 50% of the preventable fraction of cardiovascular mortality (Patel et al., 2015), although, as we'll see, there are other factors that may be important in preventing and treating heart disease. This chapter will cover a broad range of topics related to basic heart functioning and factors related to different forms of arterial and coronary diseases, and given the connection to circulatory disorders, we'll also consider the factors that lead to stroke and processes that can limit the damaging effects that would otherwise occur. These topics will be accompanied by an overview of psychosocial and environmental factors that can instigate poor heart health and, conversely, of how behavioral methods can be used to enhance cardiovascular functioning or to limit heart problems. After covering this chapter, you should be familiar with:

- how the heart operates and under what conditions heart disease can develop
- psychosocial and personality factors that influence the course of chronic heart disease
- neurochemical processes and inflammatory factors linked to chronic heart disease
- the processes by which events related to circulatory accidents, such as stroke, can occur
- comorbid conditions related to heart disease
- what can be done to limit the occurrence of heart-related disturbances.

THE CARDIOVASCULAR SYSTEM

Before delving into how heart disease develops and what can be done to limit its occurrence, we'll examine how the heart operates. A cursory description of this system is provided here, and only some of the problems that can occur will be explored.

How the cardiovascular system works

The main function of the heart is to pump 4–5 liters of blood so that it circulates through arteries to all parts of the body, providing oxygen to cells of various organs, and delivering nutrients and chemicals, as well as immune factors that protect us from invading microorganisms. For this to occur, the heart's pumping capacity must be powerful, which requires that heart cells beat in sync with one another. Coordination of these cells is determined through the sinoatrial node, which acts like a symphony conductor who makes sure that all the members of the orchestra are doing what they're supposed to do at the right time. Should the activity of cells become discoordinated, *arrhythmia* may occur, usually manifesting as excessively fast heart rate (*tachycardia*) or the rate may become too slow (*bradycardia*). The palpitations that an individual feels when this occurs typically are not immediately dangerous, but arrhythmia can result in cardiac arrest or sudden death.

Some of the main arteries that take blood through the body are thick and relatively elastic, which is necessary because of the great pressure created when the heart contracts. The large arteries

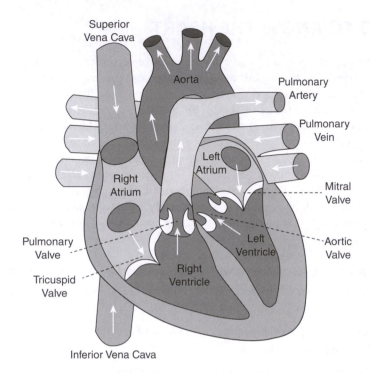

Figure 8.1   Veins throughout the body carry deoxygenated blood to the heart. Through the pulmonary circulation loop, 'dirty' or deoxygenated blood from the body enters the heart through the superior and inferior vena cavae, which then pumps it into its right ventricle and then to the lungs. The lungs remove the carbon dioxide, and oxygen is concurrently absorbed, and the cleansed blood is then returned to the left ventricle of the heart (in the diagram, the heart is facing you, so the left ventricle and left atrium are on your right). At this point, the system circulation loop comes into play in which the cleansed blood is pumped through the aorta to various parts of the body through an extensive system of arteries so that cells will stay alive and do their jobs effectively.

Source: http://www.todayifoundout.com/wp-content/uploads/2010/09/Heart-300-1.png

branch off into smaller arteries, and these, in turn, branch off into *arterioles* that carry blood to very fine *capillaries*. These small capillaries are made up of only a thin layer of *endothelial* cells, so that blood traversing through them maintains blood *platelets* (tiny blood cells that are important for clot formation and hence for wound healing) on the inside, but still permits fluids, dissolved gases and other chemicals to diffuse into cells from the surrounding tissue.

Constituents of blood

The blood circulating through our body is made up of red blood cells (*erythrocytes*), which carry oxygen, white blood cells (*leukocytes*) which include immune cells, as well as platelets that, in collaboration with coagulation factors, are responsible for clotting. About 55% of the blood is made up of a liquid, referred to as *plasma*, which contains glucose, electrolytes, nutrients, and hormones (e.g., epinephrine, *atrial natriuretic peptide* (ANP), *B-type natriuretic peptide* (BNP)) that are essential for organs to operate as they should (McGrath et al., 2005).

DISEASES OF THE HEART

Despite its usual smooth functioning, when heart problems arise they can take any of several forms. Hypertensive heart disease, which entails elevated blood pressure, appears in up to 20% of individuals, varying with factors such as age, gender, ethnicity, body size, and basal heart rate. Another frequent disturbance is coronary heart disease (CHD), also referred to as coronary artery disease (CAD), in which blood flow to the heart is diminished, leading to a lack of oxygen (*ischemia*). In still other instances, the cardiac muscle might become diseased, a condition referred to as cardiomyopathy. As well, several forms of inflammatory heart disease can occur, including inflammation of the inner layer of the heart (*endocarditis*), inflammation of the muscle portion of the heart (*myocarditis*), and *inflammatory cardiomegaly*, which is associated with enlargement of the heart. You might recognize the latter three terms as they seem to be favorites in television shows, probably because of their esoteric-sounding names.

HYPERTENSION

What is hypertension?

When the heart pumps blood the pressure created against artery walls is elevated. Thus, blood pressure rises with each heartbeat (as blood is ejected from the heart) and falls as the heart relaxes between beats. The increased pressure created by the heart pumping blood is referred to as *systolic* pressure, and the pressure that exists between beats, as the heart relaxes, is called the *diastolic* pressure. This is what is being measured when a doctor determines your blood pressure. For many years the recommendation was that systolic blood pressure should be under 140 millimeters of mercury (this is a unit of pressure: the amount of pressure required to raise the column of merccury in a glass tube), but a National Institute of Health (NIH) initiative has now suggested that health outcomes would be more positive if systolic blood pressure of 120 were the target (NIH, 2015). Ideally, systolic pressure should be about or below 120 and the diastolic pressure below 80, and they are usually described as 120 over 80. As arteries begin to block, the pressure increases (much as it does in a garden hose when your thumb partially blocks the nozzle end), and when resting blood pressure (when sitting quietly) is higher, say between 120–139 over 80–89, the individual is said to be in a pre-hypertension condition. With further elevation to about 140–159 over 90–99, hypertension (Stage 1) is diagnosed, and above these values, hypertension Stage 2 is said to be present.

Left untreated, hypertension can result in damage to the arterial walls, plaque accumulation, and hence further narrowing and hardening of arteries. Often, hypertension isn't accompanied by obvious symptoms, and thus problems aren't detected early unless individuals have periodic medical evaluations. Screening individuals at work and at community events has been useful in identifying those at risk (Alderman & Lamport, 1988), and blood pressure monitoring has been facilitated through relatively inexpensive monitors that are widely sold. No doubt these can be useful for some individuals, and may encourage them to make life-style modifications to thwart the development of this condition.

Factors associated with hypertension

The cause of hypertension is often unknown, in which case it is referred to as *essential hypertension*. In other instances, medical conditions such as thyroid or kidney disease may cause the blood pressure increase, which is classed as *secondary hypertension*.

Life-style factors

Life-styles may contribute to hypertension, and a family history of illness is predictive of this condition developing (Smith et al., 1987). Ethnicity (e.g., being African American) has also been linked to hypertension, possibly being secondary to poverty and the life-style factors that go with this (Winkleby et al., 1998). It is of practical and theoretical interest that distress, hostility and anger provoked by social alienation and discrimination were found to be linked to high blood pressure in African Americans (Blascovich et al., 2001). Although hypertension has long been known to increase as people become older, remarkably, it has also become more common in children, likely owing to a more sedentary life-style and the ease of obtaining foods high in fat or sodium, or low in potassium. Stressful events such as loneliness, especially among somewhat older individuals (50–68 years of age), may also lead to elevated blood pressure (Hawkley et al., 2006), and job strain has similarly been linked to hypertension, especially in the presence of heavy family responsibilities (Harada et al., 2006).

Emotional contributions

A disposition toward expressing anger (Harburg et al., 2003) or coming from a family environment that encouraged anger (Ewart, 1991) was accompanied by increased risk of hypertension. Conversely, conditions that reduce anger (e.g., the propensity to forgive slights) were associated with high blood pressure being less evident (May et al., 2014). Hostility was also associated with the cardiac hormone ANP being elevated in blood (Smith et al., 2013), and the combination of hostility and time urgency/impatience was predictive of later hypertension developing. Furthermore, as hostile individuals will have lost some of their social coping resources, their risk for stress-related hypertension may increase (Brondolo et al., 2003), whereas social competence, even among children, predicts reduced risk for cardiovascular illness (Chen et al., 2002).

Sleep problems

Hypertension has been linked to insomnia, short sleep duration (less than 5 hours), and early morning awakening (Meng et al., 2013), even in young adults (Chung et al., 2013). Meta-analyses of both cross-sectional and prospective studies have confirmed that short sleep duration alone was accompanied by hypertension (Wang et al., 2012), as well as coronary heart disease and stroke (Azevedo Da Silva et al., 2014). Sleeping too much has also been linked to hypertension and heart disease (Wang et al., 2012), although excessive sleep might be indicative of heart-related problems being present, possibly secondary to elevated levels of cytokines that have sleep-inducing (*soporific*) effects.

Treatment adherence

Hypertension cannot be 'cured' and remains a life-long condition that needs to be continuously monitored and dealt with, but patient compliance (adherence to treatment) can be a major problem. It's not unusual for patients to let down their guard and discontinue their life-style changes or take their meds inconsistently. As one might expect, when patients don't adhere to treatments, the risk of heart attack and stroke are greatly increased. Providing education concerning health habits may have some positive effects, even when offered through the internet (Moore et al., 2008). However, given the difficulties in maintaining life-style changes for protracted periods, too often the effectiveness of such education programs are limited over the long run.

CORONARY ARTERY DISEASE

Cardiovascular and circulatory diseases are the greatest cause of death worldwide, and poor heart functioning has many other negative effects that ought to be considered. For example, poor heart functioning alters life-styles, which encourages the development of still other illnesses, including dementia (Jefferson et al., 2010). On the positive side, across age groups, sex and education categories, heart disease has been declining in most developed countries since the 1960s. Even over the short span from 2006 to 2010, CAD declined from 6.7% to 6.0% of the population, although it was still very high among some ethnic groups, such as Native Americans (Fang et al., 2011). Moreover, CAD is at record high levels in the Russian Federation, Belarus, Ukraine, and Central Asian republics, and has been increasing in developing or transitional countries, probably owing to the life-style changes that come with industrial development (Mathers & Loncar, 2006). Thus, it is likely that cardiovascular disease will remain the leading cause of death for a few more years, unless of course something comes along that eclipses it, such as a horrid pandemic.

Development of CAD

When damage occurs on the thin layer of cells that line the inner portion of blood vessels (*endothelium*), monocytes, macrophages, and T cells infiltrate the site, where they release cytokines that promote inflammation and the formation of *plaque*, a semi-hard substance composed of cholesterol, fat, calcium, and fibrin (Hansson & Hermansson, 2011). With time, and repeated damage, plaque build-up will progress, typically covered by a thin fibrous layer of *collagen* (a component of connective tissue that holds the body together) and smooth muscle cells. Eventually, the restricted flow of blood to the heart (i.e., *atherosclerosis*) will result in symptoms becoming obvious and a formal diagnosis of CAD will follow.

Events that increase blood flow and pressure, such as exertion or stressful experiences (technically referred to as *hemodynamic stress*), may cause the plaque to rupture, resulting in a *thrombosis* or blood clot that goes into circulation, causing blockage of a main artery and the occurrence of a *myocardial infarction* (MI; heart attack) (Libby & Theroux, 2005). If the heart attack was due to partial blockage, recovery is best when *cauterization* to eliminate this is conducted within 24–48 hours of hospitalization (Khera et al., 2014), although further post-treatment methods (social and physical support, life-style changes) ought to be applied for maximal benefits to be accrued.

CAD is often asymptomatic (symptoms are not apparent) and although plaque begins to form years earlier, it's common for men and women to first be diagnosed in their 50s and 60s once blood flow is reduced by more than 75%. In general, CAD comes to attention when individuals feel chest pain (*angina pectoris*) that arises when insufficient oxygenated blood gets to the heart, which is most notable in response to physical exertion, but can also be elicited by psychological stressors (Krantz et al., 1996). In some instances myocardial ischemia and the accompanying *angina* (pressure or squeezing in the chest, pain in the shoulder, arm, neck, jaw, or back, or appearing as indigestion) is transient, resolving with discontinuation of behaviors that placed a load on the heart (*stable angina*) or through medications that increase blood supply (e.g., nitro-glycerine placed under the tongue). However, as the disease progresses, ischemia may become longer lasting (more than 10 minutes) and *unstable* angina may appear, in which symptoms occur even with minimal energy output or when individuals are at rest. Once this occurs it is predictive of *arrhythmia* (disturbed heart rhythm) and MI (Casscells et al., 2003).

If the left main coronary artery or proximal left anterior descending coronary artery is suddenly and completely blocked (occluded), a massive heart attack occurs, resulting in 'sudden death'. This can occur when a plaque ruptures and platelets that flow to the site of the rupture form a blockage. Some symptoms may precede the attack, but they proceed rapidly and in some instances there's no warning at all. This form of heart attack, sometimes referred to as the 'widow maker', tells you a fair bit about prognosis. However, contrary to some myths and expressions ('sudden death', and 's/he was dead before s/he hit the ground'), when a widow maker hits, a person can last as long as 10–20 minutes, as some oxygen is stored in the blood that keeps organs alive. Thus, with very fast action, it is possible to have individuals survive, and increasingly the appropriate equipment and trained individuals are present at public events to deal with such occurrences.

Those who die of heart attacks often do so before reaching an emergency room, owing to *ventricular fibrillation* (abnormal and irregular heart rhythm, including rapid and uncoordinated fluttering contractions of the lower ventricles of the heart), but if they successfully reach a hospital emergency room, more than 90% of individuals ought to survive. This has largely been achieved through the development of clot dissolving drugs, as well as coronary balloon angio-plasty (temporarily inserting and inflating a tiny balloon where the artery is clogged to help widen it) and coronary stents (a small wire mesh tube to keep the artery open) to permit blood to circulate and reach the heart before greater damage occurs. However, if the heart is sufficiently damaged, then other problems or death will occur soon after. Obviously, denial and procrastination are about the worst possible strategies to use in relation to heart attack.

Symptoms of heart attack

Knowing the symptoms of heart attack, provided in Table 8.1, and being able and prepared to get to a hospital emergency room are fundamental for survival. Men and women present with many similar symptoms of MI, but some distinct differences may also exist. Discomfort in the right side (opposite the heart), dull ache, and indigestion tend to be reported more by men than women, whereas the opposite generally occurs with respect to throat discomfort, pressing on the chest, and vomiting among women. Importantly, women are typically much less likely to identify their symptoms as being heart-related. As a result, women take longer than men to get to hospital, and thus may have a poorer outcome.

Table 8.1   Signs of heart attack

- pain, fullness and/or squeezing sensation of the chest
- shortness of breath
- arm pain (typically the left arm, but may appear in the right arm), jaw pain, toothache, headache, or upper back pain (women tend to experience these features more than men)
- nausea, vomiting, and/or general discomfort at the upper middle abdomen
- heartburn and/or indigestion
- breaking out in a cold sweat
- general malaise (vague feeling of illness)

FACTORS THAT PROMOTE HEART DISEASE

Many of the risk factors for heart disease are well known, such as sedentary life-style, high levels of low-density lipoprotein (LDL) cholesterol and low levels of high-density lipoprotein (HDL) cholesterol or fat, obesity and particularly abdominal fat distribution, and large waist circumference or waist–hip ratio (Kop & Mommersteeg, 2014). Thus, it is usually recommended that intake of saturated fats should be limited (to less than 7% of total calories), trans fatty acids should be avoided entirely, and daily physical activity ought to be undertaken. As blood pressure is also a primary risk factor for cardiovascular mortality as well as mortality related to other causes, it is recommended that blood pressure be lower than 140/90 mmHg, or 130/80 mmHg for high-risk patients, such as those with diabetes or chronic kidney disease.

Many factors that often aren't under our control may increase risk for heart disease. These include certain stressor experiences, coming from a lower socioeconomic class, our general social environment including social isolation and low social support, negative early adverse experiences, the occurrence of depressive illness, as well as anxiety, anger, and hostility. Each of these is an independent risk factor for the development and progression of CAD, and the risk is still greater when several risk factors are present (Steptoe & Kivimäki, 2013) as well as in the presence of gene mutations related to neurochemical functioning (Brummett et al., 2014).

Stress in relation to heart disease

In response to stressful situations, one of the many adaptive changes that occur comprises activation of the autonomic nervous system through the release of epinephrine from sympathetic nerve fibers, thus increasing heart rate so that needed supplies of oxygen by body organs and the brain are obtained. With the termination of the stressor, the parasympathetic nervous system, through the release of acetylcholine, slows heart rate. In some instances, this parasympathetic response may persist and predominate, and hence heart rate may be lowered a bit too much (*bradycardia*), possibly causing fainting, feeling light-headed or dizzy, nausea, sweating, weakness, and heart palpitations.

With the increased heart activity provoked by stressors or physical exertion, greater pressure is necessary for blood to be pushed through the heart and to various organs. In these instances, systemic *vascular resistance* (referring to resistance that needs to be overcome to push blood through the circulatory system) is elevated, but especially so if the coronary arteries are narrowed. Thus, under challenge conditions blood pressure that goes up excessively is likely a sign that a cardiovascular problem exists, which might not be detected as readily when resting blood pressure is measured. Among patients with CAD, myocardial ischemia can be induced by psychological stressors, particularly those that elicit strong emotional responses, such as a speaking assignment concerning personal faults. This is of practical significance as individuals who exhibit myocardial ischemia in response to a stressor within a laboratory were also likely to exhibit myocardial ischemia during *electrocardiogram* (ECG) monitoring over the course of daily-life activity, which predicted the occurrence of later cardiac events (Wei et al., 2014).

Acute trauma or catastrophic events can provoke MI among vulnerable individuals or those with pre-existing cardiac problems, as observed following the 1994 Los Angeles earthquake and in response to Iraqi scud missile attacks on Israel during the first Gulf war in 1991. It has been estimated that mental stress-induced cardiac events or those provoked by physical challenges account for 20% of cardiac events, particularly among individuals who are already at risk (Kop, 1999). In the main, however, chronic stressors are more responsible for the development of CAD, and although we often can't go by what people say, it seems that among people who believe that stressful events are having a negative effect on their health, the chance of heart attack doubles over a subsequent 18-year period (Nabi et al., 2013). Several prospective studies similarly indicated that new diagnoses of CAD and CAD-related mortality were elevated by about 25% among individuals who perceived particularly high levels of distress. For instance, the chronic stress associated with acting as a caregiver has been accompanied by elevated risk of hypertension, just as it has been associated with other cardiovascular illnesses (Capistrant et al., 2012). Likewise, the stress created by bereavement has been associated with a 200–300% increase of mortality in the subsequent months. As seen with so many other illnesses, adverse experiences early in life were also seen to be connected to adult atherosclerosis and heart attack (Thurston et al., 2014). Essentially, when the brain is distressed, the heart will be affected.

Job strain

Our job can serve as a source of comfort and as a way of coping with stressors, but it can also be an unbearable source of stress that disturbs psychological and physical well-being. The Whitehall studies, which began in the 1970s, indicated that within the UK civil service, individuals in more senior ranks had a lower mortality rate in relation to heart disease relative to individuals in the lower ranks (Marmot et al., 1978). The subsequent Whitehall II studies, as well as many other investigations, confirmed these findings, and indicated that lower social rank was also related to other illnesses, including certain forms of cancer, gastrointestinal illnesses, diabetes, chronic lung disease, chronic back pain, as well as depression and suicide.

Of the factors that could potentially predict aspects of the job that make it more or less stressful and more closely linked to heart disease, one that was particularly significant concerned '*job strain*', which reflects high job demands coupled with low decision latitude (not being in a position to make decisions). Subsequent meta-analyses of prospective studies also revealed that high work efforts and low rewards were associated with a 50% increase of CAD (Kivimäki et al., 2014). This bad situation was made still worse if individuals perceived a lack of justice (unfairness) (De Vogli et al., 2007), and if they experienced ongoing distress that promoted anxiety, irritability, and poor sleep. As expected, having a positive home life buffered against the adverse consequences of job strain, but if marital problems existed, then the risk for heart disease was markedly elevated.

Job strain and other job-related stressors could have negative effects on well-being as a result of stressor-provoked changes of autonomic, hormonal, and central nervous system processes as well as inflammatory factors that might affect metabolic abnormalities, inflammation, insulin resistance, dyslipidemia, and endothelial dysfunction. Moreover, this could evolve owing to altered life-styles (e.g., smoking, alcohol consumption, sleep), and by affecting compliance with recommended medications.

Socioeconomic status

It's hardly surprising that the occurrence of CAD and recovery from heart conditions is linked to low socioeconomic status (SES) (Philbin et al., 2001; Myers et al., 2014), just as low SES has been linked to other health problems. In addition, low SES may be linked to job strain, as well as life-style factors that promote heart problems, including poor food choices, smoking, and alcohol consumption, and may be accompanied by more frequent stressor encounters. It's not unusual, as well, for those in lower SES categories to have poorer access to medical care, and both preventive care and health knowledge may be limited, as is attendance and completion of cardiac rehabilitation after a cardiac event (Lemstra et al., 2013). Aside from the multiple elements that seem to conspire to undermine well-being, low SES individuals likely maintain a smaller array of coping methods and their 'resource capacity' to cope with stressors may be limited.

DOESN'T MATTER WHICH POPULATIONS ARE ASSESSED

The relationship between social status and health outcomes was even evident among the Tsimane, an egalitarian society of forager-farmers living in the Bolivian Amazon. Given the poor standards of living endemic to all people within the region, it likely isn't simply wealth or access to resources that influences health outcomes. Instead, psychosocial stress that accompanies low status, regardless of other factors, might be responsible for poor well-being (Stieglitz et al., 2014). Thus, aside from the usual suspects that have been implicated in heart disease (and other illnesses), allostatic overload may be more likely to occur among individuals of subordinate status, leading to biological changes that promote illness.

Depressive illness and heart disease

It's a bit curious that when researchers are enmeshed in a particular field they might not detect particular relations, as obvious as they might seem in retrospect. So it was with respect to the link between depressive illness and heart disease, which we know to be highly comorbid conditions.

Depression was linked to CAD, even after considering life-style factors (Baune et al., 2012), and this relationship was bidirectional as heart disease was frequently associated with subsequent depression, and depressive illness was highly predictive of later CAD, especially in the presence of hopelessness and pessimism (Kop & Mommersteeg, 2014; Nicholson et al., 2006). In fact, among women, depression was a better predictor of later heart disease than were traditional risk factors (e.g., smoking, obesity, hypertension, and diabetes). Even depression that appeared at 17–39 years of age predicted later development of heart disease (Shah et al., 2011), as did childhood depression (Rottenberg et al., 2014).

Depression isn't only associated with a doubling of heart disease; its presence is accompanied by slower recovery following cardiac events, and predicts an increase in the probability of a future heart attack. The comorbidity that exists between these illnesses might speak to the possibility that they share some biological processes, and it was suggested that depression could serve as a cogent marker for the occurrence of physical disorders (Anisman & Hayley, 2012a). Parenthetically, if depression exacerbates heart disease and limits recovery from heart problems, it might be thought that reducing depression through medications would improve heart health. As we know, however, CAD develops over many years, and modifying depressive symptoms once heart problems are already present may be way too late to reverse existent problems (the proverbial closing of barn doors after the horse is gone). This doesn't necessarily mean that treatments aimed at diminishing depression would be ineffective in preventing further damage, provided that appropriate life-style changes were also adopted. In fact, antidepressant use may diminish myocardial ischemia that can be exacerbated by psychologically stressful events (W. Jiang et al., 2013).

It's not just depression that has been linked to heart disease, but also a variety of other mental health problems. A mental illness (schizophrenia, bipolar disorder, anxiety disorder, and major depression) any time in a person's life doubled their risk for heart disease, and individuals using psychiatric medications were at three times the risk of stroke (e.g., Goldie et al., 2014). The source for this dramatic outcome may be related to several elements, including behavioral risk factors such as elevated tobacco and alcohol use, poor diet, and physical inactivity. As well, those with mental illnesses may be less likely to seek health care related to cardiovascular function, and physicians might also be less apt to detect such problems. Furthermore, many of the drugs used to treat psychiatric illnesses are accompanied by weight gain, which could potentially affect heart health.

VITAL EXHAUSTION

Feelings of excessive fatigue and lack of energy, progressively greater irritability, and feeling demoralized, sound a lot like burn-out (in a work context) and depression. These symptoms are also prominent in a syndrome known as 'vital exhaustion', which may be a predictor of subsequent cardiovascular problems, including MI, angina, and sudden cardiac death (Kop, 1999), even after apparently successful angioplasty (Kop et al., 1994). Moreover, the relation between vital exhaustion and CAD was apparent after controlling for blood pressure, cholesterol levels, smoking, and hypertensive drug usage, as well as age, gender, race, body mass index, and diabetes (J.E. Williams et al., 2010).

A strong link exists between vital exhaustion and depressive disorders, and both were predictive of mortality after myocardial infarction. This linkage was notable in relation to the somatic features of depression (sleep problems, appetite changes, and psychomotor alterations), but not to cognitive-affective symptoms, such as depressed mood, anhedonia, negative feelings about self, concentration problems, and suicidal ideation (Smolderen et al., 2009). Inflammatory processes have been linked to depressive illness, vital exhaustion, and heart disease (Meyer et al., 2010), and inflammatory factors may be a common denominator in the provocation of these conditions. Thus, vital exhaustion (or cytokine levels) might be an important and easily determined marker of heart disease.

The comorbidity that exists between depression and heart disease begs the question as to why this comorbidity occurs. As depression is a stressful condition, it may place excessive strain on the heart. This is especially the case as depression is often accompanied by antecedent negative experiences, elevated interpersonal stress responsiveness, and an internalizing coping style, which could instigate elevated HPA axis activity, sustained autonomic nervous system activation, and the promotion of inflammatory processes that promote heart disease (Kop & Mommersteeg, 2014). It is equally possible that depressed individuals might be highly reactive to stressful stimuli that favor the development of vascular alterations.

It's been known for decades that psychosocial factors, particularly supportive relationships, may have beneficial effects on various health conditions, and cardiovascular health is no exception (Albus, 2010). Having supportive relationships is particularly germane in this regard, and several studies have indicated that heart health is superior among married individuals to those who are single. Not surprisingly, having social support diminishes stress and acts against depressive disorder that may be secondary to heart failure (Graven & Grant, 2013), and may diminish the adverse effects of depression in relation to heart disease (Compare et al., 2013).

POSITIVE MOOD AND HEART HEALTH

As negative experiences and mood states are associated with increased risk for heart disease, the obvious question has been whether positive events and mood would predict enhanced heart functioning. Researchers in the field of positive psychology are fond of saying that the absence of negative events is not the same as the presence of positives. There has indeed been considerable data suggesting that positivity is associated with general well-being and improved heart health. Optimists have been found to have healthier hearts (Hernandez et al., 2015) as have individuals who tend to be high in dispositional mindfulness (Loucks et al., 2015). Relatedly, having a dog as a pet may be associated with increased heart health, either because it makes individuals happier having this unconditional adoration, or perhaps pets act a stress buffer, or get people out walking more (Levine et al., 2013).

(Continued)

(Continued)

A review of some 200 studies indicated that people with a general sense of well-being engaged in better health behaviors, which were related to enhanced physiological indices of heart health (Boehm & Kubzansky, 2012). Some of the effects of positivity could also have their effects by attenuating the adverse consequences ordinarily attributable to stressors, although a meta-analysis of retrospective and prospective studies revealed that the link between positive mood and heart disease were not simply due to the attenuation of the negative actions of emotional distress (Chida & Steptoe, 2008).

Loneliness and heart disease

As most individuals tend to be social and our social groups and networks can have important health benefits (Jetten et al., 2012), it's not surprising that loneliness can have profound negative effects, including increased morbidity and mortality (Luo et al., 2012). Although social withdrawal and isolation are part of the depressive profile, loneliness can have damaging effects beyond those associated with depression. This relationship to heart disease was appreciably more pronounced among women than men (Thurston & Kubzansky, 2009), and among older people loneliness predicted a decline in daily activities and an increased risk of death (Perissinotto et al., 2012). Loneliness in this instance should be distinguished from living alone as not all people living alone are actually lonely, and, conversely, living with others doesn't necessarily mean that loneliness isn't experienced. In fact, the best predictor of poor well-being among the elderly is not their living status, but whether they feel lonely or depressed. As the saying goes, one can feel lonely in a crowded room, and for older individuals, loneliness can be a devastating stressor. In fact, it has even been suggested that in relation to heart disease, loneliness is more dangerous than is smoking.

Sleep disturbances

Sleep disturbances as we've seen, are accompanied by numerous health impairments, including CAD (Irwin, 2015), and poor sleep during adolescence, which often appears together with other poor life-style factors, predicts the occurrence of heart disease in adulthood (Narang et al., 2012). As stressful events and depression are linked to sleep disturbances, the relationship to CAD may also operate through stress and depression as opposed to stemming directly from sleep loss. There are data, however, supporting the view that sleep disturbances, through effects on inflammatory processes, contribute to cardiovascular disease (Irwin, 2015).

Gender differences in heart disease

Heart disease is the leading cause of death in women, just as it is men, but the development and appearance of the disease varies with their age. Premenopausal women are generally less apt to develop heart disease than same-aged men, but following menopause the rate of illness equals that of men. It seems that estrogen acts as 'female protection' against heart disease, but when estrogen levels decline following menopause, or in association with menstrual irregularities, vulnerability to CAD increases (Kallen & Pal, 2011). Beyond such hormonal influences, several psychosocial variables are associated with CAD in women. By example, psychosocial stressors and depression are more closely aligned with CAD in women than in men. Moreover, low socioeconomic status is a better predictor of heart disease in women than in men, and the frequency of CAD is lower in women in administrative positions than among women in the lower ranks, but there is an important caveat to this. To a considerable extent work might serve to facilitate coping with other life stressors, although there is a limit to its protective actions. If women faced the double load of working and taking care of a family, the risk for CAD was elevated (Blom et al., 2003).

Ethnic and cultural factors

As with so many other illnesses, heart disease varies with cultural and ethnic factors. In the UK, immigrants of South Asian descent are more likely to develop CAD than are others, probably owing to factors such as elevated glucose intolerance, obesity, elevated triglycerides, and insulin levels that come from newly changed life-styles (McKeigue et al., 1991). Likewise, African American men are 30% more likely to die from heart disease relative to white males, possibly being linked to higher blood pressure, more frequent occurrence of diabetes, subclinical vascular injury, and greater risk for blood pressure-related clinical complications than in whites (Flack et al., 2014). Heart disease within the US was also marked among ethnic minority women, being related to cultural and ethnic differences in BMI, diet, and physical inactivity (Winkleby et al., 1998).

An often overlooked aspect of health care is that symptom presentation may differ across groups, and the efficacy of treatments might also vary in this regard (Chaturvedi, 2003). Further to this, the *normative* levels of blood pressure in the US were determined on the basis of white individuals, and might not be as relevant to their black counterparts, in whom hypertension treatments ought to begin at lower blood pressures (Flack et al., 2014). This important difference is not as widely known as it should be, making intercessions to improve heart health more difficult in some groups.

A PARADOX AND A PARADOX

Death as a result of ischemic heart disease in France is about 25% lower than in Britain even though the usual risk factors are present in the two countries. This so-called 'French Paradox' has often been attributed to increased red wine consumption in France (Renaud & de Lorgeril, 1992). Red wine contains resveratrol, which serves as an antioxidant and anti-inflammatory agent that acts against heart disease (although there have been questions as to whether resveratrol actually acts as an antioxidant). Alternatively, some bacteria release inflammatory factors that promote plaque formation and hence favor heart disease, but other bacteria, stimulated by red wine, make carotinoids, which serve as antioxidants, which act against heart disease and stroke. However, there is reason to believe that red wine, or at least resveratrol or the formation of carotinoids, aren't actually the link (or the only link) to reduced heart disease (Semba et al., 2014), as much as some people might wish wine to have these effects. Instead, the France–UK difference may have to do with a time lag that exists between

(Continued)

(Continued)

increases in consumption of animal fat, serum cholesterol concentrations, and the resulting increase in mortality from heart disease. High consumption of animal fat and increased serum cholesterol concentrations appeared years earlier in England than in France (Law & Wald, 1999). Thus, the reports of higher cardiac-related deaths in England may be related to the consumption of foods that led to CAD, rather than wine consumption leading to a reduction of this condition in France.

So, should red wine be consumed for its beneficial effects on heart health? Consuming alcohol in the form of red wine may have positive effects (some doubters notwithstanding) by increasing good cholesterol, although grape skin can similarly do so, as they contain flavonoids and other antioxidant substances that can protect the heart from damage created by free oxygen radicals. The American Heart Association recommends that if you drink alcohol, then this ought to be done in moderation, which comprises no more than one to two drinks per day for men and one drink per day for women. More than this increases the risk for alcoholism, as well as high blood pressure, obesity, stroke, breast cancer, suicide, and accidents.

The French paradox isn't the only one that exists in relation to heart disease. Hispanics within the US comprise multiple ethnicities with origins in Mexico, Central America, South America, the Caribbean, and other Spanish-speaking countries, and all of these groups have lower rates of vascular disease than whites or African Americans. The 'Hispanic Paradox' is that this occurs despite the fact that they generally experience more frequent psychosocial and socioeconomic risk factors for heart disease, as well as the lowest rates of screening for elevated cholesterol levels and hypertension, the lowest rates of counseling for smoking problems, as well as poor blood pressure and glycemic control. So, what features are common among Hispanic groups that make them more resilient than other groups in relation to heart disease, and what are the implications of this for the development of new intervention or treatment strategies? It would seem that this would be a natural experiment that could be conducted readily, but this population has received less research attention than others (Lopez-Jimenez & Lavie, 2014).

Genetic factors

It is difficult to identify which genetic factors are most important in determining CAD, if for no other reasons than there are so many gene variants that may be associated with the condition, and they may affect this disease through different processes. A large genome-wide association study revealed about 240 genetic signals that were tied to plaque formation, of which about one-quarter were linked to cholesterol (Deloukas et al., 2013). Other studies of CAD identified genetic variants related to low- and high-density cholesterol and triglycerides, although it was suggested that the triglyceride-related genes were especially relevant (Roberts, 2014).

A genetic variant (PCSK9), which codes for cholesterol regulation, was identified as being related to CAD, subsequently led to the development of a monoclonal antibody that had promising effects in clinical trials (Dandona & Roberts, 2014). Other genes have been identified that similarly hold important clues related to CAD. For instance, a family of genes, sirtuins, was identified that appeared to be associated with longevity. The actions of these genes can manifest in several ways that may have significant implications for heart functioning (Cencioni et al., 2015). It also appears that genes related to inflammatory processes may come to influence heart functioning, and it has likewise been reported that regions of the genome that had previously been thought to be 'junk' portions are now known to include genes that, among other actions, affect heart functioning (K.C. Yang et al., 2014). A great number of other genes have been identified that in some fashion affect heart disease, and many of these may interact with particular foods, stressors, or other life-style factors that encourage or discourage CAD.

PERSONALITY FACTORS

Type A personality, hostility, and aggression

Just as individuals with certain personality traits differ in their responses to stressful events, such factors may also dispose some individuals to heart disease. The work of Friedman and Rosenman (1971) indicated that individuals with a *Type A* personality, described as being ambitious, competitive, impatient, hostile, and rushed, were more prone to heart disease relative to Type B individuals, who were generally viewed as being relatively laid back. Although such reports were met with excitement and prompted considerable research, subsequent studies only partially confirmed these findings. While the Type A personality was not consistently associated with heart disease, an element of this personality style comprising hostility and anger was linked to coronary problems (Barefoot et al., 1983). Even this view was challenged, but a detailed meta-analysis indicated that anger and hostility were, in fact, related to heart disease, particularly in men (Chida & Steptoe, 2010).

Just as trait anger has been associated with hypertension and heart disease, so has anger suppression (Denollet et al., 2010). Likewise, anger/hostility can be outwardly directed (anger-out) or it can be directed at the self (anger-in), and individuals who exhibit an anger-in characteristic are particularly prone to CAD (Stewart et al., 2010). Anger-out, in some instances, can serve as an effective coping mechanism (Matheson & Anisman, 2012), even though it is commonly accompanied by elevated blood pressure; whereas anger suppression may be accompanied by more persistent blood pressure elevations when the stressor is encountered again subsequently (Quartana & Burns, 2010), much as if they were unable to let go of their first negative experience. As Buddha was purported to have said, "Holding onto anger is like drinking poison and expecting the other person to die".

The Type D personality

Given the link between heart disease and depression, and also between depression and stressful experiences, the view was introduced that heart disease might be linked to what was referred to as the distressed (Type D) personality (Denollet, 2000). These individuals were described as being particularly attentive to negative stimuli, and tended to express negative emotions, such as depressed mood, anxiety, anger, hostile feelings, and worrying. They were also characterized as being asocial, uncomfortable with strangers, tense, and insecure with other people, and typically inhibited self-expression in social interactions.

Heart problems among Type D individuals were seen to be markedly elevated, and among those undergoing cardiac rehabilitation further complications were particularly frequent

(Denollet et al., 2010; Grande et al., 2012). Type D individuals were generally more apt to exhibit sensitized cardiovascular responses to repeated stressors (Howard & Hughes, 2013), an exaggerated hemodynamic response to a cold stressor, and increased occurrence of ventricular arrhythmias (Einvik et al., 2014). As well, cortisol dysregulation was common in Type D individuals (Denollet & Kupper, 2007), and daily cortisol output was elevated following an acute coronary event, possibly signaling further cardiac morbidity (Molloy et al., 2008).

As in the case of other personality factors suspected of being linked to heart disease, there have been failures to detect a strong relationship between Type D personality and heart disturbances (Larson et al., 2013). Some researchers questioned whether the inclusion of Type D as a predictor variable told us more than simply assessing depressive mood. There is also the question of whether having a Type D personality actually influences the course of heart disease by affecting relevant neurobiological processes, or whether Type D personality features might simply be accompanied by more unhealthy behaviors (Ginting et al., 2014), or poorer adherence to medication (Wu & Moser, 2013). It is premature to dismiss or support the usefulness of the Type D personality as a marker of heart disease and its prognosis, and prospective analyses are needed to sort things out (Grande et al., 2012).

PHYSIOLOGICAL STRESS RESPONSES IN RELATION TO HEART DISEASE

Sympathetic nervous system hyper-responsivity

Stressful experiences, through their actions on sympathetic nervous system activity, have been implicated in hypertension and eventual atherosclerosis, left *ventricular hypertrophy* (thickening of the left ventricle that can be indicative of further cardiac problems, such as enlargement of the heart), arrhythmia, and may act as a trigger to promote adverse cardiac events, including the rupture of plaques that provoke heart attacks (Esler & Kaye, 2000). The individual differences in sympathetic responses to stressors might also contribute to differences in the emergence of pathological outcomes. Depressed individuals, for instance, may react more strongly to certain challenges, reflected by enhanced sympathetic activity and circulating norepinephrine levels. Likewise, greater sympathetic responses and higher epinephrine levels in response to mental stressors occur in Type A individuals (Howard et al., 1990), and 'hot reactors', which exhibit marked sympathetic hyper-reactivity in response to challenges, are more prone to developing atherosclerosis relative to 'cold reactors' (Eliot et al., 1982). Although these linkages may seem straightforward, still other factors could moderate stressor-related sympathetic arousal, including personality traits and diet, which can also independently influence cardiovascular illnesses.

Brain influences on cardiac functioning and disease

Receptors located in blood vessels (*baroreceptors*) are sensitive to blood pressure changes, and they send relevant information on to brain regions such as the hypothalamus, which can influence heart functioning. Drug treatments that attenuate norepinephrine activity (e.g., by blocking the β-norepinephrine receptors) reduce blood pressure, irrespective of whether the drug is administered systemically or directly into the hypothalamus, indicating that brain processes are fundamental for the blood pressure changes. Similarly, blocking excitatory glutamate receptors within the paraventricular nucleus of the hypothalamus influences sympathetic activity and heart functioning (Garcia Pelosi et al., 2009).

In addition to the involvement of the hypothalamus, heart rate and blood pressure could be affected by altering neuronal activity in cortical and limbic brain areas known to be involved in mood states (Ciriello et al., 2013). Cardiovascular activity was similarly associated with neuronal changes in brain regions implicated in decision making or processing of information relevant to stressors (cingulate cortex and insula), and those associated with vigilance under stressful situations (e.g., locus coeruleus) (e.g., Wang, Piñol et al., 2014). In essence, although cardiovascular functioning is influenced by autonomic nervous system processes together with variations of hypothalamic activity, top-down management of heart functioning also occurs, which may be affected by emotional stressors.

Inflammatory processes in heart disease

As we've seen, inflammatory processes are essential for our well-being, but they can also act in a destructive manner, including the provocation of atherosclerosis (Coggins & Rosenzweig, 2012). In this regard, CAD was seen to be accompanied by antibodies indicative of earlier (or current) pathogen presence, including *Helicobacter pylori* (more commonly associated with ulcers), *Chlamydia pneumoniae* (associated with pneumonia), and *cytomegalovirus* (associated with forms of herpes) (Kop & Mommersteeg, 2014). Moreover, socioeconomic status, coupled with an individual's *pathogen burden*, reflected by the total number of infections experienced, was related to heart disease (Steptoe et al., 2008; Zhu et al., 2000). As stressor experiences, infectious agents, and chemical or physical trauma that cause tissue damage all increase proinflammatory cytokines in blood and generally increase pathogen burden, these factors may come together in the development of heart disease (P.S. Miller et al., 2014).

GUM DISEASE AND HEART HEALTH

There are occasions where seemingly odd illness comorbidities turn out to have considerable significance. There have been reports indicating that periodontal (gum) disease is accompanied by greater incidence of heart disease (Humphrey et al., 2008) and it has been linked to the extent and severity of heart attack (Marfil-Álvarez et al., 2014). It's tempting to make causal conclusions regarding this relationship, supposing that increased inflammatory factors related to chronic periodontal disease are responsible for the developmental of heart disease. A statement from the American Heart Association has, however, made it clear that this conclusion is premature as the two disorders share other features, including age, smoking habits, and the presence of diabetes, any of which might account for the comorbidity (Lockhart et al., 2012).

Cytokines and stressors

Inflammatory factors, as described earlier, contribute to plaque formation and hence atherosclerosis. This is magnified when the immune system is in an activated state, as in the case of infection being present (Kop & Cohen, 2007). Stressful events likewise increase circulating cytokines, and might thus contribute to heart disease (Pasic et al., 2003), and the cumulative actions of severe stressors over the life time can be especially pernicious in relation to heart disease (O'Donovan et al., 2012). In line with this suggestion, protracted periods of distress that lead to PTSD (e.g., in soldiers at war) were associated with a doubling of the later development of heart disease (Vaccarino et al., 2013).

Beyond the peripheral actions of inflammatory factors in the provocation of CAD, cytokine activity in the brain may also contribute to heart-related problems. In animals, the infusion of IL-1β or TNF-α directly into the brain increases arterial blood pressure and sympathetic activity, and may promote the release of hormones that contribute to heart disease (Mollace et al., 2001). Conversely, a TNF-α antagonist administered following myocardial injury attenuated some of the effects otherwise associated with heart failure (Wang et al., 2011).

Another inflammatory cytokine, IL-18, which we haven't considered in any detail to this point, may also contribute to the development of CAD. Besides promoting the production of other cytokines, IL-18 released from *cardiomyocytes* (cardiac muscle cells) may contribute to '*vascular remodeling*' (Reddy et al., 2010). Specifically, under certain conditions, such as chronic hemodynamic stress and hormonal variations, blood vessels are able to change their geometry or configuration through cell production and growth, possibly reflecting adaptive changes to ongoing conditions (Dzau & Gibbons, 1993). During this process, however, lesions can develop that set in motion a cascade of cytokine and structural alterations that can lead to narrowing of blood vessels, acute coronary syndromes, progression of atherosclerosis, myocardial infarction, and cardiomyopathy (e.g., Lu et al., 2013).

BIOMARKERS FOR HEART DISEASE

Cardiac disturbances may be accompanied by increased cytokine levels which give rise to heart cells producing atrial natriuretic peptide (ANP) and brain natriuretic peptide (BNP), as well as C-reactive protein (CRP), the latter being released from the liver in response to inflammation (Danesh et al., 2004). Altered ANP and BNP, and elevated CRP, IL-6, and fibrinogen in older people, were associated with a propensity for fatal heart attack (and stroke) relative to non-fatal events (Sattar et al., 2009). Thus, elevated levels of these substrates have been used as markers for cardiac disease (Tavener & Kubes, 2006).

If inflammatory factors contribute to CAD, as opposed to simply being a marker for illness, then manipulating these inflammatory processes could potentially influence heart disease. In fact, however, anti-TNF-α agents, such as etanercept or infliximab, were not effective treatments of CAD and in some instances caused further problems (Cacciapaglia et al., 2011). As we saw in discussing positive psychology, these treatments were evaluated when damage to the heart had already been present, and by then it might have been too late to reap any benefits of interventions. Furthermore, as multiple processes likely contribute to heart disease, simply altering one of these might be insufficient to reverse existent damage or to get to the root of the problem.

Adiposity and cytokines in relation to heart disease

Being overweight may increase risk factors for heart disease, even if body mass index is only moderately elevated. In fact, obesity may have protracted effects so that children and adolescents who are obese may exhibit elevated biological risk factors for later heart disease (Kit et al., 2015). Is being heavy a strain that wears down the heart, or is being heavy associated with less exercise that could potentially improve heart functioning? Alternatively, does obesity actually encourage dyslipidemia (excess cholesterol and fat in blood), impaired glucose tolerance, insulin resistance, metabolic syndrome, diabetes, and hypertension, which favor the development of heart disease? Although there are multiple routes linking obesity and CAD, it is significant that heart disease occurs more readily when fat is localized around the gut. These fat cells (*adipose tissue*) are a particularly rich source for inflammatory factors, including IL-6 and TNF-α, and their sustained release might promote heart disease, as well as other illnesses (Abizaid et al., 2014).

Recovery from cardiac events

Following a heart attack or heart failure, the probability of re-hospitalization or death is about one in five, and elevated risk persists over the ensuing year (Dharmarajan et al., 2015). It is certain that an individual's behaviors following a cardiac event, such as engaging in rehabilitation and maintaining proper heart health behaviors, act against illness recurrence, whereas relatively low health literacy (ability to read, understand, and use health information) may predict heart failure (McNaughton et al., 2015). For that matter, just as a sedentary life-style such as sitting too much can ordinarily be detrimental to health, this may also influence recovery from heart problems. Similarly, recovery from heart attack is disturbed with stressor experiences (Xu et al., 2015), making stress-reduction methods especially important in fostering recovery. As indicated earlier, knowing that something is either dangerous or beneficial doesn't necessarily translate into actions that can enhance health. Knowing what most people do about basic life-style factors and heart disease, it's remarkable that in Europe about half the people who had smoked prior to an MI continued to do so afterward and frequently didn't engage in exercise needed for proper rehabilitation. Most patients who had previously been overweight or obese continued to maintain their weight, their hypertension typically persisted, and both their bad cholesterol and glucose were at risky levels (Kotseva et al., 2015).

PHARMACOLOGICAL TREATMENTS OF HEART DISEASE

Medications have been at the forefront of efforts to limit heart disease. Some drugs, such as ACE inhibitors, limit heart failure, just as they are useful in treating high blood pressure. Other treatments being developed have been directed at specific heart proteins that might be responsible for cell damage following heart attack, and novel antioxidants have been developed in an effort to 'rejuvenate' old arteries. There have even been novel gel-like materials developed that can be applied directly to damaged heart tissue that will deliver inhibitors of enzymes that otherwise promote inflammation. In line with novel approaches in the treatment of other illnesses, there has been a quest to develop gene therapies to strengthen the heart, and early success in animal studies has encouraged human trials. As described in relation to other illnesses, there has been an appreciable focus on tying the effectiveness of specific medications to particular genes in an effort to develop personalized therapy.

Treating hypertension

Treatment of hypertension ought to include life-style changes that focus on increased exercise, maintaining proper body weight, eating properly (e.g., vegetables, fruit, whole grains, low-fat and low-sodium foods), eliminating bad habits such as smoking, and adopting effective ways to diminish stress. In this regard, cognitive behavioral therapy may be useful in diminishing hypertension in some people or might reduce the drug dose required to attenuate borderline hypertension (Shapiro et al., 1997). Often, however, this might not do the trick, and specific antihypertensive medications may be prescribed.

Beta blockers

For some time a favored medication was norepinephrine beta receptor blockers (usually referred to simply as *beta blockers*), which had been developed 50 years ago, and for which hundreds of millions of prescriptions have been written. These drugs, of which there are about 20 different brands, block norepinephrine receptors of the sympathetic nervous system, and as a result the heart beats more slowly and with less force, thus reducing blood pressure. The rapid effects of beta blockers caused it to become a hit in the medical community, and its inventor, James Black, was awarded a Nobel Prize in 1988. For several reasons, however, beta blockers have run into disfavor. Aside from not getting at the source of the problem responsible for the elevated blood pressure, a 4-year prospective study indicated that beta blockers didn't reduce the risk of heart attacks, deaths from heart attacks, or stroke among individuals with a history of myocardial infarction but who were stable, or among individuals with CAD without a history of MI, or those who were only at risk for CAD (Bangalore et al., 2012). A similar study among individuals who experienced a heart attack likewise indicated that of several treatments, beta blockers were least effective in reducing mortality (Zuckerman et al., 2012), and among patients who had not experienced myocardial infarction and heart failure, the use of beta blockers in the treatment of hypertension actually increased the risk of cardiovascular events and death (Bangalore et al., 2008). The problem for beta blockers became still greater, and the controversy surrounding their use more pronounced, with the report that death following non-cardiac surgery was elevated by 27% among patients who had been using beta blockers (Bouri et al., 2013). This also raises the question as to whether the use of beta blockers in the treatment of other illnesses, such as migraine headaches (which are also associated with increased risk of stroke and myocardial infarction), should be reconsidered. At first blush these findings might seem shocking. These compounds have been around for 50 years and it's only *now* that we're learning that their effects are limited? The limited effectiveness of these agents may be thought to be less urgent because they are being overshadowed by more effective agents; but, in fact, they are still being used frequently.

ACE inhibitors

A class of drugs referred to as ACE (*angiotensin-converting enzyme*) inhibitors block the production of the hormone *angiotensin II*, thereby attenuating blood vessel constriction and permitting better flow of blood being pumped to the heart, resulting in blood pressure being lowered. Across several studies, the ACE inhibitors reduced cardiovascular death, MI, and stroke (Zuckerman et al., 2012). Likewise, angiotensin II receptor blockers (ARBs), which have their effect by limiting angiotensin II from stimulating blood vessel receptors, have been used in the treatment of hypertension. These agents are also beneficial as they decrease chemicals that promote salt and fluid build-up in the body. Other ways of diminishing the effects of heart disease have been explored, including drugs that act as *calcium channel blockers* to dilate coronary arteries, thereby enhancing blood flow to the heart (Poole-Wilson et al., 2004).

Treatments of CAD

Statins for limiting cholesterol

Statins that reduce lipids, and particularly *low-density lipoprotein* (LDL) cholesterol levels (i.e., bad cholesterol), can act against the development of CAD by about 30%, even among older individuals and in those with diabetes. A systematic review of the literature concluded that statins reduced heart disease and death among individuals with high bad cholesterol levels (Taylor et al., 2013). However, other reviews asserted that there were few benefits to the use of statins (Petretta et al., 2010), and their usefulness in women was still more uncertain. These contradictory views notwithstanding, the American College of Cardiology and the American Heart Association have come down on the side of using statins to limit or prevent cardiovascular disease among individuals with high levels of bad (LDL) cholesterol (Stone et al., 2013).

Baby aspirin

A great number of people have opted to use low dose (75–150 mg/kg day) aspirin to act against heart problems. Not everyone gains from taking aspirin, and it was indicated that beneficial effects can be predicted on the basis of about 60 genes being activated that influence blood platelets (and hence clotting) (Voora et al., 2013). For people with aspirin intolerance, other agents, such as clopidogrel and ticlopidine, are effective.

Digoxin

If heart disease is present and the heart's pumping ability has been weakened (termed *heart failure*), digoxin may be prescribed to help the weakened or injured heart pump blood through the body more efficiently. It does so by augmenting the heart's contractions and slowing heart rate.

Diuretics

With heart failure, a build up of fluids may occur that makes it more difficult for the heart to pump. Thus, diuretics are prescribed that facilitate the elimination of water and salt through increased urination.

Nitrates

In those with angina or chest pain owing to blocked arteries, nitrates are used to relax coronary arteries. They may be used in combination with other agents, such as those that reduce blood pressure (hydralazine) when congestive heart failure occurs.

ALTERNATIVE MEDICINE IN THE TREATMENT OF HEART DISEASE

The notion that supplements or alternative medicines can cure anything has become a major industry. Does this mean that once arteries are excessively clogged one can simply turn back the clock and undo the damage that's accrued over years? I suppose it depends on whom you ask. One of the more talked about supplements for good heart health is that of Omega-3 fatty acids. Some randomized clinical trials reported positive effects, including lowering of blood pressure and triglyceride levels and even reducing mortality. In fact, various governments have approved omega-3 treatment as a supplement for patients who experienced a heart attack, or to reduce triglycerides that were too high, and even for 'cardiovascular protection'. As it happens, not all randomized control studies reported positive effects with omega-3 supplements. Systematic reviews and meta-analyses, in fact, indicated that the use of omega-3 was not accompanied by altered cardiac death rates, sudden death, heart attack, stroke, or all-cause mortality (Rizos et al., 2012).

As many as half the people with heart problems use herbal or other supplements, sometimes believing that even if these 'natural' remedies don't cure them, they can't have negative effects. Wrong! Some supplements can interfere with standard medications, such as the blood thinning agent warfarin. In some instances, as described in Table 8.2. these supplements might not even be used for heart problems, but taken for other potential ailments, but might still have negative cardiac consequences (Tachjian et al., 2010).

Table 8.2   Herbal products to avoid in patients with cardiovascular diseases

Herb	Purported use	Adverse effect of interaction
Alfalfa	Arthritis, asthma, dyspepsia, hyperlipidemia, diabetes	Increases bleeding risk with warfarin
Aloe vera	Wounds (topical), diabetes (oral)	Hypokalemia causing digitalis toxicity and arrhythmia
Angelica (dong quai)	Appetite loss, dyspepsia, infection	Increases bleeding risk with warfarin
Bilberry	Circulatory disorders, local inflammation, skin conditions, diarrhea, arthritis	Increases bleeding risk with warfarin
Butcher's broom	Circulatory disorders, inflammation, leg cramps	Decreases effects of α-blockers
Capsicum	Shingles, trigeminal and diabetic neuralgia	Increases blood pressure (with MAOI)
Fenugreek	High cholesterol	Increases bleeding risk with warfarin; hypoglycemia
Fumitory	Infection, edema, hypertension, constipation	Increases effects of β-blockers, calcium channel blockers, cardiac glycosides

Herb	Purported use	Adverse effect of interaction
Garlic	High cholesterol, hypertension, heart disease	Increases bleeding risk with warfarin
Ginger	High cholesterol, motion sickness, indigestion, antioxidant	Increases bleeding risk with warfarin
Ginkgo	Poor circulation, cognitive disorder	Increases bleeding risk with warfarin, aspirin, or COX-2 inhibitors Potential risk of seizures
Ginseng	Aging, diminished immunity, improves mental and physical capacity and stress tolerance	Increases blood pressure Decreases effects of warfarin Hypoglycemia
Gossypol	Male contraceptive	Increases effects of diuretics Hypokalemia
Grapefruit juice	Weight loss, to promote cardiovascular health	Increases effects of statins, calcium channel blockers, or cyclosporines
Green tea	Improve cognitive performance, mental alertness, weight loss, diuretic	Decreases effects of warfarin (contains vitamin K)
Hawthorn	CHF, hypertension	Potentiates action of cardiac glycosides and nitrates
Irish moss	Ulcers, gastritis	Increases effects of antihypertensives
Kelp	Cancer, obesity	Increases effects of antihypertensives and anticoagulants
Khella	Muscle spasms	Increases effects of anticoagulants and calcium channel blockers
Licorice	Ulcer, cirrhosis, cough, sore throat, infections	Increases blood pressure Hypokalemia May potentiate digoxin toxicity
Lily of the valley	CHF	Increases effects of β-blockers, calcium channel blockers, digitalis, quinidine, steroids
Ma-huang (ephedra)	Obesity, cough	Increases heart rate and blood pressure
Night-blooming cereus	CHF	Increases effects of angiotension-converting enzyme inhibitors, antiarrhythmics, β-blockers, calcium channel blockers, cardiac glycosides

(Continued)

(Continued)

Herb	Purported use	Adverse effect of interaction
Oleander	Muscle cramps, asthma, cancer, CHF, hepatitis, psoriasis, arthritis	Heart block Hyperkalemia Arrhythmia Death
St. John's wort	Depression	Increases heart rate and blood pressure (with MAOI) Decreases digoxin concentration
Storphanthus	CHF	Increases effects of cardiac glycosides
Yohimbine	Impotence	Increases heart rate Increases or decreases blood pressure

Abbreviations: CHF, congestive heart failure; COX, cyclooxygenase; MAOI, monoamine oxidase inhibitor

From Tachijian et al. (2010)

CHRONIC OBSTRUCTIVE PULMONARY DISEASE

Illness etiology

Just about everyone knows that smoking tobacco products promotes heart disease and several forms of cancer, but much less attention has been devoted to chronic obstructive pulmonary diseases (COPD), of which emphysema is best known. COPD, the third leading cause of death in Western countries, is a disorder in which airflow to the lungs is impaired, typically being characterized by shortness of breath, frequent coughing, and production of sputum, with symptoms worsening with the passage of time (Vestbo et al., 2013). Although genetic factors contribute to the development of COPD, the most prominent causes of the disorder are smoking tobacco, including second-hand smoke, and industrial pollutants (dust, chemicals and fumes). Approximately 80–90% of individuals with COPD had previously smoked (or were currently smokers), and of those who still smoke, about 20% could count on developing the disorder, varying with the extent of their smoking (Ward, 2012). Not surprisingly, household air pollution has also been associated with COPD (as well as pneumonia, asthma, and lung cancer) and has been notably problematic in parts of Asia and Africa where wood, charcoal, or coals are used for cooking (Gordon et al., 2014).

A longitudinal study that spanned about 18 years pointed to still other contributing factors for COPD. The odds of developing COPD were elevated among individuals who had shown signs of vital exhaustion, had experienced a dysfunctional social network, or who had encountered economic hardships (Clark et al., 2015). As well, COPD was linked to poverty level, being frequent in poor and rural areas (Holt et al., 2011), and there have been indications that being overweight and not exercising were associated with this respiratory condition (Behrens et al., 2014).

Biological mechanisms

The development of COPD involves inflammatory responses, particularly IL-6, in response to irritants (Rubini, 2013), which may be further aggravated by oxidative stress stemming from high concentrations of free radicals released by inflammatory cells. There is also reason to believe that COPD may involve either an autoimmune response, the induction of factors in the airway wall that leads to modifications of these cells, or immune alterations stemming from epigenetic changes (Tzortzaki et al., 2013).

The diminished airflow characteristic of COPD comes about owing to lung tissue breaking down (*emphysema*) and small airways being disturbed (*obstructive bronchitis*). The inflammation and scarring that occurs narrows airways, contributing to difficulties of exhaling fully, and thus some of the air from the previous breath remains in the lungs as the next inhalation occurs (referred to as '*trapping*'). Thus, shortness of breath may occur with mild exercise simply as a result of difficulty inhaling when the lungs are already partially full (O'Donnell, 2006). In more severe cases, lung tissue may actually be modified by air pockets (bullae) leading to a disease condition referred to as *bullous emphysema*. As the disease progresses, the lung arteries may encounter increased pressure, thus straining the right ventricle ('*cor pulmonale*'), leading to bulging neck veins and leg swelling (Weitzenblum & Chaouat, 2009).

RUSSIAN ROULETTE

COPD is frequently comorbid with other illnesses, including elevated blood pressure, CAD, diabetes, lung cancer, osteoporosis, cerebral microbleeds, cognitive impairments, anxiety and depression (Decramer et al., 2012), as well as bacterially-related disturbances such as staphylococcal infections (Inghammar et al., 2014). Any of these illnesses may be the bullet that kills, and COPD may be the gun that fired the bullet.

Psychological contributions

Patients with COPD frequently perceive themselves as experiencing increased distress, usually stemming from their illness condition, being most pronounced among those with limited problem-focused coping styles (Andenæs et al., 2006). Predictably, the presence of anxiety, depression, and PTSD is accompanied by COPD symptom exacerbation (e.g., Laurin et al., 2012). In contrast, training individuals to cope with stressors, even through a tele-health program, has been shown to reduce somatic symptoms and enhance general well-being (Blumenthal et al., 2014).

Treatment

There is currently no cure for COPD, although attempts are being made to antagonize the processes that lead to activation of destructive immune responses that are elicited by cigarette smoke.

This condition, as described in Table 8.3, can be managed so that symptoms are reduced (D.E. O'Donnell et al., 2008; Puhan, 2011). Most often medications are also prescribed, comprising inhalation of bronchodilation agents, such as beta-norepinephrine receptor stimulants or those that block acetylcholine receptors (Decramer et al., 2012), sometimes accompanied by corticoid treatments. Antibiotics have also seen some use, and as the disease progresses, supplemental oxygen may be called for. Increasing research attention has focused on the possibility that manipulations of immune functioning can act against COPD, and early indications revealed this to be a promising treatment target (Ngkelo & Adcock, 2013).

Table 8.3   Preventive strategies for exacerbation of chronic obstructive pulmonary disease

- Smoking cessation
- Vaccinations

  - Influenza (annually)
  - Pneumococcal vaccine (every 5–10 years)

- Self-management education
- Regular long-acting bronchodilator therapy (for moderate or severe COPD)
- Regular therapy with a combination of inhaled corticosteroids and a long-acting beta$_2$-agonist
- Oral corticosteroid therapy
- Pulmonary rehabilitation

STROKE

Stroke subtypes

Stroke, sometimes referred to as a cerebrovascular accident (CVA) or cerebrovascular insult (CVI), comes in two basic forms. *Hemorrhagic stroke*, the less common of the two, making up 10–15% of cases, comprises a ruptured blood vessel bleeding directly into the brain or into the subarachnoid space surrounding brain tissue. The second, *ischemic strok*e, refers to the loss of brain functioning that occurs owing to a lack of blood flow and hence a lack of oxygen and glucose being provided to the brain. The ischemia can occur as a result of blood vessel blockage owing to a *thrombosis* (blod clot) or *arterial embolism* (clot, fat globule, or gas bubble) or by cerebral *hypoperfusion* (general reduction of blood supply) (Sims & Muyderman, 2009). Another form of ischemic stroke involves occlusion of a single 'deep penetrating artery' that feeds deep brain structures. These *lacunar* strokes make up about one-quarter of strokes.

The damage created by a stroke doesn't just reflect the neuronal death that occurs within minutes of a stroke occurring. Following a stroke, an excessively great release of the neurotransmitter glutamate may occur, often described as a 'glutamate storm', which is responsible for the death of neurons (Kostandy, 2012), and thus may continue to cause damage for some time. It is likewise possible that elevated cytokine levels that occur following brain injury might occur in an effort to heal the brain, but when these levels become excessive, they can be damaging (Shichita et al., 2014).

Signs of stroke

The specific physical and behavioral signs associated with stroke depend on the brain regions that are directly or indirectly affected. Obviously, the more widespread the damage, the more profound the symptoms, and new symptoms can emerge as areas secondary to the initial damage are affected. Several instruments have been devised to assess for a potential stroke quickly, such as the Cincinnati Prehospital Stroke Scale (CPSS) (Kothari et al., 1999), as well as other similar instruments. The most common signs are face weakness or facial droop (ask the person to smile or show their front teeth; if one side of the face moves less well than the other, this might signify stroke), abnormal speech (ask the person to repeat a familiar phrase, such as "You can't teach an old dog new tricks"; if the words are slurred or some words are wrong, or if the person is unable to speak, this might signify stroke), and arm drift (ask person to close their eyes and hold both arms straight out in front of them for 10 seconds; if one arm falls or drifts down more than the other, then stroke is a possibility). Some stroke symptoms are unique to women, such as dizziness, headaches, numbness over the whole body, more on one side of the body, and women more often than men will develop hiccups accompanied by unusual chest pains (most women, incidentally, are unaware of this symptom). When one or more of these symptoms appear it is essential to reach a hospital quickly, and the usual procrastination about 'maybe it'll go away' is a very bad idea.

The specific symptoms presented can reflect the brain region(s) affected by stroke. Brainstem involvement may affect responses related to the cranial nerves and so symptoms might comprise changes of smell, taste, hearing, or vision; drooping of eyelid (ptosis) and weakness of ocular muscles; disturbed gag or swallowing reflex; disturbed pupil reactivity to light; problems with balance; altered heart rate or breathing; problems or weakness within a major neck muscle so that the ability to turn the head is hampered; or difficulty moving the tongue. Should the stroke involve the cerebral cortex, the symptoms might comprise aphasia (difficulty of comprehension or expression of language), auditory comprehension, dysarthria (motor speech disturbances), apraxia (disturbed voluntary movements), memory disturbances, hemineglect (in which patients are seemingly unaware of stimuli on one side of them), and a lack of insight pertaining to their disability. Finally, if the stroke occurs within the cerebellum, then symptoms might comprise disturbed motor coordination, change in gait, and dizziness (vertigo).

It probably goes without saying that in the aftermath of stroke significant emotional and cognitive repercussions are prominent. About 30% of patients experience post-stroke psychological depression that resembles major depressive disorder (Hackett et al., 2005), but some patients will exhibit rapid shifts of emotion, and in some instances emotional changes occur entirely inappropriately. Still other patients will display anxiety, apathy, panic attacks, mania, or psychosis, presumably owing to disturbances of particular brain regions as a direct result of the stroke. The cognitive disturbances secondary to stroke also vary widely, depending on the individual's age, pre-existing neuropathology, and intellectual and cognitive functioning. These cognitive disturbances include perceptual disturbances, and problems with attention and memory (Lim & Alexander, 2009), and dementia (Leys et al., 2005).

SILENT STROKE

Unlike ischemic and hemorrhagic stroke in which symptoms and outcomes are very obvious, 'silent stroke' may occur in which outward stroke symptoms are not apparent and the individual may be unaware that they have suffered a stroke. Some damage will have accrued that can be detected through an MRI scan (Leary & Saver, 2003), and individuals may be at increased risk for a major stroke. Even though this type of stroke sounds unusual, among individuals over 65 years of age, about 30% experience such an event. The risk factors for silent stroke are much like those associated with major stroke. These include age, hypertension, cigarette smoking, diabetes, metabolic syndrome, irregular heart rate, elevated inflammatory markers – particularly C reactive protein and IL-6, anemia, and sleep apnea.

Another form of stroke that has effects that are less pronounced than those of major strokes comprises a transient ischemic attack (TIA), which is frequently thought of as a 'mini-stroke'. Although some individuals mistake these for being entirely benign, they may be warning signs of a worse stroke that might follow. Like ischemic strokes, TIA is caused by a clot, except that the blockage is temporary, after which symptoms disappear. Obviously, during the course of symptoms appearing it isn't certain how serious these are, and they ought to be considered as being of an ischemic nature, possibly reflecting stroke.

Risk factors and epidemiology

Stroke accounts for slightly more than 10% of deaths, being somewhat higher in underdeveloped countries (Feigin et al., 2014). Stroke can occur at any age, but 95% of strokes occur after the age of 45, and more than two-thirds of strokes occur after the age of 65. Although men are considerably more likely to experience strokes than women, and they occur at an earlier age, when women experience a stroke it's more likely to be fatal, possibly because of their relatively older age. In addition to age, blood pressure is predictive of stroke, as are diabetes, high cholesterol, tobacco smoking, atrial fibrillation, a history of stroke or transient ischemic attack (TIA); and anxiety, anger, hostility, depression, and PTSD are also considered risk factors (Everson-Rose et al., 2014; Hakim, 2011). Stressful experiences also increase stroke risk, and among individuals who experience a major life event, the occurrence of stroke quadruples in the ensuing year (Egido et al., 2012). Not unexpectedly, stroke is linked to socioeconomic status (SES), likely owing to life-styles endorsed, stressors experienced, and limited access to preventive care (Jaja et al., 2013). Moreover, stressors encountered early in life (e.g., abuse) may increase stroke occurrence in adulthood, possibly by altering stress responses during development and in adulthood. Prenatal stressor experiences can also influence the risk for stroke in adulthood, especially if a second hit in the form of an adult stressor is encountered (Zucchi et al., 2014).

STROKE AND DEPRESSION

Just as the occurrence of depression is a good predictor of later heart disease, it may also be linked to the occurrence of major stroke (Hakim, 2011) as well as silent stroke (Vermeer et al., 2007). The link between depression and stroke has been shown to increase with age and be more prominent among women with a history of heart problems (Hermann et al., 2008; Wassertheil-Smoller et al., 2004). It has also been reported that patients who present with depressed symptoms following stroke may exhibit a poor prognosis for functional recovery, increased risk for further stroke and greater mortality over the ensuing few years (Lichtman et al., 2014).

Depression has been associated with microstructural changes within the midbrain (Blood et al., 2010), just as such changes are associated with aging, and it is possible that these variations contribute to later stroke. As cytokines have been linked to both depression and stroke, and might constitute a clinical marker of later functional recovery, the identification of specific cytokine changes introduced by ischemic stroke might be useful in the development of novel targets to treat or limit the downstream negative consequences that are typically associated with a stroke.

Treating stroke

If an ischemic stroke is treated with 'clot busters' within a small window of only a few hours, often referred to as 'golden hours', then damage to the brain might be limited and patients may have a good recovery. *Tissue plasminogen activator* (tPA) is the class of drug that has received particular attention in conditions in which blood clots are prominent features. A systematic review and meta-analysis indicated that this compound had positive effects if delivered in the critical 3-hour window following the occurrence of a stroke (although newer guidelines suggest positive effects may be obtained up to 4.5 hours since stroke occurrence). Yet, the clot-busting capacity of tPA was also associated with increased mortality during the ensuing week owing to increased occurrence of intracranial hemorrhage (Wardlaw et al., 2012).

In some instances, where tPA is not a treatment option, surgery may be required to repair some damage attributable to stroke, or to remove blood that pooled owing to hemorrhagic stroke. A relatively new procedure has been developed for ischemic stroke, endovascular therapy (ET), that is coupled with tPA treatment. A thin tube is inserted into the artery in the groin, and then threaded through the body and up to the brain vessels where the clot is present. The clot is retrieved through a stent and once it has been removed blood flow in the brain is possible (Saver et al., 2015).

Rehabilitation

For individuals who have suffered a stroke, the battle isn't over simply by surviving, as CNS damage incurred will usually call for considerable stroke rehabilitation efforts for the person to be able to return to normal life, to the extent that this is possible. Rehabilitation ought to begin as soon as possible, and can lasts months or years, with the objective being that individuals regain the skills of everyday living to help them adapt to difficulties that might be encountered, limit or preclude complications related to the condition or its treatment, and provide training and education to family members who will probably be contributing to the patient's care and well-being. Typically, rehabilitation involves a team of individuals who have divergent but overlapping skills. Such teams comprise physiotherapists, occupational therapists, physicians with specific training in rehabilitation medicine, nursing staff, speech and language therapists, orthotists (paramedical health professionals who provide biomechanical devices to physically disabled people), and sometimes psychologists and social workers.

TAKING ADVANTAGE OF SYNAPTIC PLASTICITY IN REVERSING THE EFFECTS OF STROKE

Following stroke, astrocytes may serve in some form of reparative capacity, but studies in mice have indicated that astrocytes were doing much more than this. Astrocytes and neural *stem/progenitor* cells (NSPCs) might improve functioning following stroke by modulating inflammation, and by facilitating a new blood supply (angiogenesis) being obtained. It may be especially significant that these NSPCs may act in a neuroprotective capacity and may produce new neurons (Kokaia & Lindvall, 2012), thus playing an essential role in recovery of functions (Magnusson et al., 2014). Not all astrocytes serve identical functions, and one particular type of astrocyte, dubbed Olig2PC-Astros, seems to be able to protect neurons from oxidative stress and has been involved in rebuilding neural circuits (P. Jiang et al., 2013). Ultimately, for the potential healing abilities of astrocytes to be realized, considerable coordination between stem cell researchers and clinicians will be necessary in order to identify conditions and treatments that are ideal for stroke patients, while minimizing the risks that such procedures entail. No doubt, other stem cell therapies will emerge to diminish the effects of stroke (Savitz et al., 2011).

Based largely on animal studies, it was suggested that advantage could be taken of the brain's remarkable neuroplasticity so that functional recovery could be attained following stroke by encouraging activity-dependent rewiring and synapse strengthening (Murphy & Corbett, 2009). By engaging in particular behaviors, the synapses controlling the relearning of various skills will be augmented and thus recovery will progress more readily, and the sooner rehabilitation is initiated, the better the subsequent outcome (Weinrich et al., 2004). As Murphy and Corbett (2009) indicated, if at least partial neuronal functioning is present, the possibility of achieving restoration of neural circuit activity can be augmented in the days or even weeks following stroke through the establishment and strengthening of compensatory rewiring and remapping of the neural circuitry. They concluded, *on both animal and human studies*, that moderate to high-intensity exercise increases growth factors, such as BDNF, insulin-like growth factor, and nerve growth factor, leading to elevated synaptogenesis in several brain regions, thereby enhancing functional recovery. They cautioned, however, that animal models and clinical experiences don't always map onto one another, and issues still need to be worked out, including the timing at which exercise ought to be initiated, as well as the influence of factors such as age and gender. They nonetheless suggested that recuperation can even occur for years after the stroke, and thus "the time window for stroke recovery, as with that of normal learning, never really closes" (Murphy & Corbett, 2009: 865).

Physiotherapy and occupational therapy are major components of post-stroke rehabilitation. Physiotherapy aims at improving joint range of motion and muscle strength through specific exercises as well as by re-learning functional tasks. Occupational therapy is more concerned with having patients re-learn and perform activities of daily living (ADLs), such as eating, drinking, dressing, bathing, cooking, reading and writing, and toileting. For patients with particular problems, speech and language therapy might be called for, and likewise, specialized treatment might be necessary for impairments stemming from a neurological disturbance of the motor-speech system that appears as the inability to translate conscious speech plans into motor plans.

Aerobic exercise appears to be a potentially effective way of promoting neuroplasticity and recovery following stroke (Ploughman et al., 2015), although the magnitude of the effects obtained with fitness training are limited (Brazzelli et al., 2011). Many of the old methods used in this regard seem tired, and traditional methods of some therapies are being enhanced with new technologies that make them more interesting, motivating, and more apt to get at muscle movement difficulties. These include video games and virtual reality-based exercises (Lange et al., 2009). As well, many of these procedures facilitate therapy conducted at home, and favor social interaction, which, as we've seen, is an important component in diminishing distress and may also encourage the therapy being sustained.

SUMMARY

Heart-related ailments, COPD, circulatory problems, and stroke are responsible for more deaths than any other illnesses, and can severely limit quality of life. Heart disease is usually a progressive illness that involves numerous antecedent psychological conditions, poor life-style, work-related stressors, socioeconomic factors, the presence of other illnesses, and biological influences. Moreover, the occurrence of depression, hostility, or having a Type D personality were each predictive of increased risk of coronary heart disease and mortality, as was coming from a low socioeconomic status or experiencing low levels of social support in relation to stressor experiences.

Numerous neurobiological processes contribute to the development of CAD and related illnesses, often being influenced by psychological factors. Life challenges, including psychosocial stressors, can provoke activation of the inflammatory immune system, and the cytokine changes that occur peripherally and within the brain can influence levels and turnover of neurotransmitters, such as serotonin, CRH, and growth factors, which then favor the development of depression. As well, elevated cytokine levels or cytokine-stressor combinations can serve as a link between depressive disorders and heart disease. This said, depression and CAD involve multiple factors, and one can pretty well be assured that these links contribute to other conditions that are comorbid with these illnesses.

9 Diabetes

THE 'SUGAR DISEASE' THAT'S NOT SWEET

Diabetes comes in several forms: type 1 diabetes typically appears in the young and is managed by insulin injection; type 2 diabetes is usually first detected in older individuals, and to an extent is manageable by diet and exercise and maintaining low weight, at least when symptoms are mild. As it progresses, drug interventions are necessary to manage the illness. Diabetes has been formally recognized for only a bit more than a century, but descriptions of a condition reminiscent of diabetes have been around for centuries, having appeared in writings from Egyptian, Chinese, Greek, Japanese, Indian, Korean, and Persian cultures. A hint that this condition was related to sugar levels came a millennium ago from Indian physicians who reported a syndrome that was accompanied by sweet urine, which was attributed to the consumption of rice, flour, and foods high in sugar (to stem the readers' imaginings, it seems likely that the notion of 'sweet urine' came through the observation that the urine attracted ants). The great breakthrough in relation to diabetes came about much later, when Sir Sharpey-Schafer hypothesized the existence of a substance in the pancreas, which he named insulin, as being involved in this disorder. This was soon followed by the extraction and use of insulin by Canadian scientists Frederick Banting and Charles Best in 1921. Insulin treatment quickly became the treatment of choice for type 1 diabetes, and continues to be today. But, this treatment did not produce equally positive effects on type 2 diabetes, which was characterized by insensitivity to insulin.

Type 2 diabetes continues to be a scourge to modern societies, although there have been enormous gains in identifying and managing this disorder. This illness was taken very seriously with the recognition that it increased the risk for numerous other illnesses. Within the US, 68% of diabetes-related deaths are a result of comorbid heart disease (2–4 times higher than in the remainder of the population), and stroke likewise is relatively frequent in those with diabetes. It doesn't stop there, being the leading cause of new occurrences of blindness, kidney disease (accounting for 44% of kidney failures), neuropathy (weakness, numbness, and pain as a result of nerve damage occurs in about

65% of diabetics), vascular disease, problems with wound healing and lower limb amputations, as well as Alzheimer's disease. The incidence of type 2 diabetes has been escalating at a frightening rate, affecting hundreds of millions (about 6% of adults). In part, this stems from increased life span, which permits the emergence of diabetes, but it's certain that sedentary life-style, coupled with poor diet, obesity, poor sleep, elevated stress, and the presence of depression have contributed to the appearance of the illness.

THE BROADER HEALTH IMPACT OF DIABETES

The urgency given to treat diabetes should be appreciable given its propensity to promote multiple negative consequences. In general, diabetes reduces life span by from 6 to 10 years, and within the US diabetes kills more people each year than does breast cancer and AIDS combined. In this chapter we'll examine:

- the characteristics of type 1 and type 2 diabetes, as well as a less frequent form of this condition, gestational diabetes
- psychosocial factors that contribute to the emergence of diabetes
- some of the biological processes that contribute to the appearance of this condition, including genetic factors, inflammatory processes, and gut bacteria
- what can be done to limit the occurrence of type 2 diabetes and how to deal with it if it does develop.

TYPE 1 DIABETES

This form of diabetes is an autoimmune disorder, but unlike other such disorders, it occurs equally frequently in males and females, with the peak age of diagnosis being about 14. This illness, which may stem from genetic factors as well as chemical and environmental challenges, including viruses, occurs as a result of the dysfunction of beta cells within the pancreas, so that insulin is not produced. Insulin is essential for body cells to take up sugars from the blood, and when it is not produced, cells suffer from not receiving nutrition, and at the same time elevated sugars in the blood cause damage to cells of various organs.

Symptoms of diabetes

The most obvious symptoms of type 1 diabetes, which has also been known as either juvenile diabetes or insulin-dependent diabetes, typically comprise elevated thirst and hunger (*polydipsia* and *polyphagia*, respectively), frequent urination (*polyuria*), weight loss, and elevated blood sugar levels. Ordinarily, fasting blood sugar level should be less than 100 mg/dL (or 5.6 mmol/L). If fasting blood sugar levels range from 100 to 125 mg/dL (5.6 to 6.9 mmol/L) this is considered as pre-diabetes, whereas levels that exceed 126 mg/dL (7 mmol/L) reflect diabetes.

This is usually confirmed by a *glycated hemoglobin (A1c) test* (also referred to as HbA1c or just A1c**),** which reflects the average blood sugar level over approximately the past 3 months. An A1c level between 5.7% and 6.4% reflects pre-diabetes, whereas a level that exceeds 6.5% reflects diabetes.

Treatment of type 1 diabetes entails administration of insulin after meals through injection into stomach tissue using a small (4–6 mm) needle, or through a small pump that provides continuous flow of insulin over the day, and a patch that releases insulin is being developed. With insulin present in the body, glucose can be taken up by cells, and hence circulating sugar levels will be reduced. As a result, some negative outcomes of diabetes are diminished, such as occurrence of kidney failure, but others, such as heart disease and stroke, are not as readily precluded.

Distribution of type 1 diabetes

The incidence of type 1 diabetes has been increasing over recent decades, varying markedly across countries and cultures. This illness occurs relatively infrequently in China and Japan (less than 1 in 100,000 children), somewhat more commonly in Western Europe (10–15 cases per 100,000), and greater than 20/100,000 in Sardinia, Finland, Sweden, Norway, Portugal, the UK, Canada, and New Zealand (Kasper et al., 2005). Why these differences exist isn't certain, but genetic factors likely contribute to these variations. Moreover, as type 1 diabetes is more frequent in wealthier countries, its occurrence might be due to nutrition or specific foods eaten, or possibly the presence of environmental toxicants, including those that are used in personal care products (e.g., phthalates). With some exceptions, individuals in countries nearer the polar regions of the earth are more affected by diabetes than are those further away (Soltesz et al., 2007). It is possible that the relation between geographic latitude and type 1 diabetes is linked to the absence of vitamin D produced by the skin when exposed to sunlight (Mohr et al., 2008). Alternatively, as gut bacteria also vary geographically, the presence of these bacteria in cold climates, possibly reflecting an adaptation to climatic conditions, could influence diabetes.

TYPE 2 DIABETES

Characteristics

The symptoms of Type 2 diabetes are very much like those associated with the type 1 form, as are the glucose and A1c levels necessary for such a diagnosis. However, type 2 diabetes isn't a result of an absolute reduction of beta cells, but instead develops because insulin levels decline appreciably or when insulin resistance occurs, essentially meaning that cells within the body are less able to respond to insulin, even if insulin levels are adequate. Type 2 diabetes is fairly common, with about 360 million people being affected world-wide, and it has been projected that 550 million people will be diabetic by 2030, increasing in both developed and newly developing countries. Within the UK, for instance, this form of diabetes increased from 1.4 to 2.9 million from 1996 to 2012, and in Canada, where 2.3 million people are affected, the prevalence has increased from 3.3% to 5.6% over a 20-year period. In the US about 19 million people have been diagnosed with diabetes, disproportionally represented among Hispanics, blacks, and Indigenous peoples relative to Euro Caucasians (e.g., Dyck et al., 2010). It has been estimated that there are also about 7 million more undiagnosed cases, and pre-diabetes (high glucose levels, but not yet reaching the diagnostic level) is present in about 80 million people (Danaei et al., 2011; Diabetes in the UK, 2012; World Health Organization, 2014c). It is especially disconcerting that the incidence of type 2 diabetes has been increasing markedly (by about 30%) in young people aged 10–19 years of age (Dabelea et al., 2014). At this rate, it's a matter of only a few decades before 1 of every 3 people will be diabetic.

"MY DOCTOR TOLD ME I'VE GOT METABOLIC SYNDROME AND THAT I SHOULD BE DIETING. BUT, THE GOOD NEWS IS THAT I'M OTHERWISE HEALTHY AS AN OX"

There are probably few health-related conditions as poorly understood by the public as metabolic syndrome. This condition might not cause notable overt symptoms, and thus people are usually unaware of its existence. Yet it is a common antecedent of type 2 diabetes, being associated with elevated fasting glucose levels and insulin resistance (i.e., cells have become less responsive to insulin) and has been linked to heart disease (Ford, 2005). But that's not the end of it, as metabolic syndrome has also been linked to increased risk of cognitive impairment, depression, neuromotor dysfunction, and incontinence. Metabolic syndrome usually is diagnosed when insulin resistance is present and accompanied by at least three additional features, such as abdominal obesity, elevated blood pressure, elevated fasting blood glucose, decreased HDL cholesterol, and high triglycerides (triglycerides are a type of fat (lipid) present in the blood formed as a result of eating sufficient amounts and types of food so that calories are converted into triglycerides that are stored within fat cells).

Many of the factors that favor the development of metabolic syndrome are the same as those that lead to diabetes, including poor life-style habits, chronic stressful experiences, and the presence of elevated visceral fat (the fat present around the tummy) (e.g., Bergmann et al., 2014). These fat cells are particularly pertinent as they are a reserve for inflammatory cytokines, and their persistent cytokine release favors metabolic syndrome, as well as the development of depression, heart disease and other vascular illnesses, rheumatoid arthritis, and osteoarthritis (Paragh et al., 2014).

GENETIC CONTRIBUTIONS

Pre-diabetes and diabetes occur more often among individuals with a family history of this condition (Vaxillaire & Froguel, 2010). Several dozen genes have been linked to diabetes

(McCarthy, 2010), although they account for only a small fraction of the variance related to this disorder. This said, factors related to the development of diabetes, such as obesity, may also be regulated by genetic factors, thereby contributing indirectly to the development of this disorder.

As we've seen in relation to other disorders, knowing whether patients carry particular genes or gene polymorphisms may provide essential information that allows for treatment strategies that directly underlie diabetes. For instance, a genetic variant of the epinephrine receptor (ADRA2A) that appears in about 30% of the population was accompanied by over-expression of a particular epinephrine receptor, impaired insulin secretion, and type 2 diabetes. When this epinephrine receptor was blocked by a drug treatment, diabetic patients carrying the gene variant exhibited an increase of insulin so that levels were comparable to that of those who did not carry this gene variant (Tang et al., 2014).

ANOTHER VIEW OF GENETIC INFLUENCES ON DIABETES

The frequency of a set of 12 gene polymorphisms has been associated with type 2 diabetes incidents world-wide. Although diabetes is infrequent in sub-Saharan Africa, certainly compared to North America, the frequencies of the illness and of these polymorphisms diminished moving from West to East, from Africa to Asia, possibly reflecting the loss of polymorphisms with eastward migration (Corona et al., 2013). Intriguingly, the possibility was raised that some of these gene variants might at one time have been beneficial in so far as they could have helped maximize the appearance of sugar to create energy. Until recently, few people lived long enough or ate enough sugar and fat to develop diabetes, and thus in prehistory there wasn't a downside to consuming foods that were high in carbs and sugar, and hence there might not have been a selection pressure against this. However, as life span has increased, the adverse effects of these genes has shown up in the form of diabetes (Gibbons, 2011).

Although some diabetes-related genes might have had their origin in Africa, among individuals with a recent Native American ancestry, including Latin Americans, the presence of a particular gene, SLC16A11 (involved in carrying molecules, such as lactate and pyruvate, across membranes), increases risk for type 2 diabetes (Williams et al., 2014). Thus, while some polymorphisms might have descended from Africa, others likely developed elsewhere at a later time.

Researchers typically search for genes that increase vulnerability for illness, but in some instances the presence of particular genes may have a protective or advantageous effect. It seems that an infrequently occurring mutation in gene SLC30A8 (codes for a zinc transporter that is necessary for insulin secretion) was associated with reduced risk for type 2 diabetes (Flannick et al., 2014). In older individuals in whom diabetes is relatively frequent, the risk for diabetes was 65% lower in those carrying this mutation. If this gene could be manipulated or the protein that it produces altered, potent ways of managing or treating diabetes might be developed. Alternatively, it might be possible to use drug treatments to modify products of the gene's actions and thus influence the development of diabetes.

STRESSORS AND TYPE 2 DIABETES

Stressful events and stress-related psychological disturbances linked to diabetes

Several life stressors were associated with the appearance of metabolic disorder and type 2 diabetes, and this was particularly notable when chronically stressed individuals indulged in high-fat, high-sugar foods (Aschbacher et al., 2014). Chronic stressful experiences can also exacerbate symptoms among individuals with type 1 diabetes, but the data concerning stressor involvement in *causing* type 1 diabetes are less impressive (Cosgrove, 2004). Nevertheless, in a prospective study, serious stressful events in childhood were accompanied by a tripling of type 1 diabetes risk (Nygren et al., 2015).

The levels of A1c in a 1-year prospective study were related to the occurrence of stressful events (Lloyd et al., 1999), and stressor-related psychological disturbances, such as depression and PTSD, were linked to diabetes (Lukaschek et al., 2013). Similarly, psychosocial stressors coupled with low social support were associated with poor diabetes control among individuals with either the type 1 or type 2 form of the disorder (Chida & Hamer, 2008). Conversely, personality factors, such as high self-efficacy, self-esteem, and optimism, together with the use of effective coping strategies, were linked to better glucose control (Yi-Frazier et al., 2015).

As we saw with respect to heart disease, diabetes takes years to develop, and even if stressful life experiences contribute to this disorder, it may be difficult to identify whether certain developmental periods were critical for its appearance. To be sure, diabetes increases markedly with aging, but early life stressors, and even those experienced in utero, were associated with the development of type 2 diabetes (Eriksson et al., 2014). For instance, low childhood socioeconomic status was linked to type 2 diabetes, even after adjusting for adult socioeconomic status and obesity, and low birth weight was predictive of adult diabetes among African-American women (Ruiz-Narváez et al., 2014). Prenatal psychosocial stressors were similarly accompanied by insulin resistance in young adults, and the children of women who lost a loved one during pregnancy were more likely to develop diabetes as adults (Li et al., 2012).

Diabetes in relation to job stress

As type 2 diabetes most commonly appears in middle or older age, studies assessing the link between stressful experiences and diabetes have evaluated the contribution of job-related stressors to this disorder (Cosgrove et al., 2012). It was indeed reported that shift work as well as long working hours were linked to diabetes, primarily among individuals low in socioeconomic status (Kivimäki et al., 2014). Moreover, as in the case of heart disease, diabetes was found to be considerably more frequent among individuals experiencing high job strain (having low decision latitude and high job demands) (Heraclides et al., 2012) and among individuals who perceived a mismatch between efforts and rewards received (Li et al., 2013).

There seem to be gender-specific effects in the relation between diabetes and job-related distress. A 9-year prospective study confirmed that low levels of job control were linked to the development of diabetes, but this was only apparent in women (P.M. Smith et al., 2012).

A female-specific increase of diabetes was similarly observed among women who experienced low decision latitude at work, as well as women who engaged in shift work (Eriksson et al., 2013). Chronic workplace distress was similarly accompanied by greater risk for diabetes in women (but not men), irrespective of socioeconomic status and stressors encountered outside the workplace (Heraclides et al., 2009). Despite the greater vulnerability among women, this doesn't mean that such relations won't occur in men. Indeed, a 3–5-year prospective study among healthy individuals indicated that burnout was accompanied by increased type 2 diabetes risk (Melamed et al., 2006), and a 35-year prospective study among older men revealed that occupational class and continued work or home stress during the preceding 1–5 years predicted increased risk for diabetes (Hedén-Stahl et al., 2014). Given the many procedural differences that exists across studies, it is uncertain why the gender differences were observed. However, it is difficult to dissociate the contribution of work-related stressors and those experienced outside work, and it is possible that the double load carried by women may have contributed to risk for diabetes.

Processes linking stressors and diabetes

There are several ways through which stressful events can promote or aggravate diabetes. Stressors could influence life-style factors, such as diminishing exercise and increasing food intake among emotional eaters – particularly foods high in carbs, leading to weight gain, and ultimately metabolic syndrome and diabetes (Harding et al., 2014). Stressful events could also affect diabetes through neurobiological changes that affect glucose availability. For example, stressors can influence hormones associated with food and energy regulation, including ghrelin, leptin, and cortisol, and could potentially influence dopamine-related brain functioning associated with reward processes. Thus consumption of tasty foods, especially those that are high in carbs might be encouraged (Abizaid et al., 2006). As well, stressor-provoked cortisol release may hinder the action of insulin and thus contribute to diabetes. It seems that insulin insufficiency or insulin resistance is accompanied by diminished positive feelings associated with food, and individuals might consequently indulge themselves in an effort to gain the pleasure they had previously obtained from certain foods (Khanh et al., 2014).

INFLAMMATORY FACTORS IN TYPE 2 DIABETES

Insulin resistance might come about owing to a chronic low-level increase of inflammatory immune cells and elevated cytokine presence (McNelis & Olefsky, 2014), which can impair pancreatic beta cell functioning. The inflammatory changes leading to metabolic syndrome and diabetes may result from the presence of pathogens, stressful events, or excessive visceral fat (Strissel et al., 2014), which is a storehouse for leptin, ghrelin, and inflammatory cytokines such as TNF-α, IL-6, and IFN-α (Abizaid et al., 2014), as well as interferon regulatory factor-5 (IRF-5). It seems that IRF-5 may be especially important in obesity as mice that were engineered not to have this factor present but were subjected to a high-fat diet became obese without exhibiting the metabolic changes associated with diabetes. This led to the suggestion that IRF-5 contributes to rechanneling (reprogramming) so that excessive eating would not lead to harmful intra-abdominal fat, but would instead be redirected to subcutaneous fat (Dalmas et al., 2015).

This factor might not be alone in contributing to the development of diabetes. Excessive fat may cause the release of the inflammatory substance leukotriene B_4 (LTB4), which might not be a problem if this occurred transiently, but among obese people this goes on chronically, and could thus lead to illness. Indeed, metabolic disturbances were not apparent in obese mice that had been genetically engineered to lack the LTB4 receptor. Likewise, improved metabolic health was apparent among obese mice treated with an LTB4 receptor antagonist that had been developed as being therapeutic for inflammatory disease (Li et al., 2015).

Although high levels of visceral fat are a risk factor for diabetes, a subgroup of obese individuals was identified in whom metabolic problems are less likely to occur (Ortega et al., 2013), and in whom inflammatory factors were relatively low (Blüher, 2012). Such findings have been instrumental in propagating the erroneous belief, described in Chapter 7, that "I may be over-weight, but I'm perfectly healthy" and has fostered the continuation of poor life-style choices. This rationalization sometimes comes from relatively young people who seem to feel invulner-able to the negative consequences of obesity, even though they haven't a clue whether they're actually in the potentially healthy subgroup. As it turns out, high levels of a molecule, heme oxygenase-1 (HO-1), may be predictive of later development of diabetes in humans, and by inhibiting HO-1 in obese mice, metabolic health was augmented. Thus, HO-1 might not only predict which overweight people are at risk for diabetes, but might point to an intervention treatment to prevent its occurrence (Jais et al., 2014).

MORE THAN JUST THAT MINTY TASTE

Dentists were encouraging preventive medicine well before many practitioners in other fields of medicine were doing so ("floss and brush after every meal" has been the mantra we've heard for years). This is obviously very important to spare your teeth from decay and in preventing perio-dontal disease, which triggers the presence of inflammation of the gum around teeth. What is less well advertised is that periodontal disease has been linked to diabetes, and the severity of gum disease is directly correlated with blood sugar levels (Bascones-Martínez et al., 2014), and has also been linked to heart disease, stroke, and rheumatoid arthritis, as we learned in Chapter 8. These studies are correlational, and thus we can't be certain that gum disease 'causes' any sort of illness (Lockhart et al., 2012). Nevertheless, it was suggested that cytokines released from dis-eased gums travel through the blood, and disturb pancreatic beta cells, thus promoting increased insulin resistance, hence leading to diabetes. Predictably, periodontal treatments among diabetic patients have been accompanied by reduced A1c levels, suggesting reduced glucose over sev-eral months (Wang, Han et al., 2014). Incidentally, as prenatal stressors and inflammation can promote pre-term labor or low birth weight, the American Academy of Periodontal Health has emphasized the importance of periodontal health among pregnant women. So, besides eating right and exercising, good dental behaviors can have added benefits, not only on the individual, but on their offspring as well.

Given that adiposity is accompanied by elevated inflammatory factors, it might be expected that stressors among obese animals or humans would similarly promote exaggerated inflammatory responses, and thus could encourage diabetes, heart disease, and depression. Thus, as described in Figure 9.1, although obesity might be a sufficient condition to promote pathology, this might be helped along when coupled with other challenges, including those of a psychological nature.

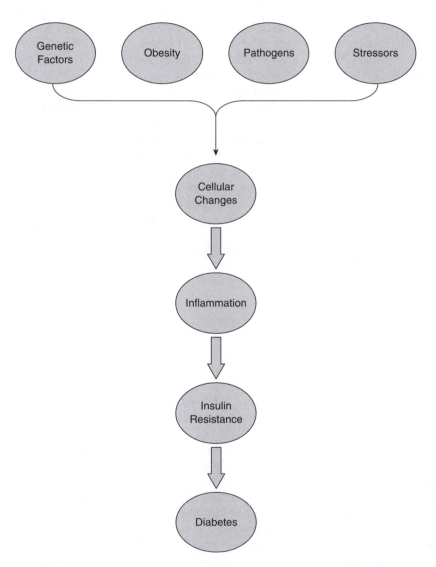

Figure 9.1 Multiple factors, including those of a genetic nature, overeating and obesity, immune pathogens, and stressors, come together to affect cellular changes and thus the activation of inflammatory processes. These, in turn, promote insulin resistance and diabetes.

Gut bacteria

As in the case of other illnesses, gut microbiota may play a significant role in the promotion of metabolic syndrome and type 2 diabetes (Shen et al., 2013), and may even play a role in determining food cravings, especially for sweets (Blaut, 2014). Thus, it was suggested that probiotics would have a beneficial effect in relation to type 2 diabetes (Gomes et al., 2014), and there have been indications that a genetically engineered form of the bacteria lactobacillus, a common gut bacteria, secretes greater amounts of *glucagon-like peptide-1* (GLP-1), which is known to reduce glucose levels among diabetics (Duan et al., 2015). As well, it was reported that diabetes was accompanied by *dysbiosis* (an imbalance between good and bad bacteria), low levels of bacteria that form butyrate (a fatty acid necessary for health of the gut), coupled with elevated levels of opportunistic bacterial pathogens (Qin et al., 2012).

Gut bacteria can affect diabetes through several routes, including activation of inflammatory processes. A high fat diet may promote altered gut homeostasis, leading to mucosal inflammation and the promotion of chronic systemic inflammation, thereby favoring the development of type 2 diabetes (Bleau et al., 2015). It was likewise suggested that among genetically susceptible individuals, inflammation related to gut bacteria might contribute to type 1 diabetes (Dunne et al., 2014), possibly by triggering an autoimmune response against beta cells. In fact, in mice, an anti-inflammatory treatment 5-aminosalicyclic acid (5-ASA), which is frequently used in the treatment of inflammatory bowel disease, effectively acted against insulin resistance that was associated with a high fat diet (Luck et al., 2015).

GESTATIONAL DIABETES

Obesity during pregnancy has been reported to increase heart disease and premature death among adult offspring (Reynolds et al., 2013). As well, diabetes can develop during pregnancy as a result of insulin receptors behaving improperly, but this gestational diabetes doesn't come with easily identifiable symptoms, and is typically detected upon health screening during pregnancy. Among women who are less likely to have an obstetrician, which is more common in poorer communities, the chance of gestational diabetes going undetected is elevated. This can lead to the development of type 2 diabetes and pre-eclampsia (characterized by high blood pressure and high levels of protein in the urine, which if left untreated can result in death). Table 9.1 provides some of the characteristics of gestational diabetes relative to that seen in the type 1 and type 2 conditions.

As observed among women who are diabetic prior to pregnancy, gestational diabetes has been associated with teratogenic effects (Allen et al., 2007) as well as childhood and adult obesity, diabetes, and cardiovascular disease (Moore, 2010). It has been suggested that epigenetic changes in the fetus that might occur during gestational diabetes in the mom could translate into later pathological conditions (Ruchat et al., 2013). Moderate exercise during pregnancy diminished the incidence of gestational diabetes by about 30% (Sanabria-Martínez et al., 2015). Likewise, adopting strategies to limit high blood sugar levels (e.g., diet, insulin therapy as needed) may limit adverse perinatal outcomes, but to what extent these procedures influence the long-term risk for metabolic syndrome, type 2 diabetes, or heart disease has been debated (Nolan, 2011).

Table 9.1   Common and differential characteristics of type 1, type 2, and gestational diabetes

	Type 1	Type 2	Gestational
Age of onset	Occurs in young individuals	Occurs in older individuals	Detected during pregnancy
Weight	Not overweight	Overweight	Overweight
Suddenness of onset	Acute onset	Insidious onset	Detected upon routine testing
Frequency	Uncommon	Common	Uncommon, but increasing
Causation	Insulin deficiency	Insulin resistance	Insulin resistance
Autoantibodies	Usually present	Absent	Usually absent
Treatment	Insulin	Diet, exercise, and medications	Diet, exercise, and medications
Familial factor	Often without family history	Presence of family history	Family history of type 2 diabetes

Several risk factors for gestational diabetes have been identified, such as ethnicity, being elevated among African Americans, Hispanics and Latinos, and American Indians and First Nations People within Canada. Women who develop this form of diabetes during the first half of pregnancy are also more likely to develop obstetric complications, recurrence of the syndrome in subsequent pregnancies, and later development of type 2 diabetes, particularly if obesity is also present (Ben-Haroush et al., 2004). In addition, a family history of diabetes may be a risk factor for gestational diabetes, and several gene variants have been linked to the development of gestational diabetes (C. Zhang et al., 2013). Gestational and type 2 diabetes share common genetic processes (Wung & Lin, 2011), hence accounting for the apparent links between the two. This risk may persist for years, calling for intensive life-style changes, and medications may be recommended, such as metformin (used to treat type 2 diabetes), which reduce the occurrence of later diabetes by about 40% (Aroda et al., 2015).

DEALING WITH DIABETES

Life-styles

Diabetes is one of the most preventable illnesses. Among individuals at high risk, intervention programs that encourage positive life-style changes, especially maintaining a proper diet, can cut the incidences of diabetes by half (Orozco et al., 2009), and may be particularly effective among those at greatest risk (Sussman et al., 2015). Despite some debate as to the most effective diet that should be undertaken, those that have a low *glycemic index* have been favored (Thomas & Elliott, 2009). Glycemic index refers to the effects of fixed amounts of different types of food on blood glucose level, generally reflecting the amount of carbohydrate present as well as the rate at which the carbohydrates are broken down and released into the bloodstream as sugar (slower breakdown produced lower sugars; Jenkins et al., 1981). Instructive tables showing the glycemic index of various foods are broadly available, indicating which foods to adopt and which to avoid. Certain foods, however, may have very little if any carbohydrates (e.g., red meats) and thus have a very low glycemic index, but some of the proteins of meat are converted into glucose and consequently carry a sugar load (DiNicolantonio et al., 2015).

One hears of various foods that can be consumed to lower type 2 diabetes risk. These have included whole fruits, especially blueberries, grapes, and apples (as opposed to fruit juices that have bad effects) (Muraki et al., 2013), and there are indications that positive effects can be obtained from fish oils through their action on inflammatory processes. As well, claims have been made that nuts, especially pistachios, may act against the negative effects of diabetes on heart functioning (Sauder et al., 2014). Although we also hear about all sorts of super foods to ward off illness (e.g., walnuts, black tea, and Chinese wolfberries), it is premature to endorse their use, certainly as a substitute for healthy diets and exercise.

Exercise is particularly important in diminishing blood sugars (exercising after supper is likely most beneficial), although it is not uncommon for diabetic individuals to focus only on diet. Dieting, for example, may directly diminish sugar levels, whereas exercise might have its positive effects through other processes, such as altering insulin insensitivity. Thus, the combination of diet and exercise provides optimal outcomes (Weiss et al., 2015).

FRUCTOSE? ISN'T THAT THE ONE THAT'S NATURAL AND SO IS GOOD FOR US?

Fructose naturally appears in fruits and vegetables, including berries, vine fruits, root vegetables, and even edible flowers. When used in moderation, it might not be as bad as other forms of sugar in aggravating diabetes (Cozma, 2012). However, fructose is added to many foods (often in the form of corn syrup) to enhance their taste, and in this way may be a prime driver of diabetes. Some health organizations suggest that sugars should not exceed 20% of our daily caloric intake, and the World Health Organization recommends a still lower level (10%). We're usually well above the WHO guidelines, and even the 20% mark, which might be OK if this came from raw whole fruits and veggies, but when they come in the form of additives or drinks (juices), their net value is particularly negative (DiNicolantonio et al., 2015).

As the appearance of type 2 diabetes may be aggravated by stressful experiences, having effective coping methods or social support could limit the actions of stressors (Maksimovic et al.,

2014), including the distress associated with being diabetic (Baek et al., 2014). Further to this, strong social support through family members was accompanied by enhanced treatment adherence, thereby improving diabetes control (Pereira et al., 2014). In fact, psychological interventions and diabetes education has proved useful in improving glycemic control, and stress management training combined with standard care has reduced glucose to levels that would be obtained through drug treatments (Surwit et al., 2002). Consistent with these reports, stress-reduction methods, such as mindfulness training, can have direct and indirect beneficial effects in controlling symptoms (Whitebird et al., 2009).

DIABETES AND ITS COMORBIDITIES

Diabetes may be comorbid with many other conditions, including heart disease, stroke, kidney disease, circulatory problems, impaired wound healing, fatty liver disease, some types of cancer, and has been associated with brain atrophy and cognitive decline (Moran et al., 2013) as well as implicated as a risk factor for the development of dementia (Ohara et al., 2011). Within just 2 years of diabetes being diagnosed, disturbances were detected in blood regulation to the brain and commensurately diminished cognitive skills (Chung et al., 2015). For that matter, even in the absence of frank diabetes, higher levels of glucose were accompanied by greater odds of dementia appearing among individuals over 65 years of age, and this risk was much greater among individuals who were both depressed and diabetic (Katon et al., 2015). The presence of metabolic syndrome, pre-diabetes or diabetes was predictive of dementia appearing among individuals presenting with a degree of cognitive decline, but this conversion to Alzheimer's features was diminished by the use of a Mediterranean diet (Cooper et al., 2015).

Of the many comorbidities associated with type 2 diabetes, depression and cardiovascular illness are likely the best known (Black, 2006). These conditions have been linked to obesity and dyslipidemia and may be tied to increased inflammatory functioning, oxidative stress, and endothelial disturbances. Predictably, when diabetes is also accompanied by depression, the risk of dying as a result of cardiovascular illness is appreciably increased (Park et al., 2013). This could reflect the conjoint actions of these different diseases, although it is possible that depressed individuals, particularly people who are older, are less likely to adhere to their treatment regimens, leading to poorer outcomes (Kimbro et al., 2014).

Medications

If exercise and diet don't yield improvement of fasting (morning) glucose levels, then medications are almost always prescribed together with diet and exercise. Drugs such as *metformin* reduce the amount of sugar formed by the liver, limit sugar absorbed into the body through foods eaten, and enhances the sensitivity of insulin receptors. Typically, this is sufficient to reduce sugar levels to a normal range, but if it is not fully effective (or its effectiveness diminishes), then additional treatments may be administered. These may include *sulfonylureas* to increase insulin release from beta cells, *alpha-glucosidase inhibitors* to prevent digestion of carbohydrates, *thiazolidinediones* that diminish insulin resistance and certain cytokines, such as IL-6, or injection of *glucagon-like peptide-1* (GLP-1), which increases insulin secretion from the pancreas and increases insulin-sensitivity (Altaf et al., 2014). A relatively new treatment has also been developed, which essentially increases glucose excretion in urine (Davidson & Kuritzky, 2014). Each treatment has its own benefits or potential side effects, and once again the ideal treatment strategy might vary across individuals. Regardless of the medication chosen, as mentioned in the context of other medical conditions, the decline of glucose levels doesn't give individuals a get-out-of-jail-free card so that they can return to poor life-style habits.

Future treatment possibilities

There are several medications in the pipeline (or close to being so) that might eventually have beneficial effects in the treatment of type 2 diabetes. It has been found that insulin is degraded by Insulin Degrading Enzyme (IDE), and when a drug was administered that inhibited this enzyme, insulin levels increased. Thus, there is the possibility that such a treatment might eventually be useful during the early stages of diabetes (Maianti et al., 2014). It was similarly shown that among diabetic mice, treatment with the growth hormone FGF-1 quickly normalized insulin responses, and there is the possibility that FGF-1 may eventually come to clinical trials in treating human diabetes (Suh et al., 2014).

An important way of potentially dealing with metabolic syndrome and diabetes is to alter the type of fat present. As we saw in Chapter 7, brown fat burns many more calories than does white fat, but as adults we have very little of this. Thus, there have been efforts to find ways of making white fat turn beige or brown with the intent of achieving calorie reductions. One approach has involved genetic engineering to circumvent the message of 'make more white fat', allowing for greater beige fat production (Bi et al., 2014). It was similarly found that a particular receptor for the hormone melanocortin, specifically the melanocortin-4 receptor, contributes to the regulation of glucose metabolism and energy expenditure, and is important for altering white fat into beige or brown fat. Thus, these receptors might also turn out to be viable targets to prevent or attenuate type 2 diabetes (Berglund et al., 2014). As insulin and leptin within the hypothalamus also contribute to the browning of white fat (Dodd et al., 2015), it might at some point be feasible to regulate these hormones in the brain, thereby affecting diabetes. There are many other ongoing treatment methods being developed for diabetes, and tests are being developed to predict impending diabetes (or identifying those at most risk for illness) so that early interventions can be undertaken. Increasingly better treatments will become available, but it would be better not to need these treatments by making healthy life-style choices.

SUMMARY

Eating foods low in carbs, exercising regularly, getting enough sleep, and being blessed with the right gene combinations may preclude the development type 2 diabetes, but once it's present, it's a difficult dragon to slay. Its management through life-style measures is obviously important, but medications are usually needed given that people are fairly fallible in the face of temptations.

Upon diabetes emerging, drug treatments are usually prescribed, but patients often fail to combine the medication with proper changes of the behaviors that led to the illness. Some patients, incorrectly believing that the drugs will control their illness, continue with their self-destructive behaviors. Others, perhaps because of ongoing stressors, will resort to feel-good foods that typically promote obesity and worsen glucose levels, and provoke hormonal changes that produce hyperglycemia. Thus, treatment ought to involve diabetes education, self-management training, social support, and coaching to diminish those factors that interfere with self-control (Laxy et al., 2014). Type 2 diabetes is a readily preventable illness for most people, but too often individuals suffer a sense of invulnerability and don't think about the harms that today's misbehaviors have on health disturbances that may appear decades down the road.

10 Immune-related Disorders

VIRAL AND BACTERIAL ILLNESS THEN AND NOW

Communicable or transmissible (contagious) diseases have been around at least since biblical times. Mummified remains from ancient Egypt indicated the presence of smallpox in the early days of that empire, but recorded descriptions of viral illnesses didn't come about until centuries later. Smallpox devastated populations in large parts of Europe, and the Europeans transmitted smallpox (and other diseases), largely eradicating Maya, Aztec, and Inca cultures, and had almost as devastating effect on Aboriginal groups in what is now Canada. In Europe, several hundred millions died as a result of smallpox before a vaccine was discovered by Edward Jenner in 1798. Still, during the twentieth century smallpox was thought to have been responsible for upward of 300 million deaths and, according to the World Health Organization, as recently as the 1960s the disease was contracted by more than 15 million people, leading to 2 million deaths. The bacterial disease bubonic plague (Black Death) also has a long history, having been recorded in Russia in the sixth century, subsequently reappearing on many occasions (Bos et al., 2011). An accurate figure of how many people died as a result of the Black Death aren't certain, but estimates have ranged from 25 million up to 200 million within Western Europe and as high as 375 million world-wide. The Black Death only obtained its wicked status as a pandemic when two mutations developed. The first allowed the development of 'pneumonic plague', a respiratory condition that permitted spread through coughs and sneezes. The second was a mutation that allowed for the high incidence and killing potency of the bacteria (Zimbler et al., 2015). Puny little mutations allowed for a disease to become a pandemic. What other little surprises will occur in the bacterial genome that could lead to another pandemic?

(Continued)

(Continued)

Viruses and bacteria are horrible enemies who don't seem to fight fairly, adopting all sorts of terrorist tactics. Viruses are able to mutate in order to avoid detection by vaccines, and every few years entirely new viruses pop up. Those that we're most familiar with now are influenza (flu) outbreaks that occur each year. Most take a toll on humans, varying from year to year, and according to the Center for Disease Control (CDC) the number of people infected in the United States (comparable numbers occur on a per capita basis in Europe, the UK, Canada, and Australia) ranges from 5% to 20% of the population, leading to more than 200,000 hospitalizations and 3,000–49,000 deaths each year (Thompson et al., 2009), but there have been more severe outbreaks. The Spanish flu (swine flu) that raged from 1918 to 1920 affected 500 million people, and was responsible for the death of more than 50 million (perhaps even as high as 130 million), which eclipsed all the deaths of World War I that preceded the outbreak. This virus originated in pigs and mutated so that it could be passed to humans, and then was spread widely by home-bound soldiers following the end of the war. Most viruses tend to have much greater effects on the young and older people, whose immune systems might be somewhat less developed or more compromised. However, the Spanish flu was an equal opportunity killer, and actually preferentially affected young adults by setting off an over-reaction of the immune system and consequently a lethal cytokine storm (Simonsen et al., 1998).

By comparison to the Spanish flu, HIV/AIDS has had a relatively modest effect, infecting about 75 million people, and causing about 36 million deaths at a time when the population is far greater and travel is much simpler. Ebola, which is the most recent mass terrorist, has frightened people around the world because of its potential, even though its passage requires contact with infected tissues, and for the moment the number of infections is still relatively small. We've had scares of many epidemics and pandemics in recent years. Bird flu, SARS, West Nile Virus, and now there's again the threat of MERS, and H5N1 as well as H7N9 lurking around the edges of our awareness. The recent version of the swine flu, H1N1, could be transmitted fairly readily, but we were lucky in that it wasn't as lethal as other diseases, although approximately 60 million people contracted the illness, 275,000 people were hospitalized, and 12,500 deaths occurred (Shrestha et al., 2011).

There is a common belief that if we receive a vaccination, then we'll be immune from a particular virus. However, vaccines aren't always effective. Some vaccines protect people 90% of the time and thus many illnesses have been largely eradicated, but they can make a comeback when people stop enjoying the advantage of vaccination, as we've seen recently in relation to measles. Other vaccines are variable in their effectiveness, largely because the virus they're meant to ward off keeps mutating. Although flu vaccines are generally effective in about 70% of people, the efficacy can drop to as low as 20%, as occurred in response to the 2014–2015 influenza outbreak. Mutations of the influenza variants are common, and it can be difficult to predict which will appear next; hence drug makers might not always get the right vaccine made, although there is some hope for a 'universal vaccine' eventually being made (Kanekiyo et al., 2013). It's also difficult to predict which mutation will make the leap from animals to humans and lead to a vicious pandemic. Even if we are successful in preventing disease 99% of the time, these successes will be historical footnotes if we're unsuccessful even once in being unable to deal with a novel and powerful virus.

IMMUNITY AND ILLNESS

Numerous factors related to our behaviors can influence immune system functioning and thus our ability to fend against challenges stemming from microorganisms. Chronic stressor experiences, an impoverished diet, or poor sleep might compromise our immune system's ability to fight off viruses or deal with bacterial insults, thus increasing illness risk. Moreover, inflammatory processes have been linked to psychological disorders, such as depressive illness, and to the development of Alzheimer's disease, and might account for the comorbidities reported between these disorders and others linked to inflammatory processes, including diabetes and heart disease. Still other illnesses may emerge owing to immune responses being turned on the self, culminating in an autoimmune disorder. In this chapter we'll consider:

- the processes that are associated with several immune-related disorders
- how immune-related illnesses occur, including those that involve allergies, those that are *infectious* (occurring owing to microscopic germs, such as bacteria or viruses), and those that are *contagious* (spreading from person to person)
- what occurs when the immune system fails to attack pathogens, and what can occur when the immune system over-reacts
- illnesses that may come about when the immune system turns against the self
- how life experiences and behavioral factors may come to affect the development and progression of viral illnesses.

ALLERGIES

What's an allergy?

Allergic responses to environmental stimuli are exceedingly common, with about 30% of people reporting some type of allergy. People likely think of *allergens* such as pollen, dust mites, or animal fur (dander) as being most common, but there are a great many other environmental compounds that elicit allergic reactions. Certain medications (e.g., penicillin), plants (poison ivy, poison sumac, poison oak), and mold lead to strong allergic reactions, and substances such as latex (e.g., in surgical gloves) can elicit fairly strong reactions, including in patients undergoing medical treatments. As well, many foods (milk or milk products, wheat, soy, eggs, peanuts, fish, and shellfish) can elicit allergic reactions. Some individuals, incidentally, are also lactose intolerant owing to the absence of a particular digestive enzyme, but this is not the same as a milk allergy, and should be considered separately.

Immunoglobulin E

Although allergic reactions have been documented for millennia, it wasn't until the early part of the twentieth century that it was discovered that they evolve as a result of individuals being exposed to environmental antigens that had previously been encountered. When allergens appear on the body's surface or in the eyes, mouth, nasal passage, throat, or gut, immune cells will act to eliminate them, and in doing so a memory of the antigen will be maintained by some cells. Having made contact with an allergen, a still stronger immune response will be elicited upon the allergen being encountered again some time later, taking the form of excessive Immunoglobulin E (IgE) activity (Gould & Ramadani, 2014). The IgE over-reaction triggers particular white blood cells, mast cells, and basophils, so that they release the hormone histamine, which causes secretions from mucus glands, coupled with nasal and/or bronchial congestion. These responses, however annoying, are typically manageable. But, in some instances, the reactions may be exceptionally marked, as seen among some individuals in response to insect (bee) stings, medications (e.g., penicillin), or particular foods (peanuts), leading to an *anaphylactic* reaction, characterized by itchy rash, throat swelling, and low blood pressure, and it can result in death. Anaphylactic reactions aren't overly common, but estimates of their occurrence have ranged from 0.5% to 2.0%, with risk for such reactions being elevated in those with asthma, eczema, or allergic rhinitis (Simons & World Allergy Organization, 2010).

Familial factors and stressors

Allergic reactions may be linked to genetic influences given that allergies run in families, and identical twins tend to be more likely than non-identical twins to exhibit the same allergies (Galli, 2000). Beyond the genetic influence, the pathophysiological profile of those with allergies is in some ways similar to that which accompanies chronic stressors (Dave et al., 2011), and stressful events, especially those encountered early in life, may contribute to the development of allergies, including particular food allergies (Schreier & Wright, 2014). Predictably, the effects of stressors on allergic reactions are especially evident in the presence of a family history of certain types of allergic reaction (Yonas et al., 2012). Presumably, the increased allergic reaction associated with stressors stems from the immunological changes that are introduced, leading to an imbalance between those attributes of the immune system that activate and those that suppress immune functioning, so that the balance rests on the side of excessive immune functioning that promotes IgG release.

GENETIC, EPIGENETIC, AND PSYCHOLOGICAL FACTORS IN ALLERGY-RELATED ILLNESSES: THE CASE OF ASTHMA

Illnesses associated with allergies, such as asthma – an inflammatory disease of airways stemming from genetic, epigenetic and environmental influences (Kabesch, 2014) – were at one time considered psychosomatic illnesses brought about principally by psychological factors, or a mix of psychological and medical problems. Asthma in children was referred to as 'asthma nervosa' because it was deemed to be a stress reaction that included neurological symptoms that stemmed from having a histrionic mother (when in doubt, blame mom). Another condition, atopic dermatitis, a form of eczema characterized by a recurring, inflammatory skin condition, had been dubbed 'neuro-dermatitis', as it was considered to be a result of strong emotional responses. In fact, stressful events can instigate the occurrence of asthmatic episodes, and attempts were made to alter the coping methods that individuals used in an effort to diminish asthmatic reactions (Barton et al., 2003). Other approaches to diminish allergic reactions included relaxation therapy, biofeedback, or mental imagery to diminish anxiety (e.g., Lehrer et al., 2004). Psychotherapy or antidepressant medications were also reported to have positive effects among asthmatic patients who were depressed (Lehrer et al., 2002).

Stressors, including family conflict, negative life events, poor social support, and the presence of ruminative behaviors, might aggravate the symptoms of atopic dermatitis and increase asthma-related hospitalization (Schreier & Wright, 2014). Such effects might come about in combination with several genes related to asthma, and may be particularly amenable to epigenetic changes in response to environmental events (e.g., prenatal maternal smoking), and risk for asthma can be passed across generations (Harb & Renz, 2015).

Microbiome involvement

Increasingly more data have pointed to the microbiome's contribution to allergies. Ordinarily, the mucosal membrane within the digestive system, together with various immune factors, limit the potential immunological effects of food antigens (they are, after all, foreign to the body), allowing tolerance for these to develop. However, problems can potentially arise owing to defects in this barrier system (Chahine & Bahna, 2010). Particular foods consumed during early life, including breast milk and solid foods that are subsequently introduced, can influence gut bacteria that lead to allergies and inflammatory illnesses (Calder et al., 2006). Indeed, the microbiome of individuals with allergies is distinguishable from those without allergies, possibly owing to diet, antibiotics, and other Western life-styles (Shreiner et al., 2008), and gut bacteria present early in life, say at 3 months of age, can predict food sensitization that appears by 1 year of age (Azad et al., 2015). The incidence of allergies has been increasing, making it likely that new external factors (possibly related to changing diets or increased use of antibiotics) are involved in disturbing balanced immune responses, and hence more frequent allergies (Belkaid & Hand, 2014).

Treating allergies

Allergic reactions can be precluded by staying away from allergens (e.g., not permitting kids access to peanuts), but some can't be avoided, thus alternative approaches are needed. Allergen immunotherapy, which comprises administration of increasing levels of an allergen over an extended period, is used in an effort to desensitize reactions to the allergen. A variant of this approach was recently adopted in which young children (1 year of age) who were at risk for allergic reactions based on the presence of other immune-related conditions (e.g., eczema present) were fed peanuts several times a week until the age of 5. At that time the incidence of peanut allergy among children who had received peanuts previously was reduced by more than 80% (Du Toit et al., 2015).

If treatments to create tolerance to allergens aren't effective, then several alternative treatments can be used to limit symptoms. Steroid hormones that reduce immune activity have served in this capacity, and medications such as antihistamines and decongestants reduce symptoms. In the case of strong anaphylactic reactions that can be life threatening, epinephrine injection is necessary should exposure occur. Those who show such reactions ought to carry an automatic injector with them (e.g., an Epipen°), but I'd guess that a few people might not have it with them just when it's needed.

CAN THINGS BE TOO CLEAN?

We hear it all the time; having kids in day care exposes them to all sorts of bacteria so that their immune systems are strengthened. The hygiene hypothesis holds that early experiences that are too sterile can result in immune tolerance to foreign substances not developing, and hence exaggerated responses (allergies) will develop to some substances that are ordinarily harmless. This view was advanced to account for the progressive growth of asthma in the last few decades (Strachan, 2000), and has been applied to other immune-related illnesses, such as multiple sclerosis (Okada et al., 2010), inflammatory bowel disease, as well as the process by which immune factors might come to promote depressive disorders (Raison et al., 2010). In fact, it has been shown that growing up in a microbially rich environment (e.g., farms) was accompanied by diminished occurrence of inflammatory bowel disorder during adulthood (Timm et al., 2014). In essence, that maxim about 'cleanliness is next to godliness' could be a little over the top, and obsessive cleanliness might be more damaging than helpful.

INFECTIOUS DISEASES

Our immune system has to deal with many viruses and bacteria, fungi, multicellular parasites, protozoa, as well prions that cause illness (prions are misfolded proteins that lead to pathogenic proteins that cause Bovine spongiform encephalopathy, more commonly known as mad cow disease, in cattle and other livestock, and Creutzfeldt-Jakob disease, which occurs in humans). The goal of these microorganisms is their own survival, and if we are the means to that end, then they just do what they have to do. Many of these agents have developed means to multiply in great numbers and to escape from our ways of combatting them. Under the right conditions bacteria can double their number every 30 minutes, but they need particular environments to flourish, including the right temperature and pH, and they need water, oxygen, and a source of energy. Some bacteria, like streptococcus, can be self-sufficient, being able to persist for some time on various external objects, such as door handles, as well as on toys and cribs, and thus can represent a fairly persistent threat.

Table 10.1   Routes of infection

Transmissible (communicable) illnesses are those that can be transmitted from one human to another or from one animal species to another member of the same species, or can be transmitted across species. These pathogenic organisms can be transmitted through several different routes.

- *Airborne transmission* – when individuals breathe, cough, or sneeze, infected droplets are placed in the air (particular dust particles can also have these droplets attached), and if these can remain suspended for long periods, another person can inhale them, leading to illnesses.
- *Droplet contact* – coughing or sneezing on another person.
- *Contact transmission (direct)* – when a disease agent is transmitted directly from an infected individual to someone else through direct physical contact, such as touching an infected person, including sexual contact.
- *Contact transmission (indirect)* – infection transmitted indirectly, for example carrying an infection on unwashed hands, depositing these on a surface, which is then touched by another person. Contact illnesses include ringworm, smallpox, scabies, scarlet fever, and impetigo.
- *Vehicle transmission* – disease agents that can be transmitted through water, ice, food, serum, plasma, or other biological products. Many diseases are passed in this manner, including cholera, dysentery, diphtheria, scarlet fever, tuberculosis, typhoid fever, and viral hepatitis.
- *Transplacental transmission (vertical disease transmission)* – diseases can be passed from a pregnant mother to her fetus, e.g., HIV, syphilis, rubella, measles, toxoplasmosis.
- *Fecal–oral transmission* – usually develops when a person doesn't take basic hygienic precautions (e.g., failing to wash their hands following a bathroom stop) so that fecal bacteria contaminate door handles, counter tops, food or water sources, thereby being passed on to others.
- *Vector transmission* – when transmission occurs indirectly through another organism, such as a mosquito, or through an intermediate host, as in the case of tapeworm being passed on through improperly cooked pork.
- *Zoonotic diseases* – infectious diseases that are transmitted from animals to humans.

Bacterial infection and antibiotic use

Bacteria can promote a range of illnesses, such as food poisoning and gastritis, upper respiratory tract infections, pneumonia, skin infections, urinary tract infections, and sinusitis. Some illnesses come about owing to a specific bacterium, whereas others can be provoked by a number of different bacteria. For instance, bacterial meningitis, which affects about 4,500 in the US and 3,200 people each year in the UK (with a 10% death rate) can arise owing to infection by streptococcus pneumonia, neisseria meningitidis, or several other bacteria. Having antibiotic agents to fight bacteria has been among the most important weapon in our arsenal to protect human health, and history tells us about the horrid consequences of not having agents that are effective in this capacity.

How antibiotic resistance develops

Unfortunately, the increasing use of antibiotics has been met by increased resistance to their effects (antimicrobial resistance), leading to ever more serious challenges in the treatment of many infectious diseases, lengthier recovery times from infection, and a greater probability of death (Maragakis, 2010). Bacteria are fairly clever little marauders, who develop their resistance through a process much like natural selection. Those hardy bacteria that aren't destroyed by the antibiotic will give rise to similarly resistant clones, and over successive generations they will be unaffected by agents attempting to destroy them. In fact, when a threat is present, as in the case of antibiotics being around, they mutate more quickly, possibly in an effort to escape the challenge (Al Mamun et al., 2012). But, they also have another skill set that makes them still more capable. Specifically, they can go dormant in the presence of an antibiotic so that they're less likely to be attacked, and with repeated antibiotic attacks they 'learn' to stay dormant for periods that match the antibiotic's actions, and then come out of this state when the antibiotics actions have dissipated (Fridman et al., 2014). If this craftiness weren't enough, it also seems that bacteria act as a team, coordinating their actions so that maximal toxic effects can be provoked, probably owing to messaging from some external source (*quorum sensing*), such as the liquid in which they rest (Ng & Bassler, 2009). Communication not only occurs within a bacterial species, but across species, so that a variety of bacteria can get into squabbles with us. Should a set of bacteria find themselves without their teammates, they begin to mutate at a greater rate, and can grow as a group rather than floating about in isolation (Krašovec et al., 2014). This is a very adaptive response on the part of the bacteria, as finding itself alone might mean that it has lost allies to some agent acting against them, and the mutations may enhance the odds of survival of that bacterial species.

Resistance to the broad-spectrum antibiotic ciprofloxacin (Cip) has been found in some forms of common bacteria, creating havoc in relation to our well-being. This is not unique to bacteria, but also occurs in relation to parasites, such as lice, which have become progressively more resilient to lice-killing chemicals (Durand et al., 2012), and it is believed that treating mosquito netting may have inadvertently increased the risk for malaria owing to insecticide-resilient mosquitos (Norris et al., 2015). Ranchers and farmers who load up their livestock with antibiotics that humans eventually ingest may be a major contributor to antibiotic resistance, although this issue is still being debated in some quarters.

Beating antibacterial resistance

Health Canada has indicated that since 2002, there has been an enormous increase of last-line (last resort) antibiotic use and that 5% of people will likely be affected by antibiotic-resistant bacteria. It's not a Canadian problem alone, as the World Health Organization has considered the issue a global emergency. Owing to the relatively rapid appearance of bacterial-resistant infections it essential for new and better antibiotic treatments to be developed. But, even if these come down the pipeline, will the same type of resistance occur again? Behavior of patients and doctors needs to change in order to prevent this. People need to be educated so that they don't ask for or obtain antibiotics every time they're ill, especially when the illness is viral, for which antibiotics aren't effective. Moreover, well-intentioned doctors need to be re-educated as they occasionally do mess up. More than two-thirds of bronchitis patients in the US received antibiotics, even though bronchitis is most often of viral origin (Barnett & Linder,

2014). Likewise, 60% of physicians prescribed antibiotics for sore throats, despite just 10% of cases being related to strep bacteria. Incidentally, doctors also had an affinity for prescribing newer broad-spectrum meds (newer must be better), even when these weren't the best medication. In light of these problems, medical agencies have been making efforts to have doctors act more responsibly and take on greater stewardship in relation to their patients' medications.

MULTIPLE COSTS OF ANTIMICROBIAL RESISTANCE

Hospital-acquired infections have been a problem for some time, and the CDC estimated that within the US, bacteria and other microorganisms are responsible for about 1.7 million hospital-associated infections and 100,000 deaths annually, with staphylococcus aureus (S. aureus) being best known. *Staph infection* is the most frequent cause of post-surgical wound infection, endocarditis (inflammation of the inner layer of the heart), bacteria in the blood (bacteremia), sepsis and whole body infection, as well as toxic shock syndrome, meningitis, and pneumonia. Although these infections could be treated with antibiotics, such as methicillin, a bacterial strain has developed, termed methicillin-resistant Staphylococcus aureus (MRSA), that has ceased responding to this agent (Chambers, 2001). Infection by S. aureus within hospitals has increased progressively over the years, doubling between 2000 and 2010 (Jarvis et al., 2012), but thankfully, owing to improved health practices, infection rates have been declining. As it turns out, however, it became progressively more common for community-acquired infection to be found in individual homes (Kassakian & Mermel, 2014) and in foods such as meat and poultry.

The occurrence of MRSA within the community, estimated to be about 12% in the US, has been linked to recent antibiotic use, people sharing contaminated items, the presence of active skin diseases or injuries, poor hygiene, and crowded living conditions. As with many illnesses, some individuals are more likely to develop S. aureus infections, including diabetics who use insulin, individuals undergoing chemotherapy, and those with HIV/AIDS or with a weakened immune system stemming from other factors. Vulnerability to infection is also elevated among individuals with burns, cuts, or lesions on the skin, as well as patients who undergo breathing intubation, or who have urinary or dialysis catheters inserted, as well as people who have medical implants such as hip replacements. Stressful experiences, presumably because of the effects on immune functioning, can also influence vulnerability to S. Aureus infection, especially in vulnerable populations such as older people (Bailey et al., 2003). Among children who have experienced trauma, hospital-associated infection could be predicted on the basis of a low and persistent immune response (Muszynski et al., 2014). MRSA also seems to thrive among smokers, and aspects of cigarette smoke may somehow protect MRSA from factors that would otherwise destroy these bacteria (McEachern et al., 2015). Evidently, the only thing that cigarette smoke doesn't harm is some things that are otherwise bad for our health.

It's not just S. aureus that has developed resistance to antibiotics. Tuberculosis has been infecting people for centuries, and was a leading cause of death in Europe in the eighteenth and nineteenth

(Continued)

(Continued)

centuries, but couldn't be treated effectively until the introduction of streptomycin in the mid-twentieth century. Tuberculosis is still around, affecting about 9 million people in 2013, and led to about 1.5 million deaths primarily in Asia and sub-Saharan Africa. This infection seems to get relatively little attention, even though a drug-resistant form of it has been spreading (World Heath Organization, 2014b). Likewise, an antibiotic-resistant form of typhoid has been spreading throughout Asia (Wong et al., 2015). This bacterial strain, dubbed H58, initially appeared several decades ago, but only recently has it become the dominant form of these bacteria. Given that typhoid affects about 30 million people each year, high levels of global surveillance will be necessary.

It so happens that yet another bacterial infection has turned up in Western countries, which seems to be treatment resistant. The usual treatment of Shigella had been ciprofloxacin, but the CDC (2015c), in their Morbidity and Mortality Weekly Report (MMWR), announced that this agent can't be counted on to treat this illness much longer. More than 500,000 people are affected by Shigella within the US on a yearly basis through the 'the fecal–oral' route. What this means is that some infected person went to the washroom, and then with disregard to basic health issues didn't bother washing their hands before exiting. They deposited their bacteria on the washroom door knob, or shook hands with you, and you may well have touched your mouth afterward. Alternatively, perhaps that person offered you half of their sandwich, which you accepted, and you thus became an unwitting consumer of poo-bacteria. Because Shigella is as infectious as it is, causing illness after ingestion of only a dozen or so bacteria, you became a victim of this chain, causing symptoms such as fever and even bloody diarrhea. You might get better on your own, or it might require antibiotics. But if Shigella is resistant to treatment, then you'll be sicker longer, and thus more likely to spread the bacteria to others. The messages here are fairly clear. Don't over-use antibiotics and wash your hands after visiting the 'washroom'. For what it's worth, I've neurotically taken to using paper towels to grab the door handle when I exit washrooms.

There have been numerous attempts to curb resistant bacteria and, as already indicated, some advances have been made by adopting simple procedures, such as hand-washing and having physicians alter their practices in doling out antibiotics. It has also been suggested that by alternating doses of antibiotics, and those that are used in successive infections, the appearance of resistance can be diminished (Fuentes-Hernandez et al., 2015). Another approach has entailed genetically altering resistant bacteria to make them more sensitive to antibiotics (Yosef et al., 2015).

Viral infection

Viruses, unlike most bacteria, can only multiply inside living cells, and they can be transmitted to other organisms in a variety of ways, as described earlier. Components of a virus (virions) attach to and penetrate a host cell, and then the virus incorporates itself into the genome of this cell. Thereafter, replication of the virus occurs within the host's DNA or RNA. After sufficient replication, the virus can force itself through the host cell's membrane or the host cell disintegrates, but either way the virus may infect other nearby cells (Dimmock et al., 2007). Viruses have been considered not to be a life form because of their inability to reproduce on their own. Instead, they have been thought of as 'organisms at the edge of life' as they possess genes and can change through natural selection, which is dictated by environmental demands (Rybicki, 1990). The most common viruses that affect humans are depicted in Figure 10.1.

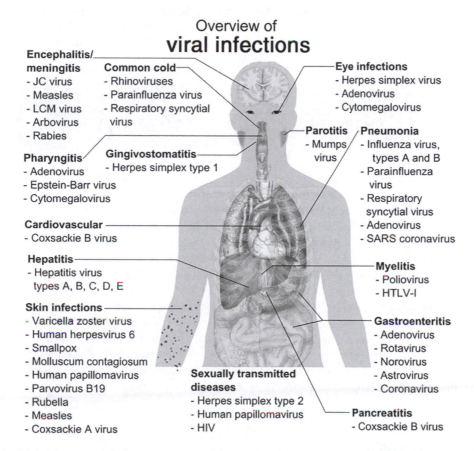

Figure 10.1   Overview of the main types of viral infection and the most notable species involved (Häggström, 2014)

The extent to which a virus spreads through a population depends on how readily it can be passed on from one person to another, the route by which it's transmitted, how readily it can penetrate the host's tissues and attach itself to cells, its ability to inhibit the host's immune defenses and to obtain nutrition from the host, and how quickly the virus kills the host. If a virus causes death of the host too rapidly, then the opportunity for the virus to be transmitted is diminished, although passage from one person to the next, as in the case of Ebola, may come about even if the host is dead. If the host doesn't die immediately, then the opportunity for viral transmission is increased, depending on the viral load being carried and whether the virus can avoid detection. Some viruses, like influenza, have further dirty tricks they use to cause illness. With the assistance of particular proteins (*neuraminidase*) they have the ability to counter the attack of natural killer cells, increasing the likelihood of the host becoming ill. As it happens, in this instance, treatments have been developed to deal with the wicked skills that viruses possess. Inhibitors of neuraminidase can be used to make natural killer cells more effective, and thus diminish flu symptoms. Antibodies have also been developed that bind to proteins that otherwise hinder natural killer cell activity, thereby allowing them to do their job more effectively (Bar-On et al., 2014).

THERE'S SOMETHING ABOUT MARY

Some individuals are 'superspreaders', seemingly infecting more than their share of people by passing on bacteria or viruses. It may be that there's something about their immune response that makes them so capable of infecting others, or they may be especially social and thus come into contact with more people than do others, or have occupations that permit them to do so. In the early 1900s, Mary Mallon, much better known as Typhoid Mary, was a cook who seemed to be a virtuoso in spreading typhoid (which comes from the bacteria salmonella), even though she never actually showed symptoms of the illness. She is credited with infecting about 50 people, eight of whom died. Poor Mary has been villainized, as she should have – not just because she spread the disease, but because she refused to alter her behaviors when suspicions arose that she was the 'spreader', and she even put herself in places (e.g., as a hospital cook) where she could do particular damage (Ram, 2014). She was eventually isolated, but she did become a bit of a celebrity thanks to the newspapers encouraging sympathy for her. The 80–20 rule (also known as the Pareto principle) may apply to viral spread in that 80% of an infectious disease is transmitted by 20% of the people. We can only hope that the potential spreaders choose to be vaccinated.

Zoonotic diseases

Viruses and bacteria can be transmitted to humans through a 'vector', such as mosquitoes or ticks (malaria, Lyme's disease, West Nile virus, dengue fever, and yellow fever), birds, pigs, or rodents and even through dogs (as in the case of rabies) and monkeys (Simian immunodeficiency virus might have been transferred to humans which then could have mutated into HIV). Over the past two decades the frequency of emerging vector-borne zoonotic diseases has been increasing (Kilpatrick & Randolph, 2012), but typically these viruses don't make the leap to being transmitted between humans. However, if a virus mutates in some way so that it can be transmitted between humans, the outcomes can be horrendous, as we've seen in the case of HIV/AIDS, as well as in the recent Ebola epidemic.

KNOWING SOMETHING ABOUT VACCINES

The best way to deal with any illness is prevention, and in the case of viral illnesses, this entails being vaccinated against them. Having encountered a foreign pathogen, T and B cells will have a memory of it so that if it is subsequently encountered again, our strong secondary immune response will sharply reduce the odds of the illness developing. Vaccines that we currently use are based on this very principle, being made up of dead, inactivated, or weakened viral particles, or products that are derived from them. The vaccine won't cause us to become ill (contrary to some of the rumors spread by anti-vaxxers), but because the dead or weakened virus will be recognized as being foreign, an immune response will be mounted, and information about this virus will be retained by immune cells. Thus, when a potentially harmful virus is later encountered, it will be eliminated by the strong immune response that occurs. It's thanks to mass vaccinations that diseases such as polio have been almost eradicated and measles, mumps, and rubella, which also caused many deaths, have been diminished (Lane, 2006).

In the case of many illnesses (e.g., measles, polio), the effectiveness of vaccines is impressive, although their effectiveness may vary somewhat across people, and may decline with age. In other instances, such as flu vaccines, their effectiveness is far more variable. Just as we keep looking for better ways to detect and destroy viruses, they make considerable efforts to avoid being detected or find ways in which the agents that we use to destroy them will not have the desired effects. One way viruses do this is through mutations so that they'll be less likely to be recognized. As influenza viruses come in a set number of formats, we can anticipate what they might look like, and thus have a head start in making supplies of vaccine. Yet, even with the best information available, vaccine producers may be fooled, and thus the effectiveness of the vaccine will be diminished. In other instances the vaccine might be an effective one, but some individuals might simply be 'nonresponders' to certain vaccines in that they don't produce sufficient antibodies to fight future infection (Osterholm et al., 2012).

The ability of a virus to affect whole populations or to turn into a pandemic is influenced by the extent to which the virus can be spread. Some viruses are effective in this capacity (e.g., when one infected person spreads it to 12 others), whereas others spread poorly and die off (1 person infects 0.5 others). When enough people in a population are vaccinated, even fairly potent viruses may have difficulty spreading, and the group as a whole will be protected (herd immunity). Ironically, this herd immunity also protects the children of parents who refuse to have their children vaccinated, which reinforces their noncompliance. However, like teeter-totters, this relationship moves up and down. When enough people within a population decide not to be vaccinated (or not have their children vaccinated), the 'tipping point' may be reached so that the herd immunity effect is no longer present, and the viral illness will spread, affecting those who hadn't been vaccinated as well as those who are vaccine nonresponders. In the case of measles, which is easily spread, the tipping point is around 92%, and in some places vaccination rates have dropped below this level, so we can pretty

(Continued)

(Continued)

much count on measles reappearing. While we're on the topic of measles, don't be misled into thinking that this is just one of those childhood illnesses that children get through. It's not a benign disease and can be very serious, leading to many hospitalizations and deaths. Moreover, following measles infection, the immune system may be altered for as long as 2–3 years so that the risk for other illnesses is increased (Mina et al., 2015). As well, among young children in whom the immune system is not fully developed the measles virus can hide in the body, even for years, and may come to infect the brain. The so-called subacute sclerosing panencephalitis (SSPE) will then manifest in the infected person years afterward as mood swings, behavioral problems, convulsions, coma and, inevitably, by death.

The effectiveness of vaccines has been enormously successful in preventing many diseases, and this very success may have bred some of the current vaccine hesitancy that has become more common. People brought up in vaccinated societies who haven't seen the horrendous impact of viruses such as measles and polio have become blasé in their attitudes.

There are many reasons why individuals might choose not to be vaccinated for common illnesses, such as influenza. Some of these have already been mentioned, such as mistrust of media and government agencies with respect to recommendations that have been made. A qualitative meta-analysis suggested that to a considerable extent individual behaviors in relation to vaccination are linked to personal experiences, such as those provided in Table 10.2 (Nowak et al., 2015).

Table 10.2   To be vaccinated or not

Factors driving choice to receive flu vaccination

- belief that individual is flu susceptible
- belief that the vaccine is effective and that being vaccinated matters
- being an older person or having an existent chronic health condition
- having had a recommendation come from a physician
- having previously experienced a bad flu or a similar illness
- having encountered active vaccination promotion indicating that it makes a difference
- easy access to vaccination

Factors driving choice to not receive flu vaccination

- belief, often based on personal experiences, that flu is a 'manageable illness'
- belief that the recommendations for vaccination don't apply to them
- belief that flu vaccines are ineffective
- hesitation based on belief that they could get the flu from the vaccine
- belief (or rationalization) that other measures are more effective
- having had some sort of negative personal experience with the vaccine

---

Neglected tropical diseases

We're all now somewhat familiar with Ebola virus, but far fewer have ever heard of hookworm, schistosomiasis, lymphatic filariasis, ascariasis, or onchocerciasis, which are a few of the '*neglected tropical diseases*' that appear primarily in Africa, Asia, and South and Central America. There are a fair number of such illnesses, stemming from protozoa, bacteria, viruses, and worms, but the World Health Organization has 17 that are most frequent, some of which are on the way to being eradicated, but there is still some distance to cover. These diseases affect more than a billion people a year, including almost half the school-aged children in sub-Saharan Africa, and a number are affected by more than one infection (Hotez & Kamath, 2009). Some of these illnesses are very treatable and inexpensive (as little as 20 cents per day in the case of schistosomiasis); others are more costly and beyond affordability for most people.

The economic and social impact of these diseases (think of responses to leprosy, which is one of these diseases) has been enormous, but they've been largely ignored. This might have occurred because of the double whammy of occurring primarily in the poorest parts of the poorest continent of the world, coupled with attention to these conditions being supplanted by HIV/AIDS, malaria, and tuberculosis. Several corporations have donated millions of dollars to deal with these conditions, as have private–public partnerships, such as the 'Global Health Innovative Technology Fund'. It is surprising, though, that the total investments in eradicating these diseases has been so limited, particularly as these emerging infections may eventually come to affect those in the West.

SEXUALLY TRANSMITTED INFECTION

Some pathogens are *endemic* to our society, meaning that they don't simply appear and then disappear, but instead are constantly present, as in the case of many sexually transmitted diseases (STDs). Some of these are more infectious than others, and some produce obvious symptoms, whereas others don't. As a result, their transmission rates differ, as does their appearance within the population. There are several STDs that are of a viral nature, including hepatitis B, Herpes simplex virus 2 (HSV-2), HIV, and Human Papillomavirus (HPV), or they may be bacterial (chlamydia, gonorrhea, syphilis, bacterial vaginosis), fungal (candidiasis), protozoal (trichomoniasis), or a result of parasites (crabs, lice, scabies).

STDs are frequent throughout the world, and in Western countries they had been increasing with changes in sexual behaviors as well as the availability of oral contraceptives. This was compounded by increased travel, which allowed the greater spread of diseases, and by the increase of drug-resistant bacteria, as in the case of those that had previously responded to penicillin. Some STDs can be treated through antibiotics (chlamydia and gonorrhea) and penicillin was the preferred treatment of syphilis, although resistant bacteria have become more common in relation to syphilis, and a resistant strain of gonorrhea (H041) has appeared that is considered a superbug (Shimuta et al., 2013). In the case of some STDs, such as hepatitis B and HPV, vaccines have been developed, although a backlash has occurred as some parents refuse to have their kids vaccinated against HPV. Still other STDs are incurable (HIV, herpes), although the length and severity of herpes outbreaks can be reduced by antivirals (e.g., Zovirax, Famvir, and Valtrex). At the moment, abstention or use of condoms, rather than cure, is the key to dealing with these illnesses.

LIFE-STYLE FACTORS IN RELATION TO IMMUNE FUNCTIONING AND WELL-BEING

The ability of our immune system to contend with a variety of insults may be influenced by genetic factors, life-style – including what we eat, our sleep, exercise, as well as by stressor experiences, and thus each of these variables may influence the emergence of illnesses. Because so many of these variables affect one another, it is difficult to dissociate the influence of any single factor from others that are concurrently present.

Diet and immunity

Considerable attention has been devoted to analyses of the processes by which eating and energy metabolism can affect immune functioning, as well as the influence of various foods and specific diets. Aside from its role in digestive processes, the gastrointestinal (GI) tract serves as a barrier to limit potential adverse effects stemming from the foods that we eat. This is no easy task, as it means that the GI tract must differentiate between those substances that are good for us and those that aren't. In part, this is accomplished by the presence of an appreciable portion of our immune system's cells being present within the gut. As well, the epithelial cells of the GI tract, together with protective mucous, diminish the passage of damaging molecules into the body while allowing passage of beneficial substances. For effective immune system functioning, several essential vitamins and minerals (e.g., zinc, selenium, iron, copper, and folic acid) need to be present, which are largely obtained from the foods we eat. Likewise, essential fatty acids and mono-unsaturated fats are required for effective functioning of immune-related processes and for the maintenance of microbial balances.

As we've seen, many systems act in opposition to one another in an effort to maintain biological equilibrium. One mechanism may be present to get things started and another to get things stopped; one system may operate in an inhibitory capacity to regulate the excitatory effects of a second system. Similarly, the presence of reactive oxygen species (by-products of cellular metabolism) and other free radicals is needed at sites of inflammation in order to facilitate the death of cells that aren't healthy. At the same time, antioxidant processes are needed to diminish the reactive oxygen species once they've done their job so that they don't create damage to healthy cells. Once again, the ingestion of particular foods (e.g., red beans, blueberries, raspberries, cranberries, artichokes) facilitates antioxidant production, thereby limiting cellular damage.

Microbiota

Gut bacteria contribute to efficient immune functioning, and the alliance between the microbiome and the immune system is fundamental in the elicitation of responses to pathogens and in maintaining tolerance to innocuous antigens so that unnecessary immune activation does not occur (Belkaid & Hand, 2014). Likewise, gut bacteria can have pronounced effects on brain functioning and thus can affect psychological well-being (Ochoa-Repáraz et al., 2011). However, over-use of antibiotics and dietary changes may have favored microbial changes that have neither the diversity nor the resilience necessary for effective and balanced immune responses to be engendered (Belkaid & Hand, 2014), thereby affecting illness vulnerability. These core microbial communities, and hence well-being, might also come to be indirectly affected by variations of socioeconomic status, cultural traditions, and increased urbanization, any of which influence diets. The repercussions of these changes may be particularly pronounced in young children given their sensitivity to foods (Jain & Walker, 2015) and may have particularly marked consequences on brain functioning among preterm infants (Sherman et al., 2015), and infants treated with antibiotics may be at increased risk of developing adult diseases (Vangay et al., 2015). It is especially interesting that a stressor in the form of repeatedly separating mouse pups from their mom during the first 3 postnatal weeks later exhibited altered gut microbiota, altered levels of the neurotransmitter acetylcholine, and displayed increased signs of anxiety and depression. When mice received the stressor treatment in germ-free conditions the microbiota and hormone changes were still apparent, but the elevated anxiety was absent. When mice were, however, colonized with bacteria from control mice, the anxiety was again apparent. Thus, it seems as if both host characteristics and microbial contributions are necessary for the adverse effects of early-life stress in the formation of psychological disturbances (De Palma et al., 2015). Beyond these effects, it also appears that gut microbes contribute to the programming and subsequent responsivity of stress systems, including those involving neuronal, hormonal, metabolic, and immune mechanisms, ultimately affecting the regulation of mood and cognitive processes (Moloney et al., 2014).

Exercise and immunity

Given all that's been said about the importance of exercise in maintaining well-being and in diminishing the impact of life stressors (Fleshner et al., 2009), it comes as no surprise that a proper exercise regimen enhances immune functioning (e.g., augmenting NK cell functioning) (McFarlin et al., 2005), and perhaps limits the immune system's decline with advancing age (*immunosenescence*). Although the available data are inconsistent in several respects, it largely appeared based on animal studies that moderate intensity exercise enhances immune functioning, and thus beneficial health effects may be accrued (Pedersen & Hoffman-Goetz, 2000).

Among humans who exercised on a regular basis (habitual-exercisers) life span was shown to have increased, and the time during which they remained healthy (*health span*) was lengthened relative to individuals who typically didn't exercise. Ordinarily a sedentary life-style may lead to increased visceral fat, and the cytokine release from *adipokines* (cytokines released from fat cells) may favor the development of illnesses. Thus, by limiting visceral fat, exercise might serve to prevent the development of these illnesses (Pedersen, 2009). This doesn't imply that more exercise is necessarily better. Unlike the positive effects of moderate exercise, excessive exercise that leads to fatigue has produced lymphocyte loss and increased illness symptoms brought on by an influenza virus (Hoffman-Goetz & Quadrilatero, 2003). Similarly, among people who engage in 'extreme exercise', which is often the behavior of high-performance athletes, immune functioning may be both impaired and accompanied by increased incidence of virally-related conditions, such as herpes virus and reactivation of Epstein-Barr virus (Walsh et al., 2011), as well as a marked increase of upper respiratory infection (Edwards et al., 2008). The health disturbances were attributed to disturbed natural killer cell functioning and reduced immunoglobulin within mucosal secretory (nasal and salivary) glands, allowing infectious molecules the opportunity to invade.

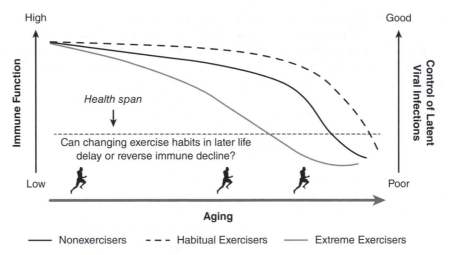

Figure 10.2 Life span and health span vary with age among individuals who maintain generally sedentary life-styles (nonexercisers), those who participate in regular exercise to enhance their health and well-being (habitual exercisers), and those who participate in extreme exercise. Whereas habitual exercisers may experience longer life and an extended health span, among extreme exercisers diminished immune functioning and poorer control in relation to viral infections may occur, and hence they will experience reductions of life span and health span. These findings raise several questions, including how being brought up with particular life-styles will affect life span and health span, and whether exercise regimens at various ages influences health disturbances that might be provoked by stressors. From Simpson & Bosch (2014).

Sleep and immunity

Sleep disorders may promote illness and may influence mortality as a result of varied disorders, often stemming from immune disturbances (Irwin, 2015). The implications of these findings are fairly significant given that 25% of individuals experience a degree of insomnia, with almost 10% meeting the criteria for chronic insomnia (LeBlanc et al., 2009).

Sleep and circadian rhythms contribute to the regulation of immune processes, and sleep disturbances are accompanied by impaired immune functioning (Irwin, 2015). As indicated earlier, sleep has profound recuperative powers, and the lack of 'restorative sleep' when accompanied by elevated inflammation may contribute to heart disease (van Leeuwen et al., 2009). Even a single night of sleep loss may be sufficient to disturb immune functioning, reflected by the diminished effects of influenza and hepatitis vaccination (Spiegel et al., 2002), and diminished sleep was associated with increased incidence of the common cold (Cohen et al., 2009). The effects of sleep loss may directly influence immune processes that affect illness vulnerability or, alternatively, the conditions that lead to sleep disturbances can elicit stress-related hormonal disturbances that could influence immune functioning (Irwin, 2015). Either way, like exercise and diet, sleep is an essential element of life-style that affects immune competence.

Stressors and viral illness

Stressful events affect immune functioning, and such experiences understandably affect susceptibility and frequency of viral illnesses (Chida & Mao, 2009), diminish the elimination of a virus, lengthen the course of illness, and favor more frequent infection-related complications (Bailey et al., 2007; Elftman et al., 2010). Among the first 'formal' demonstrations of such actions (moms were saying this for ages, but without hard evidence) was that stressful experiences were accompanied by increased occurrence of colds among individuals treated with a low dose of the virus (Cohen et al., 1993), especially if the stressor had been experienced chronically (Cohen et al., 1998). Similar outcomes were subsequently observed in relation to other types of virus, such as the response to cytomegalo-virus (CMV), and antibody production upon exposure to Epstein-Barr virus, and stressors that exist at the individual and the neighborhood level may exacerbate the progression of HIV to AIDS (Aiello et al., 2010). In addition, stressors may affect the *reactivation* of a latent virus, such as HSV-1 (the virus that causes cold sores), that had been in hiding within the trigeminal ganglion. As a result, cold sores associated with infection may recur, often at the most inopportune times. It is largely taken for granted that stressors are causally linked to viral illnesses, but it is not unusual for stressor experiences to be accompanied by other life changes, including altered diet, sleep, and exercise, and the illnesses associated with stressful experiences may reflect the interactive actions of these various factors.

AUTOIMMUNE DISORDERS

Despite the immune system being reasonably effective in protecting us from an assortment of microbes, there are occasions in which it seems confused, and instead of focusing on external challenges, it turns against us, resulting in *autoimmune disorders* in which our own organs or tissues are attacked. There are about 75–80 disorders that are known or suspected to fall into this class, with their combined overall prevalence being about 8% in developed countries. For most of these illnesses, the frequency is far greater in females (70–90%) than in males. The view is often taken that females carry particular vulnerability factors that place them at increased risk for such disorders, but it is possible instead that males carry a protective factor so that they're less likely to be affected.

The processes responsible for these disorders vary from one another, even though many are comorbid conditions, and the course of the illnesses can be exacerbated by common factors. It is possible, for instance, that autoimmune disorders involve a gene variant that influences T helper cells so that normal cells are attacked more readily, or cells that normally suppress immune functioning aren't operating efficiently. In conjunction with these operations, still other genetic variants might determine which specific aspect of the body will be attacked. In this regard, the 'autoimmune regulator' gene (AIRE) is responsible for training immune cells to ignore self-made antigens, and attack only those that are foreign. However, it was suggested that a child who inherits two mutated versions of the AIRE gene (and it seems that this may even occur with a mutation on one allele) won't have the ability to examine immune cells as to their competency, and as a result some of them may turn on the body's own organs (Oftedal et al., 2015). In essence, if immune activity persists when it should be turned off, it can ultimately lead to the immune system attacking the self. As we'll see in covering several auto-immune disorders, there is currently no cure for most of these conditions; some can be managed to an appreciable extent, whereas others seem to have so far eluded our abilities.

Sjogren's syndrome

This disorder occurs at a moderately high frequency, but estimates of its prevalence have varied widely from 400,000 to 3.1 million cases. *Sjogren's syndrome* occurs when the body's white blood cells destroy salivary and lacrimal (tear producing) glands (Borchers et al., 2003). As a result, individuals experience dry eyes and mouth, and they may also experience problems related to blood vessels, various organs (kidneys, liver, lungs, and pancreas) as well as the peripheral nervous system and the brain. The disease usually appears in mid-life (45–55), is more common in women (90%), and often appears among individuals with a rheumatic disease (e.g., rheumatoid arthritis).

The causes of this autoimmune disorder are uncertain, but seem to involve genetic and hormonal factors, such as elevated estrogen (Voulgarelis & Tzioufas, 2010), together with a constellation of environmental influences that could affect glandular infection. Psychosocial factors, such as pain catastrophizing, was related to the presence of the disorder, and occurred relatively frequently among individuals who experienced high levels of psychological stress in response to major negative life events, but lacked effective coping strategies, such as social support (Karaiskos et al., 2009). These findings raise the possibility that behavioral interventions to reduce catastrophizing and negative illness appraisals, as well as training cognitive and behavioral coping methods, might be useful in controlling some symptoms (Segal et al., 2014).

Psoriasis

Psoriasis, which affects about 2% of individuals, is a chronic, immune-mediated skin disease characterized by itchy red, scaly patches, papules, and plaques that can be localized or may extend to broad sections of the body. Unlike many other autoimmune disorders, this condition appears among males and females equally, initially when they are between 15 and 25 years of age, more commonly among Euro Caucasians than African or Native Americans, as well as among individuals with other autoimmune-based illnesses, such as ulcerative colitis or Crohn's disease (forms of inflammatory bowel disease). In psoriasis, the immune system mistakenly identifies normal skin cells as a pathogen, and overproduction of new skin cells may develop, sometimes being replaced at a rate 5–10 times faster than normal, owing to a cascade of cytokine alterations (Nestle et al., 2009). Genetic factors contribute to the emergence of psoriasis, but this alone is not sufficient to account for its occurrence, and several environmental factors also have powerful effects on this condition (Krueger & Ellis, 2005). For instance, symptoms may be aggravated by chronic infections, stress, smoking, diet, alcohol consumption, and changes in season (Nestle et al., 2009).

Inflammatory bowel disease

Inflammatory bowel disease (IBD) refers to inflammatory autoimmune conditions involving the colon and small intestine, with ulcerative colitis and Crohn's disease being the most common. Although the latter is often thought of as being restricted to the colon and small intestine, it can also affect the mouth, esophagus, stomach, and anus. These illnesses are distinct from one another, but they share many symptoms related to intestinal problems, such as abdominal pain, vomiting, diarrhea, rectal bleeding, and severe internal cramps/muscle spasms in the region of the pelvis. As well, nonbowel-related characteristics might emerge (e.g., anemia) and several other autoimmune disorders may co-occur with IBD, such as arthritis and primary sclerosing cholangitis (in which inflammation impedes the flow of bile to the gut, potentially causing cirrhosis of the liver, liver failure, and liver cancer). Recommendations have been made concerning the best foods to eat in order to limit IBD symptoms, including a diet that is limited in fermentable, poorly absorbed carbohydrates and sugar alcohols (Cuomo et al., 2014), but there is some question as to whether there is a specific diet that is most suitable (Hayes et al., 2014).

Microbial involvement

The appearance of IBD and ulcerative colitis are promoted by a large number of genes that together account for almost 10% of the variance of each disorder (Jostins et al., 2012). But, there's obviously more to their occurrence and exacerbation, including influences of gut bacteria, particularly in the form of a reduced number of different types of bacteria (Mukhopadhya et al., 2012). Gut microbiota implicated in the emergence of IBD might also contribute to the comorbidity that occurs with other conditions, even having been linked to psychiatric disorders (Collins, 2014). Epidemiologic studies have consistently indicated that diet can influence the development of intestinal inflammation, and increasingly more studies have been assessing the effects of defined diets in reducing IBD through their microbial actions (Leone et al., 2014). As important as diet alone might be in affecting the microbiota, and hence IBD, we shouldn't lose sight of the fact that the microbiota is affected by other life-style factors (antibiotic usage, infection, and stress) that ought to be considered in developing treatment strategies for this disorder (Collins, 2014).

It's still not known which bacteria are principally responsible for the seemingly excessive immune response associated with IBD, although several culprits have been identified. Microbes of a *clostridial* family, often referred to as 'clostridial clusters', act against bacteria such as C. difficile that cause inflammation, diarrhea, bleeding, and massive loss of fluids that can lead to death. It seems that these clostridial clusters also play a fundamental role in limiting immune activation that could be harmful. In 'germ-free' mice bred to provide experimental animals that were relatively uncontaminated by a dirty world, strong reactions occurred to antibiotics in that their immune suppressor cells (*Tregs*) declined precipitously, and they became exceptionally susceptible to an inflammatory bowel condition much like that of IBD in humans. However, if mice were treated with a cocktail of bacteria from the clostridial cluster, the Tregs were reinstated and the bowel disorder diminished (Nagano et al., 2012). Taking the lead from such studies, efforts have been made to deal with such diseases by altering the constituent bacteria within the gut through diet or fecal microbiota transplantation (West et al., 2015).

Analysis of factors related to the microbiome has also provided a better understanding of Crohn's disease, and has made us take a second look at how the microbiome operates. The view emerged that this disorder might evolve owing to bad gut bacteria provoking inflammation. However, in surgically removed portions of intestine from patients with Crohn's there was a considerable reduction of a particular bacterium, *Faecalibacterium prausnitzii*. This led to the view that Crohn's didn't emerge owing to the presence of bad bacteria, but instead developed owing to specific 'good' bacteria being absent (Sokol & Seksik, 2010). Indeed, when these good bacteria were transplanted into mice, positive effects emerged. The question now is what causes these good bacteria to decline to levels that favor the development of illness, and what can be done about this.

Treatment of IBD

The realization that the enteric nervous system may contribute to IBD gave rise to the development of treatments aimed at serotonergic and neurotrophic processes which are plentiful in the gut nervous system (Hansen, 2003; Wood, 2013). Likewise, benzodiazepine-sensitive receptors are present, and stress responses can alter the functioning of the gut, and thus anxiety-related treatments have been used in an effort to control IBD (Salari & Abdollahi, 2011). There have also been a fair number of studies conducted to determine whether fecal microbial transplant, antibiotics, probiotics, and prebiotics can be used to treat IBD. However, most have involved a small number of patients and the results obtained were inconsistent. As a result, there has yet to be significant acceptance of microbe-based treatments for these conditions, although it may be premature to abandon them entirely (West et al., 2015).

Treatment of ulcerative colitis and Crohn's disease are usually determined on an individual basis. The American Gastroenterological Association has provided guidelines for which treatments are most appropriate, given specific symptoms being expressed, such as presence of constipation versus diarrhea (recommendations entail linaclotide and rifaximin, respectively). When the conditions are relatively severe, immunosuppressive agents may be called for (e.g., TNF-α inhibitors, prednisone). If treatments fail, then surgical procedures may be required, involving removal of large portions or all of the large intestine. It is significant that despite these firm demarcations regarding treatment, there has been a notable increase in a push for individualized treatment of IBD (Mosli et al., 2014).

Celiac disease

Celiac disease, an autoimmune disorder involving the small intestine, affects 1.0–1.5% of Euro Caucasian people, but is infrequent among people of African, Japanese, or Chinese decent. This illness affects individuals of all ages, more commonly women than men, and has a clear genetic component (Gujral et al., 2012). Several genetic factors may contribute to the occurrence of celiac disease, although some individuals without this genetic constitution may also develop the disorder. At one time it was rarely diagnosed, but this increased as the disorder came to be understood and diagnostic procedures became available.

This disease is characterized by pain and discomfort in the digestive tract, chronic constipation and diarrhea, cramping, bloatedness and abdominal distension (owing to the production of bowel gas), weight loss or a failure to gain weight (in children), as well as fatigue and anemia. In the presence of severe celiac disease, pale, loose, and greasy stools may be present, and deficiencies of vitamins are not infrequent, likely owing to the diminished ability of the small intestine to absorb nutrients properly from foods (van der Windt et al., 2010). Typically, celiac disease is determined based on symptoms presented coupled with blood tests, endoscopy (an imaging procedure in which a tube is threaded to a hollow organ or body cavity), and through the determination of vitamin and iron deficiencies. Some patients present with atypical symptoms, but improved assessment methods have allowed for a diagnosis of this disorder to be made, although this may take some time (Pulido et al., 2013).

Symptoms of celiac disease stem from a reaction to *gliadin*, a gluten protein present in wheat and grains, such as barley and rye, which results in enzymatic changes that cause the immune system to react to small-bowel tissue, provoking an inflammatory reaction. This, in turn, causes the villi (tiny hair- or finger-like projections) lining the small intestine to become shortened, which undermines the ability of the intestine to absorb nutrients and transfer them to blood vessels to which they are connected (Guandalini & Setty, 2008). It's possible that early life consumption of wheat, barley, or rye, before barriers within the gut are fully developed, may encourage celiac disease (Akobeng et al., 2006).

Currently, the only way of managing celiac disease is through a life-long gluten-free diet (Fasano & Catassi, 2012). Depending on the degree of damage that has been created, the adoption of such a diet may allow for intestinal healing, attenuation or elimination of symptoms, and diminish the elevated risk for intestinal cancer and osteoporosis that is otherwise present. As the diet must be strictly maintained, the assistance of a dietician is highly recommended, and because the diet can be somewhat unappetizing, patients are encouraged to try new ways of preparing foods (Troncone et al., 2008). Unfortunately, among some patients, more so women than men, some symptoms may persist even with appropriate diets for several years.

GLUTEN-FREE IS THIS YEAR'S FAD

Have you noticed the very large number of people who are currently on gluten-free diets, although only a small fraction of the population suffers from celiac disease? Some individuals without celiac disease claim heightened gluten sensitivity and report feeling better when not consuming food with gluten in it, but this condition is questionable based on clinical tests (Biesiekierski et al., 2013). Regardless of how this comes about, if it works for them, even if it's a placebo effect, then that's fine provided that essential foods don't go by the wayside.

Gluten intolerance may be accompanied by skin diseases (Humbert et al., 2006), and there are individuals with psoriasis who believe that a gluten-free diet has helped control their symptoms, although it's possible that this came about owing to weight loss and the consequent decline of cytokines released from belly fat that encourages autoimmune responses (Ricketts et al., 2010).

Being on a gluten-free diet has become a fad (is craze a better term?) encouraged by books that suggest that any product with wheat in it is dangerous, even those containing whole grains. Sports figures and some Hollywood types have also had an impact on the gluten-free movement, even though they might not be the right people to believe with respect to medically-related issues. Some people on this diet feel that it improves their mood, others believe that it will help them lose weight, which might be accurate given that the food is often unappetizing. However, if it's not a medical necessity, as in those who actually are experiencing celiac disease, it's probably not useful and can even cause some harm as these diets often lack needed fiber, minerals, and vitamins, and are not fortified by nutrients, such as folate and iron (although these fortified nutrients can be obtained through sufficient intake of other foods). Gluten-free diets are having a substantial popular impact given that big business has responded in a fairly big way, just as they would to any other fad that could mean billions of dollars in sales. Check the supermarkets and you'll see gluten-free sections (is a gluten-free pizza really a pizza?), and name brand companies are advertising 'gluten-free products', even if they had never, ever had gluten in them.

Rheumatoid arthritis

Rheumatoid arthritis, which occurs in about 1% of individuals, primarily women (80%), is an autoimmune disorder that affects *synovial* joints (i.e., movable joints surrounded by a capsule containing lubricating fluid), the membrane that lines joints, tendon sheaths, and cartilage in the fingers, wrists, knees, elbows, and cervical spine. The disorder is characterized by inflammation of a single or multiple joints, joint pain, muscle aches and pains, general malaise or feelings of fatigue, and may be accompanied by weight loss and poor sleep. Although it is usually considered in terms of joint problems, it may also be accompanied by autonomic nervous system dysfunctions as well as heart problems (Adlan et al., 2014). This disorder usually appears when individuals are 40–60 years old, although systemic inflammation and autoimmunity may begin years before detectable joint inflammation is present (Demoruelle et al., 2014). Depending on the degree of inflammation present, symptoms may wax and wane, and there may be periods that can last months or years during which the symptoms seem to be in remission, only to reoccur (referred to as a *flare*).

Biological mechanisms

Rheumatoid arthritis is accompanied by the presence of specific antibodies, known as *rheumatoid factors* (RF), as well as other proteins (*citrullinated* peptides). Although these biological factors are present prior to the appearance of clinical signs of the illness, they might also be involved in illness provocation and can be used as biomarkers for disease occurrence (McInnes & Schett, 2007). The development of this disorder is also accompanied by a high load of bacterial antigens within the *periodontium* (tissue that surrounds the teeth), lung, and gut (Brusca et al., 2014), thus implicating a role for microbial factors. In addition, rheumatoid arthritis has been linked to telomere shortening, but once again it's not known whether this was a consequence of the disorder, the distress created by the illness, or in some fashion contributed to the illness (Dehbi et al., 2013).

Multiple sclerosis

Multiple sclerosis (MS) most often occurs among women, typically appearing during early adulthood. In this disorder, immune responses are directed toward myelin, the sheath that surrounds brain and spinal cord axons, resulting in the slowing of electrical signals within neurons. Thus, MS symptoms comprise sensory and motor disturbances, such as loss of sensitivity or tingling, pricking, or numbness, as well as fatigue, muscle weakness, difficulty moving, disturbed balance and coordination, and it's not unusual for cognitive impairments and depression to manifest as the disease progresses. In one form of the illness, the *relapsing-remitting* type, discrete episodes may be followed by intervals extending to months or years before another incident occurs. At these times individuals might misconstrue the illness as being on hold, or even diminishing, but unfortunately, the neurological disturbances may persist and even worsen. A variant of MS that affects 10–15% of those with the disorder, *primary progressive MS*, appears at about age 40 and is not accompanied by periods of apparent remission, often leading to disability earlier than in the relapsing–remitting form of MS. *Secondary progressive MS*, also known as 'galloping MS', appears like relapsing–remitting MS, but a progressive neurologic decline occurs between episodes (Compston & Coles, 2008).

Biological mechanisms

As in the case of other autoimmune disorders, the processes that instigate MS have yet to be fully determined. One hypothesis is that in the presence of particular genetic determinants, infections may operate as a trigger for the disease (Venkatesan & Johnson, 2014). Although several such pathogens have been suggested, Epstein-Barr virus (EBV) has received particular attention given that MS is approximately 15 times higher among individuals infected with EBV during childhood and about 30 times greater among those infected in adolescence relative to those who were not infected (Ascherio, 2013). These findings, together with detection of EBV-infected B-cells in patients' brain, have been consistent with the suggestion that immunopathology in MS stems from chronic EBV infection (Salvetti et al., 2009). Confirmation of a causal relationship between these factors, however, requires prospective studies that assess the fate of those who had (or had not) experienced EBV as well as other concordant factors (e.g., genetic profile).

Systemic lupus erythematosus (SLE)

Systemic lupus erythematosus (SLE), which is far more common in women than in men, typically appears at about 15–35 years of age and affects about 0.5% of the population, varying across ethnic populations. Lupus may affect almost any portion of the body, including joints, blood vessels, skin, liver, kidneys, heart, lungs, and the nervous system. Moreover, with disease progression, numerous comorbid illnesses may develop, ranging from infections, osteoporosis, through to cardiovascular disease and cancer, and in about half the cases it appears along with arthritis (Cervera et al., 2009). A diagnosis of lupus, at least early on, can be difficult to make because the symptoms expressed are nonspecific (e.g., joint and muscle pain, fatigue, and recurrent, unpredictable bouts of fever), and due to the fact that some symptoms might appear and then disappear, leading to it initially being mistaken for other illnesses.

As the illness progresses, flares are usually preceded by signals, such as elevated fatigue, pain, rash, fever, abdominal discomfort, headache, and dizziness. At this point, marked neurological and psychiatric manifestations of the disorder are detectable, notably white matter (referring to glia and myelinated axons) hyper-intensities in certain brain areas as well as hemorrhages, lesions, cell loss, and cell atrophy. In some instances, microstructural abnormalities can be detected in the brain that likely contribute to disturbed memory, executive functioning, and the speed of information processing. Despite the gravity of the illness, mortality attributable to lupus has been declining over the years (Bernatsky et al., 2006), particularly in developed countries. This is largely due to better health care access, education, physician availability, and treatment compliance, suggesting that the management of lupus may have to do with life-style factors rather than medications alone (Lisnevskaia et al., 2014).

Biological mechanisms

As in the case of other autoimmune disorders, several candidates have been identified that may contribute to the development and progression of lupus. There has been the suggestion that lupus arises owing to disturbances in the clearance of debris stemming from cells that have died or been destroyed, and the subsequent development of *antinuclear antibodies* (antibodies that attack inner portions of our own cells) (Lisnevskaia et al., 2014). As lupus is often associated with compromised blood–brain barrier functioning, *auto-antibodies* (self-directed antibodies) might gain access to brain sites where they can cause damage (S. Williams et al., 2010), thereby promoting the development of depressive-like symptoms and cognitive disturbances (Kowal et al., 2006). Alternatively, these auto-antibodies might cross-react with aspects of glutamate (NMDA) receptors, leading to cell death (Faust et al., 2010). Since lupus occurs primarily in women, there has also been the view that estrogen might be a causal agent for this illness and/or that testosterone has a protective effect in this regard. Finally, environmental factors may contribute to the emergence of lupus. For instance, low levels of exposure to sunlight can provoke vitamin D deficiency, which is accompanied by elevated disease activity (Kamen & Aranow, 2008). Other triggers include cigarette smoking, infection, administration of estrogen, certain drugs and pesticides, as well as phthalates, which are incorporated into plastics to increase flexibility and durability.

Factors that exacerbate autoimmune disorders

Stressors and psychosocial contributions

Despite the characteristic differences that exist across autoimmune disorders, they share several common features. Many have a genetic basis, often running in families, and those with one autoimmune disorder may also be afflicted with others. It is also thought that even if genetic factors contribute to autoimmune disorders, an external agent (a second hit) is necessary to get the process rolling. These may comprise viral infection or other illnesses, toxicants (chemicals in the environment, including the workplace, smoking, drugs, and even particular hair dyes), some foods, and traumatic events.

Life stressors are probably not responsible for the initiation of an autoimmune disorder, but such experiences have been implicated in the appearance of flares or exacerbations of the illness, and in MS patients these flares may be accompanied by an increase of brain lesions (Mohr et al., 2004). Early studies assessing these relationships involved only a small number of patients and comprised retrospective analyses of stressor experiences; however, subsequent prospective studies confirmed that flares were often preceded by stressful events (Brown et al., 2005). The important element in promoting flares wasn't necessarily the severity of the stressors, but the frequency of their occurrence. The relationship between MS symptoms and stress responses were, predictably, moderated by the coping methods that individuals adopted, being most prominent among individuals who focused on their illness through emotion-based coping, and least apparent among those who coped through avoidance/distraction (Mohr et al., 2002). Having good social support resulted in improved psychological adjustment, although full symptom remission typically was not achieved.

Like many patients with serious illness, those with rheumatoid arthritis frequently attributed their illness to stressful experiences or believed that stressful events worsened their symptoms (Affleck, Pfeiffer et al., 1987). Once again, the results of retrospective reports were confirmed through prospective studies (Evers et al., 2014). Workers with rheumatoid arthritis reported that their perceived pain was especially intense on days that involved many work-related stressors, and were most severe among individuals with jobs that entailed high 'strain'. Predictably, the negative effects of day-to-day hassles were buffered by having adequate social support (Straub et al., 2005). Given the differential actions of mild and strong stressors as well as acute and chronic stressors on circulating cytokines and corticoid functioning, it is possible that these factors play a prominent role in affecting the course of autoimmune disorders.

Eating and autoimmune disorders

Interventions based on diet have been proposed in relation to many illnesses, and autoimmune disorders are no exception. As dietary factors influence metabolic and inflammatory processes, it would be expected that diet would affect the development and/or progression of autoimmune disorders. Recommendations have been made regarding what to eat and what not to eat in relation to autoimmune disorders, including foods that could affect the microbiome, thereby influencing MS, rheumatoid arthritis, and IBD (Vieira et al., 2014; Yeoh et al., 2013). Other foods have been recommended that act against inflammation, oxidative stress, and *angiogenesis* (new blood vessel growth) that may be associated with MS. Some of the most notable are *polyphenols* (bioactive molecules found in vegetables, fruits, spices, herbs, soy, tea, wine and other fruit-based beverages), *carotenoids* that are obtained from vegetables, *omega-3 polyunsaturated fatty acids* (PUFA) from fish, and vitamins, such as vitamin D and niacin (Van Meeteren et al., 2005). It was also recommended that the diet should discourage inflammatory responding, and thus should include moderate protein and energy content, but rich in minerals (especially antioxidants) and mono/polyunsaturated fatty acids.

Contradictory evidence

Inconsistent data have been reported regarding the link between foods and autoimmune exacerbation. It is difficult to reconcile many of these findings, but it is important to bear in mind that focusing on the impact of any single dietary category may be counterproductive. Several studies have indeed examined whether broader diets would have positive effects on arthritis symptoms, and while several studies that assessed vegetarian, Mediterranean, and elemental eating plans yielded positive outcomes, they typically comprised samples that were too small to permit reliable conclusions (Smedslund et al., 2010). If nothing else, however, diet-related treatments might offer people with illness an opportunity to gain a sense of control over their condition, and thus may have important psychological benefits (Stamp et al., 2005).

Multiple sclerosis, vitamins, and dietary factors

Despite the certainty that seems to be apparent in some quarters, the links between several dietary factors and autoimmune disorders is not particularly strong. By example, the involvement of vitamin D in relation to MS has received particular attention, and there is some evidence that deficits of this vitamin may contribute to *some* autoimmune disorders (e.g., SLE, rheumatoid arthritis) and disorders that are organ-specific (i.e., type 1 diabetes, primary biliary cirrhosis) (Agmon-Levin et al., 2013). However, the research suggesting a causal link between the progression of MS and vitamin D has not been convincing (von Geldern & Mowry, 2012). Similarly, PUFAs either did not affect disease progression (Farinotti et al., 2012) or provided only small positive effects (von Geldern & Mowry, 2012). Several other nutritional factors were initially said to influence MS, including antioxidants (uric acid, vitamins A, C, and E, lipoic acid), milk proteins, probiotics, polyphenols, as well as ginkgo biloba extracts and curcumin, but once again the data have not been convincing and statements about their efficacy need to be constrained (von Geldern & Mowry, 2012).

Drug treatments of autoimmune disorders

It is unfortunate that for most autoimmune conditions a cure isn't presently available, but 'disease-modifying treatments' can often minimize symptoms or delay the illness's downhill course. In other instances, such as the progressive-remitting form of MS, positive effects in delaying illness progression have been limited. In the case of MS and rheumatoid arthritis, physiotherapy and life-style changes are sometimes recommended, but for the most part, symptoms are managed through drug treatments that reduce inflammation and by pain-relieving medications.

Like so many other illnesses, autoimmune disorders are physiologically heterogeneous, and it may be necessary to devise personalized approaches, using genetic and other markers, to provide optimal treatments for patients. For the moment, however, most patients receive a standardized course of treatments. Ordinarily, nonsteroidal anti-inflammatory drugs (e.g., prednisone) are used to deal with mild symptoms, whereas stronger drugs that affect immune functioning are used to deal with relatively severe symptoms. These include corticosteroids, and immunosuppressants such as cyclophosphamide, but because of their potential adverse effects, drug development efforts have targeted specific types of immune cell (e.g., belimumab or atacicept, which inhibit B-cell activity) rather than acting broadly on immune functioning. Treatments may also include immunosuppressive agents, or antibody immunomodulators as well as those that influence cytokine functioning (e.g., Kamal, 2014; Kaneko & Takeuchi, 2014).

Promising results in slowing down disease progression have been reported using *disease-modifying antirheumatic drugs* (DMARDs), including agents that inhibit proinflammatory cytokines (IL-1β and TNF-α), although in some instances the disease is not responsive (*refractory*) to treatments and many patients do not experience symptom remission (Polido-Pereira et al., 2011). In MS cases that are not responsive to any treatments, high dose immunotherapy may be tried in an effort to diminish the immune system's attack, although this procedure in itself can have negative consequences (Paz Soldán & Weinshenker, 2015). It is nonetheless significant that when high dose immunotherapy was followed by transplants of the patient's own *hematopoietic stem cells* (the types of cell that give rise to varied other blood cells), 75% experienced relief from relapsing–remitting MS that was still apparent 3 years later (Nash et al., 2015).

Despite the generally negative outlook regarding a cure for autoimmune disorders, occasional breakthroughs have been made that hold promise for the future. In the case of MS, by administering incrementally higher doses of specific antigens that are being attacked by immune cells, it is possible to re-educate these immune cells so that they cease attacking, but without diminishing their ability to eliminate other dangerous antigens (Burton et al., 2014). An alternative approach has been to focus on a substance, SIRT-1, that is essential in regulating the balance between T cells involved in attacking tissues and those involved in regulating the responses of other T cells (Lim et al., 2015). As multiple pathways might contribute to diseases, lupus treatment was attempted based on low dose tolerance therapy with a cocktail of several agents that activated regulatory T cells and suppressed interferon gene expression. In this way several immune-related processes related to lupus could be triggered concurrently in an effort to attenuate illness (L. Zhang et al., 2013).

Novel compounds are also being developed to provide relief from autoimmune disorders. One approach focused on reestablishing the presence of myelin on nerve fibers rather than attempting to reduce inflammatory responses (Miron et al., 2013). Another approach, so far assessed only in mice with an MS-like condition, revealed that transplantation of human embryonic stem cells (that may differentiate and repair the myelin sheath) caused a reduction of neuroinflammation and behavioral signs of MS in less than 2 weeks (L. Chen et al., 2014), and encouraging results have been reported regarding other autoimmune conditions, such as rheumatoid arthritis. Trials using gene therapy and stem cell transplantation to treat severe autoimmune conditions have been conducted across countries for more than 15 years, and some of the findings have been encouraging (Li & Sykes, 2012; Shu et al., 2014). This approach is still in its infancy and there's still much that needs to be done, including analyses of the clinical efficacy of the treatments as well as their safety, the side effects that can be expected, and the long-term benefits that are obtained. Ultimately, there is the hope that this approach would not only diminish or eliminate symptoms of autoimmune disorders, but might lead to the creation of a cure (Liao et al., 2015).

A PLACE FOR MEDICAL MARIJUANA

There is evidence that marijuana's primary active ingredient, THC, may cause epigenetic changes that act against inflammation and could thus be beneficial for a variety of autoimmune disorders (X. Yang et al., 2014). However, the anti-inflammatory effects attributable to the use of marijuana during teen years may subsequently flip, so that during later adulthood the predominance of pro-inflammatory processes might contribute to autoimmune disorders (Moretti et al., 2014).

Whether these new findings will hold up and whether there are actually negative repercussions for well-being will have to await further studies in humans. For the moment, however, there have been reports, often being played and replayed by newspapers and television, regarding 'medical marijuana' use for an assortment of illnesses, as a pain reducing agent, as a method to keep PTSD in check (Neumeister et al., 2013), to diminish intraocular pressure associated with glaucoma, as well as to diminish side effects associated with medical treatments (e.g., nausea related to cancer therapy). It was unexpectedly observed as well that individuals who experienced severe trauma were less likely to die if they had tested positive for THC (Nguyen et al., 2014), possibly owing to increased blood flow provoked by THC and hence elevated nutrients delivered to the brain, or because THC inhibits glutamate, thereby limiting neuronal damage that might otherwise have occurred.

Given increasing moves regarding the legalization of marijuana, we can pretty well count on a new arsenal of treatments becoming available for immune-related disorders as well as those related to stress and trauma. No doubt, this will require improved standardization of the product, and risk–benefit analyses will be needed considering the adverse effects that can occur regarding CNS functioning (Yadav & Narayanaswami, 2014), including stunted development of white matter associated with its early and chronic use (Filbey et al., 2014; but see Weiland et al., 2015). This will become that much more important with increased use of high-potency ('skunk-like') cannabis (Di Forti et al., 2014).

SUMMARY

The immune system is obviously tough, resilient, and well designed. But the enemy it faces is equally sly and resourceful, and as the immune system learns ways to deal with challenges, microbes learn new ways of getting around immune defenses. More than that, numerous factors can compromise the ability of the immune system to deal with threats. Eating the wrong foods or encountering chronic stressors may diminish immune functioning, thereby altering risk for the emergence of pathological conditions, more so among individuals who have inherited particular genes. The presence of toxicants can also affect immune functioning, and may create tissue disturbances or gene mutations that can cause illness. It also seems that these environmental events or our experience may cause adverse outcomes as a result of changes within the microbiome or by altering hormonal and neurochemical processes. Thus, identifying these specific mechanisms, and determining why these factors differ across individuals, could result in the development of targeted treatments to deal with a variety of challenges. This said, it would be far better to adopt behavioral strategies to prevent disease occurrence, although it is certain that there are many conditions for which this isn't possible. Besides, in relation to illnesses and its causes, we often simply don't know what we don't know, and, for this reason, maintaining healthy life-styles is a fairly good tactic.

Finally, in considering emerging threats, especially viruses and bacteria with potentially devastating outcomes, it is essential to act quickly and decisively as half measures don't work. Some diseases, such as Middle East respiratory syndrome (MERS), airborne H5N1 influenza, and H7N9 avian flu, have crossed the line to affect humans, although they haven't *yet* posed widespread threats, as they aren't being passed from human to human. In contrast, Ebola, which likely came from animals, has had profound negative effects in some parts of Africa. This disease first appeared about 40 years ago, so one has to wonder why more attention wasn't devoted to it earlier. Clearly, to deal with potentially transmissible diseases, active efforts need to be undertaken before the problems become too large to handle. Likewise, illnesses such as polio, although largely eliminated, persist in some countries, and vaccine-resistant strains have appeared (Drexler et al., 2014); and TB, which affects 8 million people yearly (and 1.3 million die), needs to be attended to more rigorously, especially as treatment-resistant forms of TB are also around. It is also essential for proper infrastructure to be present to contain viral spread, including high levels of cooperation across countries as well as among people within any particular locale. Conspiracy scenarios or false information being passed around, irrespective of whether it's Ebola or measles, are counterproductive in dealing with viral or bacterial spread.

11 Cancer

OH NO, WHY ME?

Some diseases promote much greater fear than others, sometimes without a rationale basis. Ebola, despite still being fairly limited in its spread, seems to have created broad anxiety and worry. Influenza, which causes a much greater number of deaths annually, is taken far less seriously, and some illnesses, such as measles, although it can cause death, have been diminished by some individuals as 'one of those things kids go through', reinforcing their disposition to refuse vaccination for their children.

Cancer falls into a unique class of illnesses that elicit shock and fear, possibly because it is so often fatal, has been associated with treatments that are fairly brutal, and patients are seen as being dehumanized. The very fact that 'it can come back again' even after a person has been 'successfully' treated, promotes continued anxiety, dread, and despair. In some instances, individuals may have a sense of helplessness, feeling as if they can't do much to get rid of the disease, and a pervasive sense of hopelessness may develop as they realize that their doctors, despite considerable experience and technology behind them, also seem unable to deal with the illness. For that matter, the "Big C" (the disease whose name we dare not speak) can develop owing to factors entirely out of our control, including genes we happened to have inherited, or toxicants (e.g., certain herbicides) to which we had been exposed years earlier, well before we had known that they were dangerous.

It wasn't that long ago that cancer treatments, as horrendous and stressful as they were, provided individuals with only a brief extension of their lives. Treatments comprised gross surgical procedures, strong radiation, and nonspecific chemotherapeutic agents or a cocktail of several agents. In more recent times improvements have been made on many fronts. Surgical procedures are much better, chemotherapy can often be targeted at certain types of cancer, and indeed the

(Continued)

(Continued)

specific treatments used may vary with multiple characteristics of the disease, including its genetic constitution. Likewise, radiation treatments are more targeted, and medications to limit side effects, such as nausea and pain, have improved.

For many years there had been a call for a change in the way diseases, such as cancer, were considered, but it wasn't until the 1960s and 1970s that radical and profound changes occurred so that the focus of cancer research wasn't just in finding better cures. Instead, increasingly greater efforts were made to prevent cancer occurrence. It's actually quite remarkable that it took so long for this to occur, but individuals were made increasingly aware that cancers could be provoked as a result of environmental factors, and that as a result they could diminish cancer occurrence by changing their behaviors and their environments. This comprised giving up cigarette smoking, limiting sun exposure and using sun blockers, getting rid of environmental toxicants, as well as diminishing the consumption of unhealthy foods. This said, within Western countries about 20% of people continue to smoke and within other countries, such as Russia, the number exceeds 50%. However, smoking is only one of several factors that can cause cancer, and those who self-righteously wonder why anyone would be foolish enough to take such a risk might consider to what extent they've paid attention to other factors that increase or diminish cancer risk (e.g., particular foods eaten or others being avoided). I'd bet that like cigarette smokers and sun worshippers, they think "it won't happen to me", but if cancer does hit them, the response might be "Oh no, why me?".

FILLING IN A FEW BLANKS

Cancer is among the most common ailments affecting humans and is among the top two or three (depending on the country) that lead to death among individuals beyond middle age. Although many biological and life-style factors have been implicated in the development of some types of cancer, most people are unaware of these linkages. This chapter will introduce:

- basic information related to the cancer process
- some of the presumed processes underlying cancer
- several environmental and biological factors that influence illness occurrence
- life-style factors (stress, eating, exercise, sleep) that affect the occurrence and/or progression of cancer
- the psychological consequences associated with cancer and its treatments, and what options individuals have in dealing with their distress and with the illness itself
- the impact of psychological interventions on cancer-related treatments.

WHAT IS CANCER AND HOW DOES IT DEVELOP?

The term 'cancer' is often used as if in reference to a single illness. There are, however, more than 200 forms of this illness, involving different cell types, many different organs, diverse genetic and environmental contributions, differential influences of hormonal and immunological processes, each of which may call for a different treatment. Cancers are illnesses in which cells undergo uncontrolled growth, culminating in tumor development. *Malignant* cancer cells are defined by their ability to break away from the main tumor mass and travel to distant sites through the blood or lymphatic system, where they might establish a new cancer colony. This process, referred to as *metastasis*, distinguishes malignant from *benign* tumors, which don't metastasize, although there are some exceptions (Kumar et al., 2014).

Classifications

Cancer subtypes can be broadly classified based on what types of tissue are affected (see Table 11.1) and the development/severity of the illness is usually described as falling into particular stages.

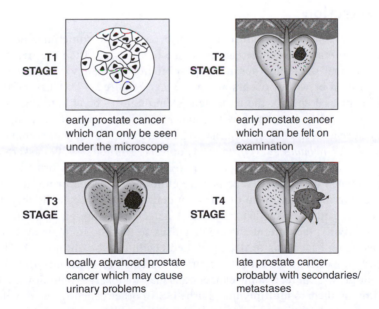

T1 STAGE
early prostate cancer which can only be seen under the microscope

T2 STAGE
early prostate cancer which can be felt on examination

T3 STAGE
locally advanced prostate cancer which may cause urinary problems

T4 STAGE
late prostate cancer probably with secondaries/ metastases

Figure 11.1   Stages of cancer development using prostate cancer as an example

Table 11.1   Cancer subtypes

- *Carcinoma*: involves the epithelial cells of tissues that line body surfaces and cavities. Cancers that affect skin and other organs, including the breast, prostate, colon, and lung are frequently carcinomas.
- *Sarcoma*: a cancer of connective tissues that includes cartilage, bone, tendons, adipose tissue, lymphatic tissue, and components of blood cells.
- *Lymphoma*: refers to blood cell tumors that originate from lymphocytes. Hodgkin lymphoma (HL) and non-Hodgkin lymphoma (NHL), as well as multiple myeloma and immunoproliferative diseases, are the primary types of lymphoma.
- *Leukemia*: involves cancers that originate in the bone marrow, culminating in abnormal white blood cells appearing in an excessively high number (e.g., leukemia cells).
- *Blastoma*: a type of cancer that involves 'blasts', comprising primitive and incompletely differentiated precursor cells. Several types of blastoma appear in children, and some forms – such as glioblastoma multiforme, which is the most aggressive brain tumor – appear in middle-aged adults.
- *Germ cell tumor*: a cancer involving germ cells (i.e., sperm or egg that unite during sexual reproduction). In essence, this type of cancer most often occurs within the ovaries or testis, and can occur in babies and children.

Avoiding detection

The battle between cancer cells and tumors can be ferocious, sometimes ending with our winning, but in too many cases, the cancers come out on top. Often the two seem to fight to a stalemate so that the tumor doesn't appear (tumor dormancy), in some cases for up to 25 years, before a break-out occurs among cancer cells (e.g., D. Chen et al., 2014). As described in Chapters 3 and 10, the immune system ought to be able to detect and destroy cancer cells fairly readily. But, being wily, cancer cells have ways of avoiding detection so that they can flourish, eventually giving rise to a constellation of cells that make up a tumor. One early view, *the immune surveillance hypothesis* (Burnett, 1970), asserted that lymphocytes were continuously on alert for the presence of newly transformed cells, and that cancer occurred when these mutated cells were either not detected or not destroyed (Dunn et al., 2004). Being a mutated form of our own cells, these cancer cells might still maintain a sufficient self-identity so that they aren't detected as foreign and thus avoid being attacked. Alternatively, they might engage disguises so that the immune system won't recognize them as being dangerous or damaged, and needing to be eliminated. There are also occasions where the effectiveness of the immune systems is compromised, thus permitting increased tumor growth. In fact, some cancer cells may themselves shut down local immune responses, allowing them to multiply undisturbed. Still other cancers may develop in places such as the brain, where the immune cells don't get to easily, and thus can grow with little interference. If all these clever devices weren't sufficient to give cancer cells an edge, it now appears that they can also influence their neighbors. Cancer cells release small vesicles called *exosomes* that were believed to be akin to garbage being tossed out. However, they also contain DNA and RNA, which can infiltrate adjacent normal cells, turning those cancerous (Melo et al., 2014). Thus, despite the capacity of the immune system to deal with dangerous invaders, disruption of its components can increase the risk of cancer developing, and this is compounded by cancer cells acting more like terrorists than a conventional army.

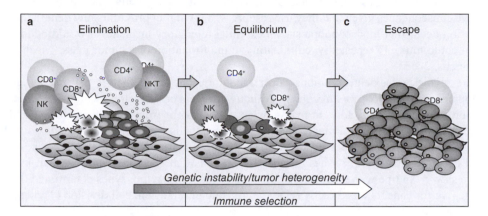

Figure 11.2   Immune system functioning could potentially affect the development of cancers. During the first of three phases, elimination, innate immune cells recognize the presence of a tumor that is growing (the immunosurveillance phase). Various components of the immune system are activated to deal with the cancer. The NK cells and macrophages stimulate one another, and through cytokine release call upon still more immune cells, including those of other varieties, to enter the battle, thereby furthering the tumor cell death. Still other factors, such as reactive oxygen species, are promoted that act against tumor cells. Dendritic cells cart off the dead tumor cells and deposit them in draining lymph nodes. In the next phase (equilibrium) various immune cells continue to be called upon (e.g., NK cells and various T cells) to deal with the threat. But, other processes are also occurring. The tumor cells present are genetically unstable and rapidly mutating, and lymphocytes and cytokines put selection pressure on them so that there is an increase in the generation of tumor cell variants that have increasingly greater capacity to escape and survive attacks by the immune system. Following the equilibrium phase, the surviving tumor cells that have escaped and are thus the most resilient are in the 'Escape' phase, during which they infiltrate the epithelium and thus continue growing in an uncontrolled fashion (shown by the large number of tumor cells over-running the T cells in the background).

Adapted from Dunn, G.P., Bruce, A.T., Ikeda, H. Old, J. & Schreiber, R.D. (2002). Cancer immunoediting: from immunosurveillance to tumor escape. *Nature Immunology 3*, 991–998.

GENETIC CONTRIBUTIONS

When we discussed DNA mutations in Chapter 3, the notion was introduced that the nucleotide sequence of a gene could be altered, even slightly, and these mutations could then appear in daughter cells of the initially mutated cell. Proofreading and editing occurs within cells so that these errors are relatively limited, but some mutations still sneak through. These mutations often appear in a portion of the DNA strand that has limited significance; however, they can also occur in aspects of genes that have much to say about the appearance of pathology. Our genes ordinarily contain a section which, upon being activated or expressed, initiates a constellation of biochemical changes that result in *apoptosis* (the cell's death). This is a natural and beneficial process as the presence of damaged or unhealthy cells could potentially have negative consequences given that they use resources, but without providing any benefit. Should a mutation occur that hinders apoptosis, an essential regulatory mechanism would be lost and the cell could multiply repeatedly, culminating in the formation of a tumor mass (Macheret & Halazonetis, 2015).

To a significant extent mutations occur randomly, but many factors can encourage the development of mutations (*mutagenesis*). Although cancers can develop owing to specific lifestyles or environmental factors, in many instances they stem from a random process and are akin to 'winning' the wrong lottery. The longer certain cells live and the more divisions they undergo, the more likely it is that a cancer-producing mutation will evolve. As such, cancer should be more frequent in tissues that have stem cells that reproduce quickly than in those that are slower. In line with this supposition, an analysis of 31 tumor types determined that the lifetime risk for cancers was directly related to the rate of total stem cell division (Tomasetti & Vogelstein, 2015).

UNDOING PUZZLES

There are many puzzles concerning the processes by which cancers evolve and why some individuals are more likely to develop a cancer than others. When individual differences emerge in a relatively systematic way, it can give us important clues as to the processes leading to illness. Often, we can attribute the individual variability to life-style factors, exposure to environmental toxicants, or having inherited particular genes. So, it's with some surprise that the occurrence of cancer among people with Alzheimer's disease is about half the number expected based on simple probabilities, and, conversely, the risk of Alzheimer's was diminished by 35% in people with some form of cancer. This seemed not to be a result of people dying of one disease before the other had an opportunity to emerge, nor a result of one illness obscuring symptoms of the other (Musicco et al., 2013). The source for this inverse relationship is presently hard to decipher, but it may have implications for determining preventive measures for both illnesses.

A second puzzling finding is that if cancer development is largely due to random mutations, then why is it so often the case that those people struck with one type of cancer may in the end be affected by several types of cancer? It turns out that those individuals who seem to be affected by several types of cancer carry a genetic marker, dubbed the KRAS-variant. Among people with cancer 25% will carry this mutation, and of this group more than 50% will develop more than one cancer, usually of an aggressive variety (Chin et al., 2008). It seems that the presence of the KRAS mutation can be used to predict the occurrence of some types of cancer (e.g., Ratner et al., 2010), and a blood test to detect this variant is now possible, which can inform doctors and patients about the risk for particular types of cancer. So, while this puzzle has come to a good resolution, there are many other puzzles that have yet to be tackled.

Gene × environment interactions

There are other ways in which inherited genes contribute to the development of cancer. For instance, the presence of BRCA1 and BRCA2 genes is involved in repair of chromosomal damage, and in this sense is involved in a tumor-suppressing capacity. However, when particular mutations occur in these genes, the risk for breast and ovarian cancer increases and the presence of these mutations thus serves as a formidable predictor of treatment outcomes (Zhong et al., 2014). These mutations have been associated with increased risk for the development of breast and ovarian cancer (55–65% of women with the BRCA1 mutation, and 45% with the BRCA2 mutation will likely develop breast cancer; Chen & Parmigiani, 2007). At the same time, as some women with a BRCA mutation might not develop cancer, suggests that additional factors contribute to illness development, including other gene mutations, the presence of certain hormones or immune factors, or environmental toxicants. It also appears that increased breast cancer risk is present among some women who use oral contraceptives, and hormone replacement therapy (estrogen plus progesterone) following menopause was likewise accompanied by increased cancer risk. Several other life-style variables, including drinking alcohol, being overweight following menopause, and low levels of physical activity promoted a small increase in the chance of cancer occurring, and while each of these has only a slight relation to the development of breast cancer, together they become a cause for concern, and it is possible that one or more of these variables interact with genetic factors in promoting cancer. As in the case of other illnesses we've discussed, it has been suspected that cancer has developed in response to several mutations and/or environmental contributions occurring concurrently or sequentially (a multi-hit hypothesis; Dent, 2013). One hit, for instance, might stimulate *proto-oncogenes* (a normal gene that has mutated and may become a cancer gene), which promotes cell proliferation, whereas a second mutation might inhibit tumor suppressing genes. Figure 11.3 depicts a possible sequence of events in which successive mutations lead to cells becoming cancerous.

Ethnic and racial variations

Appreciable differences exist across cultural groups with respect to the presence of the BRCA mutation. Among Ashkenazi Jews (i.e., primarily those of European descent) the mutation occurs in about 8% of women, whereas it occurs at a rate of 0.5% among Asian American women and 3.5% among Hispanic individuals (John et al., 2007). Ethnic differences have also been reported in relation to early detection of cancers. For instance, black and South Asian women are diagnosed with breast cancer later than white or Japanese women, and mortality rates have varied along these lines as well. Similarly, these differences were not accounted for by income or estrogen receptor status, but might reflect intrinsic differences in the features of tumors across ethnic groups (Iqbal et al., 2015).

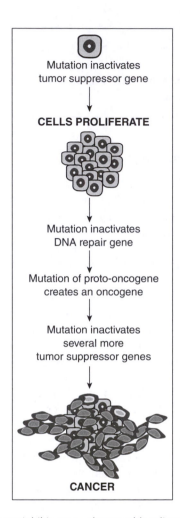

Figure 11.3   An initial mutation may inhibit genes that would ordinarily act against the development of factors that suppress tumor production, followed by a second mutation that limits DNA repair of damaged genes. This might lead to yet another mutation that favors a proto-oncogene becoming an oncogene, and when coupled with further activation of genes involved in tumor suppression, cancerous cells may develop. Ordinarily, proto-oncogenes have several different functions, such as providing signals that lead to cell division, or they may be involved in regulating programmed cell death (apoptosis). When a proto-oncogene is defective (referred to as an oncogene), unregulated cell division may occur, even in the absence of common growth signals that are normally provided by growth factors. In fact, even a single altered copy of an oncogene can instigate unregulated growth.

Source: "Cancer requires multiple mutations from NIHen". Licensed under Public Domain via Wikimedia Commons -http:// commons.wikimedia.org/wiki/File:Cancer_requires_multiple_mutations_from_NIHen.png#/media/File:Cancer_ requires_multiple_mutations_from_NIHen.png

WHAT TO DO WHEN....

When women test positive for the mutated forms of BRCA1 or BRCA2 they have several decisions and behaviors that ought to be made. They might begin screening for breast cancer earlier, but among these women mammography itself might pose a risk for cancer development, and MRI determinations might miss some types of cancer. Moreover, this gene also disposes women toward ovarian cancer, which is difficult to catch early (Evans et al., 2009). A second option is to have a double mastectomy to limit breast cancer, and removal of the ovaries and fallopian tubes to diminish risk of ovarian cancer, although these procedures don't guarantee that cancer won't develop (Domchek et al., 2010). Women can use an estrogen receptor antagonist (e.g., tamoxifen used in cancer treatment) to diminish the risk of breast cancer in those with a BRCA mutation (Phillips et al., 2013), although such agents don't eliminate the risk of cancer developing.

Deciding to undergo mastectomy to prevent cancer is obviously a tough decision to make, but most individuals subsequently tend to be at peace with their decision (Boughey et al., 2015). Likewise, if a tumor is found to be present, the choice between mastectomy (with or without reconstructive procedures) versus breast-conserving surgery (e.g., lumpectomy) is also taxing. Following surgery, pain and fatigue may persist for some time, and women may be affected by changes of their body image and perceived stigma. With breast reconstruction, later body image has proved comparable to that of women who had breast-conserving surgery and better than that of women with mastectomy without this procedure (Fang et al., 2013). Individual differences regarding psychological consequences of surgery are pronounced, and what to do to diminish negative psychological states ought to be considered on an individual basis.

ENVIRONMENTAL CONTRIBUTIONS

There is a long list of carcinogen-provoked mutations that favor the development of several types of cancer. Particular living conditions or certain occupations, which bring people into contact with specific chemicals (e.g., endocrine disruptors or carcinogens), are associated with increased cancer incidence. Thus, even if it was observed that cancer runs through families, this wouldn't necessarily mean that this cancer was due to genetic inheritance. Instead it might reflect a shared environment, such as living downwind from a carcinogen spewing factory or continued exposure to second-hand or even third-hand tobacco smoke comprising gases and particles that end up as dust within a room (Ramírez et al., 2014).

Carcinogens

Numerous environmental chemicals and stimuli (*carcinogens*) may cause cancer through their metabolic actions, or alternatively through the instigation of DNA mutations, interference with

DNA repair processes, or the disruption of tumor suppressor genes. It is equally possible that carcinogens serve as a second hit that functions to promote cancer, disturb a cell's ability to correct errors (mutations), or increase aging processes that could lead to pathologic outcomes (Pfeifer, 2015). Cigarettes have the worst reputation in this regard, while ultraviolet radiation from the sun is a distant second, followed by the many pollutants that we encounter daily. There are a great number of other carcinogens, such as asbestos, benzene, vinyl chloride, and gasoline, which we hear less about but which nonetheless can have powerful effects.

Carcinogens may appear in the form of manufactured, synthetic, or natural products, such as aristolochic acid found in certain herbal medicines that have been linked to urothelial carcinomas (Pfeifer, 2015). The International Agency for Research on Cancer (IARC) has also warned that glyphosate, the most widely used herbicide world-wide, is "probably carcinogenic to humans". Moreover, radiation (radium and plutonium, ionizing radiation such as that from X-rays and gamma rays) as well as immune-suppressing treatments, many of which are used during the course of medical treatments, can also promote different types of cancer. We're obviously affected wherever we are, including at home and at work, despite the government legislation to protect us from these hazards.

Epigenetics

Just as random mutations can be instrumental in the production of tumors, so can epigenetic modifications of genes brought about by environmental toxicants, although it can be difficult to identify whether a particular epigenetic change is causally related to the appearance of a given type of cancer. In this regard, the 'pattern' of methylation that occurred in cancer cells was found to be in much greater disarray than in non-cancerous cells (many epigenetic changes occur concurrently, but without a systematic pattern). This diversity might not only help cancer cells deal with the multiple challenges that they encounter, but might also make it more difficult to target therapeutics at specific epigenetic marks (Landau et al., 2014). This roadblock in the treatment of cancer aside, considerable evidence has pointed to certain epigenetic modifications promoting the initial appearance and metastases of some types of cancer. Thus, it has become ever more important to identify these epigenetic marks so that classification systems can be established to determine prognosis and treatments of particular types of cancer (Szyf, 2012). Stressor experiences and diet can also affect epigenetic processes, which are being considered in the evolution of cancer occurrence and progression, as well as in the development of treatment strategies that target specific epigenetic processes (Day & Bianco-Miotto, 2013).

VIRAL FACTORS

In addition to carcinogens, several viruses have been implicated in the development of some cancers (*oncovirus*). Human papillomavirus (HPV) has been associated with cervical carcinoma, but it is also tied to cancer of the vagina, anus, penis, and throat (Schiffman et al., 2007). Considerable attention has been given to HPV because it is possible to immunize young women (and men) against this virus (Markowitz et al., 2007). Still other viruses, including hepatitis B and hepatitis C, have been linked to liver cancer, Epstein-Barr virus has been associated with several different types of cancer (Burkitt's lymphoma, Hodgkin's lymphoma, post-transplant lymphoproliferative disease, and nasopharyngeal carcinoma), and human T-cell leukemia virus-1, as the name implies, has been associated with leukemia. Moreover, Kaposi's sarcoma herpes virus, an opportunistic infection often seen in patients with HIV/AIDS, has been associated with cancer development (Pagano et al., 2004).

A STRESS–CANCER LINK

Stressful events in predicting cancer

The notion has been tossed around for years that cancer might develop as a result of stressful experiences. Perhaps individuals who were diagnosed with cancer, seeking a reason for their misfortune, ended up blaming past experiences for their lot, but there have been few scientific reports that support that contention. Although studies in animals have suggested that stressful experiences could modify the growth of induced or transplanted tumors, possibly owing to altered hormonal functioning or diminished immune responses against these tumor cells (Sklar & Anisman, 1979), there has been no convincing evidence of cancer being *caused* by stressors.

Inflammatory responses have been implicated as important factors within the local environments in which cancer cells grow (Mantovani et al., 2008). Such inflammatory processes are thought to be linked to 15–20% of all deaths from cancer, and were associated with several different types of cancer, such as the incidence of breast cancer (Touvier et al., 2013), and breast cancer recurrence (Cole, 2009). Elevated levels of C-reactive protein (CRP) and other markers of inflammation have also been associated with increased mortality related to lung, colorectal, liver, and prostate cancer, and this is further exacerbated by smoking (Shiels et al., 2013). As stressors have the propensity to increase circulating cytokines and encourage inflammatory processes, they may also promote the progression of cancer growth.

Several studies in humans have shown that stressful experiences were accompanied by increased cancer progression and cancer-related mortality (Hamer et al., 2009), and earlier death following stem cell transplantation applied in an effort to beat the disease (Park et al., 2010). It was likewise demonstrated in animal models that chronic stressors can diminish the effectiveness of treatments used to deal with prostate cancer (Hassan et al., 2013), and in humans stress-related psychological disorders (e.g., anxiety and depression) were predictive of a poorer response to neoadjuvant therapy (e.g., chemotherapy or hormone treatments) prior to the primary treatment being administered. The case has been made that stressful events, through their actions on hormones, neurotransmitters (particularly responses of epinephrine receptors), immune system functioning, as well as changes in tumor biology itself, could influence virtually every stage in the growth of existent tumors (Powell et al., 2013).

IS THERE A LINK BETWEEN STRESSORS AND METASTASES?

During the course of fetal development, cells differentiate so that they can form particular organs and engage in particular functions. There's a sense of order and organization of body cells, so that pancreatic cells know that they are part of the pancreas and they function in a predictable way (except when they

(Continued)

(Continued)

don't). Cells of the liver, or the breast or bone, don't suddenly decide that they'd be more content as kidney or brain cells and then up and move. Cancer cells, in contrast, seem to be rebellious and travel to distant sites, where a new colony is established. So, what is it about them that supports their inclination to migrate and how is it that they survive? Do they have some sort of coating so that they aren't recognized by immune cells that would otherwise destroy them? Or do they have protective factors that give them pardon to avoid proteins known as metastasis suppressors? Alternatively, are they politically astute to the extent that they hold hands with regular cells, fooling the immune cells which might react with 'a friend of my friend is also my friend' and thus won't destroy these cancerous cells. It's also possible that cancer cells use substances in the body, such as neurotransmitters, in an effort to 'fit in', or they might actually adopt the identity of other cells (e.g., expressing certain receptors on their surface), thereby going undetected. It also appears that lymphocytes can secrete a web of sticky DNA that captures cancer cells in circulation, but instead of killing these cells, they end up making them stronger and more aggressive, and more likely to reach organs that can then be colonized. Despite the science-fiction quality of these various alternatives, each has been advanced as a possible way by which cancer cells avoid detection and facilitate metastasis.

In theory, dietary factors or stressors could affect tumor growth and metastases through hormones (e.g., cortisol) that diminish immune functioning, thus allowing for less restrained tumor growth and metastases (Moreno-Smith et al., 2010; Reiche et al., 2004) or by stimulation of norepinephrine receptors, which encourages cancer growth (Campbell et al., 2012). It is equally possible that metastasis can be facilitated through stressor-elicited hormonal changes. The migration and invasion of cancer cells could, for instance, be provoked by the release of epinephrine and norepinephrine following stressor exposure. When breast cancer cells were injected into the hearts of mice (thus simulating cancer cells that have left the main tumor mass), these cells increased subsequent cancer lesions on bones to a greater extent among stressed than nonstressed mice. However, when sympathetic activity was reduced by administration of the norepinephrine receptor blocker propranolol, the frequency of cancer lesions was attenuated. In line with these studies, there have been an increasing number of reports (albeit the number is still modest) suggesting that treatments in humans that interfere with norepinephrine functioning can limit metastasis (e.g., Ganz, 2011).

Not every environment is a welcoming one for cancer cells, but metastasis may be accompanied by the growth of a new network of blood vessels (angiogenesis) that feed the tumor cells, and it is possible that stress hormones could contribute to this process (Thaker et al., 2006). Indeed, pulmonary metastases have been seen to increase 5-fold among mice that had been exposed to a social stressor and later re-exposed to the negative event shortly after tumor cell inoculation, and these cancer-promoting effects of the stressor could be attenuated by pretreating mice with a drug that blocked the actions of epinephrine.

Stressor-related biological changes associated with cancer

The vast majority of studies that assessed the link between stressful events and cancer relied on retrospective procedures, which, as already detailed, can have serious limitations. The few studies that prospectively assessed this relationship, as in the case of a 20-year prospective study in Israeli individuals who had lost a son in war or by accident, revealed that this link-age was a weak one and could have been secondary to other factors related to the trauma, including life-style changes, rather than the distress experienced (Reiche et al., 2004). There have also been prospective reports indicating that appropriate coping and social support was predictive of slower cancer progression, but, once again, the data were not strong (Chida et al., 2008).

While these findings suggest that stressors might not contribute to the emergence of cancer, data are available indicating that stressors may influence the course of cancer that is present or affect recovery from the illness. Consistent with the stress–cancer link, NK cell functioning was disturbed among breast cancer patients reporting high levels of psycholog-ical stress. Over the course of an 18-month period following surgery, women who indicated greater levels of distress exhibited diminished NK cell activity and reduced lymphocyte proliferative responses (Varker et al., 2007). As well, men who received stress management training exhibited enhanced mood following radical prostatectomy, coupled with recovery of NK cell activity (Thornton et al., 2007). As expected, coping indices, including social support, benefit finding, and optimism, were also directly related to NK cell activity and lymphocyte proliferative responses among individuals being treated for breast, gyneco-logic, prostate, gastrointestinal, digestive tract, and liver malignancies. A meta-analysis indeed confirmed that increased distress was accompanied by poorer survival across dif-ferent types of cancer (Chida et al., 2008), and having a stress-prone personality, negative emotional responses, poor coping styles, or poor quality of life were related to higher cancer mortality.

Owing to the difficulty of conducting prospective studies, another approach was adopted to determine whether stressful events were linked to cancer appearance. In this instance the patients' stressor history was obtained when a tumor was first suspected and a biopsy performed, but before the biopsy results were available. As predicted, the appearance of malignant tumors (but not benign tumors) occurred more often in association with greater past stressors. Had the reported stressor experiences reflected biased appraisals on the part to those being assessed for possible cancer, then elevated negative life events would have been reported irrespective of whether the lump turned out to be benign or malignant, as both sets of women ought to have been equally distressed by the prospect of the cancer being malignant (Weinrib et al., 2010). In fact, however, vegetative and affective depressive symptoms were increased, as were nocturnal plasma cortisol among women with ovarian cancer relative to that which occurred among women with a benign disease (Lutgendorf et al., 2008), and diur-nal cortisol levels among individuals with metastatic breast cancer predicted earlier mortality (Sephton et al., 2000). Although these findings support the view that stressful experiences, psychological changes, and cancer occurrence might be linked, there have also been reports that have been inconsistent with this perspective. As already indicated, the data supporting a causal connection between stressful experiences and the development of cancer have not been persuasive, whereas the findings pointing to stressor-elicited exacerbation of already-existent cancer have been more telling.

LOOKING FOR STRESSORS AT THE WRONG TIME AND THE WRONG PLACE

When researchers conducted retrospective analyses in an effort to link stress and cancer, they typically focused on stressors experienced in recent years (e.g., the past 2 years), although in some studies lengthy time frames were assessed (20 years) in predicting later cancer occurrence. But let's consider to what extent these are appropriate in the context of diseases such as cancer. The cancer process is a lengthy one, and cancer cells can be around for a long time before they go into a relatively rapid multiplication phase. The question that should be addressed is not whether there is an association with the relatively recent stressor experiences that could be recalled, but instead whether stressors preceded the first mutations that got the processes going or, alternatively, the events that occurred soon after a mutation appeared so that the growth and survival of those first malignant cells were enhanced. Early-life and prenatal stressful experiences cause multiple changes in the developmental course of many hormonal, neurochemical, and immunological systems, and may influence the response to later challenges encountered in adulthood. From this perspective, the root of stressor effects on pathology, including cancer, could potentially stem from these early experiences. Thus, trying to find a link between the occurrence of cancer and stressors experienced in the past few years might simply reflect looking in the wrong place at the wrong time.

Influence of early-life stressors on cancer

Adverse early-life experiences in humans have been associated with increased incidence of breast cancer, just as this relationship was observed with other psychological and physical disorders. For instance, loss of a parent or poverty during early development was predictive of increased adult cancer incidence (Schuler & Auger, 2011), as were stressors that comprised physical or emotional abuse. Once again, these findings don't point to causal relations; stressors, such as loss of a parent or poverty, can have multiple downstream consequences (altered diet or health-seeking behaviors) that could favor the development of cancer.

Stressor-provoked modification of therapeutic treatment responses

It is of theoretical and practical importance that stressors may influence the effectiveness of treatments used in cancer therapy. As cancer patients typically experience considerable strain, it is conceivable that the beneficial effects of their treatment are limited owing to stressor-elicited epinephrine changes or variations of other hormones or immune factors. Moreover, it might be considered that treatment with a beta norepinephrine blocker, by reducing distress, might enhance the effectiveness of their cancer treatment. Consistent with this perspective, the effectiveness of the anti-cancer treatment bicalutamide in reducing prostate tumors in mice was diminished by a chronic stressor regimen, an outcome that could be attenuated by treatment with a β-norepinephrine blocker (Hassan et al., 2013).

THE CHILD'S EXTRA BURDEN

Most severe, chronic illnesses, particularly if they involve intense treatment, can lead to PTSD symptoms. Among women with breast cancer, 1 in 4 developed signs of PTSD, and among children with cancer, 1 in 5 were at increased vulnerability to develop this disorder (Graf et al., 2013). Moreover, the risk for PTSD persists among childhood cancer survivors so that as adults new stressor experiences will be more likely to promote PTSD (Stuber et al., 2010). Beyond these psychological consequences, 60% of children treated for cancer experienced adult impairment of cardiac, pulmonary, endocrine, and nervous system disturbances, neurocognitive and auditory system problems, as well as other negative outcomes that likely came about owing to the treatments themselves, as well as to uncertainties and the development of PTSD (Lee et al., 2009). Overall, virtually all survivors of childhood cancer had at least one type of ongoing disturbance (Hudson et al., 2013), which could have encouraged the development of PTSD. While it might be important for all patients to receive stress reduction therapies as a part of their cancer treatment, this is especially true for children, who might not fully understand what is occurring and who probably don't have effective ways of coping. Cognitive behavioral therapy has been found to be effective in children (Gillies et al., 2013) and could potentially serve in this capacity among children in cancer treatment.

Hormones and hormone receptors in cancer

Cancers may differ widely in their basic characteristics and the genes associated with the cancer, making them differentially amenable to particular types of treatment. Factors that influence reproductive hormones (use of oral contraceptives, pregnancy, having children, age when first child was born, breast feeding practice, age at first menstruation, age of menopause) can influence the occurrence and progression of some cancers, and thus therapy for some forms of breast and prostate cancer will include treatments that affect estrogen or testosterone functioning (e.g., Ricci et al., 2014). However, there are types of cancer that are less readily treatable in this manner. One form of breast cancer, referred to as triple-negative breast cancer, does not express the genes for the estrogen receptor (ER), progesterone receptor (PR), or HER2 (Hudis & Gianni, 2011), and treatment success is generally lower than in triple-positive instances. This said, even though there is a certain amount of uniformity to triple-negative cancers, they may actually comprise diverse attributes. Specifically, in most instances triple-negative breast cancers have a poor prognosis and require more aggressive therapy, but in others, oddly, prognosis may be as good as in hormone receptor positive breast cancers (Cheang et al., 2008).

Given the link between hormones and some types of cancer, it would be expected that experiences that affect hormones, including eating, exercise, as well as medications being taken, could potentially influence cancer risk or progression. Hormone replacement therapy (HRT) among women in menopause, particularly if it involved a combination of estrogen and progesterone, increased the risk of breast cancer, and declined among women who had stopped using HRT

(Narod, 2011). As stressful events influence multiple hormonal processes, including estrogen, it would be reasonable to suppose that such experiences could influence the progression of breast cancer, particularly among women using HRT.

CANCER AND THE PILL

Oral contraceptives come in two forms: the mini-pill contains only progesterone, whereas the combined pill, the far more popular of the two, contains both estrogen and progesterone. Not long after oral contraceptives were first introduced, it was argued that the hormonal changes provoked could favor the development of some cancers. However, with the concentrations of the hormones being reduced, the risk was diminished. Almost 20 years ago, a report from the Collaborative Group on Hormonal Factors in Breast Cancer (1996) and a subsequent study that tracked over 116,000 female nurses (Emons et al., 2000; Hunter et al., 2010) indicated that women using oral contraceptives were still at somewhat elevated risk of developing breast cancer, but after stopping its use the risk declined, so that after 10 years the increased risk was entirely absent. One form of oral contraceptive in which the dose of hormones is changed in three stages during monthly cycles ('triphasic pill') was accompanied by higher risk for breast cancer (Hunter et al., 2010). Like breast cancer, cervical cancer was elevated among women using oral contraceptives, and then declined after termination of their use (Appleby et al., 2007).

In line with other studies, oral contraceptive use, even for as long as 10 years, was not associated with an increase of breast cancer (Hankinson et al., 1997) and actually offered some protection against ovarian cancer (Hankinson et al., 1992). These findings were subsequently observed in other studies that involved varied hormone formulations. Hormonal treatments can have many benefits, some of which are related to certain forms of cancer, whereas others are unrelated to cancer. However, we don't hear much about these beneficial actions of hormonally-related contraceptive methods (Bahamondes et al., 2015).

EATING AND CANCER

Linking the consumption of particular foods to the development of cancer is difficult, just as it is in relation to heart disease. Given how many different foods we eat, how does one identify which, if any, are causing problems and which are simply bystanders? As well, the foods we eat may be influenced by other variables that could directly or indirectly influence the cancer process (e.g., living in poverty can influence the foods eaten). Finding answers to such issues obviously can't be done through retrospective studies (do you remember what you ate 2 days ago, let alone 2 weeks ago?), and even prospective studies (e.g., using a food diary) can be unreliable.

Despite these research limitations, it is thought that foods eaten or the accumulation of fat can affect cancer processes. According to Cancer Research UK (2014), some forms of cancer, including breast (among women after menopause), bowel, uterine, esophageal, gastric, pancreatic, renal, and gallbladder cancers, are connected to obesity in about 5% of cases. Some of these cancers might be exacerbated because fat tissues release cytokines that elicit inflammation, and our diet can also affect hormones (e.g., estrogen and testosterone) that in turn affect cell functioning and immune activity. Beyond these factors, certain foods may negatively interact with the stomach lining or, alternatively, the stomach doesn't receive the stimulation it needs from certain chemicals, eventually favoring cancer development. Aspects of the diet also affect gut microbiota which can influence some cancers, such as colorectal cancer (Walsh et al., 2014). In this regard, the gut microbiota can either act against or aggravate cancer development, and may contribute to complications related to cancer treatment (Garrett, 2015). Perhaps it is especially significant that forms of bacteria Providencia and Fusobacterium may be linked to colon cancer and that identifying bacterial genes may be useful in predicting the occurrence of this type of cancer (M.B. Burns et al., 2015). It has also been maintained that certain foods, such as daily consumption of nuts, can reduce cancer risk somewhat (Bao et al., 2014), and some types of cancer, notably that of the mouth, esophagus, stomach and bowel, can be diminished by eating foods high in fiber as well as fruits and vegetables, and avoiding salt, red meat, and processed meats (Corpet, 2011). We occasionally hear about 'superfoods' that ward off multiple diseases, but these claims typically sound too good to be true, and typically have no scientific backing.

As indicated in discussing the positive influence of particular diets, foods associated with cancer risk or benefits have been claimed far too often, and, as indicated earlier, it has been argued that many of these single studies offered "implausibly large effects" (Schoenfeld & Ioannidis, 2013). This doesn't mean that particular foods don't have positive attributes, nor that 'biotherapeutics' can't be developed to prevent or treat certain cancers (Prakash et al., 2011) or modify responses to other therapies (Iida et al., 2013). However, it should be understood that complex interactions probably exist between gut bacteria, genetic, epigenetic, and immunologic factors, diet and age (Serban, 2014).

EXERCISE AND CANCER

Given the positive effects of exercise on so many of our functions, including immune processes, there has been the question of whether an exercise regimen can influence quality of life among cancer patients, attenuate the development of cancer, or alter its course. There have been many scientific reports claiming the positive effects of exercise on factors secondary to cancer or its treatment (e.g., quality of life, diminished fatigue, improved muscle strength), which can diminish morbidity and mortality (Eyigor & Kanyilmaz, 2014). Positive outcomes might vary with numerous features and the type of cancer being assessed, as exercise interventions seem not to have particularly beneficial effects in the case of some cancers, such as colorectal cancer (Cramer et al., 2014). For other types of cancer, combined aerobic and resistance exercise regimens may diminish the fatigue that is otherwise common (Meneses-Echávez et al., 2015), and exercise can act against cancer *cachexia* (progressive weight loss, anorexia, and wasting) (Grande et al., 2014) and enhance health-related quality of life (Mishra et al., 2014). Although some of the positive attributes of exercise having been mentioned, but it should also be considered that different amounts of exercise can have varied health effects in patients, just as in non-ill individuals. Thus, it needs to be established whether certain doses of exercise are most practical and beneficial among those with cancer or those who have previously been treated.

There is little information as to whether exercise can play some role in preventing the development of cancer, although there have been suggestions to this effect (Abioye et al., 2015). Studies still need to be conducted prospectively over extended periods, and once more, they need to distinguish between different types of cancer as they might not all be governed by the same processes. Furthermore, it is often difficult to establish whether the effects attributable to exercise in this context can be dissociated from related positive life-style factors (diet, stress experiences, sleep).

SLEEP AND CANCER

Sleep disturbances are accompanied by altered activity of inflammatory immune processes, and it might be expected that sleep alterations would influence cancer risk. This linkage has, however, received very limited support, although work-related variations of sleep patterns (e.g., among shift workers) have been proposed as a modest risk factor for breast, prostate, colon, and uterine malignancies as well as non-Hodgkin's lymphoma (Haus & Smolensky, 2013). Although increased risk of prostate cancer was observed among men who had difficulties falling and staying asleep (Sigurdardottir et al., 2013), an association between sleep complaints or sleep duration and risk of breast cancer was not observed (Vogtmann et al., 2013). In still other studies, both short sleep (less than 5 hours) and long sleep (more than 9 hours) were associated with elevated colorectal cancer risk (Jiao et al., 2013). The data currently available are too scant and not sufficiently consistent to make causal connection between sleep disorders and cancer, or whether any effects of sleep disturbances are specific to only some types of cancer.

CANCER TREATMENT AND PSYCHOLOGICAL FACTORS

Some types of cancer have been treated more successfully than others, potentially owing to improved early detection methods or to improved treatment (or illness management). It is also possible that improvements in general patient care and greater focus on psychological health might have contributed in this regard.

The strain of cancer treatment

Cancer treatment can be arduous, beset by obstacles, stumbles, and even backward steps. Soon after cancer is suspected, the individual is subjected to multiple tests, including biopsies; the treatments themselves can be exceptionally stressful, and both behavior and identity might change from one of an independent, self-sufficient person to that of a 'victim'. Patients may have to undergo surgical procedures that range from limb amputation to removal of organs or parts of organs. As well, chemotherapeutic agents are highly toxic, killing healthy cells along with those that are cancerous, and many adverse outcomes can be expected. Normal fast-growing cells that are not cancerous, especially in the mouth, stomach, and intestines, will be most affected, as will blood cells and hair follicle cells (the latter is responsible for hair loss that occurs during treatment). The treatments may suppress the immune system (at times to dangerously low levels), provoke anemia and severe fatigue, and cause nausea and vomiting, anorexia, diarrhea, abdominal cramps, as well as constipation. Chemotherapy may also engender heart problems, infertility, peripheral neuropathy (pain, tingling, or numbness, usually in the hands and feet, that may not be reversible), and secondary neoplasms, such as acute myeloid leukemia. In addition, cognitive impairments may develop (sometimes referred to as chemo-brain), including disturbances of memory functioning (e.g., Paquet et al., 2013). These outcomes, as well as depression and PTSD that occur as a result of treatments, are all stressors that could potentially influence the effectiveness of the treatments themselves, and long-term disturbances (e.g., cardiovascular problems) aren't uncommon (Yeh et al., 2004).

THE STRESS OF SURGERY

Many people are frequently fearful of medical procedures. For some, even a needle or the sight of blood makes them woozy; others are concerned with surgical procedures, either because of uncertainties regarding what things will be like after the surgery, or simply because when anaesthetized they would lose all control over the situation. There's little question that surgical procedures and tools have become more precise. By example, in many instances large incisions to reach the abdominal cavity are replaced by keyhole (laparoscopic) surgery involving only a small incision, which allows for more rapid healing. For instance, patients who had a laproscopic procedure for gall bladder cancer had a longer survival than those who received other forms of surgery (Goetze & Paolucci, 2006). Still, cancer-related surgery is an invasive procedure, recovery isn't always easy, and the procedures themselves aren't always as successful as one would hope or may uncover still other problems. Despite the improvements, for many people surgery is a major stressor, which can disturb immune functioning (e.g., Rosenberger et al., 2009). For that matter, simply treating patients with anesthetic or creating any sort of wound might affect the tumor process, and thus there's something to be said for the use of immune-enhancing agents following surgery (Whelan, 2001).

To improve surgical accuracy and diminish patient distress, robotic surgery has become increasingly well developed, and in many instances has yielded especially positive outcomes (e.g., Broholm et al., 2015). Novel approaches have also been proposed so that surgical procedures can be achieved through natural orifices (e.g., transluminal endoscopic surgery), which can also be enhanced through robotic control (Azizi Koutenaei et al., 2014). There's the important issue of how comfortable patients will be in placing their trust in a heartless, soul-less robot in comparison to an understanding and compassionate human. Of course, the argument will also be made that human judgment is often necessary for complex decisions that need to be made during surgery, even if the surgeon graduated 94th in their class of 100, and miserably bombed the section on spleen because they didn't think it would be on the exam.

There's another issue that needs to be considered in the context of surgical procedures. Given the distress and uncertainties that accompany surgery, it might seem surprising that such procedures are undertaken in patients with Stage 4 (metastasized) cancer. Sometimes this is done to relieve pain caused by obstructions, but at other times it might be to calm family members who demand something be done. Surely, the oncologists know that the patient's case is terminal and not much can provide enhanced quality of life. However, the serious discussions that need to be undertaken with the patient and the family might not have occurred. In fact, only a small fraction of patients had issued a 'Do Not Resuscitate' order, possibly suggesting that a number still expected positive outcomes (Bateni et al., 2015).

Despite the hardships of treatment, the procedures will hopefully have positive effects and the patient will survive and resume their previous lives. To some extent, post-treatment symptoms, such as depression, have been related to trait optimism and how threatening individuals perceived their situation to be (Levkovich et al., 2014). However, even under ideal circumstances one shouldn't be misled to believe that the patient can now feel entirely relieved. Getting to this point beats the alternative, but the battle isn't over. Patients often have to spend time in physical or occupational rehabilitation, which in itself limits their usual activities, and additional tests are needed every few months to determine whether other adverse effects (e.g., cardiovascular problems) have emerged as a result of the treatment or whether the cancer has returned or metastasized. Understandably, these tests bring with them considerable distress as patients wait for the other shoe to drop. Being seen as a 'cancer survivor' doesn't necessarily mean that the patient returns to their previous life exactly as it had been, and they soon realize that life has taken on a 'new normal'. Thus, although the cancer survivors may develop a better appreciation for the good aspects of life, they often experience enormous strain and uncertainty about the future.

Psychological impact

Being informed that one is stricken with cancer is distressing and may be associated with the subsequent development of depression, anxiety, and PTSD. When faced with such an experience, some individuals will succumb and remain depressed or anxious, whereas others might find effective ways of coping, and may even be able to find positive aspects from bad experiences (finding meaning). Considerable success has been achieved in the treatment of psychological disturbances secondary to cancer (Barrera & Spiegel, 2014), although it's clear that there is still room for improvement (Galway et al., 2012). For many cancer patients collaborative care models, which included screening for depression and linking depression treatment programs, were found to be beneficial (Walker & Sharpe, 2014). Stress reduction treatments, such as cognitive behavioral therapy (CBT) and mindfulness-based stress reduction (MBSR), may also reduce distress and depression associated with cancer. Supportive group therapy likewise extended survival time among women with malignant melanoma (Fawzy et al., 1993), and similar findings were reported by a combination of psychotherapy and antidepressant drug treatments in relation to metastatic breast and gastrointestinal cancer. The enhanced subjective indices of psychological well-being may be accompanied by altered neuroendocrine functioning, lymphocyte proliferation, and pro-inflammatory cytokine production, as well as lengthening of telomeres (Matchim et al., 2011; McGregor & Antoni, 2009).

Although psychological treatments often have positive effects on the individual's psychological state, the benefits on the cancer process and survival have not always been realized. Some cancers might be entirely independent of stress-related processes, and in other instances it may have progressed to a point where psychological interventions were provided too late to have any effect. As indicated earlier, however, even if a psychological intervention doesn't influence tumor progression, for many people it may help in coping with day-to-day burdens, and perhaps promote benefit finding that will allow them to consider their life experiences from a positive perspective.

Given how devastating depression can be, coupled with reports that emotional factors can undermine cancer treatment, it is more than a bit surprising that 73% of cancer patients who experience depression are not treated for this (Walker et al., 2014).

TELOMERES FROM A DIFFERENT PERSPECTIVE

The finding that shortened telomeres were associated with poor health and earlier death prompted researchers to attempt to determine whether telomere length was simply a marker of poor well-being or was in some way causally related to the development of illness. In conducting such studies it was unexpectedly found that longer telomeres obtained from white blood cells were associated with an increased proclivity of dying from cancer. It is thought that people have long telomeres when their physical system is adept at repairing them. However, this very same process may act against our well-being when they serve to maintain and repair cancer cells. If this turns out to be correct, then it might be possible to limit cancer growth by undermining the ability of telomeres to maintain their length (Rode et al., 2015). There have been suggestions that telomeres may be involved in the development of cancer, and it was demonstrated that normal cell death, and by extension death of cells that may become cancer cells, can be manipulated by altering telomeres so that they lose their ability to protect cells (Hayashi et al., 2015).

Social support

Support from friends is especially valuable in cancer recovery, enhancing quality of life and improving adherence to treatment protocols (Le et al., 2014), and having larger social networks of friends and social support has been linked to reduced mortality following a diagnosis of breast cancer (Kroenke et al., 2012). Being married has likewise been associated with fewer health problems and greater longevity relative to being unmarried (or presumably individuals who are unhappily married), and this has also been observed in relation to some types of cancer (Inverso et al., 2014). A study of more than 734,000 patients diagnosed with the 10 leading types of cancer revealed that metastasis was lower by 17% among patients who were married than in those who were not (Aizer et al., 2013).

There is, at times, the misconception that once a patient has gone through the rigors of cancer treatment and the primary tumor is no longer evident, that the battle has been won. Thus, it's not unusual for social support that had been available from good friends to diminish, as these friends have their own problems to deal with. This is perfectly understandable, but as we've already seen, for many patients considerable uncertainty still remains as to whether the cancer will 'come back' in the next few months or years. Moreover, the distress experienced during the preceding months, coupled with the physical and psychological toll of the treatments, may leave patients drained, albeit happy that it seems over, even for the moment. These 'cancer survivors' need continued support, and other effective ways of coping with the ensuing months and years of uncertainty.

Psychooncology

The 1970s and 1980s saw the evolution of programs to link immune disturbances to psychological factors and specific brain processes. Some researchers focused on how psychosocial factors might influence the growth of an already existent cancer, whereas others considered the psychological ramifications of cancer and how to modify these outcomes. As already described, for many people psychological interventions enhanced quality of life, even if these treatments didn't affect the course of the illness.

Perhaps because clinical oncologists have witnessed repeated failures to develop cancer cures based on a standard medical model, there has been increased consideration that psychological treatments may have a role to play in extending life. Others, of course, continue to view the link between psychological processes and cancer as an interesting epiphenomenon, but might not consider it useful in achieving positive treatment outcomes. Nonetheless, it is being accepted that life-style and stressful experiences could negatively influence the course of cancer progression, and could potentially influence the treatment efficacy. As we'll see in ensuing chapters concerning how to deal with illness as well as end-of-life treatments, enormous progress has been made in developing adjunctive psychosocial treatments in dealing with cancer-related well-being (Artherholt & Fann, 2012).

While not necessarily diminishing the importance of psychological processes, some physicians feel that they should be doing what they were trained to do, namely treat the patient's cancer and other aspects of the patient's physical well-being, whereas psychological health should be dealt with by experts best suited to doing precisely that. It's difficult to argue with this perspective, especially if the oncologists hadn't received training to deal with the patients' psychological issues. Yet the oncologist ought to appreciate that gravely ill patients are likely to look to their primary treating physician for signs of positive change and for support, and thus casting aside this responsibility is counterproductive.

Being distraught and even desperate, some patients have opted for alternatives to standard medical treatments, even resorting to the most unlikely and ineffective therapies. 'Natural medicines' or 'alternative medicines' have been used as an adjunct to standard remedies or as a replacement for these procedures. It's difficult to say to what extent these alternative approaches reflect hocus-pocus, and how much is real, but every time one turns around another odd treatment seems to appear. These range from imaging Pac-man-like characters gobbling up cancer cells, through to consumption of apricot pits or shark cartilage in the hope that these would provide a cure. Fasting for several days has been offered as a way to fight cancer, allegedly because this 'kick-starts' our immune system. Likewise, ancient Chinese medicines, green tea, red wine extracts, and herbal tonics including ginko biloba have all been suggested to either enhance standard cancer treatment or attenuate the side effects that might otherwise occur. This is not only worrisome because these treatments might not have any positive effect, but also because they might be used instead of possibly effective approaches. Moreover, some of these pseudo-treatments may actually have a negative influence on the actions of chemotherapy, or may increase risk of some cancers, as reported with respect to high levels of vitamin E or supplements containing selenium (Kristal et al., 2014).

DEALING WITH CANCER-RELATED PAIN

Aside from so many other problems for the cancer patient, many cancers cause terrible pain. This may come about due to the growing tumor compressing or infiltrating sensitive regions of the body (e.g., bone), causing inflammation, or the release of chemicals that increase pain sensitivity. The intensity of pain increases with advanced cancers and more than 50% of individuals report pain sufficiently severe to disrupt day-to-day functioning. Thankfully, in most cases the degree of pain can be controlled by medications (e.g., opioids when the pain is severe), although these can also produce uncomfortable side effects. As well, various psychosocial and pain management techniques can be used, allowing for doses of medication to be reduced, and antidepressant drugs have also been found to be helpful.

Despite the low cost of pain medications, patients in large portions of the world (e.g., in parts of the Middle East, Africa, Asia, Latin America, and the Carribean) do not receive pain medications, either because of medicines not reaching their target audience, or because of over-regulation limiting their legitimate use (e.g., Cleary et al., 2013). These countries have serious challenges in relation to drug use, and a multipronged effort will be needed to alter regulatory policies and to provide educational reforms regarding the use of opioid acting agents.

Patient decisions regarding treatments

The shock of a cancer diagnosis sets most people into a shock reaction, and yet they are asked soon afterward what their wishes are concerning treatments they're prepared to receive. Understandably, this is exceptionally difficult, and to facilitate this process the Mayo Clinic has offered a series of guidelines for patients that will help them make these decisions in collaboration with their doctor, who ought to be their partner in this process (see Table 11.2) (Mayo Clinic, 2015).

Table 11.2   Recommended steps for patients in treatment (Mayo Clinic, 2015)

Step 1: Setting ground rules: Patients ought to establish an appreciation of what they are willing or comfortable with in relation to several aspects of the disease and its treatment. Only then can decisions be made.

- **How much you want to know?** How much do you want to know about the treatment? Most people want to know as much as they can about the treatment and the chances of success, whereas others might be more comfortable not knowing. It's up to the patient to let the doctor know what they're most comfortable with.

(Continued)

Table 11.2   (Continued)

- **How will treatment decisions be made?** Some patients want to be a full partner in decision making and even take the lead in this process. Others may want to leave it to the doctors to decide. Again, patients ought to inform the doctor what they prefer.
- **Having realistic expectations.** Doctors can provide 'estimates' concerning the efficacy of various treatments, and what side effects might occur. Patients need to be realistic concerning what side effects they can endure relative to the potential success of treatments. Once again, this needs to be communicated clearly to the doctor.
- **Accept help.** As with other illness, support from friends, family and the treatment team will be necessary, so patients need to be prepared to seek and accept help.

Step 2: Deciding on a goal. Given the type of cancer and its stage, patients need to define their goals, which can then inform their decisions. Is the patient expecting or hoping for a cure, stabilization of the disease, or just symptom relief?

- **Cure.** Following initial diagnosis, individuals will want a cure for the illness, and may be willing to endure more intense and broad side effects to achieve this end.
- **Control.** If the cancer is relatively advanced, or if earlier treatments have not been successful, goals might be changed. Full cure may be an unlikely outcome, and patients might aim for just have the cancer shrink or stop growing. Once more, this may dictate how willing the patient is to endure side effects of harsh treatments.
- **Comfort.** In the case of advanced cancer or when treatments haven't provided the outcomes that had been hoped, comfort and pain reduction may be of greatest importance to the patient.

Step 3: Research your treatment options: Having the essential information is crucial for proper decision making, and it also helps individuals feel as if they have a semblance of control over their destiny. The doctor or other members of the treatment team may be able to provide trustworthy websites, books and educational materials.

Step 4: Analyze the benefits versus the risks. Once information has been obtained from the doctor and from other resources, patients may be in a better position to assess the benefits and risks of different treatments and how these map onto the goals they had set out. Particular consideration should be given to:

- **Side effects.** What are the side effects of each treatment? How commonly do they occur? What are the options for managing these side effects? Is it worth enduring these side effects?
- **Quality of life.** Consideration should be given to the effects of treatment on quality of everyday life. Will work or family life be affected? Will travel be needed for treatment?
- **Financial costs.** Determine the treatments that will be covered by insurance, and if certain treatments aren't covered, what can the individual afford. The position of the insurance company should be determined in advance of treatment.
- **Other health conditions.** Cancer treatments may produce other health problems or might in some fashion exacerbate existing illnesses.
- **Maintaining a decision.** Remember that once a decision has been made, it isn't fixed in stone. Patients can change their mind over the course of treatment. In this regard, patients may choose not to have any treatment, but can change their mind subsequently.

Step 5: Patient–doctor communication. Effective communication between the patient and the doctor is critical for decision making. A connection between doctor and patients might not occur after a single meeting and may require several meetings. To facilitate communication, the following need to be kept in mind:

- **Indicate when something is unclear.** If patients say nothing, doctors may assume that they understand what was said to them. If clarifications or explanations are needed, patients need to say so.

- **Write your questions in advance.** As some individuals may be distressed at appointments and less able to articulate their thoughts, it may be useful for patients to write down their questions, expectations and preferences before appointments.

- **Recording conversations.** If possible, keep track of conversations with the doctor by taking notes or, with permission, recording the conversations. Owing to distress, patients may not accurately recall the information received and would not be in a good position to make informed decisions. It may be possible to bring a friend or family member along for support and for taking notes, as well as for subsequent decision making.

- **Pressure.** Unless your decisions are very bad, doctors will typically agree to your wishes. Patients should not feel that they are being pressured into particular treatments, and should select treatment options that they're most comfortable with. Usually, there isn't an incredible rush to do so, and the patient should take adequate time make their decisions.

- **Keeping medical records.** Obtain copies of medical records and bring them to appointments.

- **Seeking a second opinion.** Most physicians appreciate the tough situation the patient is in, and likely won't be offended if you indicate that you'd like a second opinion.

BROAD CONSIDERATION REGARDING CANCER TREATMENT

There are many reasons why cancer treatments might not work as well as one would hope. As we've already seen, aside from cancer cells' ability to avoid detection by the body's own immune cells, the treatment may not be attacking the root cause of the disease (e.g., the right gene or growth factors). As well, a second cancer-promoting mutation may develop so that a drug that targets the first mutation won't be effective. It also seems that characteristics of cells that serve as a target for a chemotherapeutic agent may disappear (be suppressed), only to reappear again when the coast is clear and the drug is gone (Nathanson et al., 2014). A drug's high toxicity may also limit its use, and its effectiveness may be compromised by the tumor's ability to develop resistance to it. Treatments may also adversely influence normal cells in parts of the body beyond those affected by the cancer, which also limits their use. Efforts have been made to overcome these problems, such as nanotechnologies to deliver medicines to where they are needed (Wicki et al., 2014), thereby allowing low doses to be used to avoid toxic side effects and to eliminate the potential for tolerance to the drugs actions. However, given that for most cancers the treatments have been only moderately successful, much more effective methods are needed to outwit the cells working to harm us.

CANCER SCREENING

The earlier cancer is detected the more likely that it can be treated successfully. Thus, it is essential that individuals are aware of their own bodies and symptoms, and when appropriate that they engage in screening for cancers. However, there have been divergent views concerning the effectiveness of some screening methods, and how often these should be conducted. As indicated in earlier chapters, there have also been concerns about the sensitivity and specificity of these screens, as false alarms or failures to detect cancers are not infrequent.

Guidelines for mammograms (an x-ray of the breast) to catch breast cancer early have been revised so that it's now recommended that routine screening begins at age 50 (instead of 40), is done every two years (instead of yearly), and is discontinued at age 74. This cut-off was based on the assumption that older women might not be able to handle the difficulties of cancer treatment, but if they are in good condition, then mammograms can be done. Reading an x-ray of the breast isn't as simple as it sounds, and varies with the density of the breast, although newer technologies (e.g., molecular breast imaging; MBI) have been handling this effectively. There are occasions where false positives occur (i.e., the radiologist says that cancer is present when there isn't actually any cancer), which can promote considerable distress and anxiety, sometimes persisting for several years. False negatives occur (i.e., saying there is no cancer when there actually is) in about 20% of cases (Mandelblatt et al., 2009), and the consequences are predictably deadly. Mammograms have advantages over no screening, but finding cancers early doesn't necessarily lead to better outcomes, largely depending on the nature of the cancer. New screening strategies are being developed, including biomarkers from a blood test which predicted breast cancer appearance 2–5 years down the road. This test still needs improved sensitivity, but with increasing biomarkers becoming available this problem could be diminished (Bro et al., 2015).

The usefulness of screening for prostate cancer, one of the leading causes of cancer death in men, has also been problematic. For years the standard approach was for the physician to assess enlargement of the prostate, or the presence of hard, lumpy, or abnormal areas through a digital rectal exam. As this didn't allow for evaluation on the side of the prostate that was inaccessible to the doctor's gloved finger, the prostate-specific antigen (PSA) test was developed, wherein the presence of this protein released from the prostate into the bloodstream was indicative of prostate cancer being present (Catalona et al., 1994). Although it had been widely used for more than two decades, elevated PSA levels were also associated with inflammation of the prostate (prostatitis) and enlargement of the prostate (benign prostatic hyperplasia), neither of which is predictive of cancer (Velonas et al., 2013). As a result, in many instances further invasive procedures were unnecessarily adopted, which often caused considerable distress. Proponents of PSA testing point out that we can't afford not to do this testing given that the incidence of prostate cancer has been increasing, but this is not surprising as more cancers are being detected simply because more men are tested. It has also been suggested that the survival rate of men has increased with early testing, but it could equally be due to better treatment methods having become available. The fact is that while some prostate tumors are aggressive and lead to death relatively quickly, most grow slowly. Currently, the United States Preventive Services Task Force (USPSTF, 2012) and the Canadian Task Force on Preventive Health Care recommend against PSA testing as the harm it can create exceeds the possible good.

Screening for other forms of cancer, such as colorectal cancer, should also be conducted among individuals over 50 years of age, especially given the frequency of this type of cancer. According to the Centers for Disease Control, the frequency of people being screened for colorectal cancer through colonoscopy is still low, and those with mental health or physical disabilities receive still less attention in this regard (Ouellette-Kuntz et al., 2015). The procedure is intrusive, and it's understandable that people are uncomfortable with having tubes travel around their intestine looking for abnormalities. However, the procedure is not painful and more often than not intravenous valium injection has the patient tripping slightly. Admittedly, the procedure necessary to void the bowel the day before a colonoscopy is no picnic, but things should be OK if individuals stay home with a clear path to the washroom.

Typically, screening methods have focused on identifying the possibility of a type of cancer being present and following this up with further tests to establish whether it was actually malignant and what specific type of malignancy it was. Another potentially useful approach has emerged in which the full population of antibodies present in an individual's blood is profiled, and based on this 'immunosignature' the presence of particular diseases can be determined with a high degree of accuracy (Stafford et al., 2014).

Individualized treatment strategies

The battle against some forms of cancer has recorded a number of wins over the past decades. Particular tumor types were linked to specific genes, hormones, or growth factors, leading to treatments based on the characteristics of the cancer, as in the case of estrogen sensitive HER2 positive breast cancer that is responsive to a drug cocktail that includes Herceptin (Trastuzumab). It likewise appears that a small molecule that fits precisely into a component of complex androgen receptors could have positive therapeutic effects in treating prostate cancer (Kulik, 2014). New treatments, such as those that target specific factors such as increasing AIM2, which ordinarily limits colon cancer growth, may serve to attenuate colon cancer (Wilson et al., 2015), although it will be some time before such compounds reach the clinic. Other cancers that had been considered a death sentence, such as chronic myelogenous leukemia, can frequently be treated successfully with Imatinib (Gleevec; Stenehjem et al., 2014), and newer compounds based on this agent are being developed (Wehrle et al., 2014). Pitted against such success stories are the many types of cancer for which the effectiveness of treatments have been limited, often adding only a few months to life. Lung and bronchial cancer, colon and rectal cancer, non-Hodgkin's lymphoma, pancreatic, liver, and intrahepatic bile duct cancer are only a few of the many that haven't realized the hoped for cure.

Even when patients seemingly have the same type of cancer, there may be marked differences between them. Genetically and hormonally they may be worlds apart, and focused individualized treatment strategies based on such considerations have become common (e.g., Tuxen et al., 2014). This entails linking particular cancers to specific gene mutations that could potentially inform treatment strategies. However, because many mutations can contribute to the appearance of cancers, the connections between specific genes and the use of particular treatment strategies might not be obvious. Furthermore, the recurrence of cancer after initial treatment may involve the presence of still other characteristics, possibly resulting from epigenetic changes or the occurrence of multiple mutations, thus making the cancer, as in the case of non-Hodgkin's lymphoma, non-responsive to chemotherapy (Pan et al., 2015). Despite these difficulties, there is the belief that advances will be seen as unique molecular genetic features of each cancer are identified (e.g., through the International Cancer Genome Consortium). In the interim, analyses of the individual differences related to psychological processes are necessary so that patients are emotionally and cognitively best equipped to deal with the illness.

TREATMENT METHODS

The amount of research concerning cancer treatments is staggering. Some of the research has focused on improvements of earlier treatments that are known to kill cancer cells, whereas others have focused on developing new approaches. These have ranged from immunotherapeutic and vaccine-based methods, attempts to use viruses (such as polio virus) to destroy some types of cancer, or offering a Trojan horse in which tumor cells take up nanoparticles that eventually cause their death. Still other methods have focused on finding weak spots on cancer cells that might make them more vulnerable to destruction. In this section we'll consider some of the common methods currently used to treat cancers, and point to a few recent approaches being adopted.

Chemotherapy

Chemotherapy has long been a primary treatment method to deal with many cancers. These agents are effective because they influence the machinery responsible for cell division (Malhotra & Perry, 2003), and thus fast-growing types of tumor (e.g., acute myelogenous leukemia and aggressive lymphomas) are more likely to be altered by chemotherapy than relatively slow-growing cancers or slower dividing, non-cancerous cells. Typically, *induction chemotherapy* begins with the intent of achieving remission. This entails a combination chemotherapy in which a cocktail of several agents is administered, depending on the specific type of cancer being dealt with. Because each of the agents in this cocktail is used at a relatively moderate dosage, drug toxicity and the chances of resistance developing are diminished. Should a good response be achieved, with patients developing remission, the same chemotherapy may be continued (*consolidation chemotherapy*) in an effort to prolong the overall disease-free time and thus enhance survival. In other instances, *intensification chemotherapy* may be used to this same end, but using drugs different from those that had initially been employed. Too often, however, the treatments fail to produce remission, and the goal of therapy may change to diminishing symptoms or to prolonging life, but knowing that remission will likely not occur the doses are kept low enough to avoid producing toxicity (Airley, 2009).

GETTING A BOOST FROM 'RECYCLED' AGENTS

Bringing a drug to market can take many years and is typically enormously expensive. Estrogen receptor modulators are a class of drug that acts by blocking estrogen receptors, with Tamoxifen being the poster-drug for this class. However, the effectiveness of such agents may diminish with repeated use, in part because newly formed cancer cells following treatment may not express the estrogen receptors. Occasionally, a drug that has been used for other purposes is found to have a second use, including in cancer treatment. Bazodoxifene, for instance, which was initially used for the treatment of osteoporosis, has positive effects in relation to cancer, and many other compounds have been found to be effective in a variety of other illnesses. When drugs are being 'recycled' for a second purpose, this is advantageous as the clinical testing for side effects will already have been established and perhaps the costs saved by drug companies will be passed on to consumers (maybe).

Radiation therapy

Another tool in the arsenal to deal with cancers is radiation therapy, which is generally used as a component of a broader treatment regimen, and is often adopted when the cancer is restricted (localized) to a portion of the body. It is used in the hope of eliminating the cancer, but it may be used in a palliative capacity to limit growth of the cancer and extend life. Radiation therapy destroys cancer cells by damaging their DNA (Lawrence et al., 2008), although there are some cancers that are not responsive to radiation treatment (e.g., melanoma and renal cell cancer). Typically, the treatment is applied over days to minimize radiation damage to healthy cells, and to increase the likelihood that cancer cells will be hit during parts of their cell cycle during which DNA damage is most likely to occur (Connell & Hellman, 2009). Radiation treatment may be preceded by neoadjuvant chemotherapy in an effort to shrink the size of the tumor and hence be more manageable by radiation therapy. As well, radiation therapy is often used following chemo-therapy or surgery in an effort to diminish cancer recurrence.

Because radiation therapy, like chemotherapy, operates by disrupting cell division, it may have some of the same side effects described earlier, ranging from fatigue, nausea, and vomiting to damage and sores on epithelial surfaces of the mouth, throat, and stomach, and may cause marked fluid retention and bloating. As well, the treatment may cause heart problems, bowel damage, and cognitive disturbances, and in infrequent instances radiation treatment itself may produce a secondary cancer (Lawrence et al., 2008).

Forms of radiation therapy

Several types of radiation therapy are available, and the choice of treatment depends on the type and size of the tumor, its location and proximity to normal tissues that are sensitive to radiation, as well as the distance into the body that the radiation will need to go. Of course, consideration is also given to what other treatments the patient will receive, their age, and their general health. Radiation therapy usually comprises the delivery of photon (e.g., gamma rays) or proton beams to specific sites over multiple sessions. Several beams of radiation are concurrently applied from different angles, and hence the full radiation dosage will only occur at the point at which the beams intersect, and thus the damaging effects can be limited to the site of tumor, although in some cases it is neces-sary to destroy cells along the margins of the cancer in case malignant cells have infiltrated the area. To achieve this specificity, the radiation procedure is combined with imaging procedures (e.g., *three-dimensional conformal radiation therapy*). For some procedures, the degree of sophistication is remarkable, as in the case of *intensity-modulated radiation therapy*, which delivers hundreds of small beams of radiation to maximize specificity and thus limit damage to healthy cells (Taylor & Powell, 2004). As the tumor may change over the course of treatment, variants of this procedure, such as image-guided radiation therapy (IGRT) and tomotherapy, which combine radiation therapy and imaging procedures, are used to hit cancer cells (Noda et al., 2009). When cancers are localized, yet another approach is used that consists of the insertion of radioactive pellets into the tumor area where they will kill off cancerous cells (*brachytherapy*) (Patel & Arthur, 2006).

Immunotherapy

A fundamental question in the development of some cancer therapies concerns why our immune system, which is thought to be so powerful, can't handle cancerous cells. Thus, research efforts have been made to enhance immune functioning, such as by manipulating a newly discovered protein (Lymphocyte Expansion molecule; LEM), which may be effective in providing the energy needed for the massive expansion of T cells that go into battle against cancer cells (Okoye et al., 2015). As we've discussed, cancer cells sometimes are able to evade detection, but even when these cancer cells can be identified, there is a fine line between immune activation having beneficial versus harmful effects. For instance, the immune system could promote the course of cancer development by increasing a type of sugar that accumulates in tumor cells (Pearce et al., 2014). Further, in some instances, our own immune cells simply don't do the right thing. In an effort to prevent excessive immune activity from causing an autoimmune response, regulatory T cells (Treg cells) may secrete cytokines that inhibit the actions of immune cells that could potentially destroy cancer cells. With this framework in mind, increasing research has focused on ways to facilitate the recognition and destruction of cancer cells by our own immune system, without having them 'behave irrationally'.

Vaccines

Several vaccines have been created to catch and destroy cancerous cells before they can do much harm. However, vaccines can also be used to promote an elevated immune response targeted at particular antigens. This requires that cancerous cells carry markers on their surface so that these cells can be targeted by a vaccine tailored to precisely match these characteristics on the cells' surface. The latter approach has seen some success against '*neoantigens*', in which mutations have occurred in tumors making them different from other cells, and thus they can be recognized and attacked by T cells. Positive outcomes using this approach were achieved in brain cancer models (Bunse et al., 2015) and may go to a Phase I trial. Likewise, there have been promising results in Phase II trials of melanoma treatment (Carreno et al., 2015). A degree of success was also obtained through a vaccine-like treatment for some types of lung cancer that added several months to life, and still better results were obtained when it was combined with other types of anti-cancer agent (Herrera & Ramos, 2014). Other vaccines have been created for cancers and while promising results were obtained, to a considerable degree they have been overshadowed by other immunotherapeutic approaches.

Cell-based therapy

In addition to vaccines, several other forms of immunotherapy have been used which target cancer cells based on markers present on their surface. One of these approaches, referred to as *cell-based therapies*, comprises the removal of immune cells from the patient, growing them externally, and then returning them to the patient, whereupon they attack the tumor. One therapy that uses this approach, *CAR T-cell therapy*, received 'breakthrough therapy' designation from the Food and Drug Administration (FDA) in 2014, allowing for expedited development based on indications that it has advantages over existing methods (Park & Brentjens, 2013). Early trials with such treatments yielded remarkably positive outcomes. Among 30 patients (children and adults) with acute lymphoblastic leukemia (ALL) who had not done well with other treatments, a 90% rate of remission was achieved (Maude et al., 2014), sometimes within days or weeks of treatment (Davila et al., 2014).

Given that the immune system sometimes turns itself off, an obvious (everything is obvious in retrospect) approach to cancer therapy is to prevent the immune inhibition. For instance, an antigen of T lymphocytes, dubbed CTLA-4, ordinarily resides within T cells, but when it appears on the surface of the cell, it signals immune activation to cease. Accordingly, if one could inhibit the actions of CTLA-4, then cancer treatment might be enhanced. The drug ipilimumab (an antibody for CTLA-4) inhibits the actions of this braking system, thus allowing for T cell activation and limiting the growth of late-stage melanoma (Egen et al., 2002). This treatment was effective in only a modest percentage of people, and could have side effects associated with too much immune functioning. Small trials in which this agent was combined with others that focused on pathways to take the brakes off the immune system engendered still better effects than ipilimumab (Porter et al., 2011), and could also be used in cancers other than melanoma.

Monoclonal antibodies

Another form of *antibody therapy* also targets cell surface receptors so that cancer cells can be destroyed. In this instance, antibodies are raised to specific antigens (markers) present on tumor cells, and when administered to patients the tumors can be destroyed (Scott et al., 2012). A related strategy has focused on modification of the brakes of the immune system, which ordinarily keeps immune activation in check, but in doing so also permits tumor cell growth. By engineering antibodies that shut down the proteins that form the brakes, effective treatment of one of the deadliest forms of cancer, melanoma, was observed (e.g., Tarhini et al., 2010), and positive initial results were observed in treating cancers of the lungs, bladder, and kidneys.

ONCOLYTIC VIROTHERAPY

Polio virus, the horror that affected so many people until a vaccine was developed, has now been resurrected for use in another way. A modified form of the virus, one that cannot cause the disease, has been used therapeutically in clinical trials in the treatment of solid tumors, such as glioblastoma, a brain tumor that is ordinarily untreatable. The altered polio virus is infused directly into the tumor site, and over the course of the next few months, assuming the right dosage is used and the tumor isn't too large, it may shrink and perhaps even disappear entirely. This 'oncolytic virotherapy' seems to work because the virus directly kills tumor cells and, importantly, the virus activates

(Continued)

(Continued)

our own immune system to fight the tumor (Brown et al., 2014). Essentially, following injection of the polio virus into the tumor, our immune system becomes engaged in eradicating the virus and concurrently destroys the tumor. Early data suggest that in addition to its effects on glioblastoma, this method might be effective in treating other forms of soft tissue sarcomas. A similar approach using a modified form of the herpes virus has also shown positive results in the treatment of melanoma (Andtbacka et al., 2015). Trials have now begun (e.g., at the Ottawa Hospital) in which two genetically modified viruses are used to attack cancer cells through somewhat different routes. One of the viruses being used in this trial is an adenovirus that was derived from the common cold, and the second is the Maraba virus, initially isolated from Brazilian sand flies, which has the ability to distinguish between normal cells and cancer cells that are attempting to hide from attack. Hopefully, this one-two punch will do what is hoped for.

Despite the remarkable success achieved through immunotherapy, we shouldn't be lulled into complacency in this battle, nor should we fool ourselves about how good this treatment is. The treatment still only works in a subset of patients for reasons not yet known, and in some instances side effects have been markedly elevated, requiring that treatment be discontinued (Larkin, 2015). It will be essential to find biomarkers that predict who will benefit from immunotherapy and who won't.

TOO OLD TO TREAT?

There is the question concerning at what age should a person stop making efforts to beat cancer or, framed differently, when should oncologists stop trying to cure older people? This is a disease of aging, and so the majority of cancer patients will be more than 65 years of age, and many will be quite a bit older. With increasing life span, and with baby boomers now hitting older age, the issue of treating older people will soon be acute. It had been thought at one time that elderly people couldn't withstand the hardships associated with cancer therapy, and so treatments were reluctantly administered, if at all. However, many of the newer treatments are less brutal than they had once been, and with improved life-styles many older patients, even some in their 90s, are sufficiently strong to deal with the treatments. That said, should older people receive the same treatments as those who are younger? Do we even know whether the treatments are equally effective (or ineffective) in both populations, given that older patients have been under-represented in clinical trials (Klepin et al., 2009)? In light of the concerns that may exist about whether older patients should be treated, guidelines have been created to facilitate decisions related to whether the benefits of treatment will outweigh the risks (Hurria et al., 2014). Essentially, the value of treatment for the patient needs to be considered in relation to the physical and psychological costs incurred, and this needs to be discussed in detail with patients and family members.

SUMMARY

Perspectives regarding the processes involved in cancer development and progression have evolved considerably over the past few decades, and increasingly greater attention has been devoted to cancer prevention, which had long been ignored. In this regard, there has been considerable focus on eliminating chemicals (and providing protection) that are carcinogenic, and this has been matched by efforts to change life-styles that might contribute to cancer appearance. As well, treatments have incorporated teams of health workers to deal with the multiple needs that patients might have, including efforts to maintain positive psychological health.

But, have we been winning the 'war on cancer'? I suppose that depends on whom you ask. Survivors probably think we are, and some physicians think so too, and for some types of cancer this is the case. For other types of cancer, the data haven't been encouraging. Mutations of our DNA are essential for natural selection and thus in making us what we are, but some mutations are also fundamental in producing cancers. In essence, for us to continue evolving and adapt to changing environments, mutations are necessary, and bad mutations come with the package. It could be argued that we have steadily been winning some battles in the war (e.g., against certain cancers), and will win further as more genetic mutations are identified and appropriate treatments are developed. The treatment strategies used to deal with cancer have indeed seen considerable change. Rather than using chemicals that simply poison cells, somewhat indiscriminately, individualized treatments have evolved to deal with each cancer in a specific manner.

Scientists working to treat cancer 50 years ago likely couldn't have imagined some of the current technologies and medicines, and the notion of individualized medicine based on biological characteristics of each cancer wouldn't even have been on the radar. To be sure, clinician scientists at that time would similarly have looked back 50 years and thought that their predecessors were fairly crude and naïve in their procedures. If we were to try to predict what medicine and cancer treatments would be like some years from now, we might envision that microbots the size of single cells would be used to target and destroy cancer, or methods would be available to sense the presence of a very small number of tumor cells and attack them through some form of very specific agent. Those of us who were around before computers were present in each home and office, and who preceded the genome being decoded, might be reluctant to make these predictions given that they know that there's so much that they actually don't know. Assuming that science moves at the pace that it has (and that global risks haven't materialized as global damage), it's likely that people 50 years from now will be wondering about the crude approaches that we used to deal with cancer.

12 Pain

THE UBIQUITOUS MALADY

All of us have experienced pain of some sort, and we dread impending pain to the extent that we want it over with as soon as possible. Often, painful experiences are simply part of life, increasing as we age, and for those who are very unfortunate, chronic pain becomes part of their daily lives. In this chapter we'll examine:

- several attributes of pain and how pain perceptions are altered by psychological processes
- neurobiological processes underlying pain perception
- various treatment strategies used to reduce pain, including pharmacological treatments and those that focus on psychological interventions
- the usefulness of alternative medicines and strategies to reduce pain perception.

DEFINING PAIN

Types of pain

Pain, according to the International Association for the Study of Pain (IASP, 2015), comprises "an unpleasant sensory and emotional experience associated with actual or potential tissue damage, or described in terms of such damage". Pain comes in varied forms that may be meaningful for diagnosis, treatment, and recovery processes. Different classification systems have been devised in an effort to have a uniform perspective on pain, but disagreement lingers as to the most appropriate ways of classifying pain. The approach offered by the IASP considers pain on the basis of the body region affected, how long it persist, its intensity and pattern of occurrence, how it came to occur, and the potential processes involved in producing the pain (Mersky & Bogduk, 1994), but there are other attributes of pain that ought to be considered (Woolf et al., 1998). In this respect, *nociceptive* pain can arise as a result of damage to non-neural body tissue, appearing as sharp, aching, or throbbing pain. It may emerge as a result of a pathological condition that is benign, or it may be caused by the growth and spread of tumors that crowd other parts of the body or cause blockage of blood vessels or organs, and it can occur owing to thermal stimulation (intense heat or cold), chemical stimulation (e.g., noxious substances stimulating particularly sensitive body regions, such as the lips or eyes), or mechanically induced damage (cutting, shearing, or crushing).

A second type of pain is *neuropathic*, stemming from damage to peripheral nerve endings or aspects of the somatosensory system, which may be felt as a burning or heavy sensation, or by marked numbness that follows along the course of an affected nerve. This sort of pain can develop as a result of toxins, infections, and disease processes as well as poor nutrition and excessive alcohol use. As well, injury or trauma to a limb can instigate a lasting pain condition stemming from damage to the peripheral (or central) nervous system. This condition, referred to as *complex regional pain syndrome* (CRPS), frequently appears in middle years, although it can develop much earlier (Birklein et al., 2014). Patients may report symptoms such as burning or the sensation of pins and needles, increased sensitivity to the affected area (*allodynia*), and it may spread beyond the site of injury (e.g., from a part of the hand to the entire arm). This intense and persistent pain may reflect interactions among inflammatory processes, autonomic nervous system activity, and neuroplasticity within the brain (Rockett, 2014).

Chronic pain

Chronic pain is usually defined as pain that lasts 6 months or longer, but there has been the view that chronic pain ought to be defined as any pain that lasts longer than necessary for normal healing to occur (Turk & Okifuji, 2001). Chronic pain should be distinguished from recurrent acute pain that emerges periodically over extended periods, but is not present most of the time.

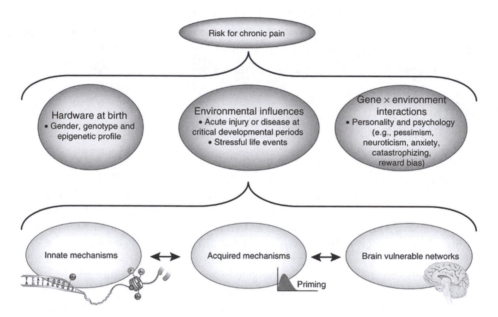

Figure 12.1   Various risk factors have been identified for chronic pain (Denk et al., 2014). Innate influences comprise the basic genetic hardware present at birth, comprising genes that are inherited, including specific polymorphisms and epigenetic processes. These genetic factors may interact with acquired processes relevant to pain perception, such as early-life pain experiences, stressful experiences, and sensitization or memory imprints of pain. Ultimately, these factors could affect numerous brain regions involved in pain regulation and perception. For instance, among patients experiencing acute pain, those with the greatest brain white matter (largely comprising glial cells and myelinated axons) connectivity between aspects of the prefrontal cortex and the nucleus accumbens were most likely to graduate to chronic pain. These characteristics may have existed before any pain was present; the presence of particular genes may have influenced the way pain messages were subsequently processed (Mansour et al., 2013). In line with this suggestion, relatively infrequent gene variants may contribute to pain sensitivity, which would also increase vulnerability to the development of chronic pain (Williams et al., 2012). It is similarly possible that cultural, social and development factors also contribute in this respect. For example, adult children of parents who dealt with pain through catastrophizing engaged in the same behaviors when they encountered pain (Kraljevic et al., 2012). From Denk et al. (2014)

Source: Denk F, McMahon SB, Tracey I. (2014). Pain vulnerability: a neurobiological perspective. *Nat Neurosci*. 17:192–200.

Migraine headaches, for instance, may occur continuously among some individuals, but most often they appear periodically, perhaps being triggered by particular foods or alcoholic beverages or following acute stressful events. In some instances, chronic pain may recede or remain stable, but in other instances '*chronic progressive pain*' may be experienced, particularly when a disease worsens with the passage of time, as in the case of rheumatoid arthritis and cancer. In the UK, Canada, and the US, about 20–30% of people suffer chronic pain, although it could actually be much higher depending on how chronic pain is defined. The economic burden this creates for government services and business is substantial, estimated at about $600 billion a year for medical treatments and lost productivity in the US (Gatchel & Okifuji, 2006).

PAIN ASSESSMENTS

For clinicians treating patients who are in pain, as well as researchers developing medications or other treatment strategies to diminish pain, having an accurate index of pain perception is essential. This ought to be fairly simple, but relying on a person's subjective appraisals might not be an ideal way of determining what's actually occurring. Aside from potential variations that exist across individuals in feeling or describing their pain, differences also exist across cultures, and even the context in which pain is assessed can influence the responses observed. Further, as there are many different types of pain (burning, throbbing, shooting, dull), comparing their relative intensities might not be meaningful. Added to this is the possibility that a given treatment might affect background pain differently from hour it influences *procedural pain* (the latter refers to pain caused by simple procedures ranging from injections or taking blood samples, through to more intense pain created by treating a wound directly). In addition to these patient-based features of pain perception, an observer's appraisal of pain others are experiencing might be inaccurate. For instance, when information about an illness was vague, health practitioners tended to discount the pain experienced by those who were least agreeable (De Ruddere et al., 2014).

A common measure to determine a patient's perceived pain involves the use of a '*visual analogue thermometer*' (VAT). Initially developed to assess pain among burn patients, it has since been used more widely (Choiniere et al., 1994). Having a visual representation of a thermometer against which pain can be plotted, including analyses of the effectiveness of pain medications, seems to be reliable and may be preferable to paper and pencil questionnaires (e.g., based on a Likert-like scale) (Huskisson, 1974). For specialized purposes, such as assessing pain in children, other simple-to-use scales have been developed, such as the University of Wisconsin Children's Hospital (UWCH) scale and the Children's Hospital of Eastern Ontario Pain Scale (CHEOPS), which are appropriate for preverbal and nonverbal children who otherwise have difficulty expressing the pain they feel (McGrath et al., 1985). There have also been pain questionnaires that explore the nature of the pain being experienced (e.g., throbbing versus burning) and scales that consider sensory and affective components related to pain (Fernandez & Turk, 1992), as well as the fear of pain (Asmundson et al., 2008). Even though these methods are all fairly good, when a patient is asked (through one of the scales) what their level of pain is at the moment, a response of, say, 'moderate pain' doesn't have much meaning given that we might not know what moderate pain means to them. Still, we can use their initial response to evaluate whether subsequent treatments have a positive effect for that particular patient.

ITCHINESS IS NO LAUGHING MATTER

You might have experienced an itch that just won't go away. Scratching gets rid of it for a brief period, but almost invariably it comes right back. When given the option between having a chronic itch and chronic pain (provided that it's not intense pain), many people would rather avoid the chronic itch. In fact, an itch (e.g., for people with eczema) can be viewed, in some respects, as being more distressing than what we usually consider a pain. As well, burns and surgical procedures are often associated with a hard-to-relieve itch, and some chronic conditions, such as kidney and liver failure, as well as diabetes and cancer, may be accompanied by incessant itchiness. Strong allergic reactions (e.g., following a bee sting) can also produce mind-breaking itchiness on the palms and soles of the feet.

It turns out that itch and pain involve the same or related mechanisms. In fact, itch is not felt by individuals who are congenitally insensitive to pain. Moreover, pain sensitivity is present around an area that is itchy, and spinal neurons respond to both pain- and itch-inducing stimuli; both are also transmitted through the spinothalamic tract, and are accompanied by activation of many of the same brain regions (Akiyama & Carstens, 2013). It is believed that we have receptors sensitive to pain, itch, or both, and while there are drugs such as antihistamines that reduce some forms of itch, they don't affect others (e.g., secondary to diabetes or kidney failure). There has been interest in determining whether drugs being developed to treat pain might also offer itch relief (Wilson et al., 2011), although it does seem that opioids which reduce pain exacerbate itch, suggesting the involvement of some independent processes.

PSYCHOLOGICAL CONSEQUENCES OF CHRONIC PAIN

Day-to-day effects of chronic pain

The negative effects of chronic pain can't be emphasized sufficiently, and those who have experienced it, or have had someone close to them go through this, will be aware of how devastating this can be. People experiencing chronic pain often must change their behavioral routines, and their life-styles necessarily change as the things they could accomplish previously might no longer be possible, such as mowing the lawn or carrying groceries, and even simple acts amounting to walking or sitting can be difficult. Some people may be unable to sleep, increasing their crankiness, and others might engage in social withdrawal, and thus find themselves with fewer social supports that might otherwise help them cope (Karoly & Ruehlman, 1996). Far too often, a person's life may revolve around their pain and how to accommodate it, and it is predictable that some might develop a pattern of negative thinking that limits their flexibility in dealing with ongoing challenges (Ruehlman et al., 2010). This catastrophizing can lead to heightened pain as well as increased risk of developing chronic pain (Khan et al., 2011). Of course, self-medication or prescribed drugs can lead to addiction, which further damages an already bad situation.

Depression and PTSD following pain experiences

The psychological cost of acute pain is profound, and even when there is an upside to painful experiences, as in the case of women giving birth, PTSD occurs in about 10–20% of people (Beck et al., 2011), varying with previous trauma experiences, coping methods, and genetic factors. The cost of chronic pain can be still steeper, particularly as it creates a psychological milieu that fosters persistent distress and feelings of being unable to determine one's own life (Maxwell et al., 1998). In some instances patients develop counterproductive methods of coping with their distress (e.g., rumination, wishful thinking, drug abuse), and the expression of pain may be socially reinforced (e.g., receiving attention from friends), which encourages the sick role being maintained (McClelland & McCubbin, 2008), particularly among individuals who catastrophize over their distress. Ultimately, chronic pain and its associated features may cause the deterioration of physical and psychological health, giving way to anxiety, anger, depression, suicidal ideation, or suicide attempts (Racine et al., 2014).

Chronic pain is apt to result in depression, especially if patients believe that they will be living in pain the rest of their lives, or if they have a history of depression (Tennen et al., 2006). Although the presence of pain tempered positive responses that could be elicited by antidepressant treatments (Bair et al., 2004), when depressive symptoms were reduced, pain reduction was also realized (Ang et al., 2010), pointing to the importance of mood state in managing chronic pain (Fishbain et al., 1998). It had been considered that antidepressants might have pain-reducing effects independent of their stress-reducing actions (e.g., in dealing with post-surgical pain), but the available data have not been sufficiently strong to support this view (Hearn et al., 2014). Interestingly, however, when given shortly after surgery to reduce pain, other agents that can affect mood (e.g., PTSD), such as pregabalin and gabapentin, can be effective in preventing later chronic post-surgical pain (Clarke et al., 2012).

Chronic pain in children

Chronic pain is not uncommon in infants, children, and adolescents, more so in girls than boys (King et al., 2011). Overall, headaches were the most frequently reported pain (23%), but musculoskeletal, back, and stomach pains occurred frequently as well, and psychosocial factors, such as depression, anxiety, low-self-esteem, and low socioeconomic status were linked to reports of pain. As stressors, including pain, experienced during infancy can have ramifications on subsequent pain hypersensitivity as well as stress responses (Victoria et al., 2013), it's all the more important to develop strategies to deal with chronic pain problems when individuals are young, rather than dismissing them as something kids go through.

PSYCHOLOGICAL FACTORS RELATED TO PAIN PERCEPTION

Pain regulation by contextual and psychological influences

An aspect of pain that makes it both interesting and puzzling is the extent to which its perception is influenced by psychological factors. Athletes, for example, may go on playing despite serious injuries, often to their own detriment, and it has been known for decades that soldiers who were wounded in combat infrequently asked for morphine, whereas civilians who experienced injuries of a similar nature were likely to request painkillers. Such effects could reflect the desire of soldiers to appear strong, or it might have stemmed from being distracted, or changes in the meaning attached to pain. Whatever the case, it is clear that psychological factors can moderate pain perceptions and reactions.

Pain perception may be dependent on the context in which it is assessed. For example, the pain of fibromyalgia was lower when measured at home than in a doctor's office (Fors et al., 2012). As well, a negative or positive experience with an analgesic influenced the behavioral responses to subsequent treatment, which was paralleled by significant differences in the activity of brain regions responsible for encoding pain and analgesia (Kessner et al., 2014). Pain perception may also be related to the perceived significance or meaningfulness of the situation. Patients who show up in hospital after a car accident or after being raped might develop a chronic pain condition that is magnified by psychological factors. This effect was more pronounced among individuals who carry a gene fundamental in regulating HPA axis functioning, leading to the suggestion that the protracted effects observed were related to psychological factors and the salience of the event that caused the pain (Bortsov et al., 2013).

Salience of pain

We saw earlier that aspects of the prefrontal cortex, notably the anterior insula together with the anterior cingulate cortex, are involved in cognitive (executive) functioning, and these regions also operate as a 'salience network' in predicting and influencing interpretations of impending pain (Wiech et al., 2010). In fact, if expectation of pain was present, even non-painful stimuli may elicit greater perceived unpleasantness coupled with increased activity within the anterior cingulate cortex and related regions associated with appraisal and decision-making processes (Sawamoto et al., 2000). In light of such findings, coupled with the powerful actions of placebo treatments, which we'll be considering shortly, there has been interest in the possibility that we can 'think pain away'. It was, indeed, demonstrated that when participants were exposed to a heat stimulus and asked to self-regulate their pain, they reported being able to do so. However, brain imaging studies indicated that when they altered their pain perception, the usual *neurological pain signature* (NPS), which is sensitive to differences in pain intensity, was unaltered. Instead, another set of connections to the nucleus accumbens and prefrontal cortex was activated (areas associated with reward and decision making), leading to the view that pain perceptions are subject to control by cognitive processes, including through connections to the prefrontal cortical regions (Woo et al., 2015).

I DON'T BELIEVE IT IF I CAN'T FEEL IT

Pain is a personal experience, so that those witnessing your pain can't feel it, despite corny expressions to the contrary ('I feel your pain'). Because pain is invisible, patients complaining about chronic, unexplainable pain, as in the case of chronic fatigue syndrome, might not be believed, even by their physician. However, a neurological pain signature has been identified, and thus it might be tempting to rely on imaging procedures (fMRI) as an indication of pain being present. An interesting review of this issue indicated that these imaging methods, as useful as they can be, can also create ethical dilemmas (Davis et al., 2012). These approaches might be useful in identifying the source of pain, especially when the person affected is unable to communicate (e.g., the very young or elderly people with dementia), and may be fundamental for personalized treatment strategies. As well, insurance companies, legal institutions, government and military organizations have the need to know whether self-reported pain is real. However, relying on imaging procedures can be risky as there are multiple types of pain and they might not all have the same reliable signatures. Moreover, different types of imaging procedure can give vastly different information, and it might not always be possible to detect a signature for certain types of pain owing to the limits of technology as well as the inability to detect subtle changes that can be present. Furthermore, a certain number of false negatives will come about (i.e., the incorrect conclusion that a person in pain is not actually having these feelings) and as a result they might not receive necessary treatments or time off from work to recover, or might be denied insurance benefits.

The placebo response

Virtually everyone has some knowledge of placebo responses in which an analgesic- or antide-pressant-like response is elicited by a treatment that can't actually have direct organic effects on physiological processes. The placebo response can be exceptionally powerful, to the extent that the efficacy of many drug treatments actually include a placebo response. Thus, many drug studies include placebo (control) treatments in order to determine the extent to which a given drug's actions are attributable to its biological effects. This said, one shouldn't be misled about the usefulness of placebo treatments as only about 25–50% of individuals exhibit such analgesic responses, although when moderate or mild levels of pain are being treated, the placebo response can be as potent as low doses of morphine. No doubt, numerous variables contribute to these individual differences, and personality factors, such as optimism and altruism, have been predictive of whether and to what extent a placebo treatment would diminish pain perception (Morton et al., 2014), as was the presence of particular genes (Hall et al., 2015).

The *expectancy* of positive effects being obtained, possibly being related to various cues surrounding the situation, may contribute to the occurrence of the placebo-related perceptual, behavioral, and clinical changes (Vase et al., 2015). The environmental features that instigate these expectancies can be subtle to the extent that individuals might not even be aware that they were being affected. Patients who were told that they would receive morphine through an automated infusion pump to alleviate post-surgical pain reported greater pain relief than did patients who were unaware when morphine treatment began (Colloca et al., 2004). As well, just seeing another patient receiving effective pain medication primed individuals to similarly show pain relief following the treatment. Remarkably, if patients exhibited a placebo response over several days, the pain reduction elicited by the treatment persisted even after they were told that they had been receiving a placebo (Schafer et al., 2015). Conversely, if patients expected that a genuine drug would not have positive effects, it was less likely to be beneficial (referred to as a *nocebo* response).

Most often, placebo effects are considered in the context of inert medications (in comparison to active drug treatments), but placebos also appear in other forms, including mechanical or electrical devices to reduce pain or muscle aches, acupuncture needles inserted into inappropriate locations, and it can be argued that faith healing reflects a placebo to encourage behavioral or physical changes. Physicians themselves are a component of a broad placebo treatment that encourages well-being, and our expectancies and trust related to the physician will thus have considerable bearing on whether prescribed treatments will be followed and positive outcomes obtained (Stewart-Williams & Podd, 2004). Predictably, the placebo response is also likely to be dependent on other factors, such as previous learning about the treatment, which encourages the belief or expectancy that the treatment will have positive effects (Kong et al., 2013). As well, social comparisons and social learning can affect placebo effects, and, like a social contagion, social interactions can affect placebo responses (Benedetti, 2014).

The effects of placebos are not restricted to agents purportedly providing pain relief, having been evident when patients are led to believe that they're receiving muscle relaxants or drugs that affect cardiac functioning (e.g., blood pressure) in programs to quit smoking, as well as treatments to diminish anxiety and depression. Indeed, a portion of antidepressant treatment responses among patients with modest levels of depression are attributable to placebo-like effects (Fournier et al., 2010), and in these instances the added value of the active drugs may have been limited (Khan et al., 2004).

Neurobiological correlates of placebo responses

How an expectancy of a particular outcome is translated into behavioral and perceptual responses has been a matter of considerable research. Placebo treatments that instigate analgesic effects are accompanied by activation of sub-cortical processes linked to pain and stress responses, including connections between the midbrain *periaqueductal gray* and *limbic brain regions* (Wager et al., 2007). More than this, however, placebo analgesia is accompanied by activation of brain regions associated with emotional and anxiety responses and to reward processes (hypothalamus, amygdala, and nucleus accumbens), as well as brain regions that support executive functioning, including the anterior cingulate, prefrontal, orbitofrontal, and insular cortices (Lidstone & Stoessl, 2007). Actually, there may not be 'a' placebo response, but rather there may be different types of placebo response, each involving different mechanisms (Benedetti, 2014). Whereas opioid-related neuronal processes or those involving endocannabinoid receptors might be involved in some placebo responses, those related to dopamine functioning might be involved in those associated with positive or rewarding feelings. Still other neurobiological mechanisms might be responsible for placebo and nocebo responses linked to 'expectancies' (Denk et al., 2014).

DON'T CARE WHY

It's not uncommon to hear "It's just a placebo effect", implying that the treatment isn't actually effective. However, given the neurobiological effects of placebos, they should be viewed as legitimate medical or psychological treatments. Many scientists, myself included, are very negative about phony treatments that are pedaled to gullible victims. Questionable herbal medicines and homeopathic treatments that are a scam seem to appear whenever there are possible financial gains in the offing. I suppose that our natural aversion to seeing a charlatan gain at the expense of those already victimized by illness makes them and their ministrations especially repugnant. Then again, it could be argued that although these treatments might not get rid of a problem, they may diminish negative mood elicited by illness, and if nothing else, might allow individuals to maintain hope (even false hope, which isn't always a bad thing). Thus, so long as it doesn't interfere with potentially effective treatments, these alternatives can be useful. At the end of the day, from the vantage of a patient in pain, it might not matter how or why a treatment has positive effects, so long as some relief is experienced.

PSYCHOSOMATIC (PSYCHOGENIC) PAIN

Given that expectancies regarding pain perception are as powerful as they are in determining placebo and nocebo responses, it isn't entirely surprising that physical pain can be provoked or exacerbated as a result of mental, emotional, or behavioral factors. This sort of *psychogenic* pain may appear as headaches, back or stomach pain, usually being diagnosed this way when other causes for the pain have been ruled out. It isn't unusual for those experiencing psychogenic pain to be stigmatized. The pain isn't a genuine one, but "it's all in your head", suggesting that the sufferer is imbalanced in some manner, despite psychogenic pain being as profound as pain that stems from other sources. It's doubly curious that although elimination of pain through psychological processes (e.g., placebo effects) carries no stigma, emergence of pain through psychological processes is stigmatizing. This aside, pain of this nature can be modified by psychosocial, experiential, and environmental factors. As we learn more about the interactions between pain processes and psychological factors, better treatments for these seemingly puzzling illnesses will emerge, but in the interim, our lack of understanding regarding illness without known etiologies should not diminish our perspectives of their seriousness.

STIGMA RELATED TO ILLNESS

It's hardly a secret that mental illnesses are associated with considerable stigma, and among some psychiatrists there is reluctance to deal with people who have been diagnosed with personality disorders (e.g., borderline, histrionic) as they are often viewed as demanding and hard to deal with. Understandably, physicians may also feel edgy about treating patients if they have come to believe that the physical symptoms expressed are due to 'untreatable' psychological causes. In fact, however, in some instances the occurrence of symptoms might not be due to psychological impairments, but simply stem from factors that haven't yet been identified.

(Continued)

(Continued)

This is what patients with chronic fatigue syndrome (CFS) seemed to face and they can end up frustrated, bitter, and reluctant to seek help. This illness has been characterized by fatigue, widespread pain, depression, and other symptoms that couldn't be attributed to any specific cause. Its diagnosis was also hampered because there wasn't an objective test that could be used, and the etiology of the disorder was uncertain (Afari & Buchwald, 2003). These patients often felt that it was bad enough not to have a treatment available, but this was compounded by the frequent beliefs of others, including some health practitioners, that affected individuals were either malingering or that the illness was a reflection of psychological instability. No wonder these individuals became increasingly depressed and suspicious of others (McInnis et al., 2014).

As it turned out, CFS was deemed to be 'a genuine disorder', likely engendered by inflammatory processes (G. Anderson et al., 2014) and might reflect an autoimmune disorder (Morris et al., 2014). Among individuals with CFS, stress-response systems are always on alert, reflected by elevated and protracted cardiac responses to cognitive challenges, leading to physical disturbances. It is accompanied by activation of inflammatory processes that stimulate the basal ganglia, a brain region involved in reward processes, cognitive functioning, and motor acts (A.H. Miller et al., 2014). In addition, CFS has been associated with bilateral white matter atrophy and what appear to be disturbances of the arcuate fasciculus (a bundle of fibers that connect the temporal and inferior parietal cortex to the frontal cortex), which could potentially be used as a biomarker of CFS (Zeineh et al., 2015). As of 2015, CFS has had its name changed to 'Systemic exertion intolerance disease'. So, those who were considered unbalanced only a few months ago have been legitimized as being physically ill.

NEUROPHYSIOLOGY OF PAIN PROCESSES

The gate control theory of pain

One of the leading perspectives on pain processes, the *gate control theory*, was developed about 50 years ago (Melzack & Wall, 1965), and still holds considerable sway on theorizing related to pain processes. An important aspect of this framework was that different types of sensory fibers, as described in Figure 12.2, were proposed to exist that could produce either fast or slow signals, and that fibers could have activating effects, inhibitory effects, and even effects that comprised inhibition of inhibitory actions. These neuronal actions would allow a 'gate' within the spinal cord to be open or closed, which would determine pain sensations.

As indicated by Braz et al. (2014), the theorizing offered by Melzack and Wall occurred well before different fiber types and neurotransmitters involved in pain had been identified, which speaks to their intuitiveness in formulating the gate theory, and their perspectives have been updated and reformulated several times. For instance, it was maintained that there are fibers that travel from a site of injury directly through the spinal cord to the brain, thus bypassing the inhibitory and excitatory transmission cells. At the same time, other brain-related processes could act downward to influence inhibitory cell activity, and hence pain perception. As well, since the initial formulations, several neurotransmitters and receptors (e.g., opioid receptors) have been identified that modulate pain perception.

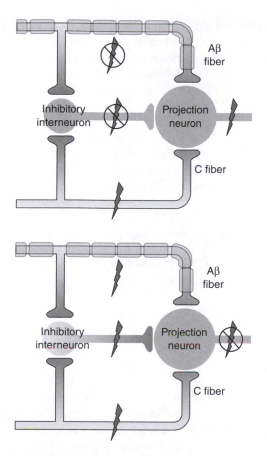

Figure 12.2 Pain perception results from activation of spinal projection neurons (right side of figure), which send messages up the spinothalamic tract to the brain. The activity of nociceptive projection neurons is dictated by two types of primary afferent fibers (carrying nerve impulses toward the spinal cord and brain), the fast transmitting Aβ fibers and the slower transmitting C fibers. These fibers carry information from the site of injury to the dorsal horn of the spinal cord (the point where sensory fibers synapse onto spinal neurons), which then send pain signals to the projection neurons that send the message to the brain. Important to this model is that connections are also present that impinge on an inhibitory interneuron that has the effect of diminishing the firing of the projection neurons (presumably being mediated by GABA activity). Thus, in addition to affecting the projection neuron, activation of C fibers will suppress (inhibit) the actions of the inhibitory interneurons, thereby having the effect of increasing activity of the projection neurons. In contrast, activation of Aβ fibers will stimulate the inhibitory neurons, thereby causing a decline of projection neuron functioning. The C fibers are thought to be preferentially stimulated by pain stimuli, whereas the Aβ fibers are stimulated by touch, pressure, or vibration. Thus, in the presence of a painful stimulus owing to C fiber activation, rubbing that site will stimulate the Aβ fibers, thereby dampening the painful sensation. This system is not independent of other processes, and the perception of painful stimuli can be moderated by a central state. Thus, when an individual is immersed in something else, they might be less aware of pain messages. In this figure, a lightning bolt signifies increased neuronal activation, whereas a crossed-out bolt signifies weakened or reduced activation.

Source: http://en.wikipedia.org/wiki/Gate_control_theory#mediaviewer/File:Gate_control_A_firing.svg

Not long after their initial breakthrough, Melzack and Casey (1968) introduced several other dimensions of pain perception processes. These included *sensory-discriminative* (intensity, location, quality, and duration), *affective-motivational* (unpleasantness), and *cognitive-evaluative* (appraisal, cultural values, context, and cognitive state) dimensions of pain. By incorporating pain and non-pain fibers, inhibitory neuronal processes, and an overarching *central state* that could influence pain perception, this theoretical perspective could explain a wide array of phenomena, such as why phantom limb pains occur, why distraction can alter pain perceptions, and why the brain might direct us to ignore the presence of pain under certain conditions (Melzack & Wall, 1996). Importantly, this multidimensional perspective reinforced the notion that pain resided in the brain, and thus pain sensations could be influenced by numerous psychological processes, which has a bearing on the usefulness of cognitive treatments in modifying pain perception (Moayedi & Davis, 2013).

REFERRED AND PHANTOM LIMB PAIN

Referred pain amounts to perceiving pain at a location other than the site of injury. Myocardial ischemia (decreased blood flow to the heart) may present with restricted feeling in the chest or as pain in the left shoulder, arm, or hand, possibly because the physical sites involved (heart/chest and left arm) share neural pathways from the periphery to the brain. For this same reason, pain in one portion of the body can be altered by stimulating another nearby area, and as we know, rubbing a wound can provide temporary pain relief. This 'counter-irritation' has become part of some pain moderating treatments and was considered in the development of gate control theory (Melzack & Wall, 1965).

Phantom limb pain, which comprises pain felt in a body part that has been lost or from which the brain no longer receives signals (e.g., following limb amputation), can be viewed as referred pain. Phantom limb pain, often described as cramping, burning, or shooting, occurs in a majority of individuals who have experienced a limb amputation (Kooijman et al., 2000). The pain may persist for many months or even years, usually emerging periodically, although it may also present on a continuous basis, and can be instigated by stress and anxiety. In some patients vibration or electrical stimulation of the stump may relieve pain, acting much like counter-irritants (Melzack & Wall, 1996).

It had been thought that nerve irritation at the stump of the amputation was responsible for the pain, but various treatments to modify this were ineffective. It subsequently appeared that phantom limb pain was accompanied with a reorganization of neural processes within the somatosensory cortex (Pons et al., 1991). Some time later several reports appeared that supported the view that phantom limb pain (and phantom limb illusions) stemmed from altered neural representations in cortical brain regions (Moseley & Brugger, 2009), and more recent fMRI analyses revealed that pain among amputees was related to the preservation of a cortical representation associated with the amputated hand (Makin et al., 2013).

These studies, in essence, suggested that phantom limb pain occurred as a result of brain processes being activated, but a study conducted at about the same time cemented a new view of phantom limb pain. In particular, it was demonstrated that a local anesthetic delivered to the place where nerves from an amputated leg entered the spinal cord rapidly diminished the phantom limb pain, suggesting that these actions involved integration of spinal neurons and brain functioning (Vaso et al., 2014). A recent perspective relevant to this is that changes in neuronal plasticity within the spinal cord form a persistent 'pain memory' at the cellular level (Bonin & De Koninck, 2014).

PAIN MANAGEMENT

The management of chronic pain within medical facilities (intensive care units, emergency departments, surgical wards) was, for some time, not nearly as effective as it could have been (Deandrea et al., 2008). Less than optimal treatment was received by individuals at all stages of life, running from neonates through to the elderly as well as during end-of-life care (e.g., Selbst & Fein, 2006), and unfortunate disparities also existed regarding under-treatment of pain on the basis of race and gender (Bonham, 2001). Currently, most hospitals (at least larger hospitals or those in large cities) have specialists or dedicated teams who focus on helping individuals diminish or deal with pain. Given the sheer number of people who experience chronic pain, and the substantial toll it takes, still greater focus is needed in relation to pain management, including the incorporation of chronic pain treatment as a specialty within medical training.

Prescription drugs and the pain ladder

Drugs prescribed to diminish pain depend on the nature and source of the pain experienced, but in all instances these are administered judiciously. For certain types of pain, such as that caused by nerve damage, compounds that affect GABA neuronal functioning, such as pregabalin (Lyrica), may be effective. For other sorts of pain, many choices of medication are available: corticoid injections at the site of musculoskeletal injuries can be used to reduce pain stemming from inflammation, muscle relaxants are administered to diminish pain in tense muscles, and anti-anxiety medications may be used to relax muscles and to reduce anxiety that aggravates pain perception.

Among patients dealing with pain from injuries, post-surgical pain, or chronic disturbances, a 'pain ladder' is often used in an effort to diminish pain, but still use the least amount of medication with the fewest aversive effects. Initially, patients receive relatively modest treatments that might comprise non-opioid drugs containing acetaminophen, or non-steroidal anti-inflammatory drugs (NSAIDs), or COX-2 inhibitors (a form of NSAID that influences inflammatory processes). If the patient first presents with relatively severe pain or if mild medications didn't do the trick, or if pain was only partially relieved, a mild opioid, such as codeine, dihydrocodeine, or Tramadol, is added to the ongoing treatment regimen. Again, if this proves insufficient to abate pain, then another step is taken on the ladder in that a stronger opioid (e.g., morphine, diamorphine (heroin), fentanyl, buprenorphine, oxymorphone, oxycodone, hydromorphone) might be used, with increasing dosage as needed. Compounds that have become available are ever stronger, containing new formulations of older drugs, or greater amounts of these drugs.

Addiction to prescription drugs

A great number of prescriptions are written each year for medications to relieve pain, and addiction to such compounds is not uncommon. This problem has been escalating, and a report from Centers for Disease Control (2010) indicated that the use of opioids doubled in about a 20-year period (some reports noted that the use of these agents has actually tripled), and the drugs used are much stronger than they used to be. For instance, a new med, Zohydro, contains 10 times as much hydrocodone as regular Vicodin (containing hydrocodone plus acetaminophen), and may thus be that much more dangerous and has predictably been met by considerable push-back.

Many factors play into whether an addiction will develop to prescription meds. Aside from the individual's personality characteristics and previous experiences with drugs, the development of addiction may be linked to the dose used, the route of administration, and thus how quickly the rewarding effects of the compound appear, and addictions may vary with other drugs that are co-administered, as synergies between them could increase addiction potential. It also seems that the development of addiction may vary with the context in which the drug is taken and the individual's expectations concerning the effects that will be obtained (Volkow & Swanson, 2003). In this regard, drugs taken for a medical condition may not have the rewarding effects that would be obtained from a drug consumed with the expectation of feeling reward, and thus the potential for addiction would differ in these scenarios. There is also the issue of attitudes concerning drug consumption. Individuals coming from a home environment where drugs are frequently used might be more cavalier about consuming them. Likewise, considerable efforts have been expended by drug companies to have people believe that pain medications are the norm and are safe, given that it is a doctor who is prescribing the meds (Compton & Volkow, 2006).

Doctors are in the unenviable position of having patients who desperately want meds to provide pain relief, yet needing to be cautious as liberally prescribing opioid-acting agents could facilitate the development of an addiction. As careful as they might be in trying to limit abuse of painkillers, chronic illnesses are common and inevitably cases of addiction will occur. Although opioids are effective in diminishing acute pain (e.g., post-surgical pain), these agents provide little benefit in alleviating chronic pain owing to the development of tolerance (Reuben et al., 2015), but given the breadth of prescription drug addictions, it's clear that these agents aren't always being used as they should be. As access to drugs is a prime mover of addiction, it has been suggested that a multipronged approach is needed to deal with this problem. In addition to improved education and the potential for addiction, access to drugs ought to be limited, monitoring services improved, and treatment programs enhanced for those who are already addicted (Kolodny et al., 2015).

Alternatives to opioid-based treatments

Because some pain medications aren't effective in dealing with several forms of chronic pain, and since opiate-based treatments have a high potential for addiction, there is a clear need for treatments that are not limited by these constraints. There have been efforts to modify oxycodone tablets so that they would be more difficult to crush or dissolve and hence less likely to be snorted or injected. Although this initially seemed to be a good option to diminish abuse, it was later found that addicted individuals had simply shifted to other opioid drugs that could more readily be used to feed their addiction.

The alternative to simply altering the form of the med has been to develop new and better treatments. This has included the development of compounds that are based on the transformation of opioid agents, but with reduced tolerance liabilities (e.g., Healy et al., 2014). Still other approaches have been based on altering nerve signals that carry pain. Especially exciting data have been reported in which calcium channels, which are essential for electrical conduction down a nerve, are blocked (Bourinet et al., 2014). By screening a large set of molecules, several were identified that could selectively have such effects, thereby diminishing pain. These seemed to act on both endocannabinoid receptors as well as certain types of calcium channel (which allow messages to be carried down an axon), and had potent effects in diminishing inflammatory pain and tactile allodynia (Bladen et al., 2015). Likewise, adenosine, a substance that plays an important role in energy processes and which acts as a signaling molecule within the nervous system, has been implicated in pain processes. By altering the activity of adenosine A3 receptors it was possible to modify chronic pain associated with several illnesses, and when adenosine receptors were stimulated the inhibitory transmitter GABA was activated, which turned off the pain signal (Ford et al., 2015).

Aside from protecting us from infection following injury, aspects of the immune system also contribute to pain processes. Glia within the spinal cord and brain release cytokines that modulate pain (Watkins & Maier, 2005), and thus cytokine therapy (e.g., anti-inflammatories or cytokine antagonists) has been considered as a way of diminishing inflammatory pain. In fact, dysregulation of glial functioning (gliopathy) within the brain, spinal cord, and peripheral nervous system might contribute to chronic pain (Ji et al., 2014). Moreover, given that chronic pain can be accompanied by brain inflammation, related processes might serve as a target for novel pain medications (Loggia et al., 2015). Yet, as neuropathic pain can also come about owing to factors other than inflammation, cytokine therapy may have positive effects only in some pain conditions (Zhang et al., 2015). Still, there are indications that pain perception could be modified by combination treatments that include blocking the activity of glial cells (rather than neurons or their receptors), which are ordinarily activated by painful stimuli (Jacobsen et al., 2014).

CANNABIS FOR PAIN RELIEF

Cannabis (marijuana) behaves like analgesics in diminishing acute nociception and clinical pain brought on by inflammation and neuropathy, and has been used in an effort to control chronic pain (Lucas, 2012). It has also been used as an adjunct treatment to deal with pain stemming from some types of cancer. It seems likely that the analgesic effects of marijuana come about owing to the activation of CB1 receptors located in portions of the nervous system (e.g., within the hippocampus) that are responsible for fear and pain processing, as well as in immune cells that regulate the neuro-immune interactions responsible for hyperalgesia provoked by inflammatory changes (Zogopoulos et al., 2013). Tolerance develops to the pain-reducing effects of CB1 activation, and studies in animals indicated that drugs can be created that target CB2 receptors and reduce pain without tolerance developing (Woodhams et al., 2015).

Surgical procedures

When all else fails, patients may opt for surgical procedures to diminish chronic pain. In the case of chronic back pain or that associated with arm or leg pain, the treatment might involve repair or replacement of discs or procedures to correct degenerative problems (e.g., osteoarthritis). In some instances, back surgery might fail to reduce pain, and procedures might be undertaken to insert activating electrodes on the spine close to where fibers would be entering from the site of the pain (Kumar et al., 2008). In severe cases, surgical treatments have been used in which CNS (mostly spinal) tissues were cut, but these are used rarely as better approaches have evolved.

Depending on the nature of the surgery undertaken, even if the procedure has positive effects, these may be relatively short-lived, and because neuronal fibers may be affected, the treatment could potentially cause other types of pain to be instigated, such as neuropathic pain. Surgery may also damage perception of other sensations, such as light touch and temperature changes, and can even cause other forms of pain to occur.

Chronic pain

In some cases devices can be implanted under the skin (or elsewhere) that will diminish pain by releasing medicines, or provoking electrical stimulation, or producing heat (Cosgrove et al., 2011). Alternatively, nerves transmitting pain signals can be destroyed chemically or mechanically in an effort to alleviate pain (Williams, 2008), and attempts to reduce pain might involve moving blood vessels or other body parts away from nerves that are being compressed. In many instances, however, treatment options are limited as the source for the pain can't be identified.

PSYCHOLOGICAL MANIPULATIONS TO DEAL WITH PAIN PERCEPTION

An important element that emerged from Melzack and Wall's (1965) theory is that pain doesn't only come from specific receptors and spinal fibers being stimulated, but also resides in the brain. Thus, various psychological factors involving limbic and cortical brain regions may influence pain perception. For instance, having effective social support can diminish the perceived pain associated with illnesses such as cancer (Zaza & Baine, 2002), just as social support can diminish the emotional pain associated with being rejected or socially excluded. Likewise, because expectancy of pain or pain relief is known to influence pain perception, as we saw in discussing placebo effects, behavioral treatment strategies to diminish pain may include altering the individual's perspectives and expectancies.

The finding that psychological processes can affect pain perception, coupled with frequent reports that chronic pain was not being well managed by medications, encouraged the development of cognitive methods to deal with pain. For these approaches to be effective, however, it is important that patients have an action-oriented attitude at the start of therapy (J.W. Burns et al., 2015). In essence, being ready for change and taking charge of pain management may go a long way in influencing the efficacy of psychologically-based treatment strategies.

I FEEL YOUR PAIN

The term 'psychological pain' is often used in the context of romantic break-ups or stemming from unsupportive social relations, such as having your two best friends turn on you like vipers, being 'excluded' from a social group, or being defriended on someone's Facebook page. Simulations of social rejection in laboratory settings have been effective in promoting negativity and rumination, accompanied by increased neuronal activity within aspects of the anterior cingulate cortex, just as physical pain influences neuronal activity within this brain region (Eisenberger et al., 2003). Based on such findings, the view was offered that the anterior cingulate cortex is part of a 'neural alarm system' that is activated in response to either physical or social threats (Eisenberger & Lieberman, 2004). In individuals who had received transcranial direct stimulation to the area approximating the right ventrolateral prefrontal cortex (a treatment that reduces depression), the pain of social rejection was diminished (Riva et al., 2015).

The effects of social exclusion in a laboratory situation are pronounced among adolescents, being particularly marked in those with high levels of rejection sensitivity, and among these individuals the rejection has also been associated with decreased neuronal activity within brain regions that support reward processes, such as the ventral tegmentum (Masten et al., 2009). As a result, these individuals would express diminished positive feelings in social interactions, which might be predictive of depression developing in the future (Masten et al., 2012).

As the dorsal anterior cingulate cortex is responsible for appraisal of information related to negative experiences and decisions regarding distress, it was suggested that poignant adverse social experiences promote negative self-referential cognitions ("I'm not well liked, and I'm a loser") and commensurate emotional responses, such as shame and humiliation (Slavich, O'Donovan et al., 2010). These negative states might also give rise to further biological stress reactions, such as altered stress hormone levels and activation of immune processes that could affect physical and psychological well-being. There have been reports that medications that diminish inflammatory responses (e.g., NSAIDs) can serve as an adjunct in the treatment of depressive disorders, and a common treatment to alleviate physical pain (acetaminophen, the essential ingredient in Tylenol) could also attenuate the psychological pain of social rejection (Dewall et al., 2010). These findings speak to the intermingling of diverse processes in pain perception.

Consistent with the effects reported concerning anterior cingulate cortex activation in response to a laboratory-based social exclusion, when individuals witnessed rejection experienced by another person (causing empathy in the witness), aspects of the cingulate cortex were also activated (Novembre et al., 2015). Likewise, following an unwanted break-up of a social relationship, people viewing a picture of their ex-partner and thinking about their rejection was accompanied by activation of regions that support physical pain (Kross et al., 2011). Here's the rub, though. When brain scans were assessed in a more sophisticated manner, it was found that although physical pain and rejection activate the same brain areas, the patterns of activity within those areas were distinguishable from one another,

(Continued)

(Continued)

as was the connectivity to other brain regions (Woo et al., 2015). Whether similar differences could potentially be discerned in the earlier studies isn't certain, but realistically it wouldn't have been expected that these very different 'pain signals' would elicit identical types of response. It's probably best to think of them as having overlapping features so that emotional pain can affect physical pain sensations, and vice versa, but their actions aren't identical.

Cognitive behavioral therapy

Mixed results have been reported concerning the effectiveness of CBT in controlling pain perception. Some patients report pain relief, but the extent of the decline is often small, and no better than alternative psychological procedures (Vlaeyen & Morley, 2005). Yet having a severe pain-promoting illness, or simply being in pain a good deal of the time, often leads to anxiety and depression (e.g., Alschuler et al., 2013), which aggravates pain perceptions. Accordingly, to achieve a reduction of pain through pharmacological treatments, some patients might need intensive psychological therapy to first diminish negative emotional states (Teh et al., 2010).

The effectiveness of pain treatments (e.g., for treatment of chronic temporomandibular disorder) varies with the patient's pain beliefs (i.e., their perceived control over pain, disability, and whether pain always signals harm), catastrophizing, as well as perceived self-efficacy in managing pain (Turner et al., 2007), and the presence of negative features at the start of treatment tends to be associated with less successful outcomes in relation to CBT (Flink et al., 2014). Yet when CBT was used as part of a chronic pain management program, positive outcomes were observed among individuals who became actively involved in their treatment (e.g., through writing, self-evaluation, and exchanges of thought with others) and who received the greatest support from other members of the group (Furnes et al., 2014). So, once again, if patients have the belief that their pain can be managed, and they are active participants in obtaining pain relief as opposed to being passive bystanders, then positive effects may occur. It is also essential that they avoid the negative cognitive frameworks that had likely been established by previous failures to diminish the pain, and when some relief is obtained through altered cognitive processes, they ought to be aware that the pain relief occurred in association with their own positive cognitions (Barlow et al., 2002).

Mindfulness

Mindful meditation has been proposed to be effective in diminishing the perception of chronic pain (Reiner et al., 2013) and may be beneficial in relation to pain acceptance, pain catastrophizing, self-efficacy, and measures of affect (M.P. Jensen et al., 2014). The efficacy of mindfulness has been shown across numerous pain conditions and appears to involve brain sites that govern elevated attention, emotional responses, and interoceptive awareness (insula and anterior cingulate cortex) (M.P. Jensen et al., 2014; Zeidan et al., 2011). The effectiveness of this procedure varies between novice and expert practitioners, but even brief periods of mindfulness training can lead to variations of brain activity and grey matter volume (e.g., within hippocampus and parietal cortical region) and a corresponding decline of pain perception (Zeiden et al., 2011). The impression might be reached from these reports that mindfulness produces pain reduction, but a systematic review and meta-analysis concluded that published reports on the topic were of mixed methodological quality and that there was actually limited evidence supporting the view that mindfulness interventions were useful for chronic pain (Bawa et al., 2015).

Relaxation training

Relaxation methods have been used to reduce chronic pain (Bradt et al., 2014), and in certain instances, such as childbirth, relaxation training was effective in diminishing pain, and increased the satisfaction with the pain relief procedures (Smith et al., 2011). In other instances, such as chronic fatigue syndrome and fibromyalgia, relaxation-related therapies were not especially effective (Meeus et al., 2015). As we've seen in other sections, these conditions are associated with several brain and inflammatory changes, coupled with psychological baggage related to stigma, and thus relaxation therapy may simply be insufficient to get the job done.

HYPNOSIS

Hypnosis has a fairly long history of being used to diminish pain, including pain associated with breast cancer and procedure-related pain among children being treated for cancer (Tomé-Pires & Miró, 2012), as well as for irritable bowel syndrome (Lee et al., 2014). Among people who are hypnotizable (not everyone is), appreciable pain reduction can be achieved, and the procedure can even have some positive effects among individuals who aren't readily hypnotizable (Jensen & Pattersen, 2014). In some instances the effects of hypnosis are superior to other psychological treatments, and even self-hypnosis may be effective (Jensen & Pattersen, 2014). The impact of hypnosis also varies with the nature of the pain being experienced, having positive effects in a minority of patients with spinal cord injuries, somewhat better actions in patients with multiple sclerosis, and still better outcomes are seen for phantom limb pain (M.P. Jensen et al., 2014).

The relaxation that stems from hypnosis may diminish anxiety and thus indirectly influence pain perception, or the hypnotic procedure itself could act as a distractor to diminish immediate pain. Alternatively, an expectation might be established so that patients might come to believe that the treatment will lead to reduced pain, and perhaps those hypnotizable individuals who are most imaginative and most suggestible would also be most likely to respond to suggestions regarding pain relief. Although the expectancy created in regard to the effectiveness of hypnosis can have pain-reducing effects just as placebos do, it has been argued that the effects of hypnosis go beyond those that can be attributed simply to placebo-like effects (M.P. Jensen et al., 2014).

CNS changes provoked by hypnosis

Altered pain perception through hypnosis is accompanied by changes in brain activity, and the effectiveness of this treatment might stem from a decline of 'connectivity' in the neural circuits associated with pain and pain perceptions (Rainville et al., 1997). Similarly, connectivity between brain regions has been diminished by hypnotic suggestion to reduce pain, whereas reduced pain that occurred following suggestions to relive positive experiences (perhaps a form of distraction) was accompanied by elevated brain connectivity (see M.P. Jensen et al., 2014). In essence, varied processes might be operating in relation to the pain-reducing effects of hypnosis, even being dependent on specific attributes of the hypnotic suggestions.

GUIDED IMAGERY

Visualize and focus intensely on a place that brings good thoughts, where you're relaxed and feel at peace. Your happy place! Doing this may diminish chronic pain for the moment, and can be used to diminish pain that is perceived to be imminent (e.g., among woman about to give birth). The positive effects of guided imagery could occur because of the relaxation it produces, or because it serves as a distractor (Bowering et al., 2013). This procedure needn't be used alone, and can have positive effects (e.g., in children and adolescents dealing with cancer, as well as in patients with fibromyalgia) when used in integrative therapies that combine music, art, massage, therapeutic play, and distraction (Thrane, 2013).

Biofeedback

In considering psychologically-based therapeutic strategies in Chapter 6, biofeedback procedures were briefly mentioned, in which individuals learned, based on feedback from the body and brain, how to control certain types of response. In addition to being used to control anxiety and heart rate, and to diminish migraine and musculoskeletal pain (Uhl et al., 2014), it has been adopted for rehabilitation purposes following injury or surgery (Giggins et al., 2013). Although biofeedback usually involves patients being hooked-up to instruments that provide feedback related to autonomic nervous system functioning (heart rate, blood pressure, galvanic skin response) or to brain activity (EEG), real-time changes of brain activity through fMRI have been used in a pain control effort (Chapin et al., 2012). By being able to evaluate brain changes in real time, the fMRI changes can be used as feedback to train healthy controls and chronic pain patients to modulate anterior cingulate cortex activity, thereby altering appraisals of pain experiences. It is still too early to predict whether this approach will become useful for pain management, particularly in light of the expense of fMRI technologies and shortages of staff with fMRI expertise.

Distraction

Perceived pain increases in intensity as people focus on it, and, conversely, pain can be diminished when they get sidetracked and distracted. Pain and anxiety associated with evaluation of the cervix, vagina, and vulva for signs of disease (colposcopy) were diminished by a simple visual distractor (Carwile et al., 2014). Likewise, diminished pain reactions occurred among young children who had a parent present to serve as a distractor or who received sweet solutions before needle-related procedural pain (Kassab et al., 2012). As effective as it might be in some circumstances, within clinical settings distraction can only be used to a limited extent, and it's probably not a treatment that should be relied upon in the absence of other treatments being applied.

Neuroimaging studies have suggested that distraction (e.g., by engaging in a memory task or solving a complex problem) and placebo treatments both activate some of the same neural circuits, including those associated with appraisals, decision making, attention, and working memory. Thus, it had been assumed that placebo effects are derived from complex cognitive functioning, and might actually be redundant with active distractions in alleviating pain. However, placebo and distraction can have additive effects so that the combination of the two yields a better outcome than either treatment alone, suggesting that their actions in the brain are not redundant (Buhle et al., 2012).

Coping effects

Poor psychosocial functioning may be accompanied by enhanced pain perception, catastrophizing increased cancer-related pain (Syrjala et al., 2014), and negative appraisal and depressive affect were related to greater pain perception, as was the tendency to inhibit the expression of anger (Burns et al., 2008). No single best method might be available to cope effectively with all pain conditions. Psychosocial interventions and empowerment has diminished pain among cancer patients (Te Boveldt et al., 2014), enhancing self-efficacy-influenced pain management associated with osteoarthritis (Allegrante & Marks, 2003), and social support has diminished chronic pain (Kerns et al., 2002). Of course, using particular coping methods to deal with pain can only go so far, and it is likely that multimodal treatment strategies, including medications and cognitive therapies, will be best for most people.

Memories of pain

Pain perception may be related to pain-related memories. Building and maintaining memories is determined by connections between neurons, which are reinforced by the presence of particular enzymes that influence protein formation (e.g., protein kinase; PKM). For instance, one form of this PKM, specifically PKMzeta, is elevated in response to painful stimulation, perhaps reflecting some type of learning about this salient stimulus. If the functioning of this protein kinase was blocked, the persistent effects of a painful stimulus were attenuated, possibly by disrupting the pain memory circuit (Laferrière et al., 2011). Findings such as these raise an important question. If pain perceptions are indeed framed as memories, can these be altered just as other types of memory are subject to change? There is evidence that features of PTSD can be 'erased' by altering trauma memories, and it might be possible to diminish pain perceptions in a similar manner.

ALTERNATIVE MEDICINE

At one time, alternative medicines were used more frequently for treating pain than for any other ailment (Astin, 1998), possibly speaking to the desperation that occurs when standard pain medications aren't as effective as one would like or when strong medications that have addiction potential aren't readily prescribed. Some alternative treatments have continued to be popular and have indeed become more popular, with acupuncture standing high within this group. This treatment is thought to have positive effects by increasing the activity of neurons within the insula and cingulate gyrus so that pain processing and perception will be altered (Theysohn et al., 2014), as well as by affecting neuronal activity within limbic regions associated with emotional components of painful stimuli (Theysohn et al., 2014). Despite the increasing popularity of acupuncture and reports consistent with a positive role for acupuncture in pain treatment, a systematic review of the effectiveness of acupuncture concluded that acupuncture only engendered small analgesic effects, possibly reflecting bias or placebo responses, and was deemed to have little clinical relevance (Madsen et al., 2009).

Analyses to assess the effectiveness (and harms) of spinal manipulation, mobilization, and massage techniques in back, neck, and thoracic pain management similarly indicated that the available data were not overly impressive. The benefits obtained from alternative medicines were generally modest and transient (Furlan et al., 2010). Reports such as these certainly don't inspire confidence in alternative medicines, but one of the positive attributes of these procedures is that they don't exclude the concurrent use of traditional medicines. Thus, so long as they produce no harm and patients engage in standard therapy, there shouldn't be a downside. However, there are many instances where patients choose one over the other, and ultimately pay the price.

Some of the procedures described earlier, including hypnosis and mindfulness meditation, differ from standard medical procedures. Some years ago they might have been viewed as 'one of those questionable alternative medicines', but with scientifically generated data, these treatment options have taken on more credibility. This is especially the case when they are combined with standard treatments, whereupon they're viewed as complementary or integrative therapies rather than alternative medicine, and they have been incorporated in treatment programs within hospital settings (although this has been infrequent).

SUMMARY

The great number of people experiencing both acute and chronic pain and the toll it takes on emotional and financial well-being makes it among the most important medical conditions to be considered. Pain processes have become increasingly better understood, and increasingly more pain medications seem to be in the pipeline. However, for the moment, the most potent/effective pain remedies are those that also have addiction potential. In some countries, patients with painful disorders, such as those involving disc problems requiring spinal surgery, encounter waiting lists many months long, and all the while addiction to pain medications becomes more prevalent. Clearly, better methods of treating pain need to be discovered, but failing this, psychological interventions ought to be provided to patients so that the drug doses (and frequency of use) can be reduced.

13 Addiction

VIEWS ON ADDICTION

The perspective people have concerning addictions varies appreciably and attitudes regarding addiction are, to some extent, molded by movies and other media sources. It may be incorrectly assumed that an addiction to heroin is something that happens to poor people, cocaine addiction is for the wealthy or upwardly mobile, gambling is for people who seem not to understand simple math (the house always wins, after all), and alcohol and tobacco, as well as gambling, are addictions that cut across lines. Internet and sex addictions have often been given the status of 'Behavioral Addictions', but in the DSM-5 (American Psychiatric Association, 2013) they are not considered addictions in the traditional sense (so-called sex addiction might simply reflect hyper-sexuality rather than a genuine addiction), nor do email, eating, and pornography 'officially' reach the status of being addictions. Incidentally, the argument can be made that 'love' is an addiction (as we hear in songs), given that it shares many of the behavioral and neuronal characteristics of other addictions, but it doesn't meet the criteria necessary to be considered as an addiction.

To achieve the status of being a genuine addiction, and thus entry into the DSM, may take years of research. This is understandable, but it's too bad that insurance companies frequently won't cover treatments that don't have the stamp of approval that comes with inclusion in the DSM. In an interesting and provocative discussion of what behaviors ought to be included in the DSM-5 as addictions, Pies (2009) provides a telling quote from Amanda Heller (*Boston Globe*, 11/02/08): "If every gratified craving from heroin to designer handbags is a symptom of 'addiction,' then the term explains everything and nothing."

Addiction is often taken to reflect a character flaw, a moral failing, or an inability to control one's own bad desires. As we'll see, however, addiction is more than any of these, and instead represents an illness like other psychological disorders, brought about by a combination of predisposing genetic factors, disturbances of particular neurobiological processes, as well as having the opportunity and the means to feed a habit.

THE BREADTH OF ADDICTION

Addiction is a complex and multidimensional problem, and although there are several fundamental similarities between different types of addiction, they also differ from one another in numerous important ways. In this chapter we'll consider several issues that are relevant in this regard, indicating that addictions are both physical and psychological disorders that aren't a disease of character or a reflection of weakness, but instead reflect a disease in which aspects of the brain have been overwhelmed so that appraisals, decision making, and judgment, and even free will, have been taken hostage. What we'll see is that:

- the factors that lead to addiction differ between individuals, and the treatments for addiction likewise may differ as a function of individual characteristics and the nature of the addiction
- dependence and addiction might arise as a response to positive feelings and perceptions that individuals attempt to re-experience. Alternatively, it can reflect a form of self-medication that reflects counterproductive efforts to cope with stressors
- neurobiological factors contribute to addiction/dependence. These may comprise neurotransmitters involved in reward processes, those involved in stress responses, and growth factors responsible for memory or habits related to addiction
- the mechanisms involved may vary over the course of an addiction. Factors that enabled the initial development of an addiction may differ from those that sustain it, those that promote binge responses, and those that cause the recurrence (*reinstatement*) of an addiction after the habit has been kicked
- environmental cues as well as stressor experiences can instigate neurochemical changes that maintain an addiction and instigate its reinstatement
- common neurobiological elements are associated with diverse forms of addiction, but marked differences also exist between them, so that the treatments to deal with one type of addiction may differ in many respects from those needed to deal with a second
- addictions can be treated, to some extent, through behavioral therapies, drug treatments, or societal influences, but will be more responsive when multiple approaches are adopted concurrently or sequentially.

DEFINING ADDICTION

The term 'addiction' can have several different meanings or connotations, but generally, it has been considered as a condition in which individuals consume a substance (e.g., alcohol, heroin, cocaine, nicotine) or engage in an activity (e.g., gambling) that is initially pleasurable or is able to diminish distress, but with continued engagement well-being is undermined. Researchers and clinicians distinguish between *abuse*, *addiction* and *dependence*, and Table 13.1 provides the DSM-5 criteria for these conditions.

Table 13.1 Addiction and dependence (American Psychiatric Association, 2013)

Abuse

- Regular and excessive use of a substance.
- Occurs despite the varied dangers that exist, including legal problems, relationships falling apart, or failures in meeting responsibilities.

Dependence

- Greater tolerance for the substance will have developed (i.e., a larger dose is necessary to obtain the effects previously elicited by a drug).
- Individuals may continue a drug binge over longer periods than intended.
- More time and effort is devoted to obtaining the drug and attention to other activities or commitments fall by the wayside.
- Physical withdrawal symptoms appear when drug use stops.

Addiction

- Person develops preoccupation and intense cravings for the substance and the inability to control their behaviors in regard to obtaining and using it.
- Individuals are compulsive in their thoughts regarding the drug, and their drug-related behaviors persist despite the knowledge of harm.
- The transition from one phase to another involves neuroplasticity within brain regions associated with reward, stress appraisals, and executive functioning (Koob & Volkow, 2010).

In addition to the primary characteristics of drug dependence and addictions, multiple secondary psychological conditions can be engendered. Alcohol abuse may encourage the emergence of depression, amphetamine and cocaine can produce symptoms very much like those associated with schizophrenia, and psychedelic agents may promote persistent delusions. Some of these features diminish once individuals abstain from drug use, but in other instances, as in the case of chronic alcohol abuse which provokes neuronal and glial damage (*Korsakoff's syndrome*), the disturbances can be permanent.

A BROAD VIEW OF ADDICTION

Addiction across countries

The frequency of addictions and dependence varies across countries, but problems exist almost everywhere. According to the National Institute on Alcohol Abuse and Alcoholism (2015), in 2013 upward of 17 million people 18 years of age and older (about 7.0% of the US population) experienced an alcohol use disorder (slightly more than twice as many men than women), leading to about 88,000 alcohol-related deaths. The incidence of alcohol use disorder within the UK, based on statistics from the National Health Service, is proportionately the same as in the US, and within Canada the rate of alcoholism is slightly higher. These figures likely represent under-reporting of the problem given that respondents to surveys might downplay their difficulties (Morral et al., 2000).

As high as alcoholism is in Western countries, it is nowhere near that evident in some former Soviet Bloc countries, such as Moldova, the Czech Republic, Hungary, Russia, and Ukraine. Alcoholism has been associated with behavioral problems (suicide, interpersonal violence, and various antisocial behaviors) and reduced life span. In his book *The Last Man in Russia* (2013: 10), Oliver Bullough points to the rate of alcoholism in Russia, stating that "One man's alcoholism is his own tragedy. A whole nation's alcoholism is a tragedy too, but also a symptom of something far larger, of a collective breakdown".

Smoking tobacco also occurs at a particularly high rate, but in the UK and the US its use has declined from above 40% to below 20% over the past two decades, although it is still seen as the most common source of preventable death. Indeed, within the US, 480,000 people die yearly as a result of cigarette smoking, and of these almost 9% occur as a result of second-hand smoke (Centres for Disease Control and Prevention, 2014). In developing countries where increased urbanization has been occurring, smoking has been increasing and the World Health Organization (2014f) indicated that 80% of smokers live in low or middle income countries, killing almost 6,000,000 people yearly. Worldwide, more than 1 billion people are smokers, but this addiction is only one of many that occupy the world stage. About 240 million people experience alcohol use disorder, and psychoactive substances (e.g., cocaine, amphetamine, opioids) are used by about 3.5% of the world's population of individuals aged 15–64 and account for 0.7% of the global burden of disease (Gowing et al., 2015; World Health Organization, 2014d).

Gender differences in addiction

Across countries, males out-drink females, and also abuse prescription and elicit drugs to a greater extent, although the difference has been diminishing. However, once on the road to addiction, the rate of drug consumption is often greater in women (Hernandez-Avila et al., 2004). Females actually should be more biologically vulnerable to some forms of addiction, including alcohol, as the female body contains less water and more fatty tissue than the male body. As fat stores alcohol, whereas water dilutes it, based on equivalent consumption, women will actually be exposed to more alcohol than men. Furthermore, *alcohol dehydrogenase* and *aldehyde dehydrogenase*, enzymes that ordinarily degrade alcohol, are lower in women than in men, and thus alcohol stays in their bodies longer, thereby increasing the proneness to addiction. Yet, in response to stressors, a key driver for increased drug use, greater effects occur in men who tend to adopt externalizing behaviors, including substance abuse (Meyers et al., 2014).

FACTORS LEADING TO ADDICTION

Numerous factors that lead to addiction, some of which are depicted in Figure 13.1 and described in various sections of this chapter. Clearly, many factors contribute to the development and maintenance of addictions, and some addictions likely share common underlying features.

Figure 13.1 The constellation of factors that promote addiction or cause its reinstatement. Some addictions arise as a result of the unfortunate confluence of negative or impoverished early-life experiences, stressors encountered in adulthood, poor social influences and life choices, and having a particular genetic constitution. But addiction can also arise owing to societal problems, including industrialization, increased stressors placed on people by business and governments, fast-paced life-styles, and governments not taking appropriate steps to curb legalized addictions.

Age and social influences

Adolescence, as we've seen, is a tough stage of development as individuals need to fit in, and there is a search for a peer group that will accept the individual. Adolescents might engage in behaviors that their group adopts, and will be especially likely to do so if this makes them appear cool and 'with-it' (Evans et al., 2006). As the forebrain is not fully developed in mid-adolescence, making for poor judgment and impulsivity and risky behaviors being adopted, the effects of social influences and pressures can be especially profound (e.g., Bricker et al., 2009). In the case of smoking, almost 80% of individuals who are smokers began before the age of 18, and although smoking initiation has steadily declined in the US since 1996, it is still a considerable problem in some countries, continuing at epidemic levels, as already indicated.

Stressful experiences

Among some individuals, addictions may develop as a result of stressor experiences, and over the course of an addiction the influence of stressors may change or they might operate in different ways (Cleck & Blendy, 2008). Negative experiences can have addictive consequences among individuals of any age, but smoking, alcohol consumption, and substance abuse were especially elevated among adolescents experiencing conflict with parents, individuals with school problems, those with low self-esteem, individuals concurrently attending school and working, and those who favor avoidant coping methods (e.g., Cooper et al., 2003). Of course, addictions were more likely to occur if several such factors were present concurrently (Hair, 2009).

In a general review of the topic, Sinha (2008) pointed to several links between stressful experiences and addictions. Specifically, addictions were tied to (a) recent stressful experiences, especially those of a psychosocial nature (the loss of a child, unfaithfulness of others, the death of a significant other, rape, being the victim of violence, witnessing violent victimization), (b) negative early-life events (e.g., emotional abuse, neglect, isolation, parental loss, divorce or conflict, or physical abuse by a parent or caretaker), (c) multiple or cumulative stressor experiences, irrespective of when they occurred, and (d) chronic psychiatric illnesses. In the face of problems, counterproductive efforts at self-medicating through alcohol or other drugs may develop in an effort to cope with emotional pain and bad memories. Unfortunately, such escape efforts work only so well and not for very long before additional stressors are generated, potentially furthering the addiction. This perspective is intuitively appealing, but the data linking stressful events and addictions are largely correlational, and it's difficult to decipher what the relationship actually implies. Table 13.2 provides a brief description of several alternative views concerning processes leading to addiction.

Table 13.2   Perspectives of factors related to addiction

Hypothesis	Description	Main factor considered
High-risk hypothesis	Certain individuals have a tendency to engage in high-risk behaviors (Brady et al., 1998)	Individual impulsivity
Susceptibility hypothesis	Drug use in certain individuals may make them more susceptible to further pathologies	Individual coping abilities
Gateway hypothesis	The use of 'soft' drugs favors the later use of more addictive ones (Kandel, 1975; Vanyukov et al., 2012)	Previous drug use
Common liability to addiction	Genetic factors or experiential processes that caused a biological change may contribute to addiction (Falconer, 1965)	Underlying biological processes

MULTIPLE NEUROCHEMICAL COMPONENTS ASSOCIATED WITH ADDICTION

Addiction has been attributed to the rewarding value obtained from drugs, or the positive feelings obtained through the reduction of anxiety and stress that might otherwise be present. As we'll see, several brain changes have been identified that occur in association with these states, which could have implications for treatments of addiction. It is important to consider, however, that addictions involve dynamic processes so that the processes operating during the initial development of drug-taking behavior can change over time. An individual might, for instance, begin using a drug because of the rewarding feelings obtained, but later drug intake may occur to diminish the negative feelings that occur when the individual does not consume the drug. Similarly, initial drug intake may stem from particular brain neurochemical changes being provoked, but this can morph into further biological changes as the addiction unfolds and becomes more entrenched (Koob & Volkow, 2010). Moreover, the reinstatement of addictive behaviors following a period of abstinence might involve still other mechanisms. As in the case of many psychiatric illnesses that involve biologically heterogeneous processes, the neurobiological elements that promote addiction in one person can differ from those that occur in a second. Thus, treatments effective for one individual may be different from those that would be most useful in a second, and these may vary yet again with the stage of addiction.

As we've seen in other contexts, features of the brain, especially neuronal connectivity, are shaped by experiences, and this also occurs as a result of addictive drugs. This is particularly apparent in brain regions related to decision-making processes and reward mechanisms. The brain's neuroplasticity allows us to acquire and remember information, and it may also be fundamental in the development of behavioral patterns related to feelings of reward that encourage the development and maintenance of addictions. As we'll discuss shortly, it might be inappropriate to consider the deeply addicted individual as acting rationally and with forethought, but instead s/he is obeying commands dictated by a combination of disturbed functioning of brain systems governing reward, decision-making ability, and impulsivity. Of course, not everyone who consumes a particular drug will end up in the same state, and there are premorbid neurobiological factors that can predict the occurrence of addiction. For instance, in non-addicted individuals at high risk (i.e., coming from a family with high drug addiction present), brain responses to a stimulant challenge could be distinguished from those who were not at high risk (Casey et al., 2014).

Dopamine

Drugs that promote positive feeling do so because they activate neural circuits associated with reward, such as dopamine and opioid peptides (Wise & Koob, 2014). The activity of neurons within the mesolimbic dopamine system, which comprises neurons traveling from cell bodies in the ventral tegmental area (VTA) to the nucleus accumbens and several forebrain cortical regions, are particularly important in relation to feelings of reward (Wise, 2004). These dopamine-rich regions contribute to reward-seeking behaviors and the formation of associations between environmental cues and reinforcing stimuli, emotions, and executive functions (Robinson & Berridge, 2003). Once an association has been formed between particular environmental cues and the reinforcing effects of a drug, which, like other learning and memory processes, involves the formation and strengthening of synaptic connections, these cues will excite reward pathways, thereby encouraging further drug use. These reward processes are seen as being integral to the development of addictions, and for recovering addicts cues associated with reward pose a significant challenge as their excitatory effects on dopamine neuronal processes can promote cravings that readily push them into relapse (Bonci & Borgland, 2009).

EVIDENCE FROM UNEXPECTED PLACES

Parkinson's disease occurs owing to a loss of dopamine neurons of a midbrain region, the substantia nigra (Blesa & Przedborski, 2014), although other processes are also involved in this disorder, including dysregulation of neurotransmitters in other brain regions that may contribute to mood and cognitive disturbances (Litteljohn & Hayley, 2012). Treatment of the disorder usually includes administration of l-DOPA, which is converted to dopamine within the brain, or other agents that influence dopamine functioning. However, the newly created dopamine doesn't just target the substantia nigra, but also affects dopamine in several other brain regions and, as a result, several behavioral changes can be introduced. For instance, the increase of dopamine in the nucleus accumbens and in forebrain regions may promote impulse control problems, compulsive buying, binge eating, hypersexuality, and addictions, such as pathological gambling (Lee & Jeon, 2014), pointing to the causal involvement of dopamine processes in relation to some addictions.

In addition to a role in determining the actions of natural reinforcers, such as food, social, and sexual interactions, dopamine activity within the nucleus accumbens is exquisitely sensitive to threatening situations (Robinson & Berridge, 2003). As we saw in Chapter 5, dopamine release at the nucleus accumbens is responsive to both rewarding stimuli and stressors. Indeed, assessments of genes activated within the nucleus accumbens have indicated that stressors and some addictive agents, such as cocaine and morphine, had similar actions, raising the possibility that the expression of these genes reflect a point of convergence between stress, reward processes, and intake of addictive drugs (Nestler, 2008). Presumably, the neuronal changes engendered by the activation of these genes serve to enhance the salience or importance of motivationally- and emotionally-relevant stimuli (or amplify their significance), irrespective of whether they're positive or negative. In this sense, this system might serve in a preparatory (or 'get ready') capacity that lets the organism know that something significant is happening or is about to happen. Thus, when a drug is consumed that stimulates dopamine activity, its salience becomes more pronounced, the link between the drug and the rewarding feelings experienced are amplified, and the synaptic connections are strengthened, thereby fostering the addiction.

NOT LEARNING FROM MISTAKES

The lateral habenula is an important brain region that hasn't received the attention that it should have. Many addictive drugs have an aversive component that limits their intake, but following destruction of the lateral habenula, alcohol consumption increased in rodents (Haack et al., 2014), possibly suggesting that this stemmed from the negative attributes of alcohol being diminished. Neurons of this region are activated in response to negative events and, through connections to reward centers in the brain, it is thought that they transmit an 'anti-reward signal' that may be fundamental in determining subjective preferences. When this region is inactivated, the ability to select between rewards that have different costs and outcomes is diminished (Stopper & Floresco, 2014). Albeit speculative, disturbed habenula functioning may affect choice behaviors and the ability to differentiate different types of negative and positive stimuli, so that individuals won't learn from past errors, which could distinguish social from problem drinkers.

The brain's neural plasticity is what underlies the enormous learning ability of humans and animals. While not dismissing the possibility that addictive drugs may co-opt the brain's normal response to rewarding stimuli and may affect judgments and decisions regarding further drug intake, epigenetic processes may influence addiction by altering positive and negative memories related to drug reward (Day et al., 2013).

Serotonin

As much as dopamine is related to reward and stimulus salience, other neurotransmitters are also likely to be involved in addiction processes (Volkow et al., 2013). Psychostimulants or opioids could influence *compulsive behaviors* associated with serotonin functioning, which might facilitate the transition from occasional to compulsive drug use (Müller & Homberg, 2015). As well, addictions may be related to impulsivity that accompanies diminished serotonin functioning (Kirby et al., 2011). In essence, if rewards are perceived to have high value, perhaps owing to dopamine functioning, and individuals are concurrently less able to inhibit risky behaviors and are motivated to obtain immediate gratification through drug use, addictions will be more likely to develop.

Corticotropin releasing hormone

Stressful events, as we saw in Chapter 5, markedly influence CRH release from the hypothalamus, thereby increasing circulating ACTH and cortisol. In addition, stressors elicit CRH changes within the amygdala and prefrontal cortex, which are associated with emotional responses (fear and anxiety) and cognitive functioning (Koob & Le Moal, 2008). These CRH responses seem to be related to addiction processes as blocking CRH1 receptors in rodents diminished the intake of cocaine, heroin, and alcohol and acted against stressor-elicited relapse (Bonci & Borgland, 2009). Likewise, polymorphisms related to CRH in humans have been associated with altered drug intake, interacting with stressor experiences in driving such outcomes (Zorrilla et al., 2014).

Of course, CRH in diverse brain regions may have very different behavioral actions. By example, stressors that promote CRH variations in aspects of the amygdala might be responsible for promoting anxiety and dampening reward processes, whereas CRH activation within the prefrontal cortex might diminish self-control (Zorrilla et al., 2014), possibly through alterations of serotonin functioning. The changes of CRH also affect the release of norepinephrine at the locus coeruleus, which influences heightened vigilance in response to potential threats (Southwick et al., 1999).

Any of these neurochemical actions might in some fashion contribute to addiction processes, although it is usually thought that anxiety stemming from stressor-provoked CRH alterations instigates drug consumption as an effort to diminish these negative mood conditions. However, CRH may have still other actions as the addiction progresses. As described earlier, either initially or during the development of addiction, the rewarding influence of dopamine functioning may encourage drug intake. But, as the addiction progresses, the processes related to drug intake may shift so that individuals no longer continue to use the drug for the reward attained, but to ward off the poor feelings that occur if the drug is not taken, which may also be mediated by elevated CRH that occurs under these circumstances (Koob, 2014).

Common elements for different addictions

Many drugs, including cocaine, heroin, and alcohol, have several common actions, and the intake of these substances can be affected by some of the same treatments; there may even be the temptation to believe that all addictions involve the same neuronal processes (e.g., those involved in reward processes or those involved in craving). In fact, these addictions are not identical, and treatments that affect one form of addiction may have no influence on others, and the impact of various treatments can vary over the course of an addiction.

As we've seen, dopamine and GABA functioning at the nucleus accumbens might contribute to the rewarding attributes of amphetamine and cocaine early in an addiction (e.g., Volkow et al., 2013), CRH functioning may be especially germane to the maintenance of alcohol dependence, and altered dopamine functioning or growth factor processes may be pivotal in accounting for drug reinstatement (Stewart, 2000). Furthermore, whereas cocaine provokes an increase of the growth factor BDNF within regions of the brain associated with reward processes (nucleus accumbens), morphine inhibits BDNF expression in a related brain region (ventral tegmentum), again pointing to the potential differences that could occur in relation to different drug addictions (Koo et al., 2012). Accordingly, different strategies might be required to treat substance abuse at different phases of the addiction. To be sure, a single treatment for all addictions might not exist, but all or most addictions may have common features, such as the involvement of reward processes, impulsivity, stressor effects, and craving, and treatments that affect these processes might conceivably be useful as adjunctive treatments, but their effectiveness may vary over the course of an addiction.

OPPONENT PROCESSES IN ADDICTION

Our body and our brain like order and balance. One system operates to increase heart rate, whereas another might kick in to prevent an excessive response. Likewise, one aspect of an immune response may favor the development of inflammation, whereas others act against this. Some of these homeostatic changes are innately driven, whereas others come about through experience-dependent processes that likely involve synaptic neuroplasticity or other biological compensatory mechanisms.

Drugs such as cocaine elicit a state of euphoria, likely through its actions on dopamine activity, but homeostatic-like opponent processes are also engendered, possibly involving CRH variations that counteract these euphoric effects (George et al., 2012). The high (euphoria) elicited by the drug wears off with the passage of time, but the opponent responses may be more persistent, so that the feelings of euphoria are replaced by more enduring dysphoria. Ultimately, drug intake might not simply occur in an effort to obtain euphoric effects, but instead may represent efforts to limit the negative affect that otherwise occurs as a result of the compensatory opponent process response (Heilig & Koob, 2007; Siegel, 1999). These opponent responses may be subject to conditioning or sensitization effects so that the dysphoria occurs progressively sooner and is greater with repeated drug use, and can also be elicited by cues that had been associated with drug intake, so that these cues themselves will encourage drug intake among those attempting to go clean.

WHY ARE ADDICTIONS AS PERSISTENT AS THEY ARE?

Neuronal memories associated with addiction

Why can addictions last as long as they do, and why can they be so readily reinstated long after the habit has been eliminated? The simplest answer, of course, is that "we like what we like, and we don't forget those things readily", even if it isn't always in our best interest. But this answer is hardly satisfying, and certainly doesn't move us forward in developing treatment strategies any more than saying that "the spirit is willing, but the flesh is weak". It might be more profitable to investigate the neurobiological processes associated with cravings and addiction-related memory processes which keep cravings at the top of the mind and encourage further drug use.

As we learn about the world around us and make associations between stimuli and what we like and what we don't, synaptic connections are being made and strengthened so that memories of these stimuli and experiences are formed. Synaptic connections are similarly formed that link emotional, perceptual, and rewarding/euphoric feelings elicited by a drug being taken, and these connections are strengthened with repeated drug use (Nestler, 2014), as are connections to specific environmental stimuli. As neuronal networks are elaborated and synapses further strengthened (Dong & Nestler, 2014), particular neurons may become more readily activated (Liu et al., 2005), encouraging memory formation related to the drug. The formation and strengthening of addiction-related synaptic connections might involve multiple neurobiological contributions, but it is likely that growth factors such as BDNF, FGF-2, and GDNF are fundamental to this process (Ghitza et al., 2010). Once these memories are well developed, contextual cues will act as secondary reinforcers that promote craving for the addictive substance. Unfortunately, even after a cognitive decision has been made to abstain, the synaptic connections still persist, and the cues that activate them promote cravings that serve to reinstate the addiction (e.g., Flores & Stewart, 2000).

PSYCHOLOGICAL DISTURBANCES ASSOCIATED WITH COCAINE ADDICTION

Chronic use of some drugs can negatively affect brain processes involved in attention and decision making. Repeated cocaine use was found to be accompanied by reduced hippocampal and cortical gray matter (Thirthalli & Benegal, 2006), and may instigate brain changes wherein the normal electrical response to rewarding stimuli is disturbed, thereby affecting decision-making

(Continued)

(Continued)

processes (Parvaz et al., 2011). In a test situation involving monetary reward, for instance, a brain electrical response (termed the P300 response) increases as monetary value does. Like most people, cocaine users indicated that the task was more interesting and exciting with greater amounts of potential winnings; however, these cognitions were not accompanied by an increase of the P300 response. The P300 response to reward in these individuals was related to the amount of gray matter present in the prefrontal cortex, which may be linked to the ability to distinguish between levels of reward. This, in turn, could alter the pleasures obtained from many aspects of life, leading to the development of depressive illness that is so often comorbid with addiction.

Processes related to drug reinstatement/relapse

One of the greatest difficulties in the treatment of addictions is that individuals who have seemingly quit their habit so often fall back. This *drug reinstatement*, as already indicated, is encouraged by the presentation of cues that had previously been linked to the addictive substance, as well as through priming by a stressor experience (Shaham et al., 2003). However, the mechanisms associated with different reinstatement stimuli might also be biologically distinct from one another (Heilig & Koob, 2007; Stewart, 2000), and reinstatement processes may vary with different drugs. For instance, reinstatement produced by alcohol-related cues was attenuated by the opioid receptor antagonist *naltrexone*, which is sometimes used in the treatment of alcoholism, but this agent did not affect stressor-provoked reinstatement (Burattini et al., 2006). In contrast, a CRH antagonist successfully diminished stressor-elicited reinstatement, but did not influence cue-elicited reinstatement (Liu & Weiss, 2003). If drug treatments are developed to diminish addictions, it will likely be necessary to deal with the cravings that may occur, and these may involve different mechanisms, depending on the type of addiction.

Epigenetic factors related to addiction

Whether or not particular behavioral changes are expressed can be influenced by experience-related epigenetic changes. Like stressors, drugs such as cocaine can promote epigenetic changes involved in the regulation of dendritic plasticity (Maze & Nestler, 2011), including neuronal processes specifically involving the nucleus accumbens, which has been associated with reward processes (Feng et al., 2014). Epigenetic effects such as these have not only been identified in relation to cocaine administration (Covington et al., 2011), but have also been reported in response to alcohol, methamphetamine, and nicotine (Krishnan et al., 2014) and could potentially contribute to addictions. It is particularly significant that although epigenetic changes are modifiable, they are usually long-lasting, possibly being responsible for the persistence of addictions (Covington et al., 2011).

TREATING WITHDRAWAL

Aside from epigenetic changes that occur during the development of an addiction, gene expression changes also occur during the course of withdrawal. Rats that had been addicted to cocaine exhibited marked drug-seeking behavior (which reflects drug craving) even a month after their last hit, possibly because of a very great number of epigenetic changes that evolved during the withdrawal period. It was reasoned that if these epigenetic marks could be diminished, the craving for the cocaine would likewise be reduced. When rats in drug withdrawal were treated with a compound (RG108) that reduced epigenetic marks just before being exposed to cues associated with cocaine, the drug-craving response was diminished. These findings point to the potential usefulness of treating individuals during withdrawal as opposed to focusing on simply getting them to stop using (Massart et al., 2015).

A LINK BETWEEN PROPENSITY FOR EATING AND DRUG ADDICTION

When overweight individuals consumed a milkshake that was high on the glycemic index, an initial surge of blood sugar occurred, followed by a sugar crash about 4 hours later. At this time participants reported intense food craving, which was accompanied by pronounced activation of neurons in the brain reward centers (Lennerz et al., 2013). As mentioned earlier, there is the view that eating, particularly yummy high-fat and high-sugar foods, might in some fashion be akin to drug addiction. However, simply because cravings occur for highly desired foods, and brain reward processes are affected, doesn't imply the presence of addiction; it simply means we like these foods and reward centers signal this.

It will be recalled that eating and addiction involve several related processes, and neurons of the ventral tegmentum that promote overeating also seem to drive the appetite for drugs such as cocaine (Hebebrand et al., 2014). Simply depriving rodents of food for 24 hours, or by chronically maintaining them on a restricted diet, increased dopamine activity within the nucleus accumbens, altered responding for rewarding brain stimulation, potentiated drug-seeking behaviors, and increased addiction relapse. It has also been known for some time that sweet preference among rats predicts their later propensity for amphetamine addiction (DeSousa et al., 2000), possibly being linked to activity of the orbital frontal cortex in response to a very sweet taste. In effect, eating processes appear to be linked to addiction-related behaviors involving reward, although the specific mechanisms mediating these relations have not been fully identified. Nonetheless, among both obese and drug-addicted individuals, impairments are present with respect to dopamine processes involved in reward sensitivity and incentive motivation, as well as memory and learning processes, impulse control, and stress reactivity (Volkow et al., 2012).

Like these other hormones, ghrelin, which is related to eating and energy regulation, could potentially be involved in drug addiction. This hormone is altered in response to social stressors

(Patterson et al., 2010), and binds to receptors at sites associated with reward processes, including the VTA, where it stimulates dopamine neuronal activity (Abizaid et al., 2006). Consistent with the suggestion that this hormone is related to the addiction process, in rodents ghrelin administered directly to the VTA enhanced alcohol intake, whereas a ghrelin antagonist elicited the opposite outcome (Davis et al., 2007). Likewise, in humans who were heavy drinkers, ghrelin administration increased alcohol cravings (Leggio et al., 2014).

There are still other eating-related factors that are tied to addictions. The hormone orexin, known for its role in food intake and arousal, may contribute in this regard as receptors for this hormone are present at the VTA, and when stimulated, they provoke the release of dopamine at the prefrontal cortex and the nucleus accumbens, culminating in increased drug-seeking behaviors (Borgland et al., 2009). In addition to orexin, neuropeptide Y (NPY), which promotes eating and is important in regulating anxiety and PTSD, may contribute to heroin and cocaine self-administration and the reinstatement of heroin intake in rats (Maric et al., 2008).

THE EATING–DRUG ADDICTION CONNECTION IS RELEVANT TO TREATMENT

It has been mentioned repeatedly that many behavioral outcomes are determined by the interactions between several neurotransmitters and hormones. Serotonin is no different in this regard, having been implicated as a contributing factor to impulsivity, mood changes, eating, and reward processes, the latter occurring through its actions on dopamine activity in the nucleus accumbens reward center. The 5-HT2C receptor agonist lorcaserin (Belviq), which is used in the treatment of obesity, is also being examined for its potential to diminish various types of addiction (Higgins et al., 2013). A set of experiments conducted by Fletcher and his associates at the Center for Addiction and Mental Health in Toronto (e.g., Higgins et al., 2012, 2013) indicated that this compound reduced the rewarding value obtained from nicotine or from cues associated with it, coupled with a decline in impulsivity, and thus disturbed nicotine self-administration in rats. Early indications are that lorcaserin may be effective in reducing smoking in humans evaluated in a 12-week trial, and it has also been reported to reduce alcohol intake and cocaine abuse (Higgins et al., 2013). Given this breadth of the drug's effects, it is possible that the 5-HT2C receptor may be a factor at the core of addiction processes, possibly by acting on craving-related processes.

PUTTING THINGS TOGETHER

Several exceptionally detailed reviews have systematically described the stages and processes involved in addiction (e.g., Koob & Volkow, 2010; Volkow et al., 2013). These reviews largely considered the neurobiological processes related to addiction without diminishing the importance of other risk factors, such as prenatal and early-life stressful experiences, gender, socioeconomic status, the occurrence of particular comorbidities (e.g., depression), disturbed self-esteem, and being relatively young (less than 16 years of age) when intoxication was initially experienced.

Euphoria and dysphoria

Among some individuals the initial consumption of a drug might have occurred for fun, curiosity, experimentation, or as a result of peer pressure. For others, especially those who ruminate over negative experiences, the drug intake might have reflected self-medication in an effort to cope with stressors. It is of particular significance that the positive feelings provoked by a drug may be associated with particular environmental stimuli (e.g., location, people who might be present, or the drug paraphernalia) so that they take on secondary positive qualities, eventually serving to promote drug craving and maintaining the addiction. Individuals who are impulsive are particularly likely to give in to the craving (just this once) even if part of their brain may be screaming that it's a bad idea.

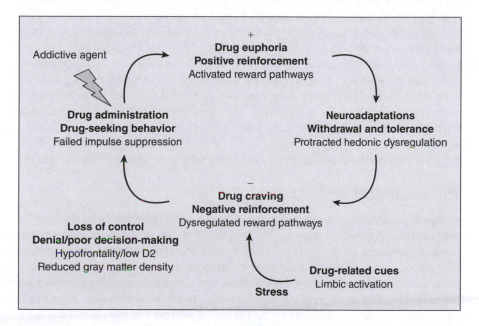

Figure 13.2   Multiple factors contribute to the development and maintenance of addiction, as well as the reinstatement of an addiction. Among individuals using a drug for pleasure (top of figure) the initial dopamine release induces euphoria and positive reinforcement through activation of dopamine-related reward pathways. But, with continued drug use, neuro-adaptations develop, the sensitivity of reward circuits may diminish, and antagonistic compensatory neurobiological responses may be provoked, and so recapitulating the initial drug-provoked euphoric experience may require progressively greater drug doses. Moreover, cues that had been associated with drug-elicited euphoria may instigate cravings so that the addiction will be maintained. At the same time, as compensatory responses become more pronounced, the waning of the euphoric effects of the drug is replaced by dysphoria, so that further drug intake may occur to ward off these negative feelings rather than simply to gain pleasure. With continued drug use, brain changes may be provoked that affect impulsivity, decision making, and judgement, furthering drug seeking and drug intake.

From Dackis, C. & O'Brien, C. (2005). Neurobiology of addiction: treatment and public policy ramifications. *Nature Neuroscience* 8, 1431–1436.

Addiction versus free will

It may be a myth that our free will or our innate strength can see us through periods of high craving. As Volkow et al. (2010) indicated, continued drug use may 'hijack' aspects of brain functioning so that neural circuits related to reward sensitivity and expectations of the drug's pleasurable effects 'overwhelm' control circuits that ought to limit compulsive drug consumption. As discussed earlier, and depicted in Figure 13.2, long-term cocaine use may be accompanied by reduced gray matter in prefrontal cortical regions associated with executive functioning and decision making (e.g., the orbitofrontal, dorsolateral prefrontal, and temporal cortex), possibly promoting impulsivity and continuation of drug use (e.g., Crunelle et al., 2014). Among individuals who had been prenatally exposed to drugs such as cocaine, these brain regions may be affected in a similar fashion, rendering them at increased risk for later addiction (Rando et al., 2013).

One might think that brain changes associated with cocaine would also occur in response to other powerful psychotropic drugs, such as amphetamine, heroin, or Percocet, but less so in relation to drugs that seem more innocuous, such as nicotine. However, nicotine biases perceptions concerning the dangers of tobacco so that upon being presented with positive and negative portrayals of smoking, brain activation patterns associated with emotional reactions differ between smokers and non-smokers (Dinh-Wiliams et al., 2014). Moreover, during periods of nicotine withdrawal, the rewarding value derived from ordinarily positive experiences or stimuli are diminished, making it that much more likely that the smoking habit will be re-engaged (Pergadia et al., 2014). Smoking is not just a bad habit; like other addictive substances it influences appraisal and reward processes.

Genetic influences

Not everyone who encounters a stressor or who experiments with drugs during adolescence will graduate to an addiction. Individuals who are generally negative, are relatively sensitive to drug-based reward, and are impulsive, might be at particular risk for addiction. Some of these features may be trait-based, perhaps evolving as a result of poor experiences, whereas others might involve a genetic component. Several genes and gene polymorphisms have been associated with various addictions (Kreek et al., 2005), and their presence might serve as biomarkers to predict treatment efficacy. For instance, the presence of a mutation of the mu opioid receptor has been associated with alcohol dependence, as have other genes, possibly by affecting the rewarding effects obtained by this substance (Nutt, 2014). Other genetic factors have similarly been identified that predict the occurrence of nicotine, amphetamine, cocaine, and alcohol addiction (e.g., Stoker & Markou, 2013). As well, epigenetic changes secondary to drug intake, as in the case of alcohol, might also come into play in favoring the development or continuation of a drug addiction (Krishnan et al., 2014)

TREATMENT STRATEGIES

There have been successes in diminishing addictions, but it isn't simple and it is obviously preferable to intercede before addictions develop. Social pressures, at least in recent years, have helped reduce smoking (in some countries), but these and other preventive measures haven't been all that successful with respect to other addictions. Moreover, individuals who are addicted often don't seek treatment either because they're content with the way things are, or they deny having a problem. Often, it's only when they're stuck at the bottom of the well that they call out hoping that someone will hear them.

GONE, BUT NOT FORGOTTEN

Once a response is sufficiently well ingrained, its repetition occurs as if the individual is flying on autopilot. These habits are exceptionally hard to break even if they have no useful function or are actually bad for us. Rats taught a particular response (e.g., turn right in a maze to receive chocolate milk) will continue to engage in this response sequence even after they become ill (owing to the food reward being laced with a substance to make them ill) and won't actually consume the chocolate milk. In essence, while the chocolate milk itself may have lost its luster, the behavioral responses still have some reward value or simply represent part of the established habit. If specific cells in the infralimbic cortex are turned off (by a technique referred to as optogenetics) as they approach the choice point of the maze, they stop turning toward the location of the treat that made them ill, suggesting that they are no longer responding on the basis of an entrenched habit. Under these conditions, animals were able to learn new alternative habits, thereby seemingly eliminating earlier responses. However, when the second habit was itself eliminated, animals immediately fell back onto their first habit. Even though it seemed to have been eliminated earlier, that habit was still there, perhaps on the fringes of conscious thought and certainly not entirely forgotten (K.S. Smith et al., 2012). Under the right circumstances, as in the case of addictions, these previous habits can emerge again, perhaps when times get tough or in response to reminder cues.

There isn't a magic elixir to treat all addictions, and not every treatment strategy is suitable for all individuals. The choice of treatment ought to depend on the nature of the addiction and its severity, but also on characteristics of the individual, particularly their readiness for treatment and their belief that certain treatments will be effective. Based on recent progress related to the analysis of gene mutations and epigenetic changes associated with addictions, these factors will likely figure in the development of individuals' treatment strategies.

COLD TURKEY OR QUITTING GRADUALLY?

"It's easy to quit smoking. I've done it dozens (hundreds) of times!" This quote, or one like it, has been attributed to Mark Twain, although some people suggest that W.C. Fields first uttered it, but in relation to alcohol. Regardless of its originator, it's usual that most people will make multiple attempts at quitting before they are successful. Anyone who has ever tried to quit smoking will tell you that the first few days are particularly stressful. For some people it seems that within hours of quitting, blood flow in the brain is diminished, cognitive functioning becomes somewhat impaired, and the associated negative feelings draw people back to the smoking fold. As it takes some time

(Continued)

(Continued)

for the brain to regulate (as occurs when individuals get off antidepressants), one approach to quit smoking might comprise withdrawing slowly, thereby getting over the initial negative hump. It's too soon to know with certainty whether this would be a useful strategy. However, just as it's hard to have just one potato chip (once brain reward circuits are activated, the relevant neurons promote further potato chip abuse), it may be difficult to sustain reduced cigarette consumption.

Checking into rehab

Rehab programs are meant to treat a variety of addictions, including alcohol, amphetamine, cocaine, heroin, as well as those involving prescription drugs. Aside from education and social support, medicinal treatments and cognitively-based therapies can be obtained in rehab. As a first step, individuals must be off drugs at the time of treatment commencement, and in many instances this will include a period of detoxification so that most of the drug has been eliminated from circulation and the brain.

Because individuals are away from their usual environment, they can begin to break the habit without having to deal with the reminder cues that would normally promote their illness. It is significant that after some period in residential care for dependence on opioid pain medication, behavioral and brain changes develop so that individuals again respond positively to cues that were ordinarily reinforcing before their addiction had developed, whereas the heightened response to drug-related cues diminishes (Bunce et al., 2015). Although this was assessed in only a small number of participants, the findings may be relevant in predicting whether individuals will be successful with their effort to go clean.

Fundamental to the success of any program, as we've seen in relation to other behavioral changes, is that the individual has to be ready to take the active steps necessary to beat an addiction, and self-efficacy is necessary to achieve this. Those who express sentiments like "They tried to make me go to rehab, but I said no, no, no", as Amy Winehouse put it, likely won't be successful within any type of program. In some instances, individuals will check into rehab as part of a plea-deal in relation to a criminal charge, or a choice made by a defendant in an effort to demonstrate their willingness to change. In other instances, the person might have come to that point without any coercion, and is taking actions with the intention of getting better. However, even if the individual is there for all the right reasons and the treatment has had positive effects, the risks for relapse are high and going back to the same old environment won't be profitable. A change of venue is often necessary and support from the right people will be vital for recovery.

As much as rehab can be an effective tool in dealing with addiction, not every rehab facility is up for the job of treating addiction. To a significant degree, rehab facilities are unregulated, yield limited improvements in the lives of the addicted individuals, but frequently charge patients and their families exorbitant amounts. A recent film, *The Business of Recovery* (Adam Finberg, Director; 2015), exposes many of the problems with the rehab business, and suggests that aside from improved government regulation and oversight, what is needed is that treatments be based on scientific evidence coupled with improved education for those who are offering the treatments. This film suggests that despite scientifically-based addiction treatments being available, many treatment facilities operate in isolation of the available data.

12-step programs

Various 12-step programs (e.g., Alcoholics Anonymous, Narcotics Anonymous) are well known and have worked for some individuals (Chappel & DuPont, 1999). Social support from others who are trying to beat the habit is fundamental to these programs, and in this sense they inherently take advantage of one of the most important ways of coping and helping people get through the rough patches, especially the frequent cravings that have to be dealt with. These programs can involve total immersion with a push to attend as many meetings as possible, to learn from others in a group-based setting, as well as on a one-on-one basis with veterans of the drug battle, and to help others beat their addiction. Yet the religious aspects that are often a component of 12-step approaches may cause some individuals to disengage from these programs. Drop-out rates are indeed common in 12-step programs (although records aren't kept at individual chapters) despite considerable efforts to encourage continued attendance. As 12-step programs alone may not be cure-alls, some of these have been integrated with other treatment strategies.

ADDICTED TO PROFITS

Gambling addiction has been a huge problem, although one doesn't hear about it nearly as much as drug addictions. Problem gamblers typically don't walk around in a drug-fueled haze, nor do they appear incoherent and they aren't violent, and so others might assume that a problem isn't present. However, a gambling addiction can be more devastating than a drug addiction. Drugs such as cocaine or alcohol can be used to a certain extent before the need is sated, at least for the moment. Similar satiety mechanisms may not exist for gambling. Individuals can gamble until they drop, and there's no shortage of different gambling venues. Cards, the ponies, football, baseball, basketball, at your buddy's house, at bars, at the casino, lottery tickets can be obtained at the gas station or the corner store, and even the internet is the gambler's best friend. It's not like the old days when the mob controlled gambling; today, governments have been reaping profits from poor sods hoping for a lucky break. In fact, in some places government agencies build and run their own casinos, or encourage privately owned casinos. Regardless of the venue they take their share in the form of taxes. This continues despite the harms done, because closing down these money pits would be politically unwise, and besides, governments have become addicted to the profits.

It is especially ironic that many government organizations responsible for the establishment of casinos also fund research to prevent or diminish addiction. Is this guilt money, a public relations

(Continued)

(Continued)

effort (look, we're doing good things!), or an effort to control what kind of research will be done? In some instances the research funded seems to be fairly reasonable, whereas in other instances it borders on silly. For instance, funds are spent to determine whether pop-up messages on slot machines to remind players to 'bet within their limits' (an oxymoron akin to 'doing irrational things rationally') will diminish gambling. Can anyone even begin to believe that this sort of messaging, particularly in the absence of other ongoing treatments, will have much of an effect on someone out to have fun at the slots, especially if that person already has a gambling problem? Given what we know about the influence of messaging and how to influence behavior, is there any hope that pop-up messages, which could be perceived as annoying, will have much of an impact on individuals hooked on gambling (even if nothing else has worked to curb this habit)? Somebody more suspicious than me would conclude that the fox is guarding the henhouse.

CBT and mindfulness

Cognitive behavioral therapy was introduced earlier as a means to treat several psychological conditions, and it is similarly used to limit relapse for drug addictions. Just as individuals being treated for depression learn to make new appraisals and deal with stressors appropriately, for those being treated for an addiction, a set of skills is learned to deal with events that would otherwise encourage recurrence. This entails acquiring new coping strategies and seeing events from a more positive perspective so that negative events won't trigger relapse. Individuals may also come to recognize when cravings are first emerging, and learn to deal with these situations (Carroll & Onken, 2005). This procedure is often used in conjunction with others and is particularly helpful given that it has persistent effects and is thus especially amenable to maintenance therapy (Carroll et al., 2004).

Mindfulness training has also seen some success in preventing addiction relapse (Witkiewitz et al., 2013), and the combination of mindfulness and CBT has been used to diminish craving and to deter prescription opioid misuse (Garland et al., 2014). When individuals were trained through mindfulness to focus on positive experiences in the moment, the need to use opioids to diminish chronic pain was reduced, as was the propensity to respond to cues that might otherwise promote opioid intake (Garland et al., 2014, 2015). Aside from opioids, mindfulness has been used to attenuate addiction to tobacco, alcohol, and other substances (Bowen et al., 2014).

Aversion therapy

Aversion therapies have been used to deal with addictions (e.g., rapid smoking in which individuals take a puff of a cigarette every few seconds, while concurrently focusing on the ill feelings created) in the hope that negative reactions will be created by engaging in unwanted behaviors. A review of this literature concluded that it might be premature to consider these to be effective approaches to reduce smoking (Hajek et al., 2013). Another procedure used in treating alcohol addiction was for individuals to take a drug, disulfiram (Antabuse), which blocks the degradation of alcohol, so if the addicted individual has a drink, the alcohol product acetaldehyde increases in the blood quickly, resulting in feelings of a hangover. Of course, this requires that individuals remember to take the drug, but those who are addicted might choose to take a brief holiday from the prescribed routine, and thus resume their addiction. However, if disulfiram is used as part of a larger treatment program, then positive results may be obtained (Krampe et al., 2006).

Transtheoretical Model of behavior change

It will be recalled that the use of the Transtheoretical Model of behavior change (TTM) considers an individual's readiness to act in particular ways and guides individuals through a series of stages to obtain behavioral change (see Chapter 6). An important aspect of this stage model is the assumption that people might encounter problems and that relapse may occur, and should this happen, they are encouraged to get back into the program and continue through the stages, eventually abstaining from drugs for long periods. This program might not be any better than others for smoking or alcohol cessation (e.g., Callaghan et al., 2007), but it can be combined with other treatments (e.g., mindfulness or CBT) to obtain still better outcomes. As with so many other therapeutic approaches, the effectiveness of this stage model is variable and it might be more beneficial if it were tailored to individual needs.

SOCIAL CURES AS MEANS TO BEAT ADDICTION

Once individuals have kicked a habit, regardless of the approach used, it's essential that they receive support from friends and family in the hope that they don't fall back. But there may be more to social influences than just helping individuals stay clean. If all my friends are dressing in a particular way, I might do so as well. Likewise, if all my friends are smoking, the odds are that I will too. But it also works the other way. If my friends all decide to stop smoking, and if they all see it as being very negative, then this might encourage me to change my behaviors. Our social identity is very powerful, and although our ingroup can influence us in negative ways, it can also be used as a social cure (Jetten et al., 2012).

Programs such as CBT, mindfulness and TTM certainly have positive effects, but it is possible that they might be more effective if they were initiated on a group basis comprising individuals who share an identity. As we've discussed, 12-step programs take advantage of social connections that can support withdrawal; perhaps other treatment strategies can similarly draw upon social support.

Government interventions

Municipal, city, regional, and federal governments have a huge sway on addictions that involve the consumption of legal substances such as tobacco, alcohol, and in some places cannabis. Despite their hazards, it's difficult for governments to make these substances illegal. Prohibition didn't work out decades ago, and it won't likely be effective now. However, governments have acted in some positive ways to discourage some unhealthy behaviors, for example by prohibiting smoking in public places, and increasing taxes on cigarettes and alcohol (Walsh & Gordon, 1986). As well, some government-funded organizations (e.g., American Cancer Society) provide valuable web pages that might be useful in helping individuals (or advising family members) to identify the correct steps to abandon addictions.

DRUG TREATMENTS TO CURB ADDICTIONS

Reducing the rewarding or euphoric effects of drugs

Various drug treatments, alone or in combination with behaviorally-based therapies, have been used to deal with addictions. For instance, methadone or buprenorphine have served as *opioid replacement therapy* for the treatment of dependence. These agents diminish the symptoms of opioid withdrawal, and at high doses diminish the euphoric effects of heroin and morphine, thereby reducing their use (Mattick et al., 2003). As much as agents such as methadone have been effective in diminishing problems related to addiction, it has not been universally accepted as an ideal treatment strategy. It was argued, for instance, that methadone doesn't actually reduce addiction, but simply keeps addicted individuals compliant and under control by authorities (Bennett, 2011). This could well be the case if methadone were used in isolation of other treatment approaches. When methadone maintenance therapy also incorporates behaviorally-based strategies to diminish addiction, it is often effective, although considerable inter-individual and sex differences exist (Bawor et al., 2014). It is of clinical relevance that the effectiveness of treatments such as methadone may be dependent on genetic variability related to the presence of particular opioid receptor genes (Bauer et al., 2014).

Several other opioid replacement therapies have been used to treat addictions, as has the opioid antagonist naltrexone in controlling alcohol addiction (Latt et al., 2002). Similarly, benzodiazepines have been utilized to limit delirium associated with alcohol withdrawal, and antiepileptic medications (gabapentin, valproate) diminish some difficulties inherent in barbiturate or benzodiazepine withdrawal. Moreover, as mentioned earlier, gene polymorphisms have been associated with various addictions, and it is possible that their presence might serve as biomarkers to predict the choice of treatments.

The most effective treatment for tobacco addiction has been nicotine replacement therapy (Elrashidi & Ebbert, 2014), but once again, no single pharmacological therapy has been effective for all individuals, and it is likely that approaches need to be adopted concurrently to obtain optimal effects. Brain imaging during peak craving periods could distinguish smokers from one another (Wilson & Sayette, 2015), and it is conceivable that such brain changes might offer clues concerning the usefulness of specific strategies in diminishing the propensity to continue smoking.

SOFT SELLING TOBACCO ADDICTION

For some time, those attempting to quit smoking have used aids in the form of gum or sprays to provide them with nicotine, but without the harmful effects stemming from the cigarette smoke. Recently, a new variation of this approach, electronic cigarettes, has made a dramatic and rapid impact on the market. The e-cigarettes dispense water vapor that has a dose of nicotine in it (and comes in a variety of flavors), thereby providing the nicotine hit and satisfying the oral habit, but without the harmful components of cigarette smoke.

Use of e-cigarettes (or vaping) could potentially be good for those who are already smokers, as it diminishes the intake of some of the bad products found in actual cigarettes (although it could serve as a cue that draws people back to real cigarettes). One supposes that for those who have repeatedly been unsuccessful in quitting this might be a realistic alternative. But there are many who worry about the downside to vaping. Young people have been catching onto this, which may be a step towards cigarette smoking. As well, e-cigarettes and genuine cigarettes share some physiological actions, such as diminishing exhaled nitric oxide, which might reflect inflammation associated with airway damage (Marini et al., 2014). As well, e-cigarettes may increase vulnerability to viral illness (Sussan et al., 2015), and nanoparticles present within e-cigarettes are able to trigger inflammatory responses that have been linked to heart disease, asthma, and diabetes (Grana et al., 2014) and may cause lung damage (Lerner et al., 2015). A solvent used to make flavored e-cigarettes produces acetaldehyde and formaldehyde, which may be carcinogenic (Kosmider et al., 2014), and even second-hand vapors from e-cigarettes, which have less particulate matter than real cigarettes, can be dangerous because of the presence of metals, such as chromium and nickel (Saffari et al., 2014).

This said, there are hundreds of e-cigarette brands, often working in different ways and delivering different toxicants. Thus, it's uncertain whether the available data are relevant to all brands or only to some. Making sense of the available data is also problematic given that many published studies were in a conflict of interest as they might have been funded by the e-cigarette producers. Furthermore, the scientific rigor of many studies is also questionable as very few assessed the effects of e-cigarettes using a double-blind procedure (two studies have adopted this approach, and the long-term effects of e-cigarettes and the influence of chronic use are simply unknown). A systematic review of the topic (Pisinger & Døssing, 2014) ended up concluding that a firm conclusion couldn't be made concerning the safety of e-cigarettes given the paucity of good, uncontaminated data, but that they should not be considered to be harmless.

Despite the potential dangers of e-cigarettes, the war for market share has become intense, and a new generation of the substitutes have been developed that burn hotter, allowing for a greater nicotine punch, but which also produce a greater amount of dangerous side products. Things will become even more intense when Big Tobacco brings out their version of smokeless cigarettes, or when legislative procedures make it sufficiently difficult and expensive for small e-cigarette manufacturers to survive, so that they'll eventually be sold to the larger competitors, namely Big Tobacco, who have the resources at hand.

Diminishing cravings

One approach to diminish addiction has been to block certain types of receptor so that illicit drugs would no longer elicit their euphoric effects. Other drugs, such as the $GABA_B$ agonist baclofen (Kemstro, Lioresal), acts to diminish drug cravings so that those who are addicted feel indifferent to addictive agents. The effectiveness of these treatments isn't unique to particular addictive substances, having been used to reduce alcohol addiction and relapse (Leggio et al., 2010) and cannabis dependence syndrome (Imbert et al., 2014). Moreover, several agents that target $GABA_B$ receptors other than baclofen have also shown promising action in relation to cocaine, nicotine, amphetamine, and alcohol dependence (Filip et al., 2015).

There are still other exciting prospects that are relevant for treatments of addiction. One of these involves changes of AMPA, a particular type of glutamate receptor. Specifically, as an addiction may represent a firmly established memory mediated by sensitized neuronal connections, it was reasoned that disrupting memory processes that involved AMPA receptors would also diminish cravings elicited by cocaine-related cues among mice in withdrawal from the drug. In line with this prediction, craving in rodents could be diminished by manipulating AMPA receptor functioning through optogenetically-provoked neuronal changes (Pascoli et al., 2014). This demonstration was exceptionally important in showing the contribution of AMPA receptors in relation to craving, but as it involved a surgical procedure to insert the probe directly into the brain, it isn't practical for human use. As it happens, however, administering a drug that altered the functioning of particular glutamate receptors, without the need for a surgical manipulation, was also able to attenuate craving, at least for short periods (Loweth et al., 2014). These findings provide an interesting target for drug treatments that might attenuate cravings during withdrawal, thereby preventing relapse.

SURPRISING WAYS OF DEALING WITH ADDICTION

We see it repeatedly. Treatments initially developed for one condition have beneficial actions for others. As we discussed earlier, in some instances the second use is more potent than that for which the drug was initially developed. It is significant that if the drug has already been approved for another condition and has been assessed with respect to safety, it can be brought to market more readily (and inexpensively for drug companies) than new drugs. This has been seen with respect to lorcaserin (Belviq), which has received approval as a weight loss remedy, and could diminish smoking. Likewise, 'topirimate', which has been used to treat epilepsy and migraine, can diminish cocaine cravings and intake (Johnson et al., 2013) and it may have such effects (based on animal studies) with respect to alcohol addiction.

Ibogaine, a psychoactive compound derived from Tabernanthe iboga, a plant used in some rituals in West Central Africa, has been said to be useful in treating addictions. It has a long history as a psychedelic agent, and isn't overly popular because of the lengthy duration of its effects. This compound may create a hallucinogenic state that lasts for several days, after which addictions may be markedly diminished, although it may take more than a single session over some months before a relatively good outcome is established (Alper et al., 1999). Although Ibogaine has been around for some time, it has been on a restricted list of drugs owing to risks associated with its use, and thus detailed analyses of its anti-addiction properties have been limited, although other related drugs are now in development.

SUMMARY

The etiological processes for addictions vary across individuals and addictions of any sort involve multiple interactive processes. Numerous psychosocial and experiential factors influence risk for addictions, ranging from stressful experiences, the desire to fit in, peer pressures, to prenatal challenges and genetic endowment. However, once established, all addictions are difficult to beat, and even after the demons have been beaten, environmental triggers, comprising stressors or reminder stimuli, readily cause the reinstatement of the addiction.

Although many addictions share common features, differences also exist between them, and treatments effective for one type of addiction might be less effective for another. It also appears that the characteristics of addiction may vary appreciably as the addiction forms and strengthens. The early desire for the rewarding effects of a drug may be superseded by the need to alleviate negative feelings associated with not hitting up. As well, the addiction may be maintained by intense craving, coupled with irrational thinking, disturbed judgment, and impulsivity.

If an addiction is provoked or fostered by stressful experiences, and this is accompanied by warped stressor appraisal processes and the use of ineffective coping strategies, then treatment strategies ought to target these maladaptive characteristics. If, instead, the addiction is related to altered reward processes, then a different therapeutic strategy would be needed. Regardless of how or why the addiction initially arose, there typically isn't just one behavior or impulse altered in an addiction, and treatment might need to be multipronged. Among other things, treatments could involve ways to reduce craving, reduce the rewarding value of secondary cues, alter memories associated with drug reward, and training in effective methods of coping with withdrawal and other stressors. At the end of the day, as with other pathological conditions, individualized treatments will likely be called for, and because biological processes associated with the addiction may be permanently altered, therapy and social support will be necessary even long after individuals have been dry.

Treatment of addiction is difficult, and it seems that prevention has been moving ahead in baby steps. There has been a search to develop a vaccine to prevent addictions from occurring (i.e., the drug would be attacked by immune factors) and there has been some success in animal models of cocaine addiction (e.g., Lockner et al., 2015). Such treatments could be useful in high-risk populations provided that people are prepared to cooperate. The perspective offered by Volkow have been especially important not only in defining the mechanisms associated with addictions, but also because her views place a humane face on addiction. As in the case of other psychological disorders, addiction might not reflect a character flaw, but an unfortunate physiological disturbance that has made it difficult for the individual to help themselves. Cravings ordinarily associated with rewarding stimuli might be dealt with through self-will and control, but when the functioning of the prefrontal cortex is disturbed, cravings will not easily be dismissed. This isn't simply the abdication of common sense, but reflects the hijacking of will by addictive drugs.

14 Major Physical Illnesses

WHAT DO YOU REALLY KNOW ABOUT YOUR ILLNESS AND YOUR DOCTOR?

Most of us have a family physician that we trust with our well-being even though we might not know anything about them other than the university that s/he graduated from (based on diplomas on their wall). When we encounter relatively severe health risks, and need to obtain specialized care, we usually obtain a referral from our primary physician and then dutifully go see the specialist, whom we also know nothing about, although given the delay encountered for an appointment, s/he must be in great demand.

Upon meeting the specialist we might want specific information about the condition and its treatment. Among other things, we want to know the chances of the recommended treatment, say complex surgery, leading to death 'on the table' or soon after surgery, the likelihood of the treatment being successful in that the problem(s) will be eliminated, the chances of complications developing following surgery, the degree of pain and discomfort that can be expected, and for how long? In response, we might be told that the pain will be controllable, but that predictions about success and complications are difficult as the statistics are based on populations and don't apply to a given individual. If we persist, we might obtain a vague response, such as "well, death or disability occurs during or soon after surgery in 10% of patients", but the surgeon might add "but, as I said, this is a population statistic. As you're young and in good shape, you're not obese and don't smoke, I expect that the risks for you are far lower". So if the physician doesn't say the latter part to me, I wonder if that means that my risk is appreciably higher than 10%. After all, for each person below an average point there ought to be one above this mark. Also, just as 'success' may vary as a function of the patient's characteristics, a degree of variance may be attributable to the surgeon. What is the success achieved by this particular surgeon? Do 19% of their patients encounter complications, or is it 1%? There are ways to find this out on your own, but most people never do. In fact, most people probably do more homework before buying a car, and finding out about servicing and advantages of each brand and model, than they do with respect to the surgeon who will be operating on them. Yes, some surgeons and GPs graduated first in their class, but some graduated last. Furthermore, in some places 'report cards' can be obtained for individual cardiac surgeons, but this likely hasn't had a great effect on referrals to particular surgeons. In fact, it seems that cardiologists might not refer patients to the best available surgeon or the surgeon to whom they would refer their own family member (Brown et al., 2013).

FEATURES OF CHRONIC ILLNESS

Each chronic illness has its own unique features and hardships, and each has the capacity to turn life upside down. When healthy, we might live under the illusion (delusion?) that life's just great, only to be shocked into reality when something occurs that quickly changes this perspective. Whether it stems from some sort of accident or the emergence of a disease, life changes are thrust upon us that we hadn't imagined or been prepared for, all in less than the blink of an eye. In this chapter we'll consider:

- distress that accompanies chronic illnesses and how this is related to psychological well-being
- quality of life (QoL), particularly as some treatments may produce recovery from illness, but at what cost?
- methods of diminishing the anxiety and depression often associated with illness, and the contribution of social and experiential factors in coping with illness
- appraisals and coping in relation to illness, including the wrong and some of the right approaches to use, and roadblocks that undermine our abilities to deal with illness.

QUALITY OF LIFE

Satisfaction with life can mean different things to various people, but we generally consider this in terms of multiple factors (health, wealth, education, living conditions, social support and feelings of belonging, leisure time activities, family, social role and functioning) that contribute to *Quality of Life* (QoL). This general well-being is sometimes considered at an individual level but, as we've already seen, QoL is not simply a reflection of what we and our close others think or do, but is also what happens within our society at large. Likewise, having adequate QoL in one domain (e.g., financial resources) doesn't ensure that other domains are similarly satisfying (Kahnemen & Deaton, 2010).

Even when healthy, an individual's quality of life may be impoverished as a result of environmental and psychosocial conditions (e.g., when poverty is a strain, when discrimination is prevalent, or when an individual's job is excessively demanding), and in the context of severe or chronic illnesses various aspects of QoL may decline. This not only occurs because of pain, discomfort, or other stressors that are present, but also because of difficulties engaging in previously cherished activities. As difficult as it might be, however, individuals may adapt to their situation, accepting that 'it is what it is', and report that their general QoL is still fairly good. Being able to accept, or at least cope with, this new situation is essential to limit psychological and physical disturbances that could ensue. For instance, among individuals who had been diagnosed with ischemic heart disease, their subsequent QoL predicted readmission to hospital owing to cardiac problems and 5-year all-cause mortality was elevated (Hansen et al., 2014). Likewise, in another study depressive symptoms prior to heart surgery predicted later cardiac hospitalization, sustained surgical pain, and failure to return to previous activity as long as 6 months after surgery (Burg et al., 2003). Table 14.1 indicates the main functions of having a QoL measure.

Table 14.1   Quality of life measures . . .

- Can tell us how the individual is generally faring
- Can tell us whether the treatments are having an impact on the individual's perceptions and satisfaction with life
- Can be used to forecast future health
- Permit the identification of specific aspects of life that may be most affected under certain conditions (Kaplan, 2003)
- Might be instrumental in providing feedback concerning which components of care are optimal in affecting well-being (Kaplan, 2003)

Measuring QoL

As QoL may vary in relation to specific health conditions, scales were developed for particular issues, such as experiences of heart disease, cancer, stroke, diabetes, or mental health difficulties, as well as various social and environmental conditions. A questionnaire developed by the World Health Organization, titled the WHOQOL-BREF, was meant to be useful across different cultures, and focuses on broad domains, including physical health, psychological health, social relationships, and environment.

Inclusion of QoL in appraisals of illness may be especially informative. A decline of symptoms might suggest that an illness is abating, but this doesn't necessarily translate as improved life satisfaction. Often, improvement of life satisfaction may lag behind symptom alleviation, and QoL instruments allow an analysis of health quality over time (Normand et al., 2005) and permit comparisons between the effectiveness of different treatment regimens (Taylor & Aspinwall, 1990).

ADJUSTMENT TO CHRONIC ILLNESS

Having been through a serious illness, some individuals are able to maintain, or regain, their physical and mental health and to experience a high level of quality of life. As described in Chapter 1, many psychosocial dimensions contribute to individuals being more or less resilient. Cognitive restructuring (e.g., finding meaning) may facilitate an individual's ability to deal with stressors related to illness (or other traumas), but for others, finding meaning isn't in the cards, and they simply feel overwhelmed and psychologically exhausted by their illness. Likewise, an earlier sickness experience, by virtue of having allowed meaning making, can engender resilience among some individuals, but others, having been worn down by the experience, might simply find it too difficult to handle yet another bout of illness (allostatic overload).

Predictors of resilience, as we discussed earlier, include personality characteristics, positive experiences, and being flexible in the coping strategies used. Moreover, a mindful and accepting orientation toward experience may facilitate psychological resilience in response to trauma and illness (Thompson et al., 2011). To be sure, it can be difficult to train individuals to become optimistic, hardy, or to have good self-esteem, so that they will become more resilient, or to translate resilience into a form that will facilitate treatment and prevention of further illness (Rutter, 2012). Nonetheless, procedures such as CBT, mindfulness training, and other psychotherapeutic methods can be adopted to enhance QoL. Such procedures may or may not have an effect on an illness, but if nothing else, they can facilitate positive self-evaluation, and encourage the feeling that life is purposeful and meaningful, that quality relations are available, continued growth and development is possible, as well as promote feelings of self-determination and the capacity to manage one's life effectively (Fava & Tomba, 2009). As in the case of many treatment and intervention strategies, optimal outcomes can be obtained through resilience-focused interventions that are tailored to specific contexts and individuals (Tol et al., 2013). Most of us will likely become ill in some manner, or we might simply wither with time, and resilience might reflect not simply the ability to prevent or overcome illness, but our ability to accept and adapt to changes.

Depression and anxiety in response to physical illness

For patients waiting for medical procedures to be performed or awaiting test results (e.g., related to cancer or genetic tests concerning risk for an illness), the anticipatory strain and anxiety can be pronounced (Kyranou et al., 2014). Besides being distressing in its own right, anxiety can also act as a stressor that aggravates illnesses and may interfere with recovery following surgery in adults (Celestin et al., 2009) and in children (Kain et al., 2006).

Individuals with physical illnesses, pain, or discomfort, who are also encountering uncertainty, and lack of control over life, might also find their other psychological coping resources strained. This is particularly apt to occur among older people, who usually have fewer methods of contending with these challenges, thereby increasing the emergence of other illnesses such as depression. It was similarly observed that depression was frequent among individuals diagnosed with rheumatoid arthritis who had been experiencing psychosocial problems and who had inflexible coping strategies (Gåfvels et al., 2014). Almost one-fifth of patients with angina, myocardial infarction, or chronic heart failure, which are usually associated with aging, subsequently developed depressive illnesses (Mavrides & Nemeroff, 2013), and a similar outcome was apparent among individuals who had suffered a stroke (Robinson, 2003) or were diagnosed with cancer (Mitchell et al., 2011). In essence, the symptoms of physical illnesses and poor psychological adjustment feed on one another to make a bad situation still worse, ultimately leading to a poorer prognosis (Lichtman et al., 2014). Table 14.2 outlines some of the consequences associated with depression that occur as a result of illness.

Table 14.2   Outcomes of depression secondary to an illness

- Diminished participation in the rehabilitation process
- Poorer treatment compliance
- Less positive functional outcomes following rehabilitation (Sinyor et al., 1986)
- More frequent and longer hospitalizations
- Elevated mortality rates
- Can be accompanied by cognitive distortions, including marked negativity and catastrophizing

---

Multiple factors play into the development of depression that occurs in response to illness. Individuals might become increasingly more aware of their own frailty and potential mortality, their lack of control in determining their own fate, increased feelings of isolation and loneliness, pain that often accompanies illness, and the obvious need to change their life-style, sometimes in very dramatic ways. Furthermore, in some instances the uncertainty about an illnesses progression and the *watchful waiting* that accompanies this has been linked to depression (Colagreco et al., 2014). Among elderly individuals who encounter chronic illnesses, the risk for depression is exceptionally high, although this is not just a result of diminished physical health and the imminence of death (Sutin et al., 2013). Decline in the meaningfulness of life, overprotection by the caregiver (which might signify a feeling of lost independence by the patient), and the individual's perceived social role functioning were also predictive of depression emerging (Schmid et al., 2012).

Depression present prior to physical illness can have profound repercussions on the course and recovery from illness. Thus, it would be of considerable value to have patients assessed for comorbid conditions upon first being admitted for treatment (Dubljanin Raspopović et al., 2014). This is especially important as depression that exists prior to an illness, or that is created by an illness, not only limits recovery, but may contribute to the appearance of still other disorders (Van Lieshout et al., 2009).

Preventing and treating illness-related depression

Depression secondary to a medical condition can evolve as a result of the neurobiological changes brought about by the stress that accompanies illness or may develop secondary to the chemical changes that are instigated by the illness itself (Anisman et al., 2008). So long as the illness is present, these neurochemical stress responses may limit the effectiveness of cognitively-based treatment strategies. Similarly, treatment may be hampered because some antidepressant drugs may not be tolerated well by patients with other illnesses. For instance, among patients with chronic liver disease, in whom depression occurs at a rate of about 30%, SSRIs and SNRIs in low doses must be used to avoid side effects (Mullish et al., 2014). Among MS patients, depression can be treated by SSRIs, which is well tolerated, but most of the SNRIs are not. Thus there needs to be selectivity in what treatments are administered, and CBT and mindfulness might be good options (Pérez et al., 2015).

Collaborative care

The view has become increasingly accepted that collaborative care (also referred to as integrative care), which involves the concurrent or sequential input of varied specialties, may be preferable to usual care procedures. Indeed, patients who received personalized psychological treatments as a component of their rehabilitation for heart or diabetes-related problems fared better than those who received usual treatment (Katon et al., 2010). Similarly, collaborative care comprising drug treatment and psychotherapy was associated with fewer subsequent heart problems relative to individuals who had received standard treatment. However, the benefits of collaborative care aren't always so straightforward. Based on a meta-analysis, it was concluded, for instance, that although collaborative care diminished depressive symptoms among diabetic patients, it did not markedly influence glycemic control, indicating that beating temptation related to food may be more of an individual endeavor (Atlantis et al., 2014). Nonetheless, it generally appears that attending to patients' psychological distress and depression associated with illness can have positive consequences for the individual's well-being, and an important by-product of this is that it may reduce the strain on stretched medical services.

Enriching environments and healing the brain

In considering recovery from stroke, Corbett and his associates (2014) made important observations that have implications that go beyond stroke itself. They suggested that following stroke and related injuries the cellular environment is reminiscent of early brain development, and is characterized by neuronal growth and neuroplasticity (perhaps in an effort on the part of the brain to heal itself). Thus, soon after stroke, environmental enrichment and task-specific therapy that can influence neuroplasticity may allow for appropriate synaptic connections to be formed and hence facilitate recovery. Although physical rehabilitation has long been at the cornerstone of improving QoL among stroke patients, it seems likely that rehabilitation programs ought to be broadened and adopted soon after injury has occurred. This brings up the issue of whether the reasoning offered by Corbett et al. (2014) can be taken further. There is broad belief that lowered growth factors are involved in several psychological disorders, such as depression, which can be instigated by stressors (Duman, 2014). As such, enriched environments and having patients as active as possible may be important tools to diminish depression associated with several physical illness, and perhaps aid in recovery of these illnesses.

APPRAISING AND COPING WITH ILLNESS

Appropriate appraisals as a good first step

Resilience in response to illnesses, such as heart disease, esophageal cancer, and traumatic brain injury, has been linked to how individuals appraise their situation (e.g., McCabe & Barnason, 2012). Analyses of patients with rheumatoid arthritis, COPD, or psoriasis indicated that having a strong illness identity (I am a sick person), belief in more severe consequences, and using passive coping strategies were associated with worse outcomes on social and disease-specific measures of functioning (Scharloo et al., 1998). These outcomes can be influenced by previous illnesses, as well as other traumatic experiences, possibly because the cognitive restructuring (e.g., finding meaning) that might have occurred in response to an earlier illness could enhance the ability to appraise and cope with a further stressor. In other instances the previous illness or other stressors could instead act against well-being as individuals may simply have experienced more than their share of distress (Kimron & Cohen, 2012).

Anticipation, uncertainty, and watchful waiting

How we generally perceive stressors, and this certainly applies to our perception of illness symptoms, is related to the presence of uncertainty and ambiguity, coupled with the anticipation of negative outcomes (Hoth et al., 2013). Severe illnesses are replete with uncertainties, as patients wonder what treatments are planned for them, whether they'll get a voice in this, and what the odds are of a successful outcome. Watchful waiting is distressing and can potentially influence the course of an illness.

With one exception, which we'll deal with later, it seems that as uncertainty diminishes, well-being improves. Conversely, those patients who are especially intolerant of uncertainty may fare relatively poorly. Greater distress and poorer emotional well-being, for instance, was reported among lung cancer patients who were intolerant of uncertainty (Kurita et al., 2013). Likewise, ambiguity regarding hepatitis C was associated with increased depressive symptoms, fatigue, and pain perception (Bailey et al., 2009), and among women anticipating breast cancer surgery, worry about the procedures, concerns regarding what would be found during surgery, and patient optimism versus pessimism, were similarly related to the distress reported (Montgomery et al., 2003). The damaging effects of uncertainty and unpredictability are common in relation to many illnesses, especially when the disease trajectory is unpredictable. Patients with HIV/AIDS, for instance, might experience periods during which they are exceptionally unwell, followed by a degree of recovery and good functioning, only to develop a further infection. Obviously, this is a terrible situation for the patient, and has serious implications for caregivers. Like uncertainty, many of the variables described in relation to stressor appraisals, such as self-efficacy and controllability, also contribute to appraisals of illness and the consequences that are seen with respect to illness progression.

Perceived control and coping with chronic illness

Many illnesses are distinct from one another in relation to the challenges experienced (e.g., with respect to pain, cognitive disturbances, treatment-related difficulties), so we can likely count on different coping strategies being involved in dealing with them. Individuals might do all the right things to maintain their well-being, or if they're already ill they might follow everything they've been instructed to do, and in this way they might feel that they can exert control over their illness. Some individuals might have the view that a belief in God and prayer will help them survive serious illness, and in this way they too are exerting a degree of control over their situation (even though they are actually abdicating control and handing this over to God). There is little doubt that self-efficacy and control have beneficial effects in relation to many illnesses, and as we saw in relation to cancer and heart disease, these beliefs can enhance poor mood that might otherwise accompany these conditions, and may even influence the course of the disease or the adjustment to it. This is not only apparent among adults, as perceived stress and control, as well as low socioeconomic status, were associated with health outcomes (e.g., pulmonary problems related to asthma) among children and adolescents (Griffin & Chen, 2006).

When faced with uncertain, uncontrollable events, some individuals fall back on emotion-focused strategies, which most often aren't particularly effective. Individuals with low grade brain tumors who adopted emotion-related strategies were most likely to become depressed and anxious (Keeling et al., 2013), and emotion-focused strategies mediated the relationship between illness perceptions and later anxiety and depression among colostomy and cardiac patients (Karademas et al., 2011; Knowles et al., 2014). In some instances, avoidant coping strategies are effective as this allows patients to continue life with fewer distressing thoughts. However, it can also be counterproductive, promoting symptom aggravation, as observed among type 1 diabetic patients (Frenzel et al., 1988), possibly because this way of coping interferes with appropriate self-management of the illness. In contrast, illness-related distress was found to be lower among individuals who adopted an active role in understanding and coping with their condition and who had a high degree of conscientiousness and self-efficacy, as well as an internal locus of control (Affleck, Tennen et al., 1987; Christensen et al., 2002). Similarly, a positive-focused coping strategy and cognitions of having control predicted enhanced psychological well-being among esophageal cancer survivors (Dempster et al., 2011).

As with most stressors, there likely isn't a single coping method that's best for all illnesses or, for that matter, one that is compatible with the characteristics of each individual. Still, from what has already been said, it seems that emotion-focused coping isn't a preferred coping strategy, and participants may be better off using active strategies or those that involve obtaining help in some fashion (e.g., information or support). However, as we also know, in some instances emotion-focused coping can be advantageous (Stanton et al., 1994), especially as it can serve as a plea for help, and simply venting frustration can have positive effects.

I'M HOME, AT LEAST FOR THE MOMENT

Patients in hospital can hardly wait to get home to enjoy their own little sanctuary. So, it's doubly distressing when shortly after being released, they find themselves readmitted to hospital. This isn't at all uncommon, with 11.8% of seriously ill patients in the US being readmitted to hospital within 30 days of initial release (Ottenbacher et al., 2014), and 20% of patients go through this experience over 3–6 months. The most common illnesses that have prompted readmission are chronic heart failure, ischemic heart disease, atrial fibrillation, diabetes, cancer, COPD, and chronic kidney disease, with 8% being avoidable conditions (Donzé et al., 2013). It is possible that some patients are released earlier than they should be because of a crunch for space, although this statement would no doubt be met with considerable disagreement from some physicians and administrators. What probably would receive little debate, in contrast, is that there is a desperate need for follow-up care, particularly for elderly patients.

Social support in the face of illness

The value of social support is especially poignant among individuals with severe illnesses, especially if they believe in the controllability/curability of the disease (Scharloo et al., 1998). Support from family members is very effective in this regard, particularly when self-reliance and personal achievement are reinforced. Conversely, critical, overprotective, controlling, and distracting family responses to illness management are more likely to be accompanied by negative outcomes for patients experiencing any of a variety of illnesses (Rosland et al., 2012).

As in so many other situations, social support from non-family members can also be exceptionally potent in helping individuals deal with illness, serving multiple functions, such as a source of distraction, encouragement, and emotional support, as well as functional support in helping to get jobs done. Support is typically received from our ingroup (friends, family) with whom we share an identity (Haslam & Reicher, 2006; Jetten et al., 2012), but positive outcomes are often most apparent when support comes from individuals who are currently dealing with similar illnesses or situations, as they have become, for all intents, the ingroup that "understands my pain" (Spiegel, 1994).

As positive as it might be, social support can be a two-edged sword in situations involving illness. Although most individuals appreciate receiving support, it can also undermine their self-esteem if they feel less competent in contending with their situation. As well, coping by seeking instrumental support has also been linked to depression, as was a perceived loss of role functioning, underscoring the view that some patients might wish not to have to rely on others, but instead may want to maintain their independence and self-efficacy (Arran et al., 2014). But these are minor issues compared to the possibility of the individual seeking support only to run into unsupportive responses from others. As we saw earlier, a single unsupportive social interaction can undo the positive effects of multiple supportive experiences and can be destructive to an individual's psychological and physical health (Ingram et al., 2001; Song & Ingram, 2002).

EXPECTING AND HAVING SUPPORT

Support is usually positive for those with illnesses, but may nonetheless vary with several factors. The type of support received is, to be sure, fundamental to its effectiveness. Wishing for emotional support but obtaining some other form of support (e.g., advice) may be seen as an unsupportive response that makes things worse. When support comes from the right people, it may be especially desirable and useful, but it is often time-limited, as those offering it might come to feel that they need to get on with their own lives. As much as this is understandable, for those who are ill and spend their time in misery, except for distraction and instrumental support obtained from friends, even modest withdrawal may be interpreted as an unsupportive response ("you know who your friends are when the chips are down"). From the perspective of the person in need of help, as my friend Aviva Freedman thoughtfully explained, "They aren't 'putting upon' you, but instead are relying on you".

Certain illnesses garner considerable support, whereas others don't, and in some cases affected individuals may be shunned. Those diagnosed with cancer typically receive considerable support. Diabetes receives some acknowledgment, but not much in the way of support. Sadly, few people gather to the side of those with a mental illness, probably fewer than to those infected with a viral illness.

STIGMA

Discrimination and its cousin stigmatization come in multiple forms, including racial, ethnic, and cultural, as well as gender and gender orientation, and they can be targeted on the basis of what a person looks like (e.g., burn victims or those who are obese), or how they behave (extremely introverted). The stigma can be blatant, or it might comprise microaggressions ("hey, for a woman, you're not half bad at math"), which are more subtle but discriminatory nonetheless (Sue et al., 2007). Regardless of the form that it takes, it can be exceedingly distressing, and can undermine psychological well-being and also influence immune disturbances, diabetes, and cardiovascular illness (Bombay et al., 2009; Thoits, 2010).

Stigma related to illness

Enacted stigma (referring to negative attitudes coming from the public, including health care professionals, clergy, or employers) has been associated with numerous illnesses. Individuals with HIV/AIDS have for years experienced discrimination and stigmatization, and having family members turn on the affected individual is obviously destructive. It has been shown that, remarkably, although the families of children with HIV/AIDS and those with cancer exhibited comparable family functioning, both coped through reframing (cognitive restructuring) and both tended to seek support from family members; the parents of children with HIV/AIDS were more reluctant to seek social support from outside the family (Martin et al., 2012). Evidently, the stigma associated with HIV/AIDS can brand whole families.

This also seems to be true of the stigma associated with mental illness despite such disorders occurring in 20% of the population, which means that there's a high likelihood that most of us have someone close to us who is affected. The stigma among those directly affected is sufficiently powerful to undermine help-seeking, and even when help is offered it may be rejected (Roness et al., 2005). In fact, only 30% of individuals with a mental disorder seek help (Roness et al., 2005), and those who need it most, including those who are suicidal, are most apt to shy away from doing so (Wilson & Deane, 2010).

This brings us to the issue of stigma as it relates to other illnesses. I suspect that many people will respond to this statement with "what stigma?", but the sad reality is that it isn't uncommon. Enacted stigma has been associated with numerous physical illnesses. Cancer patients have reported the presence of stigma from others, which was related to poorer QoL, elevated psychological distress, and depression (Chambers et al., 2012; Gonzalez & Jacobsen, 2012). To some extent, the stigma experienced among lung cancer patients, which is generally more than that experienced by those with other types of cancer, stems from the view that patients are responsible for their illness because they smoked. Indeed, many patients who develop lung cancer feel considerable guilt and shame, to the extent that they might not fully disclose their feelings to their partner or to their physician, even though they might need psychological counseling (Dikse et al., 2014). While smoking is a great risk factor for lung cancer, there is a sizable minority that develop the disease even though they have never smoked, and they too report feeling stigmatized (Cataldo et al., 2012; Chapple et al., 2004). Other illnesses that have been associated with stigma have included hepatitis C (Marinho & Barreira, 2013) and liver cirrhosis (Vaughn-Sandler et al., 2014), possibly because they have been associated with the use of tainted needles and alcohol abuse, respectively.

Oddly, stigma has also been reported among individuals with lupus erythematosus (Sehlo & Bahlas, 2013) and inflammatory bowel disease (Taft et al., 2009), even though nobody would argue that these individuals bore any responsibility for their illness. Likewise, it is not uncommon for individuals with neurological conditions, such as epilepsy and amyotrophic lateral sclerosis (ALS), to experience stigmatization (e.g., Molina et al., 2013). Elderly people often have such experiences as well, especially if their condition is viewed as a 'nuisance', as in the case of elderly women with urinary incontinence (Heintz et al., 2013). These are a few examples of stigma experienced by individuals with a variety of medical conditions, but there are many others. People with illnesses have so much they have to contend with, it is regrettable they should have to go through any further strain emanating from others.

Self-stigma

It's unfortunate that in addition to the stigma expressed by other people (*public stigma*), individuals may come to apply it to themselves (*self-stigma*) when they become aware of the negative stereotype applied to them. This may, in turn, foster a decline of self-esteem and self-efficacy, as well as promote shame, self-blame, fear of the judgment of others, and a need to maintain and cope with secrecy (Corrigan et al., 2011). Predictably, the development of self-stigma may result in diminished efforts to reach particular goals owing to the development of the attitude of "why try?" (Corrigan et al., 2009).

Structural stigma

Stigma may be encountered within the processes and operations of institutions (*structural stigma*). Patients who are elderly or those with mental health problems don't get the same attention as those who are suffering a physical disorder, and in emergency rooms their physical symptoms may be attributed to their cognitive problems rather than being seen as genuine medical conditions that require treatment (Barney et al., 2009). Likewise, individuals with mental disorders who are at risk for type 2 diabetes are much less likely to be advised about physical activity and healthy dietary choices from their health care provider, which could be a factor that accounts for their shorter life span. In general, officials may choose to misinterpret conditions and behaviors, or they ignore or perceive symptoms as unimportant or as indices of failure, rather than deserving of intervention.

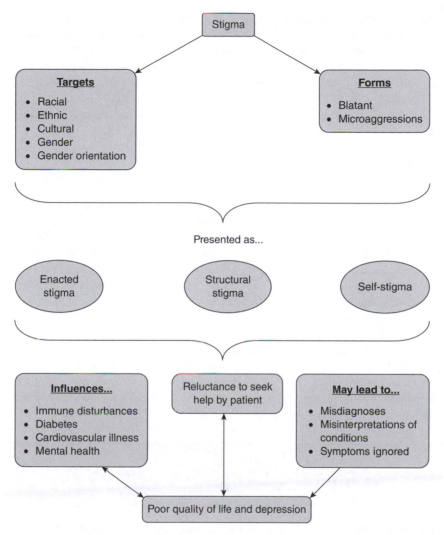

Figure 14.1   Stigma comes in different forms and can have different targets, which can be manifested at a personal level, at a structural level (organizational: governments, corporations, hospitals), and as a self-stigma. These various forms of stigma serve as powerful stressors that can influence health, help-seeking, as well as treatments received, which can undermine quality of life.

Educating people regarding stigma?

One would think that individuals could be educated so that stigma related to illness would be less common. Unfortunately, educational programs don't seem to be of much value, and even those who are or should be engaged in educating others (e.g., health professionals) sometimes carry stigmatizing attitudes (Adams et al., 2010). Indeed, when they experience mental health problems, many fail to seek help owing to the fear of being stigmatized. In reviewing the relevant literature related to different approaches to deal with this issue, Corrigan and Fong (2014) suggested that a grass-roots approach to dealing with stigma, including increased contact with individuals who are affected (which might necessarily entail stigmatized individuals coming forward), may be the way to curtail stigmatizing attitudes and behavior.

SELF-PERCEPTIONS

Although not always directly related to stigma, illness perceptions can also be affected by self-concept, stemming from an individual's social abilities, achievements, body image, and aspects of their 'private self'. Illnesses such as cancer, which might require single or double mastectomy, might radically alter a woman's self-image, and although breast reconstruction will often diminish this, the stigma associated with mastectomy can still affect self-image (Fang et al., 2013), and thus breast-conserving surgery (lumpectomy) is typically preferred over mastectomy (Sun et al., 2014). As satisfaction with treatment is related to the individual's expectations prior to breast reconstruction, it is important for them to be educated and prepared so that their expectations are in line with potential outcomes (Pusic et al., 2012).

Changes of body image and QoL aren't just seen among women who experience mastectomy, but also among those who experience limb amputation (Holzer et al., 2014), and among individuals who suffer facial burns (Hunter et al., 2013). In many instances psychotherapeutic approaches can be used to enhance self-image and self-concept, but this is more difficult and the outcomes are more variable among burn survivors (Corry et al., 2009).

IF ONLY THINGS HAD BEEN DIFFERENT

Life satisfaction and self-esteem are often tied to our work or hobbies (achieving self), as well as our connections with members of our ingroup, including family members (social self) (Brewer, 1991). Illnesses of various sorts can result in a diminution of what we're able to do, and even if employers and family members are sympathetic to the person's difficulties, the affected individual's achieving, social, and personal self may be undermined. Serious illness can obviously limit our dreams and aspirations, and too often affected individuals ruminate about 'what could have been'. A recent study, which included quantitative and qualitative analyses of women with fibromyalgia or MS, provided several interesting statements that were pertinent to the personal self (McInnis et al., 2015). One woman with fibromyalgia stated "I was an elite athlete and I had to give up my dreams of succeeding in that area of my life because my body doesn't react like a normal person's body does to exercise.

Overall, everything I've aspired to be was taken away and I've had to lower my expectations to the simple things". A second woman stated "My business clothes gather dust now, my makeup has long since dried up, and my jewelry sits in the drawers untouched. Whenever I see a smart business woman dressed in stockings, high heels and a nice suit, her hair done nice and it breaks my heart and I think 'that used to be me'. That 'me' was stolen from me. I had no choice in the matter".

SUMMARY

At some point, hopefully later rather than sooner, most of us can count on becoming seriously ill. Aside from the risks, pain, or other physical discomforts created, these illnesses can markedly affect our quality of life within one or more domains. To a considerable extent, the occurrence of illness may be due to the life-styles we have enjoyed, genetic factors, or perhaps just bad luck (fate), and getting through these illnesses will likewise be related to some of these same factors as well as our individual resilience, which comprises our appraisal and coping skills, our social support systems, having proper collaborative care, and the presence of particular personality factors (e.g., optimism, self-efficacy). Those individuals who succumb to depression or anxiety, conversely, will be less likely to recover well from illness, and mortality in some cases will occur considerably sooner. Likewise, individuals who are less capable of dealing with uncertainty or unpredictability, and instead engage in watchful waiting, will be less resilient. Clearly, stressful experiences that erode an individual's psychological and biological abilities to contend with challenges will negatively affect physical well-being, and will hinder recovery from illness.

15 Dealing with Illness

THE GOOD FIGHT VERSUS THE RIGHT FIGHT

We often hear that raging against an illness will somehow make it more likely that the affected person will overcome it. It might well be that giving up might favor a person's demise, but it's hard to know whether raging against the illness will have curative effects. As far as I know, prospective studies haven't been conducted to assess the success obtained by raging against the dying of the light, as Dylan Thomas put it.

Although a relationship has been reported between social support/social involvement and cancer survival, modest relations were apparent between survival time and the presence of depression, anxiety, hopelessness, helplessness, and hostility, and no relationship whatsoever was observed with having a fighting spirit and stoic acceptance (Petticrew et al., 2002). It's unlikely that anybody would argue against patients maintaining a positive outlook, as this may diminish their distress and allow them to maintain their quality of life. But, let's not be fooled into thinking that maintaining a fighting spirit threatens cancer cells into submission.

In some instances, it is possible that the knee-jerk reaction of friends and family to 'fight this thing' can be counterproductive, no matter how well-meaning they might be in saying this. These words can initially have positive psychological effects, but later, as recovery seems unlikely, this statement should be made with consideration to what the patient is going through and what they actually want. This means that we consider the prognosis, how long they've been ill, the pain and discomfort being experienced, loss of self, and what their short-term quality of life will be like should they survive somewhat longer. Undoubtedly, there are instances where fighting against an illness is worth it, even if the fight is unsuccessful. Yet we ought to question whether encouragement to rage against the illness is always the right thing to do. There are times and conditions in which the patient would prefer 'to go gentle into that good night', and perhaps the consent and blessing of loved ones might help this transition.

RECOGNIZING ILLNESS SYMPTOMS AND WHAT NEEDS TO BE DONE

When we're relatively young, the possibility of dying is far off; we hardly give it a thought. Even when healthy behaviors are engaged by young people, it's probably not with thoughts of living healthier or longer, but might instead have more to do with looking better. As we age, however, our mortality comes to mind more often, although few of us obsess about it unless we become ill and the end is staring at us. Of course, most people would like to extend their life, provided that they can also stay healthy, and they might often look back with regret at not having engaged in healthy behaviors and instead engaged in stupid stuff. In this chapter we'll deal with issues pertaining to illness, so that readers come away with an appreciation of:

- what to do when symptoms of illness arise
- the perspectives concerning an individual's help-seeking behaviors when health threats are present
- factors that might influence illness perception and treatment compliance
- the importance of connections between the patient and health providers
- what factors limit effective treatment.

RECOGNIZING WARNINGS AND HEALTH RISKS

Whether it's people or cars, parts wear down with age, functioning becomes less than ideal, and eventually something will fall apart (hopefully the muffler and not the engine). In some instances this might occur without adequate warning, seemingly hitting the person out of nowhere. At other times warning signs might have been present, but they were either subtle and went undetected, or, alternatively, they had been detected, but their significance was unclear, and thus they were ignored (or perhaps they were clear, but were foolishly ignored). Clearly, individuals ought to have some understanding of what's happening in their own bodies and while they might not know how to fix problems, they should be capable and willing to seek help.

Learning about illness symptoms

When fairly obvious and intense symptoms (e.g., related to heart attack or stroke) are experienced most people will take steps to reach a hospital. But, what is it that causes some people not to seek help for symptoms like intermittent pain in the chest, the presence of bloody stools, or constant phlegmy coughing. In some instances symptoms may be a bit vague and can easily be attributed to something less critical (e.g., heart attack being attributed to indigestion), perhaps leading to the adoption of counterproductive measures, such as avoidance/denial. Ignoring early warning signs in the hope that the symptoms will vanish on their own is sometimes simply not a good idea. Most people are reluctant to run to the doctor with every minor ache or pain and appear like a whiner or a hypochondriac (Lichtman et al., 2015). However, if individuals are already in a high-risk group, ignoring symptoms might only be profitable for the undertaker.

So, a good first step might be for individuals to learn something about their own bodies, and the symptoms of diseases to which they may be vulnerable (e.g., based on family history or other risk factors). The fact is that many people don't know where some of their critical organs are located (do you know where your spleen is, or where the adrenal glands lie?), even if they suffer an illness that involves that particular organ (Weinman et al., 2009). It's obviously important that individuals know that certain symptoms shouldn't be minimized and that in many cases time urgency exists as this can determine life or death or the extent of damage produced, as we saw in discussing stroke.

To be sure, there are hypochondriacs who display excessive worry or are preoccupied by having a serious illness and thus take up more than their share of medical time. Likewise, neurotic individuals will readily identify and over-report their symptoms, and they might also seek medical attention even when there's not much wrong with them (Feldman et al., 1999). However, for most individuals, symptoms are meaningful, and the obstacles that stand in the way of seeing a doctor or visiting an emergency room (laziness, avoidance coping, not wanting to be a nuisance, or fear of finding out that they're actually sick) need to be overcome. In some instances this may be difficult to achieve as other factors may get in the way. For instance, cultural differences exist in relation to illness reporting, and certain groups can be expected to show up for treatment less readily than others. Indeed, the ethnic and cross-cultural differences that exist in this regard may be sufficiently significant to have prompted the call for clinical research involving community-based ethnographic and ecological processes, so that a better picture will emerge concerning models of somatic distress that are sensitive to personal and cultural differences (Kirmayer & Sartorius, 2007).

ILLNESS PERCEPTIONS AND BELIEFS

The common-sense model of illness

Much like Lazarus's perspective regarding appraisals and coping in dealing with stressors, the *common-sense model of illness* was offered to explain the steps individuals go through in response to a perceived health threat (Leventhal et al., 1984). According to this perspective, symptoms promote both cognitive and emotional responses that are processed in parallel. Individuals initially form a representation (or schema) regarding an illness or health threat, often based on what they've read or heard, together with their own illness experiences and personal characteristics, which influence behaviors used to cope with a health threat, and appraisals of the efficacy of their behaviors (Diefenbach & Leventhal, 1996). As well, feedback loops exist between appraisals of the illness or threat coping strategies, which come to influence decision making and the behaviors adopted. In effect, through abstract and concrete information as well as emotional representations, individuals will attempt to make sense of their situation, which will inform their behavioral responses.

The emotional representations regarding an illness comprise negative reactions, such as anger, dismay, blame, and fear, and the cognitive arm of this process similarly involves several distinct components, shown in Table 15.1, that contribute to how the illness is considered. A meta-analysis of 45 studies confirmed that predictable relationships exist between illness cognitions and coping, which are linked to psychological well-being as well as social functioning (Hagger & Orbell, 2003). Furthermore, these illness perceptions can be altered (e.g., by a hospital intervention) and may improve recovery following heart attack as well as chronic illnesses such as diabetes (e.g., Petrie et al., 2003).

Table 15.1   Cognitive components of the common-sense model of illness

Identity	Label used by individuals to describe the illness, and its perceived symptoms and features
Consequences	Expected impact of the illness
Cause	Attributions concerning cause of illness
Timeline	Perception concerning how long the illness will persist
Cure/control	Beliefs regarding recovery or control over the illness
Coherence	Extent to which the symptoms are in line with one another and come together to link to an illness condition

Psychological factors influence illness perception

Just as pain perception can be influenced by a central state, day-to-day experiences can influence whether individuals will detect symptoms of illness. When individuals are caught up in activities, it's less likely that they'll attend to mild symptoms of illness. In contrast, in the absence of distractors, or when bored and engaged in mindless activities, people are more apt to notice these symptoms. Furthermore, individuals who are generally negative will usually report greater and more distressing experiences as well as poorer health (Watson & Pennebaker, 1989). Likewise, depressed or anxious individuals are more likely to report somatic symptoms, fatigue, feeling weak, headache, and multiple pain complaints.

Misattributions regarding illness

When bad things happen to people, they often want to understand why these events occurred, and sometimes they make attributions based on very little evidence. Among patients with gynecological cancers, genetics factors were perceived as being the most cogent cause of the illness. The next highest beliefs concerned the notion that the illness was related to stressor experiences, God's will, hormones, and environmental factors (Costanzo et al., 2005). Patients who made strong causal attributions concerning the influence of these uncontrollable factors in the development of their cancer were most likely to be depressed and anxious, and adopted few health behaviors. But, if they believed that the occurrence or reoccurrence of illness (e.g., cancer) was due to controllable factors, then they were more likely to adopt healthy behaviors in an effort to diminish the likelihood of the disease returning (Costanzo et al., 2005).

Patients sometimes engage in either self-blame or other-blame in relation to illnesses. In many instances illnesses develop as a result of poor health behaviors, so there may be ample reason for self-blame (not that it helps much), and there are instances where others contribute to the development of illness (e.g., companies spewing pollutants into the environment). However, the cause of an illness may not be known or be entirely out of anyone's control. Thus, other-blame isn't productive, particularly when there isn't actually anybody at fault, and self-blame is equally impractical. When patients engage in self-blame, it's more likely that they will become depressed or feel guilt (Bennett et al., 2005), which can impair healing and lengthen the course of recovery.

Illness perception and treatment compliance

Part of our illness appraisal processes includes perceptions concerning our abilities to contend with a specific illness. One would like to take the position that it's better not to catastrophize over an illness and 'stress yourself out'. At the same time, those at risk and those who are already ill should appreciate that chronic illnesses need to be taken seriously to preclude worsening of the condition; but, even when they do, treatment compliance, including intervention efforts, is among the greatest struggles that physicians have with patients. Bipolar patients might choose not to take meds because it dampens their creativity, depressed patients may take holidays from their SSRIs because they interfere with sexual gratification, and patients with diabetes might simply forget their medication or feel that they can 'cheat' every so often in relation to the foods they eat.

We saw earlier that as safety measures improved in various contexts (e.g., helmets for bicycling; seat belts in driving) people generally took more risks, thereby diminishing some of the benefits that could be derived from these safety measures. The very same thing might occur in relation to symptoms of illness and treatment compliance. When a diabetic patient is put on metformin or a patient with hypertension is given a beta blocker, their sugar levels or blood pressure hopefully normalize, but they might mistakenly believe that they can now let down their guard and return to eating the same bad foods and not exercise, forgetting that these very acts led to the illness in the first place (Hekler et al., 2008). In effect, when the signs and symptoms of illness are suppressed, this shouldn't be taken to imply 'all clear', and patients obviously need to have a proper perspective of their illness, accepting that some life-style changes are needed.

Assessing perception of illness

Based on our discussion of placebo and nocebo effects, it won't come as a surprise that perceptions of symptoms and how seriously they should be taken are influenced by the individual's expectations, which are often based on previous experiences with similar or dissimilar conditions. However, the appraisals that are made are sometimes baseless. By example, if an illness condition was thought to be one that was rare, individuals perceived it to be more dangerous than if it was relatively common (Croyle & Hunt, 1991). In addition, if a patient had previously been ill with a particular condition, they appraised the illness as being relatively common and thus less dangerous than other illnesses (Jemmott et al., 1988). Regardless of whether or not appraisals are based on factual information, they can affect health behaviors, mood related to the illness, and even the course of the illness itself. Thus, to objectively assess appraisals of illness, the Illness Perception Questionnaire (IPQ) was developed. A revision of this instrument reduced the length from 80 questions to a brief 8-item questionnaire (provided in Table 15.2) that assesses identity, timeline, consequences, personal control, treatment control, concern, emotional responses, and coherence (Broadbent et al., 2006). These factors could potentially be related to the health behaviors people adopt and whether they will adhere to prescribed treatments.

Table 15.2   The Brief Illness Perception Questionnaire

For the following questions, please circle the number that best corresponds to your views:

1. How much does your illness affect your life?

    0   1   2   3   4   5   6   7   8   9   10

    Not at all   Severely affects my life

2. How long do you think your illness will continue?

    0   1   2   3   4   5   6   7   8   9   10

    A very short time   Forever

3. How much control do you feel you have over your illness?

    0   1   2   3   4   5   6   7   8   9   10

    None at all   Extreme amount of control

4. How much do you think your treatment can help your illness?

    0   1   2   3   4   5   6   7   8   9   10

    Not at all   Extremely helpful

5. How much do you experience symptoms from your illness?

    0   1   2   3   4   5   6   7   8   9   10

    No symptoms at all   Many severe symptoms

6. How concerned are you about your illness?

    0   1   2   3   4   5   6   7   8   9   10

    Not at all   Extremely concerned

7. How well do you feel you understand your illness?

    0   1   2   3   4   5   6   7   8   9   10

    No understanding at all   Understand very clearly

8. How much do you feel your illness affects you emotionally? (e.g., does it make you angry, upset, scared or depressed?)

    0   1   2   3   4   5   6   7   8   9   10

    Not at all emotionally affected   Extremely emotionally affected

RELATION BETWEEN THE PATIENT AND THE HEALTH PROVIDER

Psychological and physical health can be influenced by the relationship between patients and health providers (physicians, nurse-practitioners, nurses, physician assistants). By informing patients about procedures they will be experiencing, these health providers can reduce the unpredictability and uncertainty being faced, and they can encourage the patients' involvement in the consultative process. As a result, patients may come to feel a greater sense of self-efficacy, and may have the opportunity to prepare themselves for possible hardships, and to spend time with those closest to them. Ultimately, patient satisfaction with the clinical treatment and services they receive can have considerable bearing on treatment adherence and on treatment outcomes.

Patient perspectives regarding physician attitudes

Some patients might feel that they want an understanding and kindly family physician over one that seems grumpy, cold, or detached. Because most people have limited medical knowledge, they might conclude that the 'nice' doctor is also competent, whereas the doctor who is aloof is less competent. Patients who perceived physicians positively and as being competent and warm, reported greater health care utilization and satisfaction and enhanced adherence to recommended treatments (Bogart et al., 2004). Thus, the well-being of patients is not only influenced by the physician's actual competence, but also by the behaviors and attitudes they express.

Most health providers are patient, thoughtful and caring. However, burn-out in health care workers is common (Sigsbee & Bernat, 2014), and on occasion patients could potentially feel the practitioner's frustration and unhappiness (Krebs et al., 2006). There are also some health providers who seem incapable of adopting appropriate behaviors despite the substantial efforts that medical schools have been making in training this aspect of patient care. Patients certainly may have the option of finding a new family physician (if one is available), but it may be more difficult finding specialists in some medical fields. Moreover, in some countries or among individuals using certain insurance plans, patients might not get a choice of specialists, instead being assigned to whichever doctors happen to be available at a given time.

The relationship between a patient and their doctor is a two-way street, and the patient ought to consider the situation the doctor is in. What sometimes bothers patients is how long they had to wait for an appointment, how long they sat in the waiting room, and how much attention they actually received when they met with the physician. Clearly, in some specialties there is a shortage of physicians, and as a result, they're backed up and have very little time with each patient. Some physicians make efforts to be accommodating and engage in a few moments of chit-chat, whereas others simply want to get down to business as quickly as possible. Thus, when the patient meets with the doctor, they should have a brief description ready concerning what brought them there, including the specific symptoms they exhibit, when the symptoms started, how intense they are, and whether certain factors promote or exacerbate these symptoms. Moreover, as certain medications, even those obtained over the counter as well as herbal remedies, can alter symptoms, patients should prepare a list of all substances that have been taken. Patients must also be prepared to answer questions accurately, even if they create a bit of embarrassment – most likely, what a patient has to say will be neither new nor shocking.

Physician–patient communication

Open communication often exists between a patient and doctor, and, as we've seen, some patients desire full disclosure from the physician, but not all patients are so inclined. Some older patients with colorectal cancer, for instance, preferred to obtain prognostic information and to have a role in deciding treatment, but an equal number preferred a more passive role (Elkin et al., 2007). These individual differences are seen in many venues. Some individuals who have the opportunity to be genetically tested to determine whether they carry a genetic trait that can potentially render them highly vulnerable to a particular illness (e.g., being BRCA1 positive) or doomed to develop an illness (e.g., Huntington's disease) will do so, whereas others might prefer not to know, even if it means going on with a sword hanging over them.

Physicians may encounter situations in which they have to juggle between maintaining their integrity and yet providing the patient with information that will allow them to make proper decisions. Sometimes, this might mean that a degree of ambiguity be maintained about the future, tempered by what the patient might want. This can certainly be challenging, especially as, at times, the physicians' perceptions may be inconsistent with those stated by the patient, and this has prompted the view that better patient–physician communication is needed. Even the way a doctor presents information may have considerable effects on how patients will respond. By example, the doctor can say "10% of patients don't do well after surgery" or they can frame it as "90% of patients do well following surgery and go on with fruitful lives"; the latter is obviously more likely to elicit a more optimistic response on the part of the patient.

OHHH, TELL ME THE GOOD NEWS FIRST; I WANT TO LIVE IN ANTICIPATION OF BAD NEWS AS LONG AS POSSIBLE

After tests are done regarding some threatening symptoms, most individuals are appropriately anxious about results, but keep hoping for the best. When the phone call arrives indicating that "the doctor would like you to come back in" or "further tests are needed", the person pretty well knows that the news they'll receive is likely not good. If the doctor has to break bad news to them, which is certainly one of the most difficult jobs they face, they must be professional and honest with patients, empathetic toward them and their family, not show their own remorse or desperation, and if there is a possible cure for the illness they need to carefully explain that this is possible and what the risks are. Understandably, most physicians (84%) expressed willingness to communicate to patients a diagnosis of a serious illness with a good prognosis, whereas far fewer (43%) were prepared to communicate a diagnosis with a poor prognosis (Wittmann et al., 2011).

So, how should the doctor deliver this news? How should it be couched? How much hope should be held out to patients? The doctor needs to get to the point fairly quickly to diminish the anxiety patients are experiencing. There are, in fact, different views concerning the best approach. Is it best to start with some good news and then follow up with the bad, or should the bad news come first and then have it tempered by some good news? Likely the best approach is to deliver the bad news initially, but couch it in as positive and empathetic a light as possible. "I hope you live a long and satisfying life, but we do have some concerns that need to be dealt with." When the full bad news follows, the patient may be too shocked to fully understand the situation, but the way this news is delivered, and even offering a vague smidgen of positivity, can potentially buffer this.

Trust in the doctor

When faced with severe illnesses, such as cancer, individuals may have to make some difficult decisions related to treatment options, despite not having an adequate knowledge base to do so. To make these intimidating decisions, they typically rely on the information provided by their physician (O'Brien et al., 2008), although increasingly more people are relying on information obtainable through internet sources. In dealing with major illnesses, such as cancer, a person's primary interest typically revolves around the skills of the oncologist or surgeon, including their trust in them (Wright et al., 2004). When the patient feels that their concerns have not been taken seriously, or when their trust in the physician is diminished, symptoms may worsen and treatments may be less effective (Greville-Harris & Dieppe, 2015).

Shared decision making and trust

It is common for patients to not only wish to know everything possible about their illness, but also to engage in shared decision making, especially if trust in the doctor is limited (Kraetschmer et al., 2004). For some patients, being able to engage in shared decision making regarding their treatment is a top priority, along with the opportunity to see the same doctor on repeated visits (Schattner et al., 2006). Typically, the desire for joint decision making is accommodated, but on occasion the barriers inherent in the doctor–patient relationship may hinder this. In some instances physicians may be relatively authoritarian and hold considerable sway over the patient. Even well educated and affluent patients might feel it necessary to simply follow old social norms of complying with whatever the doctor instructs (Frosch et al., 2012). Likewise, as indicated earlier, physicians usually have a packed schedule, and by their verbal and non-verbal statements they make it clear that there's no time for dilly-dallying and that they (the physician) call the shots, making patients reluctant to even venture into the realm of shared decision making.

When patients had a say over their options, they reported increased satisfaction with care, and they sensed greater improvements in healing, even if the course of improvement or pain reduction was no greater than it would have been otherwise. It's not infrequent, however, for patients to indicate that their desired treatment options were not always reflected in the treatment they received (Keating et al., 2002), and this was often related to regret that they later expressed regarding their decisions (Lantz et al., 2005). Of course, when asked about regret over previous decisions, hindsight bias, low overall quality of life, or poor physical and psychological health outcomes may have contributed to increased levels of regret (Sheehan et al., 2008), even when the decisions made were perfectly appropriate under the conditions.

At one time, the general attitude of "doctor knows best" was pervasive, but has since come to be replaced by a greater emphasis on what the patients' needs and goals are in the context of treatments that will be obtained. In the face of a serious illness, patients may be consulted about the treatment options available to them, but since they typically have little knowledge about the relevant issues, making decisions is both frightening and difficult. As a result, many patients simply prefer to leave decisions to the physician. Others, in contrast, will thoroughly examine their options, checking the internet for solutions, asking their friends, and seeking opinions from other physicians (although some might not be inclined to seek a second opinion because they think the physician might be upset by this). They might well conclude that they're best off following the advice of their physician, but being involved in this decision might leave them with the feeling that they aren't simply a victim of the situation and that they have a degree of control over their own destiny, as illusory as this might be.

Of course, there are many cases in which patients choose not to take the advice of physicians, opting for some alternative medicines (e.g., treating cancer through consumption of apricot pits, shark cartilage, or ridiculous homeopathic solutions) or culturally-based treatments that might (or not) have beneficial effects. This is their option, but in the case of parents making choices for children, legal agencies may step in on behalf of the child's best interests, although courts may find in favor of the family's right to determine treatment.

Not every decision made by the patient and/or the physician works out well, and although patients want to be involved in making decisions regarding their treatment, they may be less inclined to accept responsibility for adverse outcomes (Deadman et al., 2001). Patients sometimes have the unrealistic expectation that the doctor will always be able to cure them, and when things turn sour, some patients will point to the doctor as being responsible. In essence, physicians need to be aware that patient trust is a sword that cuts both ways. With the benefits of trust that physicians receive from patients comes the possibility of blame when positive outcomes aren't realized. Indeed, the increasingly more frequent malpractice lawsuits might reflect the erosion of trust between patients and their doctors (Peters, 2000), or might stem from patients who trust their doctors developing expectations that can't possibly be met (Hill & O'Hara, 2006).

PATIENT OPTIONS

An alliance between the patient and the therapist means that the patient has trust and confidence in the therapist's actions. As already indicated, a match between the patient's treatment preference and the treatment offered is accompanied by enhanced adherence, diminished attrition (drop-out), and moderately superior outcomes (Kwan et al., 2010). This raises the obvious question as to what can be expected when there's a mismatch between the patient's preferred treatment and the procedure recommended. Ordinarily, patients are consulted about treatment preferences, as these might be influenced by previous experiences with medications or other forms of treatment, and they tend to fare moderately better when provided with their preferred treatment (Dunlop et al., 2011). It could be argued that patients will not receive treatments that they don't want, given that physicians need patient consent to administer treatments. Yet, when the patient signs an 'informed consent' for certain procedures, they might not fully understand what they're signing. Besides, patients might be reluctant to contradict their physicians, and to do so might have them labeled as a 'difficult patient'.

In relation to patient options, there is another consideration that is fairly important. Specifically, in studies regarding mental health, patients are often more positive about doctors of their own ethnic/racial group, with this being particularly strong among African Americans (Cabral & Smith, 2011). However, as African Americans make up only 5% of doctors, much lower than the percentage of African Americans in the general population, many individuals won't receive their preferred doctor. It is uncertain whether this has any relevance to individual well-being, but given the importance of trust in the doctor–patient relationship, more training of doctors from varied minority groups would be desirable. This isn't a matter of affirmative action, but one of meeting patient desires.

Table 15.3   Patient decisions regarding cancer treatment

When faced with a severe illness, and multiple decisions have to be made, patients are often intimidated and confused by what's ahead of them. They need to be able to weigh their options, but they might also feel a sense of pressure to make their decision. The Mayo Clinic (2013) has offered a series of steps that ought to be taken in this decision making process.

Cardinal to these decision steps is that patients (a) take their time in making a decision, (b) not be concerned about seeking a second opinion on important issues, (c) understand that after a decision has been made that they can still change their mind, (d) appreciate that they don't have to be involved in decision making and can simply leave it to the doctor, and (e) can also decide not to have any treatment, although they can have a change of heart later.

Step 1. Setting ground rules

- Individuals need to decide on how much information they want concerning their illness as well as the treatment consequences. Ordinarily, the oncologist can provide estimates regarding what can be expected from different types of treatment, but the patient needs to communicate to the doctor the extent that they're willing to experience negative side effects given the potential benefits of the treatment.
- Patients should consider whether they want to be in control of treatment decisions, whether the doctor should make the final call, or that these decisions be shared. The patient is the final decision-maker in most regards, and shouldn't feel pressure in selecting a given treatment.

Step 2. Deciding on a goal

Patients ought to have a goal in relation to the treatment, which may vary with the cancer type and stage. Upon first being diagnosed, patients may aim for a cure, and thus would be willing to endure marked short-term side effects. At a later stage, the goal might be shrinking the cancer or stopping its growth. In this instance, patients might be more reluctant to endure harsh treatments. In advanced stages of cancer, or if treatments haven't been successful, the patient might simply want comfort and the absence of pain, and thus might want limited treatment.

Step 3. Researching treatment options

In order for an informed decision to be made, varied treatment options should be explored in the context of the type of cancer and the stage. Consulting with the oncologist in order to obtain information regarding trusted websites is a good option. Similarly, consultations regarding side effects and pain medications should be considered.

Step 4. Analyzing the benefits and risks associated with treatments

Depending on the type and stage of cancer, patients ought to consider both the benefits and the hardships that come with treatments.

- *Side effects.* Consider what side effects can be expected (based on the physician's comments) and to what extent they can be managed.
- *Quality of life.* To what extent will life be affected? Will treatments require time off from work, alter general capabilities, or affect the individual's social role?

- *Financial costs.* Are treatments covered by insurance, and if not, can the patient afford the treatment? Find out before treatment rather than afterward.

- *General health.* Among patients with other health conditions, it is important to consider whether some cancer treatments may have effects on these conditions.

Step 5. Communication with the doctor

It is obviously essential to be able to communicate with a doctor so that a proper decision regarding treatment can be made.

- *Saying something when you don't understand.* If individuals say nothing, it is usually assumed that they understand. So, if explanations are unclear, the patient needs to speak up.

- *Writing question.* Interviews with a doctor under these circumstances can be distressing and patients may lose track of their thoughts. Writing questions down in advance can be helpful.

- *Bringing someone along.* Bringing a family member or friend to an interview can be helpful to remember what was said, and in later decision making.

- *Recording the conversation.* Ask the doctor whether it's OK to take notes or record the conversations so that you can subsequently replay it to yourself.

- *Keep copies of health records.* Obtain a copy of your health record, and bring it to each appointment.

Best practices from a physician's perspective

Guidelines have been offered outlining best practices for physicians. Among other things, it was suggested that physicians ought to share prognostic information, actively elicit decision-making preferences from the patient (and their family members), understand fully patient fears and goals, as well as define and explore (on the basis of fears, goals, and other relevant information) the trade-offs that exist between getting well and possible impaired functioning as a result of the treatment (Bernacki & Block, 2014). Patient concerns vary widely and are not limited to the possibility of death, often comprising the potential for disability or mutilation, loss of independence, role, or status, and even fear of leaving home (Teutsch, 2003). These issues need to be explored in the dialogue between the physician and the patient. In the absence of good communication between physicians and patients (or surrogates, such as family members) it is more likely that patients will not receive the care they might wish for, and they might even receive non-beneficial treatments (Cooper et al., 2014).

It's unfortunate that even with the knowledge that is available regarding the importance of the patient–physician alliance, and the need for physicians to understand more about their patients, physicians frequently don't have time to make these accommodations. As a result, some physicians might not understand or appreciate what patients tell them, leading to 'silent misdiagnosis' (Mulley et al., 2012). In one study 71% of physicians came to the conclusion that their patients with breast cancer had 'keeping their breast' as a main priority, whereas only 7% of patients actually felt this way. Optimal care requires that physicians understand their patient's desire, which means engaging properly with the patient and the family, providing patients with options based on hard scientific data, and working as a team in the decision-making process.

A final point needs to be made on this issue. Sometimes, exigencies exist where a decision-making role on the part of the patient needs to be abrogated (e.g., emergency situations, or when the patient engages in behaviors that are counterproductive). It is also the case that although a physician is generally not permitted to administer treatments without the patient's consent, the reverse is also true in the sense that the physician isn't obliged to administer treatments simply because the patient desires them. Based on training and practical experiences, the physician has the right and obligation to make the call, as he or she perceives the situation. Patients might request surgery to remove a tumor in the hope that it will do some good, but the physician may feel that this might not be useful (particularly if the cancer has already metastasized) and so will deny this treatment. In fact, performing the surgery can have negative repercussions, such as limiting the opportunity to administer other treatments that could be beneficial. Of course, there may be instances where a physician at one facility may choose not to engage in certain procedures, but a physician at a second facility may see the situation differently and thus agree to perform the treatment requested.

Despite efforts to deliver best services, sometimes events conspire to provide patients with less than optimal care. Hospitals on some occasions might simply not be hospitable. Perhaps that motivates people to get out as soon as possible. However, in the interim, patients spend their time intractably bored, often immobile, kept awake and maintained under bright lights, often stuck and prodded, and deprived of their privacy and often their dignity. Sounds more like Guantanamo than a place to get better, doesn't it? These factors may well contribute to long-term health problems, especially in older individuals.

Table 15.4   Taking care of the older hospitalized patient (Pearl, 2015)

- Health care staff should be made more aware of patient needs and how to prevent, recognize, and manage delirium as well as post-hospital syndrome (generalised risk for a range of adverse health outcomes) in returning patients.
- Identify patients at risk for these conditions, including those at advanced age, patients with cognitive problems, and certainly those with a history of delirium or post-hospital syndrome.
- Augment caloric intake and diminish delays of procedures wherein patients take nothing by mouth.
- Diminish the amount of blood drawn daily, and avoid multiple needle sticks (NB: among older people with fragile veins, have a specialist do the blood draw and not a member of staff in training who may require multiple jabs).
- Patients should have family and friends present (to the extent that they can handle this).
- Hospital rooms should be bright during the day and properly dark at night and permit patients to obtain proper sleep.
- Patients' glasses and hearing aids should be available and functional.
- Patients should move about (walk) as much as possible to maintain muscle strength, even when this means carting around a stand with intravenous equipment or breathing tubes.
- Managing pain is essential and whenever possible this should be done using non-sedating non-opioid medications, and by avoiding sedatives (e.g., benzodiazepines) or other drugs that can disturb cognitive and mental function.

About half of elderly patients in hospital will develop delirium, which comprises confusion, disordered speech, and hallucinations, often developing within hours or days, although it seems to come and go. It may be brought on by medications, but the distressing environment may contribute as well. In some instances it is misdiagnosed as being symptomatic of dementia being present or developing, even though the symptoms will disappear with appropriate treatments. Unfortunately, delirium, according to the American Delerium Society, is not properly recognized in about 60% of cases, leading to extended hospital stays.

Yet another severe condition is post-hospital syndrome (Krumholz, 2013), which refers to the frequent occurrence of patients leaving hospital, only to return not long afterward with a new illness, possibly because of inadequate care at home (e.g., lack of exercise) that produces overall weakness. In fact, older patients often develop lung problems or general weakness, and may never return to their pre-treatment condition. An excellent opinion piece by Robert Pearl on this very topic offers a number of suggestions regarding what can be done to improve patients' lives while in care (see Table 15.4; Pearl, 2015).

IATROGENIC ILLNESS

Wearing a starched white coat, looking knowledgeable and confident, a doctor inspires trust. A doctor can act as a powerful placebo that can make us feel better. As their job is to heal us, and a fundamental aspect of medical treatment is that they do no harm, we generally follow their advice, expecting that whatever ails us will resolve. However, there are times when outcomes aren't in line with our expectations, and negative outcomes are experienced. In some instances, this might not have to do with a particular treatment not being effective, but may instead be related to 'something having gone wrong'. Often, these unintended events are readily overcome, but there are instances in which negative outcomes of treatment may actually be more severe than the condition that was being treated.

Let's face it, medicine isn't magic. Illness diagnoses can be difficult given the frequent ambiguity of symptoms and because many illnesses share features with one another. Likewise, many procedures, particularly surgical interventions, can be complex. In the case of high-risk surgical procedures, success isn't guaranteed, and a certain number of patients may not gain relief from their problems. Depending on the nature of the procedures being performed or the health of the individual, but not because any errors occurred, some patients will not survive surgery or will die soon afterward. As well, unforeseen events can be encountered during the surgery or can develop afterward, such as infection. Some treatments might also come with negative side effects, but it might not be known in advance who will react in one way or another. In essence, negative outcomes may arise, but there's nobody that can or should be blamed.

Complications of medical procedures, including those involving either diagnostic errors or those stemming from treatment, irrespective of whether they are actually known risks or occur as a result

(Continued)

(Continued)

of errors of omission or commission, are referred to as 'iatrogenic illnesses'. In some instances, strains of bacteria resistant to antibiotic treatments can cause infection that can't be attributed to any single person, although procedures can be adopted to minimize risk. Likewise, unexpected allergic reactions to drugs may occur. These are obviously unintended events, but they are nevertheless considered to be iatrogenic conditions. Aside from events that occur during surgery, post-operative complications, including those related to anaesthesia, are a major source of problems for patients, but thankfully these have declined significantly with improved procedures over the last few decades.

Diagnostic errors, perhaps understandably, are all too common, amounting to about 5% in outpatient clinics, and in the US this may account for as many as 80,000–160,000 deaths or disabilities each year. An analysis of malpractice suits conducted over a 25-year period revealed that diagnostic errors, more than medication overdoses or surgical errors, accounted for the greatest number of claims (Tehrani et al., 2013). Naïvely, we often assume that something like reading various types of scan, including those from imaging procedures (MRI, PET) and breast mammograms, is simple and straightforward, much like describing a scene in a photograph. However, interpreting these scans can be very complicated, and will vary with the experience of the person doing the analysis, and the presence of subtle problems can be missed. Predictably, a large number of diagnostic errors stem from these difficulties.

Iatrogenic illnesses also occur in relation to psychiatric illnesses. Mental illnesses are often difficult to diagnose, especially early on, and bipolar disorder may be diagnosed as depression or schizophrenia. As well, physical illness among mentally ill patients may be misattributed to psychological issues. We also know that therapists can harm patients by offering inappropriate advice or, as in some notorious cases, they can facilitate the creation of false memories that can affect patients and devastate families (Loftus & Davis, 2006).

There have been occasions where negative outcomes have occurred that could (or should) have been foreseen, as well as negative outcomes that have developed due to frank negligence. The frequency of medical errors isn't certain, and we can pretty well be assured that not every instance of such events will be discovered or disclosed (sorry if I sound like a conspiracy nut, but I'd have to be fairly naïve to believe otherwise). Some sources have estimated that serious iatrogenic illnesses in hospital settings occur in about 14.4% of cases, of which 5.2% were considered to be preventable errors. Of these, 34% were judged to be of moderate severity, 10.4% severe, and 3.6% were fatal (Anderson et al., 2013). In pediatric surgery, the statistics are also a bit discouraging. A 6-year audit of about 331,000 surgeries revealed that 30-day incidence of any adverse event was 10.3%, including errors related to transfusions or wound complications, although only a modest number of the procedures accounted for over 60% of the problems (Rice-Townsend et al., 2010). It also appears that a large number of adverse drug events occur that comprise the use of inappropriate drugs or a failure to properly monitor patients (Thomsen et al., 2007). Given the huge number of hospitalizations that take place yearly, even the most conservative estimates would yield millions of cases of 'medical misadventure', many of which could have been avoided. What we hear of most through the media are 'never events' that usually comprise inexcusable procedures that one would imagine to be rare events, but actually aren't. By example, many instruments are used during complicated surgery, and while all instruments should be accounted for, surgical instruments (clamps, tweezers, forceps, needles, safety pins, scalpels, knife blades, scissors, sponges, towels, suction tips and tubes, towels) have been left behind in patients' bodies. On a fair number of occasions the wrong procedure is conducted on a patient, or the wrong person is operated on, and in mental health facilities it isn't all that infrequent that patients receive incorrect medications for other illnesses that they might have been suffering from. It has been estimated that surgical 'never events' occur at least 4,000 times each year within the US, leading to death 6.6% of the time, and permanent injury was reported in 32.9% of these cases (Mehtsun et al., 2013).

The intent of bringing up this issue isn't to get a reaction based on sensationalism, nor is it to undermine trust in physicians. Iatrogenic illness can occur that isn't the fault of a physician, and even if it were, we ought to consider that humans are fallible, and errors will occur despite physicians' best efforts. But, the occurrence of preventable medical errors is sufficiently frequent to endorse a call for greater transparency, hopefully leading to improved medical conditions. As well, there ought to be concern regarding what is included as an iatrogenic error. Specifically, an iatrogenic error includes not just 'errors of commission', but also 'errors of omission' (i.e., not doing something that should have been done). Depending on where you live, medical treatments, even for serious conditions, may take weeks or months to be obtained. When a medical system fails people in this way, shouldn't this be considered an iatrogenic error, and if so, does it reflect negligence?

What patients know, what they need to know, and what they have a right to know

There was a time when there was debate as to what a patient should be told if they had a serious illness, the notion being that if the picture was grim, then there might not be any point in telling them as this would only create additional, unnecessary distress. In my immigrant community about 50 years ago, one would occasionally hear about so-and-so having "the real thing" or "the big C". After some head shaking and sighing, the second person might inquire "Does he know?". In those days patients often weren't told about their disease or its prognosis, although it's hardly likely that this secret was maintained for very long. In most Western countries this is rarely the case any longer, as patients are typically provided with fundamental information (if this is their preference), but in other places, such as in parts of Asia, Latin America, and the Middle East, some physicians are less likely to discuss an illness that has a poor prognosis.

Often, with the best intentions, physicians believe that negative information should be withheld so that patients can live with less anxiety and greater hope for the future (Montazeri et al., 2009). However, as patients might figure things out, this can exacerbate uncertainty, anxiety, and dissatisfaction, and it can also affect the patient–doctor relationship and influence the quality of terminal care (Nakajima et al., 2013). There is also the view that although the physician needs to be truthful with the patient, there ought to be at least a bit of wiggle room. After all, there are reports of the spontaneous disappearance of cancers, even if they are exceptionally rare. Indeed, some patients with terminal illnesses survive much longer than expected, whereas others take sudden, unexpected downturns. As already said, medicine isn't a precise science and making projections is risky.

In this debate there is yet another position that seems to bridge the gap between the various perspectives (Mishel, 1999). Being confronted with a fatal illness, some people will simply give up all hope and sink into despair. However, if uncertainty exists, individuals may have the opportunity to construe this negative situation so that a glimmer of hope prevails despite the negative odds. Even if events are spiraling downward, patients can capitalize on uncertainty and put a more positive spin on the situation, allowing them to recognize that the worst is likely and to make necessary preparations, but hoping for the best allows them the opportunity to function as well as possible.

OBTAINING MEDICAL CARE

Health delivery

Delivery of health services has been changing over the years, and promises to change still more. Unfortunately, efficiency isn't always the friend of compassion and caring. At one time, as seen in old movies or TV reruns, doctors would visit the sick person at their home, which made a lot of sense as the sick person might have trouble getting around. This was replaced by patients visiting the physician, just as they did the dentist or optometrist. Thus, many people have ended up sitting in waiting rooms, desperately trying to dodge invisible germs that might be emanating from others.

Universal health care

Today most Western countries have a universal health care system in which all individuals are eligible to receive medical services without a fee. The specific benefits covered may vary from country to country and 'allowable' options vary as well (e.g., Are second opinions covered? Are dental and optometry services covered? Are meds covered?). Thus, private insurance (often obtained through the workplace) may be necessary to supplement services that aren't covered by government-run programs. As well, to different degrees, two-tiered health care systems appear across countries so that those who can afford it are able to obtain additional coverage that allows them faster access, and perhaps better treatment, through private clinics.

There is little question that having universal health care is enormously beneficial, especially for those less able to afford medical treatments and those who experience severe or chronic illnesses that can deplete financial savings. It is often thought that these systems are too expensive, but several reports from diverse organizations have indicated that the US, which until recently did not have a universal health care system (it seems to have the beginnings of one now, but it will need to evolve further), had higher per capita health care costs (almost double) relative to other Western countries. Yet, it also had the highest infant mortality rate, the highest number of preventable deaths per capita, and a somewhat lower life expectancy.

Down side of universal health care

Universal health care has had an excellent reputation in most quarters, but this hasn't been the rule. In some countries the cost of the medical system is thought to be too high, and despite the expenditures, the resources available for ambulatory care and preventive medicine (health check-ups, outpatient rehabilitation, psychosocial and psychotherapeutic care, and nursing) have been deemed to be inadequate. This was coupled with social inequalities in the use of medical services, including preventive health check-ups, immunization, and dentistry, as well as attention to the prevention of illness (Hofmarcher & Quentin, 2013). In some countries problems have been encountered ensuring sustainability of health care financing and sufficient human resources, greater integration of health and social services, prioritizing patient-centered health care, ensuring the encouragement of healthy behavior, and assuring health care access for lower socioeconomic groups. The issue frequently comes up that the common complaints comprising long wait lists for critical services could be modified through private insurance (a two-tiered health care system), but this could, in the long run, present a burden for those with low incomes (Schoen & Doty, 2004).

LOOPHOLES IN COVERAGE

One of the most overlooked aspects of health care systems is that medications often aren't covered by government programs, and unless individuals have private insurance, which the poor often don't have, they go with unmet needs. By example, the cost of a medication for type 2 diabetes, a GLP-1 agonist (e.g., Victoza) that is prescribed when drugs like metformin don't do the trick, amounts to about $4,000 yearly. In addition, a relatively new and very effective treatment for hepatitis C, Sofosbuvir (Cholongitas & Papatheodoridis, 2014), can run around $80,000 for a 12-week course of treatment, and many cancer drugs exceed $100,000 each year and their effectiveness is often limited.

Pharmaceutical companies have maintained that getting drugs through development and clinical trials is enormously expensive, which is absolutely true, but for patients to cough up $13,000 or $14,000 a month for life-saving medicines is over the top when universal health is purportedly the norm. Protestation regarding drug prices rings hollow when instances are uncovered where drug companies increase the price of their products simply because they're able to do so in the absence of competition. In some instances prices of drugs seem to double for no apparent reasons; others sky-rocket when one company takes over another or when a company buys a particular product from another company so that they become the only game in town. Insurers often cover drug charges (as much as 80%), but those without insurance end up not being able to afford them. It is ironic as well that insurance companies often don't cover weight loss treatments, as in the case of a relatively new medication, Saxenda, even though obesity can have health consequences that will be very expensive for insurers down the road. Their notion, however, is that by the time individuals get sick as a result of obesity, they might well have other insurance carriers.

Over-treatment

We saw in Chapter 6 that overdiagnosis of illness has been a problem, and hand-in-hand with this is the issue of over-treatment. Indeed, according to the NHS in the UK, 1 in 7 treatments has been unnecessary, leading to a considerable cost for the individual's well-being, and an enormous financial cost that could have been used in the treatment of others and in intervention strategies.

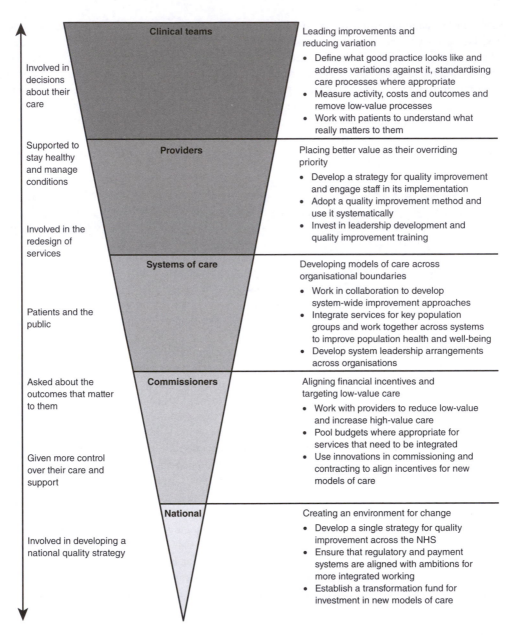

Figure 15.1   A provisional approach to the development of a strategy to improve health care and to offer patients what is actually needed and at the lowest cost. As shown in this figure, effective health delivery requires a contribution from all sectors.

Source: The King's Fund (2015) Better value in the NHS. http://www.kingsfund.org.uk/publications/better-value-nhs/summary

Among other things, medications have been prescribed unnecessarily, as in the case of antibiotics being used for the common cold, inappropriate or inadequate care leading to complications, as well as too many missed opportunities to catch illness early. A significant contributor to over-spending has come from the failure to treat people through day-care procedures rather than in patient admittance. Figure 15.1 provides a model that has been offered to develop priorities and strategies that can be used to address varied health care issues.

Patient equality

Children and older people are generally at increased risk for numerous illnesses, and hence they use medical services more than do others. Wealthier people and those with better education tend to be relatively healthy (and live longer), so it might be expected that they would not be frequent users of health services. However, it's actually the poor who use medical facilities least often (Meara et al., 2008), and health inequalities are also related to race and cultural differences (e.g., Kennedy, 2013). Living in disadvantaged areas is accompanied by diminished *preventive* health services, and increased likelihood of having unmet medical needs (Fiscella & Williams, 2004). As a result, poverty is accompanied by earlier death and an assortment of illnesses, many of which could have been limited by enhanced preventive medicine. So, as much as universal health care is desirable, greater access to these health programs is needed, especially for those people least likely to have access to these health care benefits.

In addition to these factors playing into health care, individuals with physical or psychological disabilities also encounter disparities. Understandably, they experience more distress than most people, encounter many more illnesses than others, and are less likely to receive treatment for their psychological distress (Okoro et al., 2014). Irrespective of whether this occurs owing to stigma versus other causes, those with psychological problems (leaving aside those with addiction-related problems where the severity of the issue is still greater) are frequently shunted aside, their physical illnesses are often incorrectly attributed to mental health problems, and their life span is shortened by about 10 years.

Delayed presentation of illness

The procrastination that exists in relation to seeking medical attention for physical or psychological problems may entail several components. Individuals may initially exhibit '*appraisal delay*', which reflects how long it takes for individuals to acknowledge and accept that whatever symptoms they have should be of concern. Individuals may also display '*illness delay*', reflecting the time to accept that serious symptoms need medical attention. But even when a decision to seek medical attention has been accepted, '*behavioral delay*' may be evident. Remarkably, even after having been told that something might be amiss and that further tests will be needed, some individuals will still delay in obtaining these tests.

At each of these stages, numerous factors can operate to create delays. In contrast to older people, who tend to respond quickly to relatively serious symptoms (and even to those that aren't serious), some individuals tend not to seek help and don't even have a personal physician. They might be reluctant visit doctors because of a lack of trust, or they might have beliefs that are unfounded or extreme ("if you let them look long enough, those quacks are bound to find something even if you're not sick"). Still others have a fear of doctors (going beyond 'white coat syndrome' in which blood pressure rises in response to the situation), or they might not wish to disclose embarrassing symptoms, or perhaps admit to poor health behaviors that carry stigma (e.g., smoking). Of course, symptoms that appear fairly innocuous and don't seem to be getting worse are most likely to receive limited attention and it's far simpler to prevaricate in relation to seemingly benign symptoms. Obviously, this isn't wise as some illnesses don't show up with pronounced symptoms until things have gotten out of hand (e.g., in the case of CAD) and some symptoms aren't painful (e.g., early stages of cancer) and thus are easy to dismiss or forget.

Sex differences

Women tend to be more inclined to seek medical attention when it's needed, possibly because they might be more sensitive to body changes when they occur, or because they are more social and hence accepting of help relative to men. Alternatively, the sex difference may stem from men shying away from seeking help (much as they won't seek directions when they get lost driving), possibly because of a need to feel strong and in control. The 'delayed presentation' of symptoms (i.e., a lengthy period between self-detection of symptoms and seeking help) among men might be due to their ineptness in identifying symptoms as being serious, elevated procrastination, or perhaps their anxiety about illness may interfere with proper judgment related to obtaining medical attention (Ristvedt & Trinkaus, 2008).

Delayed presentation of symptoms also occurs among a moderate number of women. It has been shown that most women who discovered signs of breast cancer visited their physician within 1 month, but almost 25% of women delayed such a visit for 1–3 months or longer (O'Mahony & Hegarty, 2009). Furthermore, many individuals, men and women alike, delayed seeking treatment for head, neck, and oral cancers. This was more common in the poor, those living alone, alcohol consumers, and individuals who favored avoidance coping strategies or who simply misinterpreted symptoms (Noonan, 2014). In some instances, as in the case of seeking help for symptoms for acute heart attack, women were less likely to do so than men, being especially notable among women 65 years of age or older. In part, this appeared to stem from low self-perceived vulnerability to heart attack and the presence of other chronic illnesses that might have provoked confusion related to symptoms. As well, the perceived seriousness of the situation may have been miscalculated as the symptoms of heart attack in women are sometimes more subtle and easily mistaken than in men (symptoms in women might comprise pain in the neck or jaw, stomach pain, shortness of breath and nausea, fatigue, and breaking out in a cold sweat).

SUMMARY

There are enough illnesses to go around so most of us will have to deal with our fair share. These illnesses might have evolved owing to fate (defined in terms of factors or events over which we had little control or because we were not even aware of their existence) or our actions (or inactions). Either way, it's up to individuals to make an initial appraisal as to whether they have symptoms that warrant medical attention, but too often people find reasons not to do so, often experiencing still further negative consequences.

Fundamental to a person's well-being is that they have a doctor (or clinic) that they can consult, rather than waiting until symptoms appear before searching for a doctor who might be available. Just as every lawyer or dentist might not be a right fit for a particular client or patient, this also holds for personal physicians. However, when there is a shortage of physicians, and those available have long backlogs, it may not be possible to pick and choose. I recall a friend who needed a specialist in a particular field of medicine saying to me "I was going to call around and see if anyone had room for me. Well, the third guy I called not only had room, but could see me the next day. At first I thought I had lucked out, and then got to thinking 'why is this guy available, when everyone had line-ups months long?' Anyway, I got an appointment with another doctor and waited my turn." As it happened, the doctor who could accommodate him quickly had a reputation that was very bad, and having alienated patients, he had lots of time on his hands. The point is that despite a shortage of physicians, it's up to individuals to find medical health professionals with whom they click and who are knowledgeable. Aside from this, it probably would be good if people understood what their rights were as a patient, and equally, they ought to be aware of the physician's rights and obligations.

16 Caregiving, Death, and Grief

TURNING BACK THE CLOCK

With improved medications to keep us well, and health practices being taken more seriously, life span has increased. Eventually, however, despite all best efforts, the clock does run down. With increasing life span and health span, retirement age should also be extended, but some people choose 65 years of age (or less) to drop work, hoping to be one of those well-preserved handsome people they see on commercials walking down sunny beaches. The number of individuals, usually beginning at middle or late-middle age, interested in 'successful' aging will continue to transform the retail market that caters to aging populations. There is even an industry in which telomere length is measured so that people can know whether their biological clocks are running down too quickly.

The obsession some people have with aging doesn't stop at determining 'biological aging', but may be accompanied by a desire or need to turn back the clock. With age, the levels of some hormones decline, so it was thought that replacing these hormones ought to make people feel younger. The primary hormone consumed for this purpose included human growth hormone (HGH), which is converted into insulin-like growth factor (IGF-1) as well as dehydroepiandrosterone (DHEA). These compounds can have modest effects in augmenting bone density and muscle strength and influence immune functioning (Rutkowski et al., 2014), but they can also have several adverse effects. Moreover, there haven't been adequate, long-term prospective studies conducted to assess the positive versus negative effects that might be attributable to DHEA replacement therapy in older individuals. In fact, a good deal of the excitement regarding the anti-aging effects of HGH was based on a single study conducted in 1990 using a small number of participants that showed that HGH treatment for 6 months increased lean body mass and reduced adipose tissue mass (Rudman et al., 1990). It seems that those in the 'business' of exploiting hormone-related findings put their own spin on these data, helped along by the media, to suggest that this hormone could be used to extend life. In an editorial in the *New England Journal of Medicine,* the same Journal in which Rudman's work was published, Vance (2003) chastised those who sought to use HGH as an anti-aging treatment. They were being misled. In fact, it seems that living long is accompanied by low HGH levels, which is the opposite to that which might be expected if HGH favored longevity.

It has been reported that transfusions of blood from a young to an old mouse could attenuate and even reverse aspects of aging. One explanation offered for this outcome was that this blood contains a protein, GDF11, which ordinarily diminishes as we age, and increasing its presence may enhance brain functioning and that of most body organs (Katsimpardi et al., 2014; Villeda et al., 2014). The "vampire therapy" has been used only in mice, but we can pretty well bet that the restorative power of young blood will be assessed to determine its effectiveness in the treatment of illnesses ranging from heart disease through to Alzheimer's, and perhaps other stress-related disorders.

Every so often we hear of the fountain of youth appearing in the form of particular genes. In this regard, members of the sirtuin deacetylase/ADP-ribosyltransferase/deacylase family (fortunately, it's usually referred to simply as sirtuin) may increase longevity through both indirect and direct processes. Sirtuins could be doing this by limiting the occurrence of illnesses such as cancer and diminishing lung inflammation and the development of COPD (Guarente, 2014; Yao et al., 2014). These sirtuins might also have their positive effects, by influencing glucose and fat oxidation (Verdin, 2014), increasing resveratrol, which is the substrate important for the beneficial effects of red wine (Howitz et al., 2003), or perhaps by inhibiting the multiplication of viruses and inflammation that otherwise take a toll on various organ systems (Koyuncu et al., 2014). At the moment, the causal link between this family of genes and longevity, if there is one, remains uncertain (Dang, 2014).

A commentary published in the prestigious journal *Nature* made the point that our current approach to health care isn't sustainable given that success in keeping people alive longer simply translates into the accumulation of more diseases (and medical costs) that are related to aging. Better strategies are clearly needed to deal with the inevitable financial and health care crisis that will emerge. Most chronic illnesses, as indicated earlier, take many years to develop, and perhaps the best strategy to adapt for longer life is to consider, a priori, that individuals will also have a healthier life. What a treatment strategy will then amount to is one that entails simple interventions to assure that people engage in better life-styles (Fontana et al., 2014).

LOOKING AT END OF LIFE

We start off naïve, perky, and wide-eyed, and eventually become wise, but somewhat fatigued, and perhaps a bit too skeptical. We can come to the end of our days content with what we've accomplished, or we can get there miserably and discontented. In this chapter we'll examine several issues related to the dying process from the perspective of caregivers and family members, as well as from those who are doing the dying. To this end, we'll consider:

- the burdens of taking on the role of a caregiver
- the psychological processes related to dying
- end-of-life care and the right to die
- the loss and grieving experienced by family members.

CAREGIVING

Taking on the role of a caregiver is fairly common within Western countries, with almost 30% of individuals acting in this capacity at some point in time. This often comprises caring for older people who have lost the ability to care for themselves, but can also involve victims of accidents, those with unfortunate illnesses or severe mental or physical disabilities, and the care of children with serious physical or mental problems. Whatever the case, serving as a caregiver can be emotionally draining, often compounded by individuals having other responsibilities that need to be met.

The caregiver's burden

Not every person is psychologically prepared to serve as a caregiver, lacking the skills or disposition to undertake this role, or they might be in a position that limits how much help they can actually offer. For some individuals, the shock of their loved one encountering an illness (or accident) and then finding themselves in a new role adds to their distress, and interpersonal disruptions that occur may be a strain on coping resources (King et al., 2010). Although caregiving of older people often falls to adult children of the recipient, the caregiver can also be an elderly spouse who isn't physically prepared or able to engage in this strenuous job, and it may have pronounced ramifications on their own well-being. Among spouses who act in a caregiving capacity for partners with some illnesses (such as dementia), their own risk for this illness increases six-fold (Norton et al., 2010). Perhaps owing to the distress of caregiving among older individuals, when one partner becomes ill, the risk for divorce increases appreciably, particularly if it's the wife who becomes ill (Karraker & Latham, 2015).

The caregiver faces an additional burden if she has children of her own who must be tended to (the pronoun 'she' is used deliberately as most caregivers typically are women, although some men take on this task). This has become more common as the great number of babies born in the late 1940s (the baby boomers) are now in their later 60s, and while some are already in need of care, others may be soon enough. The distress of the caregiver is amplified if the care recipient lives with them, as well as with increased time spent in this capacity, feelings of social isolation, financial hardship, and the perception that there is no option other than acting in this capacity (Adelman et al., 2014).

The strain on the caregiver will likely vary with various attributes of the situation, and may vary over time with changes in the needs of the care recipient. The many uncertainties, the frequent ups and downs, and sometimes having to witness the dehumanizing conditions faced by their loved one, makes the caregiving role particularly distressing. Predictably, being in this position may promote the development of anxiety, depression, PTSD, as well as endocrine and immune disturbances (Lovell & Wetherell, 2011), particularly among individuals who had experienced childhood adversity (Kiecolt-Glaser et al., 2011).

Caring for the caregiver

In view of the load on caregivers and the adverse effects that can ensue, what should be done to diminish these outcomes? As indicated earlier, not all individuals are suitable to serve in a caregiving role, and having personality characteristics that include high levels of mastery, optimism, self-efficacy, and a tendency toward problem-focused coping methods might be ideal

(Roepke et al., 2010). In some instances, the use of religion and spirituality has been instrumental in dealing with the distress associated with caregiving (Sun & Hodge, 2014), and finding meaning in a caregiving role can be an important method of maintaining well-being for some individuals (McLennon et al., 2011).

For a caregiver, the load carried is often unrelenting; one day runs into the next, and the job is unremitting. Caregivers need time away to recuperate, they need social support, and other family members or professional caregivers need to step in to help (Koerner et al., 2010). Too often, those who ought to be helping let the 'willing horse do the work' and feel that their duty is done by visiting on odd occasions, while the daily caregiver broods about the unfairness of the situation. There is little doubt that for so difficult a job, one of the most important factors concerns the caregiver's motivation to engage in this task. Caregivers who were intrinsically motivated (i.e., motivation driven by interest and/or reward derived from the activity) fared well in this capacity, whereas those who were extrinsically motivated (derived from external pressures) were most apt to experience negative outcomes, such as depression and anger (Romero-Moreno et al., 2011). Obviously, caregivers need to engage in this activity for the right reasons, rather than taking on unwanted obligations or succumbing to the demands (perceived or real) of others.

In light of the multiple adverse consequences on health that can develop through improperly supported caregiving, Collins and Swartz (2011) indicated that more attention ought to be focused on the care of caregivers. Doing otherwise will not only enhance the likelihood of poor outcomes among the caregivers, but might also influence the well-being of the recipient. Indeed, even a few days of care through a hospice service has shown to be sufficient to make an enormous difference in the life of the caregiver (Ornstein et al., 2015). It's not one of those dirty little secrets that can be hidden away, but many individuals suffer elder abuse, possibly stemming from frustrations experienced by family members, including those acting in a caregiving role. The problem was sufficiently serious and widespread to have prompted the American Academy of Neurology to advise clinical neurologists to screen patients for abuse to determine whether their problems might be secondary to such experiences.

SOMETHING ELSE THEY'RE NOT TELLING US, BUT SHOULD

Elderly people, even if they aren't at the point of dementia (but experiencing mild cognitive impairments), are vulnerable to still greater cognitive disturbances following a stressor experience. Among patients hospitalized with respiratory failure, septic shock, or cardiogenic shock, which are powerful stressors in their own right, 74% experienced delirium (a confusional state that occurs due to organic factors), and even several months later, 40% exhibited signs like those of people who had suffered traumatic brain injury (Pandharipande et al., 2014). Anesthetics associated with surgical procedures likewise produce prominent confusion and memory loss that can last for extended periods following return from hospital. In rodents the injectable anesthetic etomidate, as well as the inhaled anesthetic isoflurane, altered GABA functioning, and did so for

(Continued)

(Continued)

about a week. During this time synaptic plasticity within the hippocampus was disrupted and memory was impaired, but could be attenuated by inhibiting particular types of GABA receptors. It is conceivable that these same processes operate to provoke memory loss in human patients undergoing surgery requiring an anesthetic (Zurek et al., 2014). It may be beneficial to monitor and attempt to shorten periods of delirium, perhaps by shortening the time patients receive sedatives and increasing their mobility.

In view of the frequency of cognitive disturbances associated with illness requiring hospitalization and anesthetics, it's remarkable that patients and their families typically aren't forewarned of this (does it even appear on consent forms?) so that they aren't gobsmacked by this development.

THE DYING PROCESS

Life span has been increasing over the years, and the causes of death as well as the burden of disease have changed remarkably. As the saying goes, "none of us gets out of this alive", but there are many ways to die, and they have different implications on the psychological well-being and QoL among those in the dying process as well as on those left behind. The primary causes of death varies across countries world-wide (Murray et al., 2012), and also differs across age groups. In most Western countries, the main causes of death among children less than 1 year of age comprise congenital anomalies, premature birth, sudden infant death syndrome (SIDS), pregnancy complications, and unintentional injury. Death is less frequent over the ensuing years, up to middle adolescence, with accidents being the most common cause of death. From then through to the middle 30s, accidents (largely automobile accidents, but also stemming from high-risk behaviors) continue to be the most likely cause of death. Suicide also ranks highly, and in some communities homicide is a major cause of death. With further aging, heart disease, cancer, and COPD take the front spots, but illnesses such as diabetes, cerebrovascular events (e.g., stroke), and accidental injury also account for many deaths.

Data such as these might inform policy makers whether there needs to be a push for the adoption of healthy behaviors, development of methods for dealing with particular diseases, or diminishing the influence of environmental factors (e.g., water safety issues that lead to diarrheal diseases) that can lead to illness and death. As well, the patterns seen over years may also help predict what prophylactic measures will be needed at the moment and what resources will be necessary in coming years. This is the case in both developing countries and in Western nations which could do with enhanced preventive services as well as improved community resources, especially with the marked increase of chronic diseases (Bauer et al., 2014).

The meaning of death in relation to age

How people diagnosed with a terminal illness deal with this news varies with many factors, including the individual's age. Young children may not understand the meaning of death, or they might envision it as a long sleep, possibly even one they could come back from when Prince

Charming arrives. By about 9 or 10 years of age, the meaning of death becomes more tangible, with children coming to the understanding that death has finality (Kastenbaum & Costa, 1977). Some adolescents dealing with a fatal illness, such as cancer, might react with shock, anger, and the feeling that this is unjust, whereas others seem to believe that the illness is less severe than it actually is, possibly reflecting an avoidance strategy (Schowalter, 1977). As people reach middle age, and the imminence of death becomes more real, even if vaguely shaped, health concerns generally increase. Still, death isn't common at this age, and such a diagnosis is hard for individuals to deal with, and the news may be met in any number of ways. Following the initial shock of learning of a fatal condition, distress may emerge with the thoughts of leaving behind a partner or children, regret may emerge as they think of things that they wanted to do but hadn't, and in some instances hopelessness and despair may occur among individuals who perceive their lives as lacking meaning and purpose (Kissane et al., 2001). Typically, having appropriate support from family and friends will be helpful in coping with this form of distress (Ringdal et al., 2007), but again, individuals may differ in the kind of support that's best, and when it should be offered.

A diagnosis that an illness is terminal might not come as a surprise to an old person, but may be distressing nonetheless. Knowing that death won't be far away, older individuals may express intense feelings of regret over things left unfinished, which may be accompanied by various physical and sleep problems. Many of the variables that predict resilience in relation to illness (having strong social support, having a purpose in life, close relations with adult children) are particularly pertinent for individuals dealing with the dying process.

Stages in adjustment to dying

A once popular conception of the dying process, advanced by Kubler-Ross (1969), was that this involved five stages: denial, anger, bargaining, depression, and acceptance. Initially, individuals tend not to accept the notion that their illness is terminal (denial), and may experience a shock reaction, disorientation, and an inability to form a cohesive picture of their situation. Typically, within a few days, the reality is absorbed, but otherwise counseling may be needed since denial may interfere with obtaining and adhering to treatments.

In the second stage, anger appears at what might be perceived as the unfairness regarding their situation, and often they ask "why me?". I've said it before, but it bears repeating, even if it sounds heartless. Specifically, in answer to "why me" all that one can really say is "why not you?". If the average life span is 80 years old, then we don't all get to live to or beyond 80. Some obviously will die earlier, and as unfair as it is, "bad things even happen to good people" (Kushner, 1981). At this stage, some individuals are able to moderate their anger, whereas others may become embittered, negative, and passive aggressive, and as a result their social alliances and support may wither. As the anger phase diminishes, it may be replaced by bargaining, in which individuals might make deals with God indicating that if they get to stay alive they'll engage in all sorts of charitable works and kind acts (never mind that they reneged on many previous deals and would probably do so again).

If bargaining seems not to have worked out, and the person realizes that their options are limited, which may occur with a worsening of physical symptoms, depression and *anticipatory grief* may follow. Individuals might initially focus on the losses of past pleasurable experiences, followed by anticipation of future losses ("I loved this spring, the sun was just right, it wasn't too hot and the flowers came out as if newly awakened. I sure wish I would have had the opportunity of experiencing that again"). In the final stage, when the individual has tired of fighting or being angry, acceptance of the inevitability of death will likely occur. At this point, provided that they have the strength to do so, they will be in a better position to make arrangements that need to be made, talk to old friends, make sure that their legal issues (e.g., their will) are in order, and then allow themselves the luxury of going peacefully.

SO, WHAT'S ON THE OTHER SIDE?

Most people, upon reaching a certain age, might wonder "what's on the other side?". They might be especially taken by people who report about 'near-death experiences', and it's hardly a wonder that books on the topic, written by apparently credible people, end up as best sellers. Feeling calm and serene, and floating toward a bright light at the end of a tunnel-like structure, makes death sound less frightening. But, what is actually occurring when people have these near-death visions that some-times are taken as epiphanies? Does a lack of oxygen during a heart attack cause hallucinations, and do they only occur in those who 'come back'? When brain signaling was measured in rats at a time near death, rather than seeing a large decline of neuronal functioning that one might have expected to occur with loss of consciousness, this period was accompanied by 'a storm' of brain activity, which also involved elevated communication with the heart that actually hastened a decline of heart func-tioning (D. Li et al., 2015). This may give us a hint that the storm of neuronal activity in rats might similarly be involved in altered perceptions that people have in association with near-death expe-riences. But, it doesn't tell us about the specific cognitions or memories that have been reported. In a study of 2,060 people who experienced cardiac arrest, more than 100 who were interviewed, and of these individuals 46% reported memories of their experience. These memories fell into sev-eral themes beyond those reported in relation to near-death experiences. These cognitive themes included fear, animals/plants, bright light, violence/persecution, deja-vu, family, recall of events, and a small number reported awareness and 'seeing' and 'hearing' actual events related to their resus-citation. There was, however, one individual who seemed to have a verifiable period of conscious awareness at a time when cerebral function ought to have been absent (Parnia et al., 2015).

Often, near-death experiences that have been reported have taken on religious overtones. Indeed, these religious aspects for those who nearly died can serve as a way of coping with these potentially traumatizing experiences, just as religion can be used by some people to cope with immi-nent death. Individuals with a religious bent might find comfort in the thought of an after-life, or the thought of going to heaven. However, coping through religion isn't meant for everybody. Obviously, atheists won't use religion in this capacity, and those who haven't decided about the existence of a God might start moving toward a religious belief as death comes closer. Over the years, I've had agnostic friends confronted with the prospect of dying soon, owing to one form of cancer or another. During the course of our conversations the topic arose about the view of some physicists concerning the existence of multiple universes, possibly lying in parallel with this one. We considered the notion that these universes could potentially be connected by wormholes, and what could pass through them.

Might one of these universes be the collection point for souls? None of us knew diddly about string theory, multiple universes, or wormholes, but perhaps because the conversation had a scientific feel, my friends were very positive about the slim possibility of something being on the other side. As negative as uncertainty may be, hopefulness can go a long way in diminishing distress.

Critiques of the Stage model

The views of Kubler-Ross opened the dialogue on a topic that hadn't received wide attention, and those dealing with palliative care recognized specific stages from their experiences with patients. However, there have been detractors of this model and others like it. These models usually consider one stage naturally leading to the next, but individuals frequently differ appreciably in the behaviors and attitudes associated with dying. Not every person necessarily goes through the stages described by Kubler-Ross, but even if they do, the order may differ (Silver & Wortman, 2007). Furthermore, the model hardly considers other aspects that affect the dying process, most notably whether individuals are feeling pain or discomfort related to a disease or its treatment.

The reality is that people differ in so many ways and have had so many different experiences that there isn't a single model that fits everyone. Will a person who reached all or most of their goals have the same attitude toward dying as the person who never achieved or perhaps never even had specific goals? Similarly, is it reasonable to expect similar processes or stages to appear in a person who has faced a lonely or unhappy existence relative to one who only intermittently encountered bad breaks? We all live differently, and it's likely that this will also be reflected in the process that accompanies dying.

END-OF-LIFE CARE

Palliative and hospice care

If one were to ask where people prefer to die, the vast majority would say that they want to die at home, in their own bed, surrounded by their loved ones. Within the UK, 18% of people died at home, whereas 64% died in hospitals or nursing homes. The figures are somewhat different within the US, where about 33.5% of Medicare beneficiaries died at home in 2009, representing a 10% increase over a 10-year period, whereas 24.6% died in the hospital and 42% died in hospice care, double that of 10 years earlier. For many, this certainly wasn't what they wanted or expected.

Palliative care comprises a team-based approach to providing optimal care for patients with severe illnesses to attenuate their symptoms, pain, and distress, and to generally improve their QoL, as well as that of family members. For palliative care to be obtained, it is not a requirement that death be close at hand, nor is it necessarily supplied in specialized centers, often being delivered at home. Aside from being cared for by specialists, palliative care has the broader advantage of diminishing use of hospital, emergency department, or ambulatory care services, which are far more expensive but not necessarily better for the patient.

Hospice care is a related procedure that is adopted once a person has exhausted all medical treatments and accepts the imminence of death. The increase in the number of older individuals dying in a hospice with good care available should be encouraging, but this isn't always so. Some people in hospice care have experienced many moves from one institution to another, including frequent intensive care unit admissions and multiple hospitalizations over a relatively brief period before dying (Teno et al., 2013). Such experiences were especially common among individuals with cognitive disturbances (Gozalo et al., 2011), which might have further impaired their functioning. Despite best intentions, the process of dying can be much more difficult than it ought to be, even when apparently appropriate arrangements have been made for end-of-life care.

EXTENDING THE DYING PROCESS

In a fascinating essay, entitled "Why I hope to die at 75", Ezekiel J. Emanuel (2014) indicated that "living too long is a loss". Aside from the frailty and multiple illnesses that are encountered, aging is often accompanied by the loss of creativity and abilities. But more than this, it affects how others see us and how they will remember us. Instead of the once vibrant person we had once been, they will recall us as feeble and ineffectual, and worse still, they may even perceive us as pathetic. With aging, QoL declines profoundly. The things that could be done when we were younger are now out of our reach as our physical, and often our mental, capacity declines. As well, aging is accompanied by more frequent chronic illnesses, ranging from heart disease, stroke, COPD, and cancer to dementia, and, as Emanuel put it, "health care hasn't slowed the aging process so much as it has slowed the dying process".

The reality is, as Gawande (2014) indicated, the ability of medicine to fend off death is limited, and some procedures are conducted even though they will impair QoL in the short time the person will stay alive. If seriously ill patients, especially those who are experiencing chronic pain, could look into the future, there's a fair chance that they wouldn't choose the route being offered. Simply put, death needn't be so brutal.

End-of-life care might involve taking medications to reduce pain and discomfort, which may include 'just in case' or 'anticipatory medications' to diminish pain as it starts to appear (Tjia et al., 2013). As well, emotional care may be critical for the patient, and the specific care delivered to any given patient is influenced by multiple psychosocial experiences, and might need to vary across different settings (Skilbeck & Payne, 2003). As individuals exhibit many different behaviors and express different needs as the end approaches, it is difficult to define what a 'good death' comprises. Based on observations of patients, care providers, and family members, several fundamental features were seen to be particularly important in this regard: diminished pain, being able to prepare for death, having a feeling of 'completion', being able to make clear and proper decisions, self-affirmation, and the feeling of having made a contribution to others (Steinhauser et al., 2000). For these outcomes to be realized, it's likely that better coordination is needed with family members, especially if the patient may not be capable of communicating or making decisions. Moreover, by working with patients, front-line care providers can offer innovative and creative approaches to ensure that patient needs are met (Skilbeck & Payne, 2005).

Communications concerning end-of-life care

Patients, families, and doctors ought to have discussions concerning the individual's end-of-life care, which may enhance relationships and encourage well-being (Scott & Caughlin, 2014). The Canadian Medical Association (CMA) has indicated that although 95% of individuals believe that end-of-life plans for care should be discussed with family members, only 30% actually do so. The CMA has thus recommended that physicians should work with patients and families in developing advanced care planning, and whatever plans are established, these should be honored unless there are legitimate and reasonable grounds not to engage in these plans. However, it isn't unusual for the essential components regarding patient desires to be missed. In this regard, the issues identified as most important by both patients and families entail the patient's care preference, the patient's values, illness prognosis, concerns and fears, and issues regarding care. However, a study revealed that few of these were discussed with the attending physician (You et al., 2014). Fortunately, front-line hospital or palliative care staff might actually have a good idea of patient needs and desires and may be instrumental in these needs being met.

PHYSICIAN-ASSISTED DEATH

There are many reasons why individuals might have lost the desire to live. Often it occurs among individuals who are severely depressed, and in those experiencing PTSD, schizophrenia, or bipolar disorder. It may be precipitated by financial problems, relationship break-ups, or loneliness, and can also be instigated by shame and humiliation, bullying, feeling trapped or helpless, or being victimized (e.g., in an abusive relationship). Suicide is the second or third leading cause of death among young people and the fourth leading cause of death among those who are in the 25–54 year-old age group. In the UK, 5,500–6,000 die by suicide on a yearly basis, and in the USA and Canada, suicide accounted for 30,000 and 3,600 deaths a year, respectively. These numbers are likely underestimates, as stigma related to suicide might act against accurate reporting. This is obviously terribly sad. Sad not only because of the emotional pain that people are experiencing, but sad because the emotional state that led to suicide might have been transient and individuals could have been helped so that they could have subsequently enjoyed happy lives.

Suicidal intentions may also occur when an individual learns that they have a progressive, incurable illness that might involve extreme pain or loss of self, as in the case of diseases such as cancer, Alzheimer's, or amyotrophic lateral sclerosis (ALS). People might choose to wait until they near the point where they would lose the ability to take their own life, but for whatever reason they might not be able to take the final step, and need help in doing so, and thus would prefer physician-assisted death. Physicians dealing with people who are seriously ill, such as those with cancer, frequently receive such requests from patients (Meier et al., 1998), but it is only recently that this has become legal in some places. In many instances, when patients have the opportunity of physician-assisted death they ultimately chose not to take this route. Simply feeling that they are in a position to determine their own destiny may offset some of the distress they had been experiencing.

Positions and counter-positions

Many reasons have been given for keeping assisted dying illegal. These have comprised the religious belief that suicide is a sin (as is facilitating suicide), it goes against the Hippocratic oath (do no harm), it's a slippery slope that could lead to the abuse of the most vulnerable, and possibly even euthanasia without patient consent. There is also the issue of who gets to choose who dies and at what point will children with disabilities be euthanized? As well, it has been argued that legislation to permit euthanasia could limit developments to improving care for those who are dying, as advocating assisted suicide or euthanasia would be "quicker and easier" than conducting palliative care research. The position has also been adopted that social values and respect for life ought to be maintained. Ironically, this last point is exactly what those in favor of doctor-assisted death are saying. There is also evidence that assisted dying can lead to a contagion in which others choose this method of death, well before it makes sense to do so. Advocates of assisted death have maintained that respect for life means not being kept on gurneys within hospital corridors because all beds are taken, not being kept alive in a comatose state as organs whither, not being maintained in a drug stupor because of intractable pain, not being in a situation where individuals are unable to control any aspect of their lives, including bowel movements. Those promoting assisted dying are saying that respect for life includes dying with dignity. When the issue of assisted dying came before the Supreme Court within Canada, Gloria Taylor, who was in a late stage of ALS, indicated "What I fear is a death that negates, as opposed to concludes, my life. I do not want to die slowly, piece by piece. I do not want to waste away unconscious in a hospital bed. I do not want to die wracked with pain".

MEANINGFUL WORDING

Incidentally, some of us prefer terms such as 'assisted dying' or 'dying with dignity', as 'physician-assisted suicide' carries so much stigma. A 2013 Gallup poll in the US indicated that 70% of people were in support of allowing a doctor to "end the [terminally ill] patient's life by some painless means", whereas only 51% supported doctors helping patients 'commit suicide'.

Whether or not assisted dying should be legalized has been fiercely debated for years, and general acceptance of the principle has slowly increased, but for this to become more widely adopted, it is essential that physicians and nurses be in favor of the procedures, especially as they will necessarily be involved in their implementation. In the UK and several other European countries, as well as Canada, most physicians did not want current laws regarding assisted dying to be altered, and in the US, the American Medical Association has not been in favor of assisted dying, largely because it challenges the physician's ethical integrity. But, more than half of US physicians surveyed supported physician-assisted dying, and a poll conducted more than a decade ago indicated that at that time US physicians felt that it was morally permissible under specific conditions (Emanuel, 2002). Moreover, it wasn't unusual, even two decades ago, for nurses to favor assisted dying, possibly because of their closeness to patients and their understanding of what patients might genuinely want (Asch & DeKay, 1997).

DO NOT RESUSCITATE

Patients often have the option of signing a declaration that in case of emergency they do not want to be placed on advanced life support or to be resuscitated (DNR) (an alternative recent term is 'allowing a natural death'; AND), particularly as survival wouldn't be for long even if they were successfully resuscitated (Zoch et al., 2000). In essence, taking active steps to hurry inevitable death is often forbidden, but withholding treatment is seen as being legal even though this means the patient will die, but will do so slowly. The British Medical Association (2007), together with the Resuscitation Council and the Royal College of Nursing, has provided guidelines as to when resuscitation can be withheld, and what the limits to this should be. However, within the US, the nature of the procedures used in relation to patients who request DNR varies appreciably across hospitals, often being greatly out of sync with the patient's desires (Hart et al., 2015).

In 2015, the Supreme Court of Canada legalized physician-assisted death, the fifth country to do so. It was suggested that this ought to be allowable when "the person affected clearly consents to the termination of life" and is suffering from a "grievous and irremediable medical condition". Legislation such as this might spell relief for those who suffer horrid physical illnesses, or those in intractable pain, permitting personal autonomy and freedom of choice for all individuals (psychological illness, such as depression, isn't considered to fall into this group, but some have argued that it should). To do otherwise would, in effect, allow for able-bodied people to die by suicide, but this option wouldn't be possible in those with physical limitations, which was considered a clear violation of equality. Furthermore, this legislation recognizes that despite its earlier illegality, assisted suicide occurred, but without adequate measures being taken to assure that it was being done under appropriate conditions. Finally, it tacitly acknowledges that the distinction between withholding or withdrawing treatment and assisted dying is wholly artificial and there is no moral significance or justification for the distinction between acts of commission and omission that lead to patient deaths (Butler et al., 2013).

LOSS AND GRIEVING

Coping with loss

Regardless of the cause of death, the impact on family members is typically traumatic, differing as a function of who it was that died (parent, child, sibling), how old they were at the time of death, whether death occurred after a prolonged struggle allowing those left behind the opportunity to prepare, and there may even be relief in seeing an end to the misery endured by the person who passed. Likewise, the consequences on survivors may vary as a function of whether someone was to blame for the death (e.g., in an accident) or whether it was an event that couldn't be predicted and couldn't be attributed to a given person or organization. Sometimes, self-blame, even if it's inappropriately directed, can have an enormous impact on those left behind. Parents who lost a child owing to drug-related events may experience exceptional grief and mental health problems, which may be compounded by limited compassion from others (Feigelman et al., 2011). The impact on family members who have experienced loss by suicide is usually particularly profound. Parents will ask what triggered the suicide. Did it occur as a result of bullying that led to despair, and what could the parents have done differently? As well, the response of others to the surviving family members may vary as a function of the characteristics of the person that died, and what prompted the suicide (Calhoun & Allen, 1991).

There isn't a simple solution to facilitate the grieving process that is applicable to everyone. Some people might benefit from support groups comprising similarly affected individuals, but others might be inclined to maintain their own counsel or that of close family members and not want their problems and grief out in the open. As we've seen in the case of other traumatic stressors, for some individuals, finding meaning in the loss might be effective (Davis et al., 1998), whereas others might be more comfortable using religion or other ways of coping to find solace.

Following from the work of Jetten and colleagues (2012) concerning the importance of social identity as a cure for distress, we can pretty well count on social support from people who share a particular identity as being exceptionally important in dealing with loss. Once again, identity in this regard is broadly defined and might consist of our ingroup (culture, religion, work, friends), but often the groups that are most helpful are those who share particular problems (e.g., support groups wherein members have encountered losses in the same way). Online grief communities have also evolved (Swartwood et al., 2011) and these can be helpful, but obviously care needs to be exercised in doing this given the online predators that seem to lurk about.

Grieving as a process

Grief is a natural reaction in response to the loss of a loved person (as well as a beloved pet), and it may take as long as 3–5 years for people to adjust to loss, often being related to factors that had been present prior to the loss, such as the presence of psychological problems, the individual's culture, and their attachment style (Shah & Meeks, 2011). The grieving process may also be related to appraisals, coping and emotional regulation, the availability and perception of social support, financial issues, beliefs concerning death and loss (including religious beliefs), positive emotions, and comfort obtained from positive memories (Mancini et al., 2012). Ordinarily, grief doesn't require clinical intervention, although it isn't unusual for anti-anxiety medication to be prescribed for the short term. Among some people, however, acute grief can morph into a chronic and debilitating condition, referred to as *complicated grief*, which can promote physical illnesses, psychological problems, cognitive disturbances, and elevated mortality (Shear et al., 2011). In these instances, specialized therapy is needed (Wittouck et al., 2011), and in some instances antidepressant medication is used to attenuate depression and anxiety (Hensley et al., 2009).

Grieving had been viewed as a process involving several stages that individuals had to work through (Maciejewski et al., 2007), but this perspective was challenged and alternative positions offered. One especially influential perspective, the dual process model, proposed that two types of bereavement-related coping processes can be engaged to deal with loss (Stroebe & Schut, 1999). *Loss-orientation* considers an individual's internal experience regarding the loss, focusing on the attachment the individual had with the person who had passed together with the emotions triggered by the loss, including rumination, yearning, despair, loneliness, but also positive reminiscing. The second, *restoration-orientation*, is concerned with the emerging challenges stemming from the loss (changes in quality of life and living style, and being able to build a second identity independent of the person who was lost). Initially, loss orientation predominates, but with time, the balance ought to shift to the more functionally effective restoration-orientation (Stroebe, 2001).

It is likely that problem- and emotion-focused coping contribute to successful transitioning from a loss- to a restoration-orientation perspective. Bereaved individuals with a negative-ruminative coping style were found to be more likely to be depressed for extended periods (Nolen-Hoeksema et al., 1994), and benefited from social support (Nolen-Hoeksema & Davis, 1999). It is of particular significance that beyond any single specific coping method, being flexible was accompanied by greatest resilience in response to loss (Burton et al., 2011).

SUMMARY

The process of dying may be shockingly brief, or it can be long and emotionally painful. In the former instance, individuals may not have many options available to them, and sorting out obligations and preparing for an end may be rushed, and sometimes impossible. Older individuals may have prepared for this possibility, whereas those who are not at that point might not have had the forethought to make these arrangements.

Different perspectives have been offered concerning the cognitive and emotional processes associated with dying. However, contrary to beliefs of several decades ago, it seems that there isn't 'a' process, and considerable differences occur across individuals in this respect, depending on their past experiences, support network, life satisfaction, what they feel they've accomplished, the cause of their dying, and who they're leaving behind. As well, while some individuals experience a relatively peaceful departure, for others it's fraught with anxiety and physical pain, and some would prefer to make this departure on their own terms rather than leaving it up to fate or orders of the state.

17 From Molecules, to Individuals, to Communities, to Policy

SHOCKING REALIZATION

I suppose that I shouldn't be surprised by the weird views that have been attributed to science, or those that purposefully ignore scientific evidence. "Humans never really landed on the moon", "fluoridation of water causes diseases", and "through the science of neuroplasticity, games that involve problem solving will act against the development of dementia". We've known for some time that people tend to be more likely to believe word-of-mouth messages or those that they are predisposed to believe than information obtained from proven reliable health organizations (Kareklas et al., 2015). The most recent reincarnation of this voodoo nonscience approach has come from the anti-vaxxer movement. In recent years, negative attitudes have been adopted toward childhood vaccination despite the fact that it has saved millions of lives and many scientific reports have indicated that there is no evidence supporting the claim that vaccines (or related agents, such as thermisol) lead to autism or any other illnesses (Jain et al., 2015). Vaccination of children may cause infrequent occurrences of adverse events, but the benefits derived by vaccination far outweigh the risks (Maglione et al., 2014). Oh sure, there are stories out there to convince people that vaccines are harmful: "So many vaccinations, especially during the early years, is bound to affect a growing brain", "science has been wrong before", "I'm not anti-vaccine, I'm pro 'safe' vaccine", "I know what's best for my own child", and the weird view that "vaccines are unnatural". Each and every one of these has been shown to be patently incorrect, but it hasn't dissuaded the true believers. One also has to wonder about parents who indicate that if everyone else vaccinates their kids, then 'herd immunity' will protect their kids from infection, seemingly not understanding that if others behave like they do, then the herd immunity will fall apart.

Even more remarkable is that the general public count on scientists to come up with cures or treatments for many illnesses and rarely express gratitude to the inventors of these cures, and even take for granted that treatments will be available for most problems that ail them. They don't see it as the least bit odd to pay a movie actor or sports figure millions of dollars a year, but would probably balk at compensating the creator of vaccines or other life-saving medical treatments (How many people even know who Jonas Salk was?). It's even more puzzling that in relation to vaccines, scientists hold little influence over public opinions, especially when they have to compete with the internet mill that spews out unverified reports and opinions disguised as data-driven. As well, it's absolutely stunning that so many people would prefer to believe the word of some Hollywood know-nothing over that of knowledgeable scientists.

Then again, as I said earlier, perhaps I shouldn't be at all shocked. Perhaps people are drawn to the fringe because it's exciting to be a 'rebel', or because there's vast mistrust of anything that's related to 'the establishment', or simply because scientists aren't sufficiently skilled to get their message across, or for the longest time hadn't been inclined to do so. Scientists have become much more aware of the importance of translating their research so that it amounts to more than speaking to other scientists, and are now more immersed in the functional and practical applications of their research. Irrespective of whether their work is meant to lead to a better understanding of disease processes so that treatments and cures can be found, scientists have taken more proactive steps toward knowledge transfer, bringing their view to the public, and potentially influencing policy. I'm not certain how scientists can get their message across most effectively (ranting as I do isn't the solution, which is why there are better spokespeople than me doing this), but it's absolutely certain that one way or another, enhanced credibility and trust of scientists needs to be established, and they need to come out of hiding in their labs and state their views. Ultimately, the trust of medical scientists needs to be greater than it is for television and movie personalities.

INTEGRATING GENETIC, NEUROBIOLOGICAL, AND PSYCHOSOCIAL PROCESSES: ELIMINATING SILOS

Even though psychiatry, neurology, and neuropsychology have all been involved in treating the broken brain, they do so through very different means, which has likely contributed to these fields residing in separate silos. Yet researchers in psychiatry have come to rely heavily on drug treatments and brain imaging as well as neuropsychological tests, and neurologists have learned the usefulness of incorporating data from other disciplines in their own treatment arsenal (Northoff, 2008). Thus, within some teaching programs the training of the three disciplines has been offered to students, while still maintaining the individual identities of each unit (Cunningham et al., 2006). The advantages of integrating these fields ought to be fairly obvious given that at their intersection considerable exchange of information is possible, combination treatments can be established, and simply understanding alternative perspectives should enhance patient treatment. As a side benefit, the emergence of '*neuropsychiatry*' as a discipline would make it more likely that people will view psychiatric disorders as medical conditions, and perhaps the stigma associated with mental disorders will be diminished.

The benefits derived from combining disciplines have also emerged within other fields of medicine. Immunology, virology, and treatment of infectious diseases obviously have much to offer one another, as do oncology, endocrinology, and psychology in providing treatment to help all aspects of the person. What has become exceptionally exciting is that the amalgam of these fields has been extended so that they have now incorporated community-based medicine, and increasingly greater translational efforts have been made so that basic and clinical research findings can influence policy and public health programs. In this chapter we'll consider several broad aspects related to health psychology and related disciplines. This will include discussion of:

- the importance of translational research, which means taking research from the lab through to treatment programs or government policies
- the barriers in translating evidence-based research to the application of interventions and treatment strategies
- the advantages of a coordinated ecosystem approach, including working across disciplines and sectors, while at the same time recognizing local priorities.

TRANSLATIONAL RESEARCH

Occasionally, scientists are perceived as hiding away in laboratories and evaluating obscure topics that are of little interest or significance to almost anyone else. This might be true in some instances, but in others it's simply wrong. I suspect that this notion has come about because many people are unaware of what scientists do, coupled with the inability of many scientists to express, in lay terms, the significance of their basic research. Beyond this, however, it might not actually be known what practical applications could eventually evolve as a result of basic science. Some guy studying pea plants might not have had a clue that his work would lead to the field of genetics, which later morphed into molecular genetics, the discovery of stem cells, and the possibility of new and better cures for a variety of illnesses. Likewise, somebody messing around with gut bacteria might have been entirely unaware that this work would eventually have implications for a huge number of physical and psychological disease conditions, and that it would eventually facilitate the development of treatments that would otherwise never even have been on the radar. This is reminiscent of what Forrest Gump's momma always said about a box of chocolates: "you never know what you're gonna get".

For many years, a death valley existed between scientific discovery and its application in some practical way. Scientists were into the science, and left it to someone else to use the data in whatever constructive way they liked. As much as basic science is fundamental for the discovery process, there came a point where more active steps were necessary for scientists to engage in the translation of research (Knowledge Translation) from the lab to the clinic and to communities. Scientists were asked to explain how their research could be used, or to actually demonstrate its practicality. Given the shortage of funding in health-based research, which is becoming scarcer each year, this was probably inevitable. As much as this move to application is laudable, there are also downsides. For example, there is concern that hampering basic science research is apt to repress creative research and inhibit curiosity, and might thus have long-term negative repercussions. In addition, science is not an outcome, but rather, it's a process. Early research findings require replication, elaboration and extension, quality checks and self-correction, along with an assessment of their generalizability. Premature application of research can have serious detrimental consequences that might be avoided with greater scrutiny by the scientific community. By its very nature, science involves tests and retests of results, challenging the interpretations of findings, and an understanding of the context in which questions are asked and findings applied.

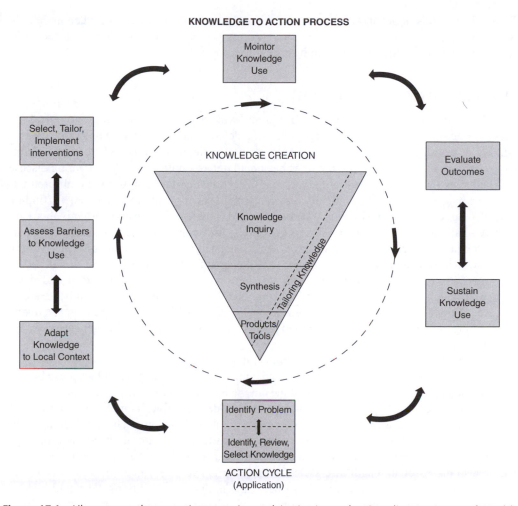

Figure 17.1   Like many other granting agencies and institutions, the Canadian Institutes of Health Research (CIHR) has developed a strong orientation toward knowledge translation, and provided a basic approach to this effort. The perspective adopted by this agency is that two multiple approaches be adopted more or less concurrently. One main theme entails knowledge creation, depicted with the triangle within the figure. The accumulation of data (Knowledge Inquiry) is essential, and this needs to be obtained at multiple levels of analysis. As the data are being collected, it needs to be synthesized and distilled (e.g., through systematic reviews or other routes), so that it can eventually provide products or tools that have applications relevant to best treatment or evidence-based practices. With the fundamental information in hand, the 'action cycle' comes into effect (the outer circle in which bidirectional movement occurs between steps). The knowledge that has been obtained can be applied to particular settings, provided that barriers to implementation are understood and dealt with (e.g., is it acceptable for individuals being treated, are community interventions appropriate, is the treatment respectful of cultural factors?) and that the strategy can be appropriately tailored to meet ongoing needs. Having reached this point, the treatment intervention can be implemented, its usefulness reassessed and modified as needed, and then incorporated into broader treatment programs.

Source: More About Knowledge Translation at CIHR (2014). http://www.cihr-irsc.gc.ca/e/39033.html#Definition

To lay people, this might appear as if scientists are contradicting one another, when in fact, this is the fundamental nature of science, and the process garners greater precision and reliability, ensuring that when evidence is applied it is actually ready to be used.

From molecules to treatment

Translation of knowledge can appear at different levels of analysis, including biological processes, environmental influences, and psychosocial determinants. There have been an increasing number of translational efforts that have gone from specific genes to the development of treatments for diseases. Stem cell research has been held out as a potential way of treating diseases that had been thought of as incurable. We've also seen that certain drugs may be differentially effective in the treatment of genetically distinct types of cancer, and molecular genetic findings may also be relevant in maximizing the number of ALS patients who can be effectively treated (Poppe et al., 2014). Likewise, aspects of genes (e.g., those that can act in silencing RNA and in the regulation of gene expression) have been associated with Parkinson's disease (Ambros, 2004), which may facilitate the development of therapeutic strategies (Sekiyama et al., 2014). Epigenetic-based research, which incorporates potential actions of psychosocial and developmental factors, may be on the cusp of being useful in the treatment of neurodegenerative diseases (Coppedè, 2014). The list of translational opportunities involving genetic discoveries is very long, and no doubt will be extended further as links between specific genes and various phenotypes are established.

With the increasing focus on intervention strategies there has also been recognition of the potential effects of environmental toxicants and climatic factors on health, and what can be done to limit such effects. These have included the emergence of diseases owing to global warming, and toxicant effects on heart disease, cancer, and neurodegenerative disorders (Litteljohn et al., 2010). Environmental agents, such as molds, can instigate inflammatory changes leading to disease states (Rand & Miller, 2011) and even very fine particulate matter in the air that we breath can increase the risk for mortality stemming from heart disease (Villeneuve et al., 2015). As we've also discussed at length, life-style factors (eating, exercise, sleep, job strain) can affect molecular biological processes that influence various disease conditions. The multiple and broad effects of environmental agents, together with human behaviors that engender disease conditions, have reinforced the importance of making individuals and communities aware of the risks that are faced daily, and of the need to have effective intervention efforts established.

As discussed earlier, treatment interventions are often more successful and treatment regimens followed more diligently when psychosocial factors are considered within the framework of knowledge translation. We know, for instance, that when strong social supports are in place, approaches to prevent disease are improved and, conversely, health can be undermined in the face of stigma and unsupportive interactions. In this regard, while neither social support nor medications are particularly effective in getting people to quit smoking, the combination of these approaches is likely to be a more effective approach. Similarly, the social context in which treatments are applied is important – if individuals are more concerned with the conditions of poverty (food, shelter, clean water), they are unlikely to put smoking cessation as a top health priority.

INCLUSION OF PARTICIPANTS IN THE RESEARCH QUESTION

Knowledge translation has often been thought of as the adoption of research findings by health practitioners in the clinical treatment of patients. However, with the importance of prevention at a population level becoming more apparent, it was realized that the hierarchical transfer of information and treatments is only a small component of the translation effort. Increasingly greater focus has been appearing in relation to population initiatives to diminish the potential adverse impacts of environmental and experiential factors. In order for positive effects to be achieved in this regard, it is necessary that there is buy-in from the public, buy-in from vulnerable populations, and buy-in from communities that show disproportionate levels of illness. Some have referred to this as the democratization of health care.

Community-based participatory research (CBPR) methods (Horowitz et al., 2009) have become more popular as a strategy for understanding and building trust with communities. It is most often the method of choice in working with marginalized groups, as it reframes individuals from being the subjects of study into being real participants in the research. In Canada, such an approach has become a requirement of working with Indigenous populations (First Nations, Inuit, and Metis). Historically, Indigenous peoples have had little reason to trust the 'establishment', be it medical, government, or even university researchers, frequently believing that they had been used for medical research in ways that showed little care for the participants. A prime example (not far removed from the Tuskegee Syphilis Experiment) were the nutritional studies conducted in Indian Residential Schools and Aboriginal communities from 1942 to 1952. Having observed starving and highly malnourished communities, medical researchers, with the endorsement of government and industry, conducted research on members of these communities to determine the effects of malnourishment on vulnerability to diseases (e.g., tuberculosis) and mortality, and to determine whether certain vitamins (riboflavin, thiamine, or ascorbic acid supplements) could attenuate the physical manifestations of disease conditions relative to an untreated, but malnourished, control group. Remarkably, the knowledge gained from these studies wasn't used for improving conditions in the communities or schools. Understandably, this kind of research has undermined the trust and cooperation of Aboriginal communities.

The goal of CBPR is to leave ownership of the research in the hands of the communities involved. Several types of research can be adopted through the CBPR approach, but at its core is the perspective that at all stages of the research an equal partnership exists between community members and researchers. Researchers typically bring sophisticated analytic and methodological tools to answer specific questions, but community partners might see some of the questions not including several main issues, and thus wish that the research be modified to address these questions. If nothing else, participants feel that their voices need to be heard in a comprehensive way (providing qualitative data through interviews, storytelling, etc.), as opposed to simply being transformed into numbers that can

(Continued)

(Continued)

be manipulated by the researchers to meet their own objectives. In the case of some community partners, such as in many Aboriginal communities, ethics review panels have been established, and there is an expectation that research complies with the principles of Ownership, Control, Access, and Possession, in order to ensure self-determination in the research. The issues raised by CBPR apply to many populations world-wide where the need for trust, cultural variations in community norms and beliefs, and historical exploitation of populations in the developing world are no less poignant. As a result, CBPR is fast becoming a best practice for conducting global health research.

From individual interventions to communities

The field of public health is founded on the premise that community interventions can go a long way in preventing and attenuating the development of illness. Whether it involves community-based efforts to clean up water systems, to reduce obesity or cigarette consumption, or to enhance the built environment, each independently (and synergistically) can have positive effects on well-being. These may comprise efforts to educate and inform individuals about vaccinating children (Saeterdal et al., 2014), or putting into practice at a community level behavioral changes aimed at diabetes self-management (Peek et al., 2014). When communities as a whole support and engage in an intervention, the collective effort can be effective in instigating and maintaining individual behavioral changes. Critical to this in some instances, whether it involves management of type 2 diabetes or efforts toward suicide prevention, is that the researchers and front-line practitioners work together with the community to understand their goals, norms, and culture (Bhattacharyya et al., 2011; Clifford et al., 2013).

Just as there has been the recognition that individualized treatments might be most productive in treating illnesses, this could also be true of communities. Two towns that are only 10 km apart, for example, might be very different from one another in multiple ways. One may be an industrial town, whereas the other may cater to retired individuals who desire a quiet life and young families wishing to escape the travails of the big city. The pollution in the towns differ as do people's life-styles, and interventions relevant to illness will necessarily be very different in these towns, and these will differ yet again for communities where poverty is endemic. Health practitioners and government officials tasked with making changes to health systems obviously need to be aware of these community-based differences, and broad policies and approaches to curing communities need to consider their individual characteristics.

INSTIGATING POLICY CHANGE

According to the World Health Organization (2014a), a decade ago infectious diseases, including HIV/AIDS, tuberculosis, and malaria combined, were responsible for around 4 million deaths. As big as that number is, chronic non-communicable diseases (e.g., heart disease, cancer) killed about 30 million people. Each of these diseases also had secondary effects, such as undermining quality of life, fostering poverty, and increasing the odds of still other diseases appearing. When diseases are present at this level, it obviously requires major investments by governments world-wide. What this amounts to is encouraging healthy life-styles, including the development of national programs to deal with specific diseases, offering education so that reforms can be undertaken at a population level, legislating actions to curb unhealthy behaviors, making the environment of cities healthier, ensuring that proper foods are available and affordable, being certain that workplaces are safe and that products developed or imported are not hazardous, and ensuring that public policies are in effect so that social justice prevails. To an extent, each of these investments seems independent of others, but there are also connections that exist between them. The built environment, as well as overpopulation and poverty within cities, encourages poor eating behaviors, limits opportunities to engage in exercise, and even reduces access to proper medical care. Sometimes the problems are endemic, and so extensive that one hardly knows where to begin to make changes. Do we start with changing school systems or do we first try to diminish poverty? Is there any point in having nicer schools when at the end of the day kids still get sent back to impoverished home environments? It's absolutely certain that multiple changes need to be made concurrently, even if this doesn't necessarily address every problem. For this to happen, multiple levels of government must work together with community organizations, and considerable help will be needed from industry and business, which also have a responsibility to maintain a healthy workforce. An African saying that found a voice through Hillary Clinton's book *It Takes a Village* (1996) suggests that raising a child is more than the job of parents or even family members, but requires the cooperation of large groups of people. This is true in so many ways, but it's not restricted to the impacts on children, but applies to whole societies.

Although necessary, the challenge with such multipronged approaches is that they are difficult to coordinate, and it is also difficult to evaluate the efficacy of any given component or their combinations. As well, isolating the causes of unintended consequences or benefits becomes virtually impossible. At the very least, however, it is essential that measurable objectives are set, and that these are scientifically evaluated in order to ensure that the investments are well justified. Such assessments need to be conducted across time and across communities, as shifts in the conditions in which interventions are operating can alter the outcomes.

Chronic diseases have become an ever greater problem within developing countries that are least able or prepared to respond to complex health challenges. This has been exacerbated owing to increased urbanization and globalization. The spread of poor health behaviors characteristic of Western countries has flourished, and at the same time traditional cultural ways that might have sustained healthier behaviors have been attenuated. Among other things, within these developing regions, globalization has led to an increase in the availability of processed foods, and foods that are unsuitable to the physiological characteristics of indigenous populations (e.g., Inuit have traditionally high fat diets, and are now exposed to high carbs that are new to their diet, possibly being a prime contributor to obesity). Even the nature of work in developing countries has shifted to being more sedentary. These negative changes have occurred without the benefits one sees in Western cultures, particularly improvements in health care and healthy behavioral alternatives.

Commendably, the WHO has taken a leading role in dealing with global health-related problems, but as with so many other issues, its effectiveness will require additional funding, and in many developing countries there are simply insufficient staff to deal with the many problems that exist. More than this, it will be necessary to have effective global responses to various challenges, and this will necessarily require coordinated policies that include partners from numerous levels of governments, and interactions between global agencies, governments, and other organizations will need to improve. We've seen too often following emergencies that bottlenecks appear that do not permit policies to be smoothly implemented (e.g., food to disaster regions sitting in warehouses because distribution is limited; illnesses such as AIDS or Ebola being spread because of a lack of personnel to bypass local customs and misinformation). In addition, the lack of understanding of communities means that interventions are attempted but are out of sync with the local priorities.

Although these global issues sound very distant from those we have in the West, they are in fact very close to home. Many diseases originate in developing countries, and through human and animal movements around the world they are often spread without discrimination between regions and countries. For this reason, global health interventions are, in fact, local health prevention strategies. The challenge in many instances is the capacity to mobilize resources quickly, as well as to ensure that trust exists to implement and partner within afflicted developing regions. Many communities have a history (perceived or real) of being test beds for Big Pharma, and so suspicions abound when they are targeted in limiting disease spread. These are not health issues in themselves, but speak to the social and cultural contexts in which knowledge translation efforts can be stymied. As Bill Gates indicated in a recent interview (McSpadden, 2015), our greatest threat is not nuclear war or devastating earthquakes, but instead comprises pandemic threats. We've had some close calls, but we've been lucky. In Western countries, Ebola was often thought to be a global threat and thus created appreciable worry. Many viruses, however, have a greater propensity to be passed from one person to another than diseases like Ebola, and one of these may, and likely will, come along that spreads as efficiently as the measles but with more deadly consequences. Algorithmic models commissioned by the Bill and Melinda Gates Foundation have indicated that with human ability to move around, the risk for massive spread is enormous. As we saw with Ebola, diseases may first appear in countries largely unprepared to deal with such threats, but if they are more infectious, their spread will not easily be contained. What happens in our neighbor's backyard will affect ours, and coordinated efforts are obviously essential in order for us to be protected.

ETHICAL DILEMMAS

Scientists conducting research with human participants are typically well versed in the ethical issues associated with such work, but research necessary for knowledge to be translated raises many further issues that need to be taken into consideration. Sound experimental design often entails having a randomized comparison control group, ideally comprising people who are matched with respect to key variables, including vulnerability to disease, but are not given the experimental treatment. Without such groups, it is difficult to know with certainty whether health improvements occur because of the treatment, or if they would simply have improved over time. The ethics of not treating people who have, or are vulnerable to, an illness are clearly of concern. Should the control group receive no treatment, or do they receive the standard treatment (treatment as usual), which is known not to have much of an effect? Of course, with new, untested treatments, there are also ethical issues associated with raising hopes and expectations, only to discover that the test treatment is less effective, or is actually detrimental to health in comparison to the standard treatment. There are also many issues regarding who should be included in clinical trials, and how to evaluate treatment effectiveness in a manner that is informative and ethical.

Often, challenges are presented when insufficient information is available concerning the effectiveness of particular treatments to proceed to the translation of information into clinical or public health protocols. Sometimes the most vulnerable populations for particular diseases are marginalized groups, and when they are targeted as priority populations for new treatments, suspicions arise, particularly when there has been a history of neglect in relation to these groups. For example, when Aboriginal communities were targeted for vaccination in anticipation of the 2009 H1N1 outbreak, some group members believed that this was just another reincarnation of past experiments conducted using Aboriginal peoples. In actuality, Aboriginal peoples might have been disproportionately affected by the H1N1 virus, and their symptoms might have been relatively severe. As a result, some Aboriginal communities strongly endorsed the vaccine, with considerable success. However, it is easy to see why health policies were met with suspicion.

Another ethical challenge of translating knowledge to marginalized populations is that interventions might heighten public awareness of the disproportionate rates of illness. In doing so, already stigmatized groups might be subject to even greater stigmatization, as the illness is seen as endemic to the group. For example, fear of the spread of HIV/AIDS meant that prevention efforts targeting gay men and drug users were justification for further social isolation and marginalization. In targeting particular populations, particularly in relation to prevention of infectious diseases, unanticipated reactions are possible that might present further challenges for the individuals involved.

SUMMARY

There is no question that moving from evidence to practice is hugely challenging, and even incremental changes can be difficult to produce. But there is also considerable evidence of such efforts having been effective. Despite the vocal anti-vaccination movement, in reality, the rate of vaccination against childhood diseases in most places has matched or exceeded the tipping point for herd immunity. Likewise, screening for illnesses has become more frequent, poor health behaviors have been declining, as have many preventable diseases. As a result, life span and health span have both been increasing. In fact, part of the reason for vaccine hesitancy today is because diseases like polio and measles haven't been experienced or even seen in the recent generation, making the need for vaccines much less salient for some people. These are success stories. Health psychology offers effective frameworks for social change, and we have the capacity to translate evidence into action and shouldn't be discouraged by the challenges involved.

References

Aberle, J., Flitsch, J., Beck, N.A. et al. (2008). Genetic variation may influence obesity only under conditions of diet: analysis of three candidate genes. *Molecular Genetics and Metabolism*, *95*, 188–191.

Abioye, A.I., Odesanya, M.O., Abioye, A.I. & Ibrahim, N.A. (2015). Physical activity and risk of gastric cancer: a meta-analysis of observational studies. *British Journal of Sports Medicine*, *49*, 224–229.

Abizaid, A. (2009). Ghrelin and dopamine: new insights on the peripheral regulation of appetite. *Journal of Neuroendocrinology*, *21*, 787–793.

Abizaid, A. & Horvath, T.L. (2008). Brain circuits regulating energy homeostasis. *Regulatory Peptides*, *149*, 3–10.

Abizaid, A., Liu, Z.W., Andrews, Z.B. et al. (2006). Ghrelin modulates the activity and synaptic input organization of midbrain dopamine neurons while promoting appetite. *Journal of Clinical Investigation*, *116*, 3229–3239.

Abizaid, A., Luheshi, G. & Woodside, B.C. (2014). Interaction between immune and energy-balance signals in the regulation of feeding and metabolism. In A.V. Kusnecov & H. Anisman (Eds.), *The Wiley-Blackwell Handbook of Psychoneuroimmunology* (pp. 488–503). Oxford, UK: Wiley-Blackwell.

Abramson, L.Y., Seligman, M.E. & Teasdale, J.D. (1978). Learned helplessness in humans: critique and reformulation. *Journal of Abnormal Psychology*, *87*, 49–74.

Adams, E.F., Lee, A.J., Pritchard, C.W. & White, R.J. (2010). What stops us from healing the healers: a survey of help-seeking behaviour, stigmatisation and depression within the medical profession. *International Journal of Social Psychiatry*, *56*, 359–370.

Adelman, R.D., Tmanova, L.L., Delgado, D. et al. (2014). Caregiver burden: a clinical review. *JAMA*, *311*, 1052–1060.

Adlan, A.M., Lip, G.Y., Paton, J.F. et al. (2014). Autonomic function and rheumatoid arthritis: a systematic review. *Seminars in Arthritis and Rheumatism*. pii: S0049–0172(14)00159-0.

Afari, N. & Buchwald, D. (2003). Chronic fatigue syndrome: a review. *American Journal of Psychiatry*, *160*, 221–236.

Affleck, G., Pfeiffer, C., Tennen, H. & Fifield, J. (1987). Attributional processes in rheumatoid arthritis patients. *Arthritis & Rheumatism*, *30*, 927–931.

Affleck, G., Tennen, H., Pfeiffer, C. & Fifield, J. (1987). Appraisals of control and predictability in adapting to a chronic disease. *Journal of Personality and Social Psychology*, *53*, 273–279.

Agmon-Levin, N., Theodor, E., Segal, R.M. & Shoenfeld, Y. (2013). Vitamin D in systemic and organ-specific autoimmune diseases. *Clinical Reviews in Allergy & Immunology*, *45*, 256–266.

Aiello, A.E., Simanek, A.M. & Galea, S. (2010). Population levels of psychological stress, herpesvirus reactivation and HIV. *AIDS and Behavior*, *14*, 308–317.

Airley, R. (2009). *Cancer Chemotherapy: basic science to the clinic*. Oxford, UK: Wiley-Blackwell.

Aizer, A.A., Chen, M.H., McCarthy, E.P. et al. (2013). Marital status and survival in patients with cancer. *Journal of Clinical Oncology*, *31*, 3869–3876.

Ajzen, I. (1991). The theory of planned behavior. *Organizational Behavior and Human Decision Processes*, *50*, 179–211.

Ajzen, I. & Fishbein, M. (1980). *Understanding Attitudes and Predicting Social Behavior*. Englewood Cliffs, NJ: Prentice-Hall.

Akiyama, T. & Carstens, E. (2013). Neural processing of itch. *Neuroscience*, *250*, 697–714.

Akl, E.A., Oxman, A.D., Herrin, J. et al. (2011). Framing of health information messages. *The Cochrane Database of Systematic Reviews*, *12*, CD006777.

Aknin, L.B., Barrington-Leigh, C.P., Dunn, E.W. et al. (2013). Prosocial spending and well-being: cross-cultural evidence for a psychological universal. *Journal of Personality and Social Psychology*, *104*, 635–652.

Aknin, L.B., Sandstrom, G.M., Dunn, E.W. & Norton, M.I. (2011). It's the recipient that counts: spending money on strong social ties leads to greater happiness than spending on weak social ties. *PLoS One*, *6*, e17018.

Akobeng, A.K., Ramanan, A.V., Buchan, I. & Heller, R.F. (2006). Effect of breast feeding on risk of coeliac disease: a systematic review and meta-analysis of observational studies. *Archives of Disease in Childhood*, *91*, 39–43.

Al Mamun, A.A., Lombardo, M.J., Shee, C. et al. (2012). Identity and function of a large gene network underlying mutagenic repair of DNA breaks. *Science*, *338*, 1344–1348.

Albus, C. (2010). Psychological and social factors in coronary heart disease. *Annals of Medicine*, *42*, 487–494.

Alda, M. (2013). Personalized psychiatry: many questions, fewer answers. *Journal of Psychiatry & Neuroscience: JPN*, *38*, 363–365.

Alderman, M.H. & Lamport, B. (1988). Treatment of hypertension at the workplace: an opportunity to link service and research. *Health Psychology*, *7*, 283.

Allegrante, J.P. & Marks, R. (2003). Self-efficacy in management of osteoarthritis. *Rheumatic Disease Clinics of North America*, *29*, 747–768.

Allen, N.J. & Barres, B.A. (2005). Signaling between glia and neurons: focus on synaptic plasticity. *Current Opinion in Neurobiology*, *15*, 542–548.

Allen, V.M., Armson, B.A., Wilson, R.D. et al. (2007). Teratogenicity associated with pre-existing and gestational diabetes. *Journal of Obstetrics and Gynaecology Canada: JOGC*, *29*, 927–944.

Alloy, L.B., Abramson, K.Y., Keyser, J. et al. (2008). Negative cognitive style. In K.S. Dobson & D.J.A. Dozois (Eds.), *Risk Factors in Depression* (pp. 237–263). New York: Academic.

Alper, K.R., Lotsof, H.S., Frenken, G. et al. (1999). Treatment of acute opioid withdrawal with ibogaine. *American Journal on Addictions*, *8*, 234–242.

Alschuler, K.N., Ehde, D.M. & Jensen, M.P. (2013). The co-occurrence of pain and depression in adults with multiple sclerosis. *Rehabilitation Psychology*, *58*, 217.

Altaf, Q.A., Barnett, A.H. & Tahrani, A.A. (2014). Novel therapeutics for type 2 diabetes: insulin resistance. *Diabetes, Obesity and Metabolism*, *17*, 319–334.

Amar, A. et al. (2012). Identity and function of a large gene network underlying mutagenic repair of DNA breaks. *Science*, *338*, 1344–1348.

Amato, L., Davoli, M., Perucci, C.A. et al. (2005). An overview of systematic reviews of the effectiveness of opiate maintenance therapies: available evidence to inform clinical practice and research. *Journal of Substance Abuse Treatment*, *28*, 321–329.

Ambros, V. (2004). The functions of animal microRNAs. *Nature*, *431*, 350–355.

American Psychiatric Association (APA) (2013). *Diagnostic and Statistical Manual of Mental Disorders* (5th ed.). Arlington, VA: American Psychiatric Publishing.

American Psychological Association (APA) (2014). Stress in America. www.apa.org/news/press/releases/stress/index.aspx (accessed March 2015).

Amitay, E.L. & Keinan-Boker, L.(2015). Breastfeeding and childhood leukemia incidence: a meta-analysis and systematic review. *JAMA Pediatrics*, *169*, e151025.

Andenæs, R., Kalfoss, M.H. & Wahl, A.K. (2006). Coping and psychological distress in hospitalized patients with chronic obstructive pulmonary disease. *Heart & Lung: The Journal of Acute and Critical Care*, *35*, 46–57.

Anderson, G., Berk, M. & Maes, M. (2014). Biological phenotypes underpin the physio-somatic symptoms of somatization, depression, and chronic fatigue syndrome. *Acta Psychiatrica Scandinavica, 129*, 83–97.

Anderson, K.N. (2014). An update in sleep neurology: the latest bedtime stories. *Journal of Neurology, 262*, 487–491.

Anderson, N.D., Damianakis, T., Kröger, E. et al. (2014). The benefits associated with volunteering among seniors: a critical review and recommendations for future research. *Psychological Bulletin, 140*, 1505–1533.

Anderson, N.D., Lau, M.A., Segal, Z.V. & Bishop, S.R. (2007). Mechanisms of mindfulness: attentional control. *Clinical Psychology and Psychotherapy, 14*, 449–463.

Anderson, O., Davis, R., Hanna, G.B. & Vincent, C.A. (2013). Surgical adverse events: a systematic review. *American Journal of Surgery, 206*, 253–262.

Andrews, Z.B. & Abizaid, A. (2014). Neuroendocrine mechanisms that connect feeding behavior and stress. *Frontiers in Neuroscience, 8*, 312.

Andtbacka, R.H., Kaufman, H.L., Collichio, F. et al. (2015). Talimogene laherparepvec improves durable response rate in patients with advanced melanoma. *Journal of Clinical Oncology*, pii: JCO.2014.58.3377. [Epub ahead of print]

Ang, D.C., Bair, M.J., Damush, T.M. et al. (2010). Predictors of pain outcomes in patients with chronic musculoskeletal pain co-morbid with depression: results from a randomized controlled trial. *Pain Medicine, 11*, 482–491.

Angelidou, A., Asadi, S., Alysandratos, K.D. et al. (2012). Perinatal stress, brain inflammation and risk of autism-review and proposal. *BMC Pediatrics,12*, 89.

Angelier, F. & Chastel, O. (2009). Stress, prolactin and parental investment in birds: a review. *General and Comparative Endocrinology, 163*, 142–148.

Anisman, H. (2014). *An Introduction to Stress and Health*. London: SAGE.

Anisman, H. (2015). *Stress and Health: From Vulnerability to Resilience*. Wiley.

Anisman, H. & Hayley, S. (2012a). Illness comorbidity as a biomarker? *Journal of Psychiatry & Neuroscience, 37*, 221–223.

Anisman, H. & Hayley, S. (2012b). Inflammatory factors contribute to depression and its comorbid conditions. *Science Signaling, 5*, pe45–pe45.

Anisman, H., Hayley, S. & Merali, Z. (2003). Cytokines and stress: sensitization and cross-sensitization. *Brain, Behavior, and Immunity, 17*, 86–93.

Anisman, H. & Matheson, K. (2005). Stress, anhedonia and depression: caveats concerning animal models. *Neuroscience & Biobehavioral Reviews, 29*, 525–546.

Anisman, H. & Merali, Z. (1999). Anhedonic and anxiogenic effects of cytokine exposure. *Advances in Experimental Medicine and Biology, 461*, 199–233.

Anisman, H., Merali, Z. & Hayley, S. (2008). Neurotransmitter, peptide and cytokine processes in relation to depressive disorder: comorbidity of depression with neurodegenerative disorders. *Progress in Neurobiology, 85*, 1–74.

Anisman, H., Zaharia, M.D., Meaney, M.J. & Merali, Z. (1998). Do early-life events permanently alter behavioral and hormonal responses to stressors? *International Journal of Developmental Neuroscience, 16*, 149–164.

Arem, H., Moore, S.C., Patel, A. et al. (2015). Leisure time physical activity and mortality: a detailed pooled analysis of the dose–response relationship. *JAMA Internal Medicine, 175*, 959–967.

Arnsten, A.F., Raskind, M.A., Taylor, F.B. & Connor, D.F. (2015). The effects of stress exposure on prefrontal cortex: translating basic research into successful treatments for post-traumatic stress disorder. *Neurobiology of Stress, 1*, 89–99.

Aroda, V.R., Christophi, C.A., Edelstein, S.L. et al. (2015). The effect of lifestyle intervention and metformin on preventing or delaying diabetes among women with and without gestational diabetes: the diabetes prevention program outcomes study 10-year follow-up. *The Journal of Clinical Endocrinology & Metabolism, 100*, 1646–1653.

Arran, N., Craufurd, D. & Simpson, J. (2014). Illness perceptions, coping styles and psychological distress in adults with Huntington's disease. *Psychology, Health & Medicine, 19*, 169–179.

Artherholt, S.B. & Fann, J.R. (2012). Psychosocial care in cancer. *Current Psychiatry Reports, 14*, 23–29.

Asch, D.A. & DeKay, M.L. (1997). Euthanasia among US critical care nurses: practices, attitudes, and social and professional correlates. *Medical Care, 35*, 890–900.

Aschbacher, K., Kornfeld, S., Picard, M. et al. (2014). Chronic stress increases vulnerability to diet-related abdominal fat, oxidative stress, and metabolic risk. *Psychoneuroendocrinology, 46,* 14–22.

Ascherio, A. (2013). Environmental factors in multiple sclerosis. *Expert Review of Neurotherapeutics, 13,* 3–9.

Asmundson, G.J., Bovell, C.V., Carleton, R.N. & McWilliams, L.A. (2008). The Fear of Pain Questionnaire–Short Form (FPQ-SF): factorial validity and psychometric properties. *Pain, 134,* 51–58.

Asnis, G.M., De La Garza, R., Kohn, S.R. et al. (2003). IFN-induced depression: a role for NSAIDs. *Psychopharmacology Bulletin, 37,* 29–50.

Astin, J.A. (1998). Why patients use alternative medicine: results of a national study. *Journal of the American Medical Association, 279,* 1548–1553.

Atlantis, E., Fahey, P. & Foster, J. (2014). Collaborative care for comorbid depression and diabetes: a systematic review and meta-analysis. *BMJ Open, 4,* e004706.

Audet, M.C. & Anisman, H. (2013). Interplay between pro-inflammatory cytokines and growth factors in depressive illnesses. *Frontiers in Cellular Neuroscience, 7,* 68.

Audet, M.C., Jacobson-Pick, S., McQuaid, R. & Anisman, H. (2014). An inflammatory perspective of stress and human depressive disorder. In A. Kusnecov & H. Anisman (Eds.), *The Wiley-Blackwell Handbook of Psychoneuroimmunology.* Hove, UK: Wiley-Blackwell.

Audet, M.C., Mangano, E.N. & Anisman, H. (2010). Behavior and pro-inflammatory cytokine variations among submissive and dominant mice engaged in aggressive encounters: moderation by corticosterone reactivity. *Frontiers in Behavioral Neuroscience, 4.*

Azad, M.B., Konya, T., Guttman, D.S. et al. (2015). Infant gut microbiota and food sensitization: associations in the first year of life. *Clinical & Experimental Allergy, 45,* 632–643.

Azevedo Da Silva M., Singh-Manoux A., Shipley M.J. et al. (2014). Sleep duration and sleep disturbances partly explain the association between depressive symptoms and cardiovascular mortality: the Whitehall II cohort study. *Journal of Sleep Research, 23,* 94–97.

Azizi, K.B., Wilson, E., Monfaredi, R. et al. (2014). Robotic natural orifice transluminal endoscopic surgery (R-NOTES): literature review and prototype system. *Minimally Invasive Therapy & Allied Technologies: MITAT: Official Journal of the Society for Minimally Invasive Therapy,* 1–6.

Bach, D.R., Seymour, B. & Dolan, R.J. (2009). Neural activity associated with the passive prediction of ambiguity and risk for aversive events. *Journal of Neuroscience, 29,* 1648–1656.

Bäckhed, F., Roswall, J., Peng, Y. et al. (2015). Dynamics and stabilization of the human gut microbiome during the first year of life. *Cell Host Microbe, 17,* 690–703.

Baek, R.N., Tanenbaum, M.L. & Gonzalez, J.S. (2014). Diabetes burden and diabetes distress: the buffering effect of social support. *Annals of Behavioral Medicine, 48,* 145–155.

Bahamondes, L., Valeria Bahamondes, M. & Shulman, L.P. (2015). Non-contraceptive benefits of hormonal and intrauterine reversible contraceptive methods. *Human Reproduction Update,* pii: dmv023. [Epub ahead of print]

Bailey, D.E. Jr., Landerman, L., Barroso, J. et al. (2009). Uncertainty, symptoms, and quality of life in persons with chronic hepatitis C. *Psychosomatics, 50,* 138–146.

Bailey, M., Engler, H., Hunzeker, J. & Sheridan, J.F. (2003). The hypothalamic-pituitary-adrenal axis and viral infection. *Viral Immunology, 16,* 141–157.

Bailey, M.T., Padgett, D.A. & Sheridan, J.F. (2007). Stress-induced modulation of innate resistance and adaptive immunity to influenza viral infection. In R. Ader (Ed.), *Psychoneuroimmunology* (pp. 1097–1124). San Diego, CA: Academic Press.

Bailey, S.M., Udoh, U.S. & Young, M.E. (2014). Circadian regulation of metabolism. *Journal of Endocrinology, 222,* R75–R96.

Bair, M.J., Robinson, R.L., Eckert, G.J. et al. (2004). Impact of pain on depression treatment response in primary care. *Psychosomatic Medicine, 66,* 17–22.

Baker, J.L., Olsen, L.W. & Sørensen, T.I. (2007). Childhood body-mass index and the risk of coronary heart disease in adulthood. *New England Journal of Medicine, 357,* 2329–2337.

Balaji, P.A., Varne, S.R. & Ali, S.S. (2012). Physiological effects of yogic practices and transcendental meditation in health and disease. *North American Journal of Medical Sciences, 4,* 442–448.

Baldwin, C.H. & Srivastava, L.K. (2015). Can the neurodevelopmental theory account for gender differences in schizophrenia? *Journal of Psychiatry and Neuroscience*, *40*, 75–77.

Balestri, M., Calati, R., Serretti, A. & De Ronchi, D. (2014). Genetic modulation of personality traits: a systematic review of the literature. *International Clinical Psychopharmacology*, *29*, 1–15.

Baliban, S.M., Michael, A., Shammassian, B. et al. (2014). An optimized, synthetic DNA vaccine encoding the toxin A and toxin B receptor binding domains of clostridium difficile induces protective antibody responses in vivo. *Infection and Immunity*, *82*, 4080–4091.

Bandura, A. (1986). *Social Foundations of Thought and Action: a social cognitive theory*. Englewood Cliffs, NJ: Prentice-Hall.

Bangalore, S., Sawhney, S. & Messerli, F.H. (2008). Relation of beta-blocker-induced heart rate lowering and cardioprotection in hypertension. *Journal of the American College of Cardiology*, *52*, 1482–1489.

Bangalore, S., Steg, G., Deedwania, P. et al. (2012). β-Blocker use and clinical outcomes in stable outpatients with and without coronary artery disease. *Journal of the American Medical Association*, *308*, 1340–1349.

Bao, Y., Rosner, B.A. & Fuchs, C.S. (2014). Nut consumption and mortality. *New England Journal of Medicine*, *370*, 882.

Barak, Y. (2006). The immune system and happiness. *Autoimmunity Reviews*, *5*, 523–527.

Barefoot, J.C., Dahlstrom, W.G. & Williams, R.B. (1983). Hostility, CHD incidence, and total mortality: a 25-year follow-up study of 255 physicians. *Psychosomatic Medicine*, *45*, 59–63.

Barel, E., Van IJzendoorn, M.H., Sagi-Schwartz, A. & Bakermans-Kranenburg, M.J. (2010). Surviving the Holocaust: a meta-analysis of the long-term sequelae of a genocide. *Psychological Bulletin*, *136*, 677–698.

Barlow, J., Wright, C., Sheasby, J. et al. (2002). Self-management approaches for people with chronic conditions: a review. *Patient Education and Counseling*, *48*, 177–187.

Barnett, M.L. & Linder, J.A. (2014). Antibiotic prescribing for adults with acute bronchitis in the United States, 1996–2010. *Journal of the American Medical Association*, *311*, 2020–2022.

Barney, L.J., Griffiths, K.M., Christensen, H. & Jorm, A.F. (2009). Exploring the nature of stigmatising beliefs about depression and help-seeking: implications for reducing stigma. *BMC Public Health*, *9*, 61.

Bar-On, Y., Seidel, E., Tsukerman, P. et al. (2014). Influenza virus uses its neuraminidase protein to evade the recognition of two activating NK cell receptors. *Journal of Infectious Diseases*, *210*, 410–418.

Barrera, I. & Spiegel, D. (2014). Review of psychotherapeutic interventions on depression in cancer patients and their impact on disease progression. *International Review of Psychiatry*, *26*, 31–43.

Barreto, G.E., Iarkov, A. & Moran, V.E. (2015). Beneficial effects of nicotine, cotinine and its metabolites as potential agents for Parkinson's disease. *Frontiers in Aging Neuroscience*, *6*, 340.

Barton, C., Clarke, D., Sulaiman, N. & Abramson, M. (2003). Coping as a mediator of psychosocial impediments to optimal management and control of asthma. *Respiratory Medicine*, *97*, 747–761.

Bascones-Martínez, A., González-Febles, J. & Sanz-Esporrín, J. (2014). Diabetes and periodontal disease: review of the literature. *American Journal of Dentistry*, *27*, 63–67.

Bastian, B., Jetten, J. & Ferris, L.J. (2014). Pain as social glue: shared pain increases cooperation. *Psychological Science*, *25*, 2079–2085.

Bateni, S.B., Meyers, F.J., Bold, R.J. & Canter, R.J. (2015). Current perioperative outcomes for patients with disseminated cancer. *Journal of Surgical Research*, *197*, 118–125.

Bauer, U.E., Briss, P.A., Goodman, R.A. & Bowman, B.A. (2014). Prevention of chronic disease in the 21st century: elimination of the leading preventable causes of premature death and disability in the USA. *The Lancet*, *384*, 45–52.

Baune, B.T., Stuart, M., Gilmour, A. et al. (2012). The relationship between subtypes of depression and cardiovascular disease: a systematic review of biological models. *Translational Psychiatry*, *2*, e92.

Bawa, F.L., Mercer, S.W., Atherton, R.J. et al. (2015). Does mindfulness improve outcomes in patients with chronic pain? Systematic review and meta-analysis. *British Journal of General Practice*, *65*, e387–400.

Bawor, M., Dennis, B.B., Anglin, R. et al. (2014). Sex differences in outcomes of methadone maintenance treatment for opioid addiction: a systematic review protocol. *Systematic Reviews*, *3*, 45.

Bazzano, L.A., Reynolds, K., Holder, K.N. & He, J. (2006). Effect of folic acid supplementation on risk of cardiovascular diseases: a meta-analysis of randomized controlled trials. *Journal of the American Medical Association*, *296*, 2720–2726.

Beals, J., Manson, S.M., Whitesell, N.R. et al. (2005). Prevalence of DSM-IV disorders and attendant help-seeking in 2 American Indian reservation populations. *Archives of General Psychiatry*, *62*, 99–108.

Beck, A.T. (1970). Cognitive therapy: nature and relation to behavior therapy. *Behavior Therapy*, *1*, 184–200.

Beck, A.T. & Dozois, D.J. (2011). Cognitive therapy: current status and future directions. *Annual Review of Medicine*, *62*, 397–409.

Beck, A.T., Rush, A.J., Shaw, B.F. & Emery, G. (1979). *Cognitive Therapy of Depression*. New York: Guilford Press.

Beck, C.T., Gable, R.K., Sakala, C. & Declercq, E.R. (2011). Posttraumatic stress disorder in new mothers: results from a two-stage US national survey. *Birth*, *38*, 216–227.

Becker, M.H. (1974). The health belief model and personal health behavior. *Health Education Monographs*, *2*, 326–473.

Becker, M.H. & Janz, N.K. (1987). On the effectiveness and utility of health hazard/health risk appraisal in clinical and nonclinical settings. *Health Services Research*, *22*, 537–551.

Begley, C.G. & Ellis, L.M. (2012). Drug development: raise standards for preclinical cancer research. *Nature*, *483*, 531–533.

Behrens, G., Matthews, C.E., Moore, S.C. et al. (2014). Body size and physical activity in relation to incidence of chronic obstructive pulmonary disease. *Canadian Medical Association Journal*, *186*, E457–E469.

Belkaid, Y. & Hand, T.W. (2014). Role of the microbiota in immunity and inflammation. *Cell*, *157*, 121–141.

Bell, J.A., Hamer, M., Sabia, S. et al. (2015). The natural course of healthy obesity over 20 years. *Journal of the American College of Cardiology*, *65*, 101–102.

Bellesi, M., Pfister-Genskow, M., Maret, S., et al. (2013). Effects of sleep and wake on oligodendrocytes and their precursors. *Journal of Neuroscience*, *33*, 14288–14300.

Belsky, J. & Pluess, M. (2013). Beyond risk, resilience, and dysregulation: phenotypic plasticity and human development. *Development and Psychopathology*, *25*, 1243–1261.

Bendix, L., Thinggaard, M., Fenger, M. et al. (2014). Longitudinal changes in leukocyte telomere length and mortality in humans. *The Journals of Gerontology Series A: Biological Sciences and Medical Sciences*, *69*, 231–239.

Benedetti, F. (2014). Placebo effects: from the neurobiological paradigm to translational implications. *Neuron*, *84*, 623–637.

Ben-Haroush, A., Yogev, Y. & Hod, M. (2004). Epidemiology of gestational diabetes mellitus and its association with type 2 diabetes. *Diabetic Medicine*, *21*, 103–113.

Bennett, C. (2011). Methadone maintenance treatment: disciplining the 'addict'. *Health and History*, *13*, 130–157.

Bennett, K.K., Compas, B.E., Beckjord, E. & Glinder, J.G. (2005). Self-blame and distress among women with newly diagnosed breast cancer. *Journal of Behavioral Medicine*, *28*, 313–323.

Berglund, E.D., Liu, T., Kong, X., et al. (2014). Melanocortin 4 receptors in autonomic neurons regulate thermogenesis and glycemia. *Nature Neuroscience*, *17*, 911–913.

Bergmann, N., Gyntelberg, F. & Faber, J. (2014). The appraisal of chronic stress and the development of the metabolic syndrome: a systematic review of prospective cohort studies. *Endocrine Connections*, *3*, R55–R80.

Bernacki, R.E. & Block, S.D. (2014). Communication about serious illness care goals: a review and synthesis of best practices. *JAMA Internal Medicine*, *174*, 1994–2003.

Bernatsky, S., Boivin, J.F., Joseph, L. et al. (2006). Mortality in systemic lupus erythematosus. *Arthritis & Rheumatism*, *54*, 2550–2557.

Bertram, J. (2000). The molecular biology of cancer. *Molecular Aspects of Medicine*, *21*, 167–223.

Best, D., I. Lubman, D., Savic, M. et al. (2014). Social and transitional identity: exploring social networks and their significance in a therapeutic community setting. *Therapeutic Communities: International Journal of Therapeutic Communities*, *35*, 10–20.

Bethell, C.D., Newacheck, P., Hawes, E. & Halfon, N. (2014). Adverse childhood experiences: assessing the impact on health and school engagement and the mitigating role of resilience. *Health Affairs*, *33*, 2106–2115.

Beydoun, H. & Saftlas, A.F. (2008). Physical and mental health outcomes of prenatal maternal stress in human and animal studies: a review of recent evidence. *Paediatric and Perinatal Epidemiology*, 438–466.

Bhattacharyya, O.K., Estey, E.A., Rasooly, I.R. et al. (2011). Providers' perceptions of barriers to the management of type 2 diabetes in remote Aboriginal settings. *International Journal of Circumpolar Health*, *70*, 552–563.

Bi, P., Shan, T., Liu, W. et al. (2014). Inhibition of Notch signaling promotes browning of white adipose tissue and ameliorates obesity. *Nature Medicine*, *20*, 911–918.

Biesiekierski, J.R., Peters, S.L., Newnham, E.D. et al. (2013). No effects of gluten in patients with self-reported non-celiac gluten sensitivity after dietary reduction of fermentable, poorly absorbed, short-chain carbohydrates. *Gastroenterology*, *145*, 320–328.

Birch, L.L. (1999). Development of food preferences. *Annual Review of Nutrition*, *19*, 41–62.

Bird, A.P. (2007). Perceptions of epigenetics. *Nature*, *447*, 396–398.

Birklein, F., O'Neill, D. & Schlereth, T. (2014). Complex regional pain syndrome: an optimistic perspective. *Neurology*, *84*, 89–96.

Biswas, A., Oh, P.I., Faulkner, G.E. et al. (2015). Sedentary time and its association with risk for disease incidence, mortality, and hospitalization in adults: a systematic review and meta-analysis. *Annals of Internal Medicine*, *162*, 123–132.

Black, P.H. (2006). The inflammatory consequences of psychologic stress: relationship to insulin resistance, obesity, atherosclerosis and diabetes mellitus, type II. *Medical Hypotheses*, *67*, 879–891.

Blackhart, G.C., Eckel, L.A. & Tice, D.M. (2007). Salivary cortisol in response to acute social rejection and acceptance by peers. *Biological Psychology*, *75*, 267–276.

Bladen, C., McDaniel, S.W., Gadotti, V.M. et al. (2015). Characterization of novel cannabinoid based T-type calcium channel blockers with analgesic effects. *ACS Chemical Neuroscience*, *6*, 277–287.

Blalock, J.E. (1994). The syntax of immune-neuroendocrine communication. *Immunology Today*, *15*, 504–511.

Blalock, J.E. (2005). The immune system as the sixth sense. *Journal of Internal Medicine*, *257*, 126–138.

Bland, S.T., Tamlyn, J.P., Barrientos, R.M. et al. (2007). Expression of fibroblast growth factor-2 and brain-derived neurotrophic factor mRNA in the medial prefrontal cortex and hippocampus after uncontrollable or controllable stress. *Neuroscience*, *144*, 1219–1228.

Bland, S.T., Twining, C., Watkins, L.R. & Maier, S.F. (2003). Stressor controllability modulates stress-induced serotonin but not dopamine efflux in the nucleus accumbens shell. *Synapse*, *49*, 206–208.

Blascovich, J., Spencer, S.J., Quinn, D. & Steele, C. (2001). African Americans and high blood pressure: the role of stereotype threat. *Psychological Science*, *12*, 225–229.

Blaut, M. (2014). Gut microbiota and energy balance: role in obesity. *Proceedings of the Nutrition Society*, *74*, 227–234.

Bleau, C., Karelis, A.D., St-Pierre, D.H. & Lamontagne, L. (2015). Crosstalk between intestinal microbiota, adipose tissue and skeletal muscle as an early event in systemic low-grade inflammation and the development of obesity and diabetes. *Diabetes/Metabolism Research and Reviews*, *31*, 545–561.

Blesa, J. & Przedborski, S. (2014). Parkinson's disease: animal models and dopaminergic cell vulnerability. *Frontiers in Neuroanatomy*, *8*, 155.

Blom, M., Janszky, I., Balog, P., et al. (2003). Social relations in women with coronary heart disease: the effects of work and marital stress. *European Journal of Cardiovascular Risk*, *10*, 201–206.

Blood, A.J., Iosifescu, D.V., Makris, N. et al. (2010). Microstructural abnormalities in subcortical reward circuitry of subjects with major depressive disorder. *PLoS One*, *5*, e13945.

Blüher, M. (2012). Are there still healthy obese patients? *Current Opinion in Endocrinology, Diabetes and Obesity*, *19*, 341–346.

Blumenthal, J.A., Emery, C.F., Smith, P.J. et al. (2014). The effects of a telehealth coping skills intervention on outcomes in chronic obstructive pulmonary disease: primary results from the INSPIRE-II study. *Psychosomatic Medicine, 76,* 581–592.

Boehm, J.K. & Kubzansky, L.D. (2012). The heart's content: the association between positive psychological well-being and cardiovascular health. *Psychological Bulletin, 138,* 655–691.

Bogart, L.M., Bird, S.T., Walt, L.C. et al. (2004). Association of stereotypes about physicians to health care satisfaction, help-seeking behavior, and adherence to treatment. *Social Science & Medicine, 58,* 1049–1058.

Bolier, L., Haverman, M., Westerhof, G.J. et al. (2013). Positive psychology interventions: a meta-analysis of randomized controlled studies. *BMC Public Health, 13,* 119.

Bolnick, D.I., Snowberg, L.K., Hirsch, P.E. et al. (2014). Individual diet has sex-dependent effects on vertebrate gut microbiota. *Nature Communications, 5,* 4500.

Bombay, A., Matheson, K. & Anisman, H. (2009). Intergenerational trauma among First Nations: communities in crisis. *Journal of Aboriginal Health, 5,* 6–47.

Bombay, A., Matheson, K. & Anisman, H. (2014a). *Origins of Lateral Violence in Aboriginal Communities: a preliminary report of student-to-student abuse in residential schools.* Ottawa, Ontario: Aboriginal Healing Foundation.

Bombay, A., Matheson, K. & Anisman, H. (2014b). The intergenerational effects of Indian Residential Schools: implications for the concept of historical trauma. *Transcultural Psychiatry, 51,* 320–338.

Bonci, A. & Borgland, S. (2009). Role of orexin/hypocretin and CRF in the formation of drug-dependent synaptic plasticity in the mesolimbic system. *Neuropharmacology, 56,* 107–111.

Bonham, V.L. (2001). Race, ethnicity, and pain treatment: striving to understand the causes and solutions to the disparities in pain treatment. *Journal of Law, Medicine & Ethics, 29,* 52–68.

Bonin, R.P. & De Koninck, Y. (2014). A spinal analog of memory reconsolidation enables reversal of hyperalgesia. *Nature Neuroscience, 17,* 1043–1045.

Booth, H., Khan, O., Prevost, A.T. et al. (2015). Impact of bariatric surgery on clinical depression: interrupted

time series study with matched controls. *Journal of Affective Disorders, 174,* 644–649.

Borchers, A.T., Naguwa, S.M., Keen, C.L. & Gershwin, M.E. (2003). Immunopathogenesis of Sjögren's syndrome. *Clinical Reviews in Allergy & Immunology, 25,* 89–104.

Borgland, S.L., Chang, S.J., Bowers, M.S. et al. (2009). Orexin A/hypocretin-1 selectively promotes motivation for positive reinforcers. *Journal of Neuroscience, 29,* 11215–11225.

Bortsov, A.V., Smith, J.E., Diatchenko, L. et al. (2013). Polymorphisms in the glucocorticoid receptor co-chaperone FKBP5 predict persistent musculoskeletal pain after traumatic stress exposure. *Pain, 154,* 1419–1426.

Bos, K.I., Schuenemann, V.J., Golding, G.B. et al. (2011). A draft genome of Yersinia pestis from victims of the Black Death. *Nature, 478,* 506–510.

Boughey, J.C., Hoskin, T.L., Hartmann, L.C. et al. (2015). Impact of reconstruction and reoperation on long-term patient-reported satisfaction after contralateral prophylactic mastectomy. *Annals of Surgical Oncology, 22,* 401–408.

Bouri, S., Shun-Shin, M.J., Cole, G.D. et al. (2013). Meta-analysis of secure randomized controlled trials of beta-blockade to prevent perioperative death in noncardiac surgery. *Heart, 100,* 456–464.

Bourinet, E., Altier, C., Hildebrand, M.E. et al. (2014). Calcium-permeable ion channels in pain signaling. *Physiological Reviews, 94,* 81–140.

Boutelle, K.N., Wierenga, C.E., Bischoff-Grethe, A. et al. (2015). Increased brain response to appetitive tastes in the insula and amygdala in obese compared with healthy weight children when sated. *International Journal of Obesity, 39,* 620–628.

Bowen, S., Witkiewitz, K., Clifasefi, S.L. et al. (2014). Relative efficacy of mindfulness-based relapse prevention, standard relapse prevention, and treatment as usual for substance use disorders: a randomized clinical trial. *JAMA Psychiatry, 71,* 547–556.

Bowering, K.J., O'Connell, N.E., Tabor, A. et al. (2013). The effects of graded motor imagery and its components on chronic pain: a systematic review and meta-analysis. *Journal of Pain, 14,* 3–13.

Bradt, J., Potvin, N., Kesslick, A. et al. (2014). The impact of music therapy versus music medicine on psychological outcomes and pain in cancer patients: a mixed methods study. *Supportive Care in Cancer, 23,* 1261–1271.

Brady, K.T., Dansky, B.S., Sonne, S.C., & Saladin, M.E. (1998). Posttraumatic stress disorder and cocaine dependence – order of onset. *American Journal on Addictions, 7,* 128–135.

Brandt, L.J., Borody, T.J. & Campbell, J. (2011). Endoscopic fecal microbiota transplantation: 'first-line' treatment for severe *Clostridium difficile* infection? *Journal of Clinical Gastroenterology, 45,* 655–657.

Branscombe, N.R. & Reynolds, K.J. (2015). Toward person plasticity: individual and collective approaches. In K.J. Reynolds & N.R. Branscombe (Eds.), *Psychology of Change: life contexts, experiences, and identities* (pp. 3–24). New York: Psychology Press.

Brave Heart, M.Y. (2003). The historical trauma response among natives and its relationship with substance abuse: a Lakota illustration. *Journal of Psychoactive Drugs, 35,* 7–13.

Braveman, P., Egerter, S. & Williams, D.R. (2011). The social determinants of health: coming of age. *Annual Review of Public Health, 32,* 381–398.

Braveman, P. & Gottlieb L. (2014). The social determinants of health: it's time to consider the causes of the causes. *Public Health Reports, 129,* 19–31.

Braz, J., Solorzano, C., Wang, X. & Basbaum, A.I. (2014). Transmitting pain and itch messages: a contemporary view of the spinal cord circuits that generate gate control. *Neuron, 82,* 522–536.

Brazzelli, M., Saunders, D.H., Greig, C.A. & Mead, G. E. (2011). Physical fitness training for stroke patients. *Cochrane Database of Systematic Reviews, 11,* CD003316.

Brewer, M. (1991). The social self: on being the same and different at the same time. *Personality and Social Psychology Bulletin, 17,* 475–482.

Bricker, J.B., Rajan, K.B., Zalewski, M. et al. (2009). Psychological and social risk factors in adolescent smoking transitions: a population-based longitudinal study. *Health Psychology, 28,* 439.

British Medical Association (2007). *Decisions relating to cardiopulmonary resuscitation: a joint statement from the British Medical Association, the Resuscitation Council (UK) and the Royal College of Nursing.* London: Resuscitation Council (UK).

Bro, R., Kamstrup-Nielsen, M.H., Engelsen, S.B. et al. (2015). Forecasting individual breast cancer risk using plasma metabolomics and biocontours. *Metabolomics, 11,* 1376–1380.

Broadbent, E., Petrie, K.J., Main, J. & Weinman, J. (2006). The Brief Illness Perception Questionnaire. *Journal of Psychosomatic Research, 60,* 631–637.

Brodal, P. (2004). *The Central Nervous System: structure and function* (3rd ed.). New York: Oxford University Press.

Broholm, M., Pommergaard, H.C. & Gögenür, I. (2015). Possible benefits of robot-assisted rectal cancer surgery regarding urological and sexual dysfunction: a systematic review and meta-analysis. *Colorectal Disease, 17,* 375–381.

Brondolo, E., Rieppi, R., Erickson, S.A. et al. (2003). Hostility, interpersonal interactions, and ambulatory blood pressure. *Psychosomatic Medicine, 65,* 1003–1011.

Brown, A.S. (2011). The environment and susceptibility to schizophrenia. *Progress in Neurobiology, 93,* 23–58.

Brown, D.L., Epstein, A.M. & Schneider, E.C. (2013). Influence of cardiac surgeon report cards on patient referral by cardiologists in New York State after 20 years of public reporting. *Circulation: Cardiovascular Quality and Outcomes, 6,* 643–648.

Brown, K.W. & Ryan, R. (2003). The benefits of being present: mindfulness and its role in psychological well-being. *Journal of Personality and Social Psychology, 84,* 822–848.

Brown, M.C., Dobrikova, E.Y. & Dobrikov, M.I. (2014). Oncolytic polio virotherapy of cancer. *Cancer, 120,* 3277–3286.

Brown, R.F., Tennant, C.C., Dunn, S.M. & Pollard, J.D. (2005). A review of stress-relapse interactions in multiple sclerosis: important features and stress-mediating and -moderating variables. *Multiple Sclerosis, 11,* 477–484.

Brug, J., Aro, A.R. & Richardus, J.H. (2009). Risk perceptions and behaviour: towards pandemic control of emerging infectious diseases. *International Journal of Behavioral Medicine, 16,* 3–6.

Brummett, B.H., Babyak, M.A. & Williams, R.B. (2014). A putatively functional polymorphism in the htr2c gene is associated with depressive symptoms in white females reporting significant life stress. *PLoS One, 9,* e114451.

Brusca, S.B., Abramson, S.B. & Scher, J.U. (2014). Microbiome and mucosal inflammation as extra-articular triggers for rheumatoid arthritis and autoimmunity. *Current Opinion in Rheumatology*, *26*, 101–107.

Brydon, L., Walker, C., Wawrzyniak, A.J. et al. (2009). Dispositional optimism and stress-induced changes in immunity and negative mood. *Brain, Behavior, and Immunity*, *23*, 810–816.

Buckman, L.B., Hasty, A.H., Flaherty, D.K. et al. (2014). Obesity induced by a high-fat diet is associated with increased immune cell entry into the central nervous system. *Brain, Behavior, and Immunity*, *35*, 33–42.

Buffie, C.G., Bucci, V., Stein, R.R. et al. (2015). Precision microbiome reconstitution restores bile acid mediated resistance to Clostridium difficile. *Nature*, *517*, 205–208.

Buhle, J.T., Stevens, B.L., Friedman, J.J. & Wager, T.D. (2012). Distraction and placebo: two separate routes to pain control. *Psychological Science*, *23*, 246–253.

Bullough, O. (2013). *The Last Man in Russia: the struggle to save a dying nation*. New York: Basic Books.

Bunce, S.C., Harris, J.D., Bixler, E.O. et al. (2015). Possible evidence for re-regulation of HPA axis and brain reward systems over time in treatment in prescription opioid-dependent patients. *Journal of Addiction Medicine*, *9*, 53–60.

Bunse, L., Schumacher, T., Sahm, F. et al. (2015). Proximity ligation assay evaluates IDH1R132H presentation in gliomas. *The Journal of Clinical Investigation*, *125*, 593–606.

Burattini, C., Gill, T.M., Aicardi, G. & Janak, P.H. (2006). The ethanol self-administration context as a reinstatement cue: acute effects of naltrexone. *Neuroscience*, *139*, 877–887.

Burg, M.M., Benedetto, M.C., Rosenberg, R. & Soufer, R. (2003). Presurgical depression predicts medical morbidity 6 months after coronary artery bypass graft surgery. *Psychosomatic Medicine*, *65*, 111–118.

Burnett, F.M. (1970). The concept of immunological surveillance. *Progress in Experimental Tumor Research*, *13*, 1–27.

Burns, J.W., Nielson, W.R., Jensen, M.P. et al. (2015). Specific and general therapeutic mechanisms in cognitive behavioral treatment of chronic pain. *Journal of Consulting and Clinical Psychology*, *83*, 1–11.

Burns, J.W., Quartana, P.J. & Bruehl, S. (2008). Anger inhibition and pain: conceptualizations, evidence and new directions. *Journal of Behavioral Medicine*, *31*, 259–279.

Burns, M.B., Lynch, J. & Starr, T.K. (2015). Virulence genes are a signature of the microbiome in the colorectal tumor microenvironment. *Genome Medicine*, *7*, 55. Doi: 10.1186/s13073-015-0177-8.

Burroughs, V.J., Maxey, R.W. & Levy, R.A. (2002). Racial and ethnic differences in response to medicines: towards individualized pharmaceutical treatment. *Journal of the National Medical Association*, *94*, 1.

Burton, B.R., Britton, G.J., Fang, H. et al. (2014). Sequential transcriptional changes dictate safe and effective antigen-specific immunotherapy. *Nature Communications*, *5*, 4741.

Burton, C.L., Yan, O.H., Pat-Horenczyk, R. et al. (2011). Coping flexibility and complicated grief: a comparison of American and Chinese samples. *Depression and Anxiety*, *29*, 16–22.

Butler, M., Tiedemann, M., Nicol, J. & Valiquet, D. (2013). Euthanasia and assisted suicide in Canada (Background Paper No. 2010-68-E.). Ottawa: Library of Parliament Research Publications.

Cabral, R.R. & Smith, T.B. (2011). Racial/ethnic matching of clients and therapists in mental health services: a meta-analytic review of preferences, perceptions, and outcomes. *Journal of Counseling Psychology*, *58*, 537–544.

Cacciapaglia, F., Navarini, L., Menna, P. et al. (2011). Cardiovascular safety of anti-TNF-alpha therapies: facts and unsettled issues. *Autoimmunity Reviews*, *10*, 631–635.

Cacioppo, J.T., Cacioppo, S., Capitanio, J.P. & Cole, S.W. (2015). The neuroendocrinology of social isolation. *Annual Review of Psychology*, *66*, 733–767.

Cahill, L. (2006). Why sex matters for neuroscience. *Nature Reviews Neuroscience*, *7*, 477–484.

Calder, P.C., Krauss-Etschmann, S., de Jong, E.C. et al. (2006). Early nutrition and immunity – progress and perspectives. *British Journal of Nutrition*, *96*, 774–790.

Calhoun, L.G. & Allen, B.G. (1991). Social reactions to the survivor of a suicide in the family: a review of the literature. *OMEGA – Journal of Death and Dying*, *23*, 95–107.

Callaghan, B.L. & Richardson, R. (2011). Maternal separation results in early emergence of adult-like fear and extinction learning in infant rats. *Behavioral Neuroscience, 125*, 20–28.

Callaghan, R.C., Taylor, L. & Cunningham, J.A. (2007). Does progressive stage transition mean getting better? A test of the Transtheoretical Model in alcoholism recovery. *Addiction, 102*, 1588–1596.

Calle, E.E., Rodriguez, C., Walker-Thurmond, K. & Thun, M.J. (2003). Overweight, obesity, and mortality from cancer in a prospectively studied cohort of US adults. *New England Journal of Medicine, 348*, 1625–1638.

Cameron, J.L. (1997). Stress and behaviorally induced reproductive dysfunction in primates. *Seminars in Reproductive Endocrinology, 15*, 37–45.

Campbell, A. (2010). Oxytocin and human social behavior. *Personality and Social Psychology Review, 14*, 281–295.

Campbell, J.P., Karolak, M.R., Ma, Y. et al. (2012). Stimulation of host bone marrow stromal cells by sympathetic nerves promotes breast cancer bone metastasis in mice. *PLoS Biology, 10*, e1001363.

Canadian Institutes of Health Research (2014). More about knowledge creation at CIHR. www.cihr-irsc.gc.ca/e/39033.html#Definition (accessed May, 2015).

Cancer Research UK. (2014). Obesity, body weight and cancer. www.cancerresearchuk.org/cancer-info/healthyliving/obesity-bodyweight-and-cancer/ (accessed May 2015).

Capistrant, B.D., Moon, J.R. & Glymour, M.M. (2012). Spousal caregiving and incident hypertension. *American Journal of Hypertension, 25*, 437–443.

Cappuccio, F.P., D'Elia, L., Strazzullo, P. & Miller, M.A. (2010). Sleep duration and all-cause mortality: a systematic review and meta-analysis of prospective studies. *Sleep, 33*, 585–592.

Capuron, L. & Miller, A.H. (2011). Immune system to brain signaling: neuropsychopharmacological implications. *Pharmacology & Therapeutics, 130*, 226–238.

Cardoso, C., Ellenbogen, M.A., Serravalle, L. & Linnen, A.M. (2013). Stress-induced negative mood moderates the relation between oxytocin administration and trust: evidence for the tend-and-befriend response to stress? *Psychoneuroendocrinology, 38*, 2800–2804.

Cardoso, C., Kingdon, D. & Ellenbogen, M.A. (2014). A meta-analytic review of the impact of intranasal oxytocin administration on cortisol concentrations during laboratory tasks: moderation by method and mental health. *Psychoneuroendocrinology, 49*, 161–170.

Cardoso, C., Orlando, M.A., Brown, C.A. & Ellenbogen, M.A. (2014). Oxytocin and enhancement of the positive valence of social affiliation memories: an autobiographical memory study. *Social Neuroscience, 9*, 186–195.

Carey, G. (2003). *Human Genetics for the Social Sciences*. London, UK: SAGE.

Carod-Artal, F.J. & Egido, J.A. (2009). Quality of life after stroke: the importance of a good recovery. *Cerebrovascular Disease, 27*, 204–214.

Carpenter, C.J. (2010). A meta-analysis of the effectiveness of health belief model variables in predicting behavior. *Health Communication, 25*, 661–669.

Carreno, B.M., Magrini, V., Becker-Hapak, M. et al. (2015). Cancer immunotherapy: a dendritic cell vaccine increases the breadth and diversity of melanoma neoantigen-specific T cells. *Science, 348*, 803–808.

Carroll, K.M., Fenton, L.R., Ball, S.A. et al. (2004). Efficacy of disulfiram and cognitive behavior therapy in cocaine-dependent outpatients: a randomized placebo-controlled trial. *Archives of General Psychiatry, 61*, 264–272.

Carroll, K.M. & Onken, L.S. (2005). Behavioral therapies for drug abuse. *American Journal of Psychiatry, 162*, 1452–1460.

Carver, C.S. & Connor-Smith, J. (2010). Personality and coping. *Annual Review of Psychology, 61*, 679–704.

Carver, C.S., Pozo, C., Harris, S.D. et al. (1993). How coping mediates the effect of optimism on distress: a study of women with early stage breast cancer. *Journal of Personality and Social Psychology, 65*, 375–390.

Carver, C.S., Scheier, M.F. & Weintraub, J.K. (1989). Assessing coping strategies: a theoretically based approach. *Journal of Personality and Social Psychology, 56*, 267–283.

Carvey, P.M., Punati, A. & Newman, M.B. (2006). Progressive dopamine neuron loss in Parkinson's disease: the multiple hit hypothesis. *Cell Transplant, 15*, 239–250.

Carwile, J.L., Feldman, S. & Johnson, N.R. (2014). Use of a simple visual distraction to reduce pain and anxiety in patients undergoing colposcopy. *Journal of Lower Genital Tract Disease*, *18*, 317–321.

Casey, B.J., Craddock, N., Cuthbert, B.N. et al. (2013). DSM-5 and RDoC: progress in psychiatry research? *Nature Reviews Neuroscience*, *14*, 810–814.

Casey, K.F., Benkelfat, C., Cherkasova, M.V. et al. (2014). Reduced dopamine response to amphetamine in subjects at ultra-high risk for addiction. *Biological Psychiatry*, *76*, 23–30.

Caspi, A., Sugden, K., Moffitt, T.E. et al. (2003). Influence of life stress on depression: moderation by a polymorphism in the 5-HTT gene. *Science*, *301*, 386–389.

Casscells, W., Naghavi, M. & Willerson, J.T. (2003). Vulnerable atherosclerotic plaque: a multifocal disease. *Circulation*, *107*, 2072–2075.

Cataldo, J.K., Jahan, T.M. & Pongquan, V.L. (2012). Lung cancer stigma, depression, and quality of life among ever and never smokers. *European Journal of Oncology Nursing*, *16*, 264–269.

Catalona, W.J., Richie, J.P., Ahmann, F.R. et al. (1994). Comparison of digital rectal examination and serum prostate specific antigen in the early detection of prostate cancer: results of a multicenter clinical trial of 6,630 men. *The Journal of Urology*, *151*, 1283–1290.

Caulfield, T. (2015). *Is Gwyneth Paltrow Wrong about Everything? When Celebrity Culture and Science Clash*. Boston, MA: Beacon Press.

Celestin, J., Edwards, R.R. & Jamison, R.N. (2009). Pretreatment psychosocial variables as predictors of outcomes following lumbar surgery and spinal cord stimulation: a systematic review and literature synthesis. *Pain Medicine*, *10*, 639–653.

Cencioni, C., Spallotta, F., Mai, A. et al. (2015). Sirtuin function in aging heart and vessels. *Journal of Molecular and Cellular Cardiology*. pii: S0022-2828(14)00435-0. [Epub ahead of print]

Centers for Disease Control and Prevention (2014). Cigarette smoking in the United States. www.cdc.gov/tobacco/campaign/tips/resources/data/cigarette-smoking-in-united-states.html (accessed March, 2015).

Centers for Disease Control and Prevention. (2015a). Life expectancy. www.cdc.gov/nchs/fastats/life-expectancy.htm (accessed May, 2015).

Centers for Disease Control and Prevention. (2015b). Non-polio enterovirus. www.cdc.gov/non-polio-enterovirus/about/EV-D68.html (accessed May, 2015).

Centers for Disease Control and Prevention. (2015c). Importation and domestic transmission of Shigella sonnei resistant to ciprofloxacin: United States, May 2014–February 2015. *Morbidity and Mortality Weekly Report (MMWR)*, *64*, 318–320.

Centers for Disease Control and Prevention. (2015d). National Center for Injury Prevention and Control: Ten leading causes of death by age group, United States–2010. www.cdc.gov/injury/wisqars/leadingcauses.html (accessed January, 2015).

Centers for Disease Control. (2010). National Center for Health Statistics (2014). Prescription Drug Use Continues to Increase: U.S. Prescription Drug Data for 2007-2008. www.cdc.gov/nchs/data/databriefs/db42.htm (accessed September 2015).

Cervera, R., Khamashta, M.A. & Hughes, G.R.V. (2009). The Euro-lupus project: epidemiology of systemic lupus erythematosus in Europe. *Lupus*, *18*, 869–874.

Chahine, B.G. & Bahna, S.L. (2010). The role of the gut mucosal immunity in the development of tolerance versus development of allergy to food. *Current Opinion in Allergy and Clinical Immunology*, *10*, 394–399.

Chambers, H.F. (2001). The changing epidemiology of Staphylococcus aureus? *Emerging Infectious Diseases*, *7*, 178–182.

Chambers, S.K., Dunn, J., Occhipinti, S. et al. (2012). A systematic review of the impact of stigma and nihilism on lung cancer outcomes. *BMC Cancer*, *12*, 184.

Chapin, H., Bagarinao, E. & Mackey, S. (2012). Real-time fMRI applied to pain management. *Neuroscience Letters*, *520*, 174–181.

Chappel, J.N. & DuPont, R.L. (1999). Twelve-step and mutual-help programs for addictive disorders. *Psychiatric Clinics of North America*, *22*, 425–446.

Chapple, A., Ziebland, S. & McPherson, A. (2004). Stigma, shame, and blame experienced by patients with lung cancer: qualitative study. *British Medical Journal, 328*, 1470.

Chaput, J.P. & Tremblay, A. (2012). Adequate sleep to improve the treatment of obesity. *Canadian Medical Association Journal*, *184*, 1975–1976.

Charney, D.S. (2004). Psychobiological mechanisms of resilience and vulnerability: implications for successful adaptation to extreme stress. *American Journal of Psychiatry*, *161*, 195–216.

Chaturvedi, N. (2003). Ethnic differences in cardiovascular disease. *Heart*, *89*, 681–686.

Cheang, M.C., Voduc, D., Bajdik, C., Leung, S. et al. (2008). Basal-like breast cancer defined by five biomarkers has superior prognostic value than triple-negative phenotype. *Clinical Cancer Research*, *14*, 1368–1376.

Chen, D., Jiao, Y. & Torquato, S. (2014). A cellular automaton model for tumor dormancy: emergence of a proliferative switch. *PLoS One*, *9*, e109934.

Chen, E., Matthews, K.A., Salomon, K. & Ewart, C.K. (2002). Cardiovascular reactivity during social and nonsocial stressors: do children's personal goals and expressive skills matter? *Health Psychology*, *21*, 16–24.

Chen, G.Y. & Nuñez, G. (2010). Sterile inflammation: sensing and reacting to damage. *Nature Reviews Immunology*, *10*, 826–837.

Chen, L., Coleman, R., Leang, R. et al. (2014). Human neural precursor cells promote neurologic recovery in a viral model of multiple sclerosis. *Stem Cell Reports*, *2*, 825–837.

Chen, S. & Parmigiani, G. (2007). Meta-analysis of BRCA1 and BRCA2 penetrance. *Journal of Clinical Oncology*, *25*, 1329–1333.

Chen, Z., Guo, L., Zhang, Y. et al. (2014). Incorporation of therapeutically modified bacteria into gut microbiota inhibits obesity. *The Journal of Clinical Investigation*, *124*, 3391–3406.

Cheng, C., Lau, H.P.B. & Chan, M.P.S. (2014). Coping flexibility and psychological adjustment to stressful life changes: a meta-analytic review. *Psychological Bulletin*, *140*, 1582–1607.

Cheng, S.T. & Li, K.K. (2010). Combining major life events and recurrent hassles in the assessment of stress in Chinese adolescents: preliminary evidence. *Psychological Assessment*, *22*, 532–538.

Chida, Y. & Hamer, M. (2008). An association of adverse psychosocial factors with diabetes mellitus: a meta-analytic review of longitudinal cohort studies. *Diabetologia*, *51*, 2168–2178.

Chida, Y., Hamer, M., Wardle, J. & Steptoe, A. (2008). Do stress-related psychosocial factors contribute to cancer incidence and survival? *Nature Clinical Practice Oncology*, *5*, 466–475.

Chida, Y. & Mao, X. (2009). Does psychosocial stress predict symptomatic herpes simplex virus recurrence? A meta-analytic investigation on prospective studies. *Brain, Behavior, and Immunity*, *23*, 917–925.

Chida, Y. & Steptoe, A. (2008). Positive psychological well-being and mortality: a quantitative review of prospective observational studies. *Psychosomatic Medicine*, *70*, 741–756.

Chida, Y. & Steptoe, A. (2010). The association of anger and hostility with future coronary heart disease: a meta-analytic review of prospective evidence. *Journal of the American College of Cardiology*, *53*, 936–946.

Chin, L.J., Ratner, E., Leng, S. et al. (2008). A SNP in a let-7 microRNA complementary site in the KRAS 3′ untranslated region increases non-small cell lung cancer risk. *Cancer Research*, *68*, 8535–8540.

Choi, J., Yoo, J., Lee, M. et al. (2014). A rapid antimicrobial susceptibility test based on single-cell morphological analysis. *Science Translational Medicine*, *6*, 267ra174.

Choiniere, M., Auger, F.A. & Latarjet, J. (1994). Visual analogue thermometer: a valid and useful instrument for measuring pain in burned patients. *Burns*, *20*, 229–235.

Cholongitas, E. & Papatheodoridis, G.V. (2014). Sofosbuvir: a novel oral agent for chronic hepatitis C. *Annals of Gastroenterology: Quarterly Publication of the Hellenic Society of Gastroenterology*, *27*, 331–337.

Chowdhury, R., Warnakula, S., Kunutsor, S. et al. (2014). Association of dietary, circulating, and supplement fatty acids with coronary risk: a systematic review and meta-analysis. *Annals of Internal Medicine*, *160*, 398–406.

Christakis, N.A. & Fowler, J.H. (2013). Social contagion theory: examining dynamic social networks and human behavior. *Statistics in Medicine*, *32*, 556–577.

Christensen, A., Dewing, P. & Micevych, P. (2011). Membrane-initiated estradiol signaling induces spinogenesis required for female sexual receptivity. *Journal of Neuroscience*, *31*, 17583–17589.

Christensen, A.J., Ehlers, S.L., Wiebe, J.S. et al. (2002). Patient personality and mortality: a 4-year prospective examination of chronic renal insufficiency. *Health Psychology*, *21*, 315–320.

Christensen, K., Ørstavik, K.H. & Vaupel, J.W. (2001). The X chromosome and the female survival advantage. In M. Weinstein, A.I. Hermalin &

M.A. Stoto (Eds.), *Population Health and Aging: strengthening the dialogue between epidemiology and demography* (pp. 175–183). New York: The New York Academy of Sciences.

Chuang, J.C. & Zigman, J.M. (2010). Ghrelin's roles in stress, mood, and anxiety regulation. *International Journal of Peptides*, 2010, pii: 460549.

Chung, C.C., Pimentel, D., Jor'dan, A.J. et al. (2015). Inflammation-associated declines in cerebral vasoreactivity and cognition in type 2 diabetes. *Neurology*, *10*, 1212.

Chung, W.S., Lin, C.L., Chen, Y.F. et al. (2013). Sleep disorders and increased risk of subsequent acute coronary syndrome in individuals without sleep apnea: a nationwide population-based cohort study. *Sleep*, *36*, 1963–1968.

Ciriello, J., Caverson, M.M. & Li, Z. (2013). Effects of hypocretin and norepinephrine interaction in bed nucleus of the stria terminalis on arterial pressure. *Neuroscience*, *255*, 278–291.

Claassen, D.O., Josephs, K.A., Ahlskog, J.E. et al. (2010). REM sleep behavior disorder preceding other aspects of synucleinopathies by up to half a century. *Neurology*, *75*, 494–499.

Clark, A.J., Strandberg-Larsen, K., Masters Pedersen, J.L. et al. (2015). Psychosocial risk factors for hospitalisation and death from chronic obstructive pulmonary disease: a prospective cohort study. *COPD: Journal of Chronic Obstructive Pulmonary Disease*, *12*, 190–198.

Clarke, H., Bonin, R.P., Orser, B.A. et al. (2012). The prevention of chronic postsurgical pain using gabapentin and pregabalin: a combined systematic review and meta-analysis. *Anesthesia & Analgesia*, *115*, 428–442.

Cleary, J., Radbruch, L., Torode, J. & Cherny, N.I. (2013). Next steps in access and availability of opioids for the treatment of cancer pain: reaching the tipping point? *Annals of Oncology*, *24*, xi60–xi64.

Cleck, J.N. & Blendy, J.A. (2008). Making a bad thing worse: adverse effects of stress on drug addiction. *Journal of Clinical Investigation*, *118*, 454–461.

Clifford, A.C., Doran, C.M. & Tsey, K. (2013). Systematic review of suicide prevention interventions targeting indigenous peoples in Australia, United States, Canada and New Zealand. *BMC Public Health*, *13*, 463.

Clinton, H.R. (1996). *It Takes a Village: and other lessons children teach us*. New York: Simon & Schuster.

Coggins, M. & Rosenzweig, A. (2012). The fire within: cardiac inflammatory signaling in health and disease. *Circulation Research*, *110*, 116–125.

Cohen, J. (1988). *Statistical Power Analysis for the Behavioral Sciences* (2nd ed.). Mahwah, NJ: Lawrence Erlbaum Associates.

Cohen, R.Y., Brownell, K.D. & Felix, M.R. (1990). Age and sex differences in health habits and beliefs of schoolchildren. *Health Psychology*, *9*, 208.

Cohen, S., Doyle, W.J., Alper, C.M. et al. (2009). Sleep habits and susceptibility to the common cold. *Archives of Internal Medicine*, *169*, 62–67.

Cohen, S., Frank, E., Doyle, W.J. & Skoner, D.P. (1998). Types of stressors that increase susceptibility to the common cold in healthy adults. *Health Psychology*, *17*, 214–223.

Cohen, S., Janicki-Deverts, D., Turner, R.B. et al. (2013). Childhood socioeconomic status, telomere length, and susceptibility to upper respiratory infection. *Brain, Behavior, and Immunity*, *34*, 31–38.

Cohen, S., Kamarck, T. & Mermelstein, R. (1983). A global measure of perceived stress. *Journal of Health and Social Behavior*, *24*, 385–396.

Cohen, S., Miller, G.E. & Rabin, B.S. (2001). Psychological stress and antibody response to immunization: a critical review of the human literature. *Psychosomatic Medicine*, *63*, 7–18.

Cohen, S., Tyrrell, D.A. & Smith, A.P. (1993). Negative life events, perceived stress, negative affect, and susceptibility to the common cold. *Journal of Personality and Social Psychology*, *64*, 131–140.

Colagreco, J.P., Bailey, D.E., Fitzpatrick, J.J. et al. (2014).Watchful waiting: role of disease progression on uncertainty and depressive symptoms in patients with chronic hepatitis C. *Journal of Viral Hepatitis*, *21*, 727–733.

Cole, S.W. (2009). Chronic inflammation and breast cancer recurrence. *Journal of Clinical Oncology*, *27*, 3418–3419.

Colen, C.G. & Ramey, D.M. (2014). Is breast truly best? Estimating the effects of breastfeeding on long-term child health and wellbeing in the United States using sibling comparisons. *Social Science & Medicine*, *109*, 55–65.

Collaborative Group on Hormonal Factors in Breast Cancer. (1996). Breast cancer and hormonal contraceptives: collaborative reanalysis of individual data on 53,297 women with breast cancer and

100, 239 women without breast cancer from 54 epidemiological studies. *The Lancet, 347,* 1713–1727.

Collins, L.G. & Swartz, K. (2011). Caregiver care. *American Family Physician, 83,* 1309.

Collins, S.M. (2014). A role for the gut microbiota in IBS. *Nature Reviews Gastroenterology & Hepatology, 11,* 497–505.

Colloca, L., Lopiano, L., Lanotte, M. & Benedetti, F. (2004). Overt versus covert treatment for pain, anxiety, and Parkinson's disease. *The Lancet Neurology, 3,* 679–684.

Compare, A., Zarbo, C., Manzoni, G.M. et al. (2013). Social support, depression, and heart disease: a ten year literature review. *Frontiers in Psychology, 4,* 384.

Compas, B.E., Connor-Smith, J.K., Saltzman, H. et al. (2001). Coping with stress during childhood and adolescence: problems, progress, and potential in theory and research. *Psychological Bulletin, 127,* 87–127.

Compston, A. & Coles, A. (2008). Multiple sclerosis. *The Lancet, 372,* 1502–1517.

Compton, W.M. & Volkow, N.D. (2006). Abuse of prescription drugs and the risk of addiction. *Drug and Alcohol Dependence, 83,* S4–S7.

Connell, P.P. & Hellman, S. (2009). Advances in radiotherapy and implications for the next century: a historical perspective. *Cancer Research, 69,* 383–392.

Connolly, H.M., Crary, J.L., McGoon, M.D. et al. (1997). Valvular heart disease associated with fenfluramine-phentermine. *New England Journal of Medicine, 337,* 581–588.

Conry, M.C., Humphries, N., Morgan, K. et al. (2012). A 10 year (2000–2010) systematic review of interventions to improve quality of care in hospitals. *BMC Health Services Research, 12,* 275.

Coomans, C.P., van den Berg, S.A., Houben, T. et al. (2013). Detrimental effects of constant light exposure and high-fat diet on circadian energy metabolism and insulin sensitivity. *The FASEB Journal, 27,* 1721–1732.

Cooper, C., Sommerlad, A., Lyketsos, C.G. & Livingston, G. (2015). Modifiable predictors of dementia in mild cognitive impairment: a systematic review and meta-analysis. *The American Journal of Psychiatry, 172,* 323–334.

Cooper, M.L., Wood, P.K., Orcutt, H.K. & Albino, A. (2003). Personality and the predisposition to engage in risky or problem behaviors during adolescence. *Journal of Personality and Social Psychology, 84,* 390–410.

Cooper, Z., Courtwright, A., Karlage, A. et al. (2014). Pitfalls in communication that lead to nonbeneficial emergency surgery in elderly patients with serious illness: description of the problem and elements of a solution. *Annals of Surgery, 260,* 949–957.

Copinschi, G., Leproult, R. & Spiegel, K. (2014). The important role of sleep in metabolism. *Frontiers of Hormone Research, 42,* 59–72.

Coppedè, F. (2014). The potential of epigenetic therapies in neurodegenerative diseases. *Frontiers in Genetics, 5,* 220.

Corbett, D., Nguemeni, C. & Gomez-Smith, M. (2014). How can you mend a broken brain? Neurorestorative approaches to stroke recovery. *Cerebrovascular Diseases, 38,* 233–239.

Corona, E., Chen, R., Sikora, M. et al. (2013). Analysis of the genetic basis of disease in the context of worldwide human relationships and migration. *PLoS Genetics, 9,* e1003447.

Corpet, D.E. (2011). Red meat and colon cancer: should we become vegetarians, or can we make meat safer? *Meat Science, 89,* 310–316.

Corrigan, P., Larson, J.E. & Rüsch, N. (2009). Self-stigma and the 'why try' effect: impact on life goals and evidence-based practices. *World Psychiatry, 8,* 75–81.

Corrigan, P.W. & Fong, M.W. (2014). Competing perspectives on erasing the stigma of illness: what says the dodo bird? *Social Science & Medicine, 103,* 110–117.

Corrigan, P.W., Rafacz, J. & Rüsch, N. (2011). Examining a progressive model of self-stigma and its impact on people with serious mental illness. *Psychiatry Research, 189,* 339–343.

Corry, N., Pruzinsky, T. & Rumsey, N. (2009). Quality of life and psychosocial adjustment to burn injury: social functioning, body image, and health policy perspectives. *International Review of Psychiatry, 21,* 539–548.

Cosgrove, M. (2004). Do stressful life events cause type 1 diabetes? *Occupational Medicine, 54,* 250–254.

Cosgrove, M.A., Towns, D.K., Fanciullo, G.J. & Kaye, A.D. (2011). Interventional pain management. In N. Vadivelu, R.D. Urman & R.L. Hines

(Eds.), *Essentials of Pain Management*. New York: Springer.

Cosgrove, M.P., Sargeant, L.A., Caleyachetty, R. & Griffin, S.J. (2012). Work-related stress and type 2 diabetes: systematic review and meta-analysis. *Occupational Medicine*, *62*, 167–173.

Costanzo, E.S., Lutgendorf, S.K., Bradley, S.L. et al. (2005). Cancer attributions, distress, and health practices among gynecologic cancer survivors. *Psychosomatic Medicine*, *67*, 972–980.

Cotman, C.W., Berchtold, N.C. & Christie, L.A. (2007). Exercise builds brain health: key roles of growth factor cascades and inflammation. *Trends in Neurosciences*, *30*, 464–472.

Covington, H.E., Maze, I., Sun, H. et al. (2011). A role for repressive histone methylation in cocaine-induced vulnerability to stress. *Neuron*, *71*, 656–670.

Cozma A.I. (2012). Effect of fructose on glycemic control in diabetes: a systematic review and meta-analysis of controlled feeding trials. *Diabetes Care*, *35*, 1611–1620.

Crabbe, J.C., Wahlsten, D. & Dudek, B.C. (1999). Genetics of mouse behavior: interactions with laboratory environment. *Science*, *284*, 1670–1672.

Cramer, H., Lauche, R., Klose, P. et al. (2014). A systematic review and meta-analysis of exercise interventions for colorectal cancer patients. *European Journal of Cancer Care*, *23*, 3–14.

Crane, J.D., Palanivel, R., Mottillo, E.P. et al. (2015). Inhibiting peripheral serotonin synthesis reduces obesity and metabolic dysfunction by promoting brown adipose tissue thermogenesis. *Nature Medicine*, *21*, 166–172.

Croyle, R.T. & Hunt, J.R. (1991). Coping with health threat: social influence processes in reactions to medical test results. *Journal of Personality and Social Psychology*, *60*, 382–389.

Crunelle, C.L., Kaag, A.M., Van Wingen, G. & van den Munkhof, H.E. (2014). Reduced frontal brain volume in non-treatment-seeking cocaine-dependent individuals: exploring the role of impulsivity, depression, and smoking. *Frontiers in Human Neuroscience*, *8*, 7.

Cruwys, T., Dingle, G.A., Haslam, C. et al. (2013). Social group memberships protect against future depression, alleviate depression symptoms and prevent depression relapse. *Social Science & Medicine*, *98*, 179–186.

Cruwys, T., Haslam, S.A., Dingle, G.A. et al. (2014). Depression and social identity: an integrative review. *Personality and Social Psychology Review*, *18*, 215–238.

Cummings, J.H. & Macfarlane, G.T. (1997). Colonic microflora: nutrition and health. *Nutrition*, *13*, 476–478.

Cunningham, M.G., Goldstein, M., Katz, D. et al. (2006). Coalescence of psychiatry, neurology, and neuropsychology: from theory to practice. *Harvard Review of Psychiatry*, *14*, 127–140.

Cuomo, R., Andreozzi, P., Zito, F.P. et al. (2014). Irritable bowel syndrome and food interaction. *World Journal of Gastroenterology*, *20*, 8837–8845.

Cupples, S.A. & Steslow, B. (2001). Use of behavioral contingency contracting with heart transplant candidates. *Progress in Transplantation*, *11*, 137–144.

Cushing, B.S. & Kramer, K.M. (2005). Mechanisms underlying epigenetic effects of early social experience: the role of neuropeptides and steroids. *Neuroscience & Biobehavioral Reviews*, *29*, 1089–1105.

Cuthbert, B.N. & Insel, T.R. (2013). Toward the future of psychiatric diagnosis: the seven pillars of RDoC. *BMC Medicine*, *11*, 126.

Cyr, A., Dunnagan, T.A. & Haynes, G. (2010). Efficacy of the health belief model for predicting intention to pursue genetic testing for colorectal cancer. *Journal of Genetic Counseling*, *19*, 174–186.

Dabelea, D., Mayer-Davis, E.J., Saydah, S. et al. (2014). Prevalence of type 1 and type 2 diabetes among children and adolescents from 2001 to 2009. *Journal of the American Medical Association*, *311*, 1778–1786.

Dacey, M.L., Kennedy, M.A., Polak, R. & Phillips, E.M. (2014). Physical activity counseling in medical school education: a systematic review. *Medical Education Online*, *19*, 24325.

Dackis, C. & O'Brien, C. (2005). Neurobiology of addiction: treatment and public policy ramifications. *Nature Neuroscience*, *8*, 1431–1436.

Daley, C., McNiel, D.E. & Binder, R.L. (2011). 'I did what?' Zolpidem and the courts. *Journal of the American Academy of Psychiatry and the Law Online*, *39*, 535–542.

Dallman, M.F. (2010). Stress-induced obesity and the emotional nervous system. *Trends in Endocrinology and Metabolism, 21*, 159–165.

Dalmas, E., Toubal, A., Alzaid, F. et al. (2015). Irf5 deficiency in macrophages promotes beneficial adipose tissue expansion and insulin sensitivity during obesity. *Nature Medicine.* [Epub ahead of print]

Danaei, G., Finucane, M.M., Lu, Y. et al. (2011). National, regional, and global trends in fasting plasma glucose and diabetes prevalence since 1980: systematic analysis of health examination surveys and epidemiological studies with 370 country-years and 2.7 million participants. *The Lancet, 378*, 31–40.

Dandona, S. & Roberts, R. (2014). The role of genetic risk factors in coronary artery disease. *Current Cardiology Reports, 16*, 479.

Danesh, J., Wheeler, J.G., Hirschfield, G.M. et al. (2004). C-reactive protein and other circulating markers of inflammation in the prediction of coronary heart disease. *New England Journal of Medicine, 350*, 1387–1397.

Dang, W. (2014). The controversial world of sirtuins. *Drug Discovery Today: Technologies, 12*, e9–e17.

Daniels, S.R., Arnett, D.K., Eckel, R.H. et al. (2005). Overweight in children and adolescents: pathophysiology, consequences, prevention, and treatment. *Circulation, 111*, 1999–2012.

Danielson, A.M., Matheson, K. & Anisman, H. (2011). Cytokine levels at a single time point following a reminder stimulus among women in abusive dating relationships: relationship to emotional states. *Psychoneuroendocrinology, 36*, 40–50.

Dantzer, R., O'Connor, J.C., Freund, G.G. et al. (2008). From inflammation to sickness and depression: when the immune system subjugates the brain. *Nature Reviews Neuroscience, 9*, 46–56.

Dantzer, R., O'Connor, J.C., Lawson, M.A. & Kelley, K.W. (2011). Inflammation-associated depression: from serotonin to kynurenine. *Psychoneuroendocrinology, 36*, 426–436.

Dave, N.D., Xiang, L., Rehm, K.E. & Marshall, G.D. (2011). Stress and allergic diseases. *Immunology and Allergy Clinics of North America, 31*, 55–68.

David, L.A., Maurice, C.F., Carmody, R.N. et al. (2014). Diet rapidly and reproducibly alters the human gut microbiome. *Nature, 505*, 559–563.

Davidson, J.A. & Kuritzky, L. (2014). Sodium glucose co-transporter 2 inhibitors and their mechanism for improving glycemia in patients with type 2 diabetes. *Postgraduate Medicine, 126*, 33–48.

Davila, M.L., Riviere, I., Wang, X. et al. (2014). Efficacy and toxicity management of 19-28z CAR T cell therapy in B cell acute lymphoblastic leukemia. *Science Translational Medicine, 6*, 224ra25.

Davis, C.G., Nolen-Hoeksema, S. & Larson, J. (1998). Making sense of loss and benefiting from the experience: two construals of meaning. *Journal of Personality and Social Psychology, 75*, 561–574.

Davis, E.P., Waffarn, F. & Sandman, C.A. (2011). Prenatal treatment with glucocorticoids sensitizes the HPA axis response to stress among full-term infants. *Developmental Psychobiology, 53*, 175–183.

Davis, K.D., Racine, E. & Collett, B. (2012). Neuroethical issues related to the use of brain imaging: can we and should we use brain imaging as a biomarker to diagnose chronic pain? *Pain, 153*, 1555–1559.

Davis, K.W., Wellman, P.J. & Clifford, P.S. (2007). Augmented cocaine conditioned place preference in rats pretreated with systemic ghrelin. *Regulatory Peptides, 140*, 148–152.

Davis, M. & Walker, D.L. (2014). Role of bed nucleus of the stria terminalis and amygdala AMPA receptors in the development and expression of context conditioning and sensitization of startle by prior shock. *Brain Structure and Function, 219*, 1969–1982.

Day, J.J., Childs, D., Guzman-Karlsson, M.C. et al. (2013). DNA methylation regulates associative reward learning. *Nature Neuroscience, 16*, 1445–1452.

Day, T.K. & Bianco-Miotto, T. (2013). Common gene pathways and families altered by DNA methylation in breast and prostate cancers. *Endocrine-Related Cancer, 20*, R215–R232.

De Dreu, C.K. (2012). Oxytocin modulates cooperation within and competition between groups: an integrative review and research agenda. *Hormones and Behavior, 61*, 419–428.

de Groote, L. & Linthorst, A.C. (2007). Exposure to novelty and forced swimming evoke stressor-dependent changes in extracellular GABA in the rat hippocampus. *Neuroscience, 148*, 794–805.

De Koning, L., Malik, V.S., Rimm, E.B. et al. (2011). Sugar-sweetened and artificially sweetened beverage consumption and risk of type 2 diabetes in men. *The American Journal of Clinical Nutrition*, *93*, 1321–1327.

De Palma, G. Blennerhassett, P., Lu, J. et al. (2015). Microbiota and host determinants of behavioural phenotype in maternally separated mice. *Nature Communications*, *6*, 7735. Doi: 10.1038/ncomms8735.

De Ruddere, L., Goubert, L., Stevens, M.A.L. et al. (2014). Health care professionals' reactions to patient pain: impact of knowledge about medical evidence and psychosocial influences. *The Journal of Pain*, *15*, 262–270.

De Vogli, R., Ferrie, J.E., Chandola, T. et al. (2007). Unfairness and health: evidence from the Whitehall II Study. *Journal of Epidemiology and Community Health*, *61*, 513–518.

De Vries, H.D. & Mudde, A.N. (1998). Predicting stage transitions for smoking cessation applying the attitude-social influence-efficacy model. *Psychology and Health*, *13*, 369–385.

Deadman, J.M., Leinster, S.J., Owens, R.G. et al. (2001). Taking responsibility for cancer treatment. *Social Science & Medicine*, *53*, 669–677.

Deandrea, S., Montanari,M., Moja, L. & Apolone, G. (2008). Prevalence of undertreatment in cancer pain: a review of published literature. *Annals of Oncology*, *19*, 1985–1991.

Deckersbach, T., Das, S.K., Urban, L.E. et al. (2014). Pilot randomized trial demonstrating reversal of obesity-related abnormalities in reward system responsivity to food cues with a behavioral intervention. *Nutrition & Diabetes*, *4*, e129.

Decramer, M., Janssens, W. & Miravitlles, M. (2012). Chronic obstructive pulmonary disease. *The Lancet*, *379*, 1341–51.

Deeks, A., Lombard, C., Michelmore, J. & Teede, H. (2009). The effects of gender and age on health related behaviors. *BMC Public Health*, *9*, 213.

Dehbi, A.Z., Radstake, T.R. & Broen, J.C. (2013). Accelerated telomere shortening in rheumatic diseases: cause or consequence? *Expert Review of Clinical Immunology*, *9*, 1193–1204.

DeLongis, A. & Holtzman, S. (2005). Coping in context: the role of stress, social support, and personality in coping. *Journal of Personality*, *73*, 1633–1656.

Deloukas, P., Kanoni, S., Willenborg, C. et al. (2013). Large-scale association analysis identifies new risk loci for coronary artery disease. *Nature Genetics*, *45*, 25–33.

Delzenne, N.M., Neyrinck, A.M. & Cani, P.D. (2011). Modulation of the gut microbiota by nutrients with prebiotic properties: consequences for host health in the context of obesity and metabolic syndrome. *Microbial Cell Factories*, *10*, S10.

Demoruelle, M.K., Deane, K.D. & Holers, V.M. (2014). When and where does inflammation begin in rheumatoid arthritis? *Current Opinion in Rheumatology*, *26*, 64–71.

Dempster, M., McCorry, N.K., Brennan, E. et al. (2011). Psychological distress among survivors of esophageal cancer: the role of illness cognitions and coping. *Diseases of the Esophagus*, *20*, 698–670.

Denk, F., McMahon, S.B. & Tracey, I. (2014). Pain vulnerability: a neurobiological perspective. *Nature Neuroscience*, 17, 192–200.

Denollet, J. (2000). Type D personality: a potential risk factor defined. *Journal of Psychosomatic Research*, *49*, 255–266.

Denollet, J., Gidron, Y., Vrints, C.J. & Conraads, V.M. (2010). Anger, suppressed anger, and risk of adverse events in patients with coronary artery disease. *The American Journal of Cardiology*, *105*, 1555–1560.

Denollet, J. & Kupper, N. (2007). Type-D personality, depression, and cardiac prognosis: cortisol dysregulation as a mediating mechanism. *Journal of Psychosomatic Research*, *62*, 607–609.

Dent, P. (2013). The multi-hit hypothesis in basal-like breast cancer. *Cancer Biology & Therapy*, *14*, 778–779.

Denzin, N.K. & Lincoln, Y.S. (Eds.). (2005). *The SAGE Handbook of Qualitative Research* (3rd ed.). Thousand Oaks, CA: SAGE.

Derry, H.M., Fagundes, C.P., Andridge, R. et al. (2013). Lower subjective social status exaggerates interleukin-6 responses to a laboratory stressor. *Psychoneuroendocrinology*, *38*, 2676–2685.

DeSousa, N.J., Bush, D.E. & Vaccarino, F.J. (2000). Self-administration of intravenous amphetamine is predicted by individual differences in sucrose feeding in rats. *Psychopharmacology*, *148*, 52–58.

DeVellis, B.M. & DeVellis, R.F. (2000). Self-efficacy and health. In A. Baum, T.A. Revenson & J.E. Singer (Eds.), *Handbook of Health Psychology* (pp. 235–247). Mahwah, NJ: Lawrence Erlbaum Associates.

Dewall, C.N., Macdonald, G., Webster, G.D. et al. (2010). Acetaminophen reduces social pain: behavioral and neural evidence. *Psychological Science*, *21*, 931–937.

Dhabhar, F.S. (2009). Enhancing versus suppressive effects of stress on immune function: implications for immunoprotection and immunopathology. *Neuroimmunomodulation*, *16*, 300–317.

Dharmarajan, K., Hsieh, A.F., Kulkarni, V.T. et al. (2015). Trajectories of risk after hospitalization for heart failure, acute myocardial infarction, or pneumonia: retrospective cohort study. *British Medical Journal*, *350*, h411.

Di Forti, M., Sallis, H., Allegri, F. et al. (2014). Daily use, especially of high-potency cannabis, drives the earlier onset of psychosis in cannabis users. *Schizophrenia Bulletin*, *40*, 1509–1517.

Diabetes in the UK (2012). www.diabetes.org.uk/Documents/Reports/Diabetes-in-the-UK-2012.pdf (accessed October 2015).

Dickerson, S. & Kemeny, M. (2004). Acute stressors and cortisol responses: a theoretical integration and synthesis of laboratory research. *Psychological Bulletin*, *130*, 355–391.

Diefenbach, M.A. & Leventhal, H. (1996). The common-sense model of illness representation: theoretical and practical considerations. *Journal of Social Distress and the Homeless*, *5*, 11–38.

Dikse, D., Lamont, L., Li, Y., Simonič, A. et al. (2014). Shame, guilt, and communication in lung cancer patients and their partners. *Current Oncology*, *21*, e718–22.

Dimmock, N.J., Easton, A.J. & Leppard, K.N. (2007). *Introduction to Modern Virology* (6th ed.). Malden, MA: Blackwell.

Dinh-Williams, L., Mendrek, A., Bourque, J. & Potvin, S. (2014). Where there's smoke, there's fire: the brain reactivity of chronic smokers when exposed to the negative value of smoking. *Progress in Neuro-Psychopharmacology & Biological Psychiatry*, *50*, 66–73.

DiNicolantonio, J.J., O'Keefe, J.H. & Lucan, S.C. (2015). Added fructose: a principal driver of type 2 diabetes mellitus and its consequences. *Mayo Clinic Proceedings*, *90*, 372–381.

Dodd, G.T., Decherf, S., Loh, K. et al. (2015). Leptin and insulin act on POMC neurons to promote the browning of white fat. *Cell*, *160*, 88–104.

Domchek, S.M., Friebel, T.M., Singer, C.F. et al. (2010). Association of risk-reducing surgery in BRCA1 or BRCA2 mutation carriers with cancer risk and mortality. *The Journal of the American Medical Association*, *304*, 967–975.

Dong, Y. & Nestler, E.J. (2014). The neural rejuvenation hypothesis of cocaine addiction. *Trends in Pharmacological Sciences*, *35*, 374–383.

Donzé, J., Lipsitz, S., Bates, D.W. & Schnipper, J.L. (2013). Causes and patterns of readmissions in patients with common comorbidities: retrospective cohort study. *BMJ: British Medical Journal*, *347*, f7171.

Drekonja, D.M., Butler, M., MacDonald, R. et al. (2011). Comparative effectiveness of Clostridium difficile treatments: a systematic review. *Annals of Internal Medicine*, *155*, 839–847.

Dresler, M., Spoormaker, V.I., Beitinger, P. et al. (2014). Neuroscience-driven discovery and development of sleep therapeutics. *Pharmacology & Therapeutics*, *141*, 300–334.

Drexler, J.F., Grard, G., Lukashev, A.N. et al. (2014). Robustness against serum neutralization of a poliovirus type 1 from a lethal epidemic of poliomyelitis in the Republic of Congo in 2010. *Proceedings of the National Academy of Sciences*, *111*, 12889–12894.

Du Toit, G., Roberts, G., Sayre, P.H. et al. (2015). Randomized trial of peanut consumption in infants at risk for peanut allergy. *New England Journal of Medicine*, *372*, 803–813.

Duan, F.F., Liu, J.H. & March, J.C. (2015). Engineered commensal bacteria reprogram intestinal cells into glucose-responsive insulin-secreting cells for the treatment of diabetes. *Diabetes*, *64*, 1793–1803.

Dube, S.R., Felitti, V.J., Dong, M. et al. (2003). The impact of adverse childhood experiences on health problems: evidence from four birth cohorts dating back to 1900. *Preventative Medicine*, *37*, 268–277.

Dubljanin Raspopović, E., Marić, N., Nedeljković, U. et al. (2014). Do depressive symptoms on hospital admission impact early functional outcome in elderly patients with hip fracture? *Psychogeriatrics*, *14*, 118–123.

Dulloo, A.G. & Montani, J.P. (2015). Pathways from dieting to weight regain, to obesity and to the metabolic syndrome: an overview. *Obesity Reviews*, *16*, 1–6.

Duman, R.S. (2014). Pathophysiology of depression and innovative treatments: remodeling glutamatergic synaptic connections. *Dialogues in Clinical Neuroscience*, *16*,11–27.

Duman, R.S. & Monteggia, L.M. (2006). A neurotrophic model for stress-related mood disorders. *Biological Psychiatry*, *59*, 1116–1127.

Dunlop, B.W., Kelley, M.E., Mletzko, T.C. et al. (2011). Depression beliefs, treatment preference, and outcomes in a randomized trial for major depressive disorder. *Journal of Psychiatric Research*, *46*, 375–381.

Dunn, G.P., Bruce, A.T., Ikeda, H. et al. (2002). Cancer immunoediting: from immunosurveillance to tumor escape. *Nature Immunology*, *3*, 991–998.

Dunn, G.P., Old, L.J. & Schreiber, R.D. (2004). The three Es of cancer immunoediting. *Annual Review of Immunology*, *22*, 329–360.

Dunne, J.L., Triplett, E.W., Gevers, D. et al. (2014). The intestinal microbiome in type 1 diabetes. *Clinical & Experimental Immunology*, *177*, 30–37.

DuPont, A.W. & DuPont, H.L. (2011). The intestinal microbiota and chronic disorders of the gut. *Nature Reviews Gastroenterology and Hepatology*, *8*, 523–531.

Durand, R., Bouvresse, S., Berdjane, Z. et al. (2012). Insecticide resistance in head lice: clinical, parasitological and genetic aspects. *Clinical Microbiology and Infection*, *18*, 338–344.

Dyck, R., Osgood, N., Lin, T.H. et al. (2010). Epidemiology of diabetes mellitus among First Nations and non-First Nations adults. *Canadian Medical Association Journal*, *182*, 249–256.

Dzau, V.J. & Gibbons, G.H. (1993). Vascular remodeling: mechanisms and implications. *Journal of Cardiovascular Pharmacology*, *21*, S1–S5.

Edwards, K.M., Burns, V.E., Adkins, A.E. et al. (2008). Meningococcal: a vaccination response is enhanced by acute stress in men. *Psychosomatic Medicine*, *70*, 147–151.

Egecioglu, E., Skibicka, K.P., Hansson, C. et al. (2011). Hedonic and incentive signals for body weight control. *Reviews in Endocrine and Metabolic Disorders*, *12*, 141–151.

Egen, J.G., Kuhns, M.S. & Allison, J.P. (2002). CTLA-4: new insights into its biological function and use in tumor immunotherapy. *Nature Immunology*, *3*, 611–618.

Egido, J.A., Castillo, O., Roig, B. et al. (2012). Is psycho-physical stress a risk factor for stroke? A case-control study. *Journal of Neurology, Neurosurgery & Psychiatry*, *83*, 1104–1110.

Eidelman, S. & Biernat, M. (2003). Derogating black sheep: individual or group protection? *Journal of Experimental Social Psychology*, *39*, 602–609.

Einvik, G., Dammen, T., Namtvedt, S.K. et al. (2014). Type D personality is associated with increased prevalence of ventricular arrhythmias in community-residing persons without coronary heart disease. *European Journal of Preventive Cardiology*, *21*, 592–600.

Eisenberg, D.M., Davis, R.B., Ettner, S.L. et al. (1998). Trends in alternative medicine use in the United States, 1990–1997: results of a follow-up national survey. *Journal of the American Medical Association*, *280*, 1569–1575.

Eisenberger, N.I. (2012). The pain of social disconnection: examining the shared neural underpinnings of physical and social pain. *Nature Reviews Neuroscience*, *13*, 421–434.

Eisenberger, N.I. (2013). An empirical review of the neural underpinnings of receiving and giving social support: implications for health. *Psychosomatic Medicine*, *75*, 545–556.

Eisenberger, N.I. & Cole, S.W. (2012). Social neuroscience and health: neurophysiological mechanisms linking social ties with physical health. *Nature Neuroscience*, *15*, 669–674.

Eisenberger, N.I. & Lieberman, M.D. (2004). Why rejection hurts: a common neural alarm system for physical and social pain. *Trends in Cognitive Sciences*, *8*, 294–300.

Eisenberger, N.I., Lieberman, M.D. & Williams, K.D. (2003). Does rejection hurt? An FMRI study of social exclusion. *Science*, *302*, 290–292.

Ekdahl, C.T., Kokaia, Z. & Lindvall, O. (2009). Brain inflammation and adult neurogenesis: the dual role of microglia. *Neuroscience*, *158*, 1021–1029.

Ekelund, U., Ward, H.A., Norat, T. et al. (2015). Physical activity and all-cause mortality across levels of overall and abdominal adiposity in European men and women: the European Prospective Investigation into Cancer and Nutrition Study (EPIC). *The American Journal of Clinical Nutrition*, *101*, 613–621.

Elder, S.J., Neale, M.C., Fuss, P.J. et al. (2012). Genetic and environmental influences on eating behavior: a study of twin pairs reared apart or reared together. *Open Nutrition Journal, 6,* 59–70.

Elftman, M.D., Hunzeker, J.T., Mellinger, J.C. et al. (2010). Stress-induced glucocorticoids at the earliest stages of herpes simplex virus-1 infection suppress subsequent antiviral immunity, implicating impaired dendritic cell function. *The Journal of Immunology, 184,* 1867–1875.

Eliot, R.S., Buell, J.C. & Dembroski, T.M. (1982). Bio-behavioural perspectives on coronary heart disease, hypertension and sudden cardiac death. *Acta Medica Scandinavica,* 211, 203–213.

Elkin, E.B, Kim, S.H., Casper, E.S. et al. (2007). Desire for information and involvement in treatment decisions: elderly cancer patients' preferences and their physicians' perceptions. *Journal of Clinical Oncology,* 25, 5275–5280.

Elledge, B.L., Brand, M., Regens, J.L. & Boatright, D.T. (2008). Implications of public understanding of avian influenza for fostering effective risk communication. *Health Promotion Practice,* 9, 54S–59S.

Ellenbogen, M.A., Linnen, A.M., Cardoso, C. & Joober, R. (2013). Intranasal oxytocin impedes the ability to ignore task-irrelevant facial expressions of sadness in students with depressive symptoms. *Psychoneuroendocrinology,* 38, 387–398.

Elrashidi, M.Y. & Ebbert, J.O. (2014). Emerging drugs for the treatment of tobacco dependence: 2014 update. *Expert Opinion on Emerging Drugs,* 19, 243–260.

Elwood, P., Galante, J., Pickering, J. et al. (2013). Healthy lifestyles reduce the incidence of chronic diseases and dementia: evidence from the Caerphilly cohort study. *PLoS One, 8,* e81877.

Emanuel, E.J. (2002). Euthanasia and physician-assisted suicide: a review of the empirical data from the United States. *Archives Of Internal Medicine, 162,* 142.

Emanuel, E.Z. (2014). Why I hope to die at 75. *The Atlantic,* September 18.

Emons, G., Fleckenstein, G., Hinney, B. et al. (2000). Hormonal interactions in endometrial cancer. *Endocrine-Related Cancer, 7,* 227–242.

Entringer, S., Epel, E.S., Kumsta, R. et al. (2011). Stress exposure in intrauterine life is associated with shorter telomere length in young adulthood. *Proceedings of the National Academy of Sciences, 108,* E513–E518.

Entringer, S., Kumsta, R., Hellhammer, D.H. et al. (2009). Prenatal exposure to maternal psychosocial stress and HPA axis regulation in young adults. *Hormones and Behavior, 55,* 292–298.

Entringer, S., Kumsta, R., Nelson, E.L. et al. (2008). Influence of prenatal psychosocial stress on cytokine production in adult women. *Developmental Psychobiology, 50,* 579–587.

Epstein, M., Hill, K.G., Bailey, J.A. & Hawkins, J.D. (2013). The effect of general and drug-specific family environments on comorbid and drug-specific problem behavior: a longitudinal examination. *Developmental Psychology, 49,* 1151–1164.

Eriksson, A.K., van den Donk, M., Hilding, A. & Östenson, C.G. (2013). Work stress, sense of coherence, and risk of type 2 diabetes in a prospective study of middle-aged Swedish men and women. *Diabetes Care, 36,* 2683–2689.

Eriksson, M., Räikkönen, K. & Eriksson, J.G. (2014). Early life stress and later health outcomes: findings from the Helsinki Birth Cohort Study. *American Journal of Human Biology, 26,* 111–116.

Ernst, E. (2002). The risk–benefit profile of commonly used herbal therapies: ginkgo, St John's wort, ginseng, echinacea, saw palmetto, and kava. *Annals of Internal Medicine, 136,* 42–53.

Esler, M. & Kaye, D. (2000). Sympathetic nervous system activation in essential hypertension, cardiac failure and psychosomatic heart disease. *Journal of Cardiovascular Pharmacology, 35,* S1–S7.

Essex, M.J., Boyce, W.T., Hertzman, C. et al. (2013). Epigenetic vestiges of early developmental adversity: childhood stress exposure and DNA methylation in adolescence. *Child Development, 84,* 58–75.

Evans, D.G., Gaarenstroom, K.N., Stirling, D. et al. (2009). Screening for familial ovarian cancer: poor survival of BRCA1/2 related cancers. *Journal of Medical Genetics, 46,* 593–597.

Evans, S.J., Choudary, P.V., Neal, C.R. et al. (2004). Dysregulation of the fibroblast growth factor system in major depression. *Proceedings of the*

National Academy of Sciences of the United States of America, *101*, 15506–15511.

Evans, W.D., Powers, A., Hersey, J. & Renaud, J. (2006). The influence of social environment and social image on adolescent smoking. *Health Psychology*, *25*, 26–33.

Evans-Campbell, T. (2008). Historical trauma in American Indian/Native Alaska communities: a multilevel framework for exploring impacts on individuals, families, and communities. *Journal of Interpersonal Violence*, *23*, 316–338.

Evers, A.W., Verhoeven, E.W., van Middendorp, H. et al. (2014). Does stress affect the joints? Daily stressors, stress vulnerability, immune and HPA axis activity, and short-term disease and symptom fluctuations in rheumatoid arthritis. *Annals of the Rheumatic Diseases*, *73*, 1683–1688.

Everson-Rose, S.A., Roetker, N.S., Lutsey, P.L. et al. (2014). Chronic stress, depressive symptoms, anger, hostility, and risk of stroke and transient ischemic attack in the multi-ethnic study of atherosclerosis. *Stroke*, *45*, 2318–2323.

Ewart, C.K., Taylor, C.B., Kraemer, H.C. & Agras, W.S. (1991). High blood pressure and marital discord: not being nasty matters more than being nice. *Health Psychology*, *10*, 155–163.

Eyigor, S. & Kanyilmaz, S. (2014). Exercise in patients coping with breast cancer: an overview. *World Journal of Clinical Oncology*, *5*, 406.

Fagman, J.B., Wilhelmson, A.S., Motta, B.M. et al. (2014). The androgen receptor confers protection against diet-induced atherosclerosis, obesity, and dyslipidemia in female mice. *The FASEB Journal*, *29*, 1540.

Falconer, D.S. (1965). The inheritance of liability to certain diseases, estimated from the incidence among relatives. *Annals of Human Genetics*, *29*, 51–76.

Falk, E.B., O'Donnell, M.B., Cascio, C.N. et al. (2015). Self-affirmation alters the brain's response to health messages and subsequent behavior change. *Proceedings of the National Academy of Sciences*, *112*, 1977–1982.

Fang, J., Shaw, K.M. & Keenan, N.L. (2011). Prevalence of coronary heart disease: United States, 2006–2010. *Morbidity and Mortality Weekly Report (MMWR)*, *60*, 1377–1381.

Fang, S., Suh, J.M., Reilly, S.M. et al. (2015). Intestinal FXR agonism promotes adipose tissue browning and reduces obesity and insulin resistance. *Nature Medicine*, *21*, 159–165.

Fang, S.Y., Shu, B.C. & Chang, Y.J. (2013). The effect of breast reconstruction surgery on body image among women after mastectomy: a meta-analysis. *Breast Cancer Research and Treatment*, *137*, 13–21.

Fanous, S., Hammer, R.P. Jr. & Nikulina, E.M. (2010). Short- and long-term effects of intermittent social defeat stress on brain-derived neurotrophic factor expression in mesocorticolimbic brain regions. *Neuroscience*, *167*, 598–607.

Farinotti, M., Vacchi, L., Simi, S. et al. (2012). Dietary interventions for multiple sclerosis. *The Cochrane Library*, *12*, CD004192.

Fasano, A. & Catassi, C. (2012). Clinical practice. Celiac disease. *The New England Journal of Medicine*, *367*, 2419–2426.

Faust, T.W., Chang, E.H., Kowal, C. et al. (2010). Neurotoxic lupus autoantibodies alter brain function through two distinct mechanisms. *Proceedings of the National Academy of Sciences*, *107*, 18569–18574.

Fava, G.A. & Tomba, E. (2009). Increasing psychological well-being and resilience by psychotherapeutic methods. *Journal of Personality*, *77*, 1903–1934.

Fawzy, F.I., Fawzy, N.W., Hyun, C.S. et al. (1993). Malignant melanoma: effects of an early structured psychiatric intervention, coping, and affective state on recurrence and survival 6 years later. *Archives of General Psychiatry*, *50*, 681–689.

Feigelman, W., Jordan, J.R. & Gorman, B.S. (2011). Parental grief after a child's drug death compared to other death causes: investigating a greatly neglected bereavement population. *Omega (Westport)*, *63*, 291–316.

Feigin, V.L., Forouzanfar, M.H., Krishnamurthi, R. et al. (2014). Global and regional burden of stroke during 1990–2010: findings from the Global Burden of Disease Study 2010. *The Lancet*, *383*, 245–255.

Feijen-de Jong, E.I., Jansen, D.E., Baarveld, F. et al. (2012). Determinants of late and/or inadequate use of prenatal healthcare in high-income countries: a systematic review. *European Journal of Public Health*, *22*, 904–913.

Feldman, P.J., Cohen, S., Doyle, W.J. et al. (1999). The impact of personality on the reporting of unfounded symptoms and illness. *Journal of Personality and Social Psychology*, *77*, 3 70–378.

Feng, J., Wilkinson, M., Liu, X. et al. (2014). Chronic cocaine-regulated epigenomic changes in mouse nucleus accumbens. *Genome Biology*, *15*, R65.

Fernandez, E. & Turk, D.C. (1992). Sensory and affective components of pain: separation and synthesis. *Psychological Bulletin*, *112*, 205–217.

Festinger, L. (1954). A theory of social comparison processes. *Human Relations*, *7*, 117–140.

Filbey, F.M., Aslan, S., Calhoun, V.D. et al. (2014). Long-term effects of marijuana use on the brain. *Proceedings of the National Academy of Sciences*, *111*, 16913–16918.

Filip, M., Frankowska, M., Sadakierska-Chudy, A. et al. (2015). GABA$_B$ receptors as a therapeutic strategy in substance use disorders: focus on positive allosteric modulators. *Neuropharmacology*, *88*, 36–47.

Firenzuoli, F. & Gori, L. (2007). Herbal medicine today: clinical and research issues. *Evidence-Based Complementary and Alternative Medicine*, *4*, 37–40.

Fiscella, K. & Williams, D.R. (2004). Health disparities based on socioeconomic inequities: implications for urban health care. *Academic Medicine*, *79*, 1139–1147.

Fishbain, D.A., Cutler, R.B., Rosomoff, H.L. & Rosomoff, R.S. (1998). Do antidepressants have an analgesic effect in psychogenic pain and somatoform pain disorder? A meta-analysis. *Psychosomatic Medicine*, *60*, 503–509.

Flack, J.M., Ference, B.A. & Levy, P. (2014). Should African Americans with hypertension be treated differently than non-African Americans? *Current Hypertension Reports*, *16*, 409.

Flannick, J., Thorleifsson, G., Beer, N.L. et al. (2014). Loss-of-function mutations in SLC30A8 protect against type 2 diabetes. *Nature Genetics*, *46*, 357–363.

Flegal, K.M., Kit, B.K., Orpana, H. & Graubard, B.I. (2013). Association of all-cause mortality with overweight and obesity using standard body mass index categories: a systematic review and meta-analysis. *The Journal of the American Medical Association*, *309*, 71–82.

Fleshner, M. (2013). Stress-evoked sterile inflammation, danger associated molecular patterns (DAMPs), microbial associated molecular patterns (MAMPs) and the inflammasome. *Brain, Behavior and Immunity*, *27*, 1–7.

Fleshner, M., Kennedy, S.L., Johnson, J.D. et al. (2009). Exercise and stress resistance: neural-immune mechanisms. In A. Siegel & S.S. Zalcman (Eds.), *Neuroimmunological Basis of Behavior and Mental Disorders* (pp. 87–107). New York: Springer.

Fletcher, J. & Patrick, K. (2014). A political prescription is needed to treat obesity. *Canadian Medical Association Journal*, *186*, 1275.

Flink, I.K., Boersma, K. & Linton, S.J. (2014). Changes in catastrophizing and depressed mood during and after early cognitive behaviorally oriented interventions for pain. *Cognitive Behaviour Therapy*, *30*, 1–10.

Flores, C. & Stewart, J. (2000). Basic fibroblast growth factor as a mediator of the effects of glutamate in the development of long-lasting sensitization to stimulant drugs: studies in the rat. *Psychopharmacology*, *151*, 152–165.

Floyd, A. & Moyer, A. (2010). Group versus individual exercise interventions for women with breast cancer: a meta-analysis. *Health Psychology Review*, *4*, 22–41.

Folkman, S. & Lazarus, R.S. (1988). *Ways of coping questionnaire*. Consulting Psychologists Press.

Fonareva, I. & Oken, B.S. (2014). Physiological and functional consequences of caregiving for relatives with dementia. *International Psychogeriatrics*, *26*, 725–747.

Fontana, L., Kennedy, B.K., Longo, V.D. et al. (2014). Medical research: treat ageing. *Nature*, *511*, 405–407.

Ford, A., Castonguay, A., Cottet, M. et al. (2015). Engagement of the GABA to KCC2 signaling pathway contributes to the analgesic effects of A3AR agonists in neuropathic pain. *Journal of Neuroscience*, *35*, 6057–6067.

Ford, E.S. (2005). Risks for all-cause mortality, cardiovascular disease, and diabetes associated with the metabolic syndrome: a summary of the evidence. *Diabetes Care*, *28*, 1769–1778.

Forgues, B. (2012). Sampling on the dependent variable is not always that bad: quantitative case-control designs for strategic organization research. *Strategic Organization*, *10*, 269–275.

Fors, E.A., Landmark, T. & Bakke, Ø. (2012). Contextual and time dependent pain in fibromyalgia: an explorative study. *BMC Research Notes*, *5*, 644.

Fournier, J.C., DeRubeis, R.J., Hollon, S.D. et al. (2010). Antidepressant drug effects and depression severity: a patient-level meta-analysis. *The Journal of the American Medical Association*, *303*, 47–53.

Fowler, S.P., Williams, K. & Hazuda, H.P. (2015). Diet soda intake is associated with long-term increases in waist circumference in a biethnic cohort of older adults: the San Antonio longitudinal study of aging. *Journal of the American Geriatrics Society*, *63*, 708–715.

Fraigne, J.J., Grace, K.P., Horner, R.L. & Peever, J. (2014). Mechanisms of REM sleep in health and disease. *Current Opinion in Pulmonary Medicine*, *20*, 527–532.

Frances, A. (2014). RDoC is necessary, but very oversold. *World Psychiatry*, *13*, 47–49.

Franklin, T.B., Russig, H., Weiss, I.C. et al. (2010). Epigenetic transmission of the impact of early stress across generations. *Biological Psychiatry*, *68*, 408–415.

Franko, D.L., Thompson, D., Affenito, S.G. et al. (2008). What mediates the relationship between family meals and adolescent health issues? *Health Psychology*, *27*, S109–S117.

Frasure-Smith, N., Lespérance, F., Irwin, M.R., et al. (2009). The relationships among heart rate variability, inflammatory markers and depression in coronary heart disease patients. *Brain, Behavior, and Immunity*, *23*, 1140–1147.

Freedman, D.S., Mei, Z., Srinivasan, S.R. et al. (2007). Cardiovascular risk factors and excess adiposity among overweight children and adolescents: the Bogalusa Heart Study. *The Journal of Pediatrics*, *150*, 12–17.

Freitas, A. & Sweeney, J.F. (2010). Bariatric surgery. In B. Banarjee (Ed.), *Nutritional Management of Digestive Disorders* (pp. 327–342). Boca Raton, FL: CRC Press.

Frenzel, M.P., McCaul, K.D., Glasgow, R.E. & Schafer, L.C. (1988). The relationship of stress and coping to regimen adherence and glycemic control of diabetes. *Journal of Social and Clinical Psychology*, *6*, 77–87.

Fridman, O., Goldberg, A., Ronin, I. et al. (2014). Optimization of lag time underlies antibiotic tolerance in evolved bacterial populations. *Nature*, *513*, 418–421.

Friedman, M. & Rosenman, R.H. (1971). Type A behavior pattern: its association with coronary heart disease. *Annals of Clinical Research*, *3*, 300–312.

Frodl, T. & O'Keane, V. (2013). How does the brain deal with cumulative stress? A review with focus on developmental stress, HPA axis function and hippocampal structure in humans. *Neurobiology of Disease*, *52*, 24–37.

Frosch, D.L., May, S.G., Rendle, K.A., et al. (2012). Authoritarian physicians and patients' fear of being labeled 'difficult' among key obstacles to shared decision making. *Health Affairs (Millwood)*, *31*, 1030–1038.

Ftouni, S., Sletten, T.L., Howard, M. et al. (2013). Objective and subjective measures of sleepiness, and their associations with on-road driving events in shift workers. *Journal of Sleep Research*, *22*, 58–69.

Fuentes-Hernandez, A., Plucain, J., Gori, F et al. (2015). Using a sequential regimen to eliminate bacteria at sublethal antibiotic dosages. *PLoS Biology*, *13*, e1002104.

Fulton, S. et al. (2006). Leptin regulation of the mesoaccumbens dopamine pathway. *Neuron*, *51*, 811–822.

Fumagalli, F., Bedogni, F., Slotkin, T.A. et al. (2005). Prenatal stress elicits regionally selective changes in basal FGF-2 gene expression in adulthood and alters the adult response to acute or chronic stress. *Neurobiology of Disease*, *20*, 731–737.

Fung, T.T., Willett, W.C., Stampfer, M.J. et al. (2001). Dietary patterns and the risk of coronary heart disease in women. *Archives of Internal Medicine*, *161*, 1857–1862.

Furlan, A.D., Yazdi, F., Tsertsvadze, A. et. al. (2010). Complementary and alternative therapies for back pain II. *Evidence Report/Technology Assessment*, *194*, 1–50.

Furnes, B., Natvig, G.K. & Dysvik, E. (2014). Therapeutic elements in a self-management approach: experiences from group participation among people suffering from chronic pain. *Patient Preference and Adherence, 8,* 1085–1092.

Gåfvels, C., Hägerström, M., Nordmark, B. & Wändell P. (2014). What predicts negative effects of rheumatoid arthritis? A follow-up two years after diagnosis. *Springerplus, 28,*118.

Galland, L. (2014). The gut microbiome and the brain. *Journal of Medicinal Food, 17,* 1261–1272.

Galli, S.J. (2000). Allergy. *Current Biology, 10,* R93–R95.

Galway, K., Black, A., Cantwell, M. et al. (2012). Psychosocial interventions to improve quality of life and emotional wellbeing for recently diagnosed cancer patients. *The Cochrane Database of Systematic Reviews, 11,* CD007064.

Ganz, P.A. (2011). Expanding our therapeutic options: beta blockers for breast cancer. *Journal of Clinical Oncology, 29,* 2612–2616.

Garcia Pelosi, G., Fiacadori Tavares, R., Barros Parron Fernandes, K. & Morgan Aguiar Corrêa, F. (2009). Cardiovascular effects of noradrenaline microinjection into the medial part of the superior colliculus of unanesthetized rats. *Brain Research, 1290,* 21–27.

García-Ruiz, A., de Llano, D.G., Esteban-Fernández, A. et al. (2014). Assessment of probiotic properties in lactic acid bacteria isolated from wine. *Food Microbiology, 44,* 220–225.

Gardner, K.L., Hale, M.W., Lightman, S.L. et al. (2009). Adverse early life experience and social stress during adulthood interact to increase serotonin transporter mRNA expression. *Brain Research, 1305,* 47–63.

Gardner, R.C., Burke, J.F., Nettiksimmons, J. et al. (2014). Dementia risk after traumatic brain injury vs nonbrain trauma: the role of age and severity. *JAMA Neurology, 71,* 1490–1497.

Garland, E.L., Froeliger, B. & Howard, M.O. (2014). Effects of mindfulness-oriented recovery enhancement on reward responsiveness and opioid cue-reactivity. *Psychopharmacology, 231,* 3229–3238.

Garland, E.L., Hanley, A.W., Thomas, E.A. et al. (2015). Low dispositional mindfulness predicts self-medication of negative emotion with prescription opioids. *Journal of Addiction Medicine, 9,* 61–67.

Garrett, W.S. (2015). Cancer and the microbiota. *Science, 348,* 80–86.

Gatchel, R.J. & Okifuji, A. (2006). Evidence-based scientific data documenting the treatment and cost-effectiveness of comprehensive pain programs for chronic nonmalignant pain. *Journal of Pain, 7,* 779–793.

Gawande, A. (2014). *Being Mortal: medicine and what matters in the end.* New York: Metropolitan Books.

Geliebter, A., Gluck, M.E. & Hashim, S.A. (2005). Plasma ghrelin concentrations are lower in binge-eating disorder. *Journal of Nutrition, 135,* 1326–1330.

George, O., Le Moal, M. & Koob, G.F. (2012). Allostasis and addiction: role of the dopamine and corticotropin-releasing factor systems. *Physiology & Behavior, 106,* 58–64.

Geraghty, A.C., Muroy, S.E., Zhao, S. et al. (2015). Knockdown of hypothalamic RFRP3 prevents chronic stress-induced infertility and embryo resorption. *Elife, 4,* e04316.

Gershon, M.D. (2000). 5-HT (serotonin) physiology and related drugs. *Current Opinion in Gastroenterology, 16,* 113–120.

Ghitza, U.E., Zhai, H., Wu, P. et al. (2010). Role of BDNF and GDNF in drug reward and relapse: a review. *Neuroscience & Biobehavioral Reviews, 35,* 157–171.

Gibb, J., Al-Yawer, F. & Anisman, H. (2013). Synergistic and antagonistic actions of acute or chronic social stressors and an endotoxin challenge vary over time following the challenge. *Brain, Behavior, and Immunity, 28,* 149–158.

Gibbons, A. (2011). Diabetes genes decline out of Africa. *Science, 334,* 583.

Giggins, O.M., Persson, U.M. & Caulfield, B. (2013). Biofeedback in rehabilitation. *Journal of Neuroengineering and Rehabilitation, 10,* 60.

Gillies, D., Taylor, F., Gray, C. et al. (2013). Psychological therapies for the treatment of post-traumatic stress disorder in children and adolescents. *Journal of Evidence-Based Medicine, 8,* 1004–1116.

Gini, G. & Pozzoli, T. (2013). Bullied children and psychosomatic problems: a meta-analysis. *Pediatrics, 132,* 720–729.

Ginting, H., van de Ven, M., Becker, E.S. & Näring, G. (2014). Type D personality is associated with health behaviors and perceived social support in individuals with coronary heart disease. *Journal of Health Psychology*, *19*, 1–11..

Girgenti, M.J., Hunsberger, J., Duman, C.H. et al. (2009). Erythropoietin induction by electroconvulsive seizure, gene regulation, and antidepressant-like behavioral effects. *Biological Psychiatry*, *66*, 267–274.

Glaser, R., Kiecolt-Glaser, J.K., Marucha, P.T. et al. (1999). Stress-related changes in proinflammatory cytokine production in wounds. *Archives of General Psychiatry*, *56*, 450–456.

Glaser, R., MacCallum, R.C., Laskowski, B.F. et al. (2001). Evidence for a shift in the Th-1 to Th-2 cytokine response associated with chronic stress and aging. *The Journals of Gerontology Series A: Biological Sciences and Medical Sciences*, *56*, M477–M482.

Glover, V. (2011). Annual research review: prenatal stress and the origins of psychopathology: an evolutionary perspective. *Journal of Child Psychology and Psychiatry*, *52*, 356–367.

Godbout, J.P. & Glaser, R. (2006). Stress-induced immune dysregulation: implications for wound healing, infectious disease and cancer. *Journal of Neuroimmune Pharmacology*, *1*, 421–427.

Goetze, T. & Paolucci, V. (2006). Does laparoscopy worsen the prognosis for incidental gallbladder cancer? *Surgical Endoscopy and other Interventional Techniques*, *20*, 286–293.

Goldie, C.L., Johnson, J.L., Ratner, P.A. & Smye, V. (2014). Utilizing the Canadian community to investigate cardiovascular risk and disease among people with mental health disorders. *Canadian Journal of Cardiology*, *10*, S120.

Goldstein, A.N. & Walker, M.P. (2014). The role of sleep in emotional brain function. *Annual Review of Clinical Psychology*, *10*, 679–708.

Goldstein, D.S. (2011). Stress, allostatic load, catecholamines, and other neurotransmitters in neurodegenerative diseases. *Endocrine Regulations*, *45*, 91–98.

Goldstein, J.M., Jerram, M., Poldrack, R. et al. (2005). Hormonal cycle modulates arousal circuitry in women using functional magnetic resonance imaging. *Journal of Neuroscience*, *25*, 9309–9316.

Gollwitzer, P.M. (1999). Implementation intentions: strong effects of simple plans. *American Psychologist*, *54*, 493–503.

Gomes, A.C., Bueno, A.A., de Souza, R.G. & Mota, J.F. (2014). Gut microbiota, probiotics and diabetes. *Nutrition Journal*, *13*, 60.

Gonzalez, B.D. & Jacobsen, P.B. (2012). Depression in lung cancer patients: the role of perceived stigma. *Psychooncology. 21*, 239–246.

Goodrich, J.K., Waters, J.L., Poole, A.C. et al. (2014). Human genetics shape the gut microbiome. *Cell*, *159*, 789–799.

Gordon, S.B., Bruce, N.G., Grigg, J. et al. (2014). Respiratory risks from household air pollution in low and middle income countries. *The Lancet Respiratory Medicine*, *2*, 823–860.

Goshen, I., Kreisel, T., Ben-Menachem-Zidon, O. et al. (2008). Brain interleukin-1 mediates chronic stress-induced depression in mice via adrenocortical activation and hippocampal neurogenesis suppression. *Molecular Psychiatry*, *13*, 717–728.

Gotink, R.A., Chu, P., Busschbach, J.J. et al. (2015). Standardised mindfulness-based interventions in healthcare: an overview of systematic reviews and meta-analyses of RCTs. *PLoS One*, *10*, e0124344.

Gottesman, I.I. & Gould, T.D. (2003). The endophenotype concept in psychiatry: etymology and strategic intentions. *American Journal of Psychiatry*, *160*, 636–645.

Gould, H.J. & Ramadani, F. (2014). IgE responses in mouse and man and the persistence of IgE memory. *Trends in Immunology*, *36*, 40–48.

Gowing, L.R., Ali, R.L., Allsop, S. et al. (2015). Global statistics on addictive behaviours: 2014 status report. *Addiction*, *110*, 904–919.

Goyal, M., Singh, S., Sibinga, E.M. et al. (2014). Meditation programs for psychological stress and well-being: a systematic review and meta-analysis. *JAMA Internal Medicine*, *174*, 357–368.

Gozalo, P., Teno, J.M., Mitchell, S.L. et al. (2011). End-of-life transitions among nursing home residents with cognitive issues. *New England Journal of Medicine*, *365*, 1212–1221.

Graf, A., Bergstraesser, E. & Landolt, M.A. (2013). Posttraumatic stress in infants and preschoolers with cancer. *Psychooncology*, *22*, 1543–1548.

Graham, D. & Becerril-Martinez, G. (2014). Surgical resilience: a review of resilience biomarkers and surgical recovery. *Surgeon*, *12*, 334–344.

Grana, R., Benowitz, N. & Glantz, S.A. (2014). E-cigarettes: a scientific review. *Circulation*, *129*, 1972–1986.

Grande, A.J., Silva, V., Riera, R. et al. (2014). Exercise for cancer cachexia in adults. *The Cochrane Database of Systematic Reviews*, *11*, CD010804.

Grande, G., Romppel, M. & Barth, J. (2012). Association between type D personality and prognosis in patients with cardiovascular diseases: a systematic review and meta-analysis. *Annals of Behavioral Medicine*, *43*, 299–310.

Grandin, L.D., Alloy, L.B. & Abramson, L.Y. (2006). The social zeitgeber theory, circadian rhythms, and mood disorders: review and evaluation. *Clinical Psychology Review*, *26*, 679–694.

Graven, L.J. & Grant, J. (2013). The impact of social support on depressive symptoms in individuals with heart failure: update and review. *Journal of Cardiovascular Nursing*, *28*, 429–443.

Greene, R.R., Hantman, S., Sharabi, A. & Cohen, H. (2012). Holocaust survivors: three waves of resilience research. *Journal of Evidence-Based Social Work*, *9*, 481–497.

Greer, S.M., Goldstein, A.N. & Walker, M.P. (2013). The impact of sleep deprivation on food desire in the human brain. *Nature Communications*, *4*, 2259.

Greville-Harris, M. & Dieppe, P. (2015). Bad is more powerful than good: the nocebo response in medical consultations. *The American Journal of Medicine*, *128*, 126–129.

Griffin, M.J. & Chen, E. (2006). Perceived control and immune and pulmonary outcomes in children with asthma. *Psychosomatic Medicine*, *68*, 493–499.

Griffith, M., Griffith, O.L., Coffman, A.C. et al. (2013). DGIdb: mining the druggable genome. *Nature Methods*, *10*, 1209–1210.

Grodstein, F., Kang, J.H., Dushkes, R. et al. (2013). Long-term multivitamin supplementation and cognitive function in men: a randomized trial. *Annals of Internal Medicine*, *159*, 806–814.

Grodstein, F., Stampfer, M.J., Colditz, G.A. et al. (1997). Post-menopausal hormone therapy and mortality. *The New England Journal of Medicine*, *336*, 1769–1775.

Grønli, J., Bramham, C., Murison, R. et al. (2006). Chronic mild stress inhibits BDNF protein expression and CREB activation in the dentate gyrus but not in the hippocampus proper. *Pharmacology Biochemistry and Behavior*, *85*, 842–849.

Grønli, J., Soulé, J. & Bramham, C.R. (2014). Sleep and protein synthesis-dependent synaptic plasticity: impacts of sleep loss and stress. *Frontiers in Behavioral Neuroscience*, *7*, 224.

Guandalini, S. & Setty, M. (2008). Celiac disease. *Current Opinion in Gastroenterology*, *24*, 707–712.

Guarente, L. (2014). The many faces of sirtuins: sirtuins and the Warburg effect. *Nature Medicine*, *20*, 24–25.

Gujral, N., Freeman, H.J. & Thomson, A.B. (2012). Celiac disease: prevalence, diagnosis, pathogenesis and treatment. *World Journal of Gastroenterology*, *18*, 6036–6059.

Gunduz-Cinar, O., Hill, M.N., McEwen, B.S. & Holmes, A. (2013). Amygdala FAAH and anandamide: mediating protection and recovery from stress. *Trends in Pharmacological Sciences*, *34*, 637–644.

Guyon, A., Balbo, M., Morselli, L.L. et al. (2014). Adverse effects of two nights of sleep restriction on the hypothalamic-pituitary-adrenal axis in healthy men. *Journal of Clinical Endocrinology & Metabolism*, *99*, 2861–2868.

Haack, A.K., Sheth, C., Schwager, A.L. et al. (2014). Lesions of the lateral habenula increase voluntary ethanol consumption and operant self-administration, block yohimbine-induced reinstatement of ethanol seeking, and attenuate ethanol-induced conditioned taste aversion. *PLoS One*, *9*, e92701.

Haasen, C., Verthein, U., Degkwitz, P. et al. (2007). Heroin-assisted treatment for opioid dependence: randomised controlled trial. *British Journal of Psychiatry*, *191*, 55–62.

Hackett, M.L., Yapa, C., Parag, V. & Anderson, C.S. (2005). Frequency of depression after stroke: a systematic review of observational studies. *Stroke*, *36*, 1330–1340.

Hagger, M.S. & Orbell, S. (2003). A meta-analytic review of the common-sense model of illness representations. *Psychology & Health*, *18*, 141–184.

Häggström, M. (2014). Medical gallery of Mikael Häggström. *Wikiversity Journal of Medicine, 1.* Doi:10.15347/wjm/2014.008. ISSN 20018762.

Hair, E.C., Park, M.J., Ling, T.J. & Moore, K.A. (2009). Risky behaviors in late adolescence: co-occurrence, predictors, and consequences. *Journal of Adolescent Health*, *45*, 253–261.

Hajek, P., Stead, L.F., West, R. et al. (2013). Relapse prevention interventions for smoking cessation. *Cochrane Database of Systematic Reviews*, *8*, CD003999.

Hakim, A.M. (2011). Depression, strokes and dementia: new biological insights into an unfortunate pathway. *Cardiovascular Psychiatry and Neurology*, *2011*, 649629.

Halaris, A. (2009). Comorbidity between depression and cardiovascular disease. *International Angiology*, *28*, 92–99.

Hall, K.T., Loscalzo, J. & Kaptchuk, T.J. (2015). Genetics and the placebo effect: the placebome. *Trends in Molecular Medicine*, *21*, 285–294.

Hamer, M., Chida, Y. & Molloy, G.J. (2009). Psychological distress and cancer mortality. *Journal of Psychosomatic Research*, *66*, 255–258.

Hamer, M., Kivimäki, M. & Steptoe, A. (2012). Longitudinal patterns in physical activity and sedentary behaviour from mid-life to early old age: a substudy of the Whitehall II cohort. *Journal of Epidemiology and Community Health*, *66*, 1110–1115.

Hamer, M., Sabia, S., Batty, G.D. et al. (2012). Physical activity and inflammatory markers over 10 years follow-up in men and women from the Whitehall II Cohort Study. *Circulation*, *126*, 928–933.

Hamer, M. & Steptoe, A. (2009). Prospective study of physical fitness, adiposity, and inflammatory markers in healthy middle-aged men and women. *The American Journal of Clinical Nutrition*, *89*, 85–89.

Hammack, S.E., Schmid, M.J., LoPresti, M.L. et al. (2003). Corticotropin releasing hormone type 2 receptors in the dorsal raphe nucleus mediate the behavioral consequences of uncontrollable stress. *Journal of Neuroscience*, *23*, 1019–1025.

Hankinson, S.E., Colditz, G.A., Hunter, D.J. et al. (1992). A quantitative assessment of oral contraceptive use and risk of ovarian cancer. *Obstetrics and Gynecology*, *80*, 708–714.

Hankinson, S.E., Colditz, G.A., Manson, J.E. et al. (1997). A prospective study of oral contraceptive use and risk of breast cancer (Nurses' Health Study, United States). *Cancer Causes & Control*, *8*, 65–72.

Hansen, M.B. (2003). The enteric nervous system III: a target for pharmacological treatment. *Pharmacology & Toxicology*, *93*, 1–13.

Hansen, T.B., Thygesen, L.C., Zwisler, A.D. et al. (2014). Self-reported health-related quality of life predicts 5-year mortality and hospital readmissions in patients with ischaemic heart disease. *European Journal of Preventive Cardiology*, *22*, 882–889.

Hanson, J.L., Nacewicz, B.M., Sutterer, M.J. et al. (2015). Behavioral problems after early life stress: contributions of the hippocampus and amygdala. *Biological Psychiatry*, *77*, 314–323.

Hansson, G.K. & Hermansson, A. (2011). The immune system in atherosclerosis. *Nature Immunology*, *12*, 204–212.

Harada, K., Karube, Y., Saruhara, H. et al. (2006). Workplace hypertension is associated with obesity and family history of hypertension. *Hypertension Research*, *29*, 969–976.

Harb, H. & Renz, H. (2015). Update on epigenetics in allergic disease. *Journal of Allergy and Clinical Immunology*, *135*, 15–24.

Harburg, E., Julius, M., Kaciroti, N. et al. (2003). Expressive/suppressive anger-coping responses, gender, and types of mortality: a 17-year follow-up (Tecumseh, Michigan, 1971–1988). *Psychosomatic Medicine*, *65*, 588–597.

Harden, A., Garcia, J., Oliver, S. et al. (2004). Applying systematic review methods to studies of people's views: an example from public health research. *Journal of Epidemiology and Community Health*, *58*, 794–800.

Harding, J.L., Backholer, K., Williams, E.D. et al. (2014). Psychosocial stress is positively associated with body mass index gain over 5 years: evidence from the longitudinal AusDiab study. *Obesity*, *22*, 277–286.

Harkness, K.L. (2008). Life events and hassles. In K.S. Dobson and D. Dozois (Eds.), *Risk Factors in Depression* (pp. 317–342). New York: Elsevier Science.

Harkness, K.L., Bruce, A.E. & Lumley, M.N. (2006). The role of childhood abuse and neglect in the sensitization to stressful life events in adolescent depression. *Journal of Abnormal Psychology*, *115*, 730–741.

Hart, J.L., Harhay, M.O., Gabler, N.B. et al. (2015). Variability among US intensive care units in managing the care of patients admitted with preexisting limits on life-sustaining therapies. *JAMA Internal Medicine*, *175,* 1019–1026.

Hartai, Z., Klivenyi, P., Janaky, T. et al. (2005). Kynurenine metabolism in plasma and in red blood cells in Parkinson's disease. *Journal of the Neurological Sciences*, *239*, 31–35.

Harvey, L. & Boksa, P. (2012). Prenatal and postnatal animal models of immune activation: relevance to a range of neurodevelopmental disorders. *Developmental Neurobiology*, *72*, 1335–1348.

Haslam, S.A. & Reicher, S. (2006). Stressing the group: social identity and the unfolding dynamics of responses to stress. *Journal of Applied Psychology, 91*, 1037.

Haslam, C., Cruwys, T. & Haslam, S.A. (2014). 'The we's have it': evidence for the distinctive benefits of group engagement in enhancing cognitive health in aging. *Social Science & Medicine*, *120*, 57–66.

Haslam, C., Holme, A., Haslam, S.A. et al. (2008). Maintaining group memberships: social identity continuity predicts well-being after stroke. *Neuropsychological Rehabilitation*, *18*, 671–691.

Hasler, G., van der Veen, J.W., Grillon, C. et al. (2010). Effect of acute psychological stress on prefrontal GABA concentration determined by proton magnetic resonance spectroscopy. *The American Journal of Psychiatry*, *167*, 1226–1231.

Hassan, S., Karpova, Y., Baiz, D. et al. (2013). Behavioral stress accelerates prostate cancer development in mice. *The Journal of Clinical Investigation*, *123*, 874–886.

Haus, E.L. & Smolensky, M.H. (2013). Shift work and cancer risk: potential mechanistic roles of circadian disruption, light at night, and sleep deprivation. *Sleep Medicine Reviews*, *17*, 273–284.

Hawkley, L.C., Masi, C.M., Berry, J.D. & Cacioppo, J.T. (2006). Loneliness is a unique predictor of age-related differences in systolic blood pressure. *Psychology and Aging*, *21*, 152–164.

Hayashi, M.T., Cesare, A.J., Rivera, T. & Karlseder, J. (2015). Cell death during crisis is mediated by mitotic telomere deprotection. *Nature*, *522*, 492–496.

Hayes, P.A., Fraher, M.H. & Quigley, E.M. (2014). Irritable bowel syndrome: the role of food in pathogenesis and management. *Gastroenterology & Hepatology*, *10*, 164–174.

Hayley, S. & Anisman, H. (2013). Neurotrophic paths in the treatment of depression. *JPN: Journal of Psychiatry & Neuroscience*, *38*, 291.

Hayley, S., Poulter, M.O., Merali, Z. & Anisman, H. (2005). The pathogenesis of clinical depression: stressor- and cytokine-induced alterations of neuroplasticity. *Neuroscience*, *135*, 659–678.

HealthyPeople.gov (2015). Healthy People 2020. www.HealthyPeople.gov (accessed May 2015).

Healy, J.R., Tonkin, J.L. & Kamarec, S.R. (2014). Evaluation of an improved sustained-release buprenorphine formulation for use in mice. *American Journal of Veterinary Research*, *75*, 619–625.

Hearn, L., Moore, R.A., Derry, S. et al. (2014). Desipramine for neuropathic pain in adults. *Cochrane Database System Review*, *9*, CD011003.

Hebebrand, J., Albayrak, Ö., Adan, R. et al. (2014). 'Eating addiction', rather than 'food addiction', better captures addictive-like eating behavior. *Neuroscience & Biobehavioral Reviews*, *47*, 295–306.

Hedén-Stahl, C., Novak, M., Hansson, P.O. et al. (2014). Incidence of type 2 diabetes among occupational classes in Sweden: a 35-year follow-up cohort study in middle-aged men. *Diabetic Medicine*, *31*, 674–680.

Heilig, M. (2004). The NPY system in stress, anxiety and depression. *Neuropeptides*, *38*, 213–224.

Heilig, M. & Koob, G.F. (2007). A key role for corticotropin-releasing factor in alcohol dependence. *Trends in Neuroscience*, *30*, 399–406.

Heim, C., Newport, D.J., Mletzko, T. et al. (2008). The link between childhood trauma and depression: insights from HPA axis studies in humans. *Psychoneuroendocrinology*, *33*, 693–710.

Heim, C., Young, L.J., Newport, D.J. et al. (2009). Lower CSF oxytocin concentrations in women with a history of childhood abuse. *Molecular Psychiatry*, *14*, 954–958.

Heinken, A. & Thiele, I. (2015). Anoxic conditions promote species-specific mutualism between gut nicrobes in silico. *Applied and Environmental Microbiology*, *81*, 4049–4061.

Heinrichs, M., Baumgartner, T., Kirschbaum, C. & Ehlert, U. (2003). Social support and oxytocin interact to suppress cortisol and subjective responses to psychosocial stress. *Biological Psychiatry, 54*, 1389-1398.

Heintz, P.A., DeMucha, C.M., Deguzman, M.M. & Softa, R. (2013). Stigma and microaggressions experienced by older women with urinary incontinence: a literature review. *Urologic Nursing*, *33*, 299–305.

Hekler, E.B., Lambert, J., Leventhal, E. et al. (2008). Commonsense illness beliefs, adherence behaviors, and hypertension control among African Americans. *Journal of Behavioral Medicine, 31,* 391–400.

Hemenover, S.H. & Dienstbier, R.A. (1996). Prediction of stress appraisals from mastery, extraversion, neuroticism, and general appraisal tendencies. *Motivation and Emotion, 20,* 299–331.

Hemmingsson, E., Johansson, K. & Reynisdottir, S. (2014). Effects of childhood abuse on adult obesity: a systematic review and meta-analysis. *Obesity Reviews, 15,* 882–893.

Hensley, P.L., Slonimski, C.K., Uhlenhuth, E.H. & Clayton, P.J. (2009). Escitalopram: an open-label study of bereavement-related depression and grief. *Journal of Affective Disorders, 113,* 142–149.

Heraclides, A.M., Chandola, T., Witte, D.R. & Brunner, E.J. (2009). Psychosocial stress at work doubles the risk of type 2 diabetes in middle-aged women evidence from the Whitehall II Study. *Diabetes Care, 32,* 2230–2235.

Heraclides, A.M., Chandola, T., Witte, D.R. & Brunner, E.J. (2012). Work stress, obesity and the risk of type 2 diabetes: gender-specific bidirectional effect in the Whitehall II Study. *Obesity, 20,* 428–433.

Hermann, L.L., Le Masurier, M. & Ebmeier, K.P. (2008). White matter hyperintensities in late life depression: a systematic review. *Journal of Neurology, Neurosurgery & Psychiatry, 79,* 619–624.

Hernán, M.A., Hernández-Díaz, S. & Robins, J.M. (2004). A structural approach to selection bias. *Epidemiology, 15,* 615–625.

Hernandez, D.C. & Pressler, E. (2015). Gender disparities among the association between cumulative family-level stress & adolescent weight status. *Preventive Medicine, 73,* 60–66.

Hernandez, R., Kershaw, K.N., Siddique, J. & Boehm, J.K. (2015). Optimism and cardiovascular health: multi-ethnic study of atherosclerosis (MESA). *Health Behavior and Policy Review, 2,* 62–73.

Hernandez-Avila, C.A., Rounsaville, B.J. & Kranzler, H.R. (2004). Opioid-, cannabis-and alcohol-dependent women show more rapid progression to substance abuse treatment. *Drug and Alcohol Dependence, 74,* 265–272.

Herrera, Z.M. & Ramos, T.C. (2014). Pilot study of a novel combination of two therapeutic vaccines in advanced non-small-cell lung cancer patients. *Cancer Immunology, Immunotherapy, 63,* 737–747.

Herzog, T.A. (2005). When popularity outstrips evidence: comment on West (2005). *Addiction, 100,* 1040–1041.

Higgins, G.A., Sellers, E.M. & Fletcher, P.J. (2013). From obesity to substance abuse: therapeutic opportunities for 5-HT 2C receptor agonists. *Trends in Pharmacological Sciences, 34,* 560–570.

Higgins, G.A., Silenieks, L.B., Roßmann, A. et al. (2012). The 5-HT2C receptor agonist lorcaserin reduces nicotine self-administration, discrimination, and reinstatement: relationship to feeding behavior and impulse control. *Neuropsychopharmacology, 37,* 1177–1191.

Hildebrand, M.E., Pitcher, G.M., Harding, E.K. et al. (2014). GluN2B and GluN2D NMDARs dominate synaptic responses in the adult spinal cord. *Scientific Reports, 4,* 4094.

Hill, A.B. (1965). The environment and disease: association or causation? *Proceedings of the Royal Society of Medicine, 58,* 295–300.

Hill, C.A. & O'Hara, E.A. (2006). A cognitive theory of trust. *Washington University Law Review, 84,* 1717–1770.

Hill, M.N., Patel, S., Campolongo, P. et al. (2010). Functional interactions between stress and the endocannabinoid system: from synaptic signaling to behavioral output. *Journal of Neuroscience, 30,* 14980–14986.

Hill, M.N. & Tasker, J.G. (2012). Endocannabinoid signaling, glucocorticoid-mediated negative feedback, and regulation of the hypothalamic-pituitary-adrenal axis. *Neuroscience, 204,* 5–16.

Hirsch, M. (2001) Surviving images: Holocaust photographs and the work of postmemory. *The Yale Journal of Criticism, 14,* 5–37.

Hjørland, B. (2011). Evidence based practice: an analysis based on the philosophy of science. *Journal of the American Society for Information Science and Technology, 62,* 1301–1310.

Hobson-West, P. (2007). Trusting blindly can be the biggest risk of all: organized resistance to childhood vaccination in the UK. *Sociology of Health and Illness, 29,* 198–215.

Hoffman, E. (2004). *After Such Knowledge: memory, history, and the legacy of the Holocaust.* New York: Public Affairs.

Hoffman-Goetz, L. & Quadrilatero, J. (2003). Treadmill exercise in mice increases intestinal lymphocyte loss via apoptosis. *Acta Physiologica Scandinavica, 179,* 289–297.

Hoffmann, T.C. & Del Mar, C. (2015). Patients' expectations of the benefits and harms of treatments, screening, and tests: a systematic review. *JAMA Internal Medicine, 175,* 274–286.

Hofmarcher, M.M. & Quentin, W. (2013). Austria: health system review. *Health Systems in Transition, 15,* 1–292.

Holmes, T.H. & Rahe, R.H. (1967). Social Readjustment rating scale. *Journal of Psychosomatic Research, 11,* 213–218.

Holt, J.B., Zhang, X., Presley-Cantrell, L. & Croft, J.B. (2011). Geographic disparities in chronic obstructive pulmonary disease (COPD) hospitalization among Medicare beneficiaries in the United States. *International Journal of Chronic Obstructive Pulmonary Disease, 6,* 321–328.

Holwerda, T.J., Deeg, D.J., Beekman, A.T. et al. (2014). Feelings of loneliness, but not social isolation, predict dementia onset: results from the Amsterdam Study of the Elderly (AMSTEL). *Journal of Neurology, Neurosurgery & Psychiatry, 85,* 135–142.

Holzer, L.A., Sevelda, F., Fraberger, G. et al. (2014). Body image and self-esteem in lower-limb amputees. *PLoS One, 9,* e92943.

Horowitz, C.R., Robinson, M. & Seifer, S. (2009). Community-based participatory research from the margin to the mainstream: are researchers prepared? *Circulation, 119,* 2633–2642.

Hotez, P.J. & Kamath, A. (2009). Neglected tropical diseases in sub-Saharan Africa: review of their prevalence, distribution, and disease burden. *PLoS Neglected Tropical Diseases, 3,* e412.

Hoth, K.F., Wamboldt, F.S., Strand, M. et al. (2013). Prospective impact of illness uncertainty on outcomes in chronic lung disease. *Health Psychology, 32,* 1170–1174.

Howard, J.H., Rechnitzer, P.A., Cunningham, D.A. et al. (1990). Type A behavior, personality, and sympathetic response. *Behavioral Medicine, 16,* 149–160.

Howard, S. & Hughes, B.M. (2013). Type D personality is associated with a sensitized cardiovascular response to recurrent stress in men. *Biological Psychology, 94,* 450–455.

Howitz, K.T., Bitterman, K.J., Cohen, H.Y. et al. (2003). Small molecule activators of sirtuins extend Saccharomyces cerevisiae lifespan. *Nature, 425,* 191–196.

Huang, E.J. & Reichardt, L.F. (2001). Neurotrophins: roles in neuronal development and function. *Annual Review of Neuroscience, 24,* 677–736.

Hudis, C.A. & Gianni, L. (2011). Triple-negative breast cancer: an unmet medical need. *The Oncologist, 16,* 1–11.

Hudson, M.M., Ness, K.K., Gurney, J.G. et al. (2013). Clinical ascertainment of health outcomes among adults treated for childhood cancer. *JAMA, 309,* 2371–2381.

Hughes, J.R. (2007). A review of sleepwalking (somnambulism): the enigma of neurophysiology and polysomnography with differential diagnosis of complex partial seizures. *Epilepsy & Behavior, 11,* 483–491.

Humbert, P., Pelletier, F., Dreno, B. et al. (2006). Gluten intolerance and skin diseases. *European Journal of Dermatology, 16,* 4–11.

Humphrey, L.L., Fu, R., Buckley, D.I. et al. (2008). Periodontal disease and coronary heart disease incidence: a systematic review and meta-analysis. *Journal of General Internal Medicine, 23,* 2079–2086.

Hunter, D.J., Colditz, G.A., Hankinson, S.E. et al. (2010). Oral contraceptive use and breast cancer: a prospective study of young women. *Cancer Epidemiology Biomarkers & Prevention, 19,* 2496–2502.

Hunter, T.A., Medved, M.I., Hiebert-Murphy, D. et al. (2013). 'Put on your face to face the world': women's narratives of burn injury. *Burns, 39,* 1588–1598.

Hurria, A., Wildes, T., Blair, S.L. et al. (2014). Senior adult oncology, version 2.2014: clinical practice guidelines in oncology. *Journal of the National Comprehensive Cancer Network, 12,* 82–126.

Huskisson, E.C. (1974). Measurement of pain. *The Lancet, 304,* 1127–1131.

Hypericum Depression Trial Study Group. (2002). Effect of Hypericum perforatum (St John's wort) in major depressive disorder: a randomized controlled trial. *The Journal of the American Medical Association*, *287*, 1807–1814.

Iida, N., Dzutsev, A., Stewart, C.A. et al. (2013). Commensal bacteria control cancer response to therapy by modulating the tumor microenvironment. *Science*, *342*, 967–970.

Imbert, B., Labrune, N., Lancon, C. & Simon, N. (2014). Baclofen in the management of cannabis dependence syndrome. *Therapeutic Advances in Psychopharmacology*, *4*, 50–52.

Imeri, L. & Opp, M.R. (2009). How (and why) the immune system makes us sleep. *Nature Reviews Neuroscience*, *10*, 199–210.

Inciardi, J.A. & Harrison, L.D. (2000). *Harm Reduction: national and international perspectives.* Thousand Oaks, CA: SAGE.

Inghammar, M., Engström, G., Ljungberg, B. et al. (2014). Increased incidence of invasive bacterial disease in chronic obstructive pulmonary disease compared to the general population: a population based cohort study. *BMC Infectious Diseases*, *14*, 163.

Ingram, K.M., Betz, N.E., Mindes, E.J. et al. (2001). Unsupportive responses from others concerning a stressful life event: development of the unsupportive social interactions inventory. *Journal of Social and Clinical Psychology*, *20*, 173–207.

Insel, T.R., Cuthbert, B., Garvey, M. et al. (2010). Research Domain Criteria (RDoC): toward a new classification framework for research on mental disorders. *American Journal of Psychiatry*, *167*, 748–751.

Insel, T.R. & Young, L.J. (2001). The neurobiology of attachment. *Nature Reviews Neuroscience*, *2*, 129–136.

International Agency for Research on Cancer (2015). IARC Monographs Volume 112: evaluation of five organophosphate insecticides and herbicides. www.iarc.fr/en/media-centre/iarcnews/pdf/MonographVolume112.pdf (accessed October 2015)

International Association for the Study of Pain (IASP) (2015). IASP taxonomy. www.iasp-pain.org/Taxonomy (accessed October, 2015).

International Collaboration of Epidemiological Studies of Cervical Cancer, Appleby, P., Beral, V., Berrington de González, A. et al. (2007). Cervical cancer and hormonal contraceptives: collaborative reanalysis of individual data for 16,573 women with cervical cancer and 35,509 women without cervical cancer from 24 epidemiological studies. *The Lancet*, *370*, 1609–1621.

Inverso, G., Mahal, B.A., Aizer, A.A. et al. (2014). Marital status and head and neck cancer outcomes. *Cancer*, *121*, 1273–1278.

Ioannidis, J.P.A. (2013). Implausible results in human nutrition research. *British Medical Journal*, *347*, f6698.

Iqbal, J., Ginsburg, O., Rochon, P.A. et al. (2015). Differences in breast cancer stage at diagnosis and cancer-specific survival by race and ethnicity in the United States. *JAMA*, *313*, 165–173.

Irwin, M.R. (2015). Why sleep is important for health: a psychoneuroimmunology perspective. *Annual Review of Psychology*, *66*, 143–172.

Ismail, N., Garas, P. & Blaustein, J.D. (2011). Long-term effects of pubertal stressors on female sexual receptivity and estrogen receptor-α expression in CD-1 female mice. *Hormones and Behavior*, *59*, 565–571.

Israel, S., Weisel, O., Ebstein, R.P. & Bornstein, G. (2012). Oxytocin, but not vasopressin, increases both parochial and universal altruism. *Psychoneuroendocrinology*, *37*, 1341–1344.

Jacobsen, J.H., Watkins, L.R. & Hutchinson, M.R. (2014). Discovery of a novel site of opioid action at the innate immune pattern-recognition receptor TLR4 and its role in addiction. *International Review of Neurobiology*, *118*, 129–163.

Jacobson-Pick, S., Elkobi, A., Vander, S. et al. (2008). Juvenile stress-induced alteration of maturation of the $GABA_A$ receptor alpha subunit in the rat. *International Journal of Neuropsychopharmacology*, *11*, 891–903.

Jäger, S., Jacobs, S., Kröger, J. et al. (2014). Breastfeeding and maternal risk of type 2 diabetes: a prospective study and meta-analysis. *Diabetologia*, *57*, 1355–1365.

Jain, A., Marshall, J., Buikema, A. et al. (2015). Autism occurrence by MMR vaccine status among US children with older siblings with and without autism. *The Journal of the American Medical Association*, *313*, 1534–1540.

Jain, N. & Walker, W.A. (2015). Diet and host-microbial crosstalk in postnatal intestinal immune homeostasis. *Nature Reviews Gastroenterology & Hepatology*, 12, 14–25.

Jais, A., Einwallner, E., Sharif, O. et al. (2014). Heme oxygenase-1 drives metaflammation and insulin resistance in mouse and man. *Cell*, *158*, 25–40.

Jaja, B.N., Saposnik, G., Nisenbaum, R. et al. (2013). Effect of socioeconomic status on inpatient mortality and use of postacute care after subarachnoid hemorrhage. *Stroke*, *44*, 2842–2847.

Janeway, C.A., Travers, P., Walport, M. & Shlomchik, M.J. (2005). *Immunobiology* (6th ed.). New York: Garland Science.

Janz, N.K. & Becker, M.H. (1984). The health belief model: a decade later. *Health Education & Behavior*, *11*, 1–47.

Jarvis, W.R., Jarvis, A.A. & Chinn, R.Y. (2012). National prevalence of methicillin-resistant Staphylococcus aureus in inpatients at United States health care facilities, 2010. *American Journal of Infection Control*, *40*, 194–200.

Jazin, E. & Cahill, L. (2010). Sex differences in molecular neuroscience: from fruit flies to humans. *Nature Reviews Neuroscience*, *11*, 9–17.

Jefferson, A.L., Himali, J.J., Beiser, A.S. et al. (2010). Cardiac index is associated with brain aging: the Framingham heart study. *Circulation*, *122*, 690–697.

Jemmott, J.B., Croyle, R.T. & Ditto, P.H. (1988). Common sense epidemiology: self-based judgments from laypersons and physicians. *Health Psychology*, *7*, 55–73.

Jenkins, D.J., Wolever, T.M., Taylor, R.H. et al. (1981). Glycemic index of foods: a physiological basis for carbohydrate exchange. *American Journal of Clinical Nutrition*, *34*, 362–366.

Jensen, M.D., Ryan, D.H., Apovian, C.M. et al. (2014). 2013 AHA/ACC/TOS guideline for the management of overweight and obesity in adults: a report of the American College of Cardiology/ American Heart Association Task Force on Practice Guidelines and The Obesity Society. *Journal of the American College of Cardiology*, *63*, 2985–3023.

Jensen, M.P., Day, M.A. & Miró, J. (2014). Neuromodulatory treatments for chronic pain: efficacy and mechanisms. *Nature Reviews Neurology*, *10*, 167–178.

Jensen, M.P. & Patterson, D.R. (2014). Hypnotic approaches for chronic pain management: clinical implications of recent research findings. *American Psychologist*, *69*, 167–177.

Jetten, J., Haslam, C. & Haslam, S.A. (2012). *The Social Cure: identity, health and well-being*. New York: Psychology Press/Taylor & Francis.

Jetten, J., Haslam, C., Haslam, S.A. et al. (2014). How groups affect our health and well-being: the path from theory to policy. *Social Issues and Policy Review*, *8*, 103–130.

Ji, R.R., Xu, Z.Z. & Gao, Y.J. (2014). Emerging targets in neuroinflammation-driven chronic pain. *Nature Reviews Drug Discovery*, *13*, 533–548.

Jiang, P., Chen, C., Wang, R. et al. (2013). hESC-derived Olig2+ progenitors generate a subtype of astroglia with protective effects against ischaemic brain injury. *Nature Communications*, *4*, 2196.

Jiang, W., Velazquez, E.J., Kuchibhatla, M. et al. (2013). Effect of escitalopram on mental stress-induced myocardial ischemia: results of the REMIT trial. *The Journal of the American Medical Association*, *309*, 2139–2149.

Jiao, L., Duan, Z., Sangi-Haghpeykar, H. et al. (2013). Sleep duration and incidence of colorectal cancer in postmenopausal women. *British Journal of Cancer*, *108*, 213–221.

Jobin, J., Wrosch, C. & Scheier, M.F. (2014). Associations between dispositional optimism and diurnal cortisol in a community sample: when stress is perceived as higher than normal. *Health Psychology*, *33*, 382–391.

John, E.M., Miron, A., Gong, G. et al. (2007). Prevalence of pathogenic BRCA1 mutation carriers in 5 US racial/ethnic groups. *The Journal of the American Medical Association*, *298*, 2869–2876.

Johnson, B.A., Ait-Daoud, N., Wang, X.Q. et al. (2013). Topiramate for the treatment of cocaine addiction: a randomized clinical trial. *JAMA Psychiatry*, *70*, 1338–1346.

Johnson, B.T., Scott-Sheldon, L.A., Huedo-Medina, T.B. & Carey, M.P. (2011). Interventions to reduce sexual risk for human immunodeficiency virus in adolescents: a meta-analysis of trials, 1985–2008. *Archives of Pediatrics & Adolescent Medicine*, *165*, 77–84.

Johnson, J.D., O'Connor, K.A., Deak, T. et al. (2002). Prior stressor exposure sensitizes LPS-induced cytokine production. *Brain, Behavior, and Immunity*, *16*, 461–476.

Johnston, B.C., Kanters, S., Bandayrel, K. et al. (2014). Comparison of weight loss among named diet programs in overweight and obese adults: a meta-analysis. *The Journal of the American Medical Association*, *312*, 923–933.

Jonas, W. & Woodside, B. (2015, in press). Physiological mechanisms and behavioral and psychological factors influencing the transfer of milk from mothers to their young. *Hormones & Behavior*.

Jones, J.M., Williams, W.H., Jetten, J. et al. (2012). The role of psychological symptoms and social group memberships in the development of post-traumatic stress after traumatic injury. *British Journal of Health Psychology*, *17*, 798–811.

Joo, E.Y., Kim, H., Suh, S. & Hong, S.B. (2014). Hippocampal substructural vulnerability to sleep disturbance and cognitive impairment in patients with chronic primary insomnia: magnetic resonance imaging morphometry. *Sleep*, *37*, 1189.

Joseph, J. (2003). *The Gene Illusion: genetic research in psychology and psychiatry under the microscope*. Ross-on-Wye, UK: PCCS Books.

Joshi, S., Jatrana, S., Paradies, Y. & Priest, N. (2014). Differences in health behaviours between immigrant and non-immigrant groups: a protocol for a systematic review. *Systematic Reviews*, *3*, 61.

Jostins, L., Ripke, S., Weersma, R.K. et al. (2012). Host-microbe interactions have shaped the genetic architecture of inflammatory bowel disease. *Nature*, *491*, 119–124.

Kabat-Zinn, J. (1990). *Full Catastrophe Living: using the wisdom of your body and mind to face stress, pain, and illness*. New York: Delacourt.

Kabesch, M. (2014). Epigenetics in asthma and allergy. *Current Opinion in Allergy and Clinical Immunology*, *14*, 62–68.

Kahneman, D. (2011). *Thinking, Fast and Slow*. New York: Farrar, Straus and Giroux.

Kahneman, D. & Deaton, A. (2010). High income improves evaluation of life but not emotional well-being. *Proceedings of the National Academy of Sciences*, *107*, 16489–16493.

Kahneman, D. & Tversky, A. (1996). On the reality of cognitive illusions. *Psychological Review*, *103*, 582–591.

Kain, Z.N., Mayes, L.C., Caldwell-Andrews, A.A. et al. (2006). Preoperative anxiety, postoperative pain, and behavioral recovery in young children undergoing surgery. *Pediatrics*, *51*, 589–596.

Kajantie, E. & Phillips, D.I. (2006). The effects of sex and hormonal status on the physiological response to acute psychosocial stress. *Psychoneuroendocrinology*, *31*, 151–178.

Kalivas, P.W. & Volkow, N.D. (2011). New medications for drug addiction hiding in glutamatergic neuroplasticity. *Molecular Psychiatry*, *16*, 974–986.

Kallen, A.N. & Pal, L. (2011). Cardiovascular disease and ovarian function. *Current Opinion in Obstetrics and Gynecology*, *23*, 258–267.

Kamal, A. (2014). The efficacy of novel B cell biologics as the future of SLE treatment: a review. *Autoimmunity Reviews*, *13*, 1094–1101.

Kamen, D. & Aranow, C. (2008). Vitamin D in systemic lupus erythematosus. *Current Opinion in Rheumatology*, *20*, 532–537.

Kandel, D. (1975). Stages in adolescent involvement in drug use. *Science*, *190*, 912–914.

Kanekiyo, M., Wei, C.J., Yassine, H.M. et al. (2013). Self-assembling influenza nanoparticle vaccines elicit broadly neutralizing H1N1 antibodies. *Nature*, *499*, 102–106.

Kaneko, Y. & Takeuchi, T. (2014). A paradigm shift in rheumatoid arthritis over the past decade. *Internal Medicine*, *53*, 1895–1903.

Kanner, A.D., Coyne, J.C., Schaefer, C. & Lazarus, R.S. (1981). Comparison of two modes of stress measurement: daily hassles and uplifts versus major life events. *Journal of Behavioral Medicine*, *4*, 239–249.

Kaplan, R.M. (2003). The significance of quality of life in health care. *Quality of Life Research*, *12*, 3–16.

Karademas, E.C., Tsalikou, C. & Tallarou, M.C. (2011). The impact of emotion regulation and illness-focused coping strategies on the relation of illness-related negative emotions to subjective health. *Journal of Health Psychology*, *16*, 510–519.

Karaiskos, D., Mavragani, C.P., Makaroni, S. et al. (2009). Stress, coping strategies and social support in patients with primary Sjögren's syndrome prior to disease onset: a retrospective case-control study. *Annals of the Rheumatic Diseases*, *68*, 40–46.

Kareklas, I., Muehling, D.D. & Weber, T.J. (2015). Reexamining health messages in the digital age: a fresh look at source credibility effects. *Journal of Advertising*, *44*, 88–104.

Karl, T.R., Melillo, J.M. & Peterson, T.C. (Eds.). (2009). *Global Climate Change Impacts in the United States.* New York: Cambridge University Press.

Karlsson, H.K., Tuominen, L., Tuulari, J.J. et al. (2015). Obesity is associated with decreased μ-opioid but unaltered dopamine d2 receptor availability in the brain. *Journal of Neuroscience*, *35*, 3959–3965.

Karoly, P. & Ruehlman, L.S. (1996). Motivational implications of pain: chronicity, psychological distress, and work goal construal in a national sample of adults. *Health Psychology*, *15*, 383–390.

Karraker, A. & Latham, K. (2015). In sickness and in health? Physical illness as a risk factor for marital dissolution in later life. *Journal of Health and Social Behavior*, *56*, 59–73.

Karsch-Völk, M., Barrett, B., Kiefer, D. et al. (2014). Echinacea for preventing and treating the common cold. *The Cochrane Database of Systematic Reviews*, *2*, CD000530.

Kasper, D.L., Fauci, A.S., Longo, D.L. et al. (2005). *Harrison's Principles of Internal Medicine* (16th ed.). New York: McGraw-Hill.

Kassab, M., Foster, J.P., Foureur, M. & Fowler, C. (2012). Sweet-tasting solutions for needle-related procedural pain in infants one month to one year of age. *The Cochrane Database of Systematic Reviews*, *12*, CD008411.

Kassakian, S.Z. & Mermel, L.A. (2014). Changing epidemiology of infections due to extended spectrum beta-lactamase producing bacteria. *Antimicrobial Resistance and Infection Control*, *3*, 9.

Kastenbaum, R. & Costa Jr, P.T. (1977). Psychological perspectives on death. *Annual Review of Psychology*, *28*, 225–249.

Katon, W.J., Lin, E.H., Von Korff, M. et al. (2010). Collaborative care for patients with depression and chronic illnesses. *New England Journal of Medicine*, *363*, 2611–2620.

Katon, W.J., Pedersen, H.S., Ribe, A.R. et al. (2015). Effect of depression and diabetes mellitus on the risk for dementia: a national population-based cohort study. *JAMA Psychiatry*, *72*, 612–619.

Katsimpardi, L., Litterman, N.K., Schein, P.A. et al. (2014). Vascular and neurogenic rejuvenation of the aging mouse brain by young systemic factors. *Science*, *344*, 630–634.

Katterman, S.N., Kleinman, B.M., Hood, M.M. et al. (2014). Mindfulness meditation as an intervention for binge eating, emotional eating, and weight loss: a systematic review. *Eating Behaviors*, *15*, 197–204.

Katz, L.Y., Kozyrskyj, A.L., Prior, H.J. et al. (2008). Effect of regulatory warnings on antidepressant prescription rates, use of health services and outcomes among children, adolescents and young adults. *Canadian Medical Association Journal*, *178*, 1005–1011.

Katz, M., Liu, C., Schaer, M. et al. (2009). Prefrontal plasticity and stress inoculation-induced resilience. *Developmental Neuroscience*, *31*, 293–299.

Keating, N.L., Guadagnoli, E., Landrum, M.B. et al. (2002). Treatment decision making in early-stage breast cancer: should surgeons match patients' desired level of involvement? *Journal of Clinical Oncology*, *20*, 1473–1479.

Keats, S. & Wiggins, S. (2014). Future diets: Implications for agriculture and food prices. Overseas development Institute. www.odi.org/sites/odi.org.uk/files/odi-assets/publications-opinion-files/8776.pdf (accessed September 2015).

Keeling, M., Bambrough, J. & Simpson, J. (2013). Depression, anxiety and positive affect in people diagnosed with low-grade tumours: the role of illness perceptions. *Psychooncology*, *22*, 1421–1427.

Kelly, O., Matheson, K., Ravindran, A. et al. (2007). Ruminative coping among patients with dysthymia before and after pharmacotherapy. *Depression and Anxiety*, *24*, 233–243.

Kelly-Irving, M., Lepage, B., Dedieu, D. et al. (2013). Adverse childhood experiences and premature all-cause mortality. *European Journal of Epidemiology*, *28*, 721–734.

Kemeny, M.E. & Schedlowski, M. (2007). Understanding the interaction between psychosocial stress and immune-related diseases: a stepwise progression. *Brain Behavior & Immunity*, *2*, 1009–1018.

Kendler, K.S., Kuhn, J.W. & Prescott, C.A. (2004). Childhood sexual abuse, stressful life events and risk for major depression in women. *Psychological Medicine*, *34*, 1475–1482.

Kendler, K.S., Thornton, L.M. & Gardner, C.O. (2000). Stressful life events and previous episodes in the etiology of major depression in women: an evaluation of the 'kindling' hypothesis. *American Journal of Psychiatry, 157,* 1243–1251.

Kendler, K.S., Thornton, L.M. & Prescott, C.A. (2001). Gender differences in the rates of exposure to stressful life events and sensitivity to their depressogenic effects. *American Journal of Psychiatry, 158,* 587–593.

Kennedy, B.R. (2013). Health inequalities: promoting policy changes in utilizing transformation development by empowering African American communities in reducing health disparities. *Journal of Cultural Diversity, 20,* 155–162.

Kerlikowske, K., Zhu, W., Tosteson, A.N. et al. (2015). Identifying women with dense breasts at high risk for interval cancer: a cohort study. *Annals of Internal Medicine, 162,* 673–681.

Kerns, R.D., Rosenberg, R. & Otis, J.D. (2002). Self-appraised problem solving and pain-relevant social support as predictors of the experience of chronic pain. *Annals of Behavioral Medicine, 24,* 100–105.

Kessner, S., Forkmann, K., Ritter, C. et al. (2014). The effect of treatment history on therapeutic outcome: psychological and neurobiological underpinnings. *PLoS One, 9,* e109014.

Khan, A., Kolts, R.L., Thase, M.E. et al. (2004). Research design features and patient characteristics associated with the outcome of antidepressant clinical trials. *American Journal of Psychiatry, 161,* 2045–2049.

Khan, K.S., Kunz, R., Kleijnen, J. & Antes, G. (2003). Five steps to conducting a systematic review. *Journal of the Royal Society of Medicine, 96,* 118–121.

Khan, R.S., Ahmed, K., Blakeway, E. et al. (2011). Catastrophizing: a predictive factor for postoperative pain. *The American Journal of Surgery, 201,* 122–131.

Khanh, D.V., Choi, Y.H., Moh, S.H. et al. (2014). Leptin and insulin signaling in dopaminergic neurons: relationship between energy balance and reward system. *Frontiers in Psychology, 5,* 846.

Khera, S., Kolte, D., Aronow, W.S. et al. (2014). Non-ST-elevation myocardial infarction in the United States: contemporary trends in incidence, utilization of the early invasive strategy, and in-hospital outcomes. *Journal of the American Heart Association, 3,* e000995.

Kiecolt-Glaser, J.K., Christian, L., Preston, H. et al. (2010). Stress, inflammation, and yoga practice. *Psychosomatic Medicine, 72,* 113–121.

Kiecolt-Glaser, J.K., Gouin, J.P., Weng, N.P. et al. (2011). Childhood adversity heightens the impact of later-life caregiving stress on telomere length and inflammation. *Psychosomatic Medicine, 73,* 16–22.

Kiecolt-Glaser, J.K., McGuire, L., Robles, T.F. & Glaser, R. (2002). Psychoneuroimmunology: psychological influences on immune function and health. *Journal of Consulting and Clinical Psychology, 70,* 537–547.

Kilpatrick, A.M. & Randolph, S.E. (2012). Drivers, dynamics, and control of emerging vector-borne zoonotic diseases. *The Lancet, 380,* 1946–1955.

Kim, E.J. & Dimsdale, J.E. (2007). The effect of psychosocial stress on sleep: a review of polysomnographic evidence. *Behavioral Sleep Medicine, 5,* 256–278.

Kim, H.S., Sherman, D.K., Mojaverian, T. et al. (2011). Gene–culture interaction: oxytocin receptor polymorphism (OXTR) and emotion regulation. *Social Psychological and Personality Science, 2,* 665–672.

Kim, J.N. & Lee, B.M. (2007). Risk factors, health risks, and risk management for aircraft personnel and frequent flyers. *Journal of Toxicology and Environmental Health Part B: Critical Reviews, 10,* 223–234.

Kim, M.J., Lee, J.H. & Duffy, J.F. (2013). Circadian rhythm sleep disorders. *Journal of Clinical Outcomes Management, 20,* 513–528.

Kimbro, L.B., Mangione, C.M., Steers, W.N. et al. (2014). Depression and all-cause mortality in persons with diabetes mellitus: are older adults at higher risk? Results from the translating research into action for diabetes study. *Journal of the American Geriatrics Society, 62,* 1017–1022.

Kimron, L. & Cohen, M. (2012). Coping and emotional distress during acute hospitalization in older persons with earlier trauma: the case of Holocaust survivors. *Quality of Life Research, 21,* 783–794.

King, R.B., Ainsworth, C.R., Ronen, M. & Hartke, R.J. (2010). Stroke caregivers: pressing problems reported during the first months of caregiving. *Journal of Neuroscience and Nursing, 42,* 302–311.

King, S., Chambers, C.T., Huguet, A. et al. (2011). The epidemiology of chronic pain in children and adolescents revisited: a systematic review. *Pain*, *152*, 2729–2738.

Kirby, E.D., Muroy, S.E., Sun, W.G. et al. (2013). Acute stress enhances adult rat hippocampal neurogenesis and activation of newborn neurons via secreted astrocytic FGF2. *eLife*, *2*, e00362.

Kirby, L.G., Zeeb, F.D. & Winstanley, C.A. (2011). Contributions of serotonin in addiction vulnerability. *Neuropharmacology*, *61*, 421–432.

Kirmayer, L.J. (2012). Cultural competence and evidence-based practice in mental health: epistemic communities and the politics of pluralism. *Social Science & Medicine*, *75*, 249–256.

Kirmayer, L.J. & Crafa, D. (2014). What kind of science for psychiatry? *Frontiers in Human Neuroscience*, *8*, 435.

Kirmayer, L.J., Gone, J.P. & Moses, J. (2014). Rethinking historical trauma. *Transcultural Psychiatry*, *51*, 299–319.

Kirmayer, L.J. & Sartorius, N. (2007). Cultural models and somatic syndromes. *Psychosomatic Medicine*, *69*, 832–840.

Kirschbaum, C., Klauer, T., Filipp, S.H. & Hellhammer, D.H. (1995). Sex-specific effects of social support on cortisol and subjective responses to acute psychological stress. *Psychosomatic Medicine*, *57*, 23–31.

Kirschbaum, C., Kudielka, B.M., Gaab, J. et al. (1999). Impact of gender, menstrual cycle phase, and oral contraceptives on the activity of the hypothalamus-pituitary-adrenal axis. *Psychosomatic Medicine*, *61*, 154–162.

Kirschbaum, C., Pirke, K.-M. & Hellhammer, D.H. (1993). The 'Trier Social Stress Test': a tool for investigating psychobiological stress responses in a laboratory setting. *Neuropsychobiology*, *28*, 76–81.

Kissane, D.W., Clarke, D.M. & Street, A.F. (2001). Demoralization syndrome: a relevant psychiatric diagnosis for palliative care. *Journal of Palliative Care*, *17*, 12–32.

Kit, B.K., Kuklina, E., Carroll, M.D. et al. (2015). Prevalence of and trends in dyslipidemia and blood pressure among US children and adolescents, 1999–2012. *JAMA Pediatrics*, *169*, 272–279.

Kivimäki, M., Virtanen, M., Kawachi, I. et al. (2014). Long working hours, socioeconomic status, and the risk of incident type 2 diabetes: a meta-analysis of published and unpublished data from 222 120 individuals. *The Lancet Diabetes & Endocrinology*, *3*, 27–34.

Klein, E.A., Thompson, I.M., Tangen, C.M. et al. (2011). Vitamin E and the risk of prostate cancer: the Selenium and Vitamin E Cancer Prevention Trial (SELECT). *JAMA*, *306*, 1549–1556.

Klepin, H., Mohile, S. & Hurria, A. (2009). Geriatric assessment in older patients with breast cancer. *Journal of the National Comprehensive Cancer Network*, *7*, 226–236.

Kliewer, K.L., Ke, J.Y., Lee, H.Y. et al. (2015). Short-term food restriction followed by controlled refeeding promotes gorging behavior, enhances fat deposition, and diminishes insulin sensitivity in mice. *Journal of Nutritional Biochemistry*, *26*, 721–728.

Knowles, S.R, Tribbick, D., Connell, W.R. et al. (2014). Exploration of health status, illness perceptions, coping strategies, and psychological morbidity in stoma patients. *Journal of Wound Ostomy & Continence Nursing*, *41*, 573–580.

Koch, S.B., van Zuiden, M., Nawijn, L. et al. (2014). Intranasal oxytocin as a strategy for medication-enhanced psychotherapy of PTSD: salience processing and fear inhibition processes. *Psychoneuroendocrinology*, *40*, 242–256.

Koerner, S.S., Shirai, Y. & Kenyon, D.B. (2010). Sociocontextual circumstances in daily stress reactivity among caregivers for elder relatives. *The Journals of Gerontology Series B: Psychological Sciences and Social Sciences*, *65*, 561–572..

Kokaia, Z. & Lindvall, O. (2012). Stem cell repair of striatal ischemia. *Progress in Brain Research*, *201*, 35–53.

Kolodny, A., Courtwright, D.T., Hwang, C.S. et al. (2015). The prescription opioid and heroin crisis: a public health approach to an epidemic of addiction. *Annual Review of Public Health*, *36*, 559–574.

Kong, J., Spaeth, R., Cook, A. et al. (2013). Are all placebo effects equal? Placebo pills, sham acupuncture, cue conditioning and their association. *PLoS ONE*, *8*, e67485.

Könner, A.C., Hess, S. & Tovar, S. (2011). Role for insulin signaling in catecholaminergic neurons in control of energy homeostasis. *Cell Metabolism*, *13*, 720–728.

Koo, J.W., Mazei-Robison, M.S., Chaudhury, D. et al. (2012). BDNF is a negative modulator of morphine action. *Science*, *338*, 124–128.

Koob, G.F. (2014). Neurocircuitry of alcohol addiction: synthesis from animal models. *Handbook of Clinical Neurology*, *125*, 33–54.

Koob, G.F. & Le Moal, M. (2008). Addiction and the brain antireward system. *Annual Review of Psychology*, *59*, 29–53.

Koob, G.F. & Volkow, N.D. (2010). Neurocircuitry of addiction. *Neuropsychopharmacology*, *35*, 217–238.

Kooijman, C.M., Dijkstra, P.U., Geertzen, J.H. et al. (2000). Phantom pain and phantom sensations in upper limb amputees: an epidemiological study. *Pain*, *87*, 33–41.

Koolhaas, J.M., Bartolomucci, A., Buwalda, B. et al. (2011). Stress revisited: a critical evaluation of the stress concept. *Neuroscience & Biobehavioral Reviews*, *35*, 1291–1301.

Kop, W.J. (1999). Chronic and acute psychological risk factors for clinical manifestations of coronary artery disease. *Psychosomatic Medicine*, *61*, 476–487.

Kop, W.J., Appels, A.P., De Leon, C.M. et al. (1994). Vital exhaustion predicts new cardiac events after successful coronary angioplasty. *Psychosomatic Medicine*, *56*, 281–287.

Kop, W.J. & Cohen, N. (2007). Psychoneuroimmunological pathways involved in acute coronary syndromes. In R. Ader (Ed.), *Psychoneuroimmunology* (4th ed., pp. 921–943). Amsterdam, Boston, MA: Academic Press.

Kop, W.J. & Mommersteeg, P.M.C. (2014). Psychoneuroimmunological processes in coronary artery disease and heart failure. In A. Kusnecov & H. Anisman (Eds.), *Handbook of Psychoneuroimmunology*. London: Wiley-Blackwell.

Kosfeld, M., Heinrichs, M., Zak, P.J. et al. (2005). Oxytocin increases trust in humans. *Nature*, *435*, 673–676.

Kosmider, L., Sobczak, A., Fik, M. et al. (2014). Carbonyl compounds in electronic cigarette vapors: effects of nicotine solvent and battery output voltage. *Nicotine & Tobacco Research*, *16*, 1319–1326.

Kostandy, B.B. (2012). The role of glutamate in neuronal ischemic injury: the role of spark in fire. *Neurological Sciences*, *33*, 223–237.

Kothari, R.U., Pancioli, A., Liu, T. et al. (1999). Cincinnati prehospital stroke scale: reproducibility and validity. *Annals of Emergency Medicine*, *33*, 373–378.

Kotseva, K., Wood, D., De Bacquer, D. et al. (2015). EUROASPIRE IV: a European Society of Cardiology survey on the lifestyle, risk factor and therapeutic management of coronary patients from 24 European countries. *European Journal of Preventive Cardiology*, pii. 2047487315569401.

Koucky, E.M., Dickstein, B.D. & Chard, K.M. (2013). Cognitive behavioral treatments for posttraumatic stress disorder: empirical foundation and new directions. *CNS Spectrums*, *18*, 73–81.

Kovalenko, I.L., Galyamina, A.G., Smagin, D.A. et al. (2014). Extended effect of chronic social defeat stress in childhood on behaviors in adulthood. *PloS One*, *9*, e91762.

Koven, N.S. & Abry, A.W. (2015). The clinical basis of orthorexia nervosa: emerging perspectives. *Neuropsychiatric Disease and Treatment*, *11*, 385–394.

Kowal, C., Degiorgio, L.A., Lee, J.Y. et al. (2006). Human lupus autoantibodies against NMDA receptors mediate cognitive impairment. *Proceedings of the National Academy of Sciences*, *103*, 19854–19859.

Koyuncu, E., Budayeva, H.G., Miteva, Y.V. et al. (2014). Sirtuins are evolutionarily conserved viral restriction factors. *MBio*, *16*, pii: e02249-14.

Kraetschmer, N., Sharpe, N., Urowitz, S. & Deber, R.B. (2004). How does trust affect patient preferences for participation in decision-making? *Health Expectations*, *7*, 317–326.

Kraljevic, S., Banozic, A., Maric, A. et al. (2012). Parents' pain catastrophizing is related to pain catastrophizing of their adult children. *International Journal of Behavioral Medicine*, *19*, 115–119.

Krampe, H., Stawicki, S., Wagner, T. et al. (2006). Follow-up of 180 alcoholic patients for up to 7 years after outpatient treatment: impact of alcohol deterrents on outcome. *Alcoholism: Clinical and Experimental Research*, *30*, 86–95.

Krantz, D.S., Kop, W.J., Santiago, H.T. & Gottdiener, J.S. (1996). Mental stress as a trigger of myocardial ischemia and infarction. *Cardiology Clinic*, *14*, 271–287.

Krašovec, R., Belavkin, R.V., Aston, J.A. et al. (2014). Mutation rate plasticity in rifampicin resistance depends on Escherichia coli cell–cell interactions. *Nature Communications*, *5*, 3742.

Krebs, E.E., Garrett, J.M. & Konrad, T.R. (2006). The difficult doctor? Characteristics of physicians who report frustration with patients: an analysis of survey data. *BMC Health Services Research, 6*, 128.

Kreek, M.J., Bart, G., Lilly, C. et al. (2005). Pharmacogenetics and human molecular genetics of opiate and cocaine addictions and their treatments. *Pharmacological Reviews, 57*, 1–26.

Krishnan, H.R., Sakharkar, A.J., Teppen, T.L. et al. (2014). The epigenetic landscape of alcoholism. *International Review of Neurobiology, 115*, 75–116.

Kristal, A.R., Till, C., Song, X. et al. (2014). Plasma vitamin D and prostate cancer risk: results from the Selenium and Vitamin E Cancer Prevention Trial. *Cancer Epidemiology Biomarkers & Prevention, 23*, 1494–1504.

Kroenke, C.H., Michael, Y., Tindle, H. et al. (2012). Social networks, social support and burden in relationships, and mortality after breast cancer diagnosis. *Breast Cancer Research and Treatment, 133*, 375–385.

Kross, E., Berman, M.G., Mischel, W. et al. (2011). Social rejection shares somatosensory representations with physical pain. *Proceedings of the National Academy of Sciences, 108*, 6270–6275.

Krueger, G. & Ellis, C.N. (2005). Psoriasis: recent advances in understanding its pathogenesis and treatment. *Journal of the American Academy of Dermatology, 53*, S94–S100.

Krumholz, H.M. (2013). Post-hospital syndrome: an acquired, transient condition of generalized risk. *New England Journal of Medicine, 368*, 100–102.

Krumholz, H.M., Normand, S.L. & Wang, Y. (2014). Trends in hospitalizations and outcomes for acute cardiovascular disease and stroke, 1999–2011. *Circulation, 130*, 966–975.

Kubany, E.S., Hanes, S.N., Leisen, M.B. et al. (2000). Development and preliminary validation of a brief broad-spectrum measure of trauma exposure: the traumatic life events questionnaire. *Psychological Assessment, 12*, 210–224.

Kubler-Ross, E. (1969). *On Death and Dying*. New York: Scribner.

Kulik, G. (2014). Precision therapy to target apoptosis in prostate cancer. *Experimental Oncology, 36*, 226–230.

Kuller, L.H. (2004). Ethnic differences in atherosclerosis, cardiovascular disease and lipid metabolism. *Current Opinion in Lipidology, 15*, 109–113.

Kumar, K., Taylor, R.S., Jacques, L. et al. (2008). The effects of spinal cord stimulation in neuropathic pain are sustained: a 24-month follow-up of the prospective randomized controlled multicenter trial of the effectiveness of spinal cord stimulation. *Neurosurgery, 63*, 762–770.

Kumar, V., Abbas, A.K., Fausto, N. & Aster, J.C. (2014). *Robbins and Cotran Pathologic Basis of Disease (Professional Edition): expert consult-online*. Philadelphia, PA: Elsevier Health Sciences.

Kundakovic, M., Gudsnuk, K., Herbstman, J.B. et al. (2015). DNA methylation of BDNF as a biomarker of early-life adversity. *Proceedings of the National Academy of Sciences, 112*, 6807–6813.

Kurita, K., Garon, E.B., Stanton, A.L. & Meyerowitz, B.E. (2013). Uncertainty and psychological adjustment in patients with lung cancer. *Psychooncology, 22*, 1396–1401.

Kushner, H.S. (1981). *When Bad Things Happen to Good People*. New York: Anchor Books.

Kwan, B.M., Dimidjian, S. & Rizvi, S.L. (2010). Treatment preference, engagement, and clinical improvement in pharmacotherapy versus psychotherapy for depression. *Behavioral Research & Therapy, 48*, 799–804.

Kyranou, M., Puntillo, K., Dunn, L.B. et al. (2014). Predictors of initial levels and trajectories of anxiety in women before and for 6 months after breast cancer surgery. *Cancer Nursing, 37*, 406–417.

Labonté, B., Suderman, M., Maussion, G. et al. (2013). Genome-wide methylation changes in the brains of suicide completers. *The American Journal of Psychiatry, 170*, 511–520.

Laferrière, A., Pitcher, M.H., Haldane, A. et al. (2011). PKMζ is essential for spinal plasticity underlying the maintenance of persistent pain. *Molecular Pain, 7*, 99.

Lam, V. et al. (2012). Intestinal microbiota determine severity of myocardial infarction in rats. *Journal of the Federation of American Societies for Experimental Biology, 26*, 1727–1735.

Landau, D.A., Clement, K., Ziller, M.J. et al. (2014). Locally disordered methylation forms the basis of intratumor methylome variation in chronic lymphocytic leukemia. *Cancer Cell, 26*, 813–825.

Lane, J.M. (2006). Mass vaccination and surveillance/containment in the eradication of smallpox. *Current Topics in Microbiology and Immunology, 304*, 17–29.

Lange, B., Flynn, S. & Rizzo, A. (2009). Initial usability assessment of off-the-shelf video game consoles for clinical game-based motor rehabilitation. *Physical Therapy Reviews, 14,* 355–362.

Lantz, P.M., Janz, N.K., Fagerlin, A. et al. (2005). Satisfaction with surgery outcomes and the decision process in a population-based sample of women with breast cancer. *Health Services Research, 40,* 745–768.

Larkin, J., Chiarion-Sileni, V., Gonzalez, R. et al. (2015). Combined nivolumab and ipilimumab or monotherapy in untreated melanoma. *New England Journal of Medicine, 373,* 23–34.

Larson, H.J., Schulz, W.S., Tucker, J.D. & Smith, D.M. (2015). Measuring vaccine confidence: introducing a global vaccine confidence index. *PLoS Currents, 7.*

Larson, N.C., Barger, S.D. & Sydeman, S.J. (2013). Type D personality is not associated with coronary heart disease risk in a North American sample of retirement-aged adults. *International Journal of Behavioral Medicine, 20,* 277–285.

Lashinger, L.M., Rossi, E.L. & Hursting, S.D. (2014). Obesity and resistance to cancer chemotherapy: interacting roles of inflammation and metabolic dysregulation. *Clinical Pharmacology & Therapeutics, 96,* 458–463.

Latt, N.C., Jurd, S., Houseman, J. & Wutzke, S.E. (2002). Naltrexone in alcohol dependence: a randomised controlled trial of effectiveness in a standard clinical setting. *Medical Journal of Australia, 176,* 530–534.

Laurin, C., Moullec, G., Bacon, S.L. & Lavoie, K.L. (2012). Impact of anxiety and depression on chronic obstructive pulmonary disease exacerbation risk. *American Journal of Respiratory and Critical Care Medicine, 185,* 918–923.

Law, M. & Wald, N. (1999). Why heart disease mortality is low in France: the time lag explanation. *BMJ: British Medical Journal, 318,* 1471–1480.

Lawrence, T.S., Ten Haken, R.K. & Giaccia, A. (2008). Principles of radiation oncology. In V.T. DeVita Jr., T.S. Lawrence & S.A. Rosenberg (Eds.), *Cancer: principles and practice of oncology* (8th ed.). Philadelphia, PA: Lippincott Williams and Wilkins.

Laxy, M., Mielck, A., Hunger, M. et al. (2014). The association between patient-reported self-management behavior, intermediate clinical outcomes, and mortality in patients with Type 2 Diabetes: results from the KORA-A Study. *Diabetes Care, 37,* 1604–1612.

Lazarus, R.S. & Folkman, S. (1984). *Stress, Appraisal, and Coping.* New York: Springer.

Le, D., Holt, C.L., Pisu, M. et al. (2014). The role of social support in posttreatment surveillance among African American survivors of colorectal cancer. *Journal of Psychosocial Oncology, 32,* 245–263.

Leary, M.C. & Saver, J.L. (2003). Annual incidence of first silent stroke in the United States: a preliminary estimate. *Cerebrovascular Diseases, 16,* 280–285.

LeBlanc, M., Merette, C., Savard, J. et al. (2009). Incidence and risk factors of insomnia in a population-based sample. *Sleep, 32,* 1027–1037.

LeDoux, J.E. (2000). Emotion circuits in the brain. *Annual Review of Neuroscience, 23,* 155–184.

Lee, H.H., Choi, Y.Y. & Choi, M.G. (2014). The efficacy of hypnotherapy in the treatment of irritable bowel syndrome: a systematic review and meta-analysis. *Journal of Neurogastroenterology and Motility, 20,* 152–162.

Lee, J.Y. & Jeon, B.S. (2014). Maladaptive reward-learning and impulse control disorders in patients with Parkinson's disease: a clinical overview and pathophysiology update. *Journal of Movement Disorders, 7,* 67–76.

Lee, P.R., Brady, D.L., Shapiro, R.A. et al. (2007). Prenatal stress generates deficits in rat social behavior: reversal by oxytocin. *Brain Research, 1156,* 152–167.

Lee, Y. & Davis, M. (1997). Role of the hippocampus, the bed nucleus of the stria terminalis, and the amygdala in the excitatory effect of corticotropin-releasing hormone on the acoustic startle reflex. *Journal of Neuroscience, 17,* 6434–6446.

Lee, Y.L., Gau, B.S., Hsu, W.M. & Chang, H.H. (2009). A model linking uncertainty, post-traumatic stress, and health behaviors in childhood cancer survivors. *Oncology Nursing Forum, 36,* 20–30.

Leggio, L., Garbutt, J.C. & Addolorato, G. (2010). Effectiveness and safety of baclofen in the treatment of alcohol dependent patients. *CNS & Neurological Disorders Drug Targets, 9,* 33–44.

Leggio, L., Zywiak, W.H., Fricchione, S.R. et al. (2014). Intravenous ghrelin administration increases alcohol craving in alcohol-dependent heavy drinkers: a preliminary investigation. *Biological Psychiatry, 76,* 734–741.

Lehrer, P., Feldman, J., Giardino, N. et al. (2002). Psychological aspects of asthma. *Journal of Consulting and Clinical Psychology, 70,* 691.

Lehrer, P.M., Vaschillo, E., Vaschillo, B. et al. (2004). Biofeedback treatment for asthma. *Chest, 126,* 352–361.

Lemos, J.C., Wanat, M.J., Smith, J.S. et al. (2012). Severe stress switches CRF action in the nucleus accumbens from appetitive to aversive. *Nature, 490,* 402–406.

Lemstra, M.E., Alsabbagh, W., Rajakumar, R.J. et al. (2013). Neighbourhood income and cardiac rehabilitation access as determinants of nonattendance and noncompletion. *Canadian Journal of Cardiology, 29,* 1599–1603.

Lennerz, B.S., Alsop, D.C., Holsen, L.M. et al. (2013). Effects of dietary glycemic index on brain regions related to reward and craving in men. *The American Journal of Clinical Nutrition, 98,* 641–647.

Leone, V.A., Cham, C.M. & Chang, E.B. (2014). Diet, gut microbes, and genetics in immune function: can we leverage our current knowledge to achieve better outcomes in inflammatory bowel diseases? *Current Opinion in Immunology, 31,* 16–23.

Lerner, C.A., Sundar, I.K., Yao, H. et al. (2015). Vapors produced by electronic cigarettes and e-juices with flavorings induce toxicity, oxidative stress, and inflammatory response in lung epithelial cells and in mouse lung. *PLoS One, 10,* e0116732.

Levenson, J.L. (2006). *Essentials of Psychosomatic Medicine.* Washington, DC: American Psychiatric Publishing.

Leventhal, H., Nerenz, D.R. & Steele, D.J. (1984). Illness representations and coping with health threats. In A. Baum, S.E. Taylor & J.E. Singer (Eds.), *Handbook of Psychology and Health, Volume IV: Social psychological aspects of health* (pp. 219–252). Hillsdale, NJ: Lawrence Erlbaum Associates.

Levine, G.N., Allen, K., Braun, L.T. et al. (2013). Pet ownership and cardiovascular risk: a scientific statement from the American Heart Association. *Circulation, 127,* 2353–2363.

Levkovich, I., Cohen, M., Pollack, S. et al. (2014). Cancer-related fatigue and depression in breast cancer patients postchemotherapy: different associations with optimism and stress appraisals. *Palliative and Supportive Care, 13,* 1141–1151.

Leys, D., Hénon, H., Mackowiak-Cordoliani, M.A. & Pasquier, F. (2005). Poststroke dementia. *The Lancet Neurology, 4,* 752–759.

Li, D., Mabrouk, O.S., Liu, T. et al. (2015). Asphyxia-activated corticocardiac signaling accelerates onset of cardiac arrest. *Proceedings of the National Academy of Sciences, 112,* E2073–E2082.

Li, H.W. & Sykes, M. (2012). Emerging concepts in haematopoietic cell transplantation. *Nature Reviews Immunology, 12,* 403–416.

Li, J., Jarczok, M.N., Loerbroks, A. et al. (2013). Work stress is associated with diabetes and prediabetes: cross-sectional results from the MIPH Industrial Cohort Studies. *International Journal of Behavioral Medicine, 20,* 495–503.

Li, J., Olsen, J., Vestergaard, M. et al. (2012). Prenatal exposure to bereavement and type-2 diabetes: a Danish longitudinal population based study. *PloS one, 7,* e43508.

Li, J., Zhang, J.H., Yi, T. et al. (2014). Acupuncture treatment of chronic low back pain reverses an abnormal brain default mode network in correlation with clinical pain relief. *Acupuncture in Medicine, 32,* 102–108.

Li, P., Bandyopadhyay, G., Lagakos, W.S. et al. (2015). LTB4 promotes insulin resistance in obese mice by acting on macrophages, hepatocytes and myocytes. *Nature Medicine, 21,* 239–247.

Liao, G.Y., An, J.J., Gharami, K. et al. (2012). Dendritically targeted Bdnf mRNA is essential for energy balance and response to leptin. *Nature Medicine, 18,* 564–571.

Liao, J., Chang, C., Wu, H. & Lu, Q. (2015). Cell-based therapies for systemic lupus erythematosus. *Autoimmunity Reviews, 14,* 43–48.

Libby, P. & Theroux, P. (2005). Pathophysiology of coronary artery disease. *Circulation, 111,* 3481–3488.

Lichtman, J.H., Froelicher, E.S., Blumenthal, J.A. et al. (2014). Depression as a risk factor for poor prognosis among patients with acute coronary syndrome: systematic review and recommendations. A scientific statement from the American Heart Association. *Circulation, 129,* 1350–1369.

Lichtman, J.H., Leifheit-Limson, E.C., Watanabe, E. et al. (2015). Symptom recognition and healthcare experiences of young women with acute myocardial infarction. *Circulation: Cardiovascular Quality and Outcome, 8,* S31–S38.

Lidstone, S.C. & Stoessl, A.J. (2007). Understanding the placebo effect: contributions from neuro-imaging. *Molecular Imaging and Biology*, *9*, 176–185.

Liebsch, G., Landgraf, R., Engelmann, M. et al. (1999). Differential behavioural effects of chronic infusion of CRH 1 and CRH 2 receptor antisense oligonucleotides into the rat brain. *Journal of Psychiatric Research*, *33*, 153–163.

Ligibel, J.A., Alfano, C.M., Courneva, K.S. et al. (2014). American Society of Clinical Oncology position statement on obesity and cancer. *Journal of Clinical Oncology*, *32*, 3568–3574.

Lilienfeld, S.O. (2014). The Research Domain Criteria (RDoC): an analysis of methodological and conceptual challenges. *Behaviour Research and Therapy*, *62*, 129–139.

Lillycrop, K.A. (2011). Effect of maternal diet on the epigenome: implications for human metabolic disease. *Proceedings of the Nutrition Society*, *70*, 64–72.

Lim, C. & Alexander, M.P. (2009). Stroke and episodic memory disorders. *Neuropsychologia*, *47*, 3045–3058.

Lim, H.W., Kang, S.G., Ryu, J.K. et al. (2015). SIRT1 deacetylates RORγt and enhances Th17 cell generation. *The Journal of Experimental Medicine*, *212*, 607–617.

Lin, T.K., Man, M.Q., Santiago, J.L. et al. (2014). Paradoxical benefits of psychological stress in inflammatory dermatoses models are glucocorticoid mediated. *Journal of Investigative Dermatology*, *134*, 2890–2897.

Linde, K., Berner, M., Egger, M. & Mulrow, C. (2005). St John's wort for depression. *The British Journal of Psychiatry*, *186*, 99–107.

Lisnevskaia, L., Murphy, G. & Isenberg, D. (2014). Systemic lupus erythematosus. *The Lancet*, *384*, 1878–1888.

Litteljohn, D. & Hayley, S. (2012). Cytokines as potential biomarkers for Parkinson's disease: a multiplex approach. *Methods in Molecular Biology*, *934*, 121–144.

Litteljohn, D., Mangano, E., Clarke, M. et al. (2010). Inflammatory mechanisms of neurodegeneration in toxin-based models of Parkinson's disease. *Parkinson's Disease*, *2011*, 713517.

Liu, Q.S., Pu, L. & Poo, M.M. (2005). Repeated cocaine exposure in vivo facilitates LTP induction in midbrain dopamine neurons. *Nature*, *437*, 1027–1031.

Liu, X. & Weiss, F. (2003). Stimulus conditioned to foot-shock stress reinstates alcohol-seeking behavior in an animal model of relapse. *Psychopharmacology*, *168*, 184–191.

Lleo, A., Battezzati, P.M., Selmi, C. et al. (2008). Is autoimmunity a matter of sex? *Autoimmunity Reviews*, *7*, 626–630.

Lloyd, C.E., Dyer, P.H., Lancashire, R.J. et al. (1999). Association between stress and glycemic control in adults with type 1 (insulin-dependent) diabetes. *Diabetes Care*, *22*, 1278–1283.

Locke, A.E., Kahali, B., Berndt, S.I. et al. (2015). Genetic studies of body mass index yield new insights for obesity biology. *Nature*, *518*, 197–206.

Lockhart, P.B., Bolger, A.F., Papapanou, P.N. et al. (2012). Periodontal disease and atherosclerotic vascular disease: does the evidence support an independent association? A scientific statement from the American Heart Association. *Circulation*, *125*, 2520–2544.

Lockner, J.W., Eubanks, L.M., Choi, J.L. et al. (2015). Flagellin as carrier and adjuvant in cocaine vaccine development. *Molecular Pharmaceutics*, *12*, 653–662.

Loftus, E. (2005). Planting misinformation in the human mind: a 30-year investigation of the malleability of memory. *Learning & Memory*, *12*, 361–366.

Loftus, E.F. & Davis, D. (2006). Recovered memories. *Annual Review of Clinical Psychology*, *2*, 469–498.

Loggia, M.L., Chonde, D.B., Akeju, O. et al. (2015). Evidence for brain glial activation in chronic pain patients. *Brain*, *138*, 604–615.

Lopez-Jimenez, F. & Lavie, C.J. (2014). Hispanics and cardiovascular health and the 'Hispanic paradox': what is known and what needs to be discovered? *Progress in Cardiovascular Diseases*, *57*, 227–229.

Loucks, E.B., Britton, W.B., Howe, C.J. et al. (2015). Positive associations of dispositional mindfulness with cardiovascular health: the New England Family Study. *International Journal of Behavioral Medicine*, *22*, 540–550..

Louis, P., Hold, G.L. & Flint, H.J. (2014). The gut microbiota, bacterial metabolites and colorectal cancer. *Nature Reviews Microbiology*, *12*, 661–672.

Lovell, B. & Wetherell, M.A. (2011). The cost of caregiving: endocrine and immune implications in elderly and non elderly caregivers. *Neuroscience & Biobehavioral Reviews*, *35*, 1342–1352.

Loweth, J.A., Scheyer, A.F., Milovanovic, M. et al. (2014). Synaptic depression via mGluR1 positive allosteric modulation suppresses cue-induced cocaine craving. *Nature Neuroscience*, *17*, 73–80.

Lu, X.T., Zhao, Y.X., Zhang, Y. & Jiang, F. (2013). Psychological stress, vascular inflammation, and atherogenesis: potential roles of circulating cytokines. *Journal of Cardiovascular Pharmacology*, *62*, 6–12.

Luby, J., Belden, A., Botteron, K. et al. (2013). The effects of poverty on childhood brain development: the mediating effect of caregiving and stressful life events. *JAMA Pediatrics*, *167*, 1135–1142.

Lucas, P. (2012). It can't hurt to ask: a patient-centered quality of service assessment of Health Canada's medical cannabis policy and program. *Harm Reduction Journal*, *9*, 2.

Luck, H., Tsai, S., Chung, J. et al. (2015). Regulation of obesity-related insulin resistance with gut anti-inflammatory agents. *Cell Metabolism*, *21*, 527–542.

Ludlow, A.T., Ludlow, L.W. & Roth, S.M. (2013). Do telomeres adapt to physiological stress? Exploring the effect of exercise on telomere length and telomere-related proteins. *BioMed Research International*, 2013: 601368.

Lukaschek, K., Baumert, J., Kruse, J. et al. (2013). Relationship between posttraumatic stress disorder and type 2 diabetes in a population-based cross-sectional study with 2970 participants. *Journal of Psychosomatic Research*, *74*, 340–345.

Luo, Y., Hawkley, L.C., Waite, L.J. & Cacioppo, J.T. (2012). Loneliness, health, and mortality in old age: a national longitudinal study. *Social Science & Medicine*, *74*, 907–914.

Lutgendorf, S.K., Weinrib, A.Z., Penedo, F. et al. (2008). Interleukin-6, cortisol, and depressive symptoms in ovarian cancer patients. *Journal of Clinical Oncology*, *26*, 4820–4827.

Luy, M. (2003). Causes of male excess mortality: insights from cloistered populations. *Population and Development Review*, *29*, 647–676.

Lynch, W.J., Roth, M.E. & Carroll, M.E. (2002). Biological basis of sex differences in drug abuse: preclinical and clinical studies. *Psychopharmacology*, *164*, 121–137.

Macheret, M. & Halazonetis, T.D. (2015). DNA replication stress as a hallmark of cancer. *Annual Review of Pathology*, *10*, 425–448.

Maciejewski, P.K., Zhang, B., Block, S.D. & Prigerson, H.G. (2007). An empirical examination of the stage theory of grief. *JAMA*, *21*, 716–723.

Mackenzie, S., Wiegel, J.R., Mundt, M. et al. (2011). Depression and suicide ideation among students accessing campus health care. *American Journal of Orthopsychiatry*, *81*, 101–107.

Macpherson, H., Pipingas, A. & Pase, M.P. (2013). Multivitamin-multimineral supplementation and mortality: a meta-analysis of randomized controlled trials. *The American Journal of Clinical Nutrition*, *97*, 437–444.

Madsen, M.V., Gøtzsche, P.C. & Hróbjartsson, A. (2009). Acupuncture treatment for pain: systematic review of randomised clinical trials with acupuncture, placebo acupuncture, and no acupuncture groups. *British Medical Journal*, *338*, a3115.

Madva, E.N. & Granstein, R.D. (2013). Nerve-derived transmitters including peptides influence cutaneous immunology. *Brain, Behavior, and Immunity*, *34*, 1–10.

Maes, M., Van Bockstaele, D.R., Gastel, A. et al. (1999). The effects of psychological stress on leukocyte subset distribution in humans: evidence of immune activation. *Neuropsychobiology*, *39*, 1–9.

Maglione, M.A., Das, L., Raaen, L. et al. (2014). Safety of vaccines used for routine immunization of US children: a systematic review. *Pediatrics*, *134*, 325–337.

Magnusson, J.P., Göritz, C., Tatarishvili, J. et al. (2014). A latent neurogenic program in astrocytes regulated by Notch signaling in the mouse. *Science*, *346*, 237–241.

Maguire, J. & Mody, I. (2007). Neurosteroid synthesis-mediated regulation of GABA(A) receptors: relevance to the ovarian cycle and stress. *Journal of Neuroscience*, *27*, 2155–2162.

Maianti, J.P., McFedries, A., Foda, Z.H. et al. (2014). Anti-diabetic activity of insulin-degrading enzyme inhibitors mediated by multiple hormones. *Nature*, *511*, 94–98.

Maier, S.F. (2001). Exposure to the stressor environment prevents the temporal dissipation of behavioral depression/learned helplessness. *Biological Psychiatry*, *49*, 763–773.

Maier, S.F. & Seligman, M.E.P. (1976). Learned helplessness: theory and evidence. *Journal of Experimental Psychology: General*, *105*, 3–46.

Maier, S.F. & Watkins, L.R. (1998). Cytokines for psychologists: implications of bidirectional immune-to-brain communication for understanding behavior, mood, and cognition. *Psychological Review*, *105*, 83–107.

Maier, S.F. & Watkins, L.R. (2005). Stressor controllability and learned helplessness: the roles of the dorsal raphe nucleus, serotonin, and corticotropin-releasing factor. *Neuroscience & Biobehavioral Reviews*, *29*, 829–841.

Makin, T.R., Scholz, J., Filippini, N. et al. (2013). Phantom pain is associated with preserved structure and function in the former hand area. *Nature Communications*, *4*, 1570.

Maksimovic, J.M., Vlajinac, H.D., Pejovic, B.D., et al. (2014). Stressful life events and type 2 diabetes. *Acta Clinica Belgica*, *69*, 273–276.

Malhotra, V. & Perry, M.C. (2003). Classical chemotherapy: mechanisms, toxicities and the therapeutc window. *Cancer Biology & Therapy*, *2*, S2–S4.

Mancini, A.D., Griffin, P. & Bonanno, G.A. (2012). Recent trends in the treatment of prolonged grief. *Current Opinion in Psychiatry*, *25*, 46–51.

Mandelblatt, J.S., Cronin, K.A., Bailey, S. et al. (2009). Effects of mammography screening under different screening schedules: model estimates of potential benefits and harms. *Annals of Internal Medicine*, *151*, 738–747.

Mander, B.A., Marks, S.M., Vogel, J.W. et al. (2015). β-amyloid disrupts human NREM slow waves and related hippocampus-dependent memory consolidation. *Nature Neuroscience*. [Epub ahead of print]

Manikkam, M., Haque, M.M., Guerrero-Bosagna, C. et al. (2014). Pesticide methoxychlor promotes the epigenetic transgenerational inheritance of adult-onset disease through the female germline. *PLoS One*, *9*, e102091.

Mann, T., Tomiyama, A.J., Westling, E. et al. (2007). Medicare's search for effective obesity treatments: diets are not the answer. *American Psychologist*, *62*, 220.

Mannes, A.E. & Moore, D.A. (2013). A behavioral demonstration of overconfidence in judgment. *Psychological Science*, *24*, 1190–1197.

Mansour, A.R., Baliki, M.N., Huang, L. et al. (2013). Brain white matter structural properties predict transition to chronic pain. *Pain*, *154*, 2160–2168.

Mantovani, A., Allavena, P., Sica, A. & Balkwill, F. (2008). Cancer-related inflammation. *Nature*, *454*, 436–444.

Maragakis, L.L. (2010). Recognition and prevention of multidrug-resistant Gram-negative bacteria in the intensive care unit. *Critical Care Medicine*, *38*, S345–S351.

Marfil-Álvarez, R., Mesam, F., Arrebola-Morenom, A. et al. (2014). Acute myocardial infarct size is related to periodontitis extent and severity. *Journal of Dental Research*, *93*, 993–998.

Maric, T., Tobin, S., Quinn, T. & Shalev, U. (2008). Food deprivation-like effects of neuropeptide Y on heroin self-administration and reinstatement of heroin seeking in rats. *Behavioural Brain Research*, *194*, 39–43.

Marinho, R.T. & Barreira, D.P. (2013). Hepatitis C, stigma and cure. *World Journal of Gastroenterology*, *19*, 6703–6709.

Marini, S., Buonanno, G., Stabile, L. & Ficco, G. (2014). Short-term effects of electronic and tobacco cigarettes on exhaled nitric oxide. *Toxicology and Applied Pharmacology*, *278*, 9–15.

Markle, J.G., Frank, D.N., Mortin-Toth, S. et al. (2013). Sex differences in the gut microbiome drive hormone-dependent regulation of autoimmunity. *Science*, *339*, 1084–1088.

Markowitz, L.E., Dunne, E.F., Saraiya, M. et al. (2007). Cervical cancer screening among vaccinated females. quadrivalent human papillomavirus vaccine: recommendations of the advisory committee on immunization practices (ACIP). *Morbidity and Mortality Weekly Report*, *56*, 1–24.

Marmot, M.G., Rose, G., Shipley, M. & Hamilton, P.J. (1978). Employment grade and coronary heart disease in British civil servants. *Journal of Epidemiology and Community Health*, *32*, 244–249.

Marrocco, J., Reynaert, M.L., Gatta, E. et al. (2014). The effects of antidepressant treatment in prenatally stressed rats support the glutamatergic hypothesis of stress-related disorders. *Journal of Neuroscience, 34,* 2015–2024.

Marshall, B.J. (1990). Campylobacter pylori: its link to gastritis and peptic ulcer disease. *Review of Infectious Diseases, 12,* S87–S93.

Martin, L.J., Tuttle, A.H. & Mogil, J.S. (2014). The interaction between pain and social behavior in humans and rodents. *Current Topics in Behavioral Neurosciences, 20,* 233–250.

Martin, S., Calabrese, S.K., Wolters, P.L. et al. (2012). Family functioning and coping styles in families of children with cancer and HIV disease. *Clinical Pediatrics, 51,* 58–64.

Martinowich, K. & Lu, B. (2008). Interaction between BDNF and serotonin: role in mood disorders. *Neuropsychopharmacology, 33,* 73–83.

Martins, R.C., Andersen, M.L. & Tufik S. (2008). The reciprocal interaction between sleep and type 2 diabetes mellitus: facts and perspectives. *Brazilian Journal of Medical Biological Research, 41,*180–187.

Massart, R., Barnea, R., Dikshtein, Y. et al. (2015). Role of DNA methylation in the nucleus accumbens in incubation of cocaine craving. *Journal of Neuroscience, 35,* 8042–8058.

Masten, C.L., Eisenberger, N.I., Borofsky, L.A. et al. (2009). Neural correlates of social exclusion during adolescence: understanding the distress of peer rejection. *Social Cognition and Affective Neuroscience, 4,* 143–157.

Masten, C.L., Telzer, E.H., Fuligni, A.J. et al. (2012). Time spent with friends in adolescence relates to less neural sensitivity to later peer rejection. *Cognition and Affective Neuroscience, 7,* 106–114.

Mastorci, F., Vicentini, M., Viltart, O. et al. (2009). Long-term effects of prenatal stress: changes in adult cardiovascular regulation and sensitivity to stress. *Neuroscience & Biobehavioral Reviews, 33,* 191–203.

Matarazzo, J.D. (1980). Behavioral health and behavioral medicine: frontiers for a new health psychology. *American Psychologist, 35,* 807–817.

Matchim, Y., Armer, J.M. & Stewart, B.R. (2010). Effects of mindfulness-based stress reduction (MBSR) on health among breast cancer survivors. *Western Journal of Nursing Research, 33,* 996–1016.

Mathers, C.D. & Loncar, D. (2006). Projections of global mortality and burden of disease from 2002 to 2030. *PLoS Medicine, 3,* e442.

Matheson, K. & Anisman, H. (2003). Systems of coping associated with dysphoria, anxiety and depressive illness: a multivariate profile perspective. *Stress, 6,* 223–234.

Matheson, K. & Anisman, H. (2012). Biological and psychosocial responses to discrimination. In J. Jetten, C. Haslam, & S.A. Haslam (Eds.), *The Social Cure* (pp. 133–154). New York: Psychology Press.

Matheson, K., Skomorovsky, A., Fiocco, A. & Anisman, H. (2007). The limits of 'adaptive' coping: well-being and affective reactions to stressors among women in abusive dating relationships. *Stress, 10,* 75–92.

Mattick, R.P., Breen, C., Kimber, J. & Davoli, M. (2003). Methadone maintenance therapy versus no opioid replacement therapy for opioid dependence. *Cochrane Database of Systematic Reviews,* CD002209.

Maude, S.L., Frey, N., Shaw, P.A. et al. (2014). Chimeric antigen receptor T cells for sustained remissions in leukemia. *New England Journal of Medicine, 371,* 1507–1517.

Mavrides, N. & Nemeroff, C. (2013). Treatment of depression in cardiovascular disease. *Depression and Anxiety, 30,* 328–341.

Maxwell, T.D., Gatchel, R.J. & Mayer, T.G. (1998). Cognitive predictors of depression in chronic low back pain: toward an inclusive model. *Journal of Behavioral Medicine, 21,* 131–143.

May, R.W., Sanchez-Gonzalez, M.A., Hawkins, K.A. et al. (2014). Effect of anger and trait forgiveness on cardiovascular risk in young adult females. *The American Journal of Cardiology, 114,* 47–52.

Mayo Clinic (2013). Cancer treatment decisions: 5 steps to help you decide. www.mayoclinic.org/diseases-conditions/cancer/in-depth/cancer-treatment/art-20047350?linkId=14804359&pg=1 (accessed March, 2015).

Maze, I., & Nestler, E. J. (2011). The epigenetic landscape of addiction. *Annals of the New York Academy of Sciences, 1216,* 99–113.

Maze, I., Covington, H.E., Dietz, D.M. et al. (2010). Essential role of the histone methyltransferase G9a in cocaine-induced plasticity. *Science, 327,* 213–216.

Mazure, C.M., Bruce, M.L., Maciejewski, P.K. & Jacobs, S.C. (2000). Adverse life events and cognitive-personality characteristics in the prediction of major depression and antidepressant response. *American Journal of Psychiatry, 157*, 896–903.

McArdle, W.D., Katch, F.I. & Katch, V.L. (2006). *Essentials of Exercise Physiology.* Philadelphia, PA: Lippincott Williams & Wilkins.

McAuley, P.A., Artero, E.G., Sui, X. et al. (2012). The obesity paradox, cardiorespiratory fitness, and coronary heart disease. *Mayo Clinic Proceedings, 87*, 443–451.

McCabe, P.J. & Barnason, S.A. (2012). Illness perceptions, coping strategies, and symptoms contribute to psychological distress in patients with recurrent symptomatic atrial fibrillation. *Journal of Cardiovascular Nursing, 27*, 431–444.

McCarthy, M.I. (2010). Genomics, type 2 diabetes, and obesity. *New England Journal of Medicine, 363*, 2339–2350.

McClelland, L.E. & McCubbin, J.A. (2008). Social influence and pain response in women and men. *Journal of Behavioral Medicine, 31*, 413–420.

McCormick, C.M., Thomas, C.M., Sheridan, C.S. et al. (2011). Social instability stress in adolescent male rats alters hippocampal neurogenesis and produces deficits in spatial location memory in adulthood. *Hippocampus, 22*, 1300–1312.

McCoy, J.G. & Strecker, R.E. (2011). The cognitive cost of sleep lost. *Neurobiology of Learning and Memory, 96*, 564–582.

McEachern, E.K., Hwang, J.H., Sladewski, K.M. et al. (2015). Analysis of the effects of cigarette smoke on staphylococcal virulence phenotypes. *Infection and Immunity, 83*, 2443–52.

McEwen, B.S. (2000). Allostasis and allostatic load: implications for neuropsychopharmacology. *Neuropsychopharmacology, 22*, 108–124.

McEwen, B.S. (2007). Physiology and neurobiology of stress and adaptation: central role of the brain. *Physiological Reviews, 87*, 873–904.

McEwen, B.S. & Gianaros, P.J. (2011). Stress- and allostasis-induced brain plasticity. *Annual Review of Medicine, 62*, 431–445.

McEwen, B.S. & Morrison, J.H. (2013). The brain on stress: vulnerability and plasticity of the prefrontal cortex over the life course. *Neuron, 79*, 6–29.

McEwen, B.S. & Wingfield, J.C. (2003). The concept of allostasis in biology and biomedicine. *Hormones and Behavior, 43*, 2–15.

McFarlin, B.K., Flynn, M.G., Phillips, M.D. et al. (2005). Chronic resistance exercise training improves natural killer cell activity in older women. *The Journals of Gerontology Series A: Biological Sciences and Medical Sciences, 60*, 1315–1318.

McGonagle, K.A. & Kessler, R.C. (1990). Chronic stress, acute stress, and depressive symptoms. *American Journal of Community Psychology, 18*, 681–706.

McGowan, P.O. & Szyf, M. (2010). The epigenetics of social adversity in early life: implications for mental health outcomes. *Neurobiology of Disease, 39*, 66–72.

McGrath, M.F., de Bold, M.L. & de Bold, A.J. (2005). The endocrine function of the heart. *Trends in Endocrinology and Metabolism, 16*, 469–477.

McGrath, P.J., Johnson, G., Goodman, J.T. et al. (1985). CHEOPS: a behavioral scale for rating postoperative pain in children. In H.L. Fields, R. Dubner & F. Cervero (Eds.), *Advances in Pain Research and Therapy* (pp. 395–402). New York: Raven Press.

McGregor, B.A. & Antoni, M.H. (2009). Psychological intervention and health outcomes among women treated for breast cancer: a review of stress pathways and biological mediators. *Brain, Behavior, and Immunity, 23*, 159–166.

McInnes, I.B. & Schett, G. (2007). Cytokines in the pathogenesis of rheumatoid arthritis. *Nature Reviews Immunology, 7*, 429–442.

McInnis, O.A., Matheson, K. & Anisman, H. (2014). Living with the unexplained: coping, distress, and depression among women with chronic fatigue syndrome (CFS) and/or fibromyalgia compared to an autoimmune disorder. *Anxiety, Stress, and Coping, 27*, 601–618.

McInnis, O.A., McQuaid, R.J., Bombay, A. et al. (2015). Finding benefit in stressful uncertain circumstances: relations to social support and stigma among women with unexplained illnesses. *Stress, 18*, 169–177.

McKeigue, P.M., Shah, B. & Marmot, M.G. (1991). Relation of central obesity and insulin resistance with high diabetes prevalence and cardiovascular risk in South Asians. *The Lancet, 337*, 382–386.

McLennon, S.M., Habermann, B. & Rice, M. (2011). Finding meaning as a mediator of burden on the health of caregivers of spouses with dementia. *Aging & Mental Health*, *15*, 522–530.

McNaughton, C.D., Cawthon, C., Kripalani, S. et al. (2015). Health literacy and mortality: a cohort study of patients hospitalized for acute heart failure. *Journal of the American Heart Association*, *4*, e001799.

McNelis, J.C. & Olefsky, J.M. (2014). Macrophages, immunity, and metabolic disease. *Immunity*, *41*, 36–48.

McQuaid, R.J., McInnis, O.A., Abizaid, A. & Anisman, H. (2014). Making room for oxytocin in understanding depression. *Neuroscience & Biobehavioral Reviews*, *45*, 305–322.

McQuaid, R.J., McInnis, O.A., Matheson, K. & Anisman, H. (2015). Distress of ostracism: xytocin receptor gene polymorphism confers sensitivity to social exclusion. *Social Cognitive and Affective Neuroscience*, nsu166. [Epub ahead of print]

McQuaid, R.J., McInnis, O.A., Stead, J.D. et al. (2013). A paradoxical association of an oxytocin receptor gene polymorphism: early-life adversity and vulnerability to depression. *Frontiers in Neuroscience*, *7*, 128.

McSpadden, K. (2015). Bill Gates thinks this is the deadliest threat to humankind. *Time Magazine*, http://time.com/3899414/bill-gates-disease-epidemic-ebola-threat-to-humanity-disaster/ (accessed October, 2015).

Meara, E.R, Richards, S. & Cutler, D.M. (2008). The gap gets bigger: changes in mortality and life expectancy, by education, 1981–2000. *Health Affairs (Millwood)*, *27*, 350–360.

Medzhitov, R. (2007). Recognition of microorganisms and activation of the immune response. *Nature*, *449*, 819–826.

Meeus, M., Nijs, J., Vanderheiden, T. et al. (2015). The effect of relaxation therapy on autonomic functioning, symptoms and daily functioning, in patients with chronic fatigue syndrome or fibromyalgia: a systematic review. *Clinical Rehabilitation*, *29*, 221–233.

Mehta, D., Klengel, T., Conneely, K.N. et al. (2013). Childhood maltreatment is associated with distinct genomic and epigenetic profiles in posttraumatic stress disorder. *Proceedings of the National Academy of Sciences*, *110*, 8302–8307.

Mehtsun, W.T., Ibrahim, A.M., Diener-West, M. et al. (2013). Surgical never events in the United States. *Surgery*, *153*, 465–472.

Meichenbaum, D. (1977). *Cognitive-Behavior Modification: an integrative approach*. New York: Springer.

Meichenbaum, D. & Cameron, R. (1974). The clinical potential of modifying what clients say to themselves. *Psychotherapy: Theory, Research & Practice*, *11*, 103.

Meier, D.E., Emmons, C.A., Wallenstein, S. et al. (1998). A national survey of physician-assisted suicide and euthanasia in the United States. *New England Journal of Medicine*, *338*, 1193–1201.

Melamed, B.G. (1995). The interface between physical and mental disorders: the need to dismantle the biopsychosocialneuroimmunological model of disease. *Journal of Clinical Psychology in Medical Settings*, *2*, 225–231.

Melamed, S., Shirom, A., Toker, S. & Shapira, I. (2006). Burnout and risk of type 2 diabetes: a prospective study of apparently healthy employed persons. *Psychosomatic Medicine*, *68*, 863–869.

Melo, S.A., Sugimoto, H., O'Connell, J.T. et al. (2014). Cancer exosomes perform cell-independent microRNA biogenesis and promote tumorigenesis. *Cancer Cell*, *26*, 707–721.

Melzack, R. & Casey, K.L. (1968). Sensory, motivational, and central control determinants of pain. In D.R. Kenshalo (Ed.), *The Skin Senses* (pp. 423–439). Springfield, IL: Charles C. Thomas.

Melzack, R. & Wall, P.D. (1965). Pain mechanisms: a new theory. *Science*, *150*, 971–979.

Melzack, R. & Wall, P.D. (1996). *The Challenge of Pain* (2nd ed.). London: Penguin.

Mendelsohn, A.R. & Larrick, J.W. (2013). Sleep facilitates clearance of metabolites from the brain: glymphatic function in aging and neurodegenerative diseases. *Rejuvenation Research*, *16*, 518–523.

Meneses-Echávez, J.F., González-Jiménez, E. & Ramírez-Vélez, R. (2015). Effects of supervised multimodal exercise interventions on cancer-related fatigue: systematic review and meta-analysis of randomized controlled trials. *BioMed Research International*, 2015: 328636.

Meng, L., Zheng, Y. & Hui, R. (2013). The relationship of sleep duration and insomnia to risk of hypertension incidence: a meta-analysis of prospective cohort studies. *Hypertension Research*, *36*, 985–995.

Mente, A., de Koning, L., Shannon, H.S. & Anand, S.S. (2009). A systematic review of the evidence supporting a causal link between dietary factors and coronary heart disease. *Archives of Internal Medicine*, *169*, 659–669.

Merali, Z., Bédard, T., Andrews, N. et al. (2006). Bombesin receptors as novel anti-anxiety therapeutic target: non-peptide antagonist PD 176252 reduces anxiety and 5-HT release through BB_1 receptor. *Journal of Neuroscience*, *26*, 10387–10396.

Merali, Z., Khan, S., Michaud, D.S. et al. (2004). Does amygdaloid corticotropin-releasing hormone (CRH) mediate anxiety-like behaviors? Dissociation of anxiogenic effects and CRH release. *European Journal of Neuroscience*, *20*, 229–239.

Merali, Z., McIntosh, J., Kent, P. et al. (1998). Aversive and appetitive events evoke the release of corticotropin-releasing hormone and bombesin-like peptides at the central nucleus of the amygdala. *Journal of Neuroscience*, *18*, 4758–4766.

Mergl, R., Henkel, V., Allgaier, A.K. et al. (2011). Are treatment preferences relevant in response to serotonergic antidepressants and cognitive-behavioral therapy in depressed primary care patients? Results from a randomized controlled trial including a patients' choice arm. *Psychotherapy and Psychosomatics*, *80*, 39–47.

Merskey, H. & Bogduk, N. (1994). *Classification of Chronic Pain* (2nd ed.). Seattle, WA: International Association for the Study of Pain.

Merton, R.K. (1936). The unanticipated consequences of purposive social action. *American Sociological Review*, *1*, 894–904.

Meyer, T., Stanske, B., Kochen, M.M. et al. (2010). Elevated serum levels of interleukin-10 and tumor necrosis factor are both associated with vital exhaustion in patients with cardiovascular risk factors. *Psychosomatics*, *51*, 248–256.

Meyer, U. & Feldon, J. (2009). Prenatal exposure to infection: a primary mechanism for abnormal dopaminergic development in schizophrenia. *Psychopharmacology*, *206*, 587–602.

Meyer, U., Nyffeler, M., Schwendener, S. et al. (2008). Relative prenatal and postnatal maternal contributions to schizophrenia-related neurochemical dysfunction after in utero immune challenge. *Neuropsychopharmacology*, *33*, 441–456.

Meyers, J.L., Salvatore, J.E., Vuoksimaa, E. et al. (2014). Genetic influences on alcohol use behaviors have diverging developmental trajectories: a prospective study among male and female twins. *Alcoholism: Clinical and Experimental Research*, *38*, 2869–2877.

Michaud, K., Matheson, K., Kelly, O. & Anisman, H. (2008). Impact of stressors in a natural context on release of cortisol in healthy adult humans: a meta-analysis. *Stress*, *11*, 177–197.

Miller, A.H., Jones, J.F., Drake, D.F. et al. (2014). Decreased basal ganglia activation in subjects with chronic fatigue syndrome: association with symptoms of fatigue. *PLoS One*, *9*, e98156.

Miller, A.H., Maletic, V. & Raison, C.L. (2009). Inflammation and its discontents: the role of cytokines in the pathophysiology of major depression. *Biological Psychiatry*, *65*, 732–741.

Miller, G.E., Chen, E. & Parker, K.J. (2011). Psychological stress in childhood and susceptibility to the chronic diseases of aging: moving toward a model of behavioral and biological mechanisms. *Psychological Bulletin*, *137*, 959–997.

Miller, G.E., Cohen, S. & Ritchey, A.K. (2002). Chronic psychological stress and the regulation of pro-inflammatory cytokines: a glucocorticoid-resistance model. *Health Psychology*, *21*, 531–541.

Miller, L., Bansal, R., Wickramaratne, P. et al. (2014). Neuroanatomical correlates of religiosity and spirituality: a study in adults at high and low familial risk for depression. *JAMA Psychiatry*, *71*, 128–35.

Miller, P.S., Evangelista, L.S., Giger, J.N. et al. (2014). Exhaustion, immuno-inflammation, and pathogen burden after cardiac surgery: an exploratory study. *European Journal of Cardiovascular Nursing*, *13*, 211–220.

Milne, S., Sheeran, P. & Orbell, S. (2000). Prediction and intervention in health-related behavior: a meta-analytic review of protection motivation theory. *Journal of Applied Social Psychology*, *30*, 106–143.

Mina, M.J., Metcalf, C.J., de Swart, R.L. et al. (2015). Vaccines: long-term measles-induced immuno-modulation increases overall childhood infectious disease mortality. *Science*, *348*, 694–699.

Miron, V.E., Boyd, A., Zhao, J.W. et al. (2013). M2 microglia and macrophages drive oligodendrocyte differentiation during CNS remyelination. *Nature Neuroscience*, *16*, 1211–1218.

Mishel, M.H. (1999). Uncertainty in acute illness. *Annual Review of Nursing Research*, *17*, 269–294.

Mishra, S.I., Scherer, R.W., Snyder, C. et al. (2014). Are exercise programs effective for improving health-related quality of life among cancer survivors? A systematic review and meta-analysis. *Oncology Nursing Forum*, *41*, E326–E342.

Mitchell, A.J., Chan, M., Bhatti, H. et al. (2011). Prevalence of depression, anxiety, and adjustment disorder in oncological, haematological, and palliative-care settings: a meta-analysis of 94 interview-based studies. *The Lancet Oncology*, *12*, 160–174.

Moayedi, M. & Davis, K.D. (2013). Theories of pain: from specificity to gate control. *Journal of Neurophysiology*, *109*, 5–12.

Mohr, D.C., Goodkin, D.E., Nelson, S. et al. (2002). Moderating effects of coping on the relationship between stress and the development of new brain lesions in multiple sclerosis. *Psychosomatic Medicine*, *64*, 803–809.

Mohr, D.C., Hart, S.L., Julian, L. et al. (2004). Association between stressful life events and exacerbation in multiple sclerosis: a meta-analysis. *British Medical Journal*, *328*, 731.

Mohr, S.B., Garland, C.F., Gorham, E.D. & Garland, F.C. (2008). The association between ultraviolet B irradiance, vitamin D status and incidence rates of type 1 diabetes in 51 regions worldwide. *Diabetologia*, *51*, 1391–1398.

Moisan, A., Lee, Y.K., Zhang, J.D. et al. (2015). White-to-brown metabolic conversion of human adipocytes by JAK inhibition. *Nature Cell Biology*, *17*, 57–67.

Molina, Y., Choi, S.W., Cella, D. & Rao, D. (2013). The stigma scale for chronic illnesses 8-item version (SSCI-8): development, validation and use across neurological conditions. *International Journal of Behavioral Medicine*, *20*, 450–460.

Mollace, V., Muscoli, C., Palma, E. et al. (2001). Central cardiovascular responses induced by interleukin 1 beta and tumor necrosis factor alpha infused into nucleus tractus solitarii, nucleus parabrachialis medialis and third cerebral ventricle of normotensive rats. *Neuroscience Letters*, *314*, 53–56.

Molloy, G.J., Perkins-Porras, L., Strike, P.C. & Steptoe, A. (2008). Type-D personality and cortisol in survivors of acute coronary syndrome. *Psychosomatic Medicine*, *70*, 863–868.

Moloney, R.D., Desbonnet, L., Clarke, G. et al. (2014). The microbiome: stress, health and disease. *Mammalian Genome*, *25*, 49–74.

Mols, F., Haslam, S.A., Jetten, J. & Steffens, N.K. (2014). Why a nudge is not enough: a social identity critique of governance by stealth. *European Journal of Political Research*, *54*, 81–98.

Molteni, R. et al. (2001). Modulation of fibroblast growth factor-2 by stress and corticosteroids: from developmental events to adult brain plasticity. *Brain Research Reviews*, *37*, 249–258.

Monroe, S.M. & Harkness, K.L. (2005). Life stress, the 'kindling' hypothesis, and the recurrence of depression: considerations from a life stress perspective. *Psychological Review*, *112*, 417–445.

Montazeri, A., Tavoli, A., Mohagheghi, M.A. et al. (2009). Disclosure of cancer diagnosis and quality of life in cancer patients: should it be the same everywhere? *BMC Cancer*, *9*, 39.

Montgomery, G.H., David, D., Goldfarb, A.B. et al. (2003). Sources of anticipatory distress among breast surgery patients. *Journal of Behavioral Medicine*, *26*, 153–164.

Moody, T.W. & Merali, Z. (2004). Bombesin-like peptides and associated receptors within the brain: distribution and behavioral implications. *Peptides*, *25*, 511–520.

Moore, T.J., Alsabeeh, N., Apovian, C.M. et al. (2008). Weight, blood pressure, and dietary benefits after 12 months of a web-based nutrition education program (DASH for health): longitudinal observational study. *Journal of Medical Internet Research*, *10*, e52.

Moore, T.R. (2010). Fetal exposure to gestational diabetes contributes to subsequent adult metabolic syndrome. *American Journal of Obstetrics and Gynecology*, *202*, 643–649.

Moos, R.H. (1981). *Work Environment Scale Manual*. Palo Alto, CA: Consulting Psychologists Press.

Moos, R.H. & Moos, B.S. (1981). *Family Environment Scale Manual*. Palo Alto, CA: Consulting Psychologists Press.

Moran, C., Phan, T.G., Chen, J. et al. (2013). Brain atrophy in type 2 diabetes: regional distribution and influence on cognition. *Diabetes Care*, *36*, 4036–4042.

Moreno-Smith, M., Lutgendorf, S.K. & Sood, A.K. (2010). Impact of stress on cancer metastasis. *Future Oncology*, *6*, 1863–1881.

Moretti, S., Castelli, M., Franchi, S. et al. (2014). Δ9-Tetrahydrocannabinol-induced anti-inflammatory responses in adolescent mice switch to proinflammatory in adulthood. *Journal of Leukocyte Biology*, *96*, 523–534.

Morgenstern, M., Wang, J., Beatty, N. et al. (2014). Obstructive sleep apnea: an unexpected cause of insulin resistance and diabetes. *Endocrinology and Metabolism Clinics of North America*, *43*, 187–204.

Morral, A.R., McCaffrey, D. & Iguchi, M.Y. (2000). Hardcore drug users claim to be occasional users: drug use frequency underreporting. *Drug and Alcohol Dependence*, *57*, 193–202.

Morris, G., Berk, M., Galecki, P. & Maes, M. (2014). The emerging role of autoimmunity in myalgic encephalomyelitis/chronic fatigue syndrome (ME/cfs). *Molecular Neurobiology*, *49*, 741–756.

Morton, D.L., El-Deredy, W. & Jones, A.K. (2014). Placebo analgesia: cognition or perception. *Handbook of Experimental Pharmacology*, *225*, 71–80.

Moseley, G.L. & Brugger, P. (2009). Interdependence of movement and anatomy persists when amputees learn a physiologically impossible movement of their phantom limb. *Proceedings of the National Academy of Sciences*, *106*, 18798–18802.

Moser, J.S., Hartwig, R., Moran, T.P. et al. (2014). Neural markers of positive reappraisal and their associations with trait reappraisal and worry. *Journal of Abnormal Psychology*, *123*, 91–105.

Mosli, M.H., Sandborn, W.J., Kim, R.B. et al. (2014). Toward a personalized medicine approach to the management of inflammatory bowel disease. *The American Journal of Gastroenterology*, *109*, 994–1004.

Moynihan, R., Henry, D. & Moons, K.G. (2014). Using evidence to combat overdiagnosis and overtreatment: evaluating treatments, tests, and disease definitions in the time of too much. *PLoS Medicine*, *11*, e1001655.

Mraz, M. & Haluzik, M. (2014). The role of adipose tissue immune cells in obesity and low-grade inflammation. *Journal of Endocrinology*, *222*, R113–R127.

Mukherjee, S. (2010). *The Emperor of All Maladies: a biography of cancer*. New York: Simon & Schuster.

Mukhopadhya, I., Hansen, R., El-Omar, E.M. & Hold, G.L. (2012). IBD: what role do proteobacteria play? *Nature Reviews Gastroenterology & Hepatology*, *9*, 219–230.

Mulick, J.A. (2006). Positive behavior support and applied behavior analysis. *The Behavior Analyst*, *29*, 51–74.

Müller, C.P. & Homberg, J.R. (2015). The role of serotonin in drug use and addiction. *Behavioural Brain Research*, *277*, 146–192.

Muller, M.B., Zimmermann, S., Sillaber, I. et al. (2003). Limbic corticotropin-releasing hormone receptor 1 mediates anxiety-related behavior and hormonal adaptation to stress. *Nature Neuroscience*, *6*, 1100–1107.

Mulley, A.G., Trimble, C. & Elwyn, G. (2012). Stop the silent misdiagnosis: patients' preferences matter. *BMJ: British Medical Journal*, *345*, e6572.

Mullish, B.H., Kabir, M.S., Thursz, M.R. & Dhar, A. (2014). Review article: depression and the use of antidepressants in patients with chronic liver disease or liver transplantation. *Alimentary Pharmacology & Therapeutics*, *40*, 880–892.

Muraki, I., Imamura, F., Manson, J.E. et al. (2013). Fruit consumption and risk of type 2 diabetes: results from three prospective longitudinal cohort studies. *BMJ: British Medical Journal*, *347*, f5001.

Murphy, T.H. & Corbett, D. (2009). Plasticity during stroke recovery: from synapse to behaviour. *Nature Reviews Neuroscience*, *10*, 861–872.

Murray, C.J. (1994). Quantifying the burden of disease: the technical basis for disability-adjusted life years. *Bulletin of the World Health Organization*, *72*, 429.

Murray, C.J., Ortblad, K.F., Guinovart, C. et al. (2014). Global, regional, and national incidence and mortality for HIV, tuberculosis, and malaria during 1990–2013: a systematic analysis for the Global Burden of Disease Study 2013. *The New England Journal of Medicine, 342*, 1045–1047.

Murray, C.J., Vios, T., Lozano, R. (2012). Disability-adjusted life years (DALYs) for 291 diseases and injuries in 21 regions, 1999–2010: a systematic analysis for the Global Burden of Disease Study 2010. *The Lancet, 380*, 2197–2123.

Mursu, J., Robien, K., Harnack, L.J. et al. (2011). Dietary supplements and mortality rate in older women: the Iowa Women's Health Study. *Archives of Internal Medicine, 171*, 1625–1633.

Musazzi, L., Treccani, G., Mallei, A. & Popoli, M. (2013). The action of antidepressants on the glutamate system: regulation of glutamate release and glutamate receptors. *Biological Psychiatry, 73*, 1180–1188.

Musicco, M., Adorni, F., Di Santo, S. et al. (2013). Inverse occurrence of cancer and Alzheimer disease: a population-based incidence study. *Neurology, 81*, 322–328.

Muszynski, J.A., Nofziger, R., Greathouse, K. et al. (2014). Innate immune function predicts the development of nosocomial infection in critically injured children. *Shock, 42*, 313–321.

Mychasiuk, R., Schmold, N., Ilnytskyy, S. et al. (2011). Prenatal bystander stress alters brain, behavior, and the epigenome of developing rat offspring. *Developmental Neuroscience, 33*, 159–169.

Myers, V., Drory, Y., Goldbourt, U. & Gerber, Y. (2014). Multilevel socioeconomic status and incidence of frailty post myocardial infarction. *International Journal of Cardiology, 170*, 338–343.

Nabi, H., Kivimäki, M., Batty, G.D. et al. (2013). Increased risk of coronary heart disease among individuals reporting adverse impact of stress on their health: the Whitehall II prospective cohort study. *European Heart Journal, 34*, 2697–2705.

Nadeau, S. & Rivest, S. (1999). Effects of circulating tumor necrosis factor on the neuronal activity and expression of the genes encoding the tumor necrosis factor in the rat brain: a view from the blood-brain barrier. *Neuroscience, 93*, 1449–1464.

Nagano, Y., Itoh, K. & Honda, K. (2012). The induction of Treg cells by gut-indigenous Clostridium. *Current Opinion in Immunology, 24*, 392–397.

Nagler, R.H. (2014). Adverse outcomes associated with media exposure to contradictory nutrition messages. *Journal of Health Communication, 19*, 24–40.

Nakajima, N., Hata, Y., Onishi, H. & Ishida, M. (2013). The evaluation of the relationship between the level of disclosure of cancer in terminally ill patients with cancer and the quality of terminal care in these patients and their families using the Support Team Assessment Schedule. *The American Journal of Hospice & Palliative Care, 30*, 370–376.

Narang, I., Manlhiot, C., Davies-Shaw, J. et al. (2012). Sleep disturbance and cardiovascular risk in adolescents. *Canadian Medical Association Journal, 184*, E913–E920.

Narod, S.A. (2011). Hormone replacement therapy and the risk of breast cancer. *Nature Reviews Clinical Oncology, 8*, 669–676.

Nash, R.A., Hutton, G.J., Racke, M.K. et al. (2015). High-dose immunosuppressive therapy and autologous hematopoietic cell transplantation for relapsing-remitting multiple sclerosis (HALT-MS): a 3-year interim report. *JAMA Neurology, 72,* 159–169.

Nathanson, D.A., Gini, B.Y., Mottahedeh, J. et al. (2014). Targeted therapy resistance mediated by dynamic regulation of extrachromosomal mutant EGFR DNA. *Science, 343*, 72–76.

National Institute of Alcohol Abuse and Alcoholism (2015). Alcohol facts and statistics. http://pubs.niaaa.nih.gov/publications/AlcoholFacts%26Stats/AlcoholFacts%26Stats.htm (accessed September 2015).

National Institute of Allergy and Infectious Diseases (NIAID). (2015). Emerging and Re-emerging Infectious Diseases. niaid.nih.gov/news/news releases/topics/Pages/emergingReleases.aspx (accessed April 2015).

National Institute of Health (NIH) (2015). Landmark NIH study shows intensive blood pressure management may save lives. http://www.nhlbi.nih.gov/news/press-releases/2015/landmark-nih-study-shows-intensive-blood-pressure-management-may-save-lives (accessed September 2015).

Nei, M. (2013). *Mutation-Driven Evolution*. New York: Oxford University Press.

Nelson, L.R. & Bulun, S.E. (2001). Estrogen production and action. *Journal of the American Academy of Dermatology*, *45*, S116–S124.

Nestle, F.O., Kaplan, D.H. & Barker, J. (2009). Psoriasis. *New England Journal of Medicine*, *361*, 496–509.

Nestle, M. (2006). Food industry and health: mostly promises, little action. *The Lancet*, *368*, 564–565.

Nestler, E.J. (2008). Transcriptional mechanisms of addiction: role of DeltaFosB. *Philosophical Transactions of the Royal Society of London. Series B: Biological Sciences*, *363*, 3245–3255.

Nestler, E.J. (2014). Δ FosB: a transcriptional regulator of stress and antidepressant responses. *European Journal of Pharmacology*, *753*, 66–72.

Neumaier, J.F., Petty, F., Kramer, G.L. et al. (1997). Learned helplessness increases 5-hydroxytryptamine 1B receptor mRNA levels in the rat dorsal raphe nucleus. *Biological Psychiatry*, *41*, 668–674.

Neumeister, A., Normandin, M.D., Pietrzak, R.H. et al. (2013). Elevated brain cannabinoid CB1 receptor availability in post-traumatic stress disorder: a positron emission tomography study. *Molecular Psychiatry*, *18*, 1034–1040.

Newman, E.A. (2003). New roles for astrocytes: regulation of synaptic transmission. *Trends in Neurosciences*, *10*, 536–542.

Ng, W.L. & Bassler, B.L. (2009). Bacterial quorum-sensing network architectures. *Annual Review of Genetics*, *43*, 197–222.

Ngkelo, A. & Adcock, I.M. (2013). New treatments for COPD. *Current Opinion in Pharmacology*, *13*, 362–369.

Nguyen, B.M., Kim, D., Bricker, S. et al. (2014). Effect of marijuana use on outcomes in traumatic brain injury. *The American Surgeon*, *80*, 979–983.

Nicholson, A., Kuper, H. & Hemingway, H. (2006). Depression as an aetiologic and prognostic factor in coronary heart disease: a meta-analysis of 6362 events among 146 538 participants in 54 observational studies. *European Heart Journal*, *27*, 2763–2774.

Nielsen, N.M., Hansen, A.V., Simonsen, J. & Hviid, A. (2011). Prenatal stress and risk of infectious diseases in offspring. *American Journal of Epidemiology*, *173*, 990–997.

Noda, S.E., Lautenschlaeger, T., Siedow, M.R. et al. (2009). Technological advances in radiation oncology for central nervous system tumors. *Seminars in Radiation Oncology*, *19*, 179–186.

Nolan, C.J. (2011). Controversies in gestational diabetes. *Best Practice & Research Clinical Obstetrics & Gynaecology*, *25*, 37–49.

Nolen-Hoeksema, S. (1998). Ruminative coping with depression. In J. Heckhausen & C.S. Dweck (Eds.), *Motivation and Self-Regulation across the Life Span* (pp. 237–256). Cambridge, UK: Cambridge University Press.

Nolen-Hoeksema, S. & Davis, C.G. (1999). 'Thanks for sharing that': ruminators and their social support networks. *Journal of Personality and Social Psychology*, *77*, 801–814.

Nolen-Hoeksema, S., Parker, L.E. & Larson, J. (1994). Ruminative coping with depressed mood following loss. *Journal of Personality and Social Psychology*, *67*, 92–104.

Noonan, B. (2014). Understanding the reasons why patients delay seeking treatment for oral cancer symptoms from a primary health care professional: an integrative literature review. *European Journal of Oncology Nursing*, *18*, 118–124.

Normand, S.L., Rector, T.S., Neaton, J.D. et al. (2005). Clinical and analytical considerations in the study of health status in device trials for heart failure. *Journal of Cardiac Failure*, *11*, 396–403.

Norris, L.C., Main, B.J., Lee, Y. et al. (2015). Adaptive introgression in an African malaria mosquito coincident with the increased usage of insecticide-treated bed nets. *Proceedings of the National Academy of Sciences*, *112*, 815–820.

Northoff, G. (2008). Neuropsychiatry: an old discipline in a new gestalt bridging biological psychiatry, neuropsychology, and cognitive neurology. *European Archives of Psychiatry and Clinical Neuroscience*, *258*, 226–238.

Norton, M.C., Smith, K.R., Østbye, T. et al. (2010). Greater risk of dementia when spouse has dementia? The Cache County study. *Journal of the American Geriatrics Society*, *58*, 895–900.

Novembre, G., Zanon, M. & Silani, G. (2015). Empathy for social exclusion involves the sensory-discriminative component of pain: a within-subject fMRI study. *Social Cognitive and Affective Neuroscience*, *10*, 153–164.

Nowak, G.J., Sheedy, K., Bursey, K. et al. (2015). Promoting influenza vaccination: insights from a qualitative meta-analysis of 14 years of influenza-related communications research by US Centers for Disease Control and Prevention (CDC). *Vaccine*, *33*, 2741–2756.

Nutt, D.J. (2014). The role of the opioid system in alcohol dependence. *Journal of Psychopharmacology*, *28*, 8–22.

Nygren, M., Carstensen, J., Koch, F. et al. (2015). Experience of a serious life event increases the risk for childhood type 1 diabetes: the ABIS population-based prospective cohort study. *Diabetologia*, *58*, 1188–1197.

Nyhan, B., Reifler, J., Richey, S. & Freed, G.L. (2014). Effective messages in vaccine promotion: a randomized trial. *Pediatrics*, *133*, e835–e842.

O'Brien, M.A., Whelan, T.J., Charles, C. et al. (2008). Women's perceptions of their treatment decision-making about breast cancer treatment. *Patient Education and Counseling*, *73*, 431–436.

Ochoa-Repáraz, J., Mielcarz, D.W., Begum-Haque, S. & Kasper, L.H. (2011). Gut, bugs, and brain: role of commensal bacteria in the control of central nervous system disease. *Annals of Neurology*, *69*, 240–247.

O'Donnell, D.E. (2006). Hyperinflation, dyspnea, and exercise intolerance in chronic obstructive pulmonary disease. *Proceedings of the American Thoracic Society*, *3*, 180–184.

O'Donnell, D.E., Hernandez, P., Kaplan, A. et al. (2008). Canadian Thoracic Society recommendations for management of chronic obstructive pulmonary disease: 2008 update – highlights for primary care. *Canadian Respiratory Journal: Journal of the Canadian Thoracic Society*, *15*, 1A.

O'Donnell, K., Brydon, L., Wright, C.E. & Steptoe, A. (2008). Self-esteem levels and cardiovascular and inflammatory responses to acute stress. *Brain, Behavior, and Immunity*, *22*, 1241–1247.

O'Donovan, A., Neylan, T.C., Metzler, T. & Cohen, B.E. (2012). Lifetime exposure to traumatic psychological stress is associated with elevated inflammation in the Heart and Soul Study. *Brain, Behavior, and Immunity*, *26*, 642–649.

Organization for Economic Co-operation and Development (OECD). (2013). *Health at a Glance 2013: OECD indicators*. Paris: OECD Publishing. http://dx.doi.org/10.1787/health_glance-2013-en (accessed January 2015).

Oftedal, B.E., Hellesen, A., Erichsen, M.M. et al. (2015). Dominant mutations in the autoimmune regulator AIRE are associated with common organ-specific autoimmune diseases. *Immunity*, *42*, 1185–1196.

Ogden, C.L., Carroll, M.D., Kit, B.K. & Flegal, K.M. (2014). Prevalence of childhood and adult obesity in the United States, 2011–2012. *The Journal of the American Medical Association*, *311*, 806–814.

Ogino, S., Fuchs, C.S. & Giovannucci, E. (2012). How many molecular subtypes? Implications of the unique tumor principle in personalized medicine. *Expert Review of Molecular Diagnostics*, *12*, 621–628.

Ogino, S., Lochhead, P., Chan, A.T. et al. (2013). Molecular pathological epidemiology of epigenetics: emerging integrative science to analyze environment, host, and disease. *Modern Pathology*, *26*, 465–484.

O'Hara, A.M. & Shanahan, F. (2006). The gut flora as a forgotten organ. *EMBO Reports*, *7*, 688–693.

Ohara, T., Doi, Y., Ninomiya, T. et al. (2011). Glucose tolerance status and risk of dementia in the community: the Hisayama Study. *Neurology*, *77*, 1126–1134.

Öhman, H., Savikko, N., Strandberg, T.E. & Pitkälä, K.H. (2014). Effect of physical exercise on cognitive performance in older adults with mild cognitive impairment or dementia: a systematic review. *Dementia and Geriatric Cognitive Disorders*, *38*, 347–365.

Okada, H., Kuhn, C., Feillet, H. & Bach, J.F. (2010). The 'hygiene hypothesis' for autoimmune and allergic diseases: an update. *Clinical & Experimental Immunology*, *160*, 1–9.

Okoro, C.A., Dhingra, S.S. & Li, C. (2014). A triple play: psychological distress, physical comorbidities, and access and use of health services among US adults with disabilities. *Journal of Health Care for the Poor and Underserved*, *25*, 814–836.

Okoye, I., Wang, L. & Pallmer, K. (2015). The protein LEM promotes CD8+ T cell immunity through effects on mitochondrial respiration. *Science*. pii: aaa7516. [Epub ahead of print]

O'Mahony, M. & Hegarty, J. (2009). Factors influencing women in seeking help from a health care professional on self discovery of a breast symptom, in an Irish context. *Journal of Clinical Nursing, 18,* 2020–2029.

Oraby, T., Thampi, V. & Bauch, C.T. (2014). The influence of social norms on the dynamics of vaccinating behaviour for paediatric infectious diseases. *Proceedings of the Royal Society B: Biological Sciences, 281,* 20133172.

Ornstein, K.A., Aldridge, M.D., Garrido, M.M. et al. (2015). Association between hospice use and depressive symptoms in surviving spouses. *JAMA Internal Medicine.* [Epub ahead of print]

Orozco, L.J., Buchleitner, A.M., Gimenez-Perez, G. et al. (2009). Exercise or exercise and diet for preventing type 2 diabetes mellitus. *Cochrane Database of Systematic Reviews,* CD003054.

Ortega, F.B., Lee, D.C., Katzmarzyk, P.T. et al. (2013). The intriguing metabolically healthy but obese phenotype: cardiovascular prognosis and role of fitness. *European Heart Journal, 34,* 389–397.

O'Shea, J.J. & Murray, P.J. (2008). Cytokine signaling modules in inflammatory responses. *Immunity, 28,* 477–487.

Osterholm, M.T., Kelley, N.S., Sommer, A. & Belongia, E.A. (2012). Efficacy and effectiveness of influenza vaccines: a systematic review and meta-analysis. *The Lancet Infectious Diseases, 12,* 36–44.

Ottenbacher, K.J., Karmarkar, A., Graham, J.E. et al. (2014). Thirty-day hospital readmission following discharge from postacute rehabilitation in fee-for-service Medicare patients. *JAMA, 311,* 604–614.

Ouellette-Kuntz, H., Coo, H., Cobigo, V. & Wilton, A.S. (2015). Uptake of colorectal cancer screening among Ontarians with intellectual and developmental disabilities. *PLoS One, 10,* e0118023.

Owen, A.D., Hayward, R.D., Koenig, H.G. et al. (2011). Religious factors and hippocampal atrophy in late life. *PLoS One, 6,* e17006.

Pace, T.W., Mletzko, T.C., Alagbe, O. et al. (2006). Increased stress-induced inflammatory responses in male patients with major depression and increased early life stress. *American Journal of Psychiatry, 163,* 1630–1633.

Pagano, J.S., Blaser, M., Buendia, M.A. et al. (2004). Infectious agents and cancer: criteria for a causal relation. *Seminars in Cancer Biology, 14,* 453–471.

Pan, H., Jiang, Y., Tabbò, F. et al. (2015). Epigenomic evolution in diffuse large B-cell lymphomas. *Nature Communications, 6,* 6921.

Pancer, Z. & Cooper, M.D. (2006). The evolution of adaptive immunity. *Annual Review of Immunology, 24,* 497–518.

Pandharipande, P.P., Girard, T.D. & Ely, E.W. (2014). Long-term cognitive impairment after critical illness. *New England Journal of Medicine, 370,* 185–186.

Papadopoulos, A.S. & Cleare, A.J. (2012). Hypothalamic-pituitary-adrenal (HPA) axis dysfunction in chronic fatigue syndrome. *Nature Reviews Endocrinology, 8,* 22–32.

Paquet, L., Collins, B., Song, X. et al. (2013). A pilot study of prospective memory functioning in early breast cancer survivors. *Breast, 22,* 455–461.

Paragh, G., Seres, I., Harangi, M. & Fülöp, P. (2014). Dynamic interplay between metabolic syndrome and immunity. *Advances in Experimental Medicine and Biology, 824,* 171–190.

Parazzini, F., Chatenoud, L., Surace, M. et al. (2003). Moderate alcohol drinking and risk of preterm birth. *European Journal of Clinical Nutrition, 57,* 1345–1349.

Pargament, K.I. (2001). *The Psychology of Religion and Coping: theory, research, practice.* New York: Guilford Press.

Park, C.L. (2010). Making sense of the meaning literature: An integrative review of meaning making and its effects on adjustment to stressful life events. *Psychological Bulletin, 136,* 257–301.

Park, J.E., Kim, K.I., Yoon, S.S. et al. (2010). Psychological distress as a negative survival factor for patients with hematologic malignancies who underwent allogeneic hematopoietic stem cell transplantation. *Pharmacotherapy, 30,* 1239–1246.

Park, J.H. & Brentjens, R.J. (2013). Immunotherapies in CLL. *Advances in Experimental Medicine and Biology, 792,* 241–257.

Park, M., Katon, W.J. & Wolf, F.M. (2013). Depression and risk of mortality in individuals with diabetes: a meta-analysis and systematic review. *General Hospital Psychiatry, 35,* 217–225.

Parks-Stamm, E.J., Gollwitzer, P.M. & Oettingen, G. (2007). Action control by implementation intentions: effective cue detection and efficient response initiation. *Social Cognition*, *25*, 248–266.

Parnia, S., Spearpoint, K., de Vos, G. et al. (2014). AWARE – AWAreness during REsuscitation: a prospective study. *Resuscitation*, *85*, 1799–1805.

Partinen, M., Kornum, B.R., Plazzi, G. et al. (2014). Narcolepsy as an autoimmune disease: the role of H1N1 infection and vaccination. *The Lancet Neurology*, *13*, 600–613.

Parvaz, M.A., Konova, A.B., Tomasi, D. et al. (2011). Structural integrity of the prefrontal cortex modulates electrocortical sensitivity to reward. *Journal of Cognitive Neuroscience*, *24*, 1560–1570.

Pascoli, V., Terrier, J., Espallergues, J. et al. (2014). Contrasting forms of cocaine-evoked plasticity control components of relapse. *Nature*, *509*, 459–464.

Pasic, J., Levy, W.C. & Sullivan, M.D. (2003). Cytokines in depression and heart failure. *Psychosomatic Medicine*, *65*, 181–193.

Patel, R.R. & Arthur, D.W. (2006). The emergence of advanced brachytherapy techniques for common malignancies. *Hematology/Oncology Clinics of North America*, *20*, 97–118.

Patel, S.A., Winkel, M., Ali, M.K. et al. (2015). Cardiovascular mortality associated with 5 leading risk factors: national and state preventable fractions estimated from survey data. *Annals of Internal Medicine*, *163*, 245–253.

Patel, S.R., Zhu, X., Storfer-Isser, A. et al. (2009). Sleep duration and biomarkers of inflammation. *Sleep*, *32*, 200–204.

Patterson, Z.R., Ducharme, R., Anisman, H. & Abizaid, A. (2010). Altered metabolic and neurochemical responses to chronic unpredictable stressors in ghrelin receptor-deficient mice. *European Journal of Neuroscience*, *32*, 632–639.

Patterson, Z.R., Khazall, R., Mackay, H. et al. (2013). Central ghrelin signaling mediates the metabolic response of C57BL/6 male mice to chronic social defeat stress. *Endocrinology*, *154*, 1080–1091.

Paykel, E.S., Prusoff, B.A. & Uhlenhuth, E.H. (1971). Scaling of life events. *Archives of General Psychiatry*, *25*, 340–347.

Paz Soldán, M.M. & Weinshenker, B.G. (2015). Moving targets for hematopoietic stem cell transplantation for multiple sclerosis. *JAMA Neurology*, *72*, 147–149.

Peacock, E.J. & Wong, P.T.P. (1990). The Stress Appraisal Measure (SAM): a multidimensional approach to cognitive appraisal. *Stress Medicine*, *6*, 227–236.

Pearce, O.M., Läubli, H.,Verhagen, A. et al. (2014). Inverse hormesis of cancer growth mediated by narrow ranges of tumor-directed antibodies. *Proceedings of the National Academy of Sciences*, *111*, 5998–6003.

Pearl, R. (2015) How hospitals can kill. Here's what we can do about it. www.kevinmd.com/blog/2015/07/how-hospitals-can-kill-heres-what-we-can-do-about-it.html (accessed June 2015).

Pedersen, B.K. (2009). The diseasome of physical inactivity: and the role of myokines in muscle–fat cross talk. *The Journal of Physiology*, *587*, 5559–5568.

Pedersen, B.K. & Hoffman-Goetz, L. (2000). Exercise and the immune system: regulation, integration, and adaptation. *Physiological Reviews*, *80*, 1055–1081.

Peek, M.E., Ferguson, M.J., Roberson, T.P. & Chin, M.H. (2014). Putting theory into practice: a case study of diabetes-related behavioral change interventions on Chicago's south side. *Health Promotion Practice*, *15*, 40S–50S.

Peeters, A., Barendregt, J.J., Willekens, F. et al. (2003). Obesity in adulthood and its consequences for life expectancy: a life-table analysis. *Annals of Internal Medicine*, *138*, 24–32.

Pepino, M.Y. & Mennella, J.A. (2005). Sucrose-induced analgesia is related to sweet preferences in children but not adults. *Pain*, *119*, 210–218.

Pereira, M.G., Pedras, S. & Machado, J.C. (2014). Family variables as moderators between beliefs towards medicines and adherence to self-care behaviors and medication in type 2 diabetes. *Families, Systems, & Health*, *32*, 198.

Pereira, O.C., Bernardi, M.M. & Gerardin, D.C. (2006). Could neonatal testosterone replacement prevent alterations induced by prenatal stress in male rats? *Life Sciences*, *78*, 2767–2771.

Pérez, L.P., González, R.S. & Lázaro, E.B. (2015). Treatment of mood disorders in multiple sclerosis. *Current Treatment Options in Neurology*, *17*, 323.

Pergadia, M.L., Der-Avakian, A., D'Souza, M.S. et al. (2014). Association between nicotine withdrawal and reward responsiveness in humans and rats. *JAMA Psychiatry*, *71*, 1238–1245.

Perissinotto, C.M., Cenzer, I.S. & Covinsky, K.E. (2012). Loneliness in older persons: a predictor of functional decline and death. *Archives of Internal Medicine, 172*, 1078–1083.

Peters, P.G., Jr. (2000). The quiet demise of deference to custom: malpractice law at the millennium. *Washington and Lee Law Review, 57*, 163–204.

Peterson, C.T., Sharma, V., Elmén, L. & Peterson, S.N. (2015). Immune homeostasis, dysbiosis and therapeutic modulation of the gut microbiota. *Clinical & Experimental Immunology, 179*, 363–377.

Petretta, M., Costanzo, P., Perrone-Filardi, P. & Chiariello, M. (2010). Impact of gender in primary prevention of coronary heart disease with statin therapy: a meta-analysis. *International Journal of Cardiology, 138*, 25–31.

Petrie, K.J., Broadbent, E. & Meechan, G. (2003). Self-regulatory interventions for improving the management of chronic illness. In L.D. Cameron & H. Leventhal (Eds.), *The Self-Regulation of Health and Illness Behaviour* (pp. 257–277). New York: Routledge.

Petticrew, M., Bell, R. & Hunter, D. (2002). Influence of psychological coping on survival and recurrence in people with cancer: systematic review. *British Medical Journal, 325*, 1066.

Petticrew, M. & Roberts H. (2006). *Systematic Reviews in the Social Sciences*. Oxford: Wiley Blackwell.

Pfeifer, G.P. (2015). How the environment shapes cancer genomes. *Current Opinion in Oncology, 27*, 71–77.

Philbin, E.F., Dec, G.W., Jenkins, P.L. & DiSalvo, T.G. (2001). Socioeconomic status as an independent risk factor for hospital readmission for heart failure. *American Journal of Cardiology, 87*, 1367–1371.

Phillips, K.A., Milne, R.L., Rookus, M.A. et al. (2013). Tamoxifen and risk of contralateral breast cancer for BRCA1 and BRCA2 mutation carriers. *Journal of Clinical Oncology, 31*, 3091–3099.

Piccinelli, M. (2000). Gender differences in depression. *British Journal of Psychiatry, 177*, 486–492.

Picorelli, A.M.A., Pereira, L.S.M., Pereira, D.S. et al. (2014). Adherence to exercise programs for older people is influenced by program characteristics and personal factors: a systematic review. *Journal of Physiotherapy, 60*, 151–156.

Pierrehumbert, B., Torrisi, R., Laufer, D. et al. (2010). Oxytocin response to an experimental psychosocial challenge in adults exposed to traumatic experiences during childhood or adolescence. *Neuroscience, 166*, 168–177.

Pies, R. (2009). Should DSM-V designate 'internet addiction' a mental disorder? *Psychiatry (Edgmont), 6*, 31–37.

Pillai, A. & Nelson, R. (2008). Probiotics for treatment of *Clostridium difficile*-associated colitis in adults. *The Cochrane Database of Systematic Reviews*, CD004611.

Pillar, G., Malhotra, A. & Lavie, P. (2000). Post-traumatic stress disorder and sleep: what a nightmare! *Sleep Medicine Reviews, 4*, 183–200.

Pinkerton, J.V. & Santoro, N. (2015). Compounded bioidentical hormone therapy: identifying use trends and knowledge gaps among US women. *Menopause*. [Epub ahead of print]

Pisinger, C. & Døssing, M. (2014). A systematic review of health effects of electronic cigarettes. *Preventive Medicine, 69*, 248–260.

Pitts, S.B.J., Keyserling, T.C., Johnston, L.F. et al. (2015). Associations between neighborhood-level factors related to a healthful lifestyle and dietary intake, physical activity, and support for obesity prevention policies among rural adults. *Journal of Community Health, 40*, 276–284.

Ploughman, M., Austin, M.W., Glynn, L. & Corbett, D. (2015). The effects of poststroke aerobic exercise on neuroplasticity: a systematic review of animal and clinical studies. *Translational Stroke Research, 6*, 13–28.

Podymow, T., Turnbull, J., Coyle, D. et al. (2006). Shelter-based managed alcohol administration to chronically homeless people addicted to alcohol. *Canadian Medical Association Journal, 174*, 45–49.

Polido-Pereira, J., Vieira-Sousa, E. & Fonseca, J.E. (2011). Rheumatoid arthritis: What is refractory disease and how to manage it? *Autoimmunity Reviews, 10*, 707–713.

Pons, T.P., Garraghty, P.E., Ommaya, A.K. et al. (1991). Massive cortical reorganization after sensory deafferentation in adult macaques. *Science, 252*, 1857–1860.

Poole-Wilson, P.A., Lubsen, J., Kirwan, B.A. et al. (2004). Effect of long-acting nifedipine on mortality and cardiovascular morbidity in patients with stable angina requiring treatment

(ACTION trial): randomised controlled trial. *The Lancet*, *364*, 849–857.

Popoli, M., Yan, Z., McEwen, B.S. & Sanacora, G. (2012). The stressed synapse: the impact of stress and glucocorticoids on glutamate transmission. *Nature Reviews Neuroscience*, *13*, 22–37.

Poppe, L., Rué, L., Robberecht, W. & Van Den Bosch, L. (2014). Translating biological findings into new treatment strategies for amyotrophic lateral sclerosis (ALS). *Experimental Neurology*, pii: S0014-4886(14)00229-5.

Porta, M. (2014). *A Dictionary of Epidemiology* (6th ed.). New York: Oxford University Press.

Porter, D.L., Levine, B.L., Kalos, M. et al. (2011). Chimeric antigen receptor–modified T cells in chronic lymphoid leukemia. *New England Journal of Medicine*, *365*, 725–733.

Poulter, M.O., Du, L., Zhurov, V. et al. (2010). Plasticity of the GABA$_A$ receptor subunit cassette in response to stressors in reactive versus resilient mice. *Neuroscience*, *165*, 1039–1051.

Powell, N.D., Tarr, A.J. & Sheridan, J.F. (2013). Psychosocial stress and inflammation in cancer. *Brain, Behavior, and Immunity*, *30*, S41–S47.

Prakash, S., Rodes, L., Coussa-Charley, M. & Tomaro-Duchesneau, C. (2011). Gut microbiota: next frontier in understanding human health and development of biotherapeutics. *Biologics: Targets & Therapy*, *5*, 71–86.

Pratchett, L.C., Pelcovitz, M.R. & Yehuda, R. (2010). Trauma and violence: are women the weaker sex? *Psychiatric Clinics of North America*, *33*, 465–474.

Preacher, K.J. & Hayes, A.F. (2008). Asymptotic and resampling strategies for assessing and comparing indirect effects in multiple mediator models. *Behavior Research Methods*, *40*, 879–891.

Pressman, S.D., Cohen, S., Miller, G.E. et al. (2005). Loneliness, social network size, and immune response to influenza vaccination in college freshmen. *Health Psychology*, *24*, 297–306.

Price, L.H., Kao, H.T., Burgers, D.E. et al. (2013). Telomeres and early-life stress: an overview. *Biological Psychiatry*, *73*, 15–23.

Prinz, F., Schlange, T. & Asadullah, K. (2011). Believe it or not: How much can we rely on published data on potential drug targets? *Nature Reviews Drug Discovery*, *10*, 712–712.

Prochaska, J.O. (1994). Strong and weak principles for progressing from precontemplation to action on the basis of twelve problem behaviors. *Health Psychology*, *13*, 47.

Puglisi-Allegra, S. & Andolina, D. (2015). Serotonin and stress coping. *Behavioural Brain Research*, *277*, 58–67.

Puhan, M.A., Gimeno-Santos, E., Scharplatz, M. et al. (2011). Pulmonary rehabilitation following exacerbations of chronic obstructive pulmonary disease. *Cochrane Database of Systematic Reviews*, CD005305.

Pulido, O., Zarkadas, M., & Dubois, S. (2013). Clinical features and symptom recovery on a gluten-free diet in Canadian adults with celiac disease. *Canadian Journal of Gastroenterology*, *27*, 449–453.

Pusic, A.L., Klassen, A.F., Snell, L. et al. (2012). Measuring and managing patient expectations for breast reconstruction: impact on quality of life and patient satisfaction. *Expert Review of Pharmacoeconomics & Outcomes Research*, *12*, 149–158.

Qin, J., Li, Y., Cai, Z. et al. (2012). A metagenome-wide association study of gut microbiota in type 2 diabetes. *Nature*, *490*, 55–60.

Quartana, P.J. & Burns, J.W. (2010). Emotion suppression affects cardiovascular responses to initial and subsequent laboratory stressors. *British Journal of Health Psychology*, *15*, 511–528.

Quirin, M., Kuhl, J. & Düsing, R. (2011). Oxytocin buffers cortisol responses to stress in individuals with impaired emotion regulation abilities. *Psychoneuroendocrinology*, *36*, 898–904.

Rabl, U., Meyer, B.M., Diers, K. et al. (2014). Additive gene–environment effects on hippocampal structure in healthy humans. *Journal of Neuroscience*, *34*, 9917–9926.

Racine, M., Choinière, M. & Nielson, W.R. (2014). Predictors of suicidal ideation in chronic pain patients: an exploratory study. *The Clinical Journal of Pain*, *30*, 371–378.

Rainville, P., Duncan, G.H., Price, D.D. et al. (1997). Pain affect encoded in human anterior cingulate but not somatosensory cortex. *Science*, *277*, 968–971.

Raison, C.L., Capuron, L. & Miller, A.H. (2006). Cytokines sing the blues: inflammation and the pathogenesis of depression. *Trends in Immunology*, *27*, 24–31.

Raison, C.L., Lowry, C.A. & Rook, G.A. (2010). Inflammation, sanitation, and consternation: loss of contact with coevolved, tolerogenic microorganisms and the pathophysiology and treatment of major depression. *Archives of General Psychiatry*, *67*, 1211–1224.

Raj, P.P. (2007). Taxonomy and classification of pain. In D. Niv, S. Kreitler, B. Diego & A. Lamberto (Eds.), *The Handbook of Chronic Pain*. New York: Nova Biomedical Books.

Rakoff-Nahoum, S., Paglino, J., Eslami-Varzaneh, F. et al. (2004). Recognition of commensal microflora by toll-like receptors is required for intestinal homeostasis. *Cell*, *118*, 229–241.

Ram, Y. (2014). 'Typhoid Mary': villainized & victimized. Retrieved from www.themicrobiologyblog.com/2014/05/typhoid-mary-villainized-victimized.html (accessed January 2015).

Ramírez, N., Özel, M.Z., Lewis, A.C. et al. (2014). Exposure to nitrosamines in thirdhand tobacco smoke increases cancer risk in non-smokers. *Environment International*, *71*, 39–47.

Rand, T.G. & Miller, J.D. (2011). Toxins and inflammatory compounds. In B. Flannigan, R.A. Samson & J.D. Miller (Eds.), *Microorganisms in Home and Indoor Work Environments: Diversity, health impacts, investigation and control* (2nd ed., pp. 209–306). New York: Taylor & Francis.

Rando, K., Chaplin, T.M., Potenza, M.N. et al. (2013). Prenatal cocaine exposure and gray matter volume in adolescent boys and girls: relationship to substance use initiation. *Biological Psychiatry*, *74*, 482–489.

Rands, C.M., Meader, S., Ponting, C.P. & Lunter, G. (2014). 8.2% of the human genome is constrained: variation in rates of turnover across functional element classes in the human lineage. *PLoS Genetics*, *10*, e1004525.

Raspopow, K., Abizaid, A., Matheson, K. & Anisman, H. (2010). Psychosocial stressor effects on cortisol and ghrelin in emotional and non-emotional eaters: influence of anger and shame. *Hormones and Behavior*, *58*, 677–684.

Ratner, E., Lu, L., Boeke, M. et al. (2010). A KRAS-variant in ovarian cancer acts as a genetic marker of cancer risk. *Cancer Research*, *70*, 6509–6515.

Ravindran, A.V., Anisman, H., Merali, Z. et al. (1999). Treatment of primary dysthymia with cognitive therapy and pharmacotherapy: clinical symptoms and functional impairments. *American Journal of Psychiatry*, *156*, 1608–1617.

Raynor, D.K., Dickinson, R., Knapp, P. et al. (2011). Buyer beware? Does the information provided with herbal products available over the counter enable safe use? *BMC Medicine*, *9*, 94.

Reddy, V.S., Prabhu, S.D., Mummidi, S. et al. (2010). Interleukin-18 induces EMMPRIN expression in primary cardiomyocytes via JNK/Sp1 signaling and MMP-9 in part via EMMPRIN and through AP-1 and NF-kappaB activation. *American Journal of Physiology – Heart and Circulatory Physiology*, *299*, H1242-H1254.

Reed, B., Villeneuve, S., Mack, W. et al. (2014). Associations between serum cholesterol levels and cerebral amyloidosis. *JAMA Neurology*, *71*, 195–200.

Reiche, E.M., Nunes, S.O. & Morimoto, H.K. (2004). Stress, depression, the immune system, and cancer. *The Lancet Oncology*, *5*, 617–625.

Reiner, K., Tibi, L. & Lipsitz, J.D. (2013). Do mindfulness-based interventions reduce pain intensity? A critical review of the literature. *Pain Medicine*, *14*, 230–242.

Renaud, S.D. & de Lorgeril, M. (1992). Wine, alcohol, platelets, and the French paradox for coronary heart disease. *The Lancet*, *339*, 1523–1526.

Reuben, D.B., Alvanzo, A.A., Ashikaga, T. et al. (2015). National institutes of health pathways to prevention workshop: the role of opioids in the treatment of chronic pain. *Annals of Internal Medicine*, *162*, 295–300.

Reynolds, R.M., Allan, K.M., Raja, E.A. et al. (2013). Maternal obesity during pregnancy and premature mortality from cardiovascular event in adult offspring: follow-up of 1 323 275 person years. *BMJ: British Medical Journal*, *347*, f4539.

Ricci, F., Buzzatti, G., Rubagotti, A. & Boccardo, F. (2014). Safety of antiandrogen therapy for treating prostate cancer. *Expert Opinion on Drug Safety*, *13*, 1483–1499.

Rice, S.M., Goodall, J., Hetrick, S.E. et al. (2014). Online and social networking interventions for the treatment of depression in young people: a systematic review. *Journal of Medical Internet Research*, *16*, e206.

Rice-Townsend, S., Hall, M., Jenkins, K.J. et al. (2010). Analysis of adverse events in pediatric surgery using criteria validated from the adult population: justifying the need for pediatric-focused outcome measures. *Journal of Pediatric Surgery*, *45*, 1126–1136.

Richter, C., Woods, I.G. & Schier, A.F. (2014). Neuropeptidergic control of sleep and wakefulness. *Annual Review of Neuroscience*, *37*, 503–531.

Ricketts, J.R., Rothe, M.J. & Grant-Kels, J.M. (2010). Nutrition and psoriasis. *Clinics in Dermatology*, *28*, 615–626.

Riemsma, R.P., Pattenden, J., Bridle, C. et al. (2003). Systematic review of the effectiveness of stage-based interventions to promote smoking cessation. *BMJ: British Medical Journal*, *326*, 1175–1177.

Rinaudo, P. & Wang, E. (2011). Fetal programming and metabolic syndrome. *Annual Review of Physiology*, *74*, 107–130.

Ringdal, G.I., Ringdal, K., Jordhøy, M.S. & Kaasa, S. (2007). Does social support from family and friends work as a buffer against reactions to stressful life events such as terminal cancer? *Palliative Support Care*, *5*, 61–69.

Ristvedt, S.L. & Trinkaus, K.M. (2008). Sex differences in responding to rectal cancer symptoms. *Psychology & Health*, *23*, 935–944.

Riva, P., Romero Lauro, L.J., Vergallito, A. et al. (2015). Electrified emotions: modulatory effects of transcranial direct stimulation on negative emotional reactions to social exclusion. *Social Neuroscience*, *10*, 46–54.

Rivest, S. (2009). Regulation of innate immune responses in the brain. *Nature Reviews Immunology*, *9*, 429–439.

Rizos, E.C., Ntzani, E.E., Bika, E. et al. (2012). Association between omega-3 fatty acid supplementation and risk of major cardiovascular disease events: a systematic review and meta-analysis. *JAMA*, *308*, 1024–1033.

Rob, J.W., Arts, R.J.W., Blok, B.A., et al. (2015). Vitamin A induces inhibitory histone methylation modifications and down-regulates trained immunity in human monocytes. *Journal of Leukocyte Biology*, *98*, 129–136.

Roberts, R. (2014). A genetic basis for coronary artery disease. *Trends in Cardiovascular Medicine*, pii: S1050-1738(14)00183-2.

Robinaugh, D.J. & McNally, R.J. (2010). Autobiographical memory for shame or guilt provoking events: association with psychological symptoms. *Behavior Research and Therapy*, *48*, 646–652.

Robinson, M., Mattes, E., Oddy, W.H. et al. (2011). Prenatal stress and risk of behavioral morbidity from age 2 to 14 years: the influence of the number, type, and timing of stressful life events. *Development and Psychopathology*, *23*, 507–520.

Robinson, R.G. (2003). Poststroke depression: prevalence, diagnosis, treatment, and disease progression. *Biological Psychiatry*, *54*, 376–387.

Robinson, T.E. & Berridge, K.C. (2003). Addiction. *Annual Review of Psychology*, *54*, 25–53.

Rockett, M. (2014). Diagnosis, mechanisms and treatment of complex regional pain syndrome. *Current Opinion in Anesthesiology*, *27*, 494–500.

Rode, L., Nordestgaard, B.G. & Bojesen, S.E. (2015). Peripheral blood leukocyte telomere length and mortality among 64 637 individuals from the general population. *Journal of the National Cancer Institute*, *107*, djv074.

Roepke, S.K., Mausbach, B.T., Patterson, T.L. et al. (2010). Effects of Alzheimer caregiving on allostatic load. *Journal of Health Psychology*, *16*, 58–69.

Rogers, R.W. (1983). Cognitive and physiological processes in fear appeals and attitude change: a revised theory of protection motivation. In J.T. Cacioppo, R.E. Petty & D. Shapiro (Eds.), *Social Psychophysiology: a sourcebook* (pp. 153–176). New York: Guilford Press.

Roh, S. & Evins, A.E. (2012). Possible role of nicotine for the treatment of mild cognitive impairment. *Expert Review of Neurotherapeutics*, *12*, 531–533.

Roitt, I., Brostoff, J. & Male, D. (2001). *Immunology* (6th ed.). St Louis. MO: Mosby.

Rolls, A., Borg, J.S. & de Lecea, L. (2010). Sleep and metabolism: role of hypothalamic neuronal circuitry. *Best Practice & Research Clinical Endocrinology & Metabolism*, *24*, 817–828.

Romero-Moreno, R., Márquez-González, M., Losada, A. & López, J. (2011). Motives for caring: relationship to stress and coping dimensions. *International Psychogeriatrics*, *23*, 573–582.

Roness, A., Mykletun, A. & Dahl, A.A. (2005). Help-seeking behaviour in patients with anxiety disorder and depression. *Acta Psychiatrica Scandinavica*, *111*, 51–58.

Ropeik, D. (2002). *Risk*. New York: Houghton Mifflin.

Rosano, G.M. & Panina, G. (1999). Oestrogens and the heart. *Therapie*, *54*, 381–385.

Rose, G. (1985). Sick individuals and sick populations. *International Journal of Epidemiology*, *14*, 32–38.

Rosenberg, S.D., Rosenberg, H.J. & Farrell, M.P. (1999). The midlife crisis revisited. In S.L. Willis & J.D. Reid (Eds.), *Life in the Middle: psychological and social development in middle age* (pp. 47–73). San Diego, CA: Academic Press.

Rosenberger, P.H., Ickovics, J.R., Epel, E. et al. (2009). Surgical stress-induced immune cell redistribution profiles predict short-term and long-term postsurgical recovery. *Journal of Bone & Joint Surgery*, *91*, 2783–2794.

Rosenkranz, M.A., Davidson, R.J., MacCoon, D.G. et al. (2013). A comparison of mindfulness-based stress reduction and an active control in modulation of neurogenic inflammation. *Brain, Behavior, and Immunity*, *27*, 174–184.

Rosenstock, I.M., Strecher, V.J. & Becker, M.H. (1988). Social learning theory and the health belief model. *Health Education & Behavior*, *15*, 175–183.

Rosenzweig, I., Glasser, M., Polsek, D. et al. (2015). Sleep apnoea and the brain: a complex relationship. *The Lancet Respiratory Medicine*, pii: S2213-2600(15)00090-9. [Epub ahead of print]

Rosland, A.M., Heisler, M. & Piette, J.D. (2012). The impact of family behaviors and communication patterns on chronic illness outcomes: a systematic review. *Journal of Behavioral Medicine*, *35*, 221–239.

Roth, T.L., Lubin, F.D., Funk, A.J. & Sweatt, J.D. (2009). Lasting epigenetic influence of early-life adversity on the BDNF gene. *Biological Psychiatry*, *65*, 760–769.

Rothwell, N.J. & Luheshi, G.N. (2000). Interleukin 1 in the brain: biology, pathology and therapeutic target. *Trends in Neurosciences*, *23*, 618–625.

Rottenberg, J., Yaroslavsky, I., Carney, R.M. et al. (2014). The association between major depressive disorder in childhood and risk factors for cardiovascular disease in adolescence. *Psychosomatic Medicine*, *76*, 122–127.

Roush, S.W., Murphy, T.V. & Vaccine-Preventable Disease Table Working Group. (2007). Historical comparisons of morbidity and mortality for vaccine-preventable diseases in the United States. *JAMA*, *298*, 2155–2163.

Ruan, H.B., Dietrich, M.O., Liu, Z.W. et al. (2014). O-GlcNAc transferase enables AgRP neurons to suppress browning of white fat. *Cell*, *159*, 306–317.

Rubini, A. (2013). Interleukin-6 and lung inflammation: evidence for a causative role in inducing respiratory system resistance increments. *Inflammation & Allergy – Drug Targets*, *12*, 315–321.

Ruchat, S.M., Hivert, M.F. & Bouchard, L. (2013). Epigenetic programming of obesity and diabetes by in utero exposure to gestational diabetes mellitus. *Nutrition Reviews*, *71*, S88–S94.

Rudman, D., Feller, A.G., Nagraj, H.S. et al. (1990). Effects of human growth hormone in men over 60 years old. *New England Journal of Medicine*, *323*, 1–6.

Ruehlman, L.S., Karoly, P. & Pugliese, J. (2010). Psychosocial correlates of chronic pain and depression in young adults: further evidence of the utility of the Profile of Chronic Pain: Screen (PCP: S) and the Profile of Chronic Pain: Extended Assessment (PCP: EA) battery. *Pain Medicine*, *11*, 1546–1553.

Ruiz-Narváez, E.A., Palmer, J.R., Gerlovin, H. et al. (2014). Birth weight and risk of type 2 diabetes in the black women's health study: Does adult BMI play a mediating role? *Diabetes Care*, *37*, 2572–2578.

Rutkowski, K., Sowa, P., Rutkowska-Talipska, J. et al. (2014). Dehydroepiandrosterone (DHEA): hypes and hopes. *Drugs*, *74*, 1195–1207.

Rutter, M. (2013). Annual research review: resilience – clinical implications. *Journal of Child Psychology and Psychiatry*, *54*, 474–487.

Ryan, B., Musazzi, L., Mallei, A. et al. (2009). Remodelling by early-life stress of NMDA receptor-dependent synaptic plasticity in a gene–environment rat model of depression. *International Journal of Neuropsychopharmacology*, *12*, 553–559.

Ryan, D.H. & Kushner, R. (2010). The state of obesity and obesity research. *JAMA*, *304*, 1835–1836.

Rybicki, E. (1990). The classification of organisms at the edge of life or problems with virus systematics. *South African Journal of Science*, *86*, 182–186.

Sack, R.L., Lewy, A.J., Blood, M.L. et al. (1992). Circadian rhythm abnormalities in totally blind people: incidence and clinical significance. *The Journal of Clinical Endocrinology & Metabolism*, *75*, 127–134.

Saeterdal, I., Lewin, S., Austvoll-Dahlgren, A. et al. (2014). Interventions aimed at communities to inform and/or educate about early childhood vaccination. *Cochrane Database of Systematic Reviews*, *11*, CD010232.

Saffari, A., Daher, N., Ruprecht, A. et al. (2014). Particulate metals and organic compounds from electronic and tobacco-containing cigarettes: comparison of emission rates and secondhand exposure. *Environmental Science: Processes & Impacts*, *16*, 2259–2267.

Sah, R., Ekhator, N.N., Jefferson-Wilson, L. et al. (2014). Cerebrospinal fluid neuropeptide Y in combat veterans with and without posttraumatic stress disorder. *Psychoneuroendocrinology*, *40*, 277–283.

Sah, R. & Geracioti, T.D. (2013). Neuropeptide Y and posttraumatic stress disorder. *Molecular Psychiatry*, *18*, 646–655.

Sakurai, M., Nakamura, K., Miura, K. et al. (2014). Sugar-sweetened beverage and diet soda consumption and the 7-year risk for type 2 diabetes mellitus in middle-aged Japanese men. *European Journal of Nutrition*, *53*, 1137–1138.

Salari, P. & Abdollahi, M. (2011). Systematic review of modulators of benzodiazepine receptors in irritable bowel syndrome: Is there hope? *World Journal of Gastroenterology*, *17*, 4251–4257.

Salmaso, N., Tomasi, S. & Vaccarino, F.M. (2014). Neurogenesis and maturation in neonatal brain injury. *Clinics in Perinatology*, *41*, 229–239.

Salmon, J., Owen, N., Crawford, D. et al. (2003). Physical activity and sedentary behavior: a population-based study of barriers, enjoyment, and preference. *Health Psychology*, *22*, 178.

Salvetti, M., Giovannoni, G. & Aloisi, F. (2009). Epstein-Barr virus and multiple sclerosis. *Current Opinion in Neurology*, *22*, 201–206.

Sanabria-Martínez, G., García-Hermoso, A., Poyatos-León, R. et al. (2015). Effectiveness of physical activity interventions on preventing gestational diabetes mellitus and excessive maternal weight gain: a meta-analysis. *BJOG: An International Journal of Obstetrics & Gynaecology*. [Epub ahead of print]

Sanacora, G., Gueorguieva, R., Epperson, C.N. et al. (2004). Subtype-specific alterations of gamma-aminobutyric acid and glutamate in patients with major depression. *Archives of General Psychiatry*, *61*, 705–713.

Sanacora, G., Treccani, G. & Popoli, M. (2012) Towards a glutamate hypothesis of depression: an emerging frontier of neuropsychopharmacology for mood disorders. *Neuropharmacology*, *62*, 63–77.

Sanders, J.L. & Newman, A.B. (2013). Telomere length in epidemiology: a biomarker of aging, age-related disease, both, or neither? *Epidemiologic Reviews*, *35*, 112–131.

Sandman, C.A., Davis, E.P., Buss, C. & Glynn, L.M. (2011). Exposure to prenatal psychobiological stress exerts programming influences on the mother and her fetus. *Neuroendocrinology*, *95*, 8–21.

Sandman, P.M. (2009). Pandemics: good hygiene is not enough. *Nature*, *459*, 322–323.

Sanz, Y., Olivares, M., Moya-Pérez, Á. & Agostoni, C. (2015). Understanding the role of gut microbiome in metabolic disease risk. *Pediatric Research*, *77*, 236–244

Sapolsky, R.M. (2005). The influence of social hierarchy on primate health. *Science*, *308*, 648–652.

Sapolsky, R.M., Romero, L.M. & Munck, A.U. (2000). How do glucocorticoids influence stress responses? Integrating permissive, suppressive, stimulatory, and preparative actions. *Endocrine Reviews*, *21*, 55–89.

Sattar, N., Murray, H.M., Welsh, P. et al. (2009). Are markers of inflammation more strongly associated with risk for fatal than for nonfatal vascular events? *PLoS Medicine*, *6*, e1000099.

Sauder, K.A., McCrea, C.E., Ulbrecht, J.S. et al. (2014). Pistachio nut consumption modifies systemic hemodynamics, increases heart rate variability, and reduces ambulatory blood pressure in well-controlled type 2 diabetes: a randomized trial. *Journal of the American Heart Association*, *3*, e000873.

Saver, J.L., Goyal, M., Bonafe, A. et al. (2015). Stent-retriever thrombectomy after intravenous t-PA vs t-PA alone in stroke. *New England Journal of Medicine*. [Epub ahead of print].

Savitz, S.I., Chopp, M., Deans, R. et al. (2011). Stem cell therapy as an emerging paradigm for stroke (STEPS) II. *Stroke*, *42*, 825–829.

Sawamoto, N., Honda, M., Okada, T. et al. (2000). Expectation of pain enhances responses to nonpainful somatosensory stimulation in the anterior cingulate cortex and parietal operculum/posterior insula: an event-related functional magnetic resonance imaging study. *Journal of Neuroscience*, *20*, 7438–7445.

Schafer, S.M., Colloca, L. & Wager, T.D. (2015). Conditioned placebo analgesia persists when subjects know they are receiving placebo. *The Journal of Pain*, pii: S1526-5900(15)00033-4.

Scharloo, M., Kaptein, A.A., Weinman, J. et al. (1998). Illness perceptions, coping and functioning in patients with rheumatoid arthritis, chronic obstructive pulmonary disease and psoriasis. *Journal of Psychosomatic Research*, *44*, 573–585.

Schattner, A., Bronstein, A. & Jellin, N. (2006). Information and shared decision-making are top patients' priorities. *BMC Health Services Research*, *28*, 21.

Schiffman, M., Castle, P.E., Jeronimo, J. et al. (2007). Human papillomavirus and cervical cancer. *The Lancet*, *370*, 890–907.

Schlotz, W., Hellhammer, J., Schulz, P. & Stone, A.A. (2004). Perceived work overload and chronic worrying predict weekend-weekday differences in the cortisol awakening response. *Psychosomatic Medicine*, *66*, 207–214.

Schluter, J. & Foster, K.R. (2012). The evolution of mutualism in gut microbiota via host epithelial selection. *PLoS Biology*, *10*, e1001424.

Schmid, A.A., Damush, T., Tu, W. et al. (2012). Depression improvement is related to social role functioning after stroke. *Archives of Physical Medicine and Rehabilitation*, *93*, 978–982.

Schmid, D.A., Held, K., Ising, M. et al. (2005). Ghrelin stimulates appetite, imagination of food, GH, ACTH, and cortisol, but does not affect leptin in normal controls. *Neuropsychopharmacology*, *30*, 1187–1192.

Schmidt-Reinwald, A., Pruessner, J.C., Hellhammer, D.H. et al. (1999). The cortisol response to awakening in relation to different challenge tests and a 12-hour cortisol rhythm. *Life Sciences*, *64*, 1653–1660.

Schoen, C. & Doty, M.M. (2004). Inequities in access to medical care in five countries: findings from the 2001 Commonwealth Fund International Health Policy Survey. *Health Policy*, *67*, 309–322.

Schoenbach, V.J. (1987). Appraising health risk appraisal. *American Journal of Public Health*, *77*, 409–411.

Schoenfeld, J.D. & Ioannidis, J.P. (2013). Is everything we eat associated with cancer? A systematic cookbook review. *The American Journal of Clinical Nutrition*, *97*, 127–134.

Schoenfeld, T.J., Rada, P., Pieruzzini, P.R. et al. (2013). Physical exercise prevents stress-induced activation of granule neurons and enhances local inhibitory mechanisms in the dentate gyrus. *Journal of Neuroscience*, *33*, 7770–7777.

Schowalter, J.E. (1977). Psychological reactions to physical illness and hospitalization in adolescence: a survey. *Journal of the American Academy of Child Psychiatry*, *16*, 500–516.

Schreier, H.M. & Wright, R.J. (2014). Stress and food allergy: mechanistic considerations. *Annals of Allergy, Asthma & Immunology*, *112*, 296–301.

Schuler, L.A. & Auger, A.P. (2010). Psychosocially influenced cancer: adverse early-life stress experiences and links to breast cancer. *Cancer Prevention Research*, *3*, 1365–1370.

Schwab, U., Lauritzen, L., Tholstrup, T. et al. (2014). Effect of the amount and type of dietary fat on cardiometabolic risk factors and risk of developing type 2 diabetes, cardiovascular diseases, and cancer: a systematic review. *Food & Nutrition Research*, *58*, 10.3402/fnr.v58.25145.

Schwartz, B. (2004). *Paradox of Choice*. New York: Harper Perennial.

Schwarzer, R. (2008). Modeling health behavior change: how to predict and modify the adoption and maintenance of health behaviors. *Applied Psychology*, *57*, 1–29.

Scientific Report of the 2015 Dietary Guidelines Advisory Committee (2015). www.health.gov/dietaryguidelines/2015-scientific-report/ (accessed May 2015).

Scott, A.M. & Caughlin, J.P. (2014). Communication nonaccommodation in family conversations about end-of-life health decisions. *Health Communication*, *30*, 144–153.

Scott, A.M., Wolchok, J.D. & Old, L.J. (2012). Antibody therapy of cancer. *Nature Reviews Cancer*, *12*, 278–287.

Sears, C.L. (2005). A dynamic partnership: celebrating our gut flora. *Anaerobe*, *11*, 247–251.

Segal, B.M., Pogatchnik, B., Rhodus, N. et al. (2014). Pain in primary Sjögren's syndrome: the role of catastrophizing and negative illness perceptions. *Scandinavian Journal of Rheumatology*, *43*, 234–241.

Segal, Z.V., Williams, J.M.G. & Teasdale, J. (2002). *Mindfulness-Based Cognitive Therapy for Depression: a new approach to preventing relapse*. New York: Guilford Press.

Segerstrom, S.C. (2000). Personality and the immune system: models, methods, and mechanisms. *Annals of Behavioral Medicine*, *22*, 180–190.

Sehlo, M.G. & Bahlas, S.M. (2013). Perceived illness stigma is associated with depression in female patients with systemic lupus erythematosus. *Journal of Psychosomatic Research*, *74*, 248–251.

Sekiyama, K., Takamatsu, Y., Waragai, M. & Hashimoto, M. (2014). Role of genomics in translational research for Parkinson's disease. *Biochemical and Biophysical Research Communications*, *452*, 226–235.

Selbst, S.M & Fein, J.A. (2006). Sedation and analgesia. In F.M. Henretig, G.R. Fleisher & S. Ludwig (Eds.), *Textbook of Pediatric Emergency Medicine*. Hagerstwon, MD: Lippincott Williams & Wilkins.

Seligman, M.E., Rosellini, R.A. & Kozak, M.J. (1975). Learned helplessness in the rat: time course, immunization, and reversibility. *Journal of Comparative and Physiological Psychology*, *88*, 542–547.

Semba, R.D., Ferrucci, L., Bartali, B. et al. (2014). Resveratrol levels and all-cause mortality in older community-dwelling adults. *JAMA Internal Medicine*, *174*, 1077–1084.

Sephton, S.E., Sapolsky, R.M., Kraemer, H.C. & Spiegel, D. (2000). Diurnal cortisol rhythm as a predictor of breast cancer survival. *Journal of the National Cancer Institute*, *92*, 994–1000.

Serafini, G.H., Howland, R., Rovedi, F. et al. (2014). The role of ketamine in treatment-resistant depression: a systematic review. *Current Neuropharmacology*, *12*, 444–461.

Serban, D.E. (2014). Gastrointestinal cancers: influence of gut microbiota, probiotics and prebiotics. *Cancer Letters*, *345*, 258–270.

Serova, L.I., Tillinger, A., Alaluf, L.G. et al. (2013). Single intranasal neuropeptide Y infusion attenuates development of PTSD-like symptoms to traumatic stress in rats. *Neuroscience*, *236*, 298–312.

Shah, A.J., Veledar, E., Hong, Y. et al. (2011). Depression and history of attempted suicide as risk factors for heart disease mortality in young individuals. *Archives of General Psychiatry*, *68*, 1135–1142.

Shah, S.N. & Meeks, S. (2011). Late-life bereavement and complicated grief: a proposed comprehensive framework. *Aging & Mental Health*, *16*, 39–56.

Shaham, Y., Shalev, U., Lu, L. et al. (2003). The reinstatement model of drug relapse: history, methodology and major findings. *Psychopharmacology*, *168*, 3–20.

Sham, H.P., Yu, E.Y.S., Gulen, M.F. et al. (2013). SIGIRR, a negative regulator of TLR/IL-1R signalling promotes microbiota dependent resistance to colonization by enteric bacterial pathogens. *PLoS Pathogens*, *9*, e1003539.

Shapiro, D., Hui, K.K., Oakley, M.E. et al. (1997). Reduction in drug requirements for hypertension by means of a cognitive-behavioral intervention. *American Journal of Hypertension*, *10*, 9–17.

Shear, M.K., Simon, N., Wall, M. et al. (2011). Complicated grief and related bereavement issues for DSM-5. *Depression and Anxiety*, *28*, 103–117.

Sheehan, J., Sherman, K.A., Lam, T. & Boyages, J. (2008). Regret associated with the decision for breast reconstruction: the association of negative body image, distress and surgery characteristics with decision regret. *Psychology and Health*, *23*, 207–219.

Sheeran, P. (2002). Intention–behavior relations: a conceptual and empirical review. In W. Stroebe & M. Hewstone (Eds.), *European Review of Social Psychology* (pp. 1–36). Hove: Psychology Press.

Shen, J., Obin, M.S. & Zhao, L. (2013). The gut microbiota, obesity and insulin resistance. *Molecular Aspects of Medicine*, *34*, 39–58.

Sherman, A.C., Simonton, S., Latif, U. & Bracy, L. (2010). Effects of global-meaning and illness-specific meaning on health outcomes among breast cancer patients. *Journal of Behavioral Medicine, 33*, 364–377.

Sherman, M.P., Zaghouani, H. & Niklas, V. (2015). Gut microbiota, the immune system, and diet influence the neonatal gut-brain axis. *Pediatric Research, 77*, 127–135.

Shichita, T., Ito, M. & Yoshimura, A. (2014). Post-ischemic inflammation regulates neural damage and protection. *Frontiers in Cellular Neuroscience, 8*, 319.

Shiels, M.S., Pfeiffer, R.M., Hildesheim, A. et al. (2013). Circulating inflammation markers and prospective risk of lung cancer. *Journal of the National Cancer Institute, 105*, 1871–1880.

Shimuta, K., Unemo, M., Nakayama, S.I. et al. (2013). Antimicrobial resistance and molecular typing of Neisseria gonorrhoeae isolates in Kyoto and Osaka, Japan, 2010 to 2012: intensified surveillance after identification of the first strain (H041) with high-level ceftriaxone resistance. *Antimicrobial Agents and Chemotherapy, 57*, 5225–5232.

Shin, H., Shin, J., Liu, P.Y. et al. (2011). Self-efficacy improves weight loss in overweight/obese post-menopausal women during a 6-month weight loss intervention. *Nutrition Research, 31*, 822–828.

Shonkoff, J.P., Boyce, W.T. & McEwen, B.S. (2009). Neuroscience, molecular biology, and the childhood roots of health disparities: building a new framework for health promotion and disease prevention. *Journal of the American Medical Association, 301*, 2252–2259.

Shreiner, A., Huffnagle, G.B. & Noverr, M.C. (2008). The 'Microflora Hypothesis' of allergic disease. *Advances in Experimental Medicine and Biology, 635*, 113–134.

Shrestha, S.S., Swerdlow, D.L., Borse, R.H. et al. (2011). Estimating the burden of 2009 pandemic influenza A (H1N1) in the United States (April 2009–April 2010). *Clinical Infectious Diseases, 52*, S75–S82.

Shu, S.A., Wang, J., Tao, M.H. & Leung, P.S. (2014). Gene therapy for autoimmune disease. *Clinical Reviews in Allergy & Immunology*, 1–14.

Shungin, D., Winkler, T.W., Croteau-Chonka, D.C. et al. (2015). New genetic loci link adipose and insulin biology to body fat distribution. *Nature, 518*, 187–196.

Siegel, S. (1999). Drug anticipation and drug addiction. The 1998 H. David Archibald Lecture. *Addiction, 94*, 1113–1124.

Sieverding, M., Matterne, U. & Ciccarello, L. (2010). What role do social norms play in the context of men's cancer screening intention and behavior? Application of an extended theory of planned behavior. *Health Psychology, 29*, 72.

Sigsbee, B. & Bernat, J.L. (2014). Physician burnout: a neurologic crisis. *Neurology, 83*, 2302–2306.

Sigurdardottir, L.G., Valdimarsdottir, U.A., Mucci, L.A., et al. (2013). Sleep disruption among older men and risk of prostate cancer. *Cancer Epidemiology Biomarkers & Prevention, 22*, 872–879.

Silver, R.C. & Wortman, C.B. (2007). The stage theory of grief. *JAMA, 297*, 2692–2694.

Simons, F.E. & World Allergy Organization. (2010). World Allergy Organization survey on global availability of essentials for the assessment and management of anaphylaxis by allergy-immunology specialists in health care settings. *Annals of Allergy, Asthma & Immunology, 104*, 405–412.

Simonsen, L., Clarke, M.J., Schonberger, L.B. et al. (1998). Pandemic versus epidemic influenza mortality: a pattern of changing age distribution. *Journal of Infectious Diseases, 178*, 53–60.

Simpson, R.J. & Bosch, J.A. (2014). Special issue on exercise immunology: current perspectives on aging, health and extreme performance. *Brain, Behavior, and Immunity, 39*, 1–7.

Sims, N.R. & Muyderman, H. (2009). Mitochondria, oxidative metabolism and cell death in stroke. *Biochimica et Biophysica Acta, 1802*, 80–91.

Sinha, R. (2008). Chronic stress, drug use, and vulnerability to addiction. *Annals of the New York Academy of Sciences, 1141*, 105–130.

Sinha, R., Dufour, S., Petersen, K.F. et al. (2002). Assessment of skeletal muscle triglyceride content by 1H nuclear magnetic resonance spectroscopy in lean and obese adolescents: relationships to insulin sensitivity, total body fat, and central adiposity. *Diabetes, 51*, 1022–1027.

Sinyor, D., Amato, P., Kaloupek, D.G. et al. (1986). Post-stroke depression: relationships to functional impairment, coping strategies, and rehabilitation outcome. *Stroke, 17,* 1102–1107.

Sjösten, N. & Kivelä, S.L. (2006). The effects of physical exercise on depressive symptoms among the aged: a systematic review. *International Journal of Geriatric Psychiatry, 21,* 410–418.

Skilbeck, J. & Payne, S. (2003). Emotional support and the role of clinical nurse specialists in palliative care. *Journal of Advanced Nursing, 43,* 521–530.

Skilbeck, J.K. & Payne, S. (2005). End of life care: a discursive analysis of specialist palliative care nursing. *Journal of Advanced Nursing, 51,* 325–34.

Skilbeck, K.J., Johnston, G.A. & Hinton, T. (2010). Stress and GABA receptors. *Journal of Neurochemistry, 112,* 1115–1130.

Sklar, L.S. & Anisman, H. (1979). Stress and coping factors influence tumor growth. *Science, 205,* 513–515.

Slavich, G.M. & Irwin, M.R. (2014). From stress to inflammation and major depressive disorder: a social signal transduction theory of depression. *Psychological Bulletin, 140,* 774–815.

Slavich, G.M., O'Donovan, A., Epel, E.S. & Kemeny, M.E. (2010). Black sheep get the blues: a psychobiological model of social rejection and depression. *Neuroscience & Biobehavioral Reviews, 35,* 39–45.

Slavich, G.M., Way, B.M., Eisenberger, N.I. & Taylor, S.E. (2010). Neural sensitivity to social rejection is associated with inflammatory responses to social stress. *Proceedings of the National Academy of Sciences, 107,* 14817–14822.

Smedslund, G., Byfuglien, M.G., Olsen, S.U. & Hagen, K.B. (2010). Effectiveness and safety of dietary interventions for rheumatoid arthritis: a systematic review of randomized controlled trials. *Journal of the American Dietetic Association, 110,* 727–735.

Smith, C.A., Levett, K.M., Collins, C.T. & Crowther, C.A. (2011). Relaxation techniques for pain management in labour. *The Cochrane Database of Systematic Reviews,* CD009514.

Smith, K.S., Virkud, A., Deisseroth, K. et al. (2012). Reversible online control of habitual behavior by optogenetic perturbation of medial prefrontal cortex. *Proceedings of the National Academy of Sciences, 109,* 18932–18937.

Smith, P.M., Glazier, R.H., Lu, H. & Mustard, C.A. (2012). The psychosocial work environment and incident diabetes in Ontario, Canada. *Occupational Medicine, 62,* 413–419.

Smith, P.M., Tuomisto, M.T., Blumenthal, J. et al. (2013). Psychosocial correlates of atrial natriuretic peptide: a marker of vascular health. *Annals of Behavioral Medicine, 45,* 99–109.

Smith, R. (2014). Are some diets 'mass murder'? *BMJ: British Medical Journal, 349,* g7654.

Smith, R.A., Manassaram-Baptiste, D., Brooks, D. et al. (2014). Cancer screening in the United States, 2014: a review of current American Cancer Society guidelines and current issues in cancer screening. *CA: A Cancer Journal for Clinicians, 64,* 30–51.

Smith, T.W., Turner, C.W., Ford, M.H. et al. (1987). Blood pressure reactivity in adult male twins. *Health Psychology, 6,* 209–220.

Smolderen, K.G., Spertus, J.A., Reid, K.J. et al. (2009). The association of cognitive and somatic depressive symptoms with depression recognition and outcomes after myocardial infarction. *Circulation: Cardiovascular Quality and Outcomes, 2,* 328–337.

Soares, J.M., Sampaio, A., Ferreira, L.M. et al. (2012). Stress-induced changes in human decision-making are reversible. *Translational Psychiatry, 2,* e131.

Sokol, H. & Seksik, P. (2010). The intestinal microbiota in inflammatory bowel diseases: time to connect with the host. *Current Opinion in Gastroenterology, 26,* 327–331.

Solomon, S. & Kington, R. (2002). National efforts to promote behavior-change research: views from the Office of Behavioral and Social Sciences Research. *Health Education Research, 17,* 495–499.

Soltesz, G., Patterson, C.C., Dahlquist, G. & EURODIAB Study Group. (2007). Worldwide childhood type 1 diabetes incidence: What can we learn from epidemiology? *Pediatric Diabetes, 8,* 6–14.

Song, Y.S. & Ingram, K. (2002). Unsupportive social interactions, availability of social support, and coping: their relationship to mood disturbance among African Americans living with HIV. *Journal of Social and Personal Relationships, 19,* 67–85.

Sorrells, S.F., Caso, J.R., Munhoz, C.D. & Sapolsky, R.M. (2009). The stressed CNS: when glucocorticoids aggravate inflammation. *Neuron, 64,* 33–39.

Southwick, S.M., Bremner, J.D., Rasmusson, A. et al. (1999). Role of norepinephrine in the pathophysiology and treatment of posttraumatic stress disorder. *Biological Psychiatry*, *46*, 1192–1204.

Specht, P.G. (2007). The Peltzman effect: Do safety regulations increase unsafe behavior? *Journal of Safety, Health and Environmental Research*, *4*, 1–2.

Spencer, S.J., Xu, L., Clarke, M.A. et al. (2012). Ghrelin regulates the hypothalamic-pituitary-adrenal axis and restricts anxiety after acute stress. *Biological Psychiatry*, *72*, 457–465.

Spencer, S.P. & Belkaid, Y. (2012). Dietary and commensal derived nutrients: shaping mucosal and systemic immunity. *Current Opinion in Immunology*, *24*, 379–384.

Spiegel, D. (1994). Health caring: psychosocial support for patients with cancer. *Cancer*, *74*, 1453–1457.

Spiegel, K., Sheridan, J.F. & Van Cauter, E. (2002). Effect of sleep deprivation on response to immunizaton. *JAMA*, *288*, 1471–1472.

Spitz, M.R., Caporaso, N.E. & Sellers, T.A. (2012). Integrative cancer epidemiology: the next generation. *Cancer Discovery*, *2*, 1087–1090.

Stafford, P., Cichacz, Z., Woodbury, N.W. & Johnston, S.A. (2014). Immunosignature system for diagnosis of cancer. *Proceedings of the National Academy of Sciences*, *111*, E3072–E3080.

Stamp, K.D., Machado, M.A. & Allen, N.A. (2014). Transitional care programs improve outcomes for heart failure patients: an integrative review. *Journal of Cardiovascular Nursing*, *29*, 140–154.

Stamp, L.K., James, M.J. & Cleland, L.G. (2005). Diet and rheumatoid arthritis: a review of the literature. *Seminars in Arthritis and Rheumatism*, *35*, 77–94.

Staneva, A., Bogossian, F., Pritchard, M. & Wittkowski, A. (2015). The effects of maternal depression, anxiety, and perceived stress during pregnancy on preterm birth: a systematic review. *Women Birth*, pii: S1871-5192(15)00030-X. [Epub ahead of print].

Stanton, A.L., Danoff-Burg, S., Cameron, C.L. & Ellis, A.P. (1994). Coping through emotional approach: problems of conceptualization and confounding. *Journal of Personality and Social Psychology*, *66*, 350–362.

Steele, C.M. (1988). The psychology of self-affirmation: sustaining the integrity of the self. *Advances in Experimental Social Psychology*, *21*, 261–302.

Steinhauser, K.E., Clipp, E.C., McNeilly, M. et al. (2000). In search of a good death: observations of patients, families, and providers. *Annals of Internal Medicine*, *132*, 825–832.

Stenehjem, D.D., Albright, F., Kuo, K.L. et al. (2014). Response monitoring, tolerability, and effectiveness of imatinib treatment for chronic myeloid leukemia in a retrospective research database. *Journal of the National Comprehensive Cancer Network*, *12*, 1113–1121.

Steptoe, A. & Kivimäki, M. (2013). Stress and cardiovascular disease: an update on current knowledge. *Annual Review of Public Health*, *34*, 337–354.

Steptoe, A., Shamaei-Tousi, A., Gylfe, Å. et al. (2008). Socioeconomic status, pathogen burden and cardiovascular disease risk. *Heart*, *93*, 1567–1570.

Sternberg, E.M. (2006). Neural regulation of innate immunity: a coordinated nonspecific host response to pathogens. *Nature Reviews Immunology*, *6*, 318–328.

Stewart, J. (2000). Pathways to relapse: the neurobiology of drug- and stress-induced relapse to drug-taking. *Journal of Psychiatry and Neuroscience*, *25*, 125–136.

Stewart, J.C., Fitzgerald, G.J. & Kamarck, T.W. (2010). Hostility now, depression later? Longitudinal associations among emotional risk factors for coronary artery disease. *Annals of Behavioral Medicine*, *39*, 258–266.

Stewart-Williams, S. & Podd, J. (2004). The placebo effect: dissolving the expectancy versus conditioning debate. *Psychological Bulletin*, *130*, 324–340.

Stieg, M.R., Sievers, C., Farr, O. et al. (2014). Leptin: a hormone linking activation of neuroendocrine axes with neuropathology. *Psychoneuroendocrinology*, *51*, 47–57.

Stieglitz, J., Schniter, E., Kaplan, H.S. et al. (2014). Functional disability and social conflict increase risk of depression in older adulthood among Bolivian forager-farmers. *The Journals of Gerontology Series B: Psychological Sciences and Social Sciences*. Doi: 10.1093/geronb/gbu080.

Stoker, A.K. & Markou, A. (2013). Unraveling the neurobiology of nicotine dependence using genetically engineered mice. *Current Opinion in Neurobiology*, *23*, 493–499.

Stone, A.A. & Neale, J.M. (1982). Development of a methodology for assessing daily experiences. In A. Baum & J.E. Singer (Eds.), *Advances in Environmental Psychology: environment and health* (pp. 49–83). Hillsdale, NJ: Lawrence Erlbaum Associates.

Stone, N.J., Robinson, J., Lichtenstein, A.H., et al. (2013). 2013 ACC/AHA guideline on the treatment of blood cholesterol to reduce atherosclerotic cardiovascular risk in adults: a report of the American College of Cardiology/American Heart Association Task Force on Practice Guidelines. *Circulation*, *129*, S1–S45.

Stopper, C.M. & Floresco, S.B. (2014). What's better for me? Fundamental role for lateral habenula in promoting subjective decision biases. *Nature Neuroscience*, *17*, 33–35.

Strachan, D.P. (2000). Family size, infection and atopy: the first decade of the 'hygiene hypothesis'. *Thorax*, *55*, S2.

Straub, R.H., Dhabhar, F.S., Bijlsma, J.W. & Cutolo, M. (2005). How psychological stress via hormones and nerve fibers may exacerbate rheumatoid arthritis. *Arthritis & Rheumatism*, *52*, 16–26.

Streeter, C.C., Gerbarg, P.L., Saper, R.B. et al. (2012). Effects of yoga on the autonomic nervous system, gamma-aminobutyric-acid, and allostasis in epilepsy, depression, and post-traumatic stress disorder. *Medical Hypotheses*, *78*, 571–579.

Strissel, K.J., Denis, G.V. & Nikolajczyk, B.S. (2014). Immune regulators of inflammation in obesity-associated type 2 diabetes and coronary artery disease. *Current Opinion in Endocrinology, Diabetes and Obesity*, *21*, 330–338.

Stroebe, M. (2001). Gender differences in adjustment to bereavement: an empirical and theoretical review. *Review of General Psychology*, *5*, 62–83.

Stroebe, M. & Schut, H. (1999). The dual process model of coping with bereavement: rationale and description. *Death Studies*, *23*, 197–224.

Stuber, M.L., Meeske, K.A., Krull, K.R. et al. (2010). Prevalence and predictors of posttraumatic stress disorder in adult survivors of childhood cancer. *Pediatrics*, *125*, e1124–e1134.

Sue, D.W., Capodilupo, C.M., Torino, G.C. et al. (2007). Racial microaggressions in everyday life: implications for clinical practice. *American Psychologist*, *62*, 271.

Suez, J., Korem, T., Zeevi, D. et al. (2014). Artificial sweeteners induce glucose intolerance by altering the gut microbiota. *Nature*, *514*, 181–186.

Sugiura, Y. (2004). Detached mindfulness and worry: a meta-cognitive analysis. *Personality and Individual Differences*, *37*, 169–179.

Suh, J.M., Jonker, J.W., Ahmadian, M. et al. (2014). Endocrinization of FGF1 produces a neomorphic and potent insulin sensitizer. *Nature*, *513*, 436–439.

Sun, F. & Hodge, D.R. (2014). Latino Alzheimer's disease caregivers and depression using the stress coping model to examine the effects of spirituality and religion. *Journal of Applied Gerontology*, *33*, 291–315.

Sun, Y., Kim, S.W., Heo, C.Y. et al. (2014). Comparison of quality of life based on surgical technique in patients with breast cancer. *Japanese Journal of Clinical Oncology*, *44*, 22–27.

Surwit, R.S., Van Tilburg, M.A., Zucker, N. et al. (2002). Stress management improves long-term glycemic control in type 2 diabetes. *Diabetes Care*, *25*, 30–34.

Sussan, T.E., Gajghate, S., Thimmulappa, R.K. et al. (2015). Exposure to electronic cigarettes impairs pulmonary anti-bacterial and anti-viral defenses in a mouse model. *PLoS One*, *10*, e0116861.

Sussman, J.B., Kent, D.M., Nelson, J.P. & Hayward, R.A. (2015). Improving diabetes prevention with benefit based tailored treatment: risk based reanalysis of Diabetes Prevention Program. *BMJ: British Medical Journal*, *350*, h454.

Sutin, A.R., Terracciano, A., Milaneschi, Y. et al. (2013). The trajectory of depressive symptoms across the adult life span. *JAMA Psychiatry*, *70*, 803–811.

Sutton, S.A. (2000). A critical review of the transtheoretical model applied to smoking cessation. In P. Norman, C. Abraham & M. Conner (Eds.), *Understanding and Changing Health Behaviour: from health beliefs to self-regulation* (pp. 207–225). Amsterdam: Harwood Academic Publishers.

Suzuki, K., Simpson, K.A., Minnion, J.S. et al. (2010). The role of gut hormones and the hypothalamus in appetite regulation. *Endocrine Journal*, *57*, 359–372.

Swartwood, R.M., Veach, P.M., Kuhne, J. et al. (2011). Surviving grief: an analysis of the exchange of hope in online grief communities. *Omega (Westport)*, *63*, 161–181.

Sweeney, A.M. & Moyer, A. (2015). Self-affirmation and responses to health messages: a meta-analysis on intentions and behavior. *Health Psychology*, *34*, 149–159.

Syrjala, K.L., Jensen, M.P., Mendoza, M.E. et al. (2014). Psychological and behavioral approaches to cancer pain management. *Journal of Clinical Oncology*, *32*, 1703–1711.

Szyf, M. (2011). The early life social environment and DNA methylation: DNA methylation mediating the long-term impact of social environments early in life. *Epigenetics*, *6*, 971–978.

Szyf, M. (2012). DNA methylation signatures for breast cancer classification and prognosis. *Genome Medicine*, *4*, 26.

Szyf, M., Weaver, I.C., Champagne, F.A. et al. (2005). Maternal programming of steroid receptor expression and phenotype through DNA methylation in the rat. *Frontiers in Neuroendocrinology*, *26*, 139–162.

Tabak, B.A., Meyer, M.L., Castle, E. et al. (2015). Vasopressin, but not oxytocin, increases empathic concern among individuals who received higher levels of paternal warmth: A randomized controlled trial. *Psychoneuroendocrinology*, *51*, 253–261.

Tachjian, A., Maria, V. & Jahangir, A. (2010). Use of herbal products and potential interactions in patients with cardiovascular diseases. *Journal of the American College of Cardiology*, *55*, 515–525.

Taft, T.H., Keefer, L., Leonhard, C. & Nealon-Woods, M. (2009). Impact of perceived stigma on inflammatory bowel disease patient outcomes. *Inflammatory Bowel Diseases*, *15*, 1224–1232.

Taha, S., Matheson, K., Cronin, T. & Anisman, H. (2014). Intolerance of uncertainty, appraisals, coping, and anxiety: the case of the 2009 H1N1 pandemic. *British Journal of Health Psychology*, *19*, 592–605.

Taha, S.A., Matheson, K. & Anisman, H. (2013). The 2009 H1N1 influenza pandemic: the role of threat, coping, and media trust on vaccination intentions in Canada. *Journal of Health Communication*, *18*, 278–290.

Taleb, N.N. (2010). *The Black Swan: the impact of the highly improbable* (2nd ed.). London: Penguin.

Talebi, M., Matheson, K. & Anisman, H. (2013). Support, depressive symptoms, and the stigma towards seeking mental health help. *International Journal of Social Science Studies*, *1*, 133–144.

Tang, Y., Axelsson, A.S., Spégel, P. et al. (2014). Genotype-based treatment of type 2 diabetes with an α2A-adrenergic receptor antagonist. *Science Translational Medicine*, *6*, 257ra139.

Tang, Y.Y., Hölzel, B.K. & Posner, M.I. (2015). The neuroscience of mindfulness meditation. *Nature Reviews Neuroscience*, *16*, 213–225.

Tannenbaum, D., Valasek, C.J., Knowles, E.D. & Ditto, P.H. (2013). Incentivizing wellness in the workplace: sticks (not carrots) send stigmatizing signals. *Psychological Science*, *24*, 1512–1522.

Tarhini, A., Lo, E. & Minor, D.R. (2010). Releasing the brake on the immune system: ipilimumab in melanoma and other tumors. *Cancer Biotherapy & Radiopharmaceuticals*, *25*, 601–613.

Tarrant, M., Hagger, M.S. & Farrow, C.V. (2012). Promoting positive orientation towards health through social identity. In J. Jetten, C. Haslam & S.A. Haslam (Eds.), *The Social Cure: identity, health and well-being* (pp. 39–54). Hove, UK: Psychology Press.

Tavener, S.A. & Kubes, P. (2006). Cellular and molecular mechanisms underlying LPS-associated myocyte impairment. *American Journal of Physiology: Heart and Circulatory Physiology*, *290*, H800–H806.

Taylor, A. & Powell, M.E. (2004). Intensity-modulated radiotherapy: What is it? *Cancer Imaging*, *4*, 68–73.

Taylor, D.J. & Pruiksma, K.E. (2014). Cognitive and behavioural therapy for insomnia (CBT-I) in psychiatric populations: a systematic review. *International Review of Psychiatry*, *26*, 205–213.

Taylor, F., Huffman, M.D., Macedo, A.F. et al. (2013). Statins for the primary prevention of cardiovascular disease. *The Cochrane Database of Systematic Reviews*, *1*, CD004816.

Taylor, L. et al. (2001). Risk factors for human disease emergence. *Philosophical Transactions of the Royal Society of London B: Biological Sciences*, *356*, 983–989.

Taylor, S.E., Burklund, L.J., Eisenberger, N.I. et al. (2008). Neural bases of moderation of cortisol stress responses by psychosocial resources. *Journal of Personality and Social Psychology*, 95, 197–211.

Taylor, S.E., Klein, L.C., Lewis, B.P. et al. (2000). Biobehavioral responses to stress in females: tend-and-befriend, not fight-or-flight. *Psychological Review*, 107, 411.

Taylor, S.E., Seeman, T.E., Eisenberger, N.I. et al. (2010). Effects of a supportive or an unsupportive audience on biological and psychological responses to stress. *Journal of Personality and Social Psychology*, 98, 47–56.

Te Boveldt, N., Vernooij-Dassen, M., Leppink, I. et al. (2014). Patient empowerment in cancer pain management: an integrative literature review. *Psychooncology*, 23, 1203–1211.

Teh, C.F., Zaslavsky, A., Reynolds III, C.F. & Cleary, P.D. (2010). Effect of depression treatment on chronic pain outcomes. *Psychosomatic Medicine*, 72, 61.

Tehrani, A.S.S., Lee, H., Mathews, S.C. et al. (2013). 25-year summary of US malpractice claims for diagnostic errors 1986–2010: an analysis from the National Practitioner Data Bank. *BMJ Quality & Safety*, 22, 672–680.

Teicholz, N. (2014). *The Big Fat Surprise: why butter, milk and cheese belong in a healthy diet.* New York: Simon & Schuster.

Teixeira, P.J., Silva, M.N., Mata, J. et al. (2012). Motivation, self-determination, and long-term weight control. *The International Journal of Behavioral Nutrition and Physical Activity*, 9, 22.

Tennen, H., Affleck, G., Armeli, S. & Carney, M.A. (2000). A daily process approach to coping: linking theory, research, and practice. *American Psychologist*, 55, 626–636.

Tennen, H., Affleck, G. & Zautra, A. (2006). Depression history and coping with chronic pain: a daily process analysis. *Health Psychology*, 25, 370–379.

Tennoune, N., Legrand, R., Ouelaa, W. et al. (2015). Sex-related effects of nutritional supplementation of Escherichia coli: relevance to eating disorders. *Nutrition*, 31, 498–507.

Teno, J.M., Gozalo, P.L., Bynum, J.P. et al. (2013). Change in end-of-life care for Medicare beneficiaries: site of death, place of care, and health care transitions in 2000, 2005, and 2009. *The Journal of the American Medical Association*, 309, 470–477.

Teutsch, C. (2003). Patient–doctor communication. *Medical Clinics of North America*, 87, 1115–1145.

Thaker, P., Han, L.Y., Kamat, A.A. et al. (2006). Chronic stress promotes tumor growth and angiogenesis in a mouse model of ovarian carcinoma. *Nature Medicine*, 12, 939–944.

Thaler, R.H. & Sunstein, C.R. (2008). *Nudge: improving decisions about health, wealth, and happiness.* New Haven, CT: Yale University Press.

The King's Fund (2015) *Better Value in the NHS*. London: The King's Fund. www.kingsfund.org.uk/publications/better-value-nhs/summary (accessed October 2015).

Theysohn, N., Choi, K.E., Gizewski, E.R. et al. (2014). Acupuncture-related modulation of pain-associated brain networks during electrical pain stimulation: a functional magnetic resonance imaging study. *The Journal of Alternative and Complementary Medicine*, 20, 893–900.

Thirthalli, J. & Benegal, V. (2006). Psychosis among substance users. *Current Opinion in Psychiatry*, 19, 239–245.

Thoits, P.A. (2010). Stress and health: major findings and policy implications. *Journal of Health and Social Behavior*, 51, S41–S53.

Thomas, D. & Elliott, E.J. (2009). Low glycaemic index, or low glycaemic load, diets for diabetes mellitus. *The Cochrane Database of Systematic Reviews*, CD006296.

Thompson, I.M., Pauler, D.K., Goodman, P.J. et al. (2004). Prevalence of prostate cancer among men with a prostate-specific antigen level≤ 4.0 ng per milliliter. *New England Journal of Medicine*, 350, 2239–2246.

Thompson, R.W, Arnkoff, D.B & Glass, C.R. (2011). Conceptualizing mindfulness and acceptance as components of psychological resilience to trauma. *Trauma Violence Abuse*, 12, 220–235.

Thompson, W.W., Moore, M.R., Weintraub, E. et al. (2009). Estimating influenza-associated deaths in the United States. *American Journal of Public Health*, 99, S225–S230.

Thomsen, L.A., Winterstein, A.G., Søndergaard, B. et al. (2007). Systematic review of the incidence and characteristics of preventable adverse drug events in ambulatory care. *Annals of Pharmacotherapy*, *41*, 1411–1426.

Thornton, L.M., Andersen, B.L., Crespin, T.R. & Carson, W.E. (2007). Individual trajectories in stress covary with immunity during recovery from cancer diagnosis and treatments. *Brain, Behavior, and Immunity*, *21*, 185–194.

Thrane, S. (2013). Effectiveness of integrative modalities for pain and anxiety in children and adolescents with cancer: a systematic review. *Journal of Pediatric Oncology Nursing*, *30*, 320–332.

Thurston, R.C., Chang, Y., Derby, C.A. et al. (2014). Abuse and subclinical cardiovascular disease among midlife women: the study of women's health across the nation. *Stroke*, *45*, 2246–2251.

Thurston, R.C. & Kubzansky, L.D. (2009). Women, loneliness, and incident coronary heart disease. *Psychosomatic Medicine*, *71*, 836–842.

Timm, S., Svanes, C., Janson, C. et al. (2014). Place of upbringing in early childhood as related to inflammatory bowel diseases in adulthood: a population-based cohort study in Northern Europe. *European Journal of Epidemiology*, *29*, 429–437.

Tindle, H.A., Davis, R.B., Phillips, R.S. & Eisenberg, D.M. (2005). Trends in use of complementary and alternative medicine by US adults: 1997–2002. *Alternative Therapies in Health and Medicine*, *11*, 42.

Tjia, J., Velten, S.J., Parsons, C. et al. (2013). Studies to reduce unnecessary medication use in frail older adults: a systematic review. *Drugs & Aging*, *30*, 285–307.

Tkachenko, O., Olson, E.A., Weber, M. et al. (2014). Sleep difficulties are associated with increased symptoms of psychopathology. *Experimental Brain Research*, *232*, 1567–1574.

Tol, W.A., Song, S. & Jordans, M.J. (2013). Annual research review: resilience and mental health in children and adolescents living in areas of armed conflict – a systematic review of findings in low- and middle-income countries. *Journal of Child Psychology and Psychiatry*, *54*, 445–460.

Tolin, D.F. & Foa, E.B. (2006). Sex differences in trauma and posttraumatic stress disorder: a quantitative review of 25 years of research. *Psychological Bulletin*, *132*, 959–992.

Tomasetti, C. & Vogelstein, B. (2015). Variation in cancer risk among tissues can be explained by the number of stem cell divisions. *Science*, *347*, 78–81.

Tomé-Pires, C. & Miró, J. (2012). Hypnosis for the management of chronic and cancer procedure-related pain in children. *International Journal of Clinical and Experimental Hypnosis*, *60*, 432–457.

Tononi, G. & Cirelli, C. (2003). Sleep and synaptic homeostasis: a hypothesis. *Brain Research Bulletin*, *62*, 143–150.

Torner, L. & Neumann, I.D. (2002). The brain prolactin system: involvement in stress response adaptations in lactation. *Stress: The International Journal on the Biology of Stress*, *5*, 249–257.

Toufexis, D., Rivarola, M.A., Lara, H. & Viau, V. (2014). Stress and the reproductive axis. *Journal of Neuroendocrinology*, *26*, 573–586.

Touvier, M., Fezeu, L., Ahluwalia, N. et al. (2013). Association between prediagnostic biomarkers of inflammation and endothelial function and cancer risk: a nested case-control study. *American Journal of Epidemiology*, *177*, 3–13.

Trochim, W. & Donnelly, J.P. (2007). *The Research Methods Knowledge Base* (3rd ed.). Mason, OH: Thomson Publishing.

Troncone, R., Ivarsson, A., Szajewska, H. & Mearin, M.L. (2008). Review article. Future research on coeliac disease: a position report from the European multistakeholder platform on coeliac disease (CDEUSSA). *Alimentary Pharmacology & Therapeutics*, *27*, 1030–1043.

Turk, D.C. & Okifuji, A. (2001). Pain terms and taxonomies. In D. Loeser, S.H. Butler, J.J. Chapman & D.C. Turk (Eds.), *Bonica's Management of Pain* (3rd ed., pp. 18–25). Philadelphia, PA: Lippincott Williams & Wilkins.

Turner, J.A., Holtzman, S. & Mancl, L. (2007). Mediators, moderators, and predictors of therapeutic change in cognitive-behavioral therapy for chronic pain. *Pain*, *127*, 276–286.

Tuxen, I.V., Jønson, L., Santoni-Rugiu, E. et al. (2014). Personalized oncology: genomic screening in phase 1. *Apmis*, *122*, 723–733.

Tversky, A. & Kahneman, D. (1974). Judgment under uncertainty: heuristics and biases. *Science*, *185*, 1124–1131.

Tzortzaki, E.G., Papi, A., Neofytou, E. et al. (2013). Immune and genetic mechanisms in COPD: possible targets for therapeutic interventions. *Current Drug Targets*, *14*, 141–148.

Udell, J.A., Zawi, R., Bhatt, D.L. et al. (2013). Association between influenza vaccination and cardiovascular outcomes in high-risk patients: a meta-analysis. *JAMA*, *310*, 1711–1720.

Uhl, R.L., Roberts, T.T., Papaliodis, D.N. et al. (2014). Management of chronic musculoskeletal pain. *Journal of the American Academy of Orthopaedic Surgeons*, *22*, 101–110.

U.S. Preventive Services Task Force (USTSPF) (2015). Prostate cancer: Screening. http://www.uspreventiveservicestaskforce.org/Page/Document/UpdateSummaryFinal/prostate-cancer-screening?ds=1&s=PSA (accessed September 2015).

Uschold-Schmidt, N., Nyuyki, K.D., Füchsl, A.M. et al. (2012). Chronic psychosocial stress results in sensitization of the HPA axis to acute heterotypic stressors despite a reduction of adrenal in vitro ACTH responsiveness. *Psychoneuroendocrinology*, *37*, 1676–1687.

Uys, J.D., Muller, C.J., Marais, L. et al. (2006). Early life trauma decreases glucocorticoid receptors in rat dentate gyrus upon adult re-stress: reversal by escitalopram. *Neuroscience*, *137*, 619–625.

Vaccarino, V., Goldberg, J., Rooks, C. et al. (2013). Post-traumatic stress disorder and incidence of coronary heart disease: a twin study. *Journal of the American College of Cardiology*, *62*, 970–978.

Vance M.L. (2003). Can growth hormone prevent aging? *New England Journal of Medicine*, *348*, 779–780.

van der Windt, D.A., Jellema, P., Mulder, C.J. et al. (2010). Diagnostic testing for celiac disease among patients with abdominal symptoms: a systematic review. *Journal of the American Medical Association*, *303*, 1738–1746.

Van Dorsten, B. & Lindley, E.M. (2011). Cognitive and behavioral approaches in the treatment of obesity. *Medical Clinics of North America*, *95*, 971–988.

van Leeuwen, W.M., Lehto, M., Karisola, P. et al. (2009). Sleep restriction increases the risk of developing cardiovascular diseases by augmenting proinflammatory responses through IL-17 and CRP. *PLoS One*, *4*, e4589.

Van Lieshout, R.J., Bienenstock, J. & MacQueen, G.M. (2009). A review of candidate pathways underlying the association between asthma and major depressive disorder. *Psychosomatic Medicine*, *71*,187–195.

Van Meeteren, M.E., Teunissen, C.E., Dijkstra, C.D. & Van Tol, E.A. (2005). Antioxidants and polyunsaturated fatty acids in multiple sclerosis. *European Journal of Clinical Nutrition*, *59*, 1347–1361.

Vangay, P., Ward, T., Gerber, J.S. & Knights, D. (2015). Antibiotics, pediatric dysbiosis, and disease. *Cell Host Microbe*, *17*, 553–564.

Vanyukov, M.M., Tarter, R.E., Kirillova, G.P. et al. (2012). Common liability to addiction and 'gateway hypothesis': theoretical, empirical and evolutionary perspective. *Drug and Alcohol Dependence*, *123*, S3–S17.

Varker, K.A., Terrell, C.E., Welt, M. et al. (2007). Impaired natural killer cell lysis in breast cancer patients with high levels of psychological stress is associated with altered expression of killer immunoglobin-like receptors. *Journal of Surgical Research*, *139*, 36–44.

Vase, L., Amanzio, M. & Price, D.D. (2015). Nocebo vs. placebo: the challenges of trial design in analgesia research. *Clinical Pharmacology & Therapeutics*, *97*, 143–150.

Vaso, A., Adahan, H.M., Gjika, A. et al. (2014). Peripheral nervous system origin of phantom limb pain. *Pain*, *155*, 1384–1391.

Vaughn-Sandler, V., Sherman, C., Aronsohn, A. & Volk, M.L. (2014). Consequences of perceived stigma among patients with cirrhosis. *Digestive Diseases and Sciences*, *59*, 681–686.

Vaxillaire, M. & Froguel, P. (2010). The genetics of type 2 diabetes: from candidate gene biology to genome-wide studies. In R.I.G. Holt, C.S. Cockram, A. Flyvbjerg & B.J. Goldstein (Eds.), *Textbook of Diabetes*. Oxford: Wiley-Blackwell.

Veldhoen, M. & Brucklacher-Waldert, V. (2012). Dietary influences on intestinal immunity. *Nature Reviews Immunology*, *12*, 696–708.

Velonas, V.M., Woo, H.H., Remedios, C.G.D. & Assinder, S.J. (2013). Current status of biomarkers for prostate cancer. *International Journal of Molecular Sciences*, *14*, 11034–11060.

Venkatesan, A. & Johnson, R.T. (2014). Infections and multiple sclerosis. *Handbook of Clinical Neurology*, *122*, 151–171.

Venkatraman, V., Chuah, Y.M., Huettel, S.A. & Chee, M.W. (2007). Sleep deprivation elevates expectation of gains and attenuates response to losses following risky decisions. *Sleep*, *30*, 603–609.

Vennelle, M., White, S., Riha, R.L. et al. (2010). Randomized controlled trial of variable-pressure versus fixed-pressure continuous positive airway pressure (CPAP) treatment for patients with obstructive sleep apnea/hypopnea syndrome (OSAHS). *Sleep*, *33*, 267.

Verdin, E. (2014). The many faces of sirtuins: coupling of NAD metabolism, sirtuins and lifespan. *Nature Medicine*, *20*, 25–27.

Vermeer, S.E., Longstreth Jr., W.T. & Koudstaal, P.J. (2007). Silent brain infarcts: a systematic review. *The Lancet Neurology*, *6*, 611–619.

Vestbo, J., Hurd, S.S., Agusti, A.G. et al. (2013). Diagnosis and assessment. Global Strategy for the Diagnosis, Management, and Prevention of Chronic Obstructive Pulmonary Disease. *American Journal of Respiratory and Critical Care Medicine*, *187*, 347–365.

Victoria, N.C., Inoue, K., Young, L.J. & Murphy, A.Z. (2013). Long-term dysregulation of brain corticotrophin and glucocorticoid receptors and stress reactivity by single early-life pain experience in male and female rats. *Psychoneuroendocrinology*, *38*, 3015–3028.

Vieira, S.M., Pagovich, O.E. & Kriegel, M.A. (2014). Diet, microbiota and autoimmune diseases. *Lupus*, *23*, 518–526.

Villeda, S.A., Plambeck, K.E., Middeldorp, J. et al. (2014). Young blood reverses age-related impairments in cognitive function and synaptic plasticity in mice. *Nature Medicine*, *20*, 659–663.

Villeneuve, P.J., Weichenthal, S., Crouse, D.L. et al. (2015). Long-term exposure to fine particulate matter air pollution and mortality among Canadian women. *Epidemiology*, 20.

Virk, J., Li, J., Vestergaard, M. et al. (2010). Early life disease programming during the preconception and prenatal period: making the link between stressful life events and type-1 diabetes. *PLoS One*, *5*, e11523.

Vlaeyen, J.W. & Morley, S. (2005). Cognitive-behavioral treatments for chronic pain: What works for whom? *The Clinical Journal of Pain*, *21*, 1–8.

Vogtmann, E., Levitan, E.B., Hale, L. et al. (2013). Association between sleep and breast cancer incidence among postmenopausal women in the women's health initiative. *Sleep*, *36*, 1437–1444.

Volkow, N.D. & Swanson, J.M. (2003). Variables that affect the clinical use and abuse of methylphenidate in the treatment of ADHD. *American Journal of Psychiatry*, *160*, 1909–1918.

Volkow, N.D., Wang, G.J., Fowler, J.S. et al. (2010). Addiction: decreased reward sensitivity and increased expectation sensitivity conspire to overwhelm the brain's control circuit. *Bioessays*, *32*, 748–755.

Volkow, N.D., Wang, G.J., Fowler, J.S. et al. (2012). Food and drug reward: overlapping circuits in human obesity and addiction. *Current Topics in Behavioral Neurosciences*, *11*, 1–24.

Volkow, N.D., Wang, G.J., Tomasi, D. & Baler, R.D. (2013). Unbalanced neuronal circuits in addiction. *Current Opinion in Neurobiology*, *23*, 639–648.

Vollrath, M. (2001). Personality and stress. *Scandinavian Journal of Psychology*, *42*, 335–347.

von Geldern, G. & Mowry, E.M. (2012). The influence of nutritional factors on the prognosis of multiple sclerosis. *Nature Reviews Neurology*, *8*, 678–689.

Voora, D., Cyr, D., Lucas, J. et al. (2013). Aspirin exposure reveals novel genes associated with platelet function and cardiovascular events. *Journal of the American College of Cardiology*, *62*, 1267–1276.

Voulgarelis, M. & Tzioufas, A.G. (2010). Pathogenetic mechanisms in the initiation and perpetuation of Sjögren's syndrome. *Nature Reviews Rheumatology*, *6*, 529–537.

Vyazovskiy, V.V. & Harris, K.D. (2013). Sleep and the single neuron: the role of global slow oscillations in individual cell rest. *Nature Reviews Neuroscience*, *14*, 443–451.

Wager, T.D., Scott, D.J. & Zubieta, J.K. (2007). Placebo effects on human mu-opioid activity during pain. *Proceedings of the National Academy of Sciences*, *104*, 11056–11061.

Wahlsten, D., Bachmanov, A., Finn, D.A. & Crabbe, J.C. (2006). Stability of inbred mouse strain differences in behavior and brain size between laboratories and across decades. *Proceedings of the National Academy of Sciences, 103*, 16364–16369.

Waldram, J.B., Herring, A. & Young, T.K. (2006). *Aboriginal Health in Canada: historical, cultural, and epidemiological perspectives*. Toronto: University of Toronto Press.

Walker, C.D. (2010). Maternal touch and feed as critical regulators of behavioral and stress responses in the offspring. *Developmental Psychobiology, 52*, 638–650.

Walker, E., Hernandez, A.V. & Kattan, M.W. (2008). Meta-analysis: its strengths and limitations. *Cleveland Clinic Journal of Medicine*, 75, 431–439.

Walker, J. & Sharpe, M. (2014). Integrated management of major depression for people with cancer. *International Review of Psychiatry, 26*, 657–668.

Walker, J., Sawhney, A., Hansen, C.H. et al. (2014). Treatment of depression in adults with cancer: a systematic review of randomized controlled trials. *Psychological Medicine, 44*, 897–907.

Walsh, C.J., Guinane, C.M., O'Toole, P.W. & Cotter, P.D. (2014). Beneficial modulation of the gut microbiota. *FEBS letters, 588*, 41204130.

Walsh, D.C. & Gordon, N.P. (1986). Legal approaches to smoking deterrence. *Annual Review of Public Health, 7*, 127–149.

Walsh, J.M. & McPhee, S.J. (1992). A systems model of clinical preventive care: an analysis of factors influencing patient and physician. *Health Education & Behavior, 19*, 157–175.

Walsh, N.P., Gleeson, M., Shephard, R.J. et al. (2011). Position statement. Part one: immune function and exercise. *Exercise Immunology Review, 17*, 6–63.

Wang, Q., Xi, B., Liu, M. et al. (2012). Short sleep duration is associated with hypertension risk among adults: a systematic review and meta-analysis. *Hypertension Research, 35*, 1012–1018.

Wang, R.P., Yao, Q., Xiao, Y.B. et al. (2011). Toll-like receptor 4/nuclear factor-kappa B pathway is involved in myocardial injury in a rat chronic stress model. *Stress, 14*, 567–575.

Wang, X., Han, X., Guo, X. et al. (2014). The effect of periodontal treatment on hemoglobin A1c levels of diabetic patients: a systematic review and meta-analysis. *PLoS One, 9*, e108412.

Wang, X., Piñol, R.A., Byrne, P. & Mendelowitz, D. (2014). Optogenetic stimulation of locus ceruleus neurons augments inhibitory transmission to parasympathetic cardiac vagal neurons via activation of brainstem α1 and β1 receptors. *Journal of Neuroscience, 34*, 6182–6189.

Wannamethee, S.G., Shaper, A.G. & Walker, M. (2000). Physical activity and mortality in older men with diagnosed coronary heart disease. *Circulation, 102*, 1358–1363.

Warburton, D.E.R., Nicol, C.W. & Bredin, S.S. (2006a). Prescribing exercise as preventive therapy. *Canadian Medical Association Journal, 174*, 961–974.

Warburton, D.E.R., Nicol, C.W. & Bredin, S.S. (2006b). Health benefits of physical activity: the evidence. *Canadian Medical Association Journal, 174*, 801–809.

Ward, H. (2012). *Oxford Handbook of Epidemiology for Clinicians*. Oxford, UK: Oxford University Press.

Wardlaw, J.M., Murray, V., Berge, E. et al. (2012). Recombinant tissue plasminogen activator for acute ischaemic stroke: an updated systematic review and meta-analysis. *The Lancet, 379*, 2364–2372.

Warziski, M.T., Sereika, S.M., Styn, M.A. et al. (2008). Changes in self-efficacy and dietary adherence: the impact on weight loss in the PREFER study. *Journal of Behavioral Medicine, 31*, 81–92.

Waselus, M., Valentino, R.J. & Van Bockstaele, E.J. (2005). Ultrastructural evidence for a role of gamma-aminobutyric acid in mediating the effects of corticotropin-releasing factor on the rat dorsal raphe serotonin system. *The Journal of Comparative Neurology, 482*, 155–165.

Wassertheil-Smoller, S., Shumaker, S. et al. (2004). Depression and cardiovascular sequelae in postmenopausal women: the Women's Health Initiative (WHI). *Archives of Internal Medicine, 164*, 289–298.

Waters, E., de Silva-Sanigorski, A., Hall, B.J. et al. (2011). Interventions for preventing obesity in children. *The Cochrane Database of Systematic Reviews, 12*.

Watkins, L.R. & Maier, S.F. (2005). Immune regulation of central nervous system functions: from sickness responses to pathological pain. *Journal of Internal Medicine, 257*, 139–155.

Watson, D. & Pennebaker, J.W. (1989). Health complaints, stress, and distress: exploring the central role of negative affectivity. *Psychological Review*, *96*, 234–254.

Weaver, I.C., Champagne, F.A., Brown, S.E. et al. (2005). Reversal of maternal programming of stress responses in adult offspring through methyl supplementation: altering epigenetic marking later in life. *Journal of Neuroscience*, *25*, 11045–11054.

Webb, T.L. & Sheeran, P. (2007). How do implementation intentions promote goal attainment? A test of component processes. *Journal of Experimental Social Psychology*, *43*, 295–302.

Weber, S.R. & Pargament, K.I. (2014). The role of religion and spirituality in mental health. *Current Opinion in Psychiatry*, *27*, 358–363.

Wegman, M.P., Guo, M., Bennion, D.M. et al. (2015). Practicality of intermittent fasting in humans and its effect on oxidative stress and genes related to aging and metabolism. *Rejuvenation Research*, *18*, 162–172..

Wehrle, J., Pahl, H.L. & von Bubnoff, N. (2014). Ponatinib: a third-generation inhibitor for the treatment of CML. *Recent Results in Cancer Research*, *201*, 99–107.

Wei, J., Rooks, C., Ramadan, R. et al. (2014). Meta-analysis of mental stress-induced myocardial ischemia and subsequent cardiac events in patients with coronary artery disease. *The American Journal of Cardiology*, *114*, 187–192.

Weiland, B.J., Thayer, R.E., Depue, B.E. et al. (2015). Daily marijuana use is not associated with brain morphometric measures in adolescents or adults. *Journal of Neuroscience*, *35*, 1505–1512.

Weiner, H.L. & Frenkel, D. (2006). Immunology and immunotherapy of Alzheimer's disease. *Nature Reviews Immunology*, *6*, 404–416.

Weinman, J., Yusuf, G., Berks, R. et al. (2009). How accurate is patients' anatomical knowledge: a cross-sectional, questionnaire study of six patient groups and a general public sample. *BMC Family Practice*, *10*, 43.

Weinrib, A.Z., Sephton, S.E., Degeest, K. et al. (2010). Diurnal cortisol dysregulation, functional disability, and depression in women with ovarian cancer. *Cancer*, *116*, 4410–4419.

Weinrich, M., Good, D.C., Reding, M. et al. (2004). Timing, intensity, and duration of rehabilitation for hip fracture and stroke: report of a workshop at the National Center for Medical Rehabilitation Research. *Neurorehabilitation and Neural Repair*, *18*, 12–28.

Weiss, E.P., Albert, S.G., Reeds, D.N. et al. (2015). Calorie restriction and matched weight loss frome: independent and additive effects on glucoregulation and the incretin system in overweight women and men. *Diabetes Care*, pii: dc142913.

Weisz, J.R., Sandler, I.N., Durlak, J.A. & Anton, B.S. (2005). Promoting and protecting youth mental health through evidence-based prevention and treatment. *American Psychologist*, *60*, 628–648.

Weitzenblum, E. & Chaouat, A. (2009). Cor pulmonale. *Chronic Respiratory Disease*, *6*, 177–185.

West, C.E., Renz, H., Jenmalm, M.C. et al. (2015). The gut microbiota and inflammatory noncommunicable diseases: associations and potentials for gut microbiota therapies. *Journal of Allergy and Clinical Immunology*, *135*, 3–13.

Wethington, E., Brown, G. & Kessler, R. (1995). Interview measurement of stressful life events. In S. Cohen, R. Kessler & L. Underwood Gordon (Eds.), *Measuring Stress* (pp. 59–79). New York: Oxford University Press.

Wheaton, B. & Gotlib, I.H. (1997). Trajectories and turning points over the life course: concepts and themes. In B. Wheaton & I.H. Gotlib, *Stress and Adversities over the Course of Life: Trajectories and turning points* (pp. 1–28). Cambridge, UK: Cambridge University Press.

Whelan, R.L. (2001). Laparotomy, laparoscopy, cancer, and beyond. *Surgical Endoscopy*, *15*, 110–115.

Whitaker, R.C., Dearth-Wesley, T., Gooze, R.A. et al. (2014). Adverse childhood experiences, dispositional mindfulness, and adult health. *Preventive Medicine*, *67*, 147–153.

Whitbeck, L.B., Adams, G.W., Hoyt, D.R. & Chen, X. (2004). Conceptualizing and measuring historical trauma among American Indian people. *American Journal of Community Psychology*, *33*, 199–130.

White, P.D., Rickards, H. & Zeman, A.Z.J. (2012). Time to end the distinction between mental and neurological illnesses. *British Medical Journal*, *344*, e3454.

Whitebird, R.R., Kreitzer, M.J. & O'Connor, P.J. (2009). Mindfulness-based stress reduction and diabetes. *Diabetes Spectrum: A Publication of the American Diabetes Association*, *22*, 226–230.

Whitehead, W.E., Palsson, O. & Jones, K.R. (2002). Systematic review of the comorbidity of irritable bowel syndrome with other disorders: What are the causes and implications? *Gastroenterology*, *122*, 1140–1156.

Wichers, M.C., Koek, G.H., Robaeys, G. et al. (2005). IDO and interferon-alpha-induced depressive symptoms: a shift in hypothesis from tryptophan depletion to neurotoxicity. *Molecular Psychiatry*, *10*, 538–544.

Wicki, A., Witzigmann, D., Balasubramanian, V. & Huwyler, J. (2014). Nanomedicine in cancer therapy: challenges, opportunities, and clinical applications. *Journal of Controlled Release*, *200*, 138.

Wiech, K., Lin, C.S., Brodersen, K.H. et al. (2010). Anterior insula integrates information about salience into perceptual decisions about pain. *Journal of Neuroscience*, *30*, 16324–16331.

Williams, A.L., Jacobs, S.B., Moreno-Macías, H. et al. (2014). Sequence variants in SLC16A11 are a common risk factor for type 2 diabetes in Mexico. *Nature*, *506*, 97–101.

Williams, F.M., Scollen, S., Cao, D. et al. (2012). Genes contributing to pain sensitivity in the normal population: an exome sequencing study. *PLoS Genetics*, *8*, e1003095.

Williams, J.E. (2008). Nerve blocks: chemical and physical neurolytic agents. In N. Sykes, M.I. Bennett & C.S.Yuan (Eds.), *Clinical Pain Management: cancer pain* (2nd ed.). London: Hodder Arnold.

Williams, J.E., Mosley, T.H., Kop, W.J. et al. (2010). Vital exhaustion as a risk factor for adverse cardiac events (from the Atherosclerosis Risk in Communities [ARIC] study). *American Journal of Cardiology*, *105*, 1661–1665.

Williams, L.M., Barton, M.J., Kemp, A.H. et al. (2005). Distinct amygdala-autonomic arousal profiles in response to fear signals in healthy males and females. *NeuroImage*, *28*, 618–626.

Williams, S., Sakic, B. & Hoffman, S.A. (2010). Circulating brain-reactive autoantibodies and behavioral deficits in the MRL model of CNS lupus. *Journal of NeuroImmunology*, *218*, 73–82.

Wilson, C.J. & Deane, F.P. (2010). Help-negation and suicidal ideation: the role of depression, anxiety and hopelessness. *Journal of Youth and Adolescence*, *39*, 291–305.

Wilson, J.E., Petrucelli, A.S. & Chen, L. (2015). Inflammasome-independent role of AIM2 in suppressing colon tumorigenesis via DNA-PK and Akt. *Nature Medicine*. [Epub ahead of print].

Wilson, S.J. & Sayette, M.A. (2015). Neuroimaging craving: urge intensity matters. *Addiction*, *110*, 195–203.

Wilson, S.R., Gerhold, K.A., Bifolck-Fisher, A. et al. (2011). TRPA1 is required for histamine-independent, Mas-related G protein-coupled receptor-mediated itch. *Nature Neuroscience*, *14*, 595–602.

Wingenfeld, K. & Wolf, O.T. (2014). Stress, memory, and the hippocampus. *Frontiers of Neurology and Neuroscience*, *34*, 109–120.

Wingfield, J.C. & Sapolsky, R.M. (2003). Reproduction and resistance to stress: when and how. *Journal of Neuroendocrinology*, *15*, 711–724.

Winkleby, M.A., Kraemer, H.C., Ahn, D.K. & Varady, A.N. (1998). Ethnic and socioeconomic differences in cardiovascular disease risk factors: findings for women from the Third National Health and Nutrition Examination Survey, 1988–1994. *Journal of the American Medical Association*, *280*, 356–362.

Wise, R.A. (2004). Dopamine, learning and motivation. *Nature Reviews Neuroscience*, *5*, 483–494.

Wise, R.A. & Koob, G.F. (2014). The development and maintenance of drug addiction. *Neuropsychopharmacology*, *39*, 254–262.

Witek-Janusek, L., Albuquerque, K., Chroniak, K.R. et al. (2008). Effect of mindfulness based stress reduction on immune function, quality of life and coping in women newly diagnosed with early stage breast cancer. *Brain, Behavior and Immunity*, *22*, 969–981.

Witkiewitz, K., Bowen, S., Douglas, H. & Hsu, S.H. (2013). Mindfulness-based relapse prevention for substance craving. *Addictive Behaviors*, *38*, 1563–1571.

Wittmann, E., Beaton, C., Lewis, W.G. et al. (2011). Comparison of patients' needs and doctors' perceptions of information requirements related to a diagnosis of oesophageal or gastric cancer. *European Journal of Cancer Care*, *20*, 187–195.

Wittouck, C., Van Autreve, S., De Jaegere, E. et al. (2011). The prevention and treatment of complicated grief: a meta-analysis. *Clinical Psychology Review*, *31*, 69–78.

Wolpe, J. (1968). Psychotheraphy by reciprocal inhibition. *Conditional Reflex: A Pavlovian Journal of Research & Therapy, 3*, 234–240.

Wong, V.K. et al. (2015). Phylogeographical analysis of the dominant multidrug-resistant H58 clade of Salmonella Typhi identifies inter- and intracontinental transmission events. *Nature Genetics, 47*, 632–639.

Woo, C.W., Roy, M., Buhle, J.T. & Wager, T.D. (2015). Distinct brain systems mediate the effects of nociceptive input and self-regulation on pain. *PLoS Biology, 13*, e1002036.

Wood, J.D. (2013). Taming the irritable bowel. *Current Pharmaceutical Design, 19*, 142–156.

Woodhams, S.G., Sagar, D.R., Burston, J.J. & Chapman, V. (2015). The role of the endocannabinoid system in pain. *Handbook of Experimental Pharmacology, 227*, 119–143.

Woolf, C.J., Bennett, G.J., Doherty, M. et al. (1998). Towards a mechanism-based classification of pain? *Pain, 77*, 227–229.

World Health Organization. (2013). *Global Status Report on Road Safety 2013*. www.who.int/violence_injury_prevention/road_safety_status/2013/en/ (accessed April, 2015).

World Health Organization. (2014a). *Health Statistics and Information Systems*. www.who.int/healthinfo/en/ (accessed February 2015).

World Health Organization. (2014b). *Global Tuberculosis Report 2014*. www.who.int/tb/publications/global_report/en/ (accessed May 2015).

World Health Organization. (2014c). *Diabetes Programme*. www.who.int/diabetes/en/ (accessed March 2015).

World Health Organization. (2014d). *Management of Substance Abuse*. www.who.int/substance_abuse/facts/en/ (accessed February 2015).

World Health Organization. (2014e). *The Top 10 Causes of Death*. Fact Sheet No. 310. Geneva: WHO. www.who.int/mediacentre/factsheets/fs310/en/ (accessed May 2015).

World Health Organization. (2014f). *Tobacco*. Fact Sheet No. 339. Geneva: WHO.

World Health Organization. (2014g). *Road Traffic Injuries*. Fact Sheet No. 358. Geneva: WHO. www.who.int/mediacentre/factsheets/fs358/en/ (accessed April 2015).

Wright, E.B., Holcombe, C. & Salmon, P. (2004). Doctors' communication of trust, care and respect in breast cancer: qualitative study. *BMJ: British Medical Journal, 328*, 864.

Wu, J.R. & Moser, D.K. (2014). Type D personality predicts poor medication adherence in patients with heart failure in the USA. *International Journal of Behavioral Medicine, 21*, 833–842.

Wung, S.F. & Lin, P.C. (2011). Shared genomics of type 2 and gestational diabetes mellitus. *Annual Review of Nursing Research, 29*, 227–260.

Xu, X., Bao, H., Strait, K. et al. (2015). Sex differences in perceived stress and early recovery in young and middle-aged patients with acute myocardial infarction. *Circulation, 131*, 614–623.

Yadav, V. & Narayanaswami, P. (2014). Complementary and alternative medical therapies in multiple sclerosis – the American Academy of Neurology guidelines: a commentary. *Clinical Therapeutics, 36*, 1972–1978.

Yan, X., Brown, A.D., Lazar, M. et al. (2013). Spontaneous brain activity in combat related PTSD. *Neuroscience Letters, 547*, 1–5.

Yang, E.V. & Glaser, R. (2002). Stress-associated immunomodulation and its implications for responses to vaccination. *Expert Review of Vaccines, 1*, 453–459.

Yang, K.C., Yamada, K.A., Patel, A.Y. et al. (2014). Deep RNA sequencing reveals dynamic regulation of myocardial noncoding RNAs in failing human heart and remodeling with mechanical circulatory support. *Circulation, 129*, 1009–1021.

Yang, P., Zhou, Y., Chen, B. et al. (2009). Overweight, obesity and gastric cancer risk: results from a meta-analysis of cohort studies. *European Journal of Cancer, 45*, 2867–2873.

Yang, X., Hegde, V.L., Rao, R. et al. (2014). Histone modifications are associated with Δ9-tetrahydrocannabinol-mediated alterations in antigen-specific T cell responses. *Journal of Biological Chemistry, 289*, 18707–18718.

Yano, J.M., Yu, K., Donaldson, G.P. et al. (2015). Indigenous bacteria from the gut microbiota regulate host serotonin biosynthesis. *Cell, 161*, 264–276.

Yao, S., Zhao, W., Cheng, R. et al. (2014). Oxytocin makes females, but not males, less forgiving following betrayal of trust. *International Journal of Neuropsychopharmacology, 17*, 1785–1792.

Yasuda, S.U., Zhang, L. & Huang, S.M. (2008). The role of ethnicity in variability in response to drugs:

focus on clinical pharmacology studies. *Clinical Pharmacology & Therapeutics, 84*, 417–423.

Yeh, E.T., Tong, A.T., Lenihan, D.J. et al. (2004). Cardiovascular complications of cancer therapy diagnosis, pathogenesis, and management. *Circulation, 109*, 3122–3131.

Yehuda, R. (2002). Current status of cortisol findings in post-traumatic stress disorder. *Psychiatric Clinics of North America, 25*, 341–368.

Yehuda, R., Halligan, S.L. & Grossman, R. (2001). Childhood trauma and risk for PTSD: relationship to intergenerational effects of trauma, parental PTSD, and cortisol excretion. *Development and Psychopathology, 13*, 733–753.

Yeoh, N., Burton, J.P., Suppiah, P. et al. (2013). The role of the microbiome in rheumatic diseases. *Current Rheumatology Reports, 15*, 1–11.

Yi-Frazier, J.P., Yaptangco, M., Semana, S. et al. (2015). The association of personal resilience with stress, coping, and diabetes outcomes in adolescents with type 1 diabetes: variable- and person-focused approaches. *Journal of Health Psychology, 20*, 1196–1206.

Yokum, S., Gearhardt, A.N., Harris, J.L. et al. (2014). Individual differences in striatum activity to food commercials predict weight gain in adolescents. *Obesity, 22*, 2544–2551.

Yonas, M.A., Lange, N.E. & Celedon, J.C. (2012). Psychosocial stress and asthma morbidity. *Current Opinion in Allergy and Clinical Immunology, 12*, 202–210.

Yoo, S.S., Gujar, N., Hu, P. et al. (2007). The human emotional brain without sleep: a prefrontal amygdala disconnect. *Current Biology, 17*, R877–R878.

Yosef, I., Manor, M., Kiro, R. & Qimron, U. (2015). Temperate and lytic bacteriophages programmed to sensitize and kill antibiotic-resistant bacteria. *Proceedings of the National Academy of Sciences, 112*, 7267–7272.

You, J.J., Dodek, P., Lamontagne, F. et al. (2014). What really matters in end-of-life discussions? Perspectives of patients in hospital with serious illness and their families. *Canadian Medical Association Journal, 186*, E679–E687.

Youm, Y.H., Nguyen, K.Y., Grant, R.W. et al. (2015). The ketone metabolite β-hydroxybutyrate blocks NLRP3 inflammasome-mediated inflammatory disease. *Nature Medicine, 21*, 263–269.

Youngster, I., Russell, G.H., Pindar, C. et al. (2014). Oral, capsulized, frozen fecal microbiota transplantation for relapsing Clostridium difficile infection. *The Journal of the American Medical Association, 312*, 1772–1778.

Ysseldyk, R., Matheson, K. & Anisman, H. (2010). Religiosity as identity: toward an understanding of religion from a social identity perspective. *Personality and Social Psychology Review, 14*, 60–71.

Zacharko, R.M. & Anisman, H. (1991). Stressor-induced anhedonia in the mesocorticolimbic system. *Neuroscience & Biobehavioral Reviews, 15*, 391–405.

Zalli, A., Carvalho, L.A., Lin, J. et al. (2014). Shorter telomeres with high telomerase activity are associated with raised allostatic load and impoverished psychosocial resources. *Proceedings of the National Academy of Sciences, 111*, 4519–4524.

Zaza, C. & Baine, N. (2002). Cancer pain and psychosocial factors: a critical review of the literature. *Journal of Pain and Symptom Management, 24*, 526–542.

Zeidan, F., Martucci, K.T., Kraft, R.A. et al. (2011). Brain mechanisms supporting the modulation of pain by mindfulness meditation. *Journal of Neuroscience, 31*, 5540–5548.

Zeineh, M.M., Kang, J., Atlas, S.W. et al. (2015). Right arcuate fasciculus abnormality in chronic fatigue syndrome. *Radiology, 274*, 517–526.

Zeitzer, J.M. (2013). Control of sleep and wakefulness in health and disease. *Progress in Molecular Biology and Translational Science, 119*, 137–154.

Zhang, C., Bao, W., Rong, Y. et al. (2013). Genetic variants and the risk of gestational diabetes mellitus: a systematic review. *Human Reproduction Update, 19*, 376–390.

Zhang, J., Echeverry, S., Lim, T. et al. (2015). Can modulating inflammatory response be a good strategy to treat neuropathic pain? *Current Pharmaceutical Design, 21*, 831–839.

Zhang, L., Bertucci, A.M., Ramsey-Goldman, R. et al. (2013). Major pathogenic steps in human lupus can be effectively suppressed by nucleosomal histone peptide epitope-induced regulatory immunity. *Clinical Immunology, 149*, 365–378.

Zhang, Y., Proenca, R., Maffei, M. et al. (1994). Positional cloning of the mouse obese gene and its human homologue. *Nature, 372*, 425–432.

Zhang, Y., Wang, Z.Z., Sun, H.M. et al. (2014). Systematic review of traditional Chinese medicine for depression in Parkinson's disease. *The American Journal of Chinese Medicine*, *42*, 1035–1051.

Zhong, Q., Peng, H.L., Zhao, X. et al. (2014). Effects of BRCA1- and BRCA2-related mutations on ovarian and breast cancer survival: a meta-analysis. *Clinical Cancer Research*, *21*, 211–220.

Zhou, W. & Wang, Y. (2014). A network-based analysis of the types of coronary artery disease from traditional Chinese medicine perspective: potential for therapeutics and drug discovery. *Journal of Ethnopharmacology*, *151*, 66–77.

Zhou, Z., Zhen, J., Karpowich, N.K. et al. (2007). LeuT-desipramine structure reveals how antidepressants block neurotransmitter reuptake. *Science*, *317*, 1390–1393.

Zhu, J., Quyyumi, A.A., Norman, J.E. et al. (2000). Effects of total pathogen burden on coronary artery disease risk and C-reactive protein levels. *American Journal of Cardiology*, *85*, 140–146.

Zhubi, A., Cook, E.H., Guidotti, A. & Grayson, D.R. (2014). Epigenetic mechanisms in autism spectrum disorder. *International Review of Neurobiology*, *115*, 203–244.

Zimbler, D.L., Schroeder, J.A., Eddy, J.L. & Lathem, W.W. (2015). Early emergence of Yersinia pestis as a severe respiratory pathogen. *Nature Communications*, *6*, 7487.

Zoccola, P.M., Figueroa, W.S., Rabideau, E.M. et al. (2014). Differential effects of post-stressor rumination and distraction on cortisol and C-reactive protein. *Health Psychology*, *33*, 1606–1609.

Zoch, T.W., Desbiens, N.A., DeStefano, F. et al. (2000). Short- and long-term survival after cardiopulmonary resuscitation. *Archives of Internal Medicine*, *160*, 1969–1973.

Zogopoulos, P., Vasileiou, I., Patsouris, E. & Theocharis, S.E. (2013). The role of endocannabinoids in pain modulation. *Fundamental & Clinical Pharmacology*, *27*, 64–80.

Zorrilla, E.P., Logrip, M.L. & Koob, G.F. (2014). Corticotropin releasing factor: a key role in the neurobiology of addiction. *Frontiers in Neuroendocrinology*, *35*, 234–244.

Zucchi, F.C., Yao, Y., Ilnytsky, Y. et al. (2014). Lifetime stress cumulatively programs brain transcriptome and impedes stroke recovery: benefit of sensory stimulation. *PLoS One*, *9*, e92130.

Zuckerman, I.H., Yin, X., Rattinger, G.B. et al. (2012). Effect of exposure to evidence-based pharmacotherapy on outcomes after acute myocardial infarction in older adults. *Journal of the American Geriatrics Society*, *60*, 1854–1861.

Zurek, A.A., Yu, J., Wang, D.S. et al. (2014). Sustained increase in α5GABAA receptor function impairs memory after anesthesia. *The Journal of Clinical Investigation*, *124*, 5437–5441.

Index

Aboriginal communities, 105–7, 144, 155–6, 259, 425–6, 429
abuse
    criteria for, 346–7
    forms of, 101
    see also child abuse; elder abuse; substance abuse
Academy of Periodontal Health, 251
acceptance, medical, 21
access to health care programs, 403
accidents, 209–10
acquired immunity, 68
acupuncture, 343–4
addiction, 153–4, 175, 190, 344–69
    age-related and social influences on, 349–50
    breadth of, 346–8
    common elements in different forms of, 354, 369
    definition of, 346–7
    drug treatments for, 366–8
    epigenetic factors in, 356
    gender differences in, 348
    neurochemical components in, 350–5
    opponent processes in, 354–5
    persistence of, 355–6
    to prescription drugs, 336–7
    processes leading to, 348–50
    rehabilitation programs, 362–3
    relapse into, 362, 364
    social cures for, 365
    treatment for, 346, 360–5
    treatments developed for one condition but later
        applied to another, 368
    withdrawal from, 357
adenosine triphosphate (ATP), 203
adherence to treatment, 217, 256
adiposity, 231

adolescence, 102–3, 192, 196–7, 349
adrenocorticotropic hormone, 57
aerobic exercise, 177–8, 243, 305
African Americans, 216, 225, 393
after-life, 412–13
aging process, 90, 104, 406, 414
alcohol consumption, 226, 347–50, 354, 356, 360, 368
alleles, 45
Allen, Woody, 87
allergies and allergic immune therapy, 261–4
allostatic overload, 89, 373
alternative medicine, 200–2, 310, 393
    for heart disease, 234–6
    for the treatment of pain, 343–4
ambiguity
    about medical prognoses, 391
    of threats, 86, 161
American Academy of Neurology, 409
American Academy of Pediatrics, 65
American Cancer Society, 365
American College of Cardiology, 233
American Delirium Society, 397
American Gastroenterological Association, 280
American Heart Association, 226, 233
American Medical Association, 416
American Psychiatric Association, 143
American Psychological Association, 14
American Society of Clinical Oncology, 186
AMPA receptors, 368
amputation, 334–5, 382
anabolic steroids, 64
anaerobic exercise, 177
'anchors', 81
Angelou, Maya, 105
anger and anger suppression, 216, 227, 343, 411

angina, 218
angiotensin-converting enzyme (ACE), 231–3
animal models of human illness, 25–8
antibiotics, 75–6, 266–8, 274–5, 403
antibody therapy, 319
antidepressant drugs, 374, 418
anxiety, 373, 387
applied behavior analysis, 168
'appraisal delay', 403
appraisals
    of illness, 375–6, 388
    of stressful events, 79–86, 110
aspirin, 154, 233
assisted dying, 416–17
associative coherence, 81
asthma, 262–4
astrocytes, 55
attitudes of physicians, patient perspectives on, 390
attribute substitution, 81
attributions related to stressors, 83–4
attrition rates
    from exercise regimes, 179
    in research, 32
autism, 101
autoimmune disorders, 68, 261, 277–87
    drug treatments for, 286–7
autonomic nervous system (ANS), 56, 219
autoreceptors, 53
aversion therapy, 364–5
avian flu, 161, 288
avoidant strategies, 91–2, 377

B cells, 69
baby boomers, 408
bacteria, 73–4, 263–8, 305; *see also* gut bacteria
bacterial illness, 259–60, 265
bad news, giving and withholding of, 391, 399–400
Bandura, A., 164
Banting, Frederick, 244
bariatric surgery, 198
basic science, 422
Bauer, U.E., 157
bazodoxifene, 317
Beck, A.T., 169
Begley, C.G., 28
behavioral change, 19–24, 141, 150–1, 155–68, 175,
    195, 211, 361
    and applied behavior analysis, 168
    and learning principles, 167
    models of, 162–7
'behavioral delay', 403
behavioral medicine, 5–6

beliefs about illness, 386–9
benzodiazepines, 366
bereavement, 418–19
    dual process model of, 418
best practice from the physician's perspective, 395–7
Best, Charles, 244
beta blockers, 232
biases in screening, 150–1
Bill and Melinda Gates Foundation, 428
biofeedback, 342
bioidentical hormones, 62
biological processes, disturbance of, 22–3
biological systems and functioning, 43–76
biomarkers, 11, 37, 143, 230, 314, 320, 366
Black, James, 232
Black Death, 259
blaming of victims, 152–3
blastoma, 292
blood, constituents of, 214–15
blood pressure, 215–16, 219, 225, 229
body mass index (BMI), 184, 189
Boksa, P., 100
brain-derived neurotrophic factor (BDNF), 66, 132, 179,
    184, 242, 354–5
brain functioning, 44, 71–3, 172
brain morphology, stressor-related changes in, 133
brain regions, 51–3, 121, 128–9, 132, 229, 239, 328–34,
    339–41, 351–3
Branscombe, N.R., 51
Braz, J., 332
breast cancer, 142, 148, 295–300, 303–4, 314–15,
    382, 395
breastfeeding, 64–5
British Medical Association, 417
British Medical Journal, 188
bubonic plague, 259
Bullough, Oliver, 348
The Business of Recovery (film), 362–3
Butlin, Henry, 140
'buy-in', 425

Caesarean delivery, 73–4
calories, 180
Canadian Institutes of Health Research (CIHR), 423
Canadian Medical Association (CMA), 415
Canadian research, 425
Canadian Supreme Court, 416–17
cancer, 85, 94, 140–3, 148–50, 181, 289–321, 379–82,
    392–6, 404
    biological changes associated with, 300–2
    in children, 303
    classifications of, 291–2

cancer *cont.*
  decision-making about, 393–4
  detection of, 292–3
  and eating, 304–5
  environmental contributions to, 297–8
  ethnic and racial variations in, 295–6
  and exercise, 305–6
  genetic contributions to, 293–7
  hormones and hormone receptors in, 303–4
  individualized treatment strategies for, 315–16, 321
  malignant cells, 291
  pain related to, 311
  physiological impact of, 308–10
  prevention of, 321
  recommended steps for patients in treatment, 311–13
  screening for, 314–15
  and sleep, 306
  strain associated with, 306–8
  and stress, 299–304
  surgery for, 307
  survivors of, 310, 321
  treatment methods, 28, 316–20
  viral factors in, 298–9
Cancer Research UK, 304
cannabis, 119, 337
carcinogens, 297–8
carcinoma, 292
cardiomyopathy, 215
cardiovascular system, 212–15
caregivers, caring for, 408–9
caregiving, 408–10
  burden of, 408
  see also end-of-life care
case control studies, 38
Casey, K.L., 334
casinos, 363
catastrophizing, 326–7, 343, 388
Caulfield, T., 20
causation as distinct from correlation, 33
C.difficile, 75
celiac disease, 280–1
cell-based therapy, 318–19
Centers for Disease Control (CDC), 161, 183–4, 260, 268, 315, 336
central nervous system (CNS), 51, 186, 341–2
changimg patterns
  in health services, 400
  in illness, 11–13
chaos theory, 97–8
charitable giving, 174
chemotherapy, 289–90, 306–7, 310, 313, 316–17
  induction-type, *consolidation*-type and *intensification*-type, 316

Cheney, Dick, 147
chikungunya virus, 18
child abuse, 130, 133
Children's Hospital of Ontario Pain Scale (CHEOPS), 325
choices, making of, 86–7
cholesterol, 233
chronic fatigue syndrome (CFS), 332
chronic illness, 1, 371–6, 388, 407, 414, 427
  adjustment to, 372–3
  coping with, 376
  features of, 371
chronic obstructive pulmonary disease (COPD), 236–8
chronic pain, 324–7, 338
  in children, 327
  psychological consequences of, 326–7
ciprofloxacin (Cip), 266
circadian rhythm sleep disorders (CRSDs), 208–9
circadian rhythms, 276
cleanliness, obsessive, 264
clinical trials, steps in, 29–30
Clinton, Hillary, 427
clonal expansion, 70
clostridial clusters, 279
cluster analysis, 34
cocaine, 355–7, 360, 369
cognitive behavioral therapy (CBT), 168–70, 308, 340, 364–5, 374
cognitive dissonance, 202, 205
cognitive restructuring, 93, 169, 376, 379
cognitive styles, 84
cohort studies, 38
'cold reactors', 228
collaborative care, 375
Collins, L.G., 409
colorectal cancer, 150, 315
comfort foods, 126–7, 182
commensal microflora, 73
common-sense model of illness, 386–7
  cognitive components of, 387
community-based participatory research (CBPR), 425–6
comorbidities, 10–11
complementary medicine, 200–1, 344
complex regional pain syndrome (CRPS), 323
complex situations, 86–7
compliance with treatment, 3, 217, 388
'complicated grief', 418
compulsive behaviors, 353
conditioned responses, 167
confirmation bias, 20
contingency contracting, 168
continuum between wellness and illness, 7–8
control groups, 428
control of illness, patients' sense of, 376–7, 387, 392–3

coordinated systems, 2–4
Coping Orientation to Problem Experience (COPE) inventory, 110–11
coping strategies, 91–4, 102, 108–11, 169, 171, 249, 343, 364, 369, 373, 376–7, 386
   male and *female*, 131
Corbett, D., 242, 375
coronary artery disease (CAD), 215–22, 225–36, 243, 404
   and depression, 243
   ethnic and cultural factors in, 225–6
   genetic factors in, 226–7
   and socioeconomic status, 221
   treatments for, 233–6
correlation matrices, 33
correlational studies, 32–3
Corrigan, P.W., 382
corticotropin releasing hormone (CRH), 57, 125–7, 192, 353–6
cortisol, 57, 71, 120–4, 126–8, 135, 301, 353
   diurnal variations in, 124
   in relations to trauma, 123–4
cost–benefit analysis, 147–8
counterfactual thinking, 24
coverage of health care systems, loopholes in, 401
cravings, 355, 357, 359, 364
   diminution of, 367–9
Crohn's disease, 279–80
cross-sectional studies, 32
cultural differences, 155–6
cultural trauma, 105
Cyberball (computer game), 97
cytokines and cytokine therapy, 70–2, 136–8, 230–1, 275, 337

Daily Life Experience (DLE) checklist, 109
Dallman, M.F., 127
damage molecular pattern molecules (DAMPs), 135
Darwin Awards, 157
data synthesis, 39–40
Davis, Bette, 104
DDT, 51
death
   main causes of, 12–17, 410
   meaning of, 410–11
   see also dying; end of life
decision-making
   abrogation of, 396
   on behalf of children, 393
   on cancer treatment, 394–5
   sharing of, 392–3
decisional balance, 166
dehydroepiandrosterone (DHEA), 406
delays in presentation of illness, 403–4

'democratization' of health care, 425
denial of particular treatments, 396
dependence, criteria for, 346–7
depression, 10, 84, 108, 128, 131–2, 327, 364, 373–5, 387–8, 417, 419
   and cancer, 309
   and cytokines, 137
   and heart disease, 221–3, 243
   and stroke, 241
developing countries, 427–8
diabetes, 244–58
   comorbidities of, 256
   genetic influences on, 247–8
   gestational, 253–4
   and stress, 249–50
   treatment for, 254–8
   type 1, 244–6, 253–4, 377
   type 2, 1, 3, 18, 244–7, 250–8, 401
Diagnostic and Statistical Manual of Mental Disorders, 143, 345
diagnostic tools, use of, 151
diet and diet-related treatments, 187–94, 274, 281, 285
diet drinks, 197–8
Dietary Guidelines Advisory Committee report (2015), 189
digestion, 182, 185
digoxin, 233
disability-adjusted life years (DALYs), 13–14
disease-modifying antirheumatic drugs (DMARDs), 286
distraction, 342–3
distress, 78
disulfiram, 364–5
diuretics, 233
DNA, 45–8, 293–8
'do not resuscitate' notices, 317, 307
doctor–patient relationship, 390–5, 399
Doll, Sir Richard, 37
dopamine, 53, 100, 126, 184, 192, 330, 351–4, 357–8
drug prices, 401
drug use, 174–5, 311, 313, 317, 335–7, 351–9
   and eating, 357–8
   reinstatement and relapse, 356
dying
   doctor-assisted, 415–17
   process of, 410–13, 419
   stages in adjustment to, 411–13
dysbiosis, 253
dysphoria, 359

early detection of disease, 150–1
early intervention, 144
early life experiences, 3, 5, 9, 23, 98, 101–2, 130, 133, 192, 262–4, 302

eating
    and cancer, 304–5
    and drug use, 357–8
    hormones involved in, 127–8
    as a means of coping, 126
    processes related to, 182–3
eating disorders, 187, 285
eating habits, 189–95
    social influences on, 190–1
    stress-related, 192–3
Ebola virus, 85, 260, 270, 273, 288–9, 428
Echinacea, 199
The Economist, 177
educational programs, 160–1, 381–2
effect size, 39
80–20 rule, 270
elder abuse, 409
elderly patients, 104–5, 320, 373–4, 380, 396–7, 403, 409
electronic cigarettes, 366–7
Ellis, L.M., 28
Emanuel, Ezekiel J., 414
emerging infectious diseases, 18
emotion-focused coping, 92–3, 377
'emotional eaters', 192–3, 250
emotional regulation through sleep, 205–6
emphysema, 236
endemic pathogens, 273
endocrine systems, 56
end-of-life care, 413–15
    communications about, 415
endophenotypic analysis, 142–4
endovascular therapy (ET), 241
enriching environments, 375
enteric nervous system, 72–4
environmental factors in health, 76, 140, 152
enzyme disturbance, 182–3
epidemiology, 13, 36–78
epigenetics, 50–1, 298, 356–7, 361, 424
epithelial cell layer, 74
Epstein-Barr virus (EBV), 283
equality for patients, 403
erring on the side of caution, 162
erythropoietin (EPO), 179
estrogens, 61–2
ethical dilemmas, 428–9
ethnic differences, 155–6
euphoria, 354, 359, 366–7
euthanasia, 416
evidence-based practice, 4
exercise, 177–80
    benefits from, 177–9
    and cancer, 305–6

exercise cont.
    and dieting, 187, 191, 194
    habitual and extreme, 275–6
    health workers' role in promotion of, 179–80
    and immune functioning, 275–6
    impediments to, 179
exocrine hormones, 56
exosomes, 292–3
expectancies, 329–31, 338, 341
experimental research studies, 29–32, 40–1
    caveats concerning, 40
    variability within, 41
exposure therapy, 167
extinction of responses, 167–8

factorial designs, 30
false alarms and 'false negatives', 149, 151, 314
family histories, medical, 262
fasting, 310
fat, brown and white, 196, 257
fetal development, 98–101
fexaramine, 187
fibroblast growth factor (FGF), 66
Fields, W.C., 361
fighting spirit, 384
Five Facet Mindfulness Questionnaire (FFMQ), 171
Fleming, Alexander, 199
Fletcher, J., 191, 358
'flooding' patients with stimuli, 167
focus groups, 38
Fong, M.W., 382
food consumption see eating
food industry, 203
food preferences, 189–90
food types, 180–1
forced exposure, 167
'framing effect' in health education, 160
Franklin, Benjamin, 140
Freedman, Aviva, 378
free-will, 360
'French paradox' with regard to heart disease, 225–6
Freud, Sigmund, 97
Friedman, M., 227
fructose, 255

GABA (γ-aminobutyric acid), 118–19
gambling, 363–4
gastric bands and gastric bypass surgery, 198
gastrointestinal (GI) tract, 274
gate control theory of pain, 332–4
Gates, Bill, 428
Gawande, A., 414

gender differences, 108, 128–31, 156–7, 224–5, 348, 404
gene–environment interactions, 47–51, 295
genetics, 44–7, 226–7, 360, 422, 424
    and cancer, 293–7
germ cell tumors, 292
ghrelin, 59–60, 127–8, 192, 357–8
gial cells and gial functioning, 55, 337
Global Burden of Disease (GBD), 13
global health interventions, 428
global warming, 18
globalization, 427
glucose, 198, 249
glutamate, 118, 238, 368
gluten intolerance, 281
glycemic index, 255, 357
'Goldilocks principle', 71
gonadal hormones, 128–9
gonadal steroids, 61
government interventions to deal with addiction, 365
Grassi, Giovanni Battista, 36
grieving process, 418–19
group therapy, 365
growth factors, 66–7, 132–3
guided imagery, 342
gum disease, 229, 251
gut bacteria, 73–4, 185, 253, 263, 274, 279, 422

habits, 361
Hahnemann, Samuel, 202
happiness, 14
harm reduction programs, 174–5
Harvey, L., 100
Haslam, C. and S.A., 418
'hassles', 108–9, 284
hazards as distinct from risks, 151
health, determinants of, 144–6
Health Belief Model, 163
Health Canada, 266
health delivery, changes in, 21
health foods, 198–201
health inequalities, 403
health promotion, 157–8
health psychology
    clinical, 5–6
    definition of, 4–6
    global perspective on, 11–18
    multidisciplinary nature of, 5
health-related behaviors, 176–7
health risk assessments, 151–2
healthy eating, 187–91
    impediments to, 187–8

heart attacks, 218–19, 404
    recovery from, 231
heart disease, 215, 219–36, 243
    alternative medicine in treatment of, 234–6
    biomarkers for, 230
    and depression, 221–3
    factors promoting, 219–27
    gender differences in, 224–5
    inflammatory processes in, 229–31
    and loneliness, 224
    and personality, 227–8
    pharmacological treatments for, 231–6
    physiological stress responses to, 228–31
heart functioning, 212–13
Heller, Amanda, 345
helplessness, sense of, 83–4, 289
herbal remedies, 199–201, 234, 331
'herd immunity', 271, 420
heritability, 47–8
H5N1 influenza, 161–2, 260, 288, 429
high-risk individuals, 8
Hill, Austin Bradford, 33, 37
Hippocrates, 36
Hippocratic oath, 416
Hirsch, Marion, 105
'Hispanic paradox' with regard to heart disease, 226
historical trauma, 105–7
HIV/AIDS, 260, 270, 273, 277, 376, 379, 429
Hoffman, E., 105
holistic perspectives on treatment of illness, 2–3
Holocaust survivors and their children, 106–7
homeopathy, 202, 331, 393
hormone disturbance, 120–5, 182–3
hormone replacement therapy (HRT), 62, 295–6, 303–4
hormones, 56–66
    and cancer, 303–4
    and eating, 58–60, 127–8
    sex-related, 61–6, 128–9
    and stress response, 57–8
hospice care, 414
hospital-acquired infections, 267
'hot reactors', 228
human growth hormone, 406–7
human papillomavirus, 298
humoral immunity, 69
'hygiene hypothesis', 264
hypertension, 215–17
    essential and *secondary*, 216
    treatment for, 232–3
hypnosis, 341–4
hypochondriacs, 386
hypothalamic-pituitary-adrenal (HPA) system, 57

iatrogenic illness, 397–9
ibogaine, 368
identical twins, 262
'illness delay', 403
Illness Perception Questionnaire (IPQ), 388–9
image-guided radiation therapy (IGRT), 318
immune functioning, 67–73, 95–6, 274–7
   and diet, 274
   and exercise, 275–6
   and life-style, 274–7
   and sleep, 276
   and stress, 134–8
'immune surveillance' hypothesis, 292
immune system, 261–2, 271–2, 288, 293
immunoglobulin E, 261–2
immunological memory, 69–70
immunotherapy, 318–20
'implementation intentions', 160
improvement of health care, strategy for, 402
incidence of disease, 38
individualized treatment strategies, 141–4, 315–16, 321,
   369, 426
infectious diseases, 264–73, 426
   emerging, 18
   routes followed by, 265
inflammatory bowel disease (IBD), 278–80
   inflammatory processes, 261
   in heart disease, 215, 229–31
   in *type 2* diabetes, 250–3
influenza vaccines, 260, 271–2
'informed consent', 393
innate immunity, 68
in situ analysis, 37
insomnia, 276
Institute of Medicine (IOM), 157
instrumental process, 164
insulin, 59–60, 127, 182–3, 244, 250, 257
insurance, 152, 191, 400–1
integration of psychiatry, neurology and psychology, 421
integrative care, 375
integrative therapies, 201, 344
intention–behavior gap, 160
intergenerational effects, 3
internal monologues, 169
International Agency for Research on Cancer, 298
International Association for the Study of Pain
   (IASP), 323
International Labour Organization (ILO), 209
intervention strategy
   stage-based, 165–6
   types of, 146
Ioannidis, J.P., 188

ipilimumab, 319
irrational behaviors, 19
itchiness, 326

Jenner, Edward, 259
Jetten, J., 173, 418
job strain/stress, 220–1, 249–50
Jonas, W., 65
'just noticeable difference' (JND) in weight, 191

Kahneman, D., 80, 86, 159
Kaposi's sarcoma, 298–9
King, Martin Luther, 96
Kington, R., 157
knowledge, translation of, 424–5, 428–9
'knowledge to action' process, 423
knowledge possessed by patients, 399–400
Kubler-Ross, E., 411, 413
Kushner, H.S., 411

lactose intolerance, 182
Lane-Claypon, Janet Elizabeth, 36–7
lawsuits, 393
lead-time bias, 150
'length bias' in illness detection, 150
leptin, 59–60, 127–8, 192
leukemia, 292
life events rated on scales, 109–10
life span and life expectancy, 17–18, 156, 275–6, 400,
   403, 406, 410–11, 429
life-style factors in health, 157, 175–7, 209–10, 274–7,
   321, 424
   interlinking of, 210
life trajectories, 97–8
locus of control, 83, 107, 377
loneliness, 103–4, 173, 224
longitudinal studies, 32
lorcaserin, 197, 368
loss, coping with, 417–19
love, 345
lung cancer, 379–80
lupus, 283–4
lymphoma, 292

McEwen, B.S., 89
McKendrick, Anderson Gray, 37
macrophages, 69
Mallon, Mary, 270
mammography, 148–9, 297, 314
marginalized social groups, 429
marijuana, 119, 337
   medical use of, 287

mastectomy, 297, 382
Mayo Clinic, 311
meaning-making efforts, 94
measles, 271–2, 289, 429
media reporting on health issues, 161–2, 187
mediated effects on relationships between variables, 34–5
Melzack, R., 332, 334, 338
memory
  neuronal, 355
  pain-related, 343
menstruation, 62–3, 128
mental illness, 54–5, 222, 331, 379–82, 403, 421
Merton, R.K., 153
meta-analysis, 39, 42
metabolic syndrome, 247, 257
metastasis, 291, 300
methadone, 366
methicillin-resistant staphyloc-occus aureus (MRSA), 267
methodological approaches to health psychology, 25–42
  caveats concerning, 40–1
microbiome, 185, 263
microbiota, 73–4, 274–5, 279, 305
microglia, 55
middle age, 103–4
migraine headaches, 325
milk, 190; *see also* breastfeeding
mindfulness, 170–2, 340–1, 344, 364–5, 374
mindfulness-based cognitive therapy (MBCT), 171
mindfulness-based stress reduction (MBSR), 171, 308
misattributions about illness, 387
MMR vaccine, 101
moderated medications, 35
moderating effects on relationships between two variables, 34–5
molecular pathological epidemiology (MPE), 37
Mols, F., 159
monoamine changes, 114–17, 138
monoclonal antibodies, 319–20
monocytes, 68–9
mood states, 223–4, 327, 331
mortality rates, 186, 295, 400
mosquito netting, 266
mosquito repellant, 154
mosquito-transmitted illness, 18
'motivational interviewing', 195
Mukherjee, Siddhartha, 140
multiple sclerosis (MS), 282–7
Murphy, T.H., 242
mutations, 48–9

narcolepsy, 207
National Academy of Sciences (NAS), US, 157
National Center for Complementary and Alternative Medicine (NCCAM), US, 201
National Health Service (NHS), UK, 347–8, 401
National Institute on Alcohol Abuse and Alcoholism, US, 347
National Institutes of Health, US, 143, 215
natural killer (NK) cells, 69, 301
natural remedies and natural food supplements, 198–201, 234, 310
'near-death experiences', 412
negative thinking, 82–5, 169, 171, 326, 387
neoantigens, 318
nervous system, 51–5; *see also* autonomic nervous system; enteric nervous system
neural adaptation, limits to, 117
neural stem/progenitor cells (NSPCs), 242
neuraminidase, 270
neurobiological processes, 26
  in addiction, 346
  in coronary artery disease, 243
  exercise-related, 178–9
  sleep-related, 203
  stress-related, 112–75
neurochemical systems, 116, 138, 350–5
neurogenic stressors, 78–9
neurological correlates of placebo responses, 330–1
neurological disorders, 54–5
neurological pain signature (NPS), 328
neuronal memories, 355
neuronal systems, 51–2
neurons, 52
neuropathic pain, 323, 337
neuropeptide Y (NPY), 125, 358
neurophysiology of pain processes, 332–5
neurotransmitters, 52–6, 64, 76, 113–17, 332, 353
neurotrophins, 66–7
neutrophils, 68–9
nicotine, 153, 358, 360, 367
nicotine replacement therapy, 366
night terrors, 207–8
nitrates, 233
nocebo responses, 329
nociceptive pain, 323
Nolen-Hoeksema, S., 88
nonalcoholic steatohepatitis (NASH), 197
norepinephrine 53, 58, 114, 228, 232, 300, 353
'nudge' strategy for changing behavior, 159
nutrition, 180–1

obesity, 126–7, 183–7, 190–2, 196–7, 202,
  251–3, 401
  in children and adolescents, 196–7
  and illness, 185–6
  neurological correlates of, 184–5
  stemming from early-life experiences, 192
obsessive compulsive disorder, 167
occupational therapy, 243
oligodendrocytes, 55
omega-3 fatty acids, 234
oncolytic virotherapy, 319–20
'one percent doctrine', 147–8
opioid replacement therapy, 175
opioids, 184, 336, 353, 364, 366
optimism, 84, 107
options for patients, 393
optogenetics, 361
oral contraceptives, 304
orexin, 358
orthorexia, 187
ostracism, 96–7
overdiagnosis, 151
overeating, 184–5, 194, 357
over-treatment, 401–3
Overseas Development Institute, UK, 184
oxytocin, 65–6, 130–2

pain, 322–44
  alternative medicine for treatment of, 343–4
  assessments of, 325
  definition of, 323–5
  and depression, 327
  and mindfulness, 340–1
  neurophysiology of, 332–5
  perceptions of, 327–31, 334, 338–43
  and post-traumatic stress disorder, 327
  psychological aspects of, 327–31
  related to cancer, 311
  relaxation training for treatment of, 341
  salience of, 328
  surgical procedures for relief of, 338
  types of, 323
  as a warning sign, 322
  see also chronic pain
'pain ladder', 335
pain management, 335–8
palliative care, 413
Paltrow, Gwyneth, 20
pandemics, 161–2, 259–60
parasomnias, 207–8
parasympathetic activity, 56
parasympathetic nervous system, 219

Pareto principle, 270
Parkinson's disease, 352
patients, focus on, 22–3
Patrick, K., 191
Pavlov, Ivan, 167
peanut allergy, 263
Pearl, Robert, 397
Peltzman effect, 154
peptic ulcers, 6
Perceived Stress Scale, 110
perceptions, patients'
  of illness, 386–9
  of physicians, 390
periodontal disease, 251
personal doctors, 405
personality, 9, 107, 137, 227–8
perverse results from medical interventions, 154
pessimism, 107
phagocytosis, 69
phantom limb pain, 334–5
pharmaceutical companies, 401
phenotypes, 44–9
phylogenetic scale, 26
physiological indices of distress, 172
physiotherapy, 243
Pies, R., 345
placebo responses, 329–31, 343
  neurological correlates of, 330–1
planned behavior, theory of, 164–5
pneumonic plague, 259
policy change, 426–8
policy makers, role of, 159
poliomyelitis (polio), 319–20, 429
polymorphisms, 48, 248, 360, 366; *see also* single
  nucleotide poly-morphisms
pop-up messages on slot machines, 364
positive psychology, 95–6
positivity, 223–4, 384
post-hospital syndrome, 397
post-traumatic growth, 93
post-traumatic stress disorder (PTSD), 51, 55, 120,
  124–5, 133, 170, 206, 230, 287, 303, 327, 343
Potts, Percival, 140
power of statistical tests, 40–1
prebehavioural strategies, 21
preclinical studies, 29
prenatal experiences, 3, 5, 98–101, 129, 133, 302
prevalence of illness, 37
prevention of illness, 140–1, 146–7
  primary, 158
  universal and *selective* programs for, 146
preventive medicine, 8, 251, 403

probiotics, 74–5
problem-solving as a method of coping, 92–3
procedural pain, 325
processing fluency, 81
program evaluation, 38
'prohibition', 365
prolactin, 64, 129
prospective studies, 32
prostate cancer, 149–50, 314–15
protection motivation theory (PMT), 163–4
pseudo-science, 202
pseudo-treatments, 310–11
psoriasis, 278
psychiatric disorders, 27, 421
psychogenic pain, 331
psychogenic stressors, 78–9
psychological aspects
  of illness, 3–6, 21–3
  of pain, 326–31
  of perception, 387–8
  of physical disorders, 178–9
psychological disorders, 7, 206
psychological disturbance, 308, 355–6
'psychological pain', 339
psychological problems, 373, 403
psychologically-based treatment, 338–40
psychooncology, 310–11
psychosocial factors, 6, 223, 249, 275, 310, 327, 343,
  372, 414, 424
psychosomatic illness and pain, 6–7, 331
psychotherapeutic approaches, 382
psychotropic drugs, 360
public health, 202–3, 426

qualitative and quantitative analysis, 4
quality of life (QoL), 371–2, 414
quasi-experimental design, 30–1
quorum sensing, 266

radiation treatments , 290, 317–18
raging against illness, 384
randomised control trials (RCTs), 29–30
rapid eye movement (REM) and non-rapid eye
  movement (NREM) sleep, 203–6
readmission to hospital after discharge, 377
reasoned action, theory of, 164
receptor functions, 53
re-emerging infections, 18
referred pain, 334
regression analysis, 32–6
  hierarchical, 34
rehabilitation programs, 375

relationships between patients and health care providers,
  389–400
relationships between variables, 34–5
relaxation training, 341
religion, 92, 94, 376, 409, 412, 416, 418
'reperceiving', 171
replication of research, 27–8, 42
reporting on illness, 386; *see also* media reporting
reproduction, human, 129
Research Domain Criteria (RDoXC) of the US National
  Institutes of Health, 143
research, translation of, 422; *see also* translational
  research
resilience, 8–9, 83, 106–8, 141–2, 373, 375
resuscitation, 317, 307
Resuscitation Council, UK, 417
retrospective analyses, 31
reuptake, 54
reward processes, 351–4, 357–60, 369
Reynolds, K.J., 51
rheumatoid arthritis, 282, 284, 373
risk appraisal and risk perception, 161
risk compensation theory, 154–5
risk and risky behavior, 38, 151–5, 385
road accidents, 209
Rosenman, R.H., 227
Ross, Ronald, 36
Royal College of Nursing, UK, 417
Rudman, D., 406
rumination, 89, 93

safety measures, 388
St John's wort, 200–1
Salk, Jonas, 421
Sapolsky, R.M., 122
sarcoma, 292
scams, 4, 202
Schoenfeld, J.D., 188
Schwartz, B., 86
science, nature of, 422–4
scientists, trust in, 20, 421
screening procedures, 148–51, 314–15, 429
  myths and misconceptions relating to, 150–1
selective serotonin reuptake inhibitors (SSRIs), 54,
  154, 374
self-affirmation, 161
self-blame by patients, 387–8
self-control and *self-reinforcement* or *self-punishment*, 168
self-efficacy, 107, 163–4, 179, 193, 195, 211, 343, 362,
  376, 378
self-initiated interventions, 148
self-monitoring, 168

self-perceptions, 382–3
self-reports, 159–60
self-stigma, 380
self-talk, 169
Semmelweis, Ignaz, 36
sensitization, 88, 116
serotonin, 54, 74, 114, 196, 203, 353, 358
sex hormones, 61–6, 128–9
sexually-transmitted diseases (STD), 273
Sharpey-Schafer, Sir Edward Albert, 244
Shigella, 268
side effects, 154
'silent stroke', 240
single nucleotide polymorphisms (SNPs), 48–9
Sinha, R., 350
sins of omission and of commission, 152–3
sirtuins, 407
Sjogren's syndrome, 278
skin blemishes, stress-related, 134
sleep, 203–9
    and eating, 207
    lack of, 205
    neurobiological aspects of, 203
    and physical illness, 206–7
sleep apnea, 208
sleep disorders, 207–9, 216, 224, 276, 306
sleep-walking, 208
sleeve gastrectomy, 198
smallpox, 259
smoking, 11, 152–3, 160–1, 236, 267, 290, 348–50,
    360–8, 380, 424
snacking, 195
Snow, John, 36
social-cognitive models of behavior change, 162–6
social factors in health, 146
social identity, 173, 190, 418
social media, 96
Social Readjustment Scale, 109–10
social rejection, 96–7, 339
social stimuli, 131
social support, 92–7, 156, 173–4, 194–6, 223, 284, 309–
    10, 338, 343, 365, 369, 378–9, 418–19, 424
Solomon, S., 157
somatoform diseases, 6–7
somnambulism, 208
Spanish flu (1918–1920), 260
specialists, medical, 370
spending on health care *per capita*, 17
spreading of infection, 270
stage-based interventions, 165–6
staphylococcus aureus (*S.aureus*), 267
statins, 233

statistical significance, 40–1
stem cell research, 424
sterile inflammation, 135
steroids, 61, 64
stigma, 1, 193, 379–82, 424, 429
    educating people about, 381–2
    related to illness, 331–2, 379–81
    structural, 380–1
stress, 77–111
    and cancer, 299–304
    and energy balances, 126–8
    and heart disease, 219–20
    and immune functioning, 134–8
    and reproduction, 129
stress appraisal measure (SAM), 110
stress interviews, 110
stress-related hormones, 57–8
stressful experiences, 72, 77–8, 82, 85, 88–90, 93–4, 97,
    108, 111, 126–9, 219–20, 227–30, 249, 262, 267,
    277, 284, 325, 350, 369
    and cancer prediction, 299–301
stressors, 77–11
    appraisal of, 79–86, 108–11
    attributes and characteristics of, 78–9, 82–8
    and brain morphology, 133
    chronic, 89–90
    controllability of, 83–4
    cumulative effect of, 90
    and cytokines, 230
    definition of, 78
    in early life, 128–9, 133
    and eating, 192–5
    effects across the life span, 97–105
    hormonal changes elicited by, 120–5
    illusions and delusions relating to, 87–8
    neurobiological changes provoked by, 113–14
    previous experience of, 88–94
    toleration of, 102
    and *type 2* diabetes, 249–50
stroke, 238–43
    and depression, 241
    rehabilitation therapy, 241–3
    risk factors and epidemiology, 240
    signs of, 239
    subtypes of, 238–9
    treatment for, 241
structural equation modeling, 35–6
subacute sclerosing panencephalitis (SSPE), 272
substance abuse, 350
sugary drinks, 197–8
suicide, 154, 415–18
support groups, 173, 418

surgery, success in, 370–1
surveillance, 37
Survey of Coping Profile Endorsement (SCOPE), 110–11
Swartz, K., 409
sympathetic activity, 56
sympathetic nervous system, 228
symptoms of illness
    delayed presentation of, 403–4
    recognition of, 385
    sufferers' ignoring of, 403–5
synaptic connections, 355, 375
synthesis of data, 39–40
systematic desensitization, 167
systematic reviews, 39–40, 42
systemic exertion intolerance disease, 332
systemic lupus erythematosus (SLE), 283–4
systemic stressors, 79

Taleb, N.N., 88
tamoxifen, 316–17
target populations, 37
Taylor, Gloria, 416
T cytotoxic cells, 69
teams of health workers, 22, 321
Teicholz, N., 189
telomere length, 90–1, 309, 406
'tend-and-befriend' and 'tend-and-defend' approaches, 131
teratogenic effects, 98–9
terminal illness, 410–11
testosterone, 61, 63–4, 108
tests, medical, 391, 403
    selectivity, sensitivity and specificity of, 149–50
theoretical models of health-related behaviors, 162
thinking systems, fast and slow, 81
Thomas, Dylan, 384
threats, ambiguity and volatility of, 87
tissue plasminogen activator (tPA), 241
Tolstoy, Leo, 1
topirimate, 368
Center for Addiction and Mental Health (Toronto), 358
toxicants and toxins, 3
traditional Chinese medicine (TCM), 201, 310
traditional healing practices, 156
trans fats, 177, 188–9, 219
transient ischemic attack, 240
transitions in life, 102–3
translational research, 422–6
transtheoretical model (TTM) of behavior change, 165–7, 365
trauma and traumatic events, 88, 105–8, 123–4
trend setters, 173

Trier Social Stress Test, 123–4
tropical diseases, 273
'true positives' and 'true negatives', 149
trust
    in doctors, 392–3
    in messages about health, 161–2
    in scientists, 20, 421
Tsimane society, 221
tuberculosis (TB), 267–8, 288
'turning points' in life, 97–8
Tversky, A., 80, 86, 159
Twain, Mark, 361
12-step programs, 363
twin studies, 47–8
two-tiered health care, 400–1
Type D personality, 227–8
typhoid, 268
Typhoid Mary, 270

uncertainty about the future, 84–6, 376–7, 400
    intolerance of, 85–6, 376
unintended consequences, 153–4
'unique disease principle', 37
United States Surgeon General, 65
universal health care, 400–1
University of Wisconsin Children's Hospital (UWCH), 325
unpredictable events, 84–5
'unsupportive' events/actions, 96

vaccination, arguments for and against, 272
vaccine hesitancy, 19–20, 162, 429
vaccines, 101, 136, 161–2, 260, 271–2, 318, 369, 420, 429
valence systems, positive and negative, 143
validity of research findings, 25–8
Vance, M.L., 406–7
'vaping', 367
variability within experiments, 41
vascular remodeling, 230
ventral tegmental area (VTA), 351, 358
viral infection, 100, 136, 259–60, 266, 268–70, 277
visual analogue thermometers (VATs), 325
'vital exhaustion', 222–3
vitamins, 181
volatility of threats, 87
Volkow, N.D., 360, 369
vulnerability to illness, 8, 141, 155, 248

Wakefield, Andrew, 101
Wall, P.D., 332, 338
warnings on health matters, 385

washrooms, use of, 268
'watchful waiting', 376, 383
'Ways of Coping' questionnaire, 110
weight loss, 191, 194–7, 211, 401
    behavioral change for promotion of, 195
    incentives for, 191
    pharmacological approaches to, 197
    products for promotion of, 201
    therapeutic approaches to, 194–5
wellness, general sense of, 7–8, 224
'white coat syndrome', 404
Whitehall studies, 220
WHOQOL-BREF questionnaire, 372
Wiesel, Elie, 96
Wilde, Oscar, 189

wine drinking, 225–6
Winehouse, Amy, 362
Wingfield, J.C., 89
Woodside, B., 65
World Health Organization (WHO), 65, 203, 209, 259, 266, 273, 348, 372, 426–7
worry, 82, 206–7

years lived with disability (YLD), 13
yoga, 172

zeitgebers, 203
zohydro, 336
zolpidem, 208
zoonotic diseases, 270–2